£18

The River Cottage Fish Book

Hugh Fearnley-Whittingstall and Nick Fisher

Photography by Simon Wheeler

Additional photography
by Paul Quagliana and Marie Derôme

B L O O M S B U R Y
LONDON · BERLIN · NEW YORK · SYDNEY

Introduction
to the revised edition

We are just as excited about catching, cooking and eating fish as we were three years ago when we wrote this book – and the recipes you'll find in these pages still represent our favourite ways to serve seafood. However, while our passion for fish and shellfish is unabated, there's something that also hasn't changed: the concern that tempers our enthusiasm. This revised edition allows us to re-emphasise a major point: namely that it's impossible – or at least unreasonable – to really enjoy fish without giving some thought to the thorny issues of sustainability which relate to sourcing it.

Since the book was first published, the outlook for the world's fish stocks has not improved a great deal. There are now more species than ever on the Marine Conservation Society's 'fish to avoid' list. That doesn't mean the story is a constant downward spiral – some stocks have rallied and UK fishing practices in general are moving, slowly, in a sustainable direction. But there is absolutely no justification for complacency.

The list of species that can be considered okay to buy is in flux. Choosing fish you can feel good about eating is sometimes quite a challenge – one that might even put you off eating it altogether. But fish remains such a wonderful, delicious, healthy food. Harvesting it from the wild can, in theory, have far less impact on the environment than raising other forms of protein, particularly meat. So we believe very strongly that fish-lovers should keep eating fish. It's just crucial not to bury our heads in the sand (or gaze stubbornly out to sea).

Thankfully, there are tools that can help conscientious fish-buyers make the right choices. The exhaustive MCS website www.fishonline.org is one (they publish a pocket fish guide, too). The Marine Stewardship Council's blue 'eco-label', to be found on a growing number of fish products, is another. Greenpeace have a very straightforward 'red list' of fish to avoid (www.greenpeace.org) – and there are other resources too. In fact, we will be launching a fish sustainability feature on our River Cottage iPhone app in early 2011.

But before you start doing your research, there are a few straightforward changes you can make in order to move towards more sustainable fish consumption. One is simply to diversify. Don't eat cod or haddock or prawns every time you fancy fish – and don't eat pollack or mussels every time either. By sampling from the very many different species on the fishmonger's slab, you will reduce your impact on all of them.

Another approach is to eat lower down the food chain – we recommend that you choose wild fish over farmed. On the whole, aquaculture is a questionable way to produce fish (mussels and oysters being honourable exceptions, as they generally require no manufactured feed and minimal inputs), and at worst, fish-farming is completely wrong-headed. Many farmed fish, particularly salmon, trout and prawns, are fed fishmeal made from small, oily fish species such as herring, sand eel, sardines, anchovies and sprats. It makes no sense at all for these fish – among the tastiest and most nutritious that swim in our waters – to be landed in huge numbers merely to fatten the aquaculture industry. Around 3kg of 'feed' fish is needed to produce just 1kg of farmed fish flesh. We would much, much rather bag those delicious little wild fish ourselves and forget the flabby farmed salmon. (There are some farmed species, such as tilapia and carp, that are herbivorous and don't need to eat fish-based food, making them a more ecologically sound choice.)

But here's a dilemma. Because of industrial fishing for fishmeal, animal feed and even fertiliser, sprats – only three years ago one of our 'fish to eat more of' and plentiful enough to be unrated by the MCS – now score a worrying 3 on their list. Yet we would argue that we should champion their value as a human food, with the long-term aim of reducing the pressure put on such bait fish by unsustainable aquaculture. Just one example of how perplexing it can get when you're attempting to be a conscientious fish eater...

Which doesn't mean you shouldn't try. Reversing the degradation of our oceans will require a consumer revolution. But that revolution will be made up of millions of small actions, millions of intelligent choices of one fish instead of another. Diversifying your fish choices in general (ideally favouring the lower-numbered species on the MCS list), and supporting certified sustainable fisheries in particular, are changes well worth making. They're hardly tedious or onerous changes; far from it. Exploring the delicious and diverse range of sustainable fish and shellfish to be had in the British Isles should be nothing but a pleasure. This book, we hope, will be your companion in that.

Hugh and Nick, October 2010

Introduction

We both love fish. And that is the overriding reason we have written this book. As anglers, cooks and (very amateur) naturalists, we've got fish under our skin. It's very hard – and rather stressful – to imagine life without them.

Over the years we've found all kinds of ways to scratch our fish itch: goldfish in a bowl, visits to aquariums, goggling at Jacques Cousteau on the telly, learning first to snorkel and then to scuba dive. Such enthusiasms have come and gone, but two have always been a constant: catching fish and eating them.

Between us, we have caught and cooked many fish. We have, of course, also caught a fair few that we haven't cooked, and cooked countless others that we haven't caught. But we are happiest when these two pursuits collide and we get to consume a fish that we have personally pulled from the deep. For both of us, our passion for fish as quarry and food began at an early age.

Hugh's first fishing expedition occurred at the age of six, when his dad took him to a stream in Richmond Park, armed with a bamboo cane, a length of string, a bent pin and a slice of bread. They actually caught a fish! Back home with his *Observer's Book of Fishes*, Hugh identified the catch as a mackerel, noting that this was a fish that was meant to live in the sea.

Being omniscient, his dad naturally had a convincing explanation: 'Er, it must have decided to swim up from the sea – like a salmon...' That was more than good enough for the young Hugh. There was no reason to be suspicious. After all, he had lifted the fish from the stream with his own hands, and watched his father knock it several times on the head with his own eyes.

Hugh's mum fried the mackerel in butter and served it with a slice of lemon. It was the first fish Hugh had ever eaten that wasn't finger-shaped, coated in breadcrumbs and doused in ketchup – and he enjoyed it very much indeed.

It was ten years before the sorry truth came out. Seeing his teenage son swearing blind to some disbelieving friends that he had once caught a mackerel in a London park with a lump of Mother's Pride on a bent pin, Hugh's dad was moved to a guilty confession. He came clean about the trip to the fishmonger's; the sleight of hand that slipped the fish on to the hook as Hugh was sent behind a bush for a much-needed pee; the ritual despatch of a fish that had, in fact, already been dead for two days...

Hugh was a little disillusioned to discover the deceit but, being sixteen, soon found other things to strop about. In the end he is, of course, eternally grateful to his dad. Grateful to be hooked on fishing, and hooked on fish.

Nick grew up in inner-city Glasgow. Other than breaking his foot with a paving slab and being made to eat mud pies by his two bossy big sisters, he doesn't remember much about being five. But what he can remember in uncanny detail is sitting on the end of a rock pier in Millport one sunny summer afternoon, holding a Winfield toy rod and catching his first totally unaided fish.

It was a wrasse. A purply-blue, mottled, spiny-finned ballan wrasse, with buck teeth and huge, rubbery lips. The fight between big fish and tiny rod had been a long one; many dads crowded round, eager to 'help' Nick land the fish. But he never did let go of that rod. Instead he dragged the wrasse up the wall on to the pier and whacked it on the head with a gaff handle.

Sadly, Nick never got to eat his first fish. In the 1960s, any fish that had the temerity not to be born a cod or a haddock was deemed 'inedible'. On the way back to their caravan, Nick's dad told him to throw the fish on the beach 'for the seagulls'. As they walked away, the beautiful creature that had lived underwater with such style and exuberance lay dead, dull and greying, speckled with grit, waiting to be pulled apart by herring gulls.

Much as he loved fishing from the start, loved eating fish, and loved the tackle, the boats, the danger and the sheer manliness of it all, what Nick realised at that moment was that there are right ways to treat fish, and there are wrong ways.

For many years, both of us carried around a kind of fat store of joy, based on happy fishy memories. Anything to do with fish was always good. Any opportunity to go fishing was always gratefully taken. And just about any piece of fish offered on a plate was gratefully devoured.

Most of the time, fish still work that simple magic for us. But they have also muscled in on our work lives – meaning that, now and again, we find ourselves taking fish and fishing quite seriously. We've both written and broadcast about them – Nick extensively, Hugh more incidentally – and it was this shared professional interest that first brought us together. Hugh was an avid fan of Nick's Channel Four series, *Screaming Reels*, and decided to stalk Nick with a view to collaborating on some fishy telly. We met, we talked, we went fishing (Hugh caught nothing, Nick a small roach) and, as we became friends, we let the telly idea drop. We enjoyed being fishing buddies too much to let work get in the way.

We've known each other for well over a decade now, and are not remotely embarrassed to admit that we have spent most of our time together if not actually fishing, then cooking, eating or talking about fish. Many of our conversations have been simply the recollection of past fish and the anticipation of future ones – you can never take the boy out of the fisherman.

One long, fishy chat ended with a joint resolution: let's do a book together. A big one. One where we celebrate the nation's fish and trumpet those species that have been 'forgotten' and ignored; where we do our best to take the fear and mystery out of handling and preparing fish, and try to communicate the tremendous pleasure and satisfaction that a few fish skills can bring; one where we don't shirk the ecological and moral issues of fishing. And, of course, one where we share all our favourite ways of cooking all our favourite fish.

Roughly three years later, here is that book. We're proud to say that, though it's taken us more time and more words than we had perhaps originally imagined, we feel we haven't flinched from our self-imposed brief. Now that we've finished the writing, we can't wait to get back to the fishing.

Hugh and Nick, Dorset, September 2007

1. Understanding fish

The nitty-gritty of this book is the delightful activity of cooking and eating fish. And we think you'll derive even more pleasure from your fish and shellfish if you understand a little, or perhaps a lot, about the business of catching and preparing them.

Besides being delicious, fish are uniquely nutritious. So you would think the very least we could do, given their contribution to our well-being, would be to nurture them in return. At this we are failing spectacularly. The prognosis is gloomy on a number of fronts, as the destructive fishing practices of the past half-century have taken their toll. The fact that we can finally acknowledge just how bad things are does offer, paradoxically, a glimmer of hope. We haven't, thank goodness, passed the point of no return; we still have a stunning range of native fish and shellfish to celebrate. We would both argue that their future lies largely in the hands of the consumer – that's every single one of us who loves to eat fish.

The angler-cook will, of necessity, prepare much of his fish from scratch, and knowing how to wield a filleting knife is clearly essential. But even the landlubber fish enthusiast may once in a while enjoy taking a live crab home or gutting a mackerel at the sink. Our two chapters covering fish and shellfish skills will show you the way.

Fish as food

Four million years ago an early prototype of the human being, Australopithecine Man, roamed across the African savannah. He walked upright, stood around 1.2 metres tall and possessed a brain about the size of a chimp's. Three million years later, on the verge of extinction, he hadn't changed much. Despite a few hundred thousand generations of hunting and eating meat, *Australopithecus* remained pretty much as intellectually and vertically challenged as he had been when he first wandered out on to the plain. He lost the battle for survival – and became just another leaf to have fallen from the evolutionary tree.

Another human forerunner, who overlapped with *Australopithecus* for the last million years of his time on the planet, was *Homo erectus*. He grew over 1.5 metres tall, and in just 200,000 years of evolution he tripled the size of his brain. Equipped with this enlarged grey matter and a range of tools, *erectus* evolved into *sapiens*. Hom sap was anatomically modern and technologically minded; in other words, he was us.

Why did one branch of proto-humans hit an evolutionary dead end while another grew bigger, stronger and – crucially – much cleverer? What made one a hopeless, doomed grunter and the other the ancestor of Leonardo da Vinci (plus you and us, of course). The answer is: fish.

Homo erectus stood up, but he didn't stand still. He wandered all over the place, in search of a better living; he left the savannah and reached the coast, where he ate fish, shellfish and seaweed for the first time (they must have made a nice change from mastodons – so much easier on the teeth). Fossil evidence shows that his burgeoning fish-eating habit coincided with his rapid cerebral growth. Scientists believe this staggering improvement came about because *Homo sapiens* was nourished by a substance previously present only in trace quantities in his diet: docohexaenoic acid, or DHA for short. Our bodies aren't able to manufacture their own DHA, so how did it end up inside them? It must have been something we ate. When it comes to identifying the 'superfood' that provided the quantities of DHA necessary for the dramatic expansion of our cranial capacity, the only serious candidate is fish.

DHA is an omega-3 essential fatty acid, of the kind we now know to be vital to brain development. The body converts it into proteins, which it uses specifically to build neurons – the conductors that manage electrochemical activity in the brain. Up to 8 per cent of our brain weight is made up of these fatty acids, so to achieve optimal brain growth we need fatty acids in our food. Put simply, the more of them we get, the better our brains develop. And there's nowhere better to get them than from fish.

So if it hadn't been for early man's trip to the seaside, we might all still be hairy bush dwellers, waiting for someone to invent the wheel (or at least the fish spear). Of course, we should remember that we didn't become piscivores in order to evolve. We weren't quite *that* clever. We ate fish because they were there, they sustained us, and perhaps because we found them delicious. It just so happens that, from a biological and evolutionary perspective, actively choosing to eat something that is so good for you makes for a fantastically virtuous circle. One that has led, down the millennia, to a culture of such stupendous sophistication that books have been written and television shows filmed about our favourite ways of eating fish (among other things).

Fish for health

A fish-rich diet continues to contribute to our well-being. Those cultures that still eat large amounts of fish and shellfish, such as the Inuits and the Japanese, have in the past consistently ranked high for good health, with far lower rates of cancer, heart disease and type-2 diabetes. But when modern, highly processed foods begin to supplant the traditional, simple, fish-rich diet of such societies, these and other health problems rapidly mount up. The rising rate of type-2 diabetes in Japan correlates nicely (or nastily) with the expansion of Western fast-food franchises in that country over the last few decades. We turn from raw fish to cheeseburgers at our peril.

The term 'health food' doesn't tend to whet our appetites but, taken at face value, it describes a piece of fish rather better than a packet of lentils. It's not just the famous omega-3s that fish have to offer. Even before you tot up the vitamins and minerals, almost all types of fish and shellfish are a superb source of first-class, low-fat, highly digestible protein. And, of course, there are so many different types of seafood – between them, they offer a whole spectrum of good things. Fin fish (i.e. fish that swim with fins) are packed with vitamins (particularly A and D but also B), plus magnesium, calcium and other trace elements. Shellfish and crustaceans are rich in other minerals, such as iodine, zinc and iron, plus vital selenium and taurine (essential for the healthy function of all human cells).

Nevertheless, it is those omega oils that really mark fish out as a fantastic food. And some fish have far more of them than others. These are the species that we refer to by the pleasingly untechnical term 'oily fish'. They include mackerel, herrings, sardines (or pilchards), sprats, scad (horse mackerel), tuna, salmon, trout and eel. All of these species are especially valuable as food because they are so rich in omega-3s – much more so than white fish. This doesn't mean that white fish, such as haddock and plaice, isn't good for you. Quite the opposite: white fish is low in fat, high in protein, a good source of vitamins and minerals, and a fabulous addition to anybody's diet. But oily fish is even better. Oily fish is essential.

Fish as brain food

The known direct health benefits of eating oily fish include a reduced risk of heart attack and type-2 diabetes; lower blood pressure and cholesterol levels; and, for expectant mothers, higher foetal birth weight, which generally correlates with more likely future good health. There is also mounting evidence of mental and psychological benefits from a fish-rich diet.

Current research into how omega-3s affect the human brain, and thus human behaviour, suggests that dramatic discoveries are just over the horizon. It dovetails neatly with our understanding of the role of fish in the evolutionary progress of *Homo sapiens*. After all, his success was surely due to the fact that he was not only clever but well adjusted too.

To recap on the brain front: essential fatty acids are necessary for optimal brain function, as they are the critical components of the neuron membranes (brain cell membranes). As we can't make fatty acids, the composition of our brains is determined by the types of fat we consume. The main dietary sources of the two types of essential fatty acid are seafood (for omega-3) and seed oils (for omega-6). For optimum biological functions, these two should be well balanced in our bodies.

Over the critical years of human evolution, the dietary ratio of omega-3 to omega-6 was generally a nice, even 1:1. But as we have turned our backs on our ancestors' diet, our consumption of omega-6 fatty acids has soared (sources include soy bean oil and corn oil as well as dairy products and red meat from grazing ruminants). In the modern Western diet, the average ratio now stands at somewhere between 15:1 to 25:1 in favour of omega-6. This staggering change cannot fail to have consequences for our brain health – and hence our mental well-being.

In 2001, a large study by Dr Antti Tanskanen and his colleagues at Finnish Psychiatric Services looked at fish consumption and depressive symptoms. It showed that the likelihood of both clinical depression and mild depressive episodes was significantly higher for those who rarely ate fish, compared to those who regularly did. It also suggested that the rise in depression rates generally might be due to the fact that our brains were built in the Paleolithic era, on a diet that offered roughly equal amounts of omega-3 and omega-6 oils. So, now that this ratio is way off kilter, our brains are prone to serious malfunction. Which is a compelling reason to eat oily fish!

And there's more. A deficiency in omega-3 oils has recently been linked to violent and criminal behaviour. In 2001, Dr Joseph Hibbeln of the United States Public Health Service published research that compared the murder rate in twenty-six different countries to local fish-eating habits. His study, 'Homicide Mortality Rates and Seafood Consumption', demonstrated that homicide rates decline as seafood consumption rises. In other words, if you eat plenty of omega-3-rich fish, you're statistically a lot less likely to kill someone.

Bernard Gesch, a senior research scientist at Oxford University, explored this idea further in a 2002 study. He enrolled 230 inmates from HM Young Offenders Institute in Aylesbury, Buckinghamshire, and divided them into two groups. Supplements that included essential fatty acids were given to one group, a placebo to the other. The researchers recorded the number of breached regulations and episodes of anti-social behaviour committed by each of the inmates in the nine months before they received the pills and in the nine months of the trial period. The group who had taken the supplements committed 25 per cent fewer offences than those who'd taken the placebo. The greatest reduction was in the number of serious offences, including violence, which fell by a staggering 40 per cent. There was no change in the behaviour of the group that took the placebo.

The results of this study suggest a probable link between anti-social behaviour and a diet that is deficient in essential fatty acids. There is clearly a compelling case that fish oil supplements make troublesome teens significantly less punchy. Making oily fish a regular item on the prison canteen menu can't be a bad plan either.

Nobody yet fully understands the reasons behind such results, but they have been consistently replicated in a whole range of studies in Europe and the United States. There certainly appears to be a relationship between a happy human brain and a diet rich in fish. This doesn't surprise us greatly. Eating fish has always made us happy – it's a spring-in-the-step kind of food. And it's good to know that scientists agree with us.

The athlete and the layabout

The difference in nutritional value between a portion of oily fish (a mackerel, say) and one of white fish (such as cod or plaice) is down to the contrasting lifestyles of these fish. The former are the long-distance runners of the ocean; the latter, frankly, its couch potatoes. These two extremes of fishy existence – constant motion versus 'just hanging out' – explain the marked difference in the physiologies of oily and white fish.

Oily fish are known as 'pelagic' (from the Greek *pelagos*, meaning ocean) because they travel far and wide. They not only swim over a considerable distance but also travel up and down the water column. They are on the move all day long, shoaling together at varying depths and across many miles, mainly in pursuit of food (while sometimes trying to avoid becoming it). It's a dynamic, high-energy existence, which requires a constant supply of fuel.

The energy these fish need is saturated throughout their body tissues in the form of oil, ready to burn. For those who eat them, getting all the goodness out of fish like mackerel is quite straightforward – it's all right there in the flesh. The reddish-brown muscle meat of oily fish is rich in blood that is in turn full of dissolved fats – you can see this in the shiny, slightly oily appearance of raw mackerel flesh. In fact, the proportion of oil contained in mackerel flesh varies throughout the year, depending on the quantity and quality of food they have been able to find. Early-spring mackerel that have endured a harsh, lean winter could contain as little as 5 per cent oil, while the plump, sprat-fed mackerel we often catch in abundance in late September ('jumbos', as we like to call them) are oozing goodness, with up to 30 per cent.

It's worth noting that the distribution of oil through the flesh of oily fish is not completely even. They have 'fat stores', which manifest themselves as a distinctly different type of flesh. The creamy pale meat that runs along the back and shoulders of a mackerel, for example, is oil-rich but not oil-saturated, while the red-brown flesh that lies directly beneath its skin on both flanks has higher concentrations of oil. This darker meat is a layer of concentrated fat, built up over the food-rich summer months to act as a long-term energy store.

Tuna, which is the most pelagic of all the pelagics, may in its lifetime swim a staggering 2 million miles – and many of those are travelled at over 30 miles per hour. (If fish *did* need bicycles, tuna would have all the latest Lycra gear – and no doubt a shiny canister of some isotonic drink mounted on the handlebars.) Tuna muscles are never at rest, and need constant fuelling – they are therefore completely saturated with blood and dissolved energy-rich oils. Hence they have the reddest flesh of any fish – and one of the most sought after for eating.

White fish, on the other hand, live their lives and store their oil very differently. They are known as 'demersal', because the area they inhabit, just above the seabed, is called the demersal zone (from the Latin *mergere, mersum* – to plunge or dive). Tidal currents and weather changes have little effect here; a pollack, haddock or cod can find a rock or wreck to hide behind and lead a relatively indolent life, simply waiting for food to be dragged past by the tide, or for smaller fish unwittingly to seek refuge near their lair. When they do move, it's in short, sharp bursts – they can pounce on prey or evade danger with phenomenal speed if they have to. But they can't keep up the pace for long.

The cod and its white-fleshed ilk keep most of their oil in their huge liver. Incidentally, in terms of omega-3, this oil is every bit as good as that of oily fish – it's just that to get at the oil, you need to get at the liver. Some white fish livers are more palatable than others – those of turbot and mullet, for example, are considered a delicacy (see page 315 for our mullet recipe), whereas those of the cod family are mostly somewhat bitter. Nonetheless, the oil has long been extracted from cod livers (and those of other members of the Gadidae family, especially ling) as a food supplement, and even as a fuel. Cod liver oil was known to benefit human health long before the modern buzz about omega-3s.

The distinction between oily and white fish is not entirely clear-cut. Some species are genuinely betwixt and between – most obviously the bass, bream and snapper (all members of the perch family). The rather unscientific term we use for them is 'semi-oily'. Their flesh looks white, or off-white, but you can tell from the taste and texture that it is richer in fish oil than that of the cod family, say, and most flatfish. You can also see, with bass in particular, those distinct areas of darker, fat-storing flesh along the lateral lines of the fish – they taste richer, too. In terms of balancing your fish consumption, there's a good case for ringing the changes between oily fish, white fish, and these in-betweenies. And if you, or your children, really find oily fish unpalatable (as some seem to), there's a good case for taking fish oil supplements.

Pollution

There's a fly in the oily fish ointment, however. The very oiliness that makes these fish such fine nutritional packages also makes them susceptible to a grievous man-made hazard: pollution. In recent years oily fish – and the oils found in white fish livers – have started to show traces of some worrying contaminants. These include dioxins (formed during the incineration of waste, as well as wood and coal), PCBs (polychlorinated biphenyls, once widely used in manufacturing electrical equipment) and brominated flame retardants (they don't sound much fun, do they?), as well as disturbingly high levels of heavy metals, including mercury. Let's not get too baffled by the scientific terminology, because there is one word that can describe all of these substances: poison.

These chemical effluents are coming back to haunt us – from polluted rivers, and rain that no longer cleanses but contaminates, they find their way into the sea and then into the food chain. They are absorbed by small fish, which are then eaten by larger fish, and so it goes on. PCBs and dioxin-like contaminants are lipophilic compounds – that is, they are at their most soluble in lipids (oils). No surprise, then, that high concentrations have been found in oily fish such as mackerel, sardines, tuna and salmon. Contaminants in the liver oil of large white fish can be removed, or reduced to harmless levels, through distillation, so if you're buying a reputable brand, you needn't worry about those cod liver oil capsules you've been taking. But no refining process will remove toxins from the oily flesh of pelagic fish.

This sorry state of affairs is why we are now advised by the Food Standards Agency (FSA) to limit our intake of oily fish to four portions a week – or two portions for pregnant women or those trying to conceive. It seems we can't be handed the good news about oily fish without being told, with a cuff round the ear from matron, not to overdo it. Because of pollution, we are being asked to keep our consumption of oily fish within 'safe levels'. If only we cleaned up our act, we could be eating this wonderful food with gay abandon.

Still, the overall advice from the Food Standards Agency is clear: the benefits of eating smaller oily fish (lower down in the food chain), such as mackerel, herring, sardines, salmon and trout, far outweigh the risks from the toxins.

Sadly, well-publicised anxieties over mercury levels have influenced some pregnant women to cut down or even cut out their intake of oily fish. However, continuing research shows that they are exactly the people who need to make sure they eat plenty of it. It's only big, top-of-the-food-chain fish such as swordfish, tuna and marlin, which may have accumulated relatively high levels of mercury, that should be completely avoided during pregnancy. So – if you're reading this and you're pregnant, please go and eat a mackerel *now*.

In a decade-long study of 9,000 British families as part of the Children of the 90s Project at Bristol University, Dr Joseph Hibbeln and his colleagues measured the amount of fish eaten by pregnant women and monitored the development of their children up to the age of eight. The results suggested that mothers whose fish consumption exceeded three portions a week had children who were more advanced socially, physically and verbally than the offspring of women who had eliminated fish from their diet while pregnant. Even given the possibility of other compounding factors, the results indicate that eating fish during pregnancy has long-term benefits for your children. The children of the no-fish mothers were 28 per cent more likely to have poor communication skills at 18 months old, 44 per cent more likely to have poor social behaviour at seven, and 48 per cent more likely to have low verbal IQs at eight. It's a daunting list of negatives. But keeping your children on the right side of the stats simply involves eating plenty of fish when you're pregnant. It's a straightforward step – although, if you're suffering from morning sickness, not necessarily an easy one. In this case, fish oil supplements offer a good alternative.

Frustratingly, as consumers, there's a limit to what we can do to help eliminate pollution from our seas, and our fish. But that doesn't mean we should give up. The FSA reports that levels of dioxins and PCBs in our food are falling (PCBs haven't been manufactured since the 1970s and are now banned worldwide). And there are choices we can make that will accelerate the departure of these toxins from our seas. Supporting cleaner industries, using ecological cleaning products, shopping locally and reducing our household waste will all make a difference. The chain from the pedal bin in your kitchen to the depths of the Atlantic is a long one – and all too easy to ignore. But that doesn't mean it isn't there.

Future sea science

Fish are not hard to see and not hard to catch. But there are other, microscopic, life forms under the sea and even under the seabed that may yet prove vital to our future. The more scientists discover about the famous 'primordial soup' that spawned life on earth, the more they reckon their findings could yet be harnessed for our benefit – particularly in the area of medicine. And the nearest thing on earth we have to the original soup is … the soup under the sea.

Those at the cutting edge of medical research are turning to sea mud and anticipating a whole raft of new discoveries. Until recently the pharmaceutical industry has relied on terrestrial micro-organisms called actinomycetes to manufacture life-saving antibiotic drugs such as penicillin. As terrestrial bacteria become increasingly resistant to existing antibiotics, researchers have searched the globe for new microbes. But the land-based microbial sources needed to produce effective new antibiotics have been dwindling alarmingly fast. It's time to look elsewhere. In research co-funded by the University of California and the pharmaceutical industry in 2002, microbiologists studied sediment samples taken from deep beneath the Pacific Ocean, the Red Sea and the Gulf of California. Bottom muds from up to a kilometre deep were found to contain up to one billion micro-organisms per cubic centimetre. From these, scientists have so far identified and studied over 100 different strains. Over 80 per cent of these produced molecules that inhibit cancer cell growth, while 35 per cent revealed the ability to destroy pathogenic bacteria and fungi. 'Never before has this level of biological activity been observed within a single group of organisms,' announced research group leader William Fenical, of the Center for Marine Biotechnology and Biomedicine in San Diego.

We scarcely understand the complexity and potential of these submarine muds, or our own influence on them. Yet there is no question that, by our hand, the marine environment is changing. Extracting vast quantities of life from it creates vacuums and imbalances; and pouring synthetic chemicals and waste materials into it must have consequences at the microscopic level. The oceanographer Sallie Chisholm, of the Massachusetts Institute of Technology, is researching the combined effect of global warming and human pollution on the marine environment – specifically how oceanic microbes react to changing sea temperatures and levels of nutrients. Her research shows that the microbial community of the sea is in a constant state of flux. It is made up of collections of mobile genes that interact to create unique combinations, depending on which microbes meet when, and under what conditions of temperature and sunlight.

These combinations of old and new genes are carried around by the mind-boggling number of viruses known to exist in seawater. Some viruses are good news, excellent news in fact, because when they infect the right microbes they create a fundamental and vital reaction – the bloom of a primitive group of photosynthesising organisms called prochlorococcus. This is the world's most abundant plankton species – the very first link in the marine food chain.

However, this good news story could take a very dark turn as a result of our meddling. According to Chisholm, these planktons could hardly be more fundamental, as they 'form an important part of the food chain in the oceans, supply some of the oxygen we breathe, and even play a role in modulating climate'. In other words, they help keep our planet on an even keel. Breaking any link in the food chain is bad enough (just look at what happens to salmon, cod and sea bass when you remove sand eels – see page 503), but taking away the very *first* link, the one that joins sunlight to sea life, would be a colossal cock-up of unimaginable consequences. But you wouldn't put it past us, would you?

If pollution was the only problem in the sea, some cautious optimism about the future might be in order. We are perhaps beginning the long and challenging process of cleaning up global industry. But there's another problem with the marine ecology, also of our own making, that runs even deeper and seems even harder to solve. It is a grim irony that our fish-built, fish-loving brains have applied themselves so thoroughly to the business of removing fish from the sea. We are now so good at it that in the case of some valuable marine species the prospect of 'total success' – i.e. extracting and killing every last one of them – is all too real. Quite how and why we are doing this, and how you as a consumer can make a difference, is the subject of the next chapter.

Sourcing fish

Like most anglers, we tend to jump for joy every time we catch a fish. And, as far as the cooking goes, we can wax lyrical till the herrings come home about the pleasures of a self-caught mackerel or a just-landed red mullet, the sweetness of a live scallop served raw, or the smoky aroma of squid over charcoal. Yet we know, in our heart of hearts, that the Big Picture doesn't look good. Our seas are in crisis. There is really no other way of putting it. According to the UN's Food and Agriculture Organisation, a quarter of the world's fish stocks are already overfished, while another half are being extracted at 'maximum biological capacity' – which basically means there is no buffer left for them between survival and eradication. They are on the brink.

In our UK fishery alone, the once seemingly inexhaustible cod stocks are close to total collapse. The common skate is as good as gone. For monkfish and bass, victims of food fashion and restaurant hype, the future is in the balance. Meanwhile, we are pouring pollutants into the ocean, wiping out whole marine habitats with destructive fishing methods, and killing countless other creatures we don't even want to eat – dolphins, turtles, albatross, to name the few we actually care about – all in our ravenous quest for more fish. How have we got ourselves into this awful mess?

In the name of 'progress'

In the past, our capacity to impact on the fish population was limited by the relative simplicity of the methods we were able to use to catch them. But today, sophisticated new methods are challenging the very concept of limits. The advances made in commercial fishing over the last few decades have been nothing short of revolutionary.

After the Second World War, the British fishing fleet (like everyone else's) was in tatters. Ancient, steam-driven tubs were all we had left – and since many of these had been requisitioned for the war effort they were in a pretty sorry state. However, since the war had all but put a stop to serious offshore fishing, the fish stocks in the North Atlantic were in excellent shape. A brave new fleet of fishing vessels was built to target these marine riches – and it was able to tap into much of the state-of-the-art technology that the conflict had spawned. All manner of military engineering was taken up by the industry. Notably, there was the Royal Navy's new echo-sounding technology, which delivered detailed three-dimensional images of the seabed, and enabled fishermen to detect vast shoals beneath their very feet. By the 1990s, affordable GPS sat-nav systems allowed any old boat to equip itself with a satellite-powered plotter that could guide it to any spot on the globe and record the exact position of successful hauls.

And so, twentieth-century fishermen were able to hunt top-grade fish with unprecedented success. Engines got faster, fuel got cheaper (and subsidised), weather forecasting became increasingly accurate, and the fishing industry entered what seemed like a golden age. The new boats could not only travel further and fish for longer than ever before, they could also fish much deeper. Dragging their gear at depths of 1,000 metres and more, they were able to exploit a whole new world of deep-dwelling fish. The sheer volume of fish that the new vessels could catch and process must have seemed like a cause for celebration. But as technology surged forward, our understanding of its effect on the marine environment lagged behind, with fatal consequences.

The trawlers' extraordinary effectiveness gave rise to a concept hitherto undreamed of: overfishing. It is simple enough. Reduce a population below a certain level (known as its 'biological limit') and it will lose the ability to reproduce itself. Every different species has what would now be called a 'tipping point'. The dwindling shoals reach a critical lower limit at which the odds are suddenly stacked massively against them. Finding each other, breeding successfully and ensuring that a significant number of young survive becomes first hard, then impossible. Species such as cod have already reached this crisis point in many areas, and plenty more are being pushed towards it.

It's not just the number of fish we catch that has damaged the health of our oceans, it's also the way we catch them. Fish are part of a highly complex ecosystem that can be harmed – even destroyed – by insensitive fishing methods. The industry euphemism for this style of fishing is 'non-selective' – but what it means is 'indiscriminate'. In the pursuit of a valued food fish, the collateral damage to other species can be immense. The (distinctly un-euphemistic) industry phrase for these is 'trash fish' – because they are literally thrown away. But mammals and birds too find themselves in the way of many commercial techniques worldwide. Even those so-called 'dolphin-friendly', 100km-long tuna long-lines still manage to snare turtles, seabirds and sharks.

There is one fishing method that perhaps more than any other symbolises the way our appetite for fish has outstripped our common sense. Beam trawling is a technique used extensively in the North Atlantic fisheries to catch bottom-dwelling 'demersal' fish (see page 21), including some particularly valuable species such as sole and monkfish. A heavy iron beam, up to 10 metres long, carries heavy chains that are dragged along the bottom to flush out fish on and under the soft seabed and scare them up into the trawl net that follows behind. Hauling the chains across miles of sea floor can be extremely destructive, ploughing up a delicate habitat of weeds and soft corals, and scooping up all manner of bottom-dwelling sea creatures such as crabs, anemones and starfish. The catch is dumped on the deck for sorting, and anything up to three-quarters of it may be discarded – dead.

Greenpeace has long been calling for a total ban on beam trawling, which it sees as a threat to one of the planet's last great strongholds of biodiversity. Its website invites us to 'think of it as driving a huge bulldozer through an unexplored, lush and richly populated forest – and being left with a flat, featureless desert'. Public awareness of the issue is gathering momentum, and in 2006 Waitrose took a lead on behalf of the consumer when it decided to stop selling beam-trawled fish in its stores.

It's easy to demonise the fishermen who practise beam trawling. But we should perhaps remember that in the 1970s, when it was first developed, the technique was viewed as a state-of-the-art solution to the challenge of catching bottom-dwelling fish. It was applauded as an efficient and highly productive method, and beam trawlers, working their new machinery in challenging conditions, were the brave pioneers of the fishing fleet. Back then, no one was really aware of the conservation issues. Thirty years later, however, scientists are measuring the destruction that beam trawling has wreaked on the seabed, and the alarm bells are clanging. It must be gutting for today's beam trawlers to be cast as the 'bad guys', when their forerunners were the heroes of the industry. Nonetheless, even they are starting to accept that their methods must be refined if beam trawling is ever to play a part in a sustainable fishery.

If we continue to mismanage our fisheries, we could effectively empty the oceans. One 2006 study by an international team of scientists even predicted a marine doomsday scenario, citing the year 2048 as the end of the line for all commercial fishing, full stop. Led by Dr Boris Worm, assistant professor in marine conservation biology at Dalhousie University in Nova Scotia, the group concluded: 'Our analyses suggest that business as usual would foreshadow serious threats to global food security, coastal water quality, and ecosystem stability, affecting current and future populations.'

Their report emphasises that the decimation of fish populations is not only disastrous for the marine ecosystem but also devastating for the human race. Worldwide, over 20 million people are employed in fishing at sea, and a billion rely on fish as their primary source of protein. If we don't look after the astonishing resources that the ocean offers us, the consequences will be grim. Not just grim in the sense that we won't be able to eat rare tuna steaks or battered cod again: grim in that we'll be faced with environmental, social and economic collapse on a global scale.

This may sound like scaremongering, but the scary precedent happened right on the research team's own doorstep. The collapse of the Grand Banks cod fishery is a classic example of how greed, political ineptness, consistent dismissal of the scientific evidence and procrastination all caused the total collapse of a 400-year-old industry that had provided a living for fishermen and fish processors in countries all around the world (see page 426).

The dreaded CFP

So, surely there must be official mechanisms to prevent the seas from commercial abuse? Measures set in law to protect our oceans and the fish that swim in them? Well, yes, there are. The problem is, they don't work.

All members of the European Union are subject to the 1983 Common Fisheries Policy (CFP). This is an agreement that aims to protect stocks from overfishing by placing an internationally agreed limit on the numbers of certain species – those considered to be under most pressure – that can be caught each year. Besides these annual 'quotas', as they are known, there are rules about the kind of gear that can be used (such as the mesh size of nets), minimum landing sizes for certain species and the amount of time allowed at sea. These rules and regulations are enforced by a clipboard-wielding inspectorate that is empowered to scrutinise catches as they are landed, enter fish processing plants and even board fishing boats at sea.

Unfortunately, it is no exaggeration to say that just about every fisherman, marine scientist and conservation campaigner from the Shetlands to the Scillies *hates* the CFP. No one trusts it; very few people within the fishing industry or even the European Parliament fully understand it. Both trade and conservation bodies see it as an unmitigated mess that is signally failing to protect our fish or, indeed, our fishermen. It is also incredibly complex. We could completely lose you, and ourselves, in the myriad contradictions and questions it provokes, but rather than tie ourselves in knots of bureaucratic red tape, we'll just highlight a few of the failings of the CFP.

How the system is supposed to work is as follows. The CFP identifies the commercially valuable species available in the overall EU fishery and then sets 'total allowable catches' (TACs). For species under particular pressure, these 'totals' are then divided into individual national quotas – each nation, in effect, is told the maximum tonnage it is allowed to land. These figures are – in theory, anyway – recommended by the scientific advisers to the EU, in the form of a body called the International Council for the Exploration of the Sea (ICES). This independent panel assesses fish populations, estimates stock sizes and proposes a sustainable TAC. So far, so good. But the theory of quotas is very hard to implement alongside the stress of international politics and the pressure of global business. In order to smooth over tensions between member states, the European Commission is allowed to adjust the scientifically recommended quotas to take on board what are known as 'socio-economic concerns'. The revised numbers are then presented to the fisheries ministers of each member state, who, after making their own further adjustments (which are almost always upwards), will set the actual quotas for their fishermen.

Those member states with massive investment in commercial fishing, such as the Spanish, Portuguese and French, have a huge vested interest in keeping political control of the seas. 'This is where the system breaks down,' says Dr Tom Pickerell, fisheries policy officer for WWF, the global conservation organisation. 'The ministers are not accountable to anyone. They can ignore all the advice if they so choose. We've analysed the quotas for the last fifteen years and they are, on average, thirty per cent higher than the ICES has recommended. Ministers are heavily influenced by sustained lobbying from the fishing industries within member states.' These fishing lobbies are far too powerful, and the politicians who wish to appease them simply ride roughshod over the ICES's recommendations.

The scandal of 'high-grading'

A system of quotas for pressurised species sounds sensible, even vital. But quotas have serious drawbacks, which can backfire on the very species they set out to protect. Jim Portus, head of the South Western Fish Producer Organisation, gives his view: 'Quotas have encouraged the race to fish and have done nothing for fisheries conservation. I can think of no reasons for praising them.'

The quotas relate to the quantity of fish that can be landed (as opposed to caught), and one of their greatest flaws is that they encourage the practice known as 'high-grading' – which is industry-speak for throwing lower-value fish back into the sea in order to boost the cash value of one's quota. If a fisherman is only allowed to land a certain tonnage of a species, he will want to make sure that those he brings in are the most valuable specimens possible. That usually means the biggest ones, as well as those in pristine condition.

So, for example, say you are a fisherman with a quota for one tonne of cod – or, to make it easier to explain, say you are allowed to catch a hundred cod on a particular day. You haul your net and find you've hit a hot spot – you catch your entire quota in one haul. Great. But half the cod are on the small side, so you decide to trawl again to see if the cod are still beneath you. They are! So you pull on board another great net of fish, most of them much better than the first haul. What do you do? It's obvious: you chuck back the smaller fish from the first haul and replace them with the best of your second haul. Your catch is now made up of big, high-value fish. But what if you trawl just once more? You might get some even bigger fish... And so it goes on.

The CFP is in effect compelling fishermen to high-grade. Many skippers find this practice appalling, but there's no advantage in refusing to high-grade as they know that most of the other boats are doing it anyway; on the contrary, they'll only lose out. But by the time a trawler returns to port after a day's high-grading, which was carried out perfectly legally, it will have killed and discarded several times more fish than its intended share of the quota. 'The CFP brings out the worst of human nature,' says Jim Portus, 'because it provides a strong incentive to throw back into the sea any fish that would waste the precious quota.'

The farce of zoning

Another area of the CFP that is in a painfully bureaucratic mess is the system of zoning that determines which country is allowed to fish where. All European waters are governed by the CFP – even the waves lapping our toes on Chesil Beach are legislated by Brussels. Each member state has its very own 'exclusion zone', extending six nautical miles from its coast. In this six-mile zone, each nation is obliged to enforce the overall regulations set by the CFP, but it can also choose to add extra regulations, over and above those directed by Brussels. The six-mile exclusion zone was devised in order to stop vessels from other states fishing in these waters and to enable the protection of inshore waters with legislation that is sensitive to specific local needs.

Between six and twelve nautical miles out to sea there exists another zone, in which not just the local vessels are allowed to fish but other nations may have 'historic fishing rights'. Belgian boats, for instance, have a legal right to catch fish in the Thames Estuary; British fishermen work in Belgian waters too. Within the twelve-mile zone, the local state has the right to enforce extra legislation upon its own boats, but not those of the sanctioned foreign visitors. This can give rise to some ridiculous situations, in which local fishermen are not allowed to catch fish in their own waters but foreign boats can come in and help themselves.

A flagrant example occurred in the Southwest bass pair-trawling fishery in 2004. Pair trawling is a highly effective way of catching large shoals of fish in huge nets strung between two trawlers (a 'pair'). Recognising that pair trawling often results in a large bycatch of dolphins and porpoises, the UK fisheries minister of the time, Ben Bradshaw, banned the British fleet from pair trawling within the twelve-mile zone off the Southwest coast. He then asked the Commission to extend this ruling to all EU boats, some of which have historic rights in this twelve-mile zone. But, bowing to pressure from the powerful French fishing lobby, it was decided that the directive should remain voluntary. So now French and Spanish boats continue to pair trawl for bass in our waters while British boats may not. It is not hard to see how bitterness brews between nations.

'The law is so complicated in this area that no one really knows what's going on,' says WWF's Dr Tom Pickerell. 'We think countries should have full control in their own twelve-mile zone. Beyond twelve miles, blanket CFP rules should apply.' We agree. Increasing a nation's control of its waters from six to twelve nautical miles would pave the way for a much-needed simplification of the rules about who fishes where and when, using which methods. The benefits would be felt in *all* European inshore waters, because it would allow for genuinely constructive local zoning and fallowing policies, steered by the local fisheries themselves, that really could help build and protect stocks.

These examples illustrate what any fisherman will tell you: the CFP doesn't work because member states wield far too much individual power within it. Apply the right pressure in the right places, or use your lobbyists wisely, and you can wriggle out of any rules that don't suit your fleet. Not only are the CFP's benefits to European fish stocks questionable, it also fosters a counterproductive and often downright ugly culture at sea, and in ports and harbours around the Union.

The fact remains, however, that the CFP is here to stay, at least for the near future. Some argue that it's better than nothing. Dr Cat Dorey, oceans researcher for Greenpeace, says that while it clearly needs a radical overhaul, we shouldn't abandon the CFP altogether: 'If nothing else, it gives us the opportunity to hold some of the most irresponsible fishing nations to account. We can learn from other countries too. Iceland, for instance, has a lot of good policies. These include a "no discarding" law, where everything that's caught must be landed. It puts paid to high-grading, as well as giving fisheries scientists a much better idea of what is actually being caught out at sea.'

So, to make the best of a bad job, we need to apply our muscle within the CFP as hard as we possibly can – and, as you'll read below, some groups of fishermen and activists are already managing to take very positive steps in the right direction, in spite of the odds stacked against them by current fisheries policy.

Some good news

'What's all this got to do with me?' you might be thinking. 'I only *shop* for fish, I don't catch them!' But remember, change does not have to come from the top down. As our political leaders fail to make a positive difference or even reach basic agreements between themselves, non-government organisations and campaign groups such as WWF and Greenpeace have stepped into the 'action vacuum'. They, more than any government, are focusing the arguments and fostering a dialogue with the consumer – all those of us who shop for fish – in the knowledge that our power, constructively harnessed, really could make a difference.

It would be easy to conclude that the current situation is so hopeless that we might as well give up eating fish altogether – or gorge ourselves on what's left while we still can. But there's more than a glimmer of hope on the horizon: there is concrete evidence that public information and concerted consumer action can play a genuine role in halting the decline of threatened species and environments and helping them to thrive again.

Slowly but surely, it's becoming easier for consumers to choose fish from sustainable, well-managed stocks. Producers and retailers have realised that it's no good simply doing the right thing, they've got to shout about it too. So, the label on your fish may now give you valuable information about how and where it was caught. By choosing such certified products over anonymous fish of unspecified origins, you are voting for better, more sustainable practice at sea.

The MSC

At the forefront of this move for clear information is the Marine Stewardship Council (MSC). This international charity promotes the certification of sustainable fisheries around the world. The 'pass' or 'fail' for a given fishery is based on an independently assessed environmental standard that measures stock levels, the fishery's impact on the marine environment and its future management plan. Any certification is purely voluntary, applied for by the fishery or local council – fisheries pursue it because they believe it will help give them a future. Certified fisheries can proudly display the MSC eco-label and logo on their products, which immediately makes them more attractive to many retailers and their customers.

There are some inspiring examples of British fisheries that have been granted MSC certification, and they are reaping financial benefits as well as conservation brownie points. They include the South West Mackerel Handline Fishery, the Hastings Fleet Dover Sole Fishery, the Burry Inlet Cockle Fishery and the Loch Torridon Nephrops (Dublin Bay Prawn) Creel Fishery. As we write, many fisheries in the UK are currently undergoing the assessment process; visit msc.org for the latest details. And wherever you buy your fish, you should start looking out for the MSC label.

At the moment, the MSC's scheme pretty much stands alone in the breadth of its application and its ease of use. There are some other, more localised, labelling initiatives that we applaud too; the South West Handline Fishermen's Association, for instance, tags all its line-caught pollack and bass so that consumers can find out when and by whom it was caught. But there is scope for far more extensive and informative labelling of fish. We don't think it's overstating the case to say that it could deliver a monumental boost to fish conservation all around the world. The time is right to kick-start a virtuous circle: the more positive choices, with ecological upsides, that can be offered to the consumer, the better.

More friends of fish

The MSC is not the only non-government organisation blazing a trail for sustainable fishing. The Marine Conservation Society (MCS), for instance, is a UK charity dedicated to the conservation of our seas and seashores. Despite their teasingly similar acronyms, the two organisations have a different emphasis, the MSC being focused on promoting more sustainable practices within the industry, and the MCS on raising awareness of marine conservation issues.

The MCS campaigns on everything from clean beaches to endangered turtles, and its website, fishonline.org, is a fantastic resource for anyone worried about the provenance of the fish they eat. It gives clear information on the conservation status of over 150 fish and shellfish species and products, with helpful 'fish to eat' and 'fish to avoid' lists. The MCS has given us invaluable assistance in our research, and you'll see its sustainability scores alongside the different species we profile in the third part of this book.

As you'd expect, WWF, being the world's largest conservation organisation, is heavily involved in marine campaigning too. It tends to operate behind the scenes and its work includes engaging with supermarkets to improve fish sourcing and influencing governments on policy initiatives. It's been a crucial catalyst for the ground-breaking Invest in Fish South West initiative that we'll come to soon.

For a more 'direct action' approach, the Greenpeace campaigns against marine pollution and overfishing are beacons of well-organised, passionate defiance. Along with newer groups such as Bite-Back, which has a particular focus on shark conservation, they are leading the fight against overtly destructive fishing practices. You will find contact details for all these groups in the Directory (see page 592).

Proof that conservation measures can work comes courtesy of the beleaguered monkfish. Let's make one thing clear. We are *not* recommending that you rush out and start buying monkfish willy nilly – many stocks are still precarious – but we feel optimistic that the advice might change in the not too distant future. By the end of the 1990s, most monkfish stocks were near collapse. Now these extraordinary creatures seem to be making tentative steps towards recovery in a few areas (see page 493), owing to tough measures taken by some fisheries. These have included the decommissioning of fishing vessels, reduced quotas and the establishment of protected areas.

Another fish that has benefited from similar measures is haddock. Once in a state almost as parlous as that of cod, its North Sea stocks are currently better than they have been for twenty years (see page 434). Both haddock and monkfish have recently been removed from the MCS's 'fish to avoid' list (though in some fisheries monkfish still scores a worrying 5).

This is a direct result of successful conservation measures and consumer pressure. Dr Bryce Beukers-Stewart, fisheries policy officer for the MCS, says: 'Over the last two years the consumer's ability to influence the sustainability of seafood, and indeed the management of fisheries, has really come to the fore.' He cites the example of Icelandic cod, the quotas for which were recently cut by a third. The Icelandic fisheries minister publicly stated that the prime motivation behind this radical move was to maintain Iceland's reputation as a source of sustainable fish for the British export market. Bryce concludes: 'This is the holy grail of the sustainable seafood movement – collective individual actions are now influencing international fisheries' management measures, and ultimately helping sustain the long-term future of our fish stocks and marine environment.'

Fish farming: the problems

Fish farming might seem like the perfect answer to the problem of plummeting fish stocks – but too often it's not, because as it turns out, it creates more ecological problems than it solves. Creating fish life in a laboratory is no longer the challenge it once was: men in white coats are now able to simulate the complex spawning processes of sought-after species, including salmon, halibut, cod, sea bass, sea trout, bream and prawns. Even the mysteries of the eel's extraordinary migratory transmogrification have been unlocked from the depths of the Sargasso Sea (see page 528).

As three decades of intensive salmon farming have shown, captive fish can be raised for market in staggering quantities. Yet, ecologically speaking, the process is fraught with difficulties: the correct location of farms, the source of the farms' feed, the waste the fish excrete, the chemicals used for treating their diseases and the fish that escape into the wild – all these are problems that have dogged the fish farming industry ever since it began, and remain a huge source of anxiety.

The main business of farming fish is feeding them – and most, being piscivores, require a constant diet of other fish in order to grow big and fat themselves. The staple diet of captive fish is 'fish meal', and it is a huge irony that this is mostly made from wild fish: species such as blue whiting, Norwegian pout, capelin and sand eel (see page 503) that have little or no value for human consumption. These are hoovered from the waters in vast quantities, in a practice known as 'industrial fishing', then turned into fish meal pellets. Inevitably this deprives already threatened wild fish of a much-needed source of protein. And it is not very efficient either: according to WWF, it takes more than three tonnes of wild fish flesh, in pellet form, to create just one tonne of farmed salmon.

After the fundamental problem of where to source their food, comes (inevitably) the ugly issue of where to put their crap. There's an awful lot of it, and without sufficient tidal flow or water depth to flush out the effluent, a fish farm can quickly wreak havoc on the local marine environment. Some sea lochs, inlets and coastal bays have seen their biodiversity crash after years of being smothered by impenetrable layers of salmon excrement. These 'mulch out' the natural flora and fauna of the sea floor to create a marine desert. They can also spread toxins to surrounding sea life – scallop fisheries along the west coast of Scotland have been suspended over the summer months for several years in succession owing to dangerous toxic algal blooms, believed by many to have been caused by fish-farm waste.

The seabed can recover from such accumulations, and in good farms a system of fallowing is used, whereby fish cages are left empty for certain periods. Siting fish farms appropriately is critical too, and can go a long way to reducing the risks. But as with all intensive farming, the commercial pressures militate in favour of corner cutting and keeping things the way they are. There are still too many fish farms that need to clean up their act.

When you farm fish, you are at the mercy of the elements – storms and high seas will inevitably cause structural damage to cages, which will lead to fish escaping. Farmed salmon escape into the wild in astonishing numbers. In 2005, almost a million salmon were reported to have escaped from salmon farms on the west coast of Scotland. Breakouts on this scale mean that farmed salmon here may outnumber wild stocks by a factor of ten – or even, in locations close to the biggest escapes, a hundred or more.

On the run, these fugitives are free to mingle with their wild brethren. Some escapees will make it into local rivers, where they can interbreed with wild stocks. But the tame salmon dilute the wild strains, creating hybrids that are less well adapted to the challenges of the open sea. They are highly unlikely to return to the rivers and breed again (they lack that essential and mysterious homing instinct). So a wild female that mates with an escaped male is effectively wasting her eggs, and her genes, for that year at least.

Escaped farm fish will also transmit diseases and parasites to wild salmon – as indeed may fish that stay in their cages. Sea lice are blood-sucking parasites that exist at generally non-threatening levels among wild sea fish populations. They are attracted to large concentrations of captive salmon and powerful chemicals are needed to kill them (usually substances that are not permitted in any other form of food production). The fall-out from these lice-exterminating treatments inevitably affects the surrounding ecosystem, killing a whole spectrum of other invertebrate aquatic life, from shrimps to anemones – creatures that many other sea dwellers rely on as food. Yet if the lice aren't treated with something toxic, not only do the farmed fish become infested but local wild fish are likely to be attacked too.

Fish farming: the possibilities

Fish farming is by no means an ecologically doomed endeavour. It still has the potential to produce fish of marketable quality in a sustainable way, and thereby give our wild fish populations a chance to recover. While examples of poor fish farming practice are all too easy to find, many fish farmers are getting their act together.

We've looked in particular at the problems of salmon farming, but some other forms of fish farming are intrinsically less intensive and less damaging. Most shellfish farming is fairly benign. Mussels, scallops and oysters need remarkably little intervention to grow successfully, as they will feed on whatever is already in the water. The farming of these bivalves involves capturing them when they are young and relocating them to a good growing site. In the case of mussels, if you choose the right site, simply providing the structures on which they can thrive will do the trick. The seed mussels will arrive of their own accord, and even create a useful habitat and nursery for other species into the bargain (see page 569).

Some freshwater fish species have the potential to be farmed with less environmental impact than sea fish. Carp, for instance, offer an opportunity for enlightened aquaculture. It may be a fringe form of fish farming right now, but it has fantastic potential for the future. Being omnivorous, these fish do not require the fish-based pellet diet of farmed salmon; instead, they will happily graze on pond vegetation, algae, zooplankton and waterbugs. All of these can be encouraged to thrive in the carp's natural environment. Supplementary feeds, such as corn or compost worms, can be produced cheaply and sustainably on site. So, the farmer is farming the feed as well as the fish, which is a pretty holistic approach. Incidentally, organic trout farming (see page 519) is based on a similarly sustainably model, where the feed is mostly natural, or at least produced on site.

In the same way that meat and vegetables are increasingly produced on small-scale farms and sold through farmers' markets, we feel there is huge potential for organic freshwater 'microfisheries' to raise modest crops of high-quality fish. It could be done with trout, carp, perch or even crayfish (provided they could be contained – see page 546). These freshwater species were once a proud part of our fish culture – and they could be again. So how about a freshwater fish box scheme? If there was one down the road, we would sign up quicker than a pike can pounce.

Even the farming of salmon *can* be done well. Better siting of farms, regular fallowing of cages and minimising of chemical inputs are the goals of a new breed of conscientious salmon farmer. Regulating the origins of the feed source has to be next on the agenda. The Soil Association has recently granted organic status to a handful of salmon farms in Scotland, based on their lower inputs and stocking densities and the sourcing of sustainable feed. The feed comes from the fish processing industry, whose leftover skeletons and fish off-cuts are 'recycled' to create fish meal without killing wild fish. There is also at least one organic cod farm, in Shetland, that now sources its feed similarly.

So, the problems of fish farming can be solved. The know-how is there for modern aquaculturists to fulfil our demand for certain fish without wreaking havoc on the environment. If this is going to happen, then the consumer must want it to happen. And that means choosing the *right* farmed fish...

Sourcing well-farmed fish

There are plenty of farms from which we would never wish to buy our meat. Five minutes in a badly run pig farm is quite long enough to tell you all you need to know about the welfare of the animals. A visit to a badly run fish farm would put you off too. The heavy smell of ammonia, the litter of feed bags, water speckled with scum, and upturned dead fish in and around the cages… You'd know it wasn't right in a minute, and be out of there in two.

Many farmers these days make a point of telling you or even showing you just how 'happy' their animals are during their lifetime, and supermarkets now display posters (of questionable veracity) of livestock contentedly grazing on lush green meadows – or at least of happy smiling farmers. But with farmed fish it's different. Sometimes a farmed fish will be labelled with some indication of its provenance – including perhaps some certification, such as the Soil Association organic logo or the RSPCA Freedom Foods logo (which indicates a limit on stocking densities). But much farmed salmon and trout is still presented fairly anonymously: all too often we know nothing of their lives before they reach the fishmonger's slab or the restaurant plate.

You're looking for fish from farms that are well sited and less intensively stocked, but in the absence of clear labelling you need to make your decision about whether or not to buy a farmed fish based largely on forensics – i.e. what its corpse can tell you. Seeing a whole dead fish is always going to tell you more about your potential dinner's life history than a couple of abstract fillets from which vital clues have already been removed.

If a farmed fish is sold without fins, tail or head, it's impossible to tell much about its past life (and you have to ask yourself why the fish was dismantled before display). A short, rounded tail is not a good sign. It is likely to have been worn down by rubbing continually against the nylon netting of its holding pen. Fins can also be rounded off, stubby or even scarred and bleeding, if the fish has been kept in overcrowded nets. There may be further signs of stress on the fish's nose. If you can see blotches or tufts of white peeling skin, then it's fair to assume it's been butting its head against other fish, and the restraining net of its cage.

As you'd expect, the good indicators are the opposite of the bad ones. Faster-flowing water from well-sited farms makes for more active, less stressed fish, which are less inclined to net rub. The wider and squarer the tail and the more developed the fins, the more active and less restricted the fish must have been. And the cleaner its nose, the less it has been butting the net and its brethren.

With salmon, trout and sea trout, the colour of the flesh reflects their diet. Wild Atlantic salmon generally have pale orange-pink flesh, coloured by the natural carotenoids in the prawns and other shellfish from their migratory feeding grounds near Greenland. But farmed salmon don't feed on crustaceans; based on their pellet diet alone, their flesh would naturally be beige or dull white. It has long been assumed that white salmon would be a marketing disaster, and so the industry has always added a dye to the feed that transforms the colour of the flesh. You can literally choose the colour you would like your fish to be from a colour swatch supplied by the feed company. Such dyes are not allowed in organic fish farming, where instead they use feeds that contain natural extracts of prawn shell. Organically farmed salmon flesh looks less appealing in comparison to dyed fish, but less colour does not mean less flavour. It is simply a more natural product.

Aside from the colour of the flesh, you should assess its texture too. The cut flesh of a farmed salmon should not look too oily – if it does, this suggests that the fish has grown too fast and exercised too little. The 'striations' – lines of white fat that run between the muscles – are another lifestyle indicator. They should be neither too white nor too wide, and are something to look out for in smoked as well as raw fish.

The future for farms

One of the main challenges for fish farming now is to achieve a healthy balance in the relationship between captive fish and wild. Aquaculture shouldn't just be a way to compensate consumers for a lack of wild fish; it should be an industry that enhances and supplements wild fish stocks, not one that bangs another nail in their coffin.

There are no black and white answers: even organic fish farming is not a simple solution. (Organic salmon farms don't seem to be any better at stopping their fish from escaping, for instance, so they still have an impact on the wild population.) But thankfully the challenges are starting to be met. In Scotland, particularly, a much more healthy dialogue between farmed and wild fish interests is now going on, with fish farm technology being adapted to help with wild fish breeding and release projects.

Well-chosen farmed fish definitely have a place in the shopping basket of the eco-conscious fish lover – but perhaps in a supporting role to wild-caught fish from sustainable sources, rather than as an outright replacement for it. After all, a wild female cod can lay up to four hundred million eggs in her lifetime. Left unmolested, in the right habitat, such wild fish can reproduce far more quickly and safely than we could ever farm them. They already have the biological equipment to fill the seas with fish, if only we would allow them to do it.

Global changes in opinion and practices often start with relatively small, local actions and it's at this level that we feel that time and energy could most usefully be directed here in the UK. With farmed fish, as with all farmed flesh, consumers are in a position to dictate the practice of farmers by the choices they make. Buy higher-welfare, organic and/or sustainably fed fish and these types of farming will gain a greater share of the market. Say no to cheap, flabby, anonymous farmed salmon – the piscine equivalent of factory-farmed chicken – and those producers will soon get the message too.

When it comes to sourcing wild fish, the same logic applies – if you only buy fish that have been sustainably sourced you cast a vote for good practice in the industry. Such votes accumulate, and lead in time to real change – bad systems will be given up in favour of better new ones (or even better old ones). But in order to cast your vote effectively, you will need to know a little about the way fish are caught in our seas.

The fishing fleet

Our domestic fleet is engaged in three main types of fishing: offshore, coastal and inshore. They're all well represented and familiar to us here in the Southwest. Our offshore fleet mostly comprises big trawlers that fish alongside French and

Spanish fleets in common European waters. Our coastal fleet is made up of smaller trawlers, scallop dredgers and large-scale crab potters – again, sharing their fishing with the rest of Europe. In both cases, fishing practice comes under the auspices of the CFP, which, as we've seen, is fraught with painful problems.

Meanwhile, the inshore fleet is made up of what are called 'polyvalent vessels' – the ones we see mostly in small harbour towns such as West Bay and Lyme Regis. These Jack-of-all-boats, normally around 10 metres long, adapt their techniques to suit the season and the target fish. These guys do a bit of everything, from potting to line fishing to seasonal sardine netting and static bottom netting. The inshore fleet is ours to shape and mould, in that it operates largely in the six-nautical-mile exclusion zone, where only UK-registered vessels are allowed to fish (see page 32). While we have to abide by the standard CFP rules that relate to all inshore fisheries in the European Union, we do have the opportunity to add extra measures to provide further protection for local fish stocks and local fishermen. So, if we want to make progress, surely this is the place to start?

However, if you spent any time hanging around harbourside, eavesdropping on the banter of your average West Country fisherman, you could be excused for believing there was a civil war raging in our inshore waters. Trawlers moaning about potters (always setting their gear in the 'wrong' place); potters moaning about trawlers and dredgers (always 'ploughing over' their pots); scallop dredgers moaning about scallop divers ('only taking the big ones'); and divers moaning about… well, just about everyone really. And so it goes on. All fishermen have a well-developed sense of grievance. It comes with the yellow oilskins.

But consumers can feel frustrated too. We constantly bemoan the fact that buying locally caught fish isn't nearly as easy as it should be. In fact, sometimes it seems almost impossible, even when you live near a port where fresh fish is regularly landed. Many coastal fishmongers, and restaurants too, find the daily vagaries of buying from the local fleet too time-consuming, and source all their fish through big markets such as Billingsgate, Brixham or Grimsby, or through the larger networked wholesalers. It's particularly dispiriting to tuck into a West Country fish supper, while actually looking out to sea, in the near certain knowledge that your fish has been driven to Brixham and back in a 48-hour 'unfreshening' round trip before being cooked and sold. Often the only solution is to buy straight from the boat yourself, which is highly satisfying for those who can manage it, but hardly practical for everybody.

However, there are encouraging signs that the political and commercial will to turn the fish situation around is genuinely there – particularly here in the Southwest. Aside from the work of conservation bodies such as the MCS, other interested parties are beginning to pool resources and come up with some practical solutions to our current crisis. A great local example is the Invest in Fish South West (IiFSW) initiative, completed in Plymouth in June 2007.

Finding a way forward

Fishermen have felt increasingly under pressure in recent years. They yo-yo from hero to zero in public perception, one day applauded for the sheer courage of their endeavours, the next vilified as dolphin killers. The quota system has often driven them to practices no good fisherman feels comfortable with, like high-grading (see page 31) or discarding bycatch. They more than anyone are ready for a change.

The IiFSW project was spawned by the climate of general discontent among fish producers and processors in the Southwest. Vitally, it has strived to bring the fishermen and their organisations on board right from the very start, as shapers of future policy, not merely recipients of the latest CFP edicts. And so it is unapologetic about taking commercial as well as ecological considerations into account. The steering group comprises a mixture of 'stakeholders' from all areas of the local and national fish industry. Fishermen, traders, retailers, restaurateurs, including a sushi chain, supermarkets, conservationists and recreational sea angler associations are all represented, and the project was co-funded through, among others, DEFRA (Department for Environment, Food and Rural Affairs), the South West Regional Development Agency and WWF.

'The concept of bringing traditionally opposing parties together to discuss common goals and seek joint solutions works – and it can translate to any fishery,' says Dr Tom Pickerell of WWF. 'Once we've actually agreed on what we all want, finding the solutions is often relatively painless.' One positive change that has emerged from the IiFSW initiative is what's known as the Trevose Closure. This refers to an agreement between local fishermen to avoid fishing off the Trevose Head area of north Cornwall during early spring, when large numbers of spawning fish are known to gather. This seasonal aggregation of fish is vital in the life cycle of a number of key Southwest species – particularly sea bass. It's a small step, but one that proves that fishermen and conservationists can work together – and one that begs to be replicated all around our coast.

But it won't always be that easy, as different interests continue to pull in different directions. The IiFSW approach is to recognise this, and to forge a path by intelligent negotiations between all parties. A good illustration is the way it is addressing the thorny problem of beam trawling (see page 29). The irony of this much criticised fishing method is that, despite the destruction it wreaks on the sea floor, it is able to deliver up some of the species that marine conservation groups are telling us to eat more of. Take megrim, for example. This sole-like fish, which lives on the seabed, partly buried in silt, is delicious to eat; what's more, all the conservation bodies agree that it's in good shape (see page 475). But the best way to catch megrim – in fact pretty much the *only* way to catch megrim – is by beam trawling. You see? A nice simple piece of advice to the consumer – 'eat more megrim' – immediately becomes compromised because the only available method to catch a 'sustainable' species is an 'unsustainable' one.

Must we be permanently stuck on the horns of such conservation dilemmas? The aim of the IiFSW is to make sure we can wrestle ourselves free. The know-how exists to make beam trawling less damaging and more selective. Jim Portus of the South Western Fish Producer Organisation explains: 'Our fishermen are using emerging technology to minimise seabed impact. A fellow member of SWFPO recently won first prize in the Clean Fishing awards. His beam trawl design incorporated a 'release panel' in the floor of the net so that organisms such as crabs, starfish and sea urchins fall out – and it's now being mimicked across the Channel fleet of beam trawlers.' Other innovations, such as large rubber wheels that lift the beam poles off the seabed to minimise damage and increase fuel efficiency, are being trialled.

Even with such innovations, the seabed will need a rest from the effects of repeated beam trawling. So fallowing is key to these discussions, and the mutual agreement of marine protected areas – patches of sea where, for years at a time, beam trawling isn't allowed – is under negotiation. It seems that even the erstwhile 'baddies' can bring positive solutions to the table.

Consumers calling the shots

In all such negotiations, the role of retailers and consumers is key. A message that fishermen really need to hear is, 'Yes, we will buy your fish if you change the way you catch it. In fact, we will buy more of it.' The South West Handline Fishery offers a great example of how good practice can be rewarded. It's a small fishery that has always used the handline technique for catching mackerel. It's sustainable (like much line fishing) because mackerel are targeted so effectively that there is no unwanted bycatch, and no damage to the marine environment. This has always been the case, and now the fishery has introduced a strict quota limit and minimum landing size. It's won them a coveted MSC label and, perhaps more importantly, legions of customers who are prepared to pay top whack for these fish they can feel good about.

The fishery is extending its methods to the line fishing of pollack and sea bass. Individual fish are now being tagged and can be traced to their source at the point of sale in fishmongers, supermarkets and restaurants. This is the ultimate in fish traceability – and consequently in consumer confidence. It's the next best thing to catching your own fish. Of course, it would be great if we could all catch our own fish, but most of us rely on retailers and restaurants for the vast majority of the fish we eat. What initiatives such as tagged fish and MSC labels tell us, however, is that we are not at the mercy of these retailers and those who supply them. Quite the opposite – we can influence their behaviour through the choices we make.

However, it is still not always easy for a shopper to identify sustainably caught fish. In the absence of labels and tags (which are found on only a tiny percentage of retailed fish), what is the eco-conscious shopper to do? Ask questions, that's what. Where was it caught, and where landed? What sort of

fishing method was used? Is it male or female (and if the latter, might it be carrying eggs?) Is it farmed or wild? If farmed, then where, and what was it fed on? Is it organic, and if so, certified by whom?

You might not manage to complete the list of questions without exasperating your fishmonger – and you might want to vary the inquisition for each visit. But it's important to let your fishmonger know that he or she has at least one customer who cares deeply about the provenance of the fish.

Of course, in order to acquire the confidence to ask such questions, and indeed to make sense of the answers, you need to know a bit about fish in the first place. It will help if you understand what a bass pair trawler does (see page 32), for instance, or why a farmed prawn is best avoided (see page 542). If you know why inshore ling is a different environmental proposition from deepwater ling (see page 441), you can make a more informed decision. It's in the hope of answering these and other questions that this book runs to more than 600 pages!

Where to get your fish

Generally, buying fish close to source should ensure that you get the maximum amount of information about it. Straight off the boat is ideal, of course, and harbourside fishmongers or stalls are often good too. With luck, such small-scale businesses will stock fish bought directly from local inshore day boats. If they do, they represent only one fairly transparent link in the chain between you and your fish. That's not to say that larger fishmongers in land-locked town centres won't know what they are selling – but in our experience, there is a greater chance there that you'll walk out feeling you are not in full possession of the facts. These guys may be buying their fish from large wholesale markets where they'd have to be asking lots of questions themselves in order to be able to pass the answers on to you.

Supermarkets are not our natural habitat, but we'd have to concede that they can be a good place to buy sustainable fish. Some supermarket fish buyers are conscientious individuals who have made pro-active choices to ban certain non-sustainable species from their fish counters. Supermarkets may be reticent about many aspects of their products' provenance but they are rarely shy of proclaiming their ecological plus points. If it's line-caught, dolphin friendly, British, or has any other positive attributes, you can be sure your supermarket will shout about it. They will also tell you its country of origin as well as whether it's been previously frozen (because they have to do that by law).

Some supermarket chains are working closely with bodies such as the MSC and MCS and are the main outlet for logo-carrying, certified sustainable fish. (Supermarkets may well be selling less ecologically acceptable stuff, too, but you shouldn't have much difficulty spotting the difference.)

If you are not well served by a local fishmonger, and supermarkets are not your thing, then the internet may prove a surprisingly useful tool for the ethically minded, adventurous fish cook. It enables you to extend your reach, as it were, into many new areas. Looking for the pollack that you know to be in season but is not to be found at your fishmonger's? Google it. The only danger here is that the internet can turn a bold shopper into a rather lazy one, tempting you to sit at home, maxing out your credit card rather than exploring your real-life local market.

The cyber-marketplace may not always compete on freshness, though some reputable sellers would claim to have the edge on freshness over supermarkets and certain fishmongers. Of course, it won't offer the pleasure of talking to the person who's selling you the fish either, though a good website will provide plenty of information and generally give a phone number for any further queries. Bear in mind also that mail-order chilled fish must be contained in large amounts of packaging – polystyrene boxes, ice packs etc – and will be transported by road to your door. So your ecologically good intentions may be offset – in the wrong direction.

Choosing the best fish

It's no good choosing the finest tagged Cornish pollack fillets if they stink to high heaven. The savvy fish shopper will always look beyond the environmental stamp of approval to the fundamental issue of freshness and quality. Choosing fish that is in really good nick is a skill that is very easy to acquire and, happily, fish quality and excellent environmental practice often (though not always) go hand in hand. Line-caught fish, for example, are often killed, packed and iced individually, so avoiding the inevitable net-crush of trawled fish, and they are usually caught by inshore day boats, so landed within hours, rather than days, of being caught.

Most whole fish are sold with the gills still in. We'd prefer them to have been removed but there is a long-established culture among fish vendors to keep them in. It is, in truth, a weight issue and an appearance issue. Fish weigh more and look better if they're intact. There's an upside, though: the condition of a fish's gills is an excellent clue to its freshness. They can be a useful tool when assessing any fish you're considering buying.

In a fresh, well-kept fish, the gills should be perky and pink or even scarlet, and the edge of the gills should be feathery and frilly, with the fronds still clearly separated. If there is any blood on the gills, it should be red and fresh looking, even if it is congealed. By contrast, the gills of a tired, stale fish will be slimy, grey-brown, with the fronds gummed together with mucus. If you ask to inspect a fish, and the fishmonger is friendly enough to agree, you should definitely check the gills.

While gummed-up gills are not a good sign, the presence of slime or mucus over the fish's body is not necessarily a bad one. In fact, if it is clear, free flowing and odourless, it is a good indicator of a fish not long dead. (If it is opaque and coagulated, on the other hand, that's less encouraging.) A lack of good clear slime is not necessarily a cause for alarm. Its presence varies from fish to fish, and depends also on how much the fish has been handled. Fish that have been rinsed several times, or re-packed from one box to another with fresh ice, will have lost much of their slime – and fish that have been scaled almost all of it.

While sizing up your fish in the shop you should, if allowed, also give it a gentle prod in the thick flesh around the lateral line. A really fresh fish is surprisingly hard and resistant to pressure; your finger should not leave a dent in the flesh. If you can also carry out a 'sniff test', so much the better: sniff the fish – first at its gills, then in its belly cavity. It really shouldn't smell of much. A mild 'fishiness' implies that the fish is perhaps not spanking – but not to be rejected out of hand. On the other hand, any whiff of genuine taint – the kind of smell that makes you wince – and you should reject the fish.

If we buy a fish direct from fishermen, we always try first to ascertain its temperature. The best turbot in the world won't taste great if it's been lying on the sunny deck of a day boat for the last four hours. A warm fish is a worrying fish. In our opinion, any boat landing fish to be sold to consumers should always carry ice on board – but not enough do.

As a fallback, you should always be ready to assess a fish by eye. Increasingly, as more fishmongers and most supermarkets won't let you handle their fish (usually on account of 'hygiene regulations'), a visual assessment is all you'll have to go on. Even without touching it, you can tell a lot. Are its scales or skin still bright and shiny, or somewhat lacklustre and dull? Does it look pumped up and hard, or is it starting to sag a bit? Is its eye lively and clear, or is it cloudy and starting to sink into its socket? It may sound odd, but you should also use your imagination when assessing a fish for freshness. If it is truly spanking fresh it will look as though, were you to drop it back in the sea, it might just swim away.

Given that recognising freshness is one of the key factors in determining that you eat good fish, the more open minded you are when shopping for it, the better. If you are over-focused on a particular recipe or species, there is a greater likelihood of disappointment. 'Today I'm going to find the freshest fish in the shop' is a much more productive attitude than 'today I am going to buy a whole John Dory of approximately 700g'.

Choosing the best shellfish

As a general rule, when it comes to buying shellfish, buy it alive. Crabs, lobsters, mussels, oysters, scallops: if they're still live and kicking at the point of sale, then at least you won't need to worry about how fresh they are. Often the shellfish on sale in this country has been boiled and 'dressed', whereas in France you'll find an array of live shellfish in even the least salubrious of supermarket chains, whilst no self-respecting Spanish fish lover would dream of buying a pre-cooked lobster.

We must confess to having both taken foolish risks with the shellfish that we have bought. On one memorably kamikaze occasion, while fishing in the Gambia, we were tempted by bags of tiny oysters cooked in their shells. Fabulously dressed women were hawking them from tiny one-umbrella pitches at the side of the road. The oysters were laid out on tin sheets on the baking-hot ground while the air temperature must have been touching 35°C. You would have thought the alarm bells would be ringing… but still we bought oysters, bags of them. And we ate them with glee, sucking the shells clean and tossing them into the sea. We couldn't help ourselves and yes, we *did* get sick, we *did* get the trots and the gloss was certainly taken off the next day's fishing, but in a funny sort of way it was worth it. Sometimes doing stupid things because of your uncontrollable love of fish and shellfish is excusable and even, we'd like to think, sort of noble… or are we just kidding ourselves?

Anyhow, here's what you *should* be looking out for:

Crabs and lobsters

Shell appearance and weight are the two most important things to look out for in brown crabs and lobsters. Don't be tempted to choose the most pristine looking; it's the shells that have the most barnacles and ingrained dirt that will provide the best meat. These are the ones that have long since moulted their shells and have been packing on flesh and weight for the last few months.

Clean crabs are ones with new shells, and most of the bulk inside is taken up with water: if you lift one up, it'll feel light and practically empty. And don't overlook the limbless. Just because a crab may have lost a claw, that doesn't mean its shell won't be crammed with the sweetest meat.

The same rules generally apply to spider crabs: look for the big, dirty, lived-in shells. On the other hand, the opposite applies regarding amputees. Since most of the best meat of the spider crab comes from its legs and claws, if it is lacking limbs you should probably give it a miss.

Mussels, oysters and scallops

When you're buying these live bivalves, you can generally assume the flesh is in good condition because it is permanently encased in its God-given armour. And if they bubble as if they're spitting foam, or you see the shell open and close, you know you have the very freshest shellfish on your hands, which you would be mad not to buy.

You might want to ask where these farmed filter feeders were gathered. Is the water in that region of good quality and free from pollution? It has to be said that in the UK any commercially produced mussels or oysters will have been subject to rigorous health checks and also ultraviolet light treatment. But if you're lucky enough to buy a bag of mussels from a waterside vendor when you're on holiday somewhere, just ask yourself a question: from what you've seen of the inshore waters and estuaries in that area, does it feel like a place that would grow healthy molluscs? When you buy fresh mussels, check that they are alive – their shells should either be firmly shut or close up if you tap them firmly.

If you can buy scallops alive in their shell, so much the better. If you live near the coast, you are in with a shout. A harbour-town fishmonger may well buy direct from a local diver and if you keep in touch you may be able to find out when a fresh batch is due. Better still, if you can pull it off, buy direct from the diver yourself. And, we hardly need to remind you – only buy dived scallops, never dredged (see page 576). Should you happen on a sack of very fresh, live scallops then you will hear, and possibly see, intermittent snapping, scraping and jostling as they open and close, moving a few millimetres each time over the shells of their companions. Close your eyes, and it could be a giant bowl of Rice Krispies in slow motion.

Once it's dead, the scallop's shell will gape open as wide as the stretched muscle will allow – a good 5cm or more – and no amount of tapping, poking or general provocation will persuade it to shut again. That doesn't necessarily mean it's no longer fresh; kept chilled, a dead scallop in its shell is good for another 24 hours. But it is certainly an early warning sign. Before buying obviously dead scallops in their shell, you really want a close look, and a good sniff – any whiff of taint and you should leave well alone.

In supermarkets (always) and fishmongers (mostly), scallops are these days sold out of their shells – the white muscles and orange corals attached or separate. This makes it hard to assess their freshness, unless a request to handle and sniff one is granted – and it probably won't be. But if it is, look for firm, close-grained muscle meat, without tears or signs of fraying on the cut surfaces, and plump, shiny corals. Even the slightest hint of an off-fish smell and you must forget them.

Squid and cuttlefish

A live or freshly dead whole squid is a wonderful thing to get your mitts on, but for most people it's a fairly rare occurrence. Whole squid can range in size from an organism no bigger than your thumb to a beast about the size of a scrum half's thigh. The ones you're most likely to see landed locally are on average about 25cm long, with a purplish membrane clinging to them. This membrane is very thin and breaks after the fish is dead, so squid can look a little tatty – but this doesn't mean they're off.

Truly off or nearly off squid have a grey, milky, wet appearance and a slimy residue that clings to the board or slab as it's lifted. At the fishmonger's, you're most likely to see squid cut into rings or sold as cleaned mantles (see pages 99–100). But whole is the only way to judge their freshness easily and visually – with rings and mantles you will have to rely on information from your fishmonger about where they came from, and when.

Cuttlefish are so rarely available in British fishmongers that we'd recommend you buy them whenever you see them. As with squid, watch out for gooey slime. If the cuttles are still covered in ink, this is usually a sign that they've been chucked in a basket on deck and died in a heap while seeping their ink over each other. We'd buy an inky mess off a fisherman who was landing his cuttle catch. But by the time a cuttle makes it to the fishmonger's slab it should be looking its best, not covered in ink.

Five rules for sustainable fish shopping

Once you've covered the freshness issue, you can start to apply your conscience to the best-looking fish on the slab. All the advice we've given on sustainability boils down to five very simple principles to keep in mind when you're out shopping:

1. BONE UP ON FISH BEFORE YOU BUY Find out how sustainable it is and which fisheries are the best managed. If you've set your heart on a particular recipe but discovered that the species in question should be avoided, then research a few substitutes (pollack for cod, lemon sole for Dover, bream for bass etc). Champion the more sustainable species; boycott those most under threat.

2. NEVER BUY FISH BLIND Question your fishmonger, or at least read the back of the packet, to make sure you know as much about it as you can. Try to find out where the fish came from, and what method was used to catch it. Favour fish and shellfish caught in the inshore fishery by local day boats.

3. SUPPORT ECO-LABELLING SCHEMES Buy their fish (see logos to look out for, opposite). This sends a powerful message to fisheries across the globe.

4. DON'T BUY UNDERSIZED FISH If fishmongers and fishermen know they can easily shift undersized fish (which may even be illegal) it 'lets them off the hook'. Delivering the message that undersized fish are unacceptable keeps the pressure on retailers to review their sources, and on fishermen to review their methods.

5. AVOID BUYING FISH DURING THEIR SPAWNING SEASON If this is hard to ascertain (different fish spawn at different times of year, and some spawn unpredictably), at least avoid 'berried' crustaceans, and try not to buy roe-carrying fish too often.

Fish to find, fish to avoid

Finally, in addition to the above 'rules', you might like to consider the following categories. Between them, they should help you to choose sustainable fish, and to enjoy some of the best seafood that our coastline has to offer.

The blacklist: ten fish to avoid

Make sure none of these fish ever passes your lips – at least for the foreseeable future – and you'll be doing a great deal to help protect our threatened species.

1   Whitebait (page 423)
2   Cod from the UK (page 426), unless MSC-certified or organically farmed
3   Hake (page 437)
4   Bluefin tuna (page 447)
5   Sharks and huss (page 452), all types except dogfish
6   Skate and rays (page 456), unless one of the three sustainable species
7   Wild halibut (page 463)
8   Sea bass (page 478), unless self-caught, line-caught and tagged, or organically farmed
9   Wild salmon (page 508)
10 Eel (page 528)

Ten most underrated sustainable seafish

These are the species we feel you can enjoy in good conscience. Fill your boots. Honestly, if we only ever ate fish from this list and nothing else, we reckon we'd be missing out on very little… provided we're allowed the Top Ten shellfish too.

1   Sprat (page 421)
2   Pollack (page 430)
3   Pouting (page 442)
4   Mackerel (page 444), ideally line-caught
5   Megrim and witch (page 475)
6   Scad or horse mackerel (page 481)
7   Black bream (page 483), especially from Cornwall, the Northwest and North Wales
8   Grey mullet (page 488)
9   Red gurnard (page 496)
10 Garfish (page 498)

Ten shellfish to seek out

In your quest for guilt-free seafood, never overlook the little guys in shells. Many are responsibly harvested from healthy stocks – or sustainably farmed.

1   Langoustines (page 546), creel-caught
2   Brown crab (page 551)
3   Blue velvet swimmer crab (page 555)
4   Spider crab (page 557)
5   Whelks (page 564)
6   Farmed mussels (page 567)
7   Dived scallops (page 574)
8   Cockles (page 578), especially MSC-certified from the Burry Inlet
9   Dived razor clams (page 582)
10 Squid (page 588), British, jig-caught

Aquaculture to feel good about

Fish farming can be bad news, but it can also offer a sustainable, high-welfare alternative to overfished wild stocks. We would happily eat the following, once in a while:

1   Organically farmed salmon
2   Organically farmed trout
3   Organically farmed cod
4   Farmed carp
5   Most farmed bivalves

Logos to look out for

When it comes to labelling schemes to identify sustainably caught or farmed fish, there's huge room for improvement. There are currently only three that we feel we can confidently endorse, but we are hoping for a labelling revolution.

1   Marine Stewardship Council eco-label for certified environmentally responsible fisheries (msc.org)
2   Soil Association organic certification for farmed fish (soilassociation.org)
3   Tagged line-caught mackerel, bass and pollack from the South West Handline Fishermen's Association (linecaught.org.uk)

Fish skills

All good ingredients are a pleasure to handle – and none more so than fish. Few amateur cooks ever get the chance to work with an entire pig, lamb or beef carcass. But taking a whole fish and dealing with it from start to finish is an act that will deepen your understanding of the animal that is going to feed you, and maybe even reconnect you with your hunter-gatherer past.

It is, of course, possible to bypass all the major elements of fish preparation by choosing either fillets or whole prepared fish that are, if you like, 'oven-ready'. One reason for doing so may be squeamishness – but a cook in a hurry may make the same choice. Few people have time to prepare all their fish from scratch. We don't. And sometimes it's pleasing to watch the fishmonger deftly gutting and descaling the fish you've chosen, performing in a few minutes a task that might take you twenty.

However, making time to do some fish prep yourself once in a while will keep you in tune with your fish and in touch with your inner fisherman (even if your outer one is still in the closet). So if you consider yourself fish phobic, we'd like to help you work through your anxieties until they evaporate, leaving you confident to deal with your fish in the future.

We know this kind of Damascene conversion can happen, because we have seen it many times. Since we've been running our Catch and Cook days at River Cottage HQ, we have fished, and cooked fish, with men and women who at the beginning of their time with us could hardly bear to touch a fish, dead or alive. By the end of the day we've had them pulling the guts out of mackerel and descaling pollack with gay abandon – happily working their way through the entire fish box and then asking for more. Learning a new skill that tears down an old barrier is one of life's great pleasures.

If you haven't handled much fish but now feel ready to confront your 'issues', may we suggest a good way to get you started: a mackerel fishing trip – the kind you can book for just an hour or two in harbour towns all around the British coast. A sympathetic skipper will provide the tackle you need, show you how to hold a live fish, unhook it, knock it on the head and, when you have recovered your composure (with a bit of luck your fish won't recover his), how to slit open its belly and remove its guts. By the time you've dealt with three of them, you'll feel like an old hand. If you enjoy the whole experience, you might consider graduating to a longer, half-day, reef or wrecking trip. With any luck you'll encounter a range of different species, and again, the best skippers will always be happy to show you the basics of on-board fish prep – not just gutting, but descaling and even filleting.

You can of course face your demons alone, at the kitchen sink, with a fish you've brought home from the fishmonger's. Read our instructions in this chapter, take a deep breath and go for it. On balance, though, we think it's good to have company when attempting breakthroughs of this kind. If you don't mind investing some time and a bit of cash in your future with fish, then we would wholeheartedly recommend a day at the Billingsgate Seafood Training School (seafoodtraining.org). You will be in the hands of serious (but good-humoured) experts, who will give you as thorough a grounding in the basic fish-prepping skills as you could wish for – and a damn fine lunch to boot. And of course it goes without saying that we'd love to see you for a River Cottage Catch and Cook day where, with a bit of luck, you will be dealing with fish you've caught yourself.

Killing fish

Let's start from first principles, in the hope that some of the fish you'll be working with will indeed be those you've caught yourself. When you've caught a fish, and decided you'd like to eat it, you should kill it without delay. This will not only minimise its suffering, it will maximise its eating qualities. Fish that thrash and gasp themselves to death on the deck or in the fish box may end up with bruised flesh.

The most effective way to kill a fish is by delivering a sharp crack across the head with a solid 'bosher', or 'priest'. You can buy these small truncheons, made from wood, plastic, metal or even the antler of a stag. Sometimes they incorporate a lead weight in the business end to give them, literally, more clout. But a well-chosen 'found object' will do just as well. Improvised priests we have encountered over the years include rolling pins, chopped-down broom handles, short lengths of steel pipe, suitably hefty bits of driftwood, small axe handles and even half a pool cue (the thicker end, of course).

It helps to hold the fish on a firm, flat surface – using a cloth, if necessary, so it doesn't slip from your hands – then crack it over the head, as if you're banging a nail in with a hammer. This should kill the fish instantly. One blow will usually be enough, but two, in rapid succession, is belt and braces. The fish may shiver or flap for a few moments – this is its nervous system playing out – but if it continues to do so for more than half a minute, another good whack may be in order. As you might imagine, the bigger the fish, the harder and more numerous the strikes required to despatch it (game-fishing boats in the tropics are often equipped with a baseball bat, to deliver the fatal blows to big fish such as dorado, wahoo, travally and tuna).

Many fishermen, particularly sea anglers, are blasé about the need to kill fish quickly once they have been caught. At the commercial end of the business, this is perhaps understandable. Fish are netted in such huge numbers that to despatch them individually would take hours – and by the time you'd dealt with a few hundred the rest would be dead anyway. But anglers don't have this excuse. They are catching fish one (or at most a few) at a time. The opportunity to give them a quick and merciful release should always be taken.

Sometimes, say in the frenzy of catching strings of mackerel in threes, fours and more, it's tempting to abandon this responsibility. On too many angling boats, it is the culture to fling the live fish in a box and let them expire in their own time. But just because this is the done thing, it doesn't mean you have to do it. You can easily kill a mackerel as you unhook it – by putting your thumb in its mouth, or gills, and pulling its head backwards to break its neck. This alternative method of despatch works for most fish under a pound.

Bleeding a fish

After you've whacked a fish and rendered it unconscious, its heart will still beat for a minute or two as the blood continues to circulate through its body. This gives you an opportunity to 'bleed' it. There are three good reasons to do this. First, it ensures the fish dies quickly. Secondly, it empties blood from the veins that weave through the fish's flesh. Bled fish have clean, translucent fillets, without vein tracks or dark patches of trapped blood, and both look and taste the better for it (this is particularly important if they are to be eaten raw as sushi and sashimi, or in a dish such as ceviche). The third reason for bleeding is to prolong shelf life. Blood attracts and nurtures bacteria much faster than flesh, so draining it off means the fish can be kept fresh for longer.

Ideally all fish, including freshwater species, should be bled. In Japan, most line-caught fish destined for the sushi markets are bled as a matter of course, in order to meet the consumers' high standards. If a fish hasn't been bled properly, its market value will be greatly reduced. In the UK, however, commercially caught fish aren't generally bled. It's simply not part of our fishing culture. But we are so convinced of the virtues of bleeding that we now do it with almost every fish we catch. By making sure a fish dies quickly and is bled thoroughly, we're not only paying our respects, we're guaranteeing it reaches the kitchen in the best possible condition – where a fitting send-off awaits...

You need to bleed a fish while its heart is still beating – so within a minute or less of that blow on the head. Cut its gills on both sides of the head with either a sharp blade or a pair of stout scissors. A major artery passes through the gills, whose job is to pass oxygen from the water. You should see the blood start to flow from the gills almost immediately. We like to bleed our fish in an empty box for ten minutes or so before rinsing them off and transferring them to the icebox. To achieve absolute optimum freshness, it's best to gut the fish before they go on ice (see page 57). But if you're too busy catching, the gutting can wait, just so long as your fish is kept cold.

Returning a live fish

If you decide you're not going to eat a fish you've just caught – it might be too small, it might be one of the less palatable, or less sustainable, species – then you should release it instead. (If it is deeply hooked or otherwise damaged, you should always kill it – and make a meal of it.) Handle a live fish that you are planning to return to the water carefully, ideally with a wet cloth or at least wet hands, to avoid rubbing off the mucus that protects its skin. Unhook the fish over the water if possible, or at least resting on a stable surface, because if you drop a fish you can damage its scales or even stun it, which greatly reduces its chances of survival.

Never carelessly fling a fish back into the sea. Treat it with respect. A fish returned in perfect condition has the potential to go forth and multiply, which is good for future fish stocks, future fish sport and future fish suppers.

Descaling

If you're keen to eat the skin of your fish (and we'd thoroughly recommend it), you may need to remove its scales. These vary in size and thickness from species to species. Mackerel have tiny, soft, inoffensive scales, most of which simply slip away as the fish is handled, rinsed and prepared. Any that remain seem to dissolve as the fish is cooked. So they don't need descaling. Bass and bream, by contrast, have coarse, fingernail-like scales, which are never pleasant to find in your mouth. If you want to make a virtue of the skin of these fish – by crisping it in your frying pan or oven – then you should definitely remove their scales.

Scales are arranged in overlapping rows, from head to tail, like the slates on a roof. The way to remove them is to scrape firmly 'uphill', from tail to head, in the opposite direction to the natural lie. The instruments that can do this effectively are many and varied, including tools especially designed for the job (see page 78). If you lack a patented descaler, you can use a blunt knife or the back of a sharp one, but you'll need to be careful.

Big bass and bream scales tend to flick and ping all over the place as you scrape; they can quickly decorate your kitchen, or boat deck, in a style that your partner, or skipper, may not appreciate. So it's a good idea to submerge such large-scaled fish in a bucket or sink while you scrape. Smaller scales, like those on trout, pollack and pouting, come off in a sort of scaly slime; you can descale them on a board and simply wipe the accumulated gunk away as you go.

Ideally you should descale your fish when it's whole. Descaling a fillet without bruising it is tricky; even descaling a gutted fish isn't as easy as one that has its belly intact. The fresher and wetter the fish, the easier it is to descale. If a fish has been in the fridge for a day or two, the mucus tends to dry, and can glue the scales together. (You can try re-wetting it, but it doesn't always work.)

Fish scales on your tongue are like toast crumbs in bed. They might not look like much, but they feel *huge*. So, before you bake or fry any fish or fillet with the skin on, always inspect it for rogue scales and eliminate any that you find.

When not to descale

It can be hard to remember which fish need descaling and which don't. Flatfish are particularly confusing – most do, but turbot and flounder don't; some, such as lemon sole, need descaling on the top skin, but not underneath. If you're not sure whether the fish you're about to cook has the kind of scales you need to remove, then test a small area around its tail – scraping towards the head, remember. If noticeable scales come away, you will need to remove them from all over the fish. If nothing much is dislodged, descaling won't be necessary.

Obviously you needn't worry about descaling a fish if you have no intention of eating its skin. In fact, if you plan to skin a fillet anyway (see page 73) it is easiest to do this with the scales on – their extra resistance will help prevent accidentally slicing through the skin. (On the other hand, if you descale and then skin a thick-skinned fish such as salmon or bass, you'll be ready to try our lovely recipe for Deep-fried fish skins on page 382.) Incidentally, any coarse-scaled fish that you're planning to fillet and skin – bass and bream in particular – should at least be descaled over the dorsal area, even if you leave the scales on over the flanks. Otherwise the heavy scales will deflect and divert the edge of the knife as you attempt the first cut.

Ready-cut fillets from a fish counter will not always have been descaled – you will need to check them before cooking. If they haven't, your best option is probably to skin them – it will be too fiddly to descale them, and you risk bruising the flesh. Fillets, cutlets and tranches that are to be added to fish soups or stews, skin on, should always be descaled, otherwise you'll end up with loose scales peppering the dish.

Here are some other occasions when we may decide not to descale a fish: if it's being barbecued, leaving the scales on will help protect its flesh from the searing heat of the coals. But it's a trade-off, as you won't be able to eat the skin. We always leave the scales on if we are baking a whole fish – usually a bass or bream – in a salt crust (see page 226), or a saltdough crust (see page 225).

The scales prevent too much salt leaching into the flesh, and again help keep the flesh tender and moist. Finally, if we know our pollack or pouting fillets are destined for the cold smoker, we'll usually leave the scales on, as we're exceedingly unlikely to want to eat the skin after the fish has been smoked.

SO THE GENERAL RULES ARE:

Keep the scales **ON** if you want to take the skin **OFF**.

Keep the scales **ON** if you intend to barbecue your fish or bake it in a salt crust.

Take the scales **OFF** in all other circumstances, *especially* if you want to eat the fish skin.

Gutting fish

The belly of a fish contains not only its vital organs but also the food it has been eating, in a partially digested state. The spectrum of bacteria present here is diverse, far more so than in the fish's flesh. Even after death, the stomach continues to be active, its enzymes breaking down any food in the gut – a process that also generates heat, aiding and abetting decay. When a fish begins to go off, it is usually from the belly out. So it is good practice to gut a fish as soon as possible after it has been killed.

When we catch a fish, we usually remove its guts within an hour or two of its death – sometimes as soon as it has been bled. A lull in the fishing action is a good opportunity to get a bit of fish prep done. On boating trips, if the day's been busy or we've been a bit lazy, we might simply kill, bleed and wash our fish, then keep them on ice until the end of the day. Then, on the ride back into port, we'll get busy gutting, descaling and sometimes, with big pollack and the like, even filleting our fish. After a day or even half a day's fishing, when you finally get back home fatigue descends in an instant. To have your fish all ready for cooking will save time, effort and even injury.

If you prep fish on the boat or the beach, the guts can be thrown back into the sea, where they will be eaten by crabs, molluscs and dogfish, provided the seagulls don't get them first. But one thing we generally don't discard is the roes of our fish, as long as they are reasonably substantial. They can be fried up fresh or, from fish such as pollack and ling, salted and smoked. From certain species, including turbot and brill, the livers also make a nice little treat, fried and served on toast.

In many commercial fisheries it is standard practice to gut fish on board the boat on which they are landed, then pack them with plenty of ice in fish boxes, ready to be transported from the quay as soon as the boat arrives. But on certain types of boat the fish may be sorted and iced without being gutted first. This isn't necessarily *bad* practice. If a freshly killed fish goes straight on to ice, even with the guts in, the onset of decay will still be arrested. And provided the fish is kept at a temperature of around 0–2°C, it will remain in good condition for several days.

So when you see a fish on the fishmonger's slab that has not yet been gutted, it is not necessarily more likely to be off than a fish that has been gutted. But it should perhaps strike a note of mild caution. If the fishmonger tells you it's just come in that morning, and it has the sheen, firmness and brightness of eye to make that claim credible, then go for it. If it looks 'borderline', then its unguttedness is definitely a point against it.

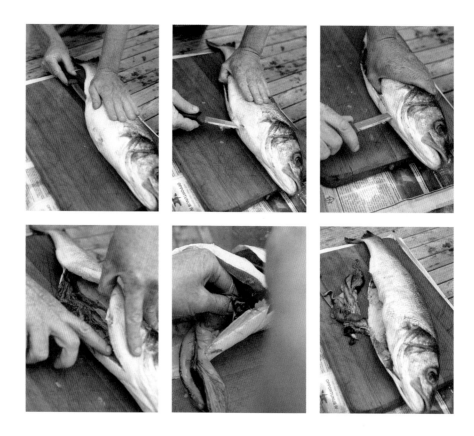

Gutting round fish

The gutting process is pretty simple. All round fish, eels and dogfish have
a clearly visible anal vent (yes, it's the fish's bumhole). This is where you
should start your cut, ideally with a short, sharp knife. Lay the fish on a board
(preferably covered with a few sheets of newspaper to prevent slipping), tail
towards you, head pointing away.

Hold the fish with one hand – keep it lying flat on its side with the anal vent
facing you – and the knife in the other. Insert the tip of the blade into the vent.
Gently slice the blade through the belly flesh, moving from the vent along the
belly of the fish in a straight line to its 'throat', to within a centimetre or so of
where the gill slits meet. The cut doesn't need to be deep; just enough to split the
belly flesh without slashing the innards.

The guts usually start to tumble out straight away, but you'll need to put your
hand inside the belly to get them all out. There's no point in doing this gingerly.
Everything that looks as if it could easily be pulled out, should be pulled out.
Sometimes, particularly on larger fish, the gullet (the fleshy tube that leads from
the throat to the stomach) is too strong and too firmly attached to come away
with a simple tug. Don't force it or you may tear the fish. Use the knife to cut it
out as close as possible to the back of the fish's mouth.

Inside the empty cavity of some fish (especially oily fish), you will find a
deposit of black gooey stuff running along below the backbone, covered by a thin

membrane. This blood-rich substance functions as the fish's kidney. Though it's perfectly benign, it's best removed, as it can accelerate spoilage and may taint the flavour of the fish. Simply slice the membrane with the tip of a knife and then scrape along the underside of the spine with your thumbnail or the handle of a spoon to remove the black gunk – perfectionists have been known to scrub it out with an old toothbrush. However you do it, working under a cold running tap will make it easier.

After a quick all-over rinse with cold water, dry both inside and outside the fish with a tea towel. Then your fish is ready to cook – or, if you're not ready to cook it, to be put back on ice, or in the fridge, or bagged for the freezer.

Once you gain confidence in handling fish, you can dispense with the board. Fish of less than a couple of kilos can easily be held belly up in one hand with a thumb in the gills to hold it steady. Then you can cut the belly from vent to throat with a knife held in the other hand, putting the knife down to free the same hand to remove the guts. Working like this you can gut a dozen mackerel, for example, in a matter of minutes.

Gutting flatfish

One of the reasons cooks love flatfish is that both flanks of flesh (upper and lower) sit on top of each other without much of a belly cavity in between. They're just pure meat – four nice fillets neatly separated by the fish's skeleton. The belly cavity of a flatfish doesn't run half the length of its body or more, as it does with a round fish. Instead it's in the 'throat' area, just below the head on one side. A quick prod with your fingers will determine where the soft innards stop and where the firm muscle flesh begins.

To gut a flatfish, stab it at the top of the soft belly area immediately below the pectoral fin and make one cut in a semicircle, following the outer contour of the gut cavity (as shown below). You only need to cut enough of a flap to get your fingers inside and pull out whatever comes away – it's usually quite a lot less than a round fish of similar size.

With most flatties, we like to leave the liver and any roe inside the cavity and cook them along with the fish, but if that doesn't bake your cake, you can remove and discard them, or give them to your cat or dog. As ever, a final rinse under a cold tap and a good wipe dry are in order.

Gutting sardines and sprats

Small oily fish, such as sprats and sardines, can easily be gutted using a stout pair of kitchen scissors. With a fish in your left hand, head pointing away from you, and the scissors in your right (or vice versa if you're left-handed), simply cut a thin strip, just a few millimetres wide, from the belly.

This will open it up and you can then simply scrape out the guts with your thumb, running the cold tap over the cavity as you do so. While you're at it, pull out the gills with your thumb and forefinger. Pat the fish dry inside and out before you cook them.

Removing gills

The gills are the feathery pink disks found immediately behind a fish's head. They are protected by the shiny gill plates, on which the scales or skin are usually extra thick and hard. Gills have a dual function: as sub-aqua 'lungs', they extract oxygen from the water and transfer it to the blood (which flows thickly through the base of each gill); and as part of the fish's filtration and desalination system, they trap potentially harmful bacteria. So, once a fish is dead, they are a hotspot for bacteria that could accelerate its decay. For this reason we often remove the gills from fish we have caught – particularly if we're likely to be keeping the fish for a few days. We usually do it at the same time as we gut them. With small mackerel, herrings and sardines, it's quite straightforward as you can usually tear them out without cutting at all.

For anything larger, a tough pair of scissors is the best tool for removing the gills, though a sharp knife will do the job. First snip or slice through the point underneath the fish's head where the gills meet – where the belly joins the 'throat' of the fish. Then cut around the base of the gills where they attach to the body and pull them away. The gills are usually discarded, but from big white fish such as pollack they may be substantial enough to be worth saving for the stockpot – provided they are extremely fresh, and thoroughly rinsed of any blood.

Handling fish with spiny fins

Bass, black bream and freshwater perch are good to look at and great to eat, but they can be a right pain to handle, literally, whether dead or alive. As part of their natural defences, they all possess sharp spines joined by fin membrane, like the webbing on a duck's feet. A spine puncture hurts a lot, both when it happens and for the rest of the day. And if it happens while you're out fishing, it will be irritated by salt water and begin to sting like a sack of nettles.

To avoid spearing yourself while you are handling (particularly descaling) a spiny species, you can either wear gloves (which we think always seem to make the job more difficult) or simply snip all the spines off first with scissors. To do this effectively, always cut from the tail towards the head, against the natural lie of the fin.

There is another neat technique for removing not only the spiny fins but also the bony structures that support them, which we often use when we are cooking whole, pan-sized bream and bass (see the recipe on page 305). With the tip of a sharp filleting knife, make a small incision just behind the head and beside the large dorsal fin. Slice into the fish to a depth of about 1cm and drag the knife all the way along the edge of the fin to the tail. Turn the fish over and repeat the process on the other side – but cutting towards the head this time. With your thumb and forefinger, take hold of the line of bones to which the fin is attached. Pull them out – the fin and a long ridge of spiky bone should come out cleanly in one piece. Use pliers if you find the fin is too tough.

Filleting fish

After you've got the hang of gutting fish, you're ready to have a stab at the next stages in its preparation: filleting, skinning, and cutting fish into various portions. Filleting first. The aim is simple: to remove two or more substantial portions of a fish from its skeleton, maximising the amount of flesh on the fillet and minimising the amount of waste on the skeleton. This may sound obvious but it's worth bearing in mind, as it informs the techniques used at all stages.

It's easy to make a mess of filleting a fish. But in the end, how much does it matter if you do? You're still going to get some kind of usable fillet, even if it's a bit raggedy and uneven. The fact that in a restaurant kitchen some psychotic chef might shout at you for such an effort need not trouble you in the least in your own kitchen. Besides, when you're filleting, always remember that the stockpot is your friend, at hand to receive any miscuts. In fact, if you make your own fish stock (see page 256), and have a good fishcake recipe up your sleeve (see pages 326, 330 and 331), you can practise filleting to your heart's content, as nothing need go to waste. All of our round fish frames (skeletons) and heads end up in the stockpot, except those from oily fish such as mackerel or herring, which don't make very good stock. These we tend to freeze and keep for bait.

Stock and fishcakes aren't the only options for trimmings and mistakes. They can be little 'fillets' in themselves. Look on them as chef's perks. From super-fresh fish, they can be trimmed as 'sashimi morsels' (see page 132) to be eaten with a dab of mustard and soy sauce. Or they can simply be flung in the pan alongside the 'senior' fillet to which, in a perfect world, they'd still be attached.

Filleting fish is quite an art, and practice doesn't always make perfect, though it does usually make competent. Of the two of us, one is much better at it than the other (strangely, he's the one who hasn't worked in a professional kitchen).

Filleting mackerel, bait-cutter style

The easiest fish to fillet, and the one with which to kick off your filleting career, is a mackerel, which lends itself to a style of filleting we call 'bait-cutter'. The reason for the name is that it's how we cut bait from a mackerel while on the boat. It's a particularly speedy way of filleting mackerel and is ideal if you've got a big catch on your hands and you want to deal with the fish quickly, or if you need lots of fillets for a recipe such as Gravad max (page 142). But it's also incredibly useful when you just want to cut and fry a few mackerel fillets for the family with minimal fuss.

It's very, very easy, as long as your blade is sharp and not too hefty. The downside is that it's not quite so neat as the standard method for other round fish (see opposite); you'll always end up leaving some bones in the flesh, or flesh on the bones. However, this may not matter that much. If, for instance, you're making Gravad max or cutting mackerel for sushi, you're probably going to trim and tidy the fillet again before serving anyway. And if it's just a quick supper you're after, picking out a bone or two will hardly spoil your evening.

Filleting bait-cutter style is best done with whole, very fresh, ungutted fish, as they stay obligingly round (but you can do it with gutted fish, too). Hold the head firmly in one hand, tail pointing away from you. Cut down into the 'armpit' (or 'fin pit') of the fish, just on the tail side of its pectoral fin (the side fin just behind the head), until you touch the spine. Then turn the blade until it lies flat on the spine, parallel to the chopping board, sharp edge pointing tailwards,

and slice along the length of the fish in as few sawing-strokes as possible. Use the full length of the blade and allow it to be guided by the backbone of the fish – always cutting away from your body.

Put the fillet to one side, flip the fish over, then repeat the procedure on the other side of the fish. The guts will remain attached to the filleted mackerel frame, so the whole lot can be chucked into the scraps bucket (or the bait box) with the minimum of mess, leaving you ready to crack on with the next fish. If the fillets are at all smeared with blood or guts, just give them a quick rinse under the cold tap and pat them dry with a clean rag.

Once you have a pair of nice clean mackerel fillets, you can give them a secondary trim, to make them completely boneless and ready for sashimi or sushi, or to be fed to small children. Deal with the belly bones first: just inside the fine dark membrane of the belly cavity, towards the head end of the fillet, will be a 'rack' of very fine bones – work the edge of the blade just beneath the line of bones and pare them out as thinly as you can.

Now for the pin bones – the row of little bones that run down the lateral line of the fillet (you will have sliced through them when you cut the fillet). Skip ahead to page 67 to find out how to remove them with pin-bone pliers. On a mackerel fillet, the whole line of pin bones can also be removed by simply slicing either side of them, as close as possible, down the length of the fillet, to create a V-shaped groove, which is an essential feature of our recipe for Mackerel stuffed with salsa verde (page 316).

Once you've removed the belly and pin bones from a good, thick mackerel fillet you have one of the most benign and diner-friendly portions of fish you could ever wish for. And the only thing between you and great homemade sashimi is the fish's skin: see page 73 for this final step.

Filleting large and medium round fish

The bait-cutter approach, handy though it is, only works *really* well with mackerel. You can certainly try it on almost any round fish, but you should expect a lot of wastage. For bigger and less round 'round' fish – bass, bream, pollack, trout, salmon and the like – the filleting technique is more refined, less gung-ho. It's not just one well-aimed slice but a series of careful cuts, focusing on following the natural bone lines of the fish to maximise the fillet portion and minimise the waste. The good news is that the same basic approach can be used for any round fish, from a 250g trout to a 5kg pollack or salmon, so it's an invaluable one to learn. We're going to describe the process in detail – read alongside the step-by-step pictures overleaf, everything should be clear.

There are different views about the best choice of knife for this kind of filleting. A fine-bladed, flexible fish filleting knife is probably the best all-rounder for the job, but many who fillet a lot of large fish, such as farmed salmon and cod, swear by stouter, wide-bladed knives, mainly because they are better at slicing through heavier pin bones. We reckon you can successfully fillet most fish with any good knife whose blade is more than 15cm long – *provided it is seriously sharp.*

REMOVING THE HEAD If the fishmonger hasn't already done so, first gut the fish (see page 58), then lay it flat on a board. You don't have to remove a round fish's head to fillet it but we think it's the best way for beginners, as once the head is out of the way it's easier to judge your first vital cut into the body. To minimise wastage, remove the head by cutting in a diagonal line from just behind the gill plate on the 'crown' of the fish (imagine where a fish king would wear his crown) to the tail side of the pectoral fin. If the fish is not too big, and your knife is a good, sharp one, you should be able to slice right through the fish flesh with a couple of sawing motions, right down through the spine, through the flesh and skin on the other side, until the blade reaches the chopping board. Then the head should come off with the 'bib front' of the fish – the fleshy bit at the head end of the belly to which the pectoral fins are attached. There's not much meat on this – except on really large fish – and the head, removed in this way, is ready for the stockpot.

If you're working on a big fish and the head end of the spine is too tough to cut through with a filleting knife, simply cut through the flesh, as above, until the edge of the knife is stopped by the spine. Then put down your filleting knife, pick up a hefty chopping knife or cleaver and place it in the cut so it rests on the spine, at a clean right angle to it. Now tap it firmly with a rolling pin to chop clean through the bone. Then pick up your filleting knife again and finish slicing through the flesh and skin on the other side of the spine.

With big (3kg-plus) white fish, particularly pollack, we'll often keep the head for roasting. When we know we are going to do this, we deliberately leave the head 'long' by cutting a few centimetres or so back towards the tail. This gives us some extra 'shoulder meat' for our lovely roast (see page 380).

FILLETING THE HEADLESS BODY There's a nice image to bear in mind when slicing fillets off the backbone of a fish. Imagine your two hands, held flat together as if in prayer, and a pair of combs, back to back, sandwiched between them. Each hand is a fillet, and the combs are the backbone. You need to slide your knife between the two hands – first one side of the combs, then the other. Start by laying your praying hands flat on a board. Your cuts will all be 'splitting' the hands, and so need to be made parallel to the board and, to minimise wastage, as close as possible to the combs.

Now, let's leave the hands-with-combs metaphor and resume business with our headless fish. With the tail pointing directly towards you, hold the knife parallel to the worktop and bring its edge to the point where the cut flesh of the head(less) end meets the skin, just above the backbone (it's the 'top corner' of your fish). Make your first cut with the edge of the blade, from the head(less) end along the entire back of the fish, passing just above the dorsal fin, in one long, controlled cut towards the tail. This first cut needn't be deep – one or two centimetres into the flesh is enough. It's really just a guide for your second (or third) cut, with which you should aim to locate, with the edge of your blade, those spiny bones that fan out from the central vertebrae towards the fish's dorsal fin (the teeth of your comb). At all times, aim for clean strokes of the knife, from head towards the tail, and avoid sawing the blade back and forth, which may tear the flesh and make it ragged.

Once you've located this line of bones, you're in the home strait, as you can allow them to guide your blade (as in picture four of the sequence), lifting the fillet as you release it from the bones. Some people like to angle their knives to use the tip more than the blade, to 'tick-tick-tick' along the bones as they go. Others are happy to go on cutting with the leading edge, drawing it lengthways through the fish.

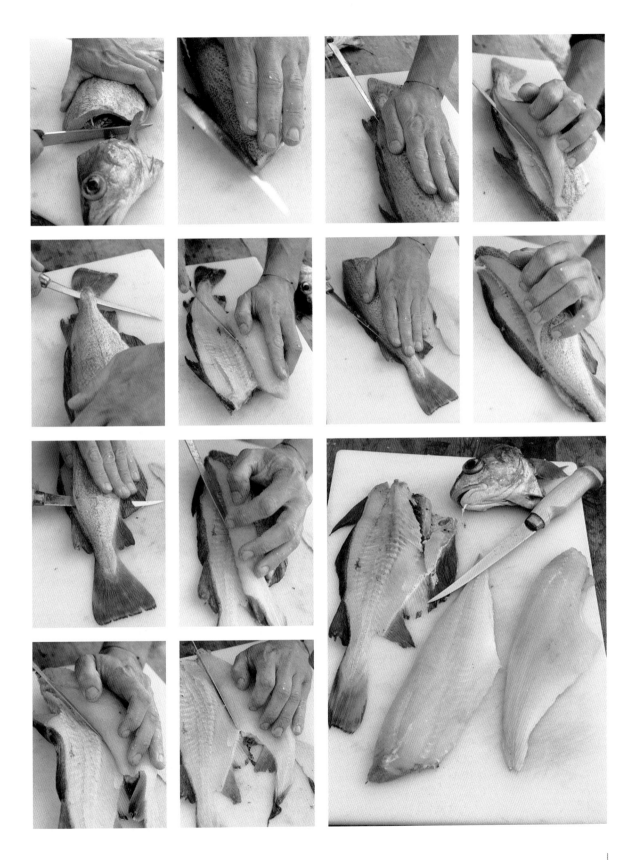

Either way, you should aim to slice tidily along the spiny bones (the teeth of the 'comb') until you get to the central bone (the back of the 'comb'). Here is where the 'ribs' that support the belly cavity start, arcing out around the belly of the fish. Leave them for a moment.

RELEASING THE TAIL FILLET You have just released the thick, dorsal part of the fillet. Now sort out the tail end. For this part of the fillet, it's almost as if you are reverting to bait-cutter style filleting (see pages 62–3) – but instead of starting right at the head, you are starting two-thirds of the way down the fish. Insert the point of the knife at a right angle to the backbone of the fish – just past the tail end of the belly cavity. Your aim is to push the point right through the flank sideways, impaling it, while passing as close as possible to the backbone, exiting somewhere around the anal vent.

The blade should end up resting across, and at a right angle to, the spine, with the meaty flank above the blade. Now cut towards the tail, scraping the blade along the spine inside the fish by tilting the leading edge down, and finishing when the blade cuts through the base (or 'wrist', as it is known) of the tail (see picture five).

THE FINAL CUTS INTO THE BELLY CAVITY The tail end of your first fillet is now free, along with everything above the central backbone. To finish off the head end around the belly cavity, essentially you have two choices.

The first option, which we tend to go for on larger fish, is to slice right through the ribs into the belly cavity so that the ribs and the flesh connecting them become part of the fillet rather than remaining on the carcass. It's better for big fish because it avoids wastage – there's really quite a lot of flesh around those ribs. To take this option, slice through the ribs all along the edge at which they join the backbone, aiming the blade directly into the top of the belly cavity. Once you've sliced through every rib, your first fillet – from head to tail – should be released. If you have not quite made a clean cut, or not quite reached the beginning of your tail cut, then there may be a point or two at which the fillet is still attached to the carcass. Just slice through any such points as cleanly as you can to release the fish.

The second choice – and the one we've shown in the picture sequence – is to guide your knife around the 'ribcage'/belly cavity instead of slicing through the bones. So, use the tip of your knife to make a series of delicate slashes guided by the ribs, releasing a few millimetres of the fillet with each cut (see picture six). When you reach the end of the ribs, simply slice away the fillet, cutting through the skin. The upside of this method is that you'll get very tidy and, with luck, completely boneless fillets. The downside is that there'll be some wastage on the carcass, but on smaller fish this isn't too much of an issue. The fillet's loss is the stockpot's gain.

THE SECOND FILLET – TAIL FIRST Your first cut on the second fillet should be the same as on the first fillet, except from tail to head instead of head to tail. So, as well as turning the fish over, rotate it 180° so that the head end is pointing towards you. Make your first cut from the tail end, along the back on the upper side of the dorsal fin, all the way to the headless shoulder. Again, a cautious centimetre or two is all that's required for the first couple of cuts, until you find those handy spine bones that can guide your knife down to the central backbone.

Detach the tail end of the fillet in much the same way as before – by skewering the knife through the fish, from back to belly, two-thirds of the way to the tail. Slice it off, keeping the knife scraping close to the bone.

Now lift as much of the fillet as you've already released to get access to those meddlesome ribs. What happens next depends on whether you've chosen to slice through, or work round, the ribcage. Either way, proceed as per the first fillet.

Finally, take a proud look at your two fillets. If their belly edges are a little ragged, give them a trim. Take a look at the remaining skeleton too: has it got anything still on it that's worth whittling off? A miniature fillet worthy of the pan or the sashimi plate?

Removing pin bones from fillets

A fillet of fish – whether it's one that you have prepared yourself or one the fishmonger has cut for you, and whether it is from a tiny little mackerel or a hulking great ling – may well contain pin bones, and you may well wish to deal with them (if the fillets are to be smoked, you can deal with them afterwards). These sharp little bones stick out sideways from the spine of the fish, so you'll find them buried in a line down the centre of the fillet, with blunt ends pointing towards you and sharp ends pointing down towards the fish skin. In big fish, pin bones can be matchstick-thick; in small ones they can be almost as fine as hairs. Either way, they are easy to remove.

To locate these tiny pin bones, run your fingertips lightly down the middle of the fish fillet from the head end to the tail end. You will feel the tips of the bones, and the movement of your fingers should pull them up towards the surface. Working methodically down the fillet, grasp the end of each bone with a pair of pin-bone pliers (see below) or stout tweezers, reserved for the purpose, and pull firmly upwards to remove it.

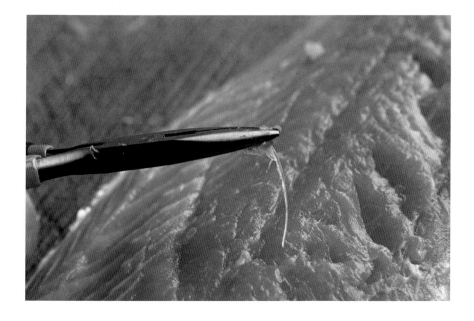

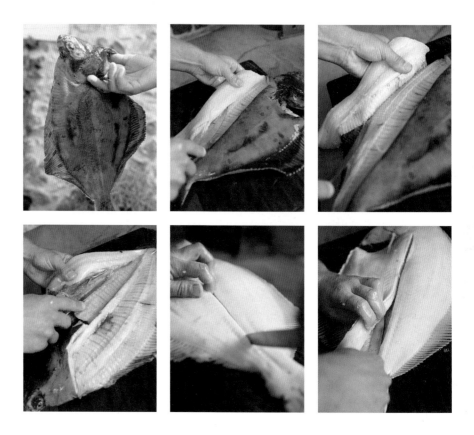

Filleting flatfish

Flatfish have two distinct sides. The upper side is camouflaged to resemble the seabed, while the lower side is virgin white. Traditionally, the white side was the 'posher' side, and some fishmongers would even charge extra for white-side fillets. We prefer the dark-side fillet, though, because it's thicker, and we're greedy.

You might imagine that flatfish are more difficult to fillet than round fish, but they're not. In fact, their generously wide skeletons will guide your filleting knife even more co-operatively. The key thing is that you are aiming not for two fillets but for four – one from each 'quarter' of the fish, or two from each side.

Take the upper, dark-side fillets off first. It's easier to tackle them because the fish will lie more naturally on its undercarriage. The fish should be gutted first if this hasn't already been done (see page 59) and, in the case of some species, descaled if you plan to cook and eat the skin (see the descale/tail test on page 56). The head can be removed before filleting if preferred, though if left on (as in this sequence) it remains conveniently attached to the skeleton for the stockpot.

THE MAIN CUTS Point the head away from you. Your first filleting cut should run from the middle just below the head, straight down through the middle of the fish to the centre of the tail. You should aim to cut all the way through the upper flesh to the bone, and with a bit of luck you'll be cutting right down the central backbone ridge of the skeleton. You're unlikely to miss it by more than a millimetre or two. From here, the spiky bones that will guide your knife radiate out to the edges of the fish.

Now you need to decide whether to take the left-hand quarter-fillet off first, or the right-hand one (left is easier for right-handers and vice versa). Slide the tip of your flexible filleting knife under the flesh on the side you've chosen, cutting sideways with the blade laying flat against the bones. Slice a couple of centimetres at a time, until you can peel back a portion of the fillet and so make it easier to work your blade deeper under the fillet, while skimming over those bones. Keep sliding the blade under the quarter-fillet from head to tail until it reaches the inside edge of the frill of fins that surrounds the fish, cutting until the point breaks through the skin.

Then peel the first quarter-fillet away from the seam along the fin, by gently tugging and cutting at the same time. Don't worry if some of the frill comes away too; fillets can always be tidied up later. Detach the other dark-side quarter-fillet in exactly the same way.

Now flip the fish over and repeat the technique on the other side, to give you two white-sided fillets. Sometimes you'll find a comet-trail-shaped lump of roe inside the gut cavity. This will usually stay attached to one of the white-side fillets; it makes a tasty little morsel when fried along with the fillet. You are now left with four fillets and a fish frame with the head attached for the stockpot.

Flatfish fillets prepared in this way do not usually have any pin bones.

'Spatchcock' filleting small oily fish

Herrings and sardines have very fine rib bones connected to a central spine. These, coupled with the fishes' diminutive size, makes filleting them in the standard, round-fish style fiddly and not very effective. Being oily, their flesh is softer and more 'congealed' than that of white fish. 'Spatchcocking' takes advantage of that, gently teasing the skeleton away from the meat rather than cutting. Herring is the best fish to practise on, and the method is easier to execute if the fish has been gutted first but its head left on.

With the fish lying on its side, extend the split in the belly down past the anal vent to the tail, so your fish is now 'unzipped' from neck to tail fin. Now flip it over on to its front with the belly flaps splayed out on either side, so the underside of the spine, which runs along the 'ceiling' of the belly cavity, is almost touching the chopping board.

In this spatchcocked position, start to press down on the back of the fish with your fingers, or the heel of your hand, to push the underside of the spine down against the board. The aim is to exert just enough pressure to cause the flesh underneath to separate partly from the skeleton. Work your way along the spine.

Now turn the fish belly up again and, by pulling on the tail, start lifting the backbone that is attached to it, teasing the whole spine structure away from the slightly flattened flesh, until you reach the head end. Snip through the bone with scissors, as close to the head as possible, and the skeleton should come away with most of the rib bones attached to it. Any fine pin bones left in the flesh can be plucked out, or simply ignored.

These fine bones present no real problem when you're eating a fresh grilled herring: they simply add a little extra crunch. But if you're using herring fillets for rollmops or an escabeche, you might want to give them a cursory pick-over with pin-bone pliers or tweezers (don't make yourself miserable over it, though – a few pin bones do not amount to a culinary disaster).

This spatchcocking technique works with small mackerel too, though not when they are super-fresh as the flesh is rather too firm and clingy. Fish that are one or two days old – still fresh enough to enjoy if they've been chilled properly – should be more obliging.

Other fish portions

Besides filleting, there are a number of other ways to cut and portion a fish – steaks, cutlets, tranches, loins and the like. They tend to involve leaving in some of the bones – otherwise they would, of course, be fillets. There are virtues to this: bones may help the fish portion keep its structure, so it does not break up in the pan. They also add body and flavour to dishes, and to the fish flesh they support.

Such portions are popular in the restaurant trade, for obvious reasons. They help a chef calculate his or her costs (it's not called portion control for nothing), and they can be cooked fairly quickly, and to order, in any number of ways: in a frying pan, char-grilled, in the oven. Most frequently, these days, they are started off in a frying pan and then finished with a few minutes in the oven (see page 215).

Cutlets and steaks

In fish apportionment parlance, these two words are more or less interchangeable, though chefs sometimes use the word 'steak' to refer to a boneless, thick portion of fillet, or a thick slice taken from the loin. The term is particularly used about tuna and swordfish, so like them, it is probably worth avoiding.

Usually, though, the words steak and cutlet refer to thick, bone-in portions that have been cut in cross-section from a round-bodied fish – classically salmon. The cutlets from any given fish will vary in shape and size according to which part of it they come from. Those cut from behind the head and across the belly cavity will be roughly crescent shaped, like a biscuit with a bite taken out, from where the belly has been split to gut the fish. Those taken from past the belly, towards the tail, will be solid ovoids of on-bone flesh – very meaty and appealing.

The technique for cutting cutlets is every bit as obvious as you'd imagine. Take a very sharp, heavy chopping knife and simply slice your fish, straight through flesh and bone, into cutlets that are 3–5cm thick. If you're trying to be fair, you'll want to make the last few tail-end cutlets thicker than the middle section ones, to compensate for the tapering body shape.

In the picture above, we've cut a lovely grey mullet into thick, roughly even cutlets from head to tail. If you want to see how we ended up cooking it, turn to page 283 for one of our favourite dishes in the book – a rich fish stew (in which we included both the head and the tail).

Cutlets also work well in the frying pan, under the grill and even, basted or marinated, baked in the oven. They are less successful on the barbecue – when laid on the hot bars, the flesh can stick something rotten.

Tranches

Tranches are flatfish cutlets – portions of a chunky flattie taken in cross section, at right angles to the lateral line and often (but not always) including some bone. This is a useful technique for portioning a large flatfish such as a brill or turbot. You don't have to remove the skin or bones, so it's pretty straightforward.

Place the gutted flatfish on a board and remove the skirt or frill around the edge. Grip the head firmly and remove it by cutting across the open edge of the belly (where the fish has been gutted) and around the head following the natural curve of the gill cover. Remove the tail too, and save it with the head for stock.

Now cut down along the length of the backbone using a large, heavy knife, following the lateral line. Ideally, you want to split the spine in half, so that each half fish has a bit of backbone running its length, helping to keep it together. To help you cut through the bone, use a heavy chopping knife or cleaver. It may even need a good tap from a rolling pin to get through.

The 'tranching' cuts are now made at right angles to the first. Try to size up roughly 200g portions, adjusting the width of each tranche according to the thickness of that part of the fish. The tail-end tranche will obviously be a triangle. The others will be roughly rectangular (with one tapering edge).

Tranches lend themselves to most forms of cooking, including shallow frying, grilling, roasting and barbecuing – but take steps to avoid sticking (see page 189).

Loins

This is a slightly cheffy term applied almost exclusively to tuna, swordfish and cod, so it's of questionable value to the environmentally conscientious fish cook. It would be nice to think that chefs might soon be boasting about the quality of their prime, line-caught pollack loins, but it would have to be a record-breaking pollack.

The loin is basically a trimmed piece from a very thick fillet from a very large fish. It comprises the main 'dorsal' (i.e. upper) section of the fillet that lies above the lateral line, starting from behind the head and ending just behind the dorsal fin. In other words, it excludes the tapering tail section and the flesh from around the belly. From a big tuna, this is a hugely impressive hunk of flesh, from which substantial thick steaks can be cut; even on a cod, it can weigh 2–3 kilos. The boneless portions cut in cross section from a cod loin might just be described as 'steaks' – if one thick slice is big enough to make a serving. But they are more likely to be called 'medallions' – like pork and lamb loins cut in a similar way.

'Saddles' of fish

This is another term borrowed by chefs from meat cookery. In the fish context, it is almost invariably applied to a headless, tail-less hunk from the middle of a cod or a salmon, usually intended as a roasting portion.

The saddle has its virtues. Being of more uniform thickness than a whole fish, it will cook nice and evenly when roasted and basted, or baked in foil. But the advantages don't, in our view, outweigh the drawbacks. We like the different textures and flavours that come with the head and tail of a roast or baked fish. And frankly, saddles of farmed salmon make us anxious: without a head or tail, it's really very hard to assess the quality of the fish.

Slashed fish

This is an excellent way of preparing a fish for roasting or grilling – usually a whole fish with the skin on, but descaled, so it can be enjoyed in its entirety and at its best. Here's what to do: take a bream or a grey mullet of a kilo or so – just the right size for two or three people. Make several slashes, a few centimetres apart, into the thickest part of the fish. Don't slash right through to the bone – go about halfway – a centimetre or two, depending on the thickness of the fish.

The virtues of slashing are quite specific: it allows the heat to get to the thicker parts of the fish quicker. And it allows your seasonings to penetrate the fish and make more contact with cut flesh. The slashed fish is a fantastic blank canvas for herb and spice mixes, marinades and rubs.

Skinning fish

Once in a while, you may wish to remove the skin from a fish or a fillet of fish. You are most likely to find yourself wanting to skin a large fillet of white fish, such as haddock or pollack (or cod, if you haven't read pages 426–9). You may be doing this so you can coat your skinless fillet in flour or batter for deep frying (though we're happy to leave the scaleless skin on – we reckon it improves the flavour), or cut it into chunks for fish pie.

Here's how to skin a fillet. Lay it skin side down on a board, pinning its tail down with the fingers of one hand and slicing, from tail to head, above the skin and below the flesh of the fillet, so that the skin is effectively 'trapped' between knife and board. This is best achieved by angling the blade ever so slightly down into the skin and towards the board – but not so much as to slice through it. If your knife is really sharp, you can almost do this by pulling the tail piece of skin back through the blade/board trap as you slice forward at the same time.

Inevitably you will occasionally manage to half-skin a fillet and end up with some (or even lots of) skin still attached. From that point you'll have to improvise – try to whittle and release another little flap of skin, then work the blade again between skin and flesh. You may eventually be reduced to turning the fillet over and trimming little bits of skin from here and there to tidy it up. It happens to the best of us.

Skinning fillets of smoked white fish is rarely necessary, as they're usually being poached in preparation for some later stage in a recipe. Once lightly poached or steamed, the flesh is easily flaked from the skin. If we're poaching a fillet of smoked pollack to enjoy, perhaps, with a poached egg and some buttered greens or spinach, we'll serve it on the skin (and eat it off the skin).

Skinning a Dover sole to cook on the bone

Who doesn't love a whole grilled Dover sole? One thing that makes it the classic it has become is a nifty bit of fish prep: the way the tough top skin is removed, leaving a fine membrane that holds the flesh neatly on the bone. The same method works with other flatties, such as megrim, witch, lemon sole and plaice, though since their skins are more delicate and less leathery, they crisp up well and make good eating. So we'd just as soon grill or roast them with the skin on.

To remove the skin from the dark, upper side of a sole, make a very shallow cut across its tail, just deep enough to nick the skin without slicing flesh. From this opening, push the blade of the knife on a couple of centimetres under the skin, further separating it from the flesh. Then jam your little finger into the gap and wiggle it from side to side, using it to separate the skin from the flesh further, until you've got enough loose skin to grab between your fingers. You can also use this flap or 'tab' to release the frill of fins that surrounds the whole fish, rather like opening an envelope: run the tip of your index finger under the edge of the skin, from the tail towards the head – first on one side, then the other. It's a knack, and you may prefer to use a knife (perhaps you prefer to use a letter opener for your mail, too).

Now the skin is ready to be stripped – ideally with a single good pull. Salting your fingers will make it easier to grip. Keeping the fish flat, hold it down with one hand while you pull the skin, almost doubled back on itself, sharply towards the head with the other. If it gets stuck or starts to tear, simply dig under the skin with your finger or the tip of your knife to tease it off the flesh again.

Once loosened, the skin should come off with a satisfying 'rip', leaving behind the membrane, known as the 'shine', that neatly holds the meat together while it cooks. Traditionally, when a Dover sole is prepared for grilling, the underside is not skinned but left as it is – the white skin here is thinner and becomes quite tender and palatable when cooked.

Skinning a dogfish

The biggest disincentive to eating a dogfish is its skin. We think people should eat more dogfish, or even just *some* dogfish, so here's how we get rid of that pesky skin. It's a quirky technique (one of many devised for skinning this fish), but if you have a dogfish in front of you as you read, these instructions should become clear. If it all sounds too complicated, get a friendly charter skipper or seasoned sea angler to show you the way.

First make sure your dogfish is dead. This species is unusually reluctant to die, so we're not being flippant. If in any doubt, hit it hard on the head, twice.

Now turn your dogfish upside down. You're going to eviscerate and behead it with one extended cut of the knife. Assuming you're right-handed, grasp both its anal fins (the ones either side of its belly) with your left hand and lift them a little. Assess the cut you're about to make for a moment or two before you make it. It should start under the anal fins just on the tail side of the anal vent. Cut down a few centimetres to begin with, but steer the blade to the horizontal as it meets the meat of the body, then slice along it, parallel to the board, up to the fish's throat, cutting the belly away.

When the blade gets close to the back of the head, stop. You'll see that by angling the knife blade down at right angles to the board, you could now simply cut off its head – so this is what you do. Slice right through to the board and pull away the head – with it will come all the guts you released as you sliced along

the belly cavity. Discard the head and guts, and the body-with-tail piece that remains will already look much more manageable. All you have to do is skin it and it will be ready for the pan. (Incidentally, you may find that, even after being boshed, beheaded and gutted, dogfish 'bodies' continue to writhe around, although they are quite clearly dead. Spooky, but it gives new meaning to the word 'fresh'.)

You're now going to peel the skin off the dogfish in two strips – one from either flank of the tapering body. You first need to slice off the dogfish's remaining fins – the dorsal fin on its back and the ventral fin underneath, near the tail. Cut a couple of extra millimetres of flesh off with each fin. Now make two body-length cuts along the skin with the tip of your knife, from tail to (missing) head. One goes right along the middle of its back (that's the cut you can see in the picture above), the other along the underside until it meets the original belly cut. Each cut should be through the skin, a few millimetres deep into the flesh.

Now use your knife to lift a little flap of the sandpapery skin from each side of the wrist of the tail. These flaps are your 'tabs' with which to grip and tear off the skin, from tail to head. One side, then the other. Grip is everything, and the best tool is a pair of wide-nosed pliers.

Hold the tail of the fish in one hand (a glove or rag will help). Grip the first tab of tail skin with pliers and pull down, stripping the skin as you go. With a bit of luck, it'll all come off in one tidy piece. If it tears, just whittle yourself another tab and pull again. Repeat the procedure on the other side. Finally, cut the tail off.

You will be left with a remarkably kitchen-friendly portion of fish. Remember, there are no bones, just that central column of spinal cartilage. This is easily removed – just slice a centimetre or so deep either side of it, from the belly side, then work underneath it with the tip of your knife to wheedle it out. You will have effectively 'butterflied' the remaining portion, which will open out into a nice fillet. You can cook it as it is, or it can be sliced almost any way you like, into smaller strips, or nuggets, for flouring, breadcrumbing or battering, then shallow or deep frying. Strips or chunks can also be dropped into soups or stews.

Fish prep kit

All of the fish skills described so far are much easier when you are working with decent tools and equipment. Here follows a quick run-down of what you need. In addition, you'll find a good supply of tea towels useful – they are the best things to use for holding a fish while you gut, clean or even skin it. To avoid undue domestic grief, and a washing basket that smells like the drains at Billingsgate, appropriate a batch of old tea towels that you keep specifically for fish work, and wash them separately.

Filleting knives

The easiest filleting knife to use is a sharp one – which is why blunt ones cause far more accidents. It is therefore essential to own not only a suitable knife but an effective sharpener, too, which should be used at the beginning of every filleting session.

Broadly speaking, there are two kinds of filleting knife we can recommend. The Scandinavian style of knife has an extremely flexible blade, 15–20cm long, which ends in a shallow, curving point with two cutting bevels, one either side of the blade. Japanese fish knives are shaped like a bread knife: long and rectangular with an angle of 45° at the tip, and a cutting bevel along only one side of the blade (you can choose left- or right-sided bevels, depending on whether you are left- or right-handed). These knives are nowhere near as flexible as the Scandinavian ones, so they are harder to use for filleting, but excellent for slicing sashimi or sushi. Japanese knives are also very sharp, and need to be sharpened only along the single bevelled side, so they require a whetstone block sharpener rather than the pull-through style, which is designed to sharpen both sides of a blade.

Some professional filleting knives fall somewhere in between the Scandinavian and Japanese styles. They have a double-bevelled edge, a wider and not very flexible blade, but they are made of very high-quality steel, which means they will normally hold an edge longer than a Scandinavian blade. They all do the job, but the Scandinavian types (which are usually on sale in our local tackle shop) are the ones we have generally adopted.

Some fishermen, and fish cooks, keep buying new knives of varying designs and end up with a collection that would scare a yakuza gang member. Yet they don't really feel comfortable with any of them. Better to choose just one type of knife and get to know it well. In fact, if you go on fishing trips yourself, buy two identical filleting knives – one for the kitchen, the other for the boat. The one you take to sea will, no matter how hard you resist, end up being abused and co-opted for cutting bait. This will inevitably dull its edge, especially if used on the gunwale or the lid of the engine box.

Keep your kitchen filleting knife as pure, clean and sharp as you can. Try to restrict its use to fish – don't be tempted to bone a leg of lamb with it – and bear in mind that it will stay sharper for longer if you fillet on a wooden block rather than a nylon cutting board.

Knife sharpeners

Even a great knife is only as good as it is sharp. There's a huge range of devices designed to give your knives an edge: butcher's steels, whetstones, strops, pull-through sharpeners, electric-powered sharpeners, diamond blocks, and even knife-holders and sheaths that contain their own built-in sharpening system.

We'd say, forget all except two of them. The safest and most efficient tool for dressing a knife with cutting bevels on both sides of the blade is the pull-through sharpener. It's hard to go wrong or to blunt your blade with one of these, whereas a single bad stroke with a butcher's steel can result in an edge you could sleep on. Such pull-through sharpeners are rather frowned upon by knife nuts and serious cheffy types. Okay, they aren't the purist's way of getting an edge and they do eat through blades a bit quicker than other techniques, but when you're starting out you can't get better. Just draw the blade through from hilt to tip (not back and forth) three or four times, pressing firmly, and the job's done.

A whetstone with a fine grain (diamond whetstones are pricy but excellent), is the only other bit of knife-sharpening kit you will ever need. These are good for knives with either a single or a double bevel. If you're deft with a whetstone, you can use it after the pull-through sharpener, to make your blade even keener. They can also be used to tweak all manner of other blades, from garden shears to African spears.

Scissors

Scissors can perform a number of fish tasks as well as or better than a knife – trimming tails and cutting off fins, removing gills, tidying up ragged fillets, snipping through the belly shell of a boiled lobster, slicing squid and cuttlefish, and even gutting small fish such as sardines, sprats and herrings. A strong, well-made pair of kitchen scissors with easy-grip handles and high-quality steel blades is as worthwhile an investment as a good filleting knife.

Descalers

These come in a variety of shapes and sizes, including fish-shaped ones, which look terribly stylish, and plastic-handled utilitarian ones, which don't. Our favourite is a cheap and cheerful design that looks a bit like a doll-sized tennis racquet without strings. It has a plastic handle and a metal bow-shaped 'blade', with one jagged, almost saw-toothed, edge and one smooth one. Fish with small scales will need attention only from the smooth edge, while fish with big scales can be given a rough pass with the jagged edge, followed by a smooth pass with the flipside. If you expect to be descaling a lot of bass and bream, then (apart from the fact that we'd like to come fishing with you) we would particularly recommend one of these, as the long handle keeps your fingers clear of the fish and its wicked spines. They cost less than a fiver from tackle shops, so it's best to buy two: one for the kitchen, the other for taking out fishing.

For the thriftily minded, an effective scaler can easily be improvised, or made at home. A discarded scallop shell does the job pretty well. Even better is a small block of wood that you can hold in one hand, with a few tacks or short nails banged into it, the heads left a few millimetres proud of the wood. But our favourite homemade version by far – based on a 'design' popular in the tropics – is the beer-bottle-top descaler. Not only is it a very satisfactory bit of recycling but it also works brilliantly. How you make one should be self-explanatory from the picture on page 55.

Pin-bone pliers

Properly designed pin-bone pliers, sold through catering outlets, can easily cost the best part of £20, which really hurts – especially as an ordinary pair of thin-nosed pliers can be bought from a hardware shop for a fraction of that. The sensible option might appear to be to buy the cheap alternative. But workshop pliers don't do the job nearly so well, for one simple reason: the handles aren't sprung, like they are on proper pin-bone pliers.

Pin boning is a tactile affair that calls for a fair amount of dexterity (see page 67). You're using the fingertips of one hand to feel the fillet and locate the pin bones, while the other hand controls the pliers. With fishmonger's pliers, you simply release the pressure after pulling out the offending bone and they'll spring open, letting the plucked bone fall from their jaws; whereas workshop pliers don't spring open, so you need to use both hands to open them and drop each bone. This means you lose your place on the fillet and have to search again for the line of pin bones. With the wrong tool it's a job that can quickly turn sticky and frustrating – and correspondingly sweary.

Pin boning should be a rhythmic task: locate, grab, pull, release; locate, grab, pull, release… The more rhythm you can establish, the better you'll do the job and the more you'll enjoy doing it.

Some consolation for the price you'll have to pay is that real pin-bone pliers have other uses too; they're perfect when you're plucking poultry and game birds, to pinch out the last few stubborn feathers, and for removing tail and wing feather stumps. Made of stainless steel and dishwasher proof, pin-bone pliers are the perfect present for a fish-loving cook (hint, hint).

Chilling and storing

As soon as a fish is dead, the onset of decay will be a direct function of time and temperature. As fish are cold-blooded, and generally live in a cool environment, the spectrum of microbes and bacteria that naturally inhabit them are active at relatively low temperatures. But while a fish is alive, its organs and cells (the gills, liver, kidneys, blood etc) regulate their levels. Once it is dead, these functions rapidly fail. The bugs will have a field day. Those with the potential to multiply, by breaking down and feeding on the flesh of the fish, do particularly well. If the temperature of the fish rises, the microbial activity will also rise. And since these processes are themselves exothermic – they generate heat – the onset of decay in a warming fish is exponential. Oily fish are particularly susceptible. A newly caught mackerel or sardine left lying under a hot sun will be spoiled within a few hours.

Commercial fishermen have long understood the importance of getting fish as cold as possible as soon as possible. The quality, and hence the market price, of their catch depends on it. They know that if they can get the fish down close to 0°C within a couple of hours of catching, and keep it there, then fish that would be spoiled within a couple of days at a mere 6–7°C will last for well over a week. At the same time, they would rather not freeze it if they don't have to. Frozen fish will keep for weeks, even months, but freezing damages the cell structure of the flesh: the water in the cells expands, rupturing them. Later, when the fish is defrosted, its flesh will be wetter and softer – more sponge-like – than it was when fresh. When it is cooked, the taste should be unimpaired but the texture will often disappoint.

Crushed or flaked ice is the magical substance that keeps fish in prime condition, and trawlers the world over carry tonnes of the stuff in their holds. It works so well because it rapidly chills the fish to around 0°C, and holds it there steadily. It is far more effective and economical than giant on-board fridges ever could be. The 'wet' contact means the chilling happens rapidly and evenly, while the way in which the ice can be shovelled around gives the fishermen maximum control. And ice, unlike fridges, cannot break down; it can only melt. Deep in the hold, insulated several feet below the deck, this happens very slowly indeed. That's why, when commercial fishing boats carry their own refrigeration units, they are usually there to make fresh ice rather than to chill and store the catch.

Ice for anglers

Some anglers are rather lackadaisical in their approach to storing the fish they have just caught. They'll leave it on the deck of a boat, or lying on the beach, for several hours after catching it (maybe partially draped with a warm wet rag to 'protect' it from the full glare of the summer sun). Back home, as often as not, they will bung it straight in the freezer – ungutted, unchilled and generally unloved. Should they ever muster the energy to defrost and attempt to cook it, they are surely destined for disappointment. No wonder so many sea anglers leave the fruits of their day's fun on the boat with the charter skipper and pick up a portion of fish and chips on the way home.

In fairness to our anglers, however, they are definitely improving in this area. If you want to catch fish, and you want to eat what you catch, then the sooner

you get an 'ice habit', the better. All the best charter skippers now carry a large icebox on board their boats. But you should take your own icebox, too, pretty much whenever you go fishing. Continuity of the chill is vital to keep your fish in good nick. It's a shame if fish that have been carefully iced all day on the boat are then transferred into a couple of bin bags in the boot of a car, so that they warm up on the drive home.

A good, 'family-sized', plastic picnic cool box is therefore an essential bit of kit for the angler-cook. In a perfect world, you'd fill it one-third full with crushed ice or ice cubes. In this less than perfect world, those blue plastic ice packs that you put in the freezer are fine. Lots of little ones are better than a couple of big ones. Once in a while, you may catch a fish that is so big it won't fit in your cool box (5kg is, we reckon, the upper limit). Frankly, that's a problem to relish, isn't it? You may have to fillet such a fish, or behead it, or betail it, to enable cold storage. Of course, it won't look so impressive when you get it home. So, just in case, make sure you remember your camera as well as your icebox.

Superstitious anglers are convinced that such scout-like preparations will guarantee a lousy day's fishing. But if you take an icebox with you *every single time you go fishing*, you will soon break the jinx.

It's not just the angler-cook who should consider using ice to transport fish back home; sometimes the shopper should, too. If you're going to be buying fish, and you know that it's likely to take an hour or three to get that fish home, then you should take a cold box, or insulated cool bag, plus ice pack, with you to the fishmonger's (or even the supermarket, if that's where you buy your fish).

Fish in the fridge

When you get your fish home, you're obviously going to put it in the fridge. Where else is there? The only drawback is that at somewhere between 5 and 10°C, most domestic fridges aren't cold enough to keep fish at its best. This is not really an issue if you are planning to consume the fish on the same day you have caught/bought it. But if you want to keep it for more than 24 hours, fridge temperature matters. Were you able to store your just-caught pollack at less than 2°C, it would keep for at least five days.

So it's worth getting to know your fridge a bit. You may be organised enough to remember to put it on maximum chill when you're 'expecting' some fish (we're not). Or you may discover that, even on its regular setting, it has a cold spot. (The Fearnley fridge, for example, has been noted for its annoying habit of lightly freezing salad leaves that were pushed too close to the back, on the middle shelf. Clearly the temperature there is close to zero…)

The best way to store whole smaller fish or fish fillets in the fridge is to dry them well, lay them on a plate, then put the plate inside a large plastic bag, which you tuck under the plate, but otherwise leave unsealed. Larger whole fish can be wrapped in a damp tea towel, then loosely in a plastic bag or two.

Smoked fish stored in the fridge should be sealed properly in a bag or cling film, or they'll permeate the whole fridge with their smoky, fishy aroma. Generally, salted, smoked and other cured fish don't thrive in the fridge for too long, unless they are vac-packed, stored in Tupperware, or fully sealed in some other way. Cured fish will dry out more quickly in chilled air, as you'll know if you've ever left a tin of anchovies open in the fridge – they quickly harden as the salty flesh reacts to the cold. So tightly wrap your leftovers of smoked fish, gravad lax/max and the like in cling film when you return them to the fridge, and make sure open jars or tins of anchovies are topped up with enough oil to cover the remaining fillets.

In the end, of course, it's you, not your fridge, who decides how fresh a fish is and how soon it has to be eaten (or whether, worst case scenario, it is time to chuck it). Use your nose and eyes to assess it, according to the criteria discussed on pages 44–5. If you deem it a bit borderline, that doesn't mean you can't eat it. But you might choose to cook it differently – maybe you'd bake it in foil with some pungent aromatics – garlic, ginger, chilli, soy – rather than steam it to serve plain, or with a very subtle sauce.

De-chilling your fish

As with meat, it's usually a good idea to remove fish from the fridge or icebox a little while before cooking it. This is particularly important with large fish that you intend to poach or bake whole, but it also applies to thick fillets, cutlets and tranches. You don't want to spend the first half of the cooking time simply driving the chill off the fish, or testing it every 5 minutes to see if it's still raw in the middle.

We are not suggesting you sit your fish on a sunny windowsill; rather, leave it loosely covered at cool room temperature, in the larder or in a shady corner of the kitchen, for perhaps an hour or two for thick fillets, three or four for a 2–3kg whole fish. Once it has lost its chill, the fish will cook a little more evenly and obligingly.

Remember that sushi and sashimi, ceviche, gravad lax/max and other marinated fish, and smoked fish and cold shellfish salads should all ideally be served and eaten cool or at room temperature – but not severely chilled. Take all such fish out of the fridge a good half hour or more before you serve them and you will experience a much fuller range of flavours when you eat them.

Freezing fish

In 1920, a field naturalist working for the US government in the Arctic Circle observed the local Inuit guides catching fish through ice-holes for camp supplies. Once caught, the fish were laid on the ice and frozen solid within minutes. Days later, the same fish were thawed out and tasted as though they were fresh.

The naturalist was Clarence Birdseye, who went on to invent techniques for commercially freezing fish, meat and vegetables. He discovered that slim, rectangular blocks of white fish froze extremely well, and he then had the brainwave of coating these piano-key-sized slabs of fish in breadcrumbs. He called them 'fish sticks', and they were a modest success. But when, in 1955, they were renamed 'fish fingers', the market took off. To date, over 15 billion fish fingers have been sold to British consumers alone.

One of Birdseye's discoveries was that white fish freeze better than oily fish. The oils in the flesh of the latter are prone to oxidation, and even while frozen they will gradually become rancid. You certainly *can* freeze oily fish: careful wrapping (or better still vac-packing) excludes air, which delays the oxidation process considerably. Nonetheless, you should consume frozen oily fish such as mackerel, sardines and herring within 3 months.

White fish, on the other hand, that is well wrapped and kept at a constant temperature, will last for at least 6 months. We have to admit we've eaten pollack, cod and even the odd bass that have lingered in the bottom of the big white box for well over a year. And, if not exactly the apex of quality, they've been quite passable.

That said, fishermen can be too cavalier about freezing fish – chucking their catch into the deep recesses of the freezer when they're knackered from a day's fishing. Months later, they discover something unidentifiable lurking behind the frozen peas, with all the culinary appeal of yellow snow. Serious fish cooks, on the other hand, can be too distrustful of the freezer, suspecting it to be a malevolent device that will ruin, or at least taint, any nice fresh piece of fish put into it.

The right attitude to fish and freezers is somewhere between that of the lazy fisherman and the paranoid cook. Yes, fish that has been frozen will never be quite as good as it was when it was spanking fresh, for the reasons explained on page 79. But a fish that was carefully frozen when still in good nick will beat an unfrozen, less-than-fresh specimen every time. If you catch your own fish – or can buy really fresh fish from close to source, then you need to make friends with your freezer. Use it correctly, and prepare your fish for freezing with a bit of care, and you're never very far away from a delicious fishy meal.

So, however obvious it may seem, it's vital to remember that frozen fish can only ever be *almost* as good as it was before it was frozen. If you freeze poor-quality fish, what you thaw out will be even worse. Therefore, how a fish is treated before it gets frozen – from the moment it's caught to the moment you slip it into the freezer – is critical. All the advice we have given you about bleeding fish, gutting them, removing the gills, wiping them and above all chilling them as soon as possible, becomes doubly important when preparing fish for the freezer, rather than for immediate consumption.

How you freeze a fish is also important. Whether it's whole or filleted, how you pack it, and how many fish you freeze in one go – all these factors will affect the quality of your eventual mouthful. Various unfortunate outcomes can result from sloppy practice:

FREEZER BURN, which is when the flesh or skin has dried out excessively and the texture of the fish has been damaged.

GAPING, which is when the muscle flakes have started to separate. It is most noticeable in frozen fillets, creating gaps that make the fillet look ragged and unappetising. When cooked, the texture may be correspondingly soft and mushy.

SHRINKAGE, which is when the defrosted fillet seems to have diminished to half the size it was when it went in the freezer.

The good news, however, is that these bad things can be avoided by following some very simple rules:

1. **DRY YOUR FISH WELL** Whether you are freezing a whole, dustbin-lid-sized turbot or a single fillet of pouting, your fish needs to be thoroughly dried with a clean tea towel first. Excess water on the fish will expand as it freezes, creating ice crystals that will penetrate the surface of the flesh and alter its texture. What's more, water clinging to the inside of the wrapping your fish is frozen in is a potential breeding ground for bacteria, which will attack the fish before, and even during, its freezer life and – most perniciously – from the moment it starts to defrost.

In this context, the natural mucus on very fresh fish is no bad thing. It actually protects the fish while it is frozen. So, when freezing a very fresh whole fish, don't feel the need to wipe away every last trace of its slime. This applies only to fish that have not been descaled, however – that process will already have removed most of the benign gunk. Freezing fish with scales (and some slime) still on is generally not a bad plan – except that you will really struggle to descale a defrosted fish. So if you know you want to end up with a nicely descaled fish, or fillets, then that's what you should put in the freezer.

2. WRAP AND BAG WITH CARE We tend to 'double wrap' most of our fish. A fairly tight binding of cling film acts as a second skin, protecting the first one and the cut surfaces of fillets from both freezer burn and condensing moisture – two or three layers will do the job. We'll then bag the wrapped fish or fillets in strong transparent freezer bags.

Don't freeze fish in carrier bags, bin bags or any other kind of bag that you lugged it home in. It doesn't matter whether you caught the fish yourself or bought it from a supermarket fish counter: you still need to unpack, dry, cling-wrap and re-pack it before freezing.

The thicker the bag, the more protection it provides. If a bag gets ripped by a sharp fin and doesn't seal properly, then air and ice crystals will get inside, causing the flesh to dehydrate. Ideally you should snip off all fins and spines before wrapping and bagging fish for the freezer.

3. DON'T FREEZE LARGE AMOUNTS OF FISH TOGETHER There is so much water within fish flesh that there is always a certain amount of 'expansion' during freezing. If you put a large single pack crammed with lots of fish into the freezer, the exterior layers will freeze first, with the centre of the pack remaining unfrozen for considerably longer. As the fish on the outside freeze and expand, they will begin to crush the unfrozen fish at the centre, and bruise and damage their flesh.

4. FREEZE QUICKLY The quicker you freeze fish, and the colder the temperature that you keep it frozen at, the longer and better it will last. If you remember, set your freezer to 'boost' or 'super-chill' a couple of hours before you put your fish in it. And ideally keep it at least −15°C at all times. Don't pile up a batch of fish to be frozen in the same part of the freezer, as the ones in the middle of the pile will freeze too slowly. Spread the bags around, amongst other items that are already frozen, to speed up the chilling.

5. LABEL, DATE, ROTATE Proper labelling is a pain, especially when you're dog-tired or in a hurry, but it's essential. You might think, 'I don't need to label this, I'll never forget what's in such a distinctive package!' Two months later, someone could beat you repeatedly around the head with the very same package and you still wouldn't have the foggiest idea what was inside. A label stating what's in the bag and when it was frozen may seem a touch obsessive for some, but you'll be glad you took the trouble.

It makes sense to use fish in the same order it went into the freezer. Once you've decided to favour an item that was only recently frozen over one that's been in there for a couple of months, the chances of your coming back to that older fish and doing something good with it are ever-diminishing.

Freezing smoked and salted fish

Both smoked and salted fish freeze, and recover from freezing, extremely well, since much of the water has been removed by these processes. So the damage done by expanding ice crystals is greatly reduced. We often lightly salt pollack fillets (see page 124) before freezing them. But smoked and salted fish still needs to be thoroughly dried and carefully packed before freezing.

Many smokers actually like to work with frozen fish, provided it has been handled and frozen with care. After defrosting, the mild damage to the cellular structure of the fish flesh is partially 'repaired' by the subsequent brining process, as it draws excess moisture from the fish, and the flesh re-contracts somewhat. Nonetheless, the resulting fillets are more open grained, and the smoke will penetrate them more effectively.

Freezing sashimi and sushi fish

Freezing is stipulated by the Food Standards Agency as a part of the preparation of fresh raw fish for commercial sashimi and sushi. Its reason is that freezing kills off any parasites in the fish, making it safer to eat raw. But such safety-conscious behaviour will always be at the expense of that fresh-fish texture. Many UK sushi chefs find the law incomprehensible and infuriating, arguing that raw fish has been served for centuries in Japan without pre-freezing.

We take our lead from the sushi chefs, and don't pre-freeze our raw fish. Our sashimi and sushi are made with super-fresh fish we've caught ourselves, or bought direct from boat or fisherman. We clean it thoroughly and prepare it with great care (see pages 130–2), and to date it's done us nothing but good.

Defrosting

The way you defrost fish has consequences for its eating quality, and the key advice is *don't rush it*. In particular, don't use warm air (i.e. a low oven) or warm water in an attempt to accelerate the process. If you do, the outer layer will defrost and even 'cook' slightly, while other parts of the fish are still frozen solid. Fish flesh is very sensitive to heat and any temperature above 50°C will actually begin to cook the fish. Once your fish is a hotchpotch of frozen/part-frozen/thawed/warm flesh, it's impossible to get it all back to an equitable state.

The two best ways to defrost any fish are to put it in the fridge overnight or to immerse it completely in a large bowl of cold water. If you use the cold water method, which is much faster, you must keep the fish completely sealed inside a plastic bag: don't expose the flesh to the water or it will start to absorb it and become soft and fragile.

The overnight fridge method, though slower, is gentler in terms of limiting collateral damage. The temperature rise from −18°C in the freezer to about 5°C in your fridge will allow the ice to melt and the flesh to thaw gradually. Take the fish out of its bag and place it in a colander inside a larger bowl or on a tray, so that it doesn't marinate in its own melt water and start to absorb it.

Thawing fish naturally at cool room temperature, or outside in a shady place, is acceptable. But avoid direct sunlight, or temperatures much in excess of 15°C, especially for really big fish. They may take several hours to defrost, and the outside of the fish may even start to go off before the centre is defrosted. Always take measures to keep flies (and cats) off your fish while it is defrosting.

Shellfish skills

If you are starting to be swayed by our thesis that handling fish is both fascinating and rewarding (as well as speaking to your inner hunter-gatherer), then be assured that the same is true of shellfish – only several times more so. Compared with fin fish, there is sometimes more work involved in preparing shellfish (think crabs), sometimes less (think mussels). But in all cases, beholding the relevant creature in its entirety (preferably while it is still alive) adds hugely to the sense of occasion. There aren't many creatures that you have an opportunity to meet and greet before you eat.

As the term shellfish implies, we're dealing with marine animals here whose defining characteristic is that they have shells. Summarising the main families, in a not overly taxonomic fashion, we have crustaceans, such as crabs, lobsters and prawns, who tend to have claws and crawl around on a generous number of legs; bivalves, such as mussels, oysters and scallops, with their two-sided castanet-style shells that hide meat of very varying flavour and texture; molluscs, such as winkles and whelks, which are clearly underwater snails; and, out on a limb (quite a few limbs, in fact), the extraordinary squid, cuttlefish and octopus – they do have shells, but they're strictly vestigial.

Another defining characteristic, we would say, is the unusually intense feelings of involvement – physical and even emotional – that are evoked by their consumption. You can't eat a bowl of mussels as you might a bowl of cereal – with casual detachment and your mind on other things. To devour them, you have to engage with them, acknowledging their form and nature. It's a form of heightened awareness that, with luck, will stimulate your appetite and increase your pleasure. But not everyone can handle the stark reality of this carnivorous behaviour (more real to some than eating a fat steak). And we all know someone who says they can't/don't/won't eat shellfish. Some people have a genuine allergic reaction, others merely a physical aversion. But there is no doubt that in many cases, whether it's acknowledged or not, the problem is all in the mind. It's all too visceral, too near the knuckle – or the shell.

This is, of course, exactly what so many of us love about shellfish. There is not much indifference around it. You don't hear people say, 'Oysters, I can take them or leave them.' They either rave or they revile.

Well, we definitely count ourselves among the ravers. And we rave about the preparation of shellfish as well as its consumption. Although it is now possible to have much of the prep work done for you, by a fishmonger or a chef, we feel strongly that if you always take this route you will be missing out. The shucking of scallops, the evisceration of squid, the cracking of crab claws, the peeling of prawns, the picking of winkles – all of these acts will heighten the anticipation and stimulate the appetite for the meal to come.

Often, the benefits of tackling whole live shellfish are practical, too. If you want to eat certain shellfish at their best, you have no choice but to engage with their natural packaging. You can't buy fresh oysters, cockles or mussels without buying the shells they come in. Yes, you can buy a ready dressed crab, and you can buy a whole pre-cooked crab. But they will never come with the same guarantee of freshness as a living creature that is defiantly waving its claws at you even as you contemplate its purchase, its despatch at your hands and its consumption at your table.

Killing and cooking a crab

Most crabs that are sold alive for cooking at home will have had their claws clipped: a membrane between the two pincers is nicked with a blade to render the claws loose and harmless. But if you are in any doubt about this – especially if you happen to be buying a crab straight from a boat – check, and if necessary ask for it to be done. As a fish shopper, it's not worth running even the slightest risk of getting pinched. Having a hand or finger crushed by a crab claw is no laughing matter – it's not just painful, it can be seriously damaging to tissue and even bone. (Should you ever decide to take up casual crab and lobster potting, get a professional to show you how to nick a crab's claws, and bind a lobster's with rubber bands.)

Crabs have a simple nervous system but we still can't be sure they don't feel pain or distress. It is considered humane to kill them quickly before putting them into a pan of boiling water. So have a large pan of well-salted water (about 10g salt per litre) ready on a full rolling boil before you kill the crab. This is most effectively done by driving a sharp spike – a small pointed screwdriver or bradawl, for instance – into one of two points on the crab's body. We always spike both points, belt and braces as it were, to be completely sure the crab is dead before we cook it. So, to kill a crab, proceed as follows:

Lay the crab on its back. The first vital point is revealed by lifting the triangular tail flap in the centre of its undercarriage. Here you'll see a cone-shaped indentation in the shell. Push the spike firmly right into the middle of it and twist it a couple of times (see top picture). This will sever vital tissues in the crab's ventral nerve centre.

Remove your spike and immediately pierce the crab a second time, this time in the head at the top of the carapace: the spike must go in through the mouth, between and below the eyes (see lower picture). Lever the spike backwards and forwards a couple of times to destroy the vital nerve tissues here.

These two moves, in quick succession, will render the crab limp and lifeless in a matter of seconds. You can then lower it gently into your pan of boiling water. One advantage of killing your crabs before boiling them is that they won't usually shed their legs when they go in the boiling water – which they almost always do if you drop them in alive.

After the water returns to the boil, cook crabs weighing up to 1kg for 10–12 minutes; for larger crabs, add 3–4 minutes to the cooking time for every extra 500g. Small crabs such as velvets will take just 5 minutes. Remove your cooked crab(s) from the pan and leave to steam off and cool. If you want to accelerate cooling, take the crab outside into a cool breeze – but for heaven's sake don't dunk it in cold water, or this will seep back into the shell and make the meat wet. With careful cooking and cooling, your home-boiled crab should be better than anything you can buy ready cooked – such crabs are usually batch boiled, dozens at a time, in big kettles, and are often overcooked.

When a boiled crab has cooled off, it is ready to crack, pick and dress – or it can be put in the fridge on a plate (no need to wrap it up). It must then be eaten within 48 hours. The instructions that follow apply to pretty much all crabs, including spiders (page 557) and velvets (page 555). There are minor anatomical differences, variations in scale of course, and in the relative quantities of white and brown meat. But generally the approach, the tools and, most importantly, the sheer tactile joy are transferable across all species.

Picking and dressing a crab

There are two approaches to dressing a crab. One is the 'eat as you go' method, in which your guests are supplied with various hammers, crackers and picks, along with buttered bread, mayonnaise and a salad or two – plus wine, of course. It's a lively affair, as claws are cracked, legs pulled and nuggets of meat teased from the shell. Everything gets eaten as it is picked (see page 351 for our serving suggestions).

Then there's the 'hoarding' approach, in which an individual or team of pickers sets out to extract and save every last morsel of white or brown meat (separate bowls laid out for each) for use in some recipe, hot or cold, simple or sophisticated. Undertaken solo, this can be an almost transcendental experience, in which the picker is transported into a crab trance, cracking, picking, twisting and scooping until all that remains is an empty carapace, the hollow tubes of leg sections, and fragments of claw shell, like broken china, orange-brown on the outside, clean white on the inside. But it is also a pleasant pastime to engage in over a glass or two with a fishing buddy, or even a spouse (not that the two are mutually exclusive). There's no question that women are better – more thorough, more patient – at crab picking than men. (Or at least Marie is much better at it than Hugh, and it consoles him to generalise the point. If there is any rule here, Nick claims vociferously that he and Helen are the exceptions.)

Whether the kind of gratification you are aiming for is instant or delayed, a certain amount of method will serve you in good stead. To tackle a whole crab, you should first take off its legs and claws. Twist the legs off at the point where they meet the body, rather than just yanking them, and try to remove the articulated socket that they sit in too. By pulling this out, you'll expose hidden pathways to the Holy Grail of white crabmeat within the body.

When the legs and claws are off, you need to open up the crab by pulling the undercarriage (or 'body shell') away from the hard-topped carapace (or 'head shell'), as shown in the picture on the left. We find the easiest way to do this is to press your thumb into the mouth, just beneath the eyes, and prise the body apart from the front end. So, using the flat of your thumb protected against the sharp shell with a scrap of cloth, or the bowl of a teaspoon, crush the mouthparts and mandibles under the eyes back against the inside of the shell. This gives you an opening into which you can insert two thumbs, while holding the carapace and undercarriage with the spread fingers of each hand. Pull the two thumbs apart from each other, levering the carapace and body apart.

Now's a good time to identify the very few parts of the crab that you cannot eat. First, look at the carapace. The only bits you need to discard, apart from the shell itself, are the mandibles – the spiny, plastic-looking bits behind the eyes and around the mouthparts – and the small, yellow-white papery sac that attaches to them, which is the crab's stomach. What remains is the brown meat (see picture five of the sequence) – the rich, creamy, brown, orange and yellow goo, which is basically the crab's internal organs. Some of the brown meat is firmly set, even moulded to the contours of the shell; but some is quite soft, even semi-liquid. It may look weird but it's all good stuff, and can be scooped out of the carapace with a dessertspoon, either for instant gratification or, if you're a 'hoarder', to put in your dedicated 'brown meat' bowl. The only other thing to look out for, and discard, is a fine papery-white membrane that sometimes clings to the edges of the brown meat.

Next, turn your attention to the undercarriage – the main body of the crab from which you have already removed the legs and claws. There's often a blob of yellowy-brown goo on top of it – this should be scraped out and added to the brown meat bowl. You'll also find, in a ring around the exposed interior, the notorious 'dead man's fingers'. All types of crab have these grey, pointed, hairy, floppy appendages. They are the crab's breathing apparatus, the equivalent of a fish's gills: their function is to filter water and extract oxygen. They aren't poisonous, but neither are they something you'd choose to eat, since they're fibrous, feathery and tough, so pull them off and discard them. Apart from the shell and a few dividing membranes, there's nothing more that needs to be thrown away.

Everyone loves the white meat (though some go quite potty for the brown) and conscientious crab picking is largely about extracting every last scrap of it. Much of the best white meat is hidden deep inside the undercarriage of the crab; compared to the claws and legs, this is the hardest white meat to extract. Twirl the whole thing around in your fingers and take a good look before you attack. Note the internal, honeycomb-like structure with 'portholes' where the legs once were. Inside these recesses are tantalising pockets of tightly packed, finely grained, sweet white meat.

Your mission is to remove as much of the white meat from the crevices as possible without damaging the delicate structure, the walls of which are made up of thin, almost translucent shell. Too much force, or careless picking, and shards of shell can easily find their way into the white meat bowl. Once you acquire a taste for crab picking, you'll find it becomes a matter of pride that you serve up white meat without shell splinters. You'll need to develop a sixth sense for spotting shards, zeroing in on the tiny fragments that dare to insult your picking prowess.

The best tool to tease out the pockets of white meat trapped within the leg sockets is a basic metal teaspoon, using the handle as the business end. You need one that comes to a fairly narrow flat end, about the width of a medium screwdriver. Once you've burrowed into each of the white-meat-yielding 'portholes' and can go no further, then it's time to chop the undercarriage in half, straight down between the two sets of leg sockets. You'll hear the shell splintering under the blade, but don't be alarmed: opening up the comb does make it possible to access a whole new cache of flesh.

Any chambers that are too small to probe with a teaspoon handle can be tackled with a shellfish pick, if you have one – they're spiky and 'picky' at one end, flat and 'scoopy' at the other. Proceed with care and you should be able pick both halves clean without too much risk of shell-shard contamination. You can, if you like, cut the halves of the body into quarters, thereby splitting open and exposing more meat-filled chambers. Again, it's an access-versus-contamination trade-off.

Now it's time to return to the legs and claws. These need to be lightly cracked – as opposed to smashed to smithereens – so the meat can be extracted in pleasingly large chunks, rather than salvaged from tiny fragments of shattered shell. You can use a small hammer if you like, provided you wield it with a degree of finesse (sharp taps are in order; swings that start behind your shoulder are not). But it is really best to use something wooden. We've tried everything from wooden spoons to small toffee mallets, meat tenderisers and rolling pins. They all work.

Whatever you choose, the force of your strike shouldn't be too great or you'll end up with a crushed mush of flesh and shell. Wrapping the claws lightly in a tea towel will help prevent chunks of shell ricocheting around your kitchen – although some would say (and not only the under-twelves) that a certain amount of flying claw is all part of the fun.

Once legs and claws have been cracked, it's just a matter of patiently picking, fiddling, probing and scraping until you have extracted every last precious flake of white meat. The super-conscientious will always double-check their personal pile of shell remnants for any shreds that evaded them first time round. On a good day for a 'hoarder', the pile of hard-to-extract white meat should be perhaps twice as big as the pile of easy-to-scoop brown (it will help to have chosen a big-clawed male – see page 554 for how to sex crabs).

If you've been eating as you pick, you may well find you've devoured the whole crab entirely *au naturel*, without so much as a squeeze or lemon or a blob of mayonnaise. And very satisfying that is, too. But if you've hoarded white meat and brown, you have a chance to 'dress' your crab: serving it up cold, but seasoned, with a few simple accompaniments – see page 350 for one of our favourite ways to dress crab.

Killing and cooking a lobster

Lobster is five times more expensive than crab, but is it five times more delicious? Of course not. To shell out a pony or more on a lobster that will barely feed two seems a bit bonkers if there's good crab to be had. On the other hand, it's hardly the lobster's fault that it is so expensive. It's still delicious, and fully deserves its reputation as one of the great shellfish treats.

So how do you reconcile the luxury of lobster with that uneasy feeling that you're getting fleeced every time you buy one? Perhaps by getting friendly with a lobster fisherman and buying live specimens straight from the boat. That way you can get lobster at half the price you'd pay in a London fishmonger's (and a quarter of what you'd pay in a restaurant.) Cooked by you, it will taste at least as good as anything a fishmonger (or chef) cooked for you.

Lobsters are even less sophisticated creatures than crabs, if you can imagine such a thing, and they do not have anything you could really call a brain. So the officially sanctioned method for killing them is less technical than it is for crabs, and involves no anatomical precision. They should simply be placed alive in a freezer for about 2 hours, until they are almost, but not quite, frozen – this will render them completely comatose.

They can then be dropped straight into a pan of rapidly boiling seawater, or well-salted fresh water (about 10g salt per litre, as for crabs). They'll be dead before they wake up. Once the water has returned to the boil, cook a lobster of 500g for 10 minutes, allow 15 minutes for one weighing 750g, and add an extra 5 minutes for every 500g after that.

The only other officially sanctioned way to kill a lobster is to split it lengthways down the middle – this is often how lobsters are prepared for a chargrill, wood oven or barbecue (see page 206). Again, it should be super-chilled first, until comatose. You can then simply bisect it lengthways with a large, heavy chopping knife (see overleaf). Less confident or more squeamish cooks may prefer to parboil it for about 5 minutes, to kill it first.

Dressing a lobster

Compared to picking a crab, a lobster is almost boringly easy to deconstruct.
This is because it is longitudinal. Once you've split it in half, the job is practically
over. Lobsters have no hidden tunnels of secret meat to excavate; what you see is
what you get.

So, to cleave a freshly boiled lobster in two, lay it belly down on a board with
its legs splayed out. Then, while holding the lobster firmly with one hand, stab
the tip of your most robust large knife into the centre of its head (with the blade
facing towards the lobster's nose – see the first two pictures above). There is a
clearly defined central 'seam' to guide your cut. Don't be gentle. Tap the handle
of your knife with the heel of your palm until the point crunches through the
shell and touches the board. With the point still resting on the block, lever the
knife blade down into the ridged seam with a firm downward cut, holding the
blade steady with the thumb and forefinger of one hand while you force down
the handle with the other. You're aiming to split the front half of the lobster's
head right down the middle, slicing through the mouthparts, until the blade hits
the board.

Now swivel the knife around 180° and following the line of your first cut in
the opposite direction, cut down through the length of the tail to split the lobster
firmly in two (see the third picture above).

Anatomically, a lobster is really just an oversized prawn. Most of its body
weight is made up of its muscle-bound tail. When cooked, this meat is firm and
white, and can be teased out of the half-shell as easily as a loaf of bread from
a well-greased tin. The only thing you need to look out for is a black vein that
runs the length of the tail. It is likely to appear on one side or other of your
longitudinal cut, though it may cross over if you haven't been super-straight.
This is the lobster's digestive tract, which should be removed and discarded.
Use the tip of a knife to ease it out.

Now you can turn your attention to the head section, which might look a bit
complicated, but isn't really. Within it, you'll see:
• A small, gritty stomach sac behind the mouth: discard this.
• The gills: these are similar to a crab's gills (or dead man's fingers), but smaller.
Chuck them, too.
• Some greyish-green or pinkish-brown, soft, smooth-textured meat: this is the
lobster's liver, and is known as the tomalley. On a raw or undercooked lobster,
it's sticky and almost jet black; cooked and set firm, it's like lobster liver pâté
– and absolutely not to be missed.

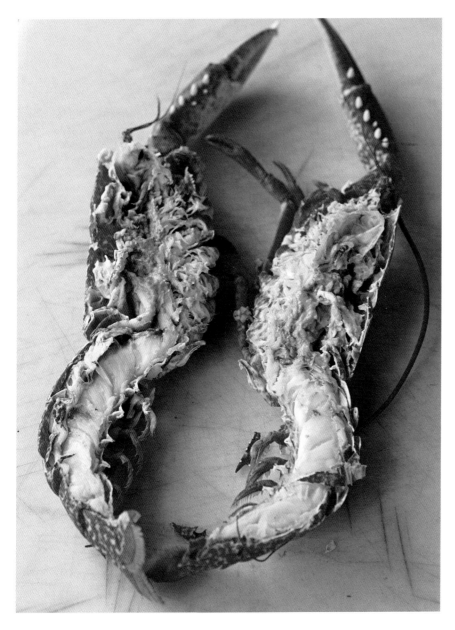

• The coral: in female lobsters, you'll find a red lump ranging from the size of a pea to the size of a prune. This is the coral, a part of the sexual organs that turns firm and scarlet on cooking. The cooked coral has a grainy texture with a bittersweet shellfish flavour – crustacean fudge! It's definitely worth eating.

The tail section, once peeled, offers a very substantial portion of firm, sweet flesh. The tomalley and the coral, on the other hand, are the nearest a lobster has to brown meat. Mixed up with a scant spoonful of good mayonnaise and maybe a dash of lemon juice and Worcestershire sauce, they will make a lively dressing to serve alongside the cooked tail.

Finally, don't forget the lobster's claws (as if you would). Provided the beast has not been overcooked, the claw meat will be sweet and juicy, with a slightly more fragile texture than that of the tail. To get at it, you will need to crack the

claws and the two jointed segments that attached them to the main body. A few quick, confident taps with the back of a heavy knife will do it, but claw crackers are also useful.

The truly dedicated will even have a go at the spindly legs. It is definitely worth pulling them from the sockets and sucking on the little scraps of flesh that come away with them. On bigger lobsters, you can snip the ends of the thicker leg sections and suck out a thin shred of white meat, as if through a straw.

When your lobster feast is over, you may want to reserve the shell and other debris for making stock (see page 257).

Cooking live shrimps, prawns and crayfish

Live prawns or shrimps, larger Dublin Bay prawns (also known as langoustines) and freshwater crayfish, can all be killed and cooked by boiling. Bring to the boil a large pan of seawater or well-salted fresh water (about 10g salt per litre). Drop the prawns, shrimps or crayfish into it. Once the water comes back to the boil, give prawns or shrimps 2 or 3 minutes and the bigger Dublin Bays and crayfish about 5 minutes. You don't need to time this to the second, but don't wander off and forget about them. Serious over-boiling will result in soft, mushy meat.

There is an ethical issue here, though, which we shouldn't duck. Prawns and shrimps are generally small enough for total immersion in rapidly boiling water to kill them almost instantly. This method of 'boiling alive' is therefore considered humane. But there's a grey area with intermediate-sized creatures, such as langoustines and freshwater crayfish, which represent the upper size limit of crustaceans that can be expected to die rapidly from this treatment. There is a case for erring on the side of mercy and giving them the anaesthetising deep-freeze treatment first. Two hours should be ample.

Peeling and preparing prawns

Once boiled, these crustaceans should be drained and left to cool. Spreading them out on a tray and taking them outside will speed this up considerably, especially if there's a breeze. Once cooled to handling temperature, they are ready to peel and eat, or can be refrigerated for 48 hours (but no more).

Prawns and shrimps are peeled with the fingers – at least we've never seen any other tools being used. One good trick for getting the tail out whole is to give the creature a little wiggle or bend in the third section from the tail end. This usually encourages the final narrow third of the tail to slip out a treat. Small prawns and brown shrimps can be eaten whole, heads, shells and all, or headless and tailless with a bit of body shell still in place. When we eat them, we like to peel a few, half peel a few and eat a few whole. And if we're feeling really greedy, we might revisit discarded heads when we've run out of whole shrimps. In fact, the heads of all prawns and shrimps should not be ignored: however small they are, they'll have a worthwhile portion of sweetly liverish goo inside, which can be scraped out with a fingernail or simply sucked from the torn end of the head.

The harder shell of a Dublin Bay prawn can be hand-peeled too, but it requires a little technique. As with the lobster, the shell on the underside of the prawn is weaker than the heavy armour over its head and back. To protect it, the hard shell of the back extends down and along the flanks of the prawn in a kind of 'skirt'. If you squeeze the two edges of the skirt together, you'll hear a popping noise as the fragile belly shell is compressed and torn. Ease them apart with your thumbs and the belly will tear open, revealing the firm tail meat, which can be teased out in a lovely two- or three-bite segment.

Alternatively, really big cooked langoustines can simply be bisected lengthways, like mini lobsters, and served in two halves. The heads of your langoustines, whether whole or split, really mustn't be overlooked – if you don't want them, someone else will (us, for instance). They have a really good dose of that tasty brown gloop that we keep banging on about. We'll scrape it out with the back of a thumbnail and suck it off (ideally when no one's looking).

Other ways of cooking prawns

Simply boiled prawns are delicious, but a charcoal fire, or a frying pan of garlicky olive oil, can add enticing flavours to their shells and flesh. If you're working with live shellfish, though, you are once again faced with a dilemma: how to kill them humanely. There are chefs who put live langoustines on the charcoal grill – or designate their underlings to do so. Pitifully they may make several attempts to crawl off, before giving up the struggle and succumbing to the heat. That may apply to both underlings and langoustines – and it isn't fair to either party.

Prawns and langoustines for the grill or barbecue should therefore be flung in rapidly boiling water, a few at a time, for a good 30 seconds to kill them before being finished over or under your fire of choice (see Garlic-sautéed Billy Winters, page 323). Really small prawns and shrimps – 4cm or less – can be thrown, a few at a time, alive into very hot oil in a pan, as they will be killed almost instantly on contact with the heat. But if in any doubt, for the sake of a humane despatch, consider the freezer for larger specimens, or a quick boil, or both.

Cleaning squid

If you are fortunate enough to catch squid (see page 588) or manage to buy fresh ones that are whole and intact, you may find yourself freaked out by the prospect of getting to grips with their weird anatomy. Don't worry: they may look as if they'll be trouble but in fact they are amazingly easy to clean. The sequence of pictures overleaf is worth a once-over before you begin – they should take most of the fear out of the process.

Over a sink or a bowl, or on a board, hold the body (known as the mantle) in one hand, then grab the head around the eyes and pull the body and head decisively apart. Most of what lurks inside the squid will be dragged out, connected to the head (see the pictures overleaf).

The quill, or part of it, may be left behind. If it hasn't appeared, feel inside to locate it. This is all that evolution has left of the squid's skeleton – a transparent, feather-shaped sliver of something that looks and feels very much like clear plastic (see right). It can usually be pulled out easily, but if it does break, put your hand in and fish out the second half. Use your fingers to pull out any more gunk that will come away easily.

If the squid doesn't appear to have shed its ink (and it will be pretty obvious if it has, as the body and tentacles are likely to be quite stained), you may be able to locate its ink sac, intact and still full of ink, among the innards attached to the head. Look for a slim, bluish-white pouch and remove it carefully. Cut

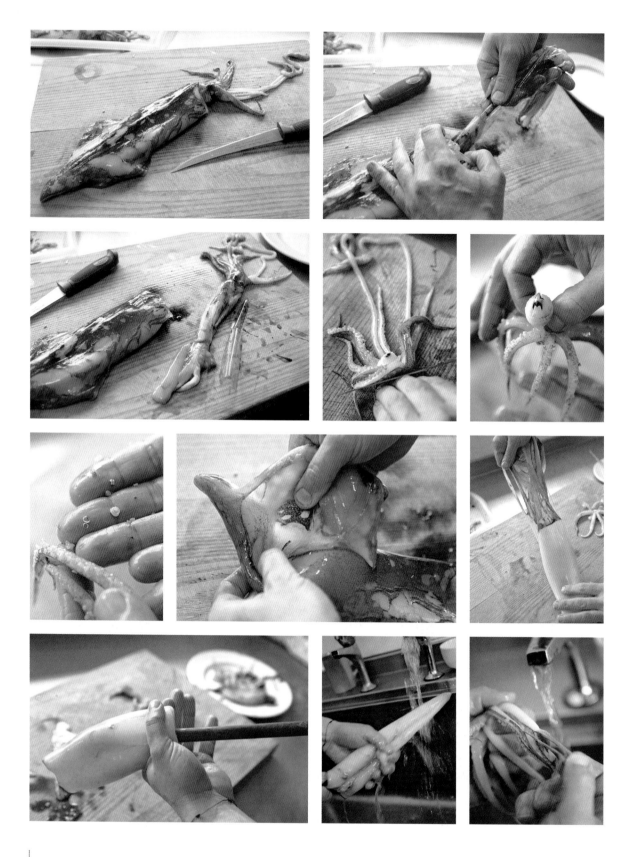

it open over a bowl to release the ink. If this amounts to more than a couple of teaspoons, it may be worth keeping for your recipe (it can be added to any 'wet' method of cooking, such as a soup, sauce or stew).

Lay the head, with its dangling entrails, on a board and push with your fingers immediately in front of the eyes and behind the beginning of the tentacles. You should feel a hard flesh ball, like a piece of gristle, under your fingers – this is the mouthparts and sharp, horny beak of the squid. Continue pushing to force this forward into the tentacles, then cut off the ring of tentacles immediately in front of the eyes. Keep the tentacles; lose the eyes and guts. Remove the hard, gristly ball and beak from just in front of the tentacles – it pulls away easily – and discard it. Give the tentacles a quick rinse and dry, removing any loose suckers, and make them the start of your 'good meat' pile.

Now return to the body. Rinse the inside of the squid under a cold running tap to get rid of any ink or remaining gloop. Pick up the body by the wings, then pull them back and press them together as if you were squeezing someone's elbows behind their back. Both wings should come off, along with some pink, patchy membrane that covers the mantle. You can get the rest of this membrane off the body and wings by rubbing with a tea towel.

The wings on medium and large squid are worth trimming and using, though they are always a mite tougher than the flesh of the body. They need to be trimmed of the thick edge by which they were attached to the mantle – feel it and you will notice the join is almost cartilaginous. Now peel off any remaining

membrane that covers the wing. The trimmed, skinned wings can then be sliced for cooking, or butterflied (see below).

The best way to clean the inside of the body properly is to turn the whole mantle cone inside out (as if you were turning a sock inside out). Do this by pushing the pointed end of the body in on itself with the handle of a wooden spoon (or a broom handle for really big squid). Then turn the squid inside out along the handle. Rinse and wipe away any guts that cling to the outside of the inside-out squid.

To make perfect squid rings (for deep frying, for instance – see page 332), you will need to cut them from a whole, intact cone – and they are best cut while it is turned inside out. This means the natural stresses in the mantle are pushing outwards, which will keep each squid ring circular while frying, rather than letting it collapse into a figure-of-eight shape (which it is inclined to do if sliced outside out).

Or, if you are going to be cutting the body open anyway, you can do that instead of turning it inside out. The best way is to slice a straight line from the edge of the mantle at the head end to the tip of it at the tail end. Feel or look for the natural ridge inside the body and make your cut more or less opposite this, not along it – it's useful to keep it as a marker for what was the inside of the squid's body.

Washed and wiped on both sides, your clean white triangle of squid flesh is now ready for slicing and cooking. Thick slices from a big squid are perfect for long, slow cooking (see the recipes on pages 284–5), but if you want to cook them fast in a pan or over charcoal, as we dearly love to do, then there's a nifty technique called 'butterflying'…

'Butterflying' squid for frying or barbecuing

Butterflying is a way of scoring the flesh in a diamond pattern. It is usually applied to medium-sized squid and has several benefits. The many cuts allow the butterflied portions to catch and hold the vital aromatics of a well-made marinade (finely chopped garlic and chilli, with a tiny trickle of olive oil, is hard to beat). Once in the pan or over the charcoal, the scoring makes the squid flesh curl up, opening the grooves still further, so the heat penetrates super-fast. A couple of minutes later, those lightly charred, curled-up, criss-crossed squid pieces will be done.

Butterflying is easy. Simply lay your opened squid cone, now a flat triangle, inside up (which means the ridge that was on the inside should now be facing up) on a board. Take a lightly serrated, but not fiercely sharp, knife (a cheap serrated table knife is ideal).

Now score the flesh as deeply as you can without cutting right through it (this is fairly easy, since the outside of the flesh is tougher than the inside). Score first at an angle of about 30° to the central ridge, with cuts about 0.5–1cm apart. Once you have a complete series of parallel cuts running across the sheet of squid, make a second set at about 45° to the first, to give a nice diamond mosaic pattern.

Cut each butterflied squid body into two to six square or triangular portions, depending on the size of the squid. Think in terms of two or three pieces, plus a few tentacles, for each serving.

To see the results of this highly satisfying (and very easy) knife work, check out the recipe and picture on pages 204–5.

Cleaning cuttlefish

If you like eating squid but you've never tasted cuttlefish, then we'd strongly recommend you try some. Many squid devotees (ourselves included) would maintain that fresh cuttlefish is, in terms of texture and flavour, every bit as good as its close relative.

There is, however, the Issue of the Ink. There's far, far more of it in your average cuttlefish than in any squid. Chefs adore cuttlefish ink for the 'essence of seafood' tang and chic black gloss that it lends – to fish stews and risottos in particular. Fishermen loathe it for the indelible stains it makes on their deck, clothes and hands, and the vicious smell that permeates the boat a couple of warm days later. Cuttlefish ink, it seems, will stain for *centuries*. We both have fishing clothes that were stained with ink umpteen hot washes ago and still sport black splatters.

On our boat, we have a strict cuttlefish landing procedure, which involves netting the cuttle, holding it out at net handle's length over the sea, then jiggling it several times. This is intended to annoy the cuttlefish, which in theory should make it fire off an angry squirt of blackness before it's brought on board. Of course, cuttlefish rarely do requests. After 5 minutes' unproductive jiggling, we assume it's already shot its load, and gingerly move it from the net towards a waiting bucket – at which moment it explodes with pent-up rage and hoses everything and everyone with tar-black, indelible ink.

If you take a whole cuttle home, ungutted, then be warned. You're carrying an ink-squirting timebomb over your threshold. Even though it's dead, the potential to wreak havoc still lurks within the pearly-grey pouch, hidden deep in the cuttle's mantle. So, always begin your cuttlefish prep in the kitchen sink, and not on a precious wooden board that you might not wish to stain. The basic procedure is similar to dealing with a squid (see pages 97–100).

Begin by separating the head and tentacles from the body, much as you would for squid, with a good firm pull on the head – only this time expect a few more of the cuttlefish's innards to be left behind in the body including, usually, the ink sac (on larger cuttles, you may have to push your hand inside the body and work it around a bit to help release the head). Put the head to one side for the moment, but do not discard it. Now have a gentle poke around inside the body and you might even locate that ink sac. If you do manage to find it, remove it with the steady dexterity of a brain surgeon, snipping it free with scissors and carefully placing it in a bowl. Add to it any loose ink that can be poured out of the body cavity.

That's the theory, anyway. Realistically, ink collecting is never quite so easy. The sac is often hard to isolate amongst the rest of the messy, soft innards. So, alternatively, you can simply scoop the entire inky contents of the cuttlefish's body into a bowl, stir them to release as much ink as possible, then strain out any 'bits' (which may include egg or sperm sacs and the membrane from the ink sac) by passing them through a sieve. What comes through is all usable ink, or other, indistinguishable, quite harmless bodily fluids. You can even rinse the body out a few times, sloshing the fluids with a couple of tablespoons of water, to maximise the inky returns.

To finish preparing the cuttlefish, take the body cavity and feel for the bony structure that keeps it rigid: grip this between finger and thumb and pull it out, encouraging it to tear through the outer skin of the cuttlefish that holds it in place between the wings. This ovoid disk – far more substantial than a squid's quill – is what they sell down the pet shop for budgies to sharpen their beaks on. Pull off the short wings from the body, taking as much of the skin with them as you can; peel off the rest of the skin with your fingers and a clean rag. What's left, when rinsed and wiped, is the clean body of the cuttlefish. The wings can be kept too, if you're planning a slow-cooked dish, but they're too tough for quick frying or grilling.

Now return to the head and attached tentacles and proceed pretty much as for squid. The bony ball of mouthparts can be squeezed out in just the same way, and the tentacles cut off just in front of the eyes, so that they remain attached to a small ring of flesh at the front of the head. Discard the rest of the head, including the eyes and any intestines attached to it. Use a knife to scrape the membrane and any tough little suckers off the tentacles. Rinse them, pat dry, and they're ready for cooking.

Preparing mussels, cockles and clams

All these smaller bivalves should be well rinsed in fresh water before use and scrubbed with a nailbrush to remove mud and sand. If, during cleaning, you come across a specimen with its shell open, give it a sharp tap on the side of the sink. If it doesn't close its shell in response to this stimulus, then discard it. It is almost certainly dead, and therefore potentially unpleasant to eat, or even harmful. For the same reason, you should throw away all bivalves with cracked or broken shells.

Removing grit

Bivalves spend most of their lives filtering water through their shells. If they live in a sandy location, as many do, some grit will often remain in the shell after you've gathered them. Cockles, clams, razor clams and wild mussels will almost certainly be at least a bit gritty, whereas rope-grown farmed mussels probably won't. Limpets are only likely to need de-gritting if they have been living on sand-fringed rocks.

Even a few grains of grit can spoil a shellfish supper. Happily, measures can be taken to eliminate it in two phases, one pre- and one post-cooking. Ideally, all bivalves gathered from the wild should be 'purged'. This means immersing them in a large bucket of clean seawater for several hours, and remembering to give them a stir from time to time.

As they filter the clean water, the bivalves should rinse out much of their grit. If you can suspend them in the upper part of the water, on a rack or colander (or a salad strainer – see the picture above right), then so much the better – the sand released will sink to the bottom of the bucket. If you think that your shellfish are really gritty, then several changes of water and a purging period of 12 hours or longer may be in order.

For some reason, the purging process can be accelerated by sprinkling a scant handful of oatmeal over the surface of the water. Why? One theory is that mussels and cockles will feed on the oatmeal, which seems plausible, particularly in Scotland (where, of course, they eat it standing up). Another is that it simply acts as an irritant and speeds up their filtration. Either way, it seems to help get them cleaner quicker.

Any remaining sand is usually released as the shellfish cook – so be warned, even if the flesh is pretty grit free, the otherwise delicious cooking juices in the bottom of the pan may contain nerve-jangling remnants. You will need to strain the juices very thoroughly. Line a sieve with a good filtering material, such as fine muslin, a thin tea towel or a piece of kitchen roll, and pour the juices through. The strained liquor can then be poured over the shellfish in the individual bowls in which you serve them (with or without further seasoning, or the addition of cream).

Debearding mussels

Before cooking, mussels require 'debearding'. The 'beard' in question is a little bundle of tough fibres (technically called byssal threads – see page 567) that the mussel uses to cling to its rock. You can simply pinch them between your thumb and the blade of a small, stout, not too sharp knife and pull them away. Use the back of the same knife to scrape away any barnacles clinging to the shell and, after a quick rinse, your mussels are ready to cook.

Shucking oysters

Shucking oysters is wonderful work once you discover your own rhythm (so says Nick, who loves it; Hugh is less keen). Sometimes it'll take half a dozen badly shucked ones before you hit your stride, but then the music starts…

Oysters are the most obstinate bivalves. They don't give it up for just anyone. But they do have an Achilles heel – or, rather, an Achilles hinge, where the two shells meet at the narrow end. This should be your first point of attack.

Hold the oyster partly wrapped in a folded thick tea towel, to give maximum grip and some protection to your hands. Those who shuck oysters by the hundred often wear a chain-mail glove – a stout gardening glove is not a bad amateur version. The vital tool you need, known as a 'shuck', is a bevel-edged, short-bladed, pointed knife, designed so that its strong, stout blade can be levered into the hinge.

Position the hinge towards you, cup the deeper side of the shell in the palm of your (cloth-covered or gloved) weaker hand and prepare to attack with the shuck held in your strongest. Go in slightly to the right of the hinge if you're right handed, slightly to the left if you favour that side.

Sometimes the oyster's shell is so craggy and crenellated that it's hard to work out where its two sides join; so you might have to gently excavate your way in. Once you've found this, be bold. If you don't dig deep enough into the hinge, you'll find the shell wall crumbles as you twist and gouge, causing gritty deposits to fall inside the shell (being too gentle can make the job worse; sometimes you have to be brutal). Excessive hand carnage can be avoided by clamping the oyster down on a chopping board (with your protected hand) rather than trying to hold it in mid-air.

Once the shell gives a little, gently prise the two sides apart. Keep the blade pressed against the upper, flatter half of the shell so as not to damage the oyster itself. The meat may still be attached to the top shell by the oyster's own little adductor muscles, in which case, use the blade to slice it free. Keep the bottom, deeper shell on the level, so you don't spill its delicious briny juices. Remove the top part of the shell and check for chef's perks – a few little smidgens of oyster frill or muscle flesh. Once you've snaffled these, you can discard this half of the shell.

You now have a whole oyster bathing obligingly in its fresh juices in the half shell. The oyster meat will still be attached to the half shell by the remainder of the adductor muscle. Some shuckers cut through this muscle now and flick the oyster over, so that it is ready to slide off the shell. But we consider this last ritual to be the prerogative of the oyster eater, not the shucker. Just check for obvious flakes of shell and flick any such contaminants away with a clean finger; it's now ready to serve.

It's always lovely to arrange a dozen oysters on a bed of crushed ice, but if this is impractical, you might still want to give them half an hour in the fridge. Oysters are best served cool or chilled, but not icy, and definitely not warm (except obviously when deliberately cooked – as, for example, on page 202). Our respective preferred accompanying condiments are described on page 574.

Shelling scallops

The white muscle inside a scallop is not just delicious, it's also enormous – bigger than any other British bivalve. This means it can muster a scary snap with its shell. It uses this reflex underwater to propel it along (scallops can actually swim – see page 576). If you stick your fingers in a live scallop's shell, it may shut sharply. This will probably make you jump, but it won't interfere with your piano playing. If the scallop won't relinquish your finger, try giving the base of its hinge a sharp tap against the sink. All such signs of life are, of course, a good indication that these hearty bivalves are as fresh as you are likely to find – unless you go and dive for them yourself.

Most scallops you handle, even if they are alive, will be partly open, allowing ready access with the tip of your knife. But if they are extremely fresh and tightly shut, this dictates a slightly different approach, which we'll come to in a moment. First, how to deal with a slightly open shell.

A scallop has two sides: one flat, one curved into a bulge. The bulge should sit comfortably in your palm, the flat side up, the hinge towards the base of your hand. Choose a flexible, fairly long-bladed knife – it doesn't have to be ultra-sharp (and if it is, since you're going to be doing some shell-scraping, it soon won't be).

The open, fanned end of the flat shell is where you need to start. Use the tip of the knife to slice between the muscle and the inside of the flat shell – scraping the shell as you go, to leave as little meat clinging to the inside face as possible. Once you get the hang of this, you can do it with a couple of quick strokes of the knife. It's most comfortable to work with the shell hinge towards you and the fanned edge of the shell away, though you might have to rotate the scallop to optimise the angle of attack.

As soon as you've completely severed the join between muscle and flat shell, it will pop open like the lid on a pedal bin. Pull the flat shell off completely and make a quick assessment of the job you've done. If there's quite a bit of muscle left clinging to it, you get a 'B minus' for your efforts and a 'try harder next time'. But you have got a little morsel that's worth scraping off, giving a quick rinse, and eating raw – chef's perks! There will probably also be a strand or two of the scallop's 'frill' – the fleshy fringe that surrounds the edge of the shell. Don't discard it; it can be put to good use, as we'll see.

So far, so easy. But what do you do if a very live scallop decides to keep its shell tightly shut? Well, in this instance, your only access is close to its hinge. To get the knife in there you will need to hold the scallop differently: hinge up, fanned end down, resting on a board or worktop, flat side facing you (see picture one, overleaf).

Poke the tip of the knife through that gap in the corner of the hinge and right across to the other side – ideally so the tip just pokes out of the opposite gap. Once again, your aim is to slide the knife between muscle and shell as close as possible to the inside surface of the flat shell. But this time you're starting from the hinge end and working towards the round, fanned end. It can be done in a single slicing motion, straight down towards the worktop, but if you put a little 'wiggle' in it, and angle the edge of the blade back towards the inside of the flat shell, you should minimise wastage. Again, as soon as the muscle is released you'll get that 'pedal bin' pop. Lift the flat shell away and look at how you've done. This method invariably leaves a little more muscle on the flat side of the shell, so don't be downhearted if this happens – slice it off, rinse and eat.

Once you've opened your scallop, you can now take a look inside the concave shell, where all the real goodies are. You'll see the big, white, cylindrical adductor muscle in the middle and, curling around it, the comma-shaped coral, which is the scallop's sexual organs and roe (see page 574). The size and condition of the coral varies at different times of the year. It may appear full, orange and ripe if the scallop is close to breeding (usually in spring and early summer), or shrivelled and dull if it has recently spawned (usually in the autumn). The plumper and brighter it is, the more you'll want to eat it – it's pretty obvious when a withered coral is not worth saving.

The muscle and coral are surrounded by a mottled, orange-brown and white skirt – more of those 'frills'. These are sometimes referred to as the scallop's 'eyes', though they are really a collection of its sensory organs combined with its filtration and breathing apparatus. Technically it's all quite edible, but it's tough, and isn't usually served up with the muscle and coral. There's a black, squidgy pouch attached near the hinge, too. This is the stomach sac – the only part of the scallop that you really need to discard. There are various ways of releasing and trimming the contents of a scallop shell but our four-step method below follows the simple principle of working from the least edible parts to the most:

1. REMOVE THE BLACK SAC This is contained within a delicate membrane, which you should be careful not to break. We lift it with thumb and first two fingers, pulling it gently away from the hinge (see picture three, above) to expose the threads attaching it to the muscle. With practice, you'll develop your own way of dealing with the black sac and its tendrils. Some commercial shuckers dig under it with a blunt knife and tear it upwards in an anti-clockwise twist, bringing out all the frills and gills too. The sac should be immediately discarded. If you tear it and spill some of its green-black waste back into the shell, remove it carefully with a teaspoon. It's not 'poisonous' in any lethal sense of the word, but should it get on to the good bits, you'd certainly want to give them a thorough rinse.

2. PULL OUT THE OUTER FRILLS Start at the left-hand top corner and, pulling in an anti-clockwise direction, simply lift and tear them out (see picture four, above). They should come away easily, but if they threaten to pull the coral with them, just nick any membrane or thread that seems to be joining them.

3. CUT OUT THE MUSCLE AND CORAL Removing the muscle and coral from the concave shell isn't difficult in itself. What is tricky is to leave the shell bare without losing even a tiny slice of prime muscle. The natural curve of the shell is the problem, and your best bet is to use the tip of your least favourite bendy filleting knife (because it'll blunt it). Try to scrape the shell rather than cut the flesh, and work from the edges of the muscle to middle, until it has been cut free.

The muscle is only attached on the right-hand side (if you're looking at the open shell with the hinge towards you), so scrape from the upper-right corner of the muscle towards the centre and it should come away cleanly. Don't worry about the coral – it's attached not to the shell but to the muscle, and should come away with it. If the two get separated, it really doesn't matter; they can still be cooked together, and reunited on the plate.

We've heard that people who open lots of scallops often use a dessertspoon with a sharpened edge, or a curved grapefruit knife. Happy amateurs that we are, though, we continue to muddle through with our best (i.e. worst) bendy knives.

4. TIDY, TRIM (AND POSSIBLY RINSE) You now have a nice, fat muscle and a juicy orange and cream coral, which may or may not still be attached. Trim away anything that is not either of the above – usually a few soft, brown, frilly scraps and the little black tube on the edge of the muscle. Nice clean scallops may not even need a rinse – just a wipe with a clean cloth. But if they are at all sandy, gritty or grubby, give them a quick one, then pat dry immediately.

5. RECYCLE OTHER PARTS (OPTIONAL) Scallop frills, along with any juices from the shell, can be used in fish stock. If you've opened more than a dozen scallops, you'll be able to make a little stock with those trimmings alone – add an onion, a stick or two of celery, both chopped fairly fine, plus a few fennel seeds or leaves and a bay leaf. Add a scant half-litre of water for each dozen scallops you've shucked, bring it all to a simmer and keep it there for just 20 minutes.

Scallop frills also make outstanding bait – packed with powerful pheromones, they are particularly effective for pouting, bream, bass and flatfish in general. They're definitely worth freezing for the next time you go sea fishing – even after defrosting, they stay on the hook for cast after cast.

Sea urchins

These stunning echinids (which is not a word we have the chance to use very often) certainly merit a mention in this book. But we haven't included them in our species profiles as they barely have a market in this country – even the dedicated forager will struggle to find them in a worthwhile quantity. Urchins must be eaten alive, and a good sign that they are not long out of the sea is that their spines will bristle slightly when touched, or even of their own accord. Should you ever get the chance, do try them. They are quite delicious.

In theory they should be opened with a *coupe oursin* – a tool specially designed for the job. Sadly, neither of us has ever actually seen one – though it's been on Hugh's Christmas present list for about a decade now. To date, we've had to make do with the kitchen scissors. Insert the tip into the mouthparts (pretty much the only way in) and cut a little piece away. Then cut around the top third of the shell, making a hole big enough for good access with a teaspoon. The parts to eat are the five pink corals of roe, sometimes called 'tongues'. They taste sweet and kelpy, and are one of the few foods whose alleged effect on body and spirit is one we'd vouch for. Hugh once ate two dozen and recalls feeling distinctly… uplifted. Aphrodisiac might be pushing it, but they're definitely a tonic.

Whelks, winkles and limpets

Like mussels, these lovely marine molluscs should be well rinsed in fresh water before use and scrubbed with a nailbrush to remove any grit or sand. Winkles and whelks shouldn't require purging, unless they've been gathered from a very sandy place. Limpets, however, should be soaked in clean seawater or a bowl of salted water for at least 30 minutes, stirring them around occasionally. Or you could suspend them in the water (as we often do with mussels, see page 103).

Everything else you really need to know about preparing and eating these univalves is revealed in their profiles: whelks, page 564; winkles, page 562; limpets, page 560. And in our recipes for them: whelks, pages 209, 328 and 364; winkles, page 277; limpets, pages 203 and 271.

One point to note, though, is that unlike most shellfish, both winkles and whelks freeze quite well, either in or out of their shells. You can freeze them alive and raw, or cooked. If the former, they won't be alive when you defrost them – which makes pre-freezing live whelks a good option for the squeamish. Some swear by this as a technique for 'improving' the texture of whelks – but this assumes you consider tenderness a virtue in a whelk.

Freezing (and frozen) shellfish

On the whole we prefer not to freeze most of our shellfish – and not to buy them frozen either. The obvious exception is prawns. As mentioned above, whelks and winkles also freeze surprisingly well. Other than that, these 'freezer notes' should all be considered to be prefaced with an 'only if you really must' caveat. Given the choice, we'd always prefer our shellfish fresh.

CRABS do not freeze very well at all, though the brown meat freezes much better than the white, which will always be watery when defrosted, and somewhat dry when the melt water has drained away. Far better to make a good crab soup (see pages 267–8) and freeze that instead.

LOBSTERS freeze fairly well, or at least their tails do, raw or lightly cooked and ideally still within the shell. But are you really going to freeze a lobster tail? Not unless you happen to have caught a bunch – or been offered a box of them down a dark alley beside some harbour pub, with a tap on the nose, and a 'You ain't seen me, right?' It's not going to happen, is it?

PRAWNS freeze very well, and certainly better than other crustaceans. Although we can only dream of catching enough prawns to consider freezing them ourselves, buying frozen shell-on coldwater prawns in a catering-size box and defrosting them 'to order', as it were, is really not a bad option. It is, after all, what the fishmonger does.

SQUID AND CUTTLEFISH both freeze moderately well, if frozen when extremely fresh. But they'll always emerge a little chewier and a touch drier from their spell in the freezer. We would therefore generally use frozen squid and cuttlefish in a slow-cooked dish rather than for flash frying or on the barbecue. The exception is the bags of tiny frozen 'party squid', which can be defrosted and fried up with no prep at all – just plenty of garlic and chilli.

If you're freezing squid you've caught or bought fresh, it's best to clean the beasts thoroughly (see pages 97–100) and freeze fully prepped bodies and tentacles, rather than whole squid with the guts in.

SCALLOPS also freeze reasonably well – again, if frozen carefully and when ultra-fresh. The flavour remains true and sweet, but they will never have the firm bite and yielding juiciness of the fresh article. Remove the corals first: these don't freeze well, but can be dried in a low oven, grated and used as a seasoning (they're very good on stir-fried spinach and greens, with a dash of garlic and soy).

Dry each scallop muscle with a tea towel and put about six at a time into small, plastic freezer bags. Suck out all the air from the bag and seal well. Once the scallops are defrosted, pat dry before cooking.

MUSSELS can be bought frozen, ready cooked and shelled, but they are not a patch on fresh ones, as they come out rather dry and crumbly after defrosting. We'd say, don't bother.

COCKLES freeze better than mussels, but once defrosted they are always a mite chewier and a shade less sweet than when fresh. You can buy frozen shucked cockles. At a pinch, they would make a not unrespectable addition to a well-flavoured chowder (page 264) or a spicy soup (page 267).

WINKLES AND WHELKS both freeze well, and freezing is rated by some professional whelkers as a good way to tenderise the flesh. They can be frozen raw (alive even) or cooked.

OYSTERS? Don't even think about it.

Refrigerating live shellfish

Most shellfish can be kept alive and moderately happy in a good cold fridge (6°C or less) for anything from 24 hours to a week, depending on the species. The golden rule is, always keep them damp, but never in water. Wet cloths, under and over, or even a few handfuls of seaweed, will help make them feel 'at home' in the salad box. Here's a quick rundown on timings:

CRABS will keep up to 48 hours, if lively when put in the fridge.

LOBSTERS can usually be kept chilled for up to 48 hours; but if they are flagging, kill and cook them.

PRAWNS will keep up to 24 hours, if very fresh and lively. They are best kept in wet seaweed.

SQUID AND CUTTLEFISH can't be stored alive, but will keep fresh for up to 3 days when dead.

SCALLOPS should be stored round side down, covered with a wet cloth, and will keep for up to 48 hours.

MUSSELS are best wrapped in a wet cloth and stored in a plastic bag (but don't allow any water to pool around them). They'll keep for 48 hours if very fresh when bought.

COCKLES will keep for about 48 hours under a wet cloth.

OYSTERS will stay alive for a week or even longer if carefully stored, round side down. There is no need to cover them, but they will become progressively drier over time. After 2 weeks they might still just be alive, but they would have little or no briny juice left.

2. Fish cookery

A good piece of fresh fish, lightly seasoned, simply and accurately cooked, with perhaps just a few drops of lemon juice, will never be dull. That's the central message of this chapter. And although we are about to embark on an examination of the various methods by which a fish may be cooked, and look at the vast array of accompanying ingredients than can increase the pleasure of eating it, at the heart of pretty much all our recipes is a simple formula: some great seasonal ingredients on or around a lovely fresh piece of fish.

Some of the recipes in the chapters that follow may appear elaborate. But even if they look long, it doesn't mean they are hard. We tend to write long, dealing with the whys as well as the hows and anticipating questions, so that provided you don't mind tackling a little more of our prose, you should be well served to approach brand new recipes with the confidence of an old hand. But we certainly don't wish to bamboozle and confuse you. So first we'll deal very clearly with the basics here.

There's one point that needs making good and early: cooking fish is easy. Some people have a problem believing that, and seem to think that fish is an ingredient designed to catch them out and expose their shortcomings in the kitchen. Such anxieties can be borne of real experiences: poached or baked fish that turns out mushy or tasteless; barbecued fish that is burned on the outside but raw in the middle; fish that just doesn't taste *right*; and let's not forget rubbery squid. Such pitfalls exist, and experiencing them can sap confidence, but we have some suggestions that might help you to avoid these mistakes.

Fear of fish cookery boils down mostly to two simple issues. The first is about the quality of the raw materials. A piece of fish that is of poor quality, damaged, or less than fresh will be at best a disappointment, at worst a heart-breaking betrayal of your efforts in the kitchen. Do everything right and it will still taste wrong. In other words, if you can't buy fish with confidence, you can't cook it with confidence. If you think that may be your problem, then it's back to page 43! Read on from there and we'll do our best to make a fearless fish shopper out of you.

The second problem arises in the kitchen. It's not that cooking fish is difficult. It's just that overcooking fish is easy – and overcooked fish can indeed be a disappointment. But there's really no reason to despair. Because *not* overcooking is easy too, and hangs on a simple understanding of what happens when you cook a piece of fish. What it amounts to is this: a fish, or piece of fish, is cooked as soon as it is hot – and only just hot – in the middle. It's as simple as that, whether you're frying, boiling, grilling, baking or poaching.

When fish gets hot

In fact, we could make it a tiny bit more complicated: it's all about the behaviour of fish proteins, particularly a substance called myosin, when exposed to heat. Myosin begins to change its form and coagulate at around 40°C, and the texture of fish flesh changes with it. Other fibre proteins in the flesh follow suit at around 50°C. The process is complete, in the flesh of most species, by 55°C (a little higher in sharks, rays and billfish such as marlin and swordfish). So when we say 'hot' (and therefore cooked), this is the temperature we mean: 55°C or a little over – 60°C tops. If you like using a temperature probe to test the doneness of meat, you can use it to test fish too. Note that the temperature at which a piece of fish is completely cooked is the same temperature at which a joint of beef is still very rare and bloody.

And this is part of the problem. If you are a keen meat cook who only rarely deals with fish, then you may easily be caught out. Really, a different mindset is in order. It's not just that fish is cooked through at a lower temperature than meat, it's also that fish flesh heats up quicker. You may well find it hard to believe just how quickly a piece of fish can be cooked. It often takes only a few minutes for the heat to travel through even quite a thick piece of fish flesh – particularly one immersed in a hot or simmering liquid.

One thing fish cookery has in its favour, though, is a degree of consistency. With meat, you may be trying to achieve different effects depending on the cut of meat, the recipe in question and even your own taste. Hours of slow braising are required to tenderise oxtail or shin of beef, but only a scant minute on either side for a thick rump steak served *bleu*, and several more minutes to get a pork chop cooked through without drying it out. With fish you are consistently aiming for the same result – that moment when it is hot in the middle.

Of course, there are exceptions. Cuttlefish and large, thick-fleshed squid behave more like mammal flesh: they can be simmered slowly for an hour or two to render them extremely tender, or they can be flash fried or grilled for just a minute or two, when they are tender by virtue of being barely cooked at all. Anywhere in between and they will, like a badly cooked steak, be quite rubbery. Similarly, if you're cooking a tuna or swordfish steak (ecologically questionable in itself), you may wish to sear it like a steak and serve it rare, or even raw, in the middle. That's because the character of the flesh of these fish is quite distinctive and some people (though by no means all) like them this way.

However, these are unusual events in the fish kitchen. In almost all the recipes that follow (and any exceptions are very well flagged), you're using a fire, a frying pan, an oven or a pot of hot liquid to heat the fish right through. The moment the heat has found its way to the centre (and not before), your fish is cooked, and it's time to stop cooking it! *Now*!

This basic principle of fish cookery, which we might summarise as '*When it's hot, it's cooked – so stop*', has given rise to some unorthodox ways of heating up fish over the years. Comic as they are, they do all actually make a strange sort of sense. You can iron a kipper, steam a salmon in the dishwasher, cook a Dover sole in a trouser press or, our favourite, hang a 'rack' of sprats, skewered through the gills, tail down into a toaster. These quirky techniques are more than mere culinary myths or cook's jokes – they are genuine options for cooking fish that you'd actually want to eat. And they work because they are all capable of generating enough heat to reach the middle of the fish in a fairly short time.

Testing for doneness

All this raises the question, 'How do you *know* when the heat has reached the middle of the fish?' – assuming you don't have a temperature probe. The answer is that there are a couple of very distinctive, easily observable physical changes that take place in the fish flesh in the critical moments. Though fish flesh comes in varying guises, its appearance always changes as it becomes hot. There is a translucency about the cold, raw flesh and an opacity or milkiness about the hot, cooked flesh (shown in the picture, opposite) that serve as a very reliable indicator as to whether a piece of fish is raw, cooked or somewhere in between. This is the visible manifestation of the coagulation of myosin and other proteins in the fish flesh.

Consequently, the briefest inspection of the thickest part of the fish should tell you straight away whether it is done or not. In the case of whole fish (round or flat, large or small) cooked on the bone, the tip of a round-ended knife or narrow palette knife is the tool for the job. Pushed through the thickest part of the flesh on the lateral line until it touches the backbone, then levered gently to one side, it will expose the flesh to the bone (illustrated on page 114). Take a look: opacity, or otherwise, and therefore doneness, or otherwise, is easily judged.

It's a physical effect, not just a visual one. The fish fibres are separating and releasing juices. The flesh has become more tender and is ready to flake. You'll also notice that the flesh, when opaque and cooked through, comes neatly away from the backbone, whereas any residual, translucent, raw flesh will cling tenaciously to it. Try serving the flesh from a whole fish when it's not cooked through and the reluctance of the uncooked middle to part from the bone will leave you in quite a mess: you start clawing cooked fish away from raw, leaving shreds of flesh on a raggedy skeleton that looks as if it's been chewed by an unusually fussy shark. And even an unusually unfussy human would be unlikely to enthuse over it. But when the moment has come, the fish flesh looks right and feels right, because it offers itself up from the bone, willing to be eaten.

In many respects this is an even more reliable indicator than a temperature probe. You can only take 55°C as a rough guide, and the exact temperature varies

according to the species, condition and freshness of the fish. But this moment, when the fish flesh becomes opaque, tender and juicy, is always the moment to stop cooking and, ideally, start eating the fish. Any more cooking and there will be further separation of the fibres, further loss of moisture, and the fish may become dry, mushy or both. So seize the moment.

Incidentally, if the fish is cooked in a hot liquid, things can speed up further. Not only that, but other ingredients in the liquid may have an effect too. In more acidic liquids, fish will cook quicker and at a lower temperature. The presence of astringents such as lemon juice, vinegar and chilli is particularly dramatic; in sufficient quantities, they may even 'cook' a fish at room temperature. We'll discuss this when we consider marinades and pickles in the next chapter.

Obviously if a fish fails the test of opacity and tenderness on the side of underdone, it needs some further cooking. So it's back in the pan, oven, court-bouillon or whatever for a few more minutes, then repeat the test. Unless, that is, the failure is really marginal – in other words, it's almost done and the flesh next to the bone is only *just* translucent and clingy. Then the best thing is simply to cover the fish and let it rest in a warm place for a couple of minutes to allow the residual heat to reach the middle.

Some cooks may worry that the knife/opacity test spoils the appearance of the fish, which they would like to present entirely unmolested. On the whole, we'd suggest that it's better to delight your guests with a perfectly cooked but lightly chef-scarred fish than to aim for top marks for presentation but serve it up raw in the middle.

However, there is a less obtrusive test of doneness, should you feel the need for it. Use a fine skewer, or thick needle, as your probe to the centre of the backbone. Hold it there for a few seconds, then draw it out and touch the tip on your lip. If it feels distinctly hot, then the fish is cooked through. If it's still cool, then the flesh by the bone is also cool, and the fish needs more cooking. If it burns your lip slightly, as it will at much over 60°C, the fish is probably a little overcooked.

When testing for doneness, fillets of fish are a slightly different proposition from whole fish. The same principle applies: as soon as the fillet is hot in the middle, it's done. But the knife test may be inappropriate, as there is no backbone to stop it, and a delicate fillet may break up (in which case at least you'll know it's done!). You can use the needle/skewer test, inserting it in the thickest part of the fillet. Realistically, the right answer to the question, 'Is this fillet done yet?' is probably 'Yes!' – unless it's a really thick fillet from a fairly hefty fish. The point being that a hot frying pan doesn't take long to send the heat through the flesh of a 2cm-thick fillet, and if you're poaching a fillet or immersing it in a bubbling soup or stew, the effect is even quicker.

Of course fish, and fish recipes, come in all shapes and sizes, and they don't all take the same time to cook. So in the interests of getting a feel for it, it seems useful to give you a few rough indications of the approximate amount of time you can expect your fish to take – so that you know when it's about the right moment for one of the above tests. See the table of fish cooking times overleaf.

Fish-related stress

Even when you've got fish cooking to a fine art, there are circumstances outside your control. The fish cook's most frequent dilemma arises whenever the dependable speed at which heat travels through a fish clashes with the wholly elastic time frame required for gathering your friends around the table. In other words: the fish is cooked, but the inconsiderate buggers are still discussing house prices in the next room. What to do? Well, don't lose your cool, for a start. Do, however, stop cooking the fish as soon as you are sure it is done. Rest it in a warm but not hot place, so that it cools only slightly and slowly, and doesn't go on cooking, while you corral your fellow diners with sticks and yells. If you end up serving it warm, or even tepid, rather than piping hot, it will still be delicious.

Picking up from that, the final important message on the subject of not overcooking fish is this: *don't worry about it too much*. With good fish in a good recipe, slight overcooking really isn't a problem – certainly not the kitchen crime of the century that some seem to think it.

A final reassurance, if you need one, may come from fast-forwarding to the recipes in the Fish thrift and standbys chapter (page 366). Many of them involve cooking leftover fish that has already been cooked and cooled once, so is bound to be a smidgeon overdone by the time it's properly heated through again. Yet herein lie some of our favourite recipes in the book – what does that tell you? If nothing else, perhaps that fish cooking really isn't that hard.

Fish cooking times

Small (plate-sized) whole bass, trout or large mackerel of around 600–700g

BAKED	BAKED/ROASTED	SHALLOW FRIED	POACHED	GRILLED/ BARBECUED
1 fish in a foil parcel at 190°C/ Gas Mark 5: 20–25 minutes	3–6 fish in a roasting tin, uncovered, at 200°C/Gas Mark 6: 12–15 minutes	in 1–2mm oil over a medium-high heat: 10–12 minutes, turning occasionally	immersed in a simmering stock, sauce, court-bouillon or plain salted water: 5–7 minutes	3–4 minutes per side

A whole salmon or sea bass of around 1.5–2kg

BAKED	POACHED	GRILLED/ BARBECUED
in a foil parcel at 190°C/Gas Mark 5: 30–35 minutes	immersed in a simmering stock, sauce or court-bouillon: 15–18 minutes	(with care) over or under a medium (not high) heat: 8–12 minutes per side

A whole small-medium flatfish of around 700g (e.g. plaice, lemon sole, megrim), on the bone

BAKED/ROASTED	SHALLOW FRIED	PAN POACHED	OVEN POACHED	GRILLED
in a lightly oiled roasting tin, uncovered, at 200°C/Gas Mark 6: 12–15 minutes	in 2mm oil over a medium heat: 5–6 minutes per side	in a simmering stock, sauce or court-bouillon in a large frying pan, covered: 6–8 minutes	in a simmering stock, sauce or court-bouillon in a large dish, covered in foil: 10–12 minutes	under a very hot grill, 10–12 minutes, turning once

A whole large flatfish of around 1.5–2kg (e.g. brill, turbot, large Dover sole, large plaice), on the bone

BAKED/ROASTED	PAN POACHED	OVEN POACHED
in a large, lightly oiled roasting tin, uncovered, at 200°C/Gas Mark 6: 25–35 minutes	immersed in a simmering stock, sauce or court-bouillon in a large frying pan or turbotière: 12–20 minutes	added to a simmering stock, sauce or court-bouillon in a large dish, covered in foil: 20–30 minutes

A chunky (3–4cm thick), skin-on fillet portion from a large salmon, bass, pollack or turbot

BAKED	BAKED/ROASTED	SHALLOW FRIED	DEEP FRIED	POACHED	GRILLED/ BARBECUED
in a foil parcel, at 190°C/Gas Mark 5: 10–12 minutes	in an oiled roasting tin, uncovered, at 200°C/Gas Mark 6: 8–10 minutes	in 1–2mm oil over a fairly high heat: 5–6 minutes skin side down, then 1–2 minutes flesh side down, giving a total of 6–8 minutes	in batter, in deep hot oil (175°C): 3–4 minutes	in a simmering stock, sauce or court-bouillon: 4–6 minutes	3–5 minutes skin side down, then 1–2 minutes flesh side down, giving a total of 4–7 minutes

Portion-sized fillets of smaller whiting, haddock or pollack, up to 2cm thick

BAKED/ROASTED	SHALLOW FRIED	DEEP FRIED	PAN POACHED	OVEN POACHED
in a lightly oiled roasting tin, uncovered, at 200°C/Gas Mark 6: 8–10 minutes	e.g. coated in breadcrumbs, in 1cm oil over a medium heat: 2–3 minutes per side	e.g. coated in breadcrumbs or batter, immersed in hot oil at 165–175°C: 3–4 minutes	in a simmering stock, sauce or court-bouillon in a large frying pan, covered with a lid: 3–4 minutes	in a simmering stock, sauce or court-bouillon in a large dish, covered in foil: 10–12 minutes

Strips/fingers of filleted, skinless bass, bream or pollack, squid or scallops, 1–2cm thick

FLASH FRIED	DEEP FRIED	POACHED
in 1mm hot oil in a frying pan over a high heat: 2–3 minutes	i.e. goujons, coated in batter or breadcrumbs: 2 minutes	i.e. dropped into a simmering sauce, stew or soup: 2–3 minutes

Thick (4–5cm) tranches of large flatfish, such as brill or turbot, or similar-sized cutlets from large round fish, such as salmon or grey mullet

BAKED/ROASTED	SHALLOW FRIED	POACHED	GRILLED/ BARBECUED
in an oiled tin, uncovered, at 200°C/Gas 6: 12–15 minutes	in 1–2mm oil over a fairly high heat: 3–4 minutes per side	in a simmering stock, sauce or court-bouillon: 5–7 minutes	3–4 minutes per side

You will come across these estimates again as you cook from the recipes that follow. But there is one important principle that you should embrace now and carry with you through all your fish cookery, forever and ever. When it comes to fish cooking times, never be a slave to a recipe – even to one of ours. Your fish may be fatter or thinner than ours. It may be warmer or cooler at the beginning of the cooking time – as indeed your frying pan or oven may be. Once you have learned to judge doneness for yourself, you're in charge.

Raw, salted and
marinated fish

Once you've got some bouncingly fresh fish in front of you – whether acquired by skilful fishing or clever shopping – one of the first questions you may want to ask yourself is, 'Am I going to eat this raw?' Taking the word 'raw' in a broad and flexible sense, there is an intriguing and exciting range of ways to answer, 'Yes'.

Your decision on whether to go the raw route will depend on many things: the type of fish you have, your mood, the weather, where you are and who's coming to dinner. Or, more practically, whether you have ready access to a bottle of soy sauce and some searingly hot wasabi (or hot English mustard – see page 130). If you decide that on this occasion you want to apply heat to the fish, then we hope you'll find inspiration elsewhere in this book. But assuming raw, or nearly raw, does take your fancy, we'll explore the possibilities here.

The raw approach

The first honourable mention should probably go to the oyster – perhaps the only item on the seafood menu for which, almost wherever you are in the world, the default setting for its preparation and consumption is raw, live, unadorned, straight from the shell. Sure, a squeeze of lemon is nice, and other embellishments – Tabasco, shallot vinegar, black pepper – are favoured by some enthusiasts, but an oyster with nothing but the briny juices of its own shell is by no means incomplete. It proves, if proof were needed, that eating seafood raw is not some folly or foible but a possibility to be taken seriously with any number of marine species – be they bivalves, crustaceans, cephalopods or fish.

When it comes to eating raw fish, some kind of seasoning undoubtedly enhances the experience. And none have come up with a better formula than the Japanese, in the form of sashimi, their purist raw fish creation. Sashimi is just neatly cut morsels of fish flesh, accompanied by two classic seasonings – wasabi and soy sauce. These are applied at the last possible moment, so there is no penetration, or marinating, of the fish. The flavours combine in the mouth as you chew the raw fish and the whole experience can be very stimulating. Paper-thin slices of pickled ginger are usually offered too, to clean the palate between mouthfuls. They literally wipe the taste slate clean, so you can start afresh with the next piece of raw fish.

Add sticky, vinegar-seasoned rice to the recipe and you find yourself in the realms of sushi. This has been one of the great cultural colonisers of the global food scene over the last twenty years – and quite rightly. At its best, it's a really outstanding way to enjoy good fish. At its worst – like so many attempts to cash in on a food phenomenon – it's awful. The only conceivable appeal of cheap smoked salmon and extruded 'ocean sticks' pressed on to lumps of fridge-cold rice must be its three-day shelf life. It really should be illegal to call that stuff sushi.

Not that we're sushi snobs. Some purists might cast aspersions on 'amateur' attempts to make sushi at home. Not us. We take the view that if you regularly catch your own fish, especially sea fish, you'd be mad not to. Fishing gives you access to fish that a master sushi chef would kill for. And simply being a good fish shopper also qualifies you to have a go – more so than any skills you may have with the filleting knife – because raw fish is all about choosing the right fish. The rest – provided you don't get stressed out by the quest for geometrical perfection in your presentation – is easy. See pages 130–7 for a relaxed River Cottage approach to sashimi and sushi preparation.

Whether or not a fish is a suitable candidate for sashimi or sushi depends on one main factor – freshness – and two lesser ones – species and size. Obviously, fish for sashimi and sushi needs to be scrupulously fresh. But just what fresh means is perhaps not quite as clear-cut as you might think. For example, a mackerel that had been caught only hours before, but left in the sun on a balmy summer's day, may be well past its sushi-by date. Whereas a sea bass or bream, killed, bled, cleaned and iced within minutes of being caught, then stored correctly at around 0–2°C, should still be in excellent nick, and quite worthy of sashimi, a full 3 days later. But you would never get 3 days' sushi life from a mackerel, however well you iced and stored it, because the oily flesh starts to soften after about 24 hours, and by 48 hours it is simply too tender and fragile to slice raw – even though it would still be perfectly good baked or barbecued.

When assessing the freshness of a given fish, the telltale signs discussed on pages 44–5, along with reliable information from a trusted supplier, provide the critical information you need. Size, on the other hand, is purely a matter of what's practical. All fish for sashimi and sushi need to be filleted and skinned, then cut neatly into one-bite or two-bite-sized pieces. With most fish of less than about half a kilo, any fillet you take off is liable to be a bit puny – too thin and frail for subdividing into sashimi-friendly slices. The exception would be the ever-obliging mackerel, so round-bodied that even a fish of a scant 250g will offer up a couple of tidy little fillets. You can see just how easy they are to fillet and trim for sashimi in the series of pictures on pages 62–3.

As to species, some fish (notably most cartilaginous species, the rays and the sharks) are just not palatable raw because the texture is too tough. We'd love to tell you that dogfish sashimi is a River Cottage revelation, a discovery worthy of export back to Japan. But we can't. Because we've tried it (inevitably, given how many 'woofs' we catch). And it isn't.

However, our favourite sashimi and sushi fish are certainly among the ones we catch or buy most often: mackerel, of course, along with bass, bream and pollack – plus scallops and squid, when we can get them super-fresh. Come to think of it, these are pretty much our favourite fish and shellfish anyway. As it happens, the first three of those fish, along with squid and scallops, are all highly favoured by classically trained sushi chefs working in the West – perhaps because they all have their equivalents, or near equivalents, in the fish markets of Japan. Pollack, by contrast, has probably never been served raw in an 'authentic' Japanese restaurant. But take it from us, if used on the same day as it's caught, it makes great sashimi. So do gurnard, coley and even zander – though we suspect these species have never met a master sushi chef.

Mackerel, beloved as it is by the Japanese, is rarely eaten completely raw in sushi restaurants. It is more often pickled, as *shimi saba*. We imagine the reason they do it like this is that they will always struggle to get a delivery of super-fresh mackerel – and even if they do, it won't keep, unpickled, for more than a day. We, on the other hand, often find ourselves in possession of mackerel caught hours or even minutes earlier, and we delight in eating it raw, as both sashimi and sushi (though we'll happily pickle it too, as you will see on page 137).

From raw to marinated

Though it may be the purest and most pared down, the Japanese approach to eating fish raw is not the only one. Other cultures eat their fish raw – in the sense of uncooked by heat – but it is usually flavoured, and sometimes preserved, by the addition of some carefully chosen, often highly acidic ingredients. You could argue that, even in the absence of heat, the application of such astringents to raw fish is tantamount to cooking it. It even results in that critical transformation from translucent to opaque. But the action of acids, such as citrus juice and vinegar, on fish flesh is not quite the same as the action of heat. It loosens the bonds between the fibres of the flesh but does not quite separate them. Hence fish prepared in a pickle or marinade, but unheated, is more tender than raw fish but does not flake in the same way as cooked fish.

In this context, the obvious next stop in a global review of raw – or nearly raw – fish is Latin America, where a citrus juice marinade enlivened with a few slivers of fresh chilli has produced the classic ceviche. Unlike the cures and pickles we will look at shortly, this is not really a way to preserve the fish (a ceviche still doesn't keep for long at ambient temperature) but rather a very clever method for making a ready supply of fresh fish tender and delicious without the use of fire.

There are many approaches to ceviche, derived from different regions of Latin America. And, as with sushi, there are also the dumbed-down, cash-in-on-the-craze bastardised versions. In the Tex-Mex restaurants of London, and no doubt other Western capitals, you will find cheap white fish slathered in ketchup, lemon juice and Tabasco and probably other, even more grisly and inauthentic condiments. Please don't go anywhere near them! Our own ceviche recipe (page 141) is based on the alchemy of fresh citrus and raw chilli with coriander leaves and thinly sliced onion. It's a sensational set of flavours, and we find that it's at its best after just 3 or 4 hours in its marinade.

Preserving fish with salt

The application of marinades and pickles also arrests the process of deterioration in raw fish flesh – we'll come to these in due course. But there is one ingredient above all others whose ability to preserve fish (and other flesh) stretches right across the globe and through the millennia. It surely ranks alongside coal, iron and even fire in its contribution to human civilisation. It is salt.

It is thought that salt – harvested from natural saltpans and the edges of briny lagoons – has been used to preserve flesh for at least 4,000 years. It remains the favoured medium, sometimes in conjunction with smoke (see next chapter), for extending the shelf life of fish in places where refrigeration still cannot be taken for granted. The effect of salt on fish is nothing short of a minor miracle, drawing out all the moisture and stopping bacteriological activity in its tracks. The result is that salted pieces of fish can be rendered so dry and inert that they may hang for years, even in a tropical climate, before being rehydrated and desalinated through soaking, then cooked and eaten.

From the sweltering humidity of West Africa or the Caribbean to the whipping wet winds of New England, salt fish has survived anything the weather could throw at it, to furnish the inhabitants with staples such as Jamaican salt fish and ackee, or a Boston salt cod dinner. No wonder this robust and versatile source of protein has stood the human race in good stead for so long. It's indestructible – and you can't say that about many foods.

Salting fish at home

Both at home and in the River Cottage kitchen, we have co-opted this traditional technique and we now do a lot of salting. There are three slightly different approaches we use, and they all aim for a different effect.

Sometimes we want to preserve fish indefinitely, by salting it right down to that state of weatherproof, leathery desiccation. We do this when we have a surfeit of white fish (mainly pollack) to deal with – but it's not merely a matter of being frugal; we could use the freezer for that. As with all preserved food, salted fish has its own unique qualities. Even when soaked and restored to palatability, it doesn't 'become fresh' again. It has its own character – a denser, more resistant texture and greater depth of flavour, quite different from that of fresh fish – that has spawned a whole range of recipes. It holds its own in robust, spicy stews, and lends its distinctive tang to starchy staples such as rice and potatoes.

As well as this full-on salting and drying, which actually preserves the fish, we use a medium- or semi-salting technique, which cures and preserves fish for a short period (i.e. a couple of weeks), after which it can be eaten without the need to soak and/or cook it further. We're in the realms of gravad lax here, and indeed Gravad max (page 142) – our mackerel-based adaptation of the classic Scandinavian cured salmon.

We also use a very light salting process on fresh fish that's to be eaten straight away. This is more about modifying the eating qualities of a piece of fish than preserving it. It works wonders with very soft-textured white fish, and is a good way to 'restore' fillets of such fish if they have been frozen.

An outline of our basic fish-salting procedures follows, in ascending order of saltiness. In all cases, we're talking about fillets rather than whole fish. Whole fish can be salted and dried too, scales on and skeletons in, and in some parts of the world this is the standard approach. But salting fillets suits us much better, as they are easier to handle and to reconstitute through soaking, and ultimately easier to cook with. Moreover, if we do the filleting ourselves, we have the bonus of fresh heads and skeletons with which to make stock (see pages 252–3).

LIGHT SALTING OF POLLACK (AND OTHER MEMBERS OF THE COD FAMILY) When you start to experiment, as every ecologically minded fish shopper should, with alternatives to cod – pollack, pouting and whiting in particular – you will find their flesh is tender and delicate. When they are super-fresh, this is undoubtedly a virtue. But once they are a day or two old, though in no sense 'off', that delicacy is in danger of being interpreted as mushiness. Here's where a quick, light salting of a whole fillet serves as an excellent remedy to revive the eating qualities of the fish.

The idea here is not to preserve the fish for any significant length of time – though a lightly salted fillet will keep for a couple of days longer than a fresh one – but to draw out a little of the moisture and firm up the texture. White fish from the cod family, including pollack, ling, pouting and whiting, can all benefit enormously from a light salting before you cook them. As the salt extracts water

from the flesh, it condenses and concentrates it, lightly seasoning it at the same time. Once this is done, the fillet can be cooked as normal – floured, crumbed or battered, shallow or deep fried, or dropped into a simmering sauce or stew – but the result will be subtly different: firmer, lightly salty (obviously), but also slightly stronger in flavour.

Salt can vary in flavour from sea-breeze sweet to fiercely caustic. Your choice will have an effect on the taste of the fish, so it is important to use a good one. For light salting, you should go for a high-quality sea salt and choose coarse crystals or flakes. These will leach water away less aggressively than fine salt and are easy to rinse off the fish when the salting time is up.

It is very important not to over-salt fresh fish that you plan to consume immediately after salting, or you'll end up with a tough and unpalatably salty result. You'll need to soak it to make it palatable again. The amount of salt applied and the salting time depend on the size of fish, but always err on the side of caution. With a small, delicate fillet of less than 100g (pouting, for example), use just a sprinkling of salt (say, 2–3 teaspoons) that will cover the fish in a thin, even layer, then rinse it off after a matter of minutes – as few as five. With fatter fillets from bigger fish, use a more generous layer and leave it for longer – up to an hour to really firm up a big fillet off a 5kg-plus pollack or ling, say. As you would imagine, there is a continuum from the 50g fillet to the 2kg fillet. For us, it's all done by hand and eye, but to get you started we'll guestimate some times and quantities. These should – of course – be taken with a pinch of salt.

Weigh the fish fillets before you salt them. You should use about 50g salt per 250g fish, though this doesn't exactly double up – i.e. for a kilo of fish, you'd get away with much less than 200g salt: about 100–150g would do it. Fillets weighing between 100 and 250g should be salted for 5–15 minutes, and those between 250 and 500g will need 15–20 minutes. Only mega fillets (weighing over a kilo) require the full hour. Obviously you don't need to weigh the salt precisely or use a stopwatch and, once you get the hang of it, you'll do the whole thing like us – by eye and feel.

Scatter half your (roughly) calculated quantity of salt over the base of a large plastic tray, Tupperware box or glass or ceramic dish (never use metal, as the salt will corrode it). Lay the fillets, skin side down, on the salt. Scatter the remaining salt evenly over the top and leave in a cool place, such as the fridge or a cool larder, for the allotted time. Then, gently rinse off the salt under the cold tap and immediately pat the fillets dry with kitchen paper. Your lightly salted fillets are ready to cook, or they can be kept in the fridge – wrapped in cling film or in a covered container – for a couple of days.

You'll see a number of recipes in this book calling for 'lightly salted white fish fillets'. Come back to this section to remind yourself what we're talking about.

MEDIUM OR 'SEMI-SALTED' FISH, INCLUDING GRAVAD LAX Somewhere between the light salting (above), which is a subtle preparation for almost immediate further cooking, and hard salting (see right), which preserves white fish in a state of virtually complete desiccation for months, if not years, is a range of medium-length salting techniques – from a few hours to a couple of days, depending on the thickness and character of the fish and the desired effect.

Whereas once these techniques were culture-specific, these days they are more or less recipe- or chef-specific – you're aiming for a particular effect with a particular kind of fish and a distinct set of accompanying ingredients. By far the best-known recipe in this category is gravad lax. The preservation technique here would once have been crude, developed as it was in medieval times or earlier to deal with the huge glut catches of spring and summer salmon in the fjords of Scandinavia. Gravad lax, which literally means 'buried salmon', was originally made by simply digging a hole in the ground, putting a layer of salmon in it, covering it with salt, then another layer of fish, and so on. But salt was scarce and relatively expensive in Scandinavia, and therefore could be used only sparingly. The burying of salmon relied on a secondary process – fermentation – to 'pickle' and preserve the fish. Indeed, covering the pit to exclude air was a vital part of getting the biochemistry right.

Fish preserved in this way was stable but very pungent. Exhumed from the pit, it may well have challenged the palates of even the hungriest members of the clan. The addition of sugar, pepper and pine needles was intended to soften the impact. One can assume it did a reasonable job – that's if you like your fish to taste of Domestos. Later, an abundant, easy-to-grow and powerfully aniseed-scented herb, dill, was increasingly used instead of pine needles. It may well have been the vital improvement that ensured the survival of gravad lax to the present day.

Over time, the recipe for gravad lax has been adapted – for pleasure and profit, as it were, rather than survival. Applying the same flavourings to thick fillets of salmon for a matter of days rather than months gives a lightly cured but highly aromatic result, without fermentation. The procedure works superbly with mackerel, too – and for us this technique serves a vital purpose whenever we are lucky enough to have a glut of these obliging fish on our hands. By making a big batch of Gravad max (page 142), we can extend the shelf life of our catch from a day or two (at most) to a couple of weeks. And indeed, since cured fish freezes so much better than fresh, we can, if it suits us, turn those weeks into months.

Gravad lax/max is not the only example of fish being preserved and presented in this way, and dill need not have a monopoly on flavouring a cure of this kind. The French love salted herrings and sardines almost as much as we love our kippers, and variations on these themes, with the semi-salted fillets of these smaller, oily fish being dressed and marinated with various exotic ingredients, are increasingly popular among chefs. Bream lends itself to this kind of treatment too, and our Marinated salt bream with roast tomatoes (page 144) is a lovely Mediterranean take on the procedure.

HARD-SALTING FISH TO PRESERVE IT LONG TERM It's always useful to have some salt fish to hand, and if ever a good catch of white fish is surplus to immediate requirements, we take off the fillets and salt them down. The heads and frames will be made into stock, which can be frozen.

Cod is the original white fish for salting – a factor that has no doubt contributed to its fragile ecological status (see page 428). However, its various relations respond to the treatment equally well. Pollack, coley and ling are all suitable, not least because of their size. We tend to give this treatment only to fish of about 2kg or more, as very small fillets are too insubstantial. Pollack of 3–6kg are our salt fish mainstays, as they yield thick fillets of 1–2kg.

Although you can salt fish in a bath of brine, we prefer the same dry-salting method we use for lightly salting – except that we use more salt and leave the fish in it for much longer. We rarely, if ever, weigh either the fish or the salt. Everything is measured by eye, and by the thickness of the fillet, and it's a very forgiving procedure, as basically you keep the fish in the salt, adding more if necessary, until the job's done. Here's how it goes:

For a decent batch you'll need at least two big fillets (total weight at least 1.5kg) from a large fish that has been descaled (see pages 55–6). And you should have a good kilo of salt to hand, though you won't need it all. You can use cheaper fine salt for this, as the process is meant to be harsh, not subtle, and you'll end up soaking away most of the salt before cooking or eating the fish.

Find yourself a deep-sided plastic or ceramic tray or container large enough to hold your fish (again, never use metal). Pour a nice, even layer of salt into the container, a good few millimetres deep, then put the fillets on top, skin side down, trying not to overlap them too much. Cover them completely with another layer of salt, making it at least 5mm–1cm deep this time. Make sure there are no air gaps. If you have lots of fillets to salt, repeat this layering until you have used all the fish.

Keep the box somewhere cool – in the fridge, if it will fit. After 24 hours, the fish will have leached quite a bit of water. Pour this off and throw on another good sprinkling of dry salt. Repeat this process every couple of days for the next

7–14 days, until the amount of water leaching out is minimal (the more fillets you have in your stack, the longer it will take). After a couple of weeks, when the salt is damp but no longer wet, the fish fillets should be fully preserved. You can leave them in their salty box for as long as you like, and they will just get drier and drier. (An early River Cottage salt pollack experiment somehow ended up staying in the salad tray of the fridge for over 2 years, by which time it was rock hard and had a slightly yellow tinge. But it was soaked for 4 days and then made into Brandade, page 150, which tasted absolutely fine.)

If the fish is taking up too much room in the fridge or larder and you want to get it out, remove the fillets from the salt, lay them out on a board and rub a little fresh, dry sea salt over them. Then tie a loop of butcher's string around the tail end (the narrowest and toughest end) of each one and hang it somewhere cool, airy and dry, such as an outdoor shed, a cool, draughty garage or a larder, until you want to use it. In persistent damp weather the fillets may sweat a bit as the salt draws moisture from the atmosphere. If the fish looks wet for more than a few days, bring it in, dry it off, then rub a little more salt on it and hang it up again.

Salt fish needs to be rehydrated before you can cook it. To do this, soak it in plenty of very cold water for at least 48 hours, changing the water at least twice a day during this period. The best way to tell if it's been soaked for long enough is to taste a little from the middle of a cut fillet (the edge will not be representative). It should still be a little salty, but not unpleasantly so.

To serve them up in the most basic (but very pleasing) form, fillets of soaked, reconstituted salt fish should be gently simmered in plenty of fresh water for about 10–15 minutes, until tender and showing some flakiness again. Drain, dress with good olive oil, black pepper and a few drops of lemon juice, then serve with plenty of rice or mash and some fried onions.

There are, of course, countless recipes from all over the world using salt cod. Brandade is our favourite, but we tend to make it with our beloved salt pollack.

Pickling by other means

There is another great preserving ingredient that has often been used to extend the life of fish: vinegar. For centuries, cheap wine vinegar and even cheaper malt vinegar, created as by-products of wine-making and brewing, served a useful purpose as alternatives to salt for preserving a harvest glut – usually of vegetables. However, the Scandinavian and Baltic countries soon took to vinegar for preserving their beloved herrings, in the form of the rollmop. Like gravad lax, this would once have been a fairly crude affair – fish submerged in a pickle severe enough to keep it almost indefinitely – but has now evolved into a delicacy, the cure adapted to suit the palates of more sophisticated consumers. These days you'll find the best rollmops in the chill cabinet, with a shelf life of weeks rather than months.

When it comes to pickling and sousing fish in vinegar at home (see pages 146–9), the aim should be to out-do even the very best of the branded commercial products, so the emphasis should be entirely on the best ingredients. The quality of the vinegar is paramount, and we have found that a good organic cider vinegar, though not strictly authentic, is very hard to beat for flavour. Good quality wine vinegars work well, too.

A range of skills for the home cook

You may begin to see why we've grouped raw and preserved fish together in this chapter. While they can represent two opposite ends of a spectrum – sashimi is as fresh as you can get, salt cod may have been stored in a state of stasis for several years – they are nevertheless on the same spectrum. It is, if you like, a spectrum of specialised processing skills enacted on raw fish that are, in our food culture at least, generally considered outside the repertoire of the home cook.

We think it shouldn't be like that. We know from experience that all these techniques are quite within the reach of any enthusiastic cook, and believe that the results you can achieve at home will be at least as good as, if not better than, those you will pay for in the market place. Having these techniques is a fantastic way to develop a holistic and respectful relationship with your fish. By embracing and practising these skills, you will not only discover some wonderful ways of eating fish but you will also never be entirely separated from the underlying motives of necessity and thrift – and that can only be a good thing.

It's an outlook we take with us every time we go fishing, even if we may be dreaming greedily of bumper catches of huge fish. And on the rare occasions when we do end up with a glut (usually of mackerel, but occasionally of pollack, or even bass), we put all the main skills of this chapter into practice, as follows:

We'll make some sashimi on the very day of the catch, maybe even on the boat before we return to port. Then back at home, we'll probably knock up a ceviche starter, before baking, frying or barbecuing as much fish as we can realistically eat. Fishermen's eyes being much bigger than their stomachs, we often have lots of leftovers – hence our extensive repertoire of recipes for leftover fish – see Fish thrift and standbys (page 366). But before the end of the day, or the next morning at the latest, we'll set about preserving the rest of the fresh fish: Gravad max (page 142) is a great favourite, as are rollmops (page 146), but we also have a souse (page 147) or escabeche (page 148) up our sleeves. Pollack fillets will be salted, some lightly, some heavily, and others will be smoked. Sea bass may be smoked too, or lightly salted in anticipation of the recipe on page 144.

Of course, we don't *need* to do this. Fish that we can't eat could simply go in the freezer, and still wouldn't be wasted. But we choose to use and manipulate these techniques because they always produce such delicious results. Salting, curing, marinating and sousing are not supplementary subjects for fish swots. They are practical and applied skills, not just for specialists but for all those who are truly enthusiastic about getting the best from their fish. If that's you, then you may well want to carry on to the next stage of the fish processing adventure, smoking your own fish at home, which is covered in the next chapter.

River Cottage sashimi and sushi

It might not sound very 'Dorset', but we eat a lot of sashimi and sushi. They are, after all, among the best ways to enjoy super-fresh fish, and we usually make them with specimens we've just caught, rather than bought. Our favourites for eating raw are mackerel, pollack, bream and bass – and, once in a while, wild salmon.

In case you were in any doubt, the difference between sashimi and sushi is simple: rice. While our sashimi is often eaten, as described below, on the hoof or on the boat, sushi is more of a sit-down affair – though some pre-made sushi rice can be taken aboard a fishing boat too, for the ultimate in fresh sushi assembly.

There is a degree of mystery associated with sushi, and it is rightly regarded as an art form when prepared by a master. However, it's unreasonable to suggest that only the highly trained professional is allowed to have a go. If you're capable of cutting a neat and skinless fillet from a fresh fish – and cutting it into a few bite-sized morsels – then you can delight your friends and family with a home-made version of this Japanese classic. And if the fish you are slicing and serving is one that you or your friends have caught within the last 24 hours, then there is every chance that you will delight them as much, or more, than any professional.

The accompaniments don't have to be super-exotic either, as you will see…

THE CORNER-SHOP SASHIMI KIT It's commonly thought that the *minimum* accompaniments to sashimi are wasabi, soy sauce and pickled ginger. In fact, only one of these is vital, and that's the soy. The ginger makes a nice palate cleanser between mouthfuls but it's not essential for flavouring the fish itself. The nose-searing, eye-watering wasabi is wonderful, of course, but the same job can be done by a properly peppy hot English mustard. So, if you take a bottle of soy sauce (light and Japanese, not heavy and Chinese – Clearspring and Kikkoman are good brands), and either a tube of wasabi or a jar of hot English mustard (good old Colman's does the trick) on a fishing trip, you are primed for some on-board Japanese raw fish action.

IMPROVISED ON-BOARD SASHIMI We almost always prepare a round or two of sashimi on the boat for our guests on every River Cottage Catch and Cook trip. Just-caught mackerel gets the most frequent outing, followed by pollack, bream and bass. Pollack is perhaps the biggest surprise. We didn't think it would be much of a sashimi fish until one day, in the absence of any alternative, we tried it more or less out of desperation. It was a knockout success.

It takes a calm, methodical approach to prepare a nice plate of sashimi on a moving boat with people fishing all around you, but it's a challenge that we now regard as a pleasure. We have devised a little system, which takes just-caught fish from a state of guts-in, scales-on wholeness to dainty finished sashimi in a few simple steps. It's called 'bucket, dirty board, clean board, plate', and it will serve you just as well in your kitchen as on the deck of a boat.

To expand: gut your fish (see pages 58–9) and rinse thoroughly in a bucket of fresh, clean seawater (or, if at home, under the cold tap in the sink). Discard the water and refill the bucket with more clean seawater. Wipe the fish with a clean cloth and put it on the 'dirty board' – it doesn't have to be dirty, of course, and should not be caked with fish guts, but it does not have to be pristine either. It's just the regular fish-prep or bait-cutting board that lives on the boat. A few sheets of wet newspaper over the board are no bad thing.

Now fillet your chosen fish as well as you are able (see page 62), on the wet paper on the dirty board. Rinse each fillet in fresh clean seawater in the bucket, pat dry with a clean cloth and place on the clean board. This really should be clean; we usually use a proper wooden or nylon chopping board that we have brought with us, wrapped in a clean tea towel, from the kitchen.

As best you can, skin the fillet (see page 73) and trim it, discarding the skin and any remaining bones or unappetising membranes, until you have a very pure, clean-looking fillet, and nothing else, on the clean board. Now start slicing the fillet into small-bite-sized strips. Roughly speaking, the best angle for each cut is at 45° to the natural grain of the fish. Place every piece you are happy with on the plate, which should also, obviously, be clean.

Once you have arranged a nice plate of sashimi with, say, two pieces for everyone on the boat, take the lid off the mustard, dab it with a clean finger, and put a light smear of mustard on every piece of fish. Shake a bit of soy over the fish, too – or pour a little into a suitable container, such as the lid, and have it on the plate for dipping. Hand the plate around.

This method can be adapted for domestic consumption, where everything will behave itself even more, and there will be clean cloths, boards and plates aplenty. It's also the basic method for prepping and trimming fish for sushi, which is, of course, simply sashimi plus rice.

Sushi rice *makes enough for 6*

At home, we stick to three basic ways of presenting our sushi but they all hinge on one constant: a quantity of perfectly seasoned sushi rice. Once you've made that, and assembled some soy sauce and wasabi (or hot English mustard, you can then choose how you'd like to proceed as far as the fish is concerned.

200g sushi rice
100ml rice wine vinegar (or cider vinegar in an emergency)

1 tablespoon sugar
¼ teaspoon salt

Rinse the rice very well under cold water until the water runs clear. Drain thoroughly, put into a large saucepan and pour over enough water to cover the rice by 3–4cm. Leave to stand for half an hour, then bring to a fast boil. Cook for 5 minutes, then turn the heat down and simmer gently for a further 15–20 minutes, until nearly all the water has been absorbed. Remove from the heat, cover the pan and leave to stand for 10 minutes.

Meanwhile, put the vinegar, sugar and salt in a small pan and heat gently until the sugar has completely dissolved. Leave to cool. Add the vinegar solution to the warm, cooked rice, combining it well. Tip the seasoned rice on to a large tray and spread it out to help it cool completely.

Finger-shaped sushi (nigiri sushi) *makes about 24*

Japanese sushi chefs train for around seven years before they are deemed competent in their art. We feel that – as long as you're not too particular about perfect symmetry – 7 minutes of practice should do it when it comes to forming these delicious morsels. The fat little pillow of rice is the perfect carrier for a mouthful of fresh fish.

400g trimmed raw fish fillets, such as
  mackerel, sea bass, black bream,
  pollack or organic farmed (or self-caught
  wild) salmon, or pickled Sushi mackerel
  (page 137)

1 quantity of Sushi rice (see left)
Wasabi or hot English mustard

TO SERVE:
Light soy sauce
Japanese pickled ginger

Cut your fish into lozenges or slightly off-kilter diamonds about 2 x 5cm, and 3–5mm thick. But don't get over-anxious about precision slicing, as long as the fish pieces more or less cover the rice pieces and are not too thick. Any leftover scraps and ends can be cut into small cubes, marinated with a little soy and wasabi, mixed with a little leftover rice and gobbled up as 'chef's perks'. See also Freestyle sushi (see page 136).

Have a small bowl of water by your side and keep your hands wet as you work (this stops the rice sticking to them). Take a roughly thumb-sized portion of cooled sushi rice and squeeze it in your palm so it sticks together in a rough cylinder. Place it on a board and carefully mould it into a smooth, neat, half-a-fat-finger (or small pillow) shape. Use your little finger to smear a touch of wasabi or mustard on the upper surface, then lay a piece of fish on top. Repeat with all the rice and fish, then serve, with the soy and ginger on the side.

To eat nigiri sushi

Really, a piece of nigiri sushi should be one good mouthful – pick it up with chopsticks, dip one end briefly in the soy, then gobble it down. If it's not punchy enough for your taste, you can add an extra smear of wasabi (or mustard) on top of each piece, or mix a little in with your dipping soy.

The ginger is strictly intended as a palate cleanser, to be eaten between mouthfuls, but some people like to put a sliver of ginger on the sushi and eat it with the fish and rice.

Drinking saki with your sushi certainly completes the experience (we prefer chilled saki to hot) but good cold beer is a very acceptable alternative.

Maki rolls *makes 30*

The extra dimension here is the dried nori seaweed in which the sushi is rolled, which adds a distinctive flavour and texture. There's more technique required here, but it isn't hard to get the knack.

Lightly oily fish, such as mackerel, salmon, trout and bass, are best for maki rolls, as very light fish can get lost among the extra flavours. You can, however, use any of the fish suitable for sashimi. You'll need a bamboo rolling mat, which you should be able to buy wherever you buy your sushi ingredients (or see the Directory, page 591, for a mail order supplier).

300g trimmed raw fish fillets, such as
  mackerel, sea bass, trout, organic farmed
  (or self-caught wild) salmon, black bream
  or pollack
5 sheets of dried nori seaweed
1 quantity of Sushi rice (see page 132)
3 teaspoons wasabi paste
½ cucumber, cut into batons, then shaved
  into thin strips (optional)

3–4 spring onions, white part only, cut into
  paper-thin ribbons (optional)
2–3 teaspoons toasted sesame seeds

TO SERVE:
Japanese pickled ginger
Light soy sauce

Prepare your chosen fish by cutting the fillets into long strips, no thicker than the top section of your little finger (or only slightly thicker than a pencil). Have the fish standing by, alongside any of the optional extra fillings you'd like to use.

Place a sheet of nori seaweed shiny side down on your bamboo rolling mat. Have a little bowl of water ready by the side of the mat. Wet your fingers and spread about a fifth of the rice over the seaweed: it should cover three-quarters to four-fifths of the sheet, leaving 1cm free on the side closest to you and a bit more than that on the side furthest away. Work quickly, using just the tips of your fingers, and aim to spread the rice only a few grains thick. Go particularly easy with the rice in the centre, as this is where the filling is also going to go. Try not to crush the grains or the finished roll will be dense and lumpy. It's a sticky, fiddly job, and it does take a bit of practice, but it pays off in the end.

Run a tiny squeeze of wasabi paste from the left side to the right, in the centre of the rice. Wasabi is incredibly, eye-poppingly hot, so use just a little if it's the first time you've done this – you can always make subsequent rolls with more fire. Now carefully lay strips of fish on top of the wasabi. Follow with some super-thin strips of cucumber, then paper-thin ribbons of spring onion, if you like. Remember, less is more. Finish off with a sprinkle of toasted sesame seeds.

Place your thumbs on the edge of the mat closest to you and lift it, supporting the filling on the other side with your fingers. Roll the rice away from you, pressing lightly as you go, using the mat to help you roll but making sure it doesn't get rolled in with the rice. You should create a neat, fat, fairly tight roll, with the far end of the seaweed adhering to the outside of the roll and making a seal. It should be 'self adhesive', as the dampness of the rice is enough to make the seaweed sticky. But if it seems reluctant to seal, then a lightly wetted finger run along the inside of the nori seaweed 'tab' should do the job. Push any loose rice lightly back into the ends of the roll to tidy them up.

You can now take the roll off the mat and cut it into 6 pieces. Use the sharpest knife you've got, and clean in hot water then wipe between every cut – if you don't do this, the sticky residue of the rice will make the knife tear the sushi rather than glide through cleanly. Repeat with the remaining rice and filling ingredients, then serve your maki rolls with pickled ginger and little bowls of soy sauce.

To eat maki rolls
Even more than nigiri sushi, these should be one-bite wonders. Just pick up with fingertips or chopsticks, dip in soy, and eat.

Freestyle sushi

Sushi purists should look away now. This serving option is somewhat inauthentic and might have a trained sushi chef committing hara-kiri with his sharpest knife. It is, however, quick, easy, delicious, and not without its own informal charms.

All you need to do is prepare some Sushi rice (page 132), spreading it out on a large platter to cool. Place this on the table, along with some wasabi or mustard, soy sauce and pickled ginger. Small pieces of prepared raw fish – sashimi-style strips (see page 132) – go on a separate plate. Everyone then simply helps themselves, making their own, slightly haphazard sushi as they go: a handful of rice, a smudge of mustard, a sliver of fish, and down the hatch.

DIY sushi rolls

Freestyle sushi meets maki rolls: you can embellish the informal proceedings described above by adding some nori seaweed, cut into 6–8cm squares, plus a few strips of spring onion, cucumber, maybe even avocado, plus sesame seeds and a pepper mill. From the fish point of view, some cooked white crabmeat or thinly sliced, super-fresh raw scallops are a fantastic addition.

The squares of nori are used for DIY rolls, no rolling mats required. These are customised by diners to their own taste, but basically involve a small handful of rice, a piece or two of fish, a smear of wasabi, plus their choice of the extras on offer. They are informally rolled into cones or short fat cheroots, dipped in soy, and gobbled in two or three mouthfuls. One option is a 'California roll': white crabmeat, avocado, cucumber and a dab of mayonnaise.

Sushi mackerel (shimi saba) *makes about 40*

This is the authentic way to pickle mackerel lightly for serving on top of sushi rice. It takes only a couple of hours, all in. So if you've had a good catch of mackerel and want to make a bit of a Japanese song and dance about it, you could prepare some of it to eat raw as sashimi (see page 132) and some pickled. The two results are quite distinct, and complement each other nicely.

Provided your mackerel has been iced and carefully stored, this recipe will work with fish up to 48 hours old.

100g fine sea salt
4 large whole mackerel fillets (about
   150g each), prepared bait-cutter style
   (see pages 62–3)

FOR THE MARINADE:
500ml rice vinegar
50ml mirin (Japanese rice wine)
10g (about 2 teaspoons) sea salt

TO ACCOMPANY:
1 quantity of Sushi rice (see page 132)
Wasabi (or hot English mustard)
Light soy sauce
Japanese pickled ginger (optional)

Sprinkle about a third of the salt over a non-metallic tray or dish. Lay the mackerel fillets on top, without overlapping them, then sprinkle over the rest of the salt in an even layer. Leave for just 5 minutes, then turn each fillet in the salt and transfer them to a bamboo basket, plastic or nylon colander or, at a pinch, simply a wooden board. Leave for another 20 minutes, so the salt continues to draw out the juices. Then quickly but thoroughly rinse each fillet in cold water and pat dry with cotton or paper towels.

Mix all the ingredients for the marinade together and place in a non-metallic container, such as a ceramic or glass gratin or pie dish, or a Tupperware box. Add the mackerel fillets and leave in the fridge for 1–1½ hours, by which time the flesh will have turned creamy-white.

Remove the fillets, shaking off the marinade back into the dish, and pat them dry again. Now carefully peel off the papery, thin outer skin from the head to the tail end. The iridescent pattern underneath should be left behind on the fillets, though a little of it may come away with the skin.

Lay the fillets skin side down again. Use tweezers (ideally special pin-bone tweezers) to remove the pin bones from the lateral line along the middle of the fillet. Do the same (or take a very fine slice with a filleting knife) to remove the belly bones in the surface of the belly edge of the fillet.

Your pickled mackerel is now ready to slice for sashimi. Cut across each fillet, at 45° or so on the bias, into slices about 2cm thick, to get slightly out-of-kilter diamond-shaped pieces. Each of these should be placed over a nicely moulded piece of sushi rice, on which you've rubbed a faint smear of wasabi (see Finger-shaped sushi, page 133).

Serve the traditional way, with soy sauce into which you've mixed a little more wasabi, and perhaps some pickled ginger, as a between-mouthfuls palate cleanser.

Salmon tartare *serves 4 as a starter*

You're probably familiar with the classic steak tartare, where finely chopped beef is combined with a range of piquant flavourings and eaten raw. You can do a very similar thing with spanking-fresh raw salmon – with excellent results. Raw salmon has a good, firm texture and eats best when cut fairly coarsely, in contrast to the almost minced texture of steak tartare.

Also works with:
• Sea trout
• Mackerel
• Scad

400g boneless, skinless organic farmed (or self-caught wild) salmon, cut into thumbnail-sized cubes
Juice of 1 lemon
A few shakes of Worcestershire sauce
A few scant shakes of Tabasco sauce

2 teaspoons finely chopped parsley
2 teaspoons finely chopped capers
2 teaspoons finely chopped gherkin
2 teaspoons very finely chopped red onion
Salt and freshly ground black pepper

Put the salmon in a large mixing bowl and squeeze over the lemon juice, followed by the Worcestershire sauce and Tabasco. Season with salt and pepper. Gently fold in the parsley, capers, gherkin and onion. Leave the mixture to stand for 10 minutes before serving, so the flavours get a chance to develop. Then mix again, leave to rest for another 10 minutes, and serve. Eat with buttered toast (granary or rye is best).

Carpaccio of bream *serves 2 as a starter*

A classic Italian carpaccio uses slivers of raw beef but this dressing of lemon juice, capers, olive oil and fennel makes the transition to fish work beautifully. Bream's firm, dense flesh makes it particularly suitable for serving raw.

Also works with:
- Sea bass
- Salmon (organic farmed or self-caught wild)
- Sea trout
- Gurnard
- Brill

1 large or 2 small fillets (about 150g in total) very fresh black bream or gilt-head bream
1 fennel bulb

Juice of ½–1 lemon
1 tablespoon baby capers, rinsed
Really good extra virgin olive oil
Salt and freshly ground black pepper

Lay the fish fillets on a board and remove any pin bones with tweezers. Make sure no bones remain, as they will make slicing the fish quite difficult.

Now slice the fish with a very sharp filleting knife, trying to make the slices as large and as thin as possible – no more than 1mm thick. Cut the bream as you might a side of smoked salmon, working gradually down towards the skin at an angle. Lay the bream slices on 1 or 2 large plates, spreading them out in an even layer so they don't overlap too much.

Cut the base from the fennel bulb and peel off the tough outer layers (the fresher the bulb, the less you'll have to discard). Slice the fennel from tip to root as finely as possible – you're aiming for what they call 'shaved' fennel. Scatter the fennel slices over the fish, then squeeze over the lemon juice, trying to get a few drops on every bit of fish. Spoon over the capers, then season the whole plate with salt and pepper. Finish with a trickle of extra virgin olive oil. Unlike a ceviche, where the fish needs at least a couple of hours to 'cook' in the marinade, this dish is all about fresh flavours combining in the mouth. So serve, and eat, immediately.

Ceviche *serves 5–6 as a starter*

This is a classic Latin American dish, where fish is marinated in citrus juice. The acid in the juice changes the chemical structure of the fish in a similar way to cooking it, so the texture and flavour cease to be 'raw' but there's still a lovely freshness on the palate. It's crucial that you start with spankingly fresh fish. Firm, well-muscled varieties such as bream and bass are ideal for ceviche, but we have had good results with gurnard and pollack as well.

There are many variations on the theme. Our tried and trusted version uses subtle flavourings that play to the strengths of the very best, freshest fish. Variations that we would sanction include the use of finely sliced fennel bulb instead of celery, and upping the heat a bit with fresh chilli and cayenne, if you like that extra zing. If finding both limes and lemons is a problem, use just one or the other. But don't miss out on the orange. We think it rather makes the dish.

500g black bream or sea bass fillets
Juice of 3 limes, 2 lemons and 1 orange
1 small red onion, sliced paper thin
2 celery sticks, finely sliced (as thick as a 10-pence piece)
½–1 mild to medium red chilli, deseeded and very finely sliced

½ teaspoon sweet unsmoked paprika
A pinch of hot unsmoked paprika or cayenne pepper
½ teaspoon soft brown sugar
A pinch of salt
1 tablespoon coarsely chopped coriander (optional)

Preparing the fish is time-consuming, but it's really worth doing it carefully. Skin the fillets (see page 73) and remove the pin bones. Work over each piece with your fingers, making sure it is completely boneless, skinless and free from the thickish membrane found around the belly area. Then slice the fish across the grain into pieces 0.5–1cm thick. Don't make them any thinner or you'll barely feel the fish in your mouth.

Pass the citrus juice through a fine sieve to remove the fibres. Then combine it with the onion, celery, chilli, spices, sugar and salt in a ceramic dish or plastic tub (not a metal container). Add the fish and mix gently, making sure it is completely submerged in the liquid. Put in the fridge to marinate for a minimum of an hour and a maximum of 12 hours; 3–4 hours is about perfect. You'll see the flesh become opaque as the juice 'cooks' it.

Taste the ceviche and adjust the seasonings, if necessary – you might feel the need for a little more cayenne pepper, sugar or salt. If you want to use the coriander, stir it in just before serving.

We like to serve the ceviche, with all its juices and aromatic flavourings, in little cups. After eating the fish, you can then drink the juice.

Also works with:
- Scallops
- Salmon (organic farmed or self-caught wild)
- Sea trout
- Brill
- Turbot
- Lemon sole
- Pollack
- Scad

Gravad max *serves 10 as a starter*

This is a real River Cottage classic, a recipe we've been enjoying for years as it uses large quantities of one of our favourite, most abundant fish – mackerel – and gives delicious results.

It is based, of course, on the Scandinavian gravad lax, a recipe originally developed to preserve salmon. That fish is no longer caught in the great hauls it once was, but mackerel remains one of the very few fish you can still experience a glut of. Since (like salmon) it has oily, sweet flesh, it makes perfect sense to adapt the old Scandinavian recipe to our needs.

It's important to use really good dill, otherwise you'll barely notice its flavour. Most supermarket dill – forced too fast in little compost pots – just doesn't cut the mustard. Grow your own, if you can, or seek out a good herb grower. Dried dill can be used in an emergency – you'll probably need the entire contents of one of those little jars.

This recipe has been adapted from one in *The River Cottage Cookbook*. These days, we tend to go for a shorter cure time (24–48 hours) and leave the fish in the juices that leach out, rather than drain them off. This gives a sweeter, more tender result – though this version won't keep quite as long as the original.

You'll need to choose a container to cure the fillets in. It can be a Tupperware box, plastic tray, or glass, terracotta or ceramic dish – anything but metal, really. Then you need to find some kind of board, lid, second dish or plate that fits fairly neatly on top of, and just inside, your chosen curing dish.

Once cured, the mackerel can be kept for 10 days in the fridge. Gravad max also freezes beautifully, so none of it need ever go to waste.

About 10 very fresh, medium-large mackerel

FOR THE CURE:
About 100g caster sugar
About 75g coarse salt
About 15g coarsely ground black or white pepper, or a mixture
A large bunch of dill, coarse stalks removed, finely chopped

FOR THE ACCOMPANYING SAUCE:
4 teaspoons English mustard
4 teaspoons golden caster sugar or light brown sugar
2 teaspoons wine vinegar
2–3 tablespoons chopped dill
6 tablespoons crème fraîche

The quickest way to prepare the mackerel is to take the fillet from either side of an ungutted fish, bait-cutter style – i.e. slicing from head to tail as close as possible to the backbone (see pages 62–3). Wipe any blood or guts from the board you are working on as you go. The whole frames (i.e. skeletons with heads and tails still on, and guts attached) from which the fillets have been taken can be kept and frozen, then used later for pot-bait.

Mix together all the ingredients for the cure. Sprinkle some cure lightly over the base of your chosen tray, box or dish, then place the first layer of fillets on it skin side down, with the thin edges just overlapping. Then sprinkle another, slightly thicker layer of cure over. Arrange the next layer of mackerel skin side up and sprinkle over another layer of cure, then place the next layer skin side down (as shown, above left). Keep going until you've used all your fish, or filled the dish.

Put the board/lid/plate on top of the final layer and weight it down with a brick, storage jar, or whatever comes to hand (see the picture on pages 118–19). Place in the fridge. You can eat the gravad max after 24 hours, but 48 is best. For really big fillets, you could wait for 72 hours. Remove the board and lift out the fillets carefully, one at a time. Give them a very quick rinse and then pat dry immediately with a clean cloth or kitchen paper.

You could serve whole fillets, leaving the problem of cutting it away from the skin and avoiding the pin-bones (which are still there, running down the middle of each fillet) to your guests. Or you could be kinder, and trim the fish before serving. So, place the cured fillet on a board, skin side down, and run a flexible filleting knife between the flesh and the skin (as shown in the lower picture on the opposite page). Alternatively you can sometimes just start the process with the knife, then peel the skin off with your fingers.

Now slice the skinless fillet either side of the pin-bone line to give you 2 long fillets – and a very thin waste piece in the middle with the pin bones in it, which you should discard. The belly-side fillet may require a final trim to remove the fine belly bones.

To make the sauce, mix the mustard, sugar and vinegar together. Add the dill, mix well and leave to macerate for a few minutes. Mix again, then stir in the crème fraîche.

Serve the mackerel – 2 whole fillets or 4 trimmed pieces per person – with the creamy sauce on the side and plenty of brown bread and butter.

VARIATION
Classic gravad lax and curing fillets of larger fish

If you'd like to make genuine gravad lax with salmon, or if you fancy curing other larger fish, such as trout or sea trout, here's the procedure.

Use 2 large fillets, ideally from a single fish weighing at least 2kg. Try to find a plastic tray or ceramic dish that will accommodate one fillet fairly snugly. Scatter a good layer of cure (exactly the same as the Gravad max cure, above) over the base of the dish, lay the first fillet on top, skin-side down, then cover with more cure. Top with the second fillet, skin side up, and cover again with cure. Put a weighted board on top and leave in a cool place. (If you don't have a suitable container for the fish, you can use cling film – lay out a sheet of it, then stack cure, fish, cure, fish and more cure on it and wrap up the whole thing tightly. Transfer to a plate or dish and put a weighted board on top.)

Leave the fish to cure for at least 3 days (for smaller fillets and/or a milder cure) and up to 7 days (for really big fillets from a 5kg salmon, or bigger). Every day, turn the 'fillet sandwich' over and baste the fish in its accumulated juices, then replace the weight. (If you've got a cling-filmed parcel, don't unwrap it – just turn the whole thing over, so the juices can run the other way.) When the fish is cured, rinse and dry the fillets as above.

Slice fairly thinly before serving. You can wrap unused or part-sliced fillets and keep them in the fridge for up to 10 days.

Marinated salt bream with roast tomatoes

serves 5–6 as a starter

This is an updated version of a lovely recipe by Adam Robinson. He used to make it with lightly salted cod at his restaurant, the Brackenbury, in Chiswick. He's upped sticks and now lives in South Africa, and we can't help wondering what local fish he might be using to make it there. Grouper perhaps?

It works beautifully with bream but a very respectable version can be made with other white fish. If you're using a larger fillet than the one specified in the recipe, you can scale up the cure time and the quantity of cure. We wouldn't recommend using smaller fillets, however, as they can easily become too salty.

Also works with:
• Sea bass
• Pollack
• Whiting
• Ling
• Coley
• Grey mullet

1 thick fillet, weighing 400–500g, from a good-sized black bream (or 2 smaller fillets), skin on
6 good ripe tomatoes – large plums or medium round ones
A few sprigs of thyme, plus some thyme leaves to finish
Olive oil
Salt and freshly ground black pepper

FOR THE CURE:
150g sea salt
50g caster sugar
2 bay leaves, finely shredded
5g freshly ground black pepper

FOR THE MARINADE:
1 small red onion or 2 shallots, finely sliced
1 tablespoon white wine vinegar or cider vinegar
4 tablespoons good-quality olive oil
1 large garlic clove, very finely sliced

Mix the ingredients for the cure together thoroughly. Choose a non-metallic tray or dish in which the fish fillet will fit neatly. Sprinkle half the cure over the base of the dish, in a layer the width of the fish. Lay the fish over the cure, skin side down, and sprinkle the rest over it. Leave the fish to cure in a cool larder, or the fridge, for 6–8 hours. You could, at a push, leave it overnight (but not if you're planning a lie-in). Beyond 10 hours, it will become unpalatably salty. Then remove the fillet, rinse thoroughly, and immediately pat dry with a clean cloth.

Meanwhile, cut the tomatoes in quarters and scoop out the seeds. Arrange the tomatoes in an ovenproof dish, sprinkle with a little salt and the thyme sprigs and trickle with olive oil. Place in the oven and roast gently, at about 140°C/Gas Mark 1 for 2–2$\frac{1}{2}$ hours, until the tomatoes are half-dried, half roasted, and nice and sweet. Remove and leave to cool completely in the dish.

Now prepare the fish by slicing from the tail end at an angle. Slice it like a side of smoked salmon, only thicker (5mm–1cm thick), cutting each slice away from the skin. Remove and discard any remaining pin or belly bones as you go.

Combine all the ingredients for the marinade. Add the pieces of sliced bream, along with the cooled roasted tomatoes and any juices from the dish, and toss together well. Leave, covered, in the fridge for at least 2 hours, and up to 4 or 5, so the flavours can marry and mingle. Remove from the fridge an hour or so before serving and toss once more. Serve, sprinkled with a few fresh thyme leaves, with crusty bread or pitta to mop up the juices.

Marinated salt bream with roasted peppers

This dish works well with roasted red peppers and/or medium-hot chillies such
as poblano or Hungarian hot wax, added instead of or as well as the tomatoes.
Roast the peppers and/or chillies in an oven preheated to 200°C/Gas Mark 6 for
about 30 minutes, until charred (either before or after roasting the tomatoes).
Then place in a bowl, cover and leave until cool enough to handle. Peel and deseed
the peppers and chillies, reserving any juices. Cut them into strips and add to
the fish instead of, or as well as, the roasted tomatoes, along with the saved
juices. Toss together and continue as for the main recipe, opposite.

Cider vinegar and orange rollmops

serves 6 as a starter or snack

Rollmops can be delicious, but they vary in quality a great deal. Bottom-of-the-range ones are cured in a harsh distilled vinegar (acetic acid) with a few onion slices and no aromatics. The best are made to more subtle, secret recipes and are a real treat. Homemade is best, of course, and this is our favoured cure. If you're preparing the herrings yourself and find they contain roe, save it to make Herring roes on toast (page 376).

6 large fresh herrings, descaled, gutted and filleted
60g salt

FOR THE MARINADE:
750ml cider vinegar
12 allspice berries

12 black peppercorns
6 bay leaves
1 tablespoon light brown sugar
Zest of one large orange, pared in wide strips, with no white pith
1 small onion, red or white, very thinly sliced

Check the herring fillets for any pin bones. Dissolve the salt in 500ml water to make a brine, then add the fillets. Leave them for 2–3 hours.

Meanwhile, make the marinade. Put all the ingredients in a saucepan, bring slowly to the boil and simmer for just 1 minute. Remove from the heat and leave to cool.

Drain the herring fillets from the brine and pat them dry with kitchen paper. Roll them up from tail end to head end, skin side out, and pack the rolls into 3 sterilised 500ml preserving jars. Pour the marinade over the herrings, making sure you get some of the spices and zest in each jar, then seal the jars.

Store in the fridge for at least 3 days before eating. They are best from 5–10 days, but will keep for up to a month. The longer you leave them, the softer and more pickled they'll get.

To serve, drain the fillets from their marinade and accompany with a little soured cream and, ideally, some rye bread.

Also works with:
· Sardines (large)
· Mackerel fillets (not the same, but still good)

Soused mackerel   *makes 24 fillets (enough for several meals)*

Sousing is a sort of cross between pickling and cooking, where the fish is poached gently in a highly spiced vinegar. It's a traditional way of preserving oily fish, particularly herring, though modern recipes use a very light pickle that extends the life of the fish for only a few days.

Soused mackerel is delicious eaten hot or cold, accompanied by a little of its aromatic liquor. The longer you store it in the fridge, the softer and more yielding the flesh will become. The liquor, too, will change, gradually jellifying as the gelatine from the fish skin works its magic.

12 mackerel
200g salt

FOR THE SOUSE:
300ml cider vinegar
150g white sugar
1 dried red chilli
½ teaspoon white peppercorns
½ teaspoon black peppercorns

½ teaspoon coriander seeds
½ teaspoon celery seeds
1 teaspoon salt
6 allspice berries
4 bay leaves, torn
3 or 4 broken parsley stalks
1 large or 2 small onions, finely sliced
2 celery sticks, finely sliced

Also works with:
• Herring
• Sardines
• Trout (small)

Fillet the fish bait-cutter style (see pages 62–3). Cut away and discard the thin sliver of brown flesh containing the belly bones. Removing the pin bones is not essential but, if you want to do so, slice carefully down each side of the pin-bone line with a very sharp knife, then remove the thin wedge of flesh with the pin bones inside it.

You need to salt the fish lightly before sousing it. Sprinkle about a third of the salt over a large plastic tray or ceramic dish. Lay half the mackerel fillets on it, skin side down, and sprinkle over another third of the salt. Add the second lot of fillets, skin side up, then sprinkle over the remaining salt. Leave for 5 minutes, then rinse off the salt quickly but thoroughly.

Combine all the ingredients for the souse in a stainless steel pan with 300ml water. Bring to the boil and simmer for 5 minutes to allow the flavours to mingle. Meanwhile, lay the rinsed mackerel fillets in a large roasting tin. They should be packed snugly together, and it doesn't matter if they are more than one fillet deep. Pour over the hot sousing liquid, which should cover, or very nearly cover, the fish. Cover the tin with foil and place in an oven preheated to 180°C/Gas Mark 4. Bake for 30 minutes, then remove from the oven and leave to cool.

Once the fish are cool, let them marinate for a minimum of 6 hours before serving. We think they taste better after at least 24 hours; you can keep them in their sousing liquor in the fridge for up to a week. Serve them at room temperature, or put a few fillets in a pan, spoon over a little of the liquor and reheat gently (don't let the liquid boil). Either way, serve with brown bread and butter or a simple potato salad.

Sardine or mackerel escabeche *serves 6*

Escabeche is simply the Spanish word for 'pickled' and usually refers to fish that's been fried first, then marinated in a flavoured vinegar. Variations of the dish, using a panoply of different spices and flavourings, can be found all over Spain and Latin America.

There's some debate – even among ourselves, it must be said – as to whether it's a dish that works best with white or with oily fish. Nick's in the white fish camp, while Hugh backs the oilies. Try it yourself with whiting or red mullet, as an alternative to sardines, and see what you think.

At River Cottage we spent years experimenting with our own escabeche recipes without feeling we'd really hit on a winner. The perfect spice combination eluded us. Eventually, we tried the dish with a set of seasonings that we always use in our merguez sausages: chilli, coriander, caraway and cumin. Known to us as the 'four c's', these are a classic combination in North African cooking. With the strong links between Spanish and Moorish food, we thought, why wouldn't it work? It certainly did, and the result is punchy, colourful, rich and intense – a dish we're truly proud of. This is how to make it.

Also works with:
- Red mullet
- Scad
- Black bream
- Grey mullet
- Pollack
- Pouting
- Whiting
- Gurnard

12 large sardines or small mackerel, carefully descaled and gutted, or large mackerel fillets
Olive oil

FOR THE DRY SPICE MIX:
2 teaspoons cumin seeds
2 teaspoons coriander seeds
2 teaspoons caraway seeds
1 teaspoon paprika
1 heaped teaspoon salt
1 heaped teaspoon sugar

FOR THE MARINADE:
A good pinch of coriander seeds
A good pinch of cumin seeds
A good pinch of caraway seeds
A good pinch of dried chilli flakes
1 large or 2 small red onions, finely sliced
2 garlic cloves, finely sliced
2 bay leaves
1 glass of white wine
½ wine glass of wine vinegar or cider vinegar

Put a heavy-based frying pan over a medium heat. Add the whole spices for the dry spice mix and toast for a few minutes, until they just start to pop. Put them in a large mortar (or a coffee or spice grinder), add the salt and sugar and grind to a fine texture.

Make sure the sardines or mackerel are dry to the touch, patting them dry with kitchen paper if necessary. Lay them on a board or large plate and dust with the spice mixture, making sure they are evenly covered – the idea is to treat the spice mix like seasoned flour.

Put a large, heavy frying pan over a medium heat and add a glug of olive oil. Add the fish (you will need to cook them in batches) and fry gently, colouring and crisping them lightly on each side – 3–4 minutes, turning occasionally, should do it, but don't fret about cooking them right through, as the cooking will be completed by the hot marinade.

Transfer the fried fish to a deep dish for marinating. If you use an ovenproof dish, you won't have to transfer the fish to another vessel when it comes to reheating them later.

Leave the frying pan on the heat and add a little more oil. Throw in the coriander, cumin, caraway and chilli for the marinade, then add the sliced onion, garlic and bay leaves. Fry for 4–5 minutes, until the onion is soft and ever so slightly coloured. Pour in the wine and vinegar, bring to a simmer and cook for 5 minutes, using a wooden spoon to scrape up any caramelised bits from the base of the pan.

Pour the hot marinade over the fish, making sure they are completely covered. Leave to cool, then chill for at least 6 hours before serving (it will keep in the fridge for a couple of days). It is best served at room temperature or slightly warm, rather than hot or cold. So either take it out of the fridge a few hours before you serve it or reheat it gently in a low oven, in its marinade.

Serve with flatbreads, such as pitta or homemade tortillas, or toasted sourdough, and perhaps a simple cucumber and lettuce salad. The flesh of whole fish will have to be wrestled off their fragile bones, but if you've used mackerel fillets, you can just eat the lot. In both cases, the skin is perfectly edible.

Brandade *serves 4 as a main course, 8 as a starter*

Brandade is a traditional Provençal dish, and a very rich and comforting one. The combination of buttery mash, salty fish and plenty of garlic really hits the spot. It's a versatile creation, too. You can serve it as a main course, accompanied by a crisp winter salad or braised greens, or turn it into a starter or snack, spreading it on slices of wholemeal toast. In fact, served in even smaller portions, it makes a lovely and very easy canapé. We also sometimes make it with smoked fish, poaching the fillet in milk until tender, then using some of the fishy, smoky milk in the mash.

250g hard-salted white fish (see page 127), such as pollack, ling, haddock, whiting or cod
500g floury potatoes, peeled and cut into chunks
25g unsalted butter

About 50ml hot milk
4–6 tablespoons olive oil
2–3 large garlic cloves, finely chopped
1–2 tablespoons double cream (optional)
Freshly ground black pepper

Soak the fish in cold water for 48 hours, changing the water at least twice a day.

Put the soaked fish in a pan, cover with fresh water and bring to a simmer. Cook gently for 10–15 minutes, until tender, then drain. Pick over the fish, discarding the skin and any bones, and break the flesh into flakes.

Boil the potatoes in lightly salted water until tender, then drain. Mash them thoroughly with the butter and hot milk to get a soft but not sloppy mash.

Heat 2–3 tablespoons of olive oil in a small pan over a low heat. Add the garlic and sweat gently in the oil for 2–3 minutes, without letting it colour.

Put the flaked fish in a food processor and pulse several times, trickling in the warm garlic and olive oil as you do so (or, more traditionally, pound everything together in a large pestle and mortar). Then add another 2–3 tablespoons olive oil, and the double cream (if you're feeling really greedy), and pulse/pound again. Transfer the puréed fish mixture to a large bowl and combine with the mashed potato, beating thoroughly so they are well mixed together (don't at any point process the potatoes in a machine, as it makes them gluey and spoils the dish). Season to taste with black pepper – you probably won't need any salt.

To heat before serving, spread the brandade in an ovenproof dish and bake for 15–20 minutes in a fairly hot oven (190°C/Gas Mark 5), until piping hot.

VARIATION
Gill's new potato brandade

This is a sort of deconstructed, summer version of brandade, invented by Gill, our chef at River Cottage, which is very simple and works particularly well with lightly salted fish (see page 124). It's one to improvise, using most or all of the following ingredients.

500g lightly salted, or smoked, white fish fillets, such as pollack, ling, haddock, whiting or cod	1–2 tablespoons olive oil
	2 garlic cloves, finely chopped
	2 tablespoons chopped parsley and/or chives
1kg new potatoes, scrubbed	
A knob of butter	Freshly ground black pepper

Poach the lightly salted fish fillets in simmering water for 3–5 minutes, just until cooked (alternatively, use rehydrated hard-salted fish, prepared and cooked as above). Drain, leave to cool, then skin the fish. Break it into flakes, removing any pin bones.

Boil the potatoes in lightly salted water until tender, then drain well.

Heat a good knob of butter and a slug of olive oil in a small pan and gently sweat the chopped garlic in it for a couple of minutes, without browning. Take off the heat and stir in the herbs. Crush the potatoes lightly in a haphazard way with a potato masher or wooden spoon, to form a rough, chunky mash. Combine with the flaked salt fish and the herby, garlicky butter and oil. Season well with black pepper and serve, with a fresh lettuce salad on the side or to follow.

Smoked fish

It seems likely that smoked fish was not so much invented as discovered. It isn't hard to imagine how that might have come about. A good catch. A celebratory gathering of the clan around a roaring fire, over which the fish were grilled and toasted. Much crunching of crisply charred skin, snaffling of tender fish flesh and sucking of sticky, smoky bones. But a few spare fish laid on a stone in the dwindling fire prove to be more than the clan members can manage (even prehistoric eyes could be bigger than stomachs). They doze off, or wander back to their huts or caves to sleep off the feast, as the fish smoulder gently above the embers. The next morning the fish, now tawny gold but somewhat dried and leathery, are still sitting among the cold cinders. Though a little chewy, they turn out to be surprisingly palatable...

Harold McGee, in the ever-fascinating *McGee on Food and Cooking* (Hodder & Stoughton, 2004), suggests another very credible ancient scenario: fishermen wishing to dry and preserve their catch might have found the usual supply of sun, wind and salt inadequate for the task. Trying to dry fish over a fire perhaps began as an act of desperation, then rapidly evolved into a favoured solution, particularly at times when one or more of the other commodities was in short supply. This could also neatly explain the close cultural relationship between salt and smoke as preservatives of fish and other flesh, which remains to this day. If salt is available in any quantity at all, then fish are invariably salted before being smoked.

In fact, many anthropologists reckon that the discovery of smoking, like the discovery of fire for cooking, was made not once but many times, by different groups of prehistoric men and women in different parts of the world at different times. In coastal communities, fish would naturally have been the food that first got the treatment. In others, among the inland hunter-gatherer tribes, it would have been meat. We can't help thinking that the early fish smokers were, gastronomically speaking, getting the slightly better deal.

The observation that fish prepared in this fashion kept for a surprisingly long time was obviously key to the way smoking permeated global food culture. Initially, this only had to be observed, not understood. Now we know that smoking improves the keeping qualities of fish by killing off bacteria and partially drying it out. The process of burning wood produces a range of chemicals, several of which have antibacterial and antioxidant properties. What this means is that salting and then smoking fish is a kind of 'belt and braces' job in terms of preserving it. It also means that if you smoke fish, you need less salt to preserve it than if you were relying on salt alone. In any culture, salt is traditionally a valuable commodity, if not an expensive one, so the economic reasons for smoking fish have long been compelling. Also, a fish that was lightly salted but heavily smoked would not have needed soaking to make it palatable – and that can only have added to its appeal.

And so, for many centuries, in many cultures, fish has been smoked mainly to preserve it, and thereby extend its ability to feed a community. But in the modern world, certainly in the West, there's no doubt that the economics of the enterprise no longer stack up. This is largely because labour costs have skewed the figures. Before they can be smoked, fish have to be cleaned, descaled, gutted, sometimes filleted, then brined, racked or strung up. Even an industrialised version of the process requires expensive machinery. Consequently smoked fish is usually somewhere between three and ten times more expensive than the equivalent fresh fish.

Nor do we need to smoke fish any more. Domestic and industrial freezers offer a far cheaper and more efficient method of preserving fish. Even frozen fish fingers with the added charms of dayglo orange breadcrumbs are, kilo for kilo, cheaper than kippers. The sheer cost of production should theoretically price smoked fish out of the modern market. And it probably would, except for one important thing. We like eating smoked fish, a lot.

There is something beguiling and irresistible about that unmistakable tang of slowly infused wood smoke, and it finds one of its happiest, most alluring partners in the flesh of fish. To appreciate this, you only have to list the dishes that would disappear from the menu should the smoking of fish somehow be maliciously uninvented. Buttered kippers, smoked mackerel pâté, smoked salmon and cream cheese bagels, taramasalata, kedgeree... surely at least one of these would rate in your top ten ways to enjoy fish? And for those prepared to go the extra fathom, there's bloater paste sandwiches, Arbroath smokies, Japanese katsuobushi...

Buying smoked fish

If you're beginning to feel that the delights of smoked fish are under-represented in your kitchen, what can you do about it? Well, at the risk of stating the obvious, you can simply go and buy it more often. The UK is a particularly good place to do so, since we have long been a nation of virtuoso fish curers. Smoked herring, haddock and salmon, in all their many guises, are among the few traditional regional foods that continue to thrive in a culture that doesn't always value such gems as it should.

If you are near the coast, it shouldn't be too hard to find authentic types of smoked herring, whether kippers, bloaters or buckling. The Arbroath smokie, a small, whole-but-headless hot-smoked haddock, is thankfully alive and well – though not literally, obviously. And you can still find really good smoked salmon all over the UK if you look hard enough (if you're looking in the supermarket, you'll have to look very hard indeed).

This is the rub. There is unquestionably some good stuff out there. But, and it's a big but, there is plenty of mediocre stuff and some downright dismal stuff too. Consider smoked salmon, which was once the patriarch of the smoked fish family. It is now mass produced, using cheap, flabby, farmed fish, whose flesh is dyed orange by artificial additives in the food they eat. They are 'smoked', thousands of fillets at a time, lying on racks in computer-controlled stainless steel 'kilns', in a process that takes only a few hours.

Contrast the brick kilns of a traditional craft smokery, where wisps of smoke from gently smouldering oak chips curl around the hanging fillets, from head to tail, for the best part of a whole day. The two processes are worlds apart, and so, inevitably, are their products. One is a greasy, pappy, fake-tan, one-dimensional, cheap sandwich filler, the fishy equivalent of plastic ham. The other can be sublime.

Nor have the other traditional smoker's favourites, the herring and the haddock, escaped industrialisation. Kippers and smoked haddock fillets are also produced in huge modern kilns. The worst of the mass-produced versions are injected with brine and finished with a smoke-flavoured glaze containing artificial colouring. They can look enticing but the taste is one-dimensional and crude, with none of the subtle, layered notes and deep, lasting flavours of the real thing.

To enjoy top-quality smoked fish, it's worth seeking out products that have been cured by dedicated artisans, who put the pursuit of excellence before the pursuit of profit (not that the two ought to be incompatible). In the fishmonger's, always ask for undyed smoked haddock and kippers, and feel entitled to enquire about the origin of any smoked products. Good fishmongers should always be proud to tell you where they source their smoked fish.

Better still, buy direct from the best artisan smokehouses. For such small businesses, the regular custom of a few dozen enthusiasts, and the ensuing word of mouth, can make all the difference. We list several excellent smokeries in the Directory (see pages 590–1), most of whom have their own websites and deliver by mail order.

Buying from those who do things properly is one way to enjoy your share of good smoked fish. Another, and one we heartily recommend, as much for the pleasures of the process as the outstanding end result you can achieve, is to smoke some fish of your own.

We'll explain the rudiments here – and you'll soon see that ours is a rough and ready approach. Nonetheless, we reckon we can guide you to some very pleasing results. But if you want to pursue the art of home smoking on a higher plane, we highly recommend the book *Home Smoking and Curing* by Keith Erlandson (Ebury Press, 2003).

Hot and cold smoking at home

Smoking has evolved into two distinct processes. It's important to distinguish between them, as they have different objectives and rely on different techniques and bits of kit.

Cold smoking is essentially a gentle drying in a cool, smoky chamber, which imparts flavour to the fish and also arrests some bacterial activity. But it does not cook it. The fish is smoked at a temperature no greater than 30°C – around 25°C is considered perfect. That's about the same as a warm room, so the flesh remains raw.

Produce for cold smoking is always salted or brined, and the dual preservative action of salt and smoke means you can keep cold-smoked fish for some time – usually a couple of weeks in the fridge. But because it is not cooked, it may need additional preparation before eating. This is particularly true of smoked white fish, such as cod or haddock – and indeed the sustainable alternative, of which we are great champions, the smoked pollack – of which more later. Usually smoked white fish finds its way into cooked dishes such as kedgeree, chowders and pies. On the other hand, cold-smoked oilier fish – notably mackerel and salmon but also bass – are usually very good without further cooking. Smoked salmon, served raw on buttered brown bread, with just a squeeze of lemon and a grinding of black pepper, is perhaps the quintessential product of the cold-smoker's art.

In contrast, hot smoking is really more a form of cooking than preserving – a light roasting, if you like – with lots of added smoke swirling around your makeshift 'oven'. Salting is usually light – intended to season the fish for better eating rather than cure it for better keeping. Consequently, hot smoking only prolongs the shelf life of the fish for a week or so, perhaps two if it's vac-packed and refrigerated.

Temperatures for hot smoking can vary considerably, according to your kit and the heat source beneath it, and are often hard to control with any precision. But they should ideally be between 80°C and 120°C, so that a thick fish fillet or small whole fish will be cooked right through in 30–45 minutes. A key indicator here is that hot-smoked fish passes the opacity test (see page 113). In contrast, cold-smoked fish stays translucent, even though it takes on a golden colour from the smoke. It only turns opaque when used in a recipe that involves heating it through – when it will flake and break, like any cooked fish.

On the whole, white fish isn't that interesting when hot-smoked (the Arbroath smokie being a notable exception), but the oilier fish, from little sprats up to great slab fillets of salmon, with handy portion-sized trout and mackerel in between, respond superbly to this treatment. Most hot-smoked fish is left to go cold before it's used. One of the joys of smoking your own is eating it hot, straight from the smoker.

Occasionally a fish may be both hot and cold smoked, and the creature that gets this treatment pretty much as standard is the beleaguered eel (see page 528). It takes the flavour of cold smoking exceptionally well, but without the hot-smoke finish, which effectively cooks the fish through, it remains chewy and not particularly appetising.

Both hot and cold smokers can easily be made at home. It is technically possible to build a smoker that will do both jobs, but it makes far more sense to have a hot smoker that is separate from your cold smoker. This is because a good hot smoker should be a portable item of kit that you can take with you to the beach or even on board a fishing boat. We think every keen fish cook should have a hot smoker, so we'll start with that, and the more refined, specialised art of cold smoking will follow.

Building a hot smoker

Making a hot smoker is *so* easy that frankly 'building' is a little flattering of the process. It can take no more than 10 minutes, and may not require any more skill than scavenging a few bits from around the house. If you can lay your hands on a suitable lidded tin, improvise some kind of rack to fit inside it (chicken wire?) and locate a small pile of sawdust, then all you need is a heat source to plonk the tin on and you're ready to hot smoke. We've even made an emergency smoker out of a flimsy old biscuit tin. The lid was too tight fitting, leading to a high risk of scalded fingers, and it was never likely to last – but it did the job.

Our own beloved hot smoker, formerly a bread bin, fits the bill admirably. The photographs (see below) were taken the first time we put it together and used it. That was a while ago, and we have used it dozens of times since, with great success. A little heavier and bigger than a biscuit tin, and with a lid that's easy to lift, it is still eminently portable, and just about perfect for the job. We reckon it has a good few years of heavy use left. The worst abuse it has received was being rinsed out in the sea without proper drying afterwards. It's since bloomed a few little spots of rust.

The only customisation was the drilling of a few holes in each side. These support four close-fitting iron rods, which in turn support the two racks. One is a roasting rack, which happened to fit inside, the other, as perhaps you can see, has been squished together from the ever-useful chicken wire.

A hot smoker uses sawdust inside the smoke box to make the smoke, and a separate heat source outside the smoke box to make the sawdust smoulder, heat up the interior of the box and cook the fish through. The most popular choice of sawdust is oak, but beech also works well, and other hardwoods and fruitwoods may be chosen for their special aromatic qualities: bay, cherry, apple and hornbeam (prevalent in West Country hedges) all work well. It's also possible to

combine whole spices and seeds with your sawdust to achieve a highly flavoured smoke. Fennel seeds, dried chillies, cloves and allspice berries are good.

To get our bread bin smoker fired up, we simply scatter a 5mm layer of our chosen sawdust over the base, put the first rack in, with the larger pieces of fish (always lightly salted, rinsed, then pressed dry) on it, then add the second rack, with smaller fish or fillets, and put the lid on. The bin is then placed on whatever heat source is available – a gas burner, barbecue or the smouldering coals of a beach or riverside fire. The base of the tin heats up and the sawdust begins to smoulder, making smoke. The inside of the tin heats up, too – not to a very predictable temperature, given that our heat source varies, but with a bit of luck it will reach more than 80°C and not much more than 120°C. Depending on this temperature, and the thickness of the fish or fillets, it may take anywhere between 15 minutes and an hour to complete the job. But 30–40 minutes would be the desired range. Your judgement as to whether the fish is ready is effectively a judgement on whether it is cooked through, so testing its opaqueness by means of the knife test (see pages 113–14) is the way to go.

If the sawdust happens to burn out before the fish is cooked, you can add some more. But you will have to remove the racks and fish – with suitably protected hands – and start again.

If you don't rate your own DIY skills, or your old enamel bread bin is too precious to pimp, you can, of course, buy portable hot smokers. They are available in all shapes and sizes, and many of them come with little meths burners to place under the base and heat the sawdust to smouldering point. However, they are of variable quality, so take a good look around, and choose one that is robust and of simple design. If it can be used over other heat sources, such as fires and gas rings, so much the better.

Building a cold smoker

This is definitely a bit more of a project, not least because a cold smoker is not readily portable, even if it can be manhandled from one place to another, and the sessions take time – up to a day or more. But that doesn't mean it's hard. To reassure yourself on this point, it's worth remembering that for centuries, cold smoking was achieved by simply hanging fish in the column of smoke above an open fire, indoors or out. And it can still be done like that.

However, a modicum of DIY skills and a keen eye for salvage can produce a dedicated cold-smoking kit that will give you years of good service, without a great deal of technical know-how. Our own cold smoker (shown on page 155), which will be described fully in due course, is a case in point. Although it is based on a reasonable understanding of the principles involved, and a clear recognition of the right end results, it does not involve a great deal of, shall we say, *calibration*. We'll start, though, with some guidelines for crude cold smoking in an existing fireplace – as practised for generations by crofters and coastal dwellers all over the British Isles.

A fireplace smoker
If you have an open fireplace at home where you regularly burn logs, you may well be able to cold smoke fish and other foods above it. It simply depends on whether you can find a way to fix your fish a reasonable height above a gently

smouldering fire, so that it hangs in the smoke without getting too hot. The ideal kind of fireplace is a big inglenook – the kind you can stand up in. A metal bar fixed across the chimney – as high as you can reasonably stretch – will allow you to hang your fillets or whole fish from string loops and butcher's hooks.

Of course few have the luxury of a walk-in fireplace. But there may be various cunning means of getting access to the flue above a much smaller domestic grate. At the original River Cottage, the fireplace in the sitting room was tiny. On the outside of the cottage, however, halfway up the chimney stack, there was an old cast-iron flue door, about 30cm square, giving access to the chimney. It required a stepladder in the flowerbed to gain access to it, but it was worth it – it went in about 3 metres above the fireplace, and was perfect for fixing a hanging bar. We smoked many a fine pollack fillet in there, as well as whole mackerel and countless sausages, and the results were always excellent.

In many houses, chimney stacks are accessed in this way, either from the outside of the house or in an upstairs room above a downstairs fireplace – so it's always worth investigating. If you are a competent builder (or know a friendly one who understands what you are trying to achieve), it may even be worth knocking a little hatch into the chimney stack to make it work as a smoker. If you can pull it off, it really is a very neat way to get a cold smoker up and running at home.

When smoking above a fire, you obviously do not want a roaring conflagration or you will roast your fish rather than smoke it. So, if the idea of your fire is to throw serious heat into the room, it may not be compatible with a smoking session. However, when you retire to bed, you can spread out the hot embers, place a large log or two over them, hang up your fish in the smoke stream and allow the fire to smoulder gently while you sleep. If you're maintaining a smoking fire during waking hours, the way to get the most smoke and the least heat is to keep it 'marginal'. Prod it now and again with the poker and push the logs apart, so it smoulders rather than blazes. Add logs to the edges rather than the middle. Incidentally, sawdust and wood chips are not that useful on an open fire. They may generate an impressive amount of smoke to begin with but, with an unrestricted supply of air, they tend to flare up after a few minutes and burn out.

So it's best to smoke over hardwood logs (such as oak, beech, bay, cherry, apple) or peat. Never use other solid fuels, such as coke or coal, as these may generate fumes that are at best unpleasant to taste, at worst poisonous to consume. And don't use firelighters or other fuels to start the fire either, as they will also taint the flavour of fish as they burn. If you do insist on using them, wait until they have burned out for at least half an hour before hanging the fish above the fire.

No two fireplaces behave in quite the same way, so in the end it's about getting to know the idiosyncrasies of your own set-up. But the best way to test the temperature in the smoking zone will always be to hold your hand above the fire exactly where the fish is going to be. Ideally it should be pleasantly warm (25–30°C). You can just about get away with 'uncomfortably warm' (35–45°C) but any hotter than that and your fish will get overdried, or even cooked.

The three-piece cold smoker
If an existing fireplace is not an option, then the fulfilment of your cold-smoking ambitions may require the construction, or at least customisation, of a special bit of kit. This can take many forms but perhaps the simplest option, unless you have space for a walk-in 'smoke-shack' (see page 165), is to construct a version

of the 'three-piece' cold smoker we now use at River Cottage. We call it this because there are three basic components, as follows:

1. **A FIREBOX** (to generate the smoke)
2. **SOME TUBING**, **PIPING OR DUCTING** (to move and cool the smoke)
3. **A SMOKE CHAMBER** (to hold the smoke and the food being smoked)

A cold smoker can either be custom built or adapted from salvaged items, so a good rummage around a tip or a junk shop is a wise first move. A few suggestions for improvised components, along with a description of our own chosen parts, follows.

1. THE FIREBOX/SMOKE GENERATOR This is where the smoke is created, by burning wood logs, chips, sawdust or a combination. The firebox can be a fixed item, made of brick or steel, permanently attached to a wall or floor, or it can be portable. It should have some basic form of ventilation to adjust the draw of the fire, and hence the intensity of the burn. It may require an external heat source, such as a gas burner, underneath to keep it going, or at least to start it off.

We use a small wood-burning stove, which can easily be moved. It was originally made from a 7kg Calor gas bottle turned on its side, with a hole cut in it for the door and another for the flue (shown on page 163). It used to live in a shepherd's hut, and it will happily burn small logs, chips or sawdust. We were given it by our builder friend, Sid, and we're lucky to have it. It doesn't need a secondary heat source to start it or keep it going and, once started, a burn of around 1kg sawdust can last for 5–7 hours, unattended. If ever you see such an item, or any miniature wood-burning stove, in a junk shop, snap it up – it's perfect for the job. You could have one made up for you by a local blacksmith or welder – you could even show him the picture.

A serviceable alternative is a small, cast-iron, potbellied barbecue with all the inner workings removed. They work best with a gas ring underneath to get the sawdust inside smouldering nicely. You'll need to improvise some kind of snug-fitting lid, with the ducting 'plumbed' into it.

Another option is a galvanised dustbin – a small, kitchen-sized bin, rather than a big outdoor one, is ideal. It's a slightly different approach here, as you don't make the fire in the base of the bin but in some kind of small, freestanding grate on the ground. A smouldering fire of wood chips and small logs is started in the grate and the bin is placed upside down over the fire. This restricts the airflow around the fire, making for a cool burn and plenty of smoke. Some kind of venting a couple of inches above ground level, adjustable if possible, is very useful – but you'll get by with a crude wedge for making a chink of air between the ground and the bottom (previously top) of the bin.

You'll definitely need to cut a hole in the base of the bin – which, being upside down, is now the top of your smoke generator – to fit the ducting neatly and duct out the smoke to your smoke chamber, supported, or wall-mounted, a few feet away and ideally higher than the top (i.e. the bottom) of the upturned bin. Heath Robinson it may be, but it works.

That's just a trio of workable suggestions – you may well find serviceable, and more ingenious, alternatives.

2. THE TUBING/PIPING/DUCTING You'll need some kind of heatproof tubing that simply leads the smoke away from the firebox and over to the smoke chamber, allowing the smoke to cool as it does so. Spare bits of galvanised drainpipes (not plastic ones) will do the job, but are rigid and hard to work with.

Flue ducting, of the kind you can see in the picture (top left, page 163), is an obvious and more practical alternative, as it's actually designed for the job of moving smoke from one place to another. It's also flexible, so can be adapted to the space you're working in, and is cheap enough to be bought and cut to the length you require. It should be at least a metre or so long – more if your firebox has a tendency to burn hot – to allow the smoke to cool as it travels to the smoke chamber.

3. THE SMOKE CHAMBER This is the space where the cooled smoke is contained, making contact with the food as it swirls lazily around. It doesn't matter if it's a bit leaky – in fact it needs to be, as if it's completely airtight it won't draw properly. In some cases a little chimney, or a least a small hole in the top of the chamber, may be necessary to help the draw.

Our smoke chamber, as you can see in the pictures on pages 155 and 163, is an old cider barrel. The fish, or whatever (we smoke a lot of bacon in it, too), is taken in and out through a lid on the top. It's usually hung on loops of string from the bars that run across the top of the barrel, though we can also put racks in, supported by some more bars across the middle, for smoking small fish, roe or fillets.

Other items we have heard of being used as smoke chambers include old filing cabinets (the drawers can be adapted to hold racks and hanging bars), fridges, wooden wardrobes (beware of toxic paint, though), large metal dustbins and – very popular these – old tea chests. You could even make a sturdy wooden box from scratch if you are up to it. Anything between the size of a tea chest and a small walk-in wardrobe will work, depending on the extent of your ambition.

With any model, the ideal finishing touch is a temperature gauge set in the wall or door of the chamber. Needless to say, we haven't got one. But we don't much feel the lack of it. In our cider barrel set-up, temperature control is crude but effective. It relies entirely on regulating the burn by adjusting the airflow. This can be done either at the door of the firebox or at the top of the chimney on the chamber. These kinds of adjustments make a difference of only a few degrees, and basically we're always trying to keep the smoke chamber as cool as possible without letting the fire go out. We do sometimes measure the temperature using an ordinary outdoor weather thermometer, placed inside the barrel for 10 minutes while we're smoking. Most of the time we're in the desired 25–30°C zone but it can head north of 35°C in there on a very hot day, or when the firebox flares up a bit.

If we were slightly more sophisticated we could introduce a more formal means of temperature control. This often involves some kind of 'baffle plate' – a heat-absorbing metal disc, perforated to allow the smoke through, placed either at the top of the firebox or in the base of the smoke chamber. Frankly, we feel that's beyond our current needs (and probably capabilities).

A single-chamber 'smoke-shack' and a brick kiln

If you have the space and the inclination to do quite a bit of smoking, a small walk-in 'smoke-shack' might suit you very well. In some respects it's even simpler than the three-piece – being a one-piece, if you like. Effectively it's a giant version of the hot smoker, in that sawdust is burned inside a sealed chamber, generating enough smoke to fill it. The essential difference is that, because of the sheer size of that chamber, the interior never gets too hot.

The classic customised smoke-shack is an old brick privy – an outdoor loo at the bottom of the garden. Bars and racks for hanging and laying food on can be arranged at approximately head height. A steel plate or solid roasting tin can be propped up on bricks on the floor. Under the bricks, and under the tray, goes a single gas ring (attached by rubber tubing to a portable gas bottle kept *outside* the shack). A pile of sawdust goes in the tray. The gas ring is lit and kept very low. The pile of sawdust is lit, too, the door is closed and the smoking begins.

The gas ring may be turned off once a good smoulder is under way, and the sawdust can be re-lit or topped up, as necessary. A small vent or chimney hole may be needed to keep the smoulder ticking over but, as often as not, a less than airtight doorframe does the job on its own.

This arrangement can be adapted for all sorts of confined spaces, provided they are *safe*. Even a small wooden garden shed will work. That may sound like madness, but provided you only ever light a small pile of sawdust in the centre of the floor space (and it must have a concrete or earth floor, not a wooden one) you'll be okay. For added peace of mind, it should be sited so that, if it *should* happen to catch fire and burn down, it can do so without putting any other buildings, objects or people at risk. And keep a fire extinguisher nearby. Of course you should never attempt to do any kind of smoking inside a house.

Not everyone has a brick privy in their back garden. But if you're handy with bricks and mortar, you can build your own dedicated brick smoking kiln, either freestanding or against the outside wall of a garage or outbuilding. This is really a compact version of the brick privy approach – and not far off the favoured kit of small-scale professional artisan smokers. Think in terms of a large, brick-sided wardrobe. The doors should be made of fairly solid metal – ideally steel plate.

The firebox/smoke generator can either be sited in the base of the kiln, in which case you will need a perforated steel baffle plate above it to reflect some of the heat back but let the smoke through. (If this is removable, or adjustable, you may be able to hot smoke in the kiln too.) Or, the firebox can be separate, purpose built of brick, steel or a combination, or a little wood-burner like ours. It should be sited below and just to one side of the kiln, with a short piece of flue ducting or drainpipe to take the smoke into the chamber.

Once you've knocked up your kit and are ready to do some cold smoking, there's just a couple more tips that will stand you in good stead.

Damp and humidity

One of the factors that most affects the success of your smoking is humidity – and therefore the weather. You need your smoke, and your smoke chamber, to be as dry as possible. The experts recommend 20 per cent humidity, and commercial smokers often have some kind of dehumidifier built in to maintain conditions close to this figure. Needless to say, we don't, and we don't worry much about it either. We find cool, dry, blue-sky autumn days are perfect for smoking, and the results are always excellent. But when we have smoked on a damp, foggy or rainy day, the results are not as good, and on the whole, we try not to do it.

There's no question that wetness is the enemy of a good smoke. Once droplets of moisture condense on the fish (or meat) being smoked, the process begins to be compromised. The smoke does not penetrate so well, but gets caught up with the moisture on the outside, producing a surface film with a slightly acrid flavour, like bitter lemon peel. It's not wholly unpleasant, but it is not the result you are looking for – and the worse the moisture problem, the more severe the taint.

For the same reason, any food you put in the smoker must itself be scrupulously dry. It should be thoroughly blotted, not just cursorily wiped, with a clean cotton cloth or paper towels.

Salting before smoking

It's crucial that almost everything that goes into a cold smoker – and certainly all fish – must be salted first, even if only lightly. This is not just because you're trying to preserve the fish – these days, as we've said, that isn't really the issue – it's also a matter of taste. Eating unsalted smoked fish is a very weird experience. You can sense that smoke is present but the flavour remains elusive, and never really kicks in. Because salting draws water from the fish, it leaves behind a greater concentration of the oils that will take on the flavour of the smoke. It also acts as a seasoning, creating the vital edge that makes the smoky flavour really come through.

There are formulae for brining whole fish and fillets, based around the weight of the fish, the strength of the brine etc, but to be honest we don't trouble ourselves with them too much, so we won't trouble you with them. We prefer to dry salt rather than brine, and we do so by eye and by feel. We use coarse sea salt or flaky salt for small, delicate fillets, but it can get expensive if you're doing a lot of smoking. Fine table salt is much cheaper and works well – but faster. We'll assume that's what you're using in the rough guide below. In each case, sprinkle half the salt over a plate or non-metallic tray. Lay the fish or fillet on it, skin side down, then sprinkle over the rest of the salt in an even layer.

SMALL FILLETS AND VERY SMALL WHOLE FISH: 150–250g (e.g. herring, mackerel and pouting). A small handful (about 30g) of salt per fillet or whole fish; leave for about 15 minutes.

FILLETS AND SMALL WHOLE FISH: 250–500g (e.g. larger mackerel, trout and small pollack). A big handful (about 50g) of salt per fillet or whole fish; leave for 15–25 minutes.

LARGER FILLETS AND MEDIUM WHOLE FISH: 750g–1.5kg (e.g. larger trout, small sea bass and medium pollack). Several handfuls (about 75g) of salt per fillet or whole fish; leave for 25–45 minutes.

VERY LARGE FILLETS AND WHOLE SIDES OF BIG FISH: 1.5–3kg (e.g. salmon, sea bass and pollack). Several large handfuls (100–125g) of salt per fillet or whole fish; leave for 45–90 minutes.

In all cases, wash off the excess salt quickly but thoroughly under a cold tap, then pat the fish dry immediately with paper towels or a cotton cloth. Ideally the dried fillets should be hung for a few hours before smoking.

Fire/smoke management

Remember that the whole point of cold smoking is to get the most possible smoke with the least possible heat – and fuel. Hence in most cases a smouldering pile of sawdust is the perfect medium. With the exception of open-fire smoking, it's what we recommend. You'll need a few good handfuls – more than you'd use for hot smoking. Although, if you achieve the slow, smouldering burn that is the ideal, you won't need kilos of it. A pile the size of a bag of sugar should last five hours or more.

Lighting a pile of sawdust isn't always easy, and keeping it smouldering steadily can be tricky too. The first tip is that you need to keep your sawdust scrupulously dry – store it in a sealed plastic bag or a dustbin with a lid on it. The second is that a blowtorch is an extremely useful item for getting reluctant sawdust to start burning! Aerating the sawdust and lighting it from within helps, too, and a favoured item with many cold smokers is a short piece of steel pipe with holes drilled in it, inserted into the bottom of the pile of sawdust. Stick the flame of your blowtorch in that and you'll soon be well away. A poor man's version, but almost as effective, is a strip of chicken wire mesh, say 15–20cm wide and two or three times as long, tightly rolled up like a fat wire cigar.

In all cases except smoking over an open fire (where logs are recommended – see page 162), you are burning your sawdust, once it's lit, with only restricted ventilation. This is essential if the sawdust is to smoulder, not flare up. But if you shut out the air entirely, the fire will soon extinguish itself. Successful

management of a burn, and hence of a cold-smoking session, is therefore more often than not down to the control of ventilation. Opening the door of the firebox a few millimetres (or the vent, if you have given it one) should increase the vigour of the burn. A small hole or little chimney in the top of the smoke chamber (if it doesn't leak already) will help draw the smoke through. Once the chamber is full of smoke, you can block it off – leaving perhaps just a tiny chink of a leak – with a smooth stone or block of wood. It's hard to be more specific than that, given that every home-built cold smoker will be different. But a decent bit of kit put together in line with the ideas described above should be fairly forgiving. A tweak here and a tweak there will see you right.

Exploring smoked fish

Whether or not you decide to explore the possibilities of home smoking, the recipes in this chapter are, we reckon, among the most tempting in the book. Good smoked fish has such a wonderful flavour and texture that it is often worth serving almost naked, save perhaps for a knob of butter. That's certainly a treatment you should try on your own first efforts – and you'll soon see how well you're getting on. It's also a great way to assess the qualities of any new piece of smoked fish that comes your way – so you may learn to appreciate the subtle, and not so subtle, differences between the various regional cures, and the different smokehouses who practise them.

Whenever you do combine good smoked fish with other ingredients, it will often have the delightful effect of seasoning them all with its mellow smokiness. This is particularly true of eggs, milk and cream, which you will see crop up regularly as companions, especially to our own favourite local cold-smoked delight – the River Cottage smoked pollack, or smollack, as we call it.

To finish, here's a quick guide to stalwart examples of smoked British fish that you might just want to track down and sample, or indeed imitate in your own home-smoking experiments. To find the best examples of each, you might also want to check out the Directory (see pages 590–1).

The herring family

KIPPER A herring that has been spatchcocked (split through the back to the belly and opened out), then cold smoked. 'Kippering' is an old name for the salting and smoking process. If you ever get the chance to eat a kipper warm off the tenterhooks, do so, because they're delicious. (Yes, that's where the expression 'on tenterhooks' comes from – and who wouldn't be in a state of excited anticipation at the prospect of a just-smoked, still-warm kipper?) Mostly though we imagine you'll get your kippers cold from the fishmonger's slab (or by mail order – for suppliers, see the Directory, pages 590–1), in which case they'll need poaching, grilling or 'jugging' (immersing in a jug of boiling water) before eating.

RED HERRING An older style of smoked herring, associated with East Anglia, on which the kipper is based. The red herring gains its mahogany colour and strong flavour from being salted and cold smoked really hard – up to 6 weeks – traditionally over oak, beech and turf.

BLOATERS Lightly cold-smoked whole herrings, which have a slightly gamey flavour because they are ungutted. Great Yarmouth has long been famous for its bloaters.

BUCKLING These are ungutted herring too, but they are hot smoked.

SMOKED SPRATS A speciality of the Suffolk coast, these are whole, ungutted and hot smoked. Sprats are related to the herring, but are only 7–10cm long. The Norwegian name for sprat is 'brisling', and you will find a product called smoked brisling, usually tinned, for sale in the UK too. The word brisling is also sometimes used to describe smoked sardines.

Haddock and cod

SMOKED HADDOCK AND COD There will be vast differences in quality between the ordinary fillets of smoked haddock you encounter in various fishmongers and supermarkets. An undyed, additive-free product is what you should be looking for. Good fishmongers usually carry information about the smokehouses whose products they sell.

FINNAN HADDIES Split, bone-in haddock, traditionally cold smoked over peat. Named after the village of Findon, near Aberdeen (one of the places they were originally produced), they're essential for proper cullen skink. A very lightly smoked version of the Finnan haddie was called the Glasgow pale.

ARBROATH SMOKIES Smaller haddock, headless and gutless, hot smoked over oak or beech. The fire is laid in a pit and covered with hessian, which is a way of controlling the heat. Arbroath smokies are also known as pinwiddies.

Salmon, trout and eels

SMOKED SALMON Generally cold smoked over oak, though sometimes peat. The cures and flavourings for smoked salmon can vary enormously – as can the overall quality of the end product (see page 157). The London cure of the old East End smoke holes is much lighter than the traditional Scottish one, and arguably superior. If you want to join that debate, we'd suggest you try wild smoked salmon from H. Forman & Son of London (cured in the same East End kiln for over a hundred years). We think it's pretty sublime – so it should be at the price. See also the various artisan smokehouses recommended in the Directory (see pages 590–1).

SMOKED TROUT As with salmon, this is hugely variable in quality, like the fish from which it is made. Hot-smoked trout is far more readily available than cold, and smoked trout pâté is very easy to find – a good one less so. Cold-smoked trout – i.e. smoked-salmon style – can be excellent. Try the one from Purely Organic, see the Directory (page 591).

SMOKED EELS First cold and then hot smoked with the skin still on, these must rank as among the very best of all smoked fish. Rich, earthy and intensely smoky, they are outstanding with a dab of grated fresh horseradish to cut the fat. However, you must wrestle with your conscience if you want to eat smoked eels; you'll find them on our blacklist of fish to avoid (see page 48).

And finally (roll of drums…)

SMOLLACK, OR COLD-SMOKED POLLACK A River Cottage favourite that we are enthusiastically championing as a sustainable alternative to smoked haddock and cod. We smoke a lot of pollack ourselves, in our good old cider barrel, but it's now also being made for us by a great local smoker. To make this plug even more shameless, we'd like to direct you to our friends at Brown and Forrest, listed on page 590 of the Directory.

Smoked pollack with poached egg *serves 2*

According to Nick, this is the one dish guaranteed to calm and soothe his wife, Helen, after a particularly stressful day. Make sure you use very fresh eggs. As well as tasting better, they form smooth, round shapes in the poaching water.

2 fillets (about 400g) smoked pollack
 (or smoked haddock)
2 bay leaves
A few black peppercorns
Up to 500ml whole milk

400g fresh spinach, washed and coarse
 stalks removed
Olive oil
2 tablespoons cider vinegar
2 large, very fresh organic eggs
Salt and freshly ground black pepper

Cut the fish fillets in half and put them in a pan. Add the bay leaves and peppercorns, then pour on enough milk just to cover the fish. Put the lid on and bring to a simmer, then remove the pan from the heat. This should be enough to cook the fish through. If it isn't quite cooked – i.e. if it doesn't break easily into flakes – turn it over, cover again and leave in the hot milk (off the heat) for a couple of minutes. Remove the fish from the milk and keep warm.

Meanwhile, put the spinach in a large pan with a little salt and pepper and a glug of olive oil. Set the pan over a medium-high heat and sweat the spinach briefly in its own juices until completely collapsed. Drain off any excess liquid.

Bring a small pan of water to the boil for poaching the eggs. Add the cider vinegar. Stir the water with a spoon to create a whirlpool. Crack the eggs into the whirlpool (or break them on to saucers first, then tip them in), turn the heat down to minimum and cook for 3–4 minutes, until the whites are set. Remove the eggs carefully with a slotted spoon and drain on kitchen paper.

Put the fish fillets on warm plates and pile the hot, wilted spinach alongside. Top with a poached egg. Take to the table and let your guest – fractious wife or otherwise – break the egg so the golden yolk spills out.

Hot-smoked sea trout with Morello cherries

serves 4

This is a great combination, the punchy cherry compote giving a beautiful edge to the salty hot-smoked trout. It's a real summer treat, as both the fish and the fruit are in season for such a short time.

Also works with:
- Salmon (organic farmed or self-caught wild)
- Trout
- Mackerel

2 wild sea trout, weighing about 1kg each, descaled and filleted
Coarse sea salt
4 sprigs of tarragon (optional)
4 sprigs of thyme (optional)
Freshly ground black pepper

FOR THE CHERRY SAUCE:
200–300g fresh Morello cherries, stoned
Up to 50g light brown sugar

Lay the fish fillets on a large board and carefully remove the pin bones with tweezers. Salt the fillets with the sea salt, as described on page 167 – they will need 15–20 minutes.

Rinse the salt from the fillets and pat them dry. Using a sharp knife, cut the fillets in half. Grind some fresh black pepper over the fish and press the herb sprigs on to the flesh, if you like.

Gently hot smoke the fish, following the technique on pages 158–60. We've had a lot of success smoking trout over oak chips but you could try cherry wood or even a blend of cherry and bay. Ensure the temperature doesn't rise much above 80°C or the fish will cook too fast and may dry out. Fillets of this size should be ready in 40–50 minutes. When the fish is just cooked through, remove it and leave to rest in a warm place.

To make the sauce, put the cherries in a pan with a tablespoon of water and 30–40g sugar. Bring to a gentle simmer, then cook for 5–6 minutes, until the fruit is soft but still retains a little shape. Taste and add more sugar if you like, but it should remain slightly tart.

Serve the smoked fish on warmed plates with a spoonful of the warm sauce. A watercress salad and a slice of toasted walnut bread go very nicely alongside.

Warm smoked fish and sausage salad *serves 4*

We used to make this salad with smoked eel, but since we are now trying to wean ourselves off this fish (see page 528), we would recommend using cold-smoked mackerel instead. It is still delicious.

½ tablespoon groundnut oil
4 organic pork sausages (big butcher's
   bangers, not chipolatas)
2 small chicory heads
300g cold-smoked mackerel (or hot-
   smoked eel) fillet, cut into chunky
   4–5cm pieces
1 small red onion, very finely sliced

FOR THE DRESSING:
1 heaped teaspoon English mustard
1 tablespoon crème fraîche
1 teaspoon sugar (or honey)
2 teaspoons cider vinegar or wine vinegar
1 tablespoon groundnut oil
Salt and freshly ground black pepper

Also works with:
• Smoked carp

Heat the groundnut oil in a frying pan over a medium heat. Add the sausages and fry them gently for 20–25 minutes, until well browned all over.

Meanwhile, break up the heads of chicory and wash them, making sure you keep the leaves whole. Spin them dry.

Remove the sausages from the pan, slice them slightly on the bias into 2cm chunks, then return them briefly to the pan to brown their cut sides (if you cut them up before you begin frying, the skins tend to come away and the sausages disintegrate). Remove from the pan and keep warm. Add the smoked fish fillets to the pan and fry lightly in the sausage fat for 1 minute on each side.

To make the dressing, put the mustard, crème fraîche, sugar, vinegar and oil in a bowl and whisk until combined. Season to taste.

Put the fish and sausages in a large bowl and add the chicory leaves and red onion. Spoon over the dressing, then mix with your hands, carefully combining all the ingredients. Divide the salad between individual plates, and serve.

Omelette Arnold Bennett

serves 2 as a main course, 4 as a starter

This rich and splendid creation is named after the writer and critic who developed a passion for it. It was dreamt up in the kitchens of London's Savoy Hotel in the 1920s, and Bennett ate it almost every day during a lengthy stay there.

There is no single, definitive recipe, as different chefs – at the Savoy and elsewhere – have made it in different ways. Smoked haddock, cheese, cream and eggs are the constants. However, we prefer to use sustainable smoked pollack instead of haddock, and Cheddar in place of the traditional Parmesan. We also add a few spring onions to cut the richness a little.

100ml double cream
100ml whole milk
250g smoked pollack (or smoked
  haddock) fillet
2 egg yolks
3–4 spring onions, finely sliced (optional)
Freshly ground black pepper

FOR THE OMELETTE:
4 eggs
A small knob of butter
Salt and freshly ground black pepper

TO FINISH:
50g mature Cheddar cheese, grated

Combine the cream and milk in a small pan and add the smoked pollack – cut it into 2 or 3 pieces, if necessary, to fit it snugly in the pan. The liquid is unlikely to cover the fish anyway, so put the lid on the pan and bring to a simmer, then take off the lid, turn the fish over, cover the pan again and simmer very gently for one more minute. Remove from the heat, strain the fish, which should be just cooked through, and reserve the poaching liquid.

Put the egg yolks into a bowl and break them up with a whisk. Slowly pour on the hot poaching liquid, whisking constantly, to form a smooth custard.

Flake the poached pollack off its skin, removing any bones you find on the way. Stir the flakes into the egg yolk and cream mixture, along with the sliced spring onions, if you're using them. Season with some black pepper.

Lightly whisk the 4 eggs together with a pinch of salt and pepper. Heat the butter in a large, non-stick frying pan over a medium heat. When the butter is foaming, pour in the beaten eggs. Cook them just as you would any omelette, moving the cooked egg around a bit to start with to allow the uncooked egg to run over the base of the pan. When the omelette is half-cooked – i.e. set on the base but still wet on top – take the pan off the heat.

Spoon the creamy smoked pollack mixture over the omelette, scatter the grated Cheddar on top and put the whole thing under a hot grill for a minute or two until golden, bubbling and slightly puffed. Let the omelette cool in the pan for a couple of minutes, then either slice it in the pan or slip it out on to a plate. Cut it in half (for a main course) or quarters (for a starter) and serve. It's rich, so a lightly dressed watercress salad cuts it nicely.

Smoked pollack soufflé *serves 6 as a starter*

A soufflé is neither complex nor particularly difficult: basically it involves folding some whisked-up egg whites into a thick, well-flavoured béchamel sauce and whacking it into a hot oven. When those flavourings are smoked white fish and tangy Cheddar, the result is arguably the best soufflé there is. If you've never attempted a soufflé before, we urge you to make this your first one. It shouldn't collapse, but even if it does, it will still be delicious.

30g unsalted butter, plus extra for greasing

2 tablespoons very fine, dry white breadcrumbs, or polenta (optional)

250g smoked pollack (or smoked haddock) fillet

1 bay leaf

300ml whole milk

30g plain flour

1 teaspoon English mustard

50g mature Cheddar cheese, grated

4 eggs, separated

Salt and freshly ground black pepper

Butter 6 individual soufflé dishes, about 200ml in capacity, and coat the inside with the dry breadcrumbs or polenta. (That's optional, but it helps the soufflé 'climb' up the inside of the dishes.)

Put the fish in a pan with the bay leaf, cutting the fish into a couple of pieces if necessary, to make it fit neatly in one layer. Pour over the milk, cover the pan and bring to a gentle simmer, then remove from the heat. This should be enough to cook the fish through. If it isn't quite cooked – i.e. if it doesn't break easily into flakes – turn it over, cover again and leave in the hot milk for a minute or two longer. Take the fish out of the milk, strain the milk and set aside. As soon as the fish is cool enough to handle, flake it off the skin in fairly small pieces, removing any pin bones.

Melt the butter in a saucepan over a medium heat and add the flour. Stir to form a roux and let it cook for about a minute. Gradually add the hot, fishy milk, beating well with each addition to make a smooth sauce. When all the milk has been added, let the sauce bubble gently, stirring often, for a minute or two. Add the mustard and Cheddar and stir until melted and smooth. Remove from the heat and leave to cool a little. Stir the egg yolks into the mixture, then fold in the smoked fish. Taste and season well with black pepper – it may not need any salt.

Now beat the egg whites until they form soft peaks. Gently fold half the beaten egg white into the cheese mixture, trying to retain as much air as possible, then fold in the rest. Pour the mixture into the soufflé dishes. Run the tip of a sharp knife around the edge of the mixture to release it from the sides of the dishes – this will help it rise.

Place in an oven preheated to 200°C/Gas Mark 6 and bake for about 10 minutes, until the soufflés are really well risen and golden on top but still have a slight wobble. Serve immediately, with a little green salad on the side.

Smoked roe

Throughout late spring and early summer, many of the female fish we catch on the boat have roe in their bellies. We use the roe rather than discard it, but we don't catch fish specifically for their roe, neither do we buy fresh roe. Roe from pollack and ling is particularly suitable for cold smoking.

A roe from a large ling caught late in the season will be pretty big – up to 2kg. Such sizeable roes are very delicate and need gentle handling, since the thin membrane that surrounds them can easily burst. Smaller roes are less fragile.

At least 500g roe or roes from large
 pollack, ling or cod, ideally whole,
 unbroken in the membrane
Fine sea salt, at least 100g per roe

You'll need a plastic tray big enough to hold all your roes. Pour salt on to the tray in an even layer about 1cm deep. Lay the roes on the salt and scatter over a further covering of salt, again about 1cm deep. Leave small roes (up to 250g) to salt for 30 minutes and large ones (up to 750g) for an hour.

Meanwhile, bring a large, deep pan of water to the boil. When the salting time is up, rinse the roes thoroughly to remove all the salt. Plunge them into the boiling water and blanch small roes for 1 minute, large ones for 3 minutes. This firms and dries the roe, making it much easier to handle.

Scoop the roe out with a slotted spoon and leave them to cool on a tray lined with kitchen paper. Make sure they are dry to the touch before smoking.

Arrange the dry roes on a rack in your smoker. Hanging them up is not advisable as they are too delicate. Smoke for 12–18 hours, depending on size, turning them over halfway through if you can. You can keep smoked roe in the fridge for up to 10 days before using, and it also freezes well.

We usually reserve the smaller smoked roes for eating as they are – perhaps sliced and served on crostini as canapés (see below). Larger roes get made into taramasalata (see page 180).

Smoked roe and lemon on toast *makes 12*

Serve these little toasts with drinks before dinner. The slivers of lemon flesh cut the salty, rich roe perfectly. For the best results, use a small, firm smoked roe that will slice easily. Those from pollack, ling and cod all work well.

12 small, thin slices of baguette or
   sourdough bread
Olive oil

About 200g cold-smoked roe
  (see opposite)
1 lemon
Freshly ground black pepper

To make the crostini, lay the slices of bread on a baking tray, trickle with olive oil and bake in an oven preheated to 190°C/Gas Mark 5 for 5–8 minutes, until crisp and golden.

Meanwhile, slice the roe with a very sharp knife into discs 2–3mm thick. Make sure you cut from the tip of each lobe inwards.

Cut the ends off the lemon so you can just see the flesh inside. Stand the lemon on one cut end on a board. Slice away the skin and pith, so you are left with just the flesh. Cut out each segment of lemon from between the membranes, then slice each segment across into 4 or 5 wedge-shaped pieces. (Alternatively, slice the whole lemon, skin on, then trim the rind and pith from each slice and cut out each little triangular wedge from its retaining membrane.)

Top each crostini with a piece of sliced roe, followed by a triangle of lemon flesh and a twist of black pepper.

River Cottage tarama *serves 6 generously*

The reputation of taramasalata has been done enormous damage by the sweet, artificially coloured gloop sold under that name in supermarkets. But make it yourself and you will rediscover its true creamy, smoky delights.

You can blend the ingredients in a food processor. However, beating by hand gives a nice, grainy texture.

Smoked cod's roe is the traditional base for taramasalata but we have made this dish very successfully with home-smoked pollack and ling roe – far better options, in fact, when you consider the environmental status of cod. Whatever you use, choose a whole roe, still in its outer membrane, which should ensure a better, moister texture.

250g smoked roe – pollack, ling or cod
  (see page 178)
1 garlic clove, peeled and mashed with
  a fork
3–4 thick slices of stale white bread
  (about 100g), crusts removed
About 200ml milk

100ml good olive oil
200ml sunflower oil
2 tablespoons lemon juice
1 tablespoon finely chopped parsley
1 tablespoon finely chopped chives
Freshly ground black pepper
Pinch of paprika, to finish

With a spoon, scrape the smoked roe out of its skin and put it in a large bowl with the garlic. Soak the bread for 2 minutes in just enough milk to cover it, then squeeze to extract most of the milk. Add the bread to the roe and mix thoroughly.

Stir the olive and sunflower oil together in a small jug; then, using a wooden spoon, beat them into the bread and roe mixture a tablespoon at a time. After you have added about half the oil, start adding the lemon juice, also a little at a time, alternating with the remaining oil. (If you prefer to use a food processor, trickle the oil on to the bread and roe through the funnel of the machine as it's running. Alternate oil and lemon juice after the first tablespoon of oil has been incorporated.) Finally mix in the parsley, chives and a few twists of pepper. Spoon into a pot and refrigerate until required.

Sprinkle with paprika and serve with hot toast, pitta or flatbreads, and/or fresh crudités such as carrots, spring onions and radishes.

Hot-smoked mackerel pâté

serves 4 as a starter, makes 12–16 canapés

Smoked mackerel pâté comes in many guises, some a bit dull and obvious. This lovely recipe is neither. It's from River Cottage refugee Emma Miles, who now cooks at the Clerkenwell Kitchen in London.

Also works with:
• Hot-smoked trout

250g hot-smoked mackerel fillet, skinned
2 teaspoons freshly grated horseradish root
1 tablespoon crème fraîche
1 teaspoon caster sugar
1 tablespoon lemon juice, or to taste

1 teaspoon coarsely ground black pepper
A handful of dill (or chives), finely chopped
½ teaspoon paprika
1 small raw beetroot, peeled and cut into matchsticks, to serve (optional)

Put half the mackerel in a food processor with the horseradish, crème fraîche, sugar and lemon juice and blend until smooth. Break up the remaining fish into flakes and stir it into the blended mixture with the pepper and dill. Add more lemon juice to taste, if necessary.

Serve the pâté on buttered rye bread. Sprinkle with paprika and accompany, if you like, with the beetroot matchsticks.

Drunken smollack rarebit *serves 4*

We love this smoky, fishy take on the Welsh Rarebit. The beer with fish is quite quirky – we think it's great, but revert to milk if it doesn't work for you. You can also serve this as a canapé if you cut the slices into smaller pieces. Smoked pollack (smollack) is our fish of choice, but smoked haddock can stand in if necessary.

500g smoked pollack (or smoked haddock) fillet
300ml whole milk
75g unsalted butter
50g plain flour
200ml beer (a good traditional ale, not cheap lager)

1 good teaspoon wholegrain mustard
75g medium-strong Cheddar cheese, grated
1 tablespoon roughly chopped flat-leaf parsley
4 large slices of wholemeal bread
Salt and freshly ground black pepper

Put the smoked fish in a large pan, cutting up the fillet if necessary so that it fits snugly, and pour the milk over (it should just cover the fish). Put the lid on the pan and bring to a simmer, then remove from the heat. This should be sufficient to cook the fish through. If it isn't quite cooked – i.e. if it does not break easily into flakes – turn the fillet over, cover again and leave in the hot milk for a couple of minutes.

Remove the fish from the pan, reserving the liquid, and set aside to cool a little. Then break it into large flakes, discarding any bones or bits of skin.

Melt the butter in a saucepan over a medium heat, stir in the flour to make a roux and cook gently for 2–3 minutes. Meanwhile, reheat the fish poaching milk if it has cooled down. Gradually add the fishy milk to the roux, followed by the beer, stirring all the time. Don't worry if it fizzes up; the bubbles soon disappear. When the sauce is thick and smooth, let it cook for a minute or two, then add the mustard, Cheddar and plenty of black pepper. Taste and add salt too, if you think it needs it, though the fish will have made the milk quite salty. Gently stir in the flaked fish and half the parsley.

Toast the bread. Spread the cheesy, fishy mixture on top and place under a hot grill until bubbling and golden. Serve straight away, with the rest of the parsley sprinkled on top.

Open-fire cooking

Barbecued fish might well be our desert-island meal – literally, perhaps, should we both one day happen to be shipwrecked during some disastrous fishing trip. In which case the island would most likely be lurking somewhere off the Dorset–Devon coast. So mackerel would certainly be on the menu and, with a bit of luck, bream or bass too, popping and hissing over a smoky driftwood fire… what could be finer?

Come to think of it, we get to enact this fantasy fairly often, albeit in a less insular way. Our beach barbecues over the years, at home and abroad, with family and friends, from early childhood until now, have pretty much fuelled this chapter.

We're hardly alone in our enthusiasm. Who doesn't enjoy the distinct flavour that wood or charcoal smoke gives to fish flesh – and most especially to fish skin? Perfection in a piece of barbecued fish is represented by moist, lightly smoky flesh and a crisp, savoury, blistered skin that you really want to eat, rather than push to the side of your plate. And if you've caught that fish yourself, then cooking it over glowing coals, unmediated by oven or frying pan, can only add to a sense of self-sufficient achievement.

However, there's no denying that this kind of cooking can be disappointing too. If you get it wrong, you may well find yourself picking bits of carbonised fish off the bars of a grill, or watching mournfully as your dinner flakes and crumbles into the ash below. That's how it is with barbecued fish: agony or ecstasy. Our mission here is to try to maximise the ecstasy and minimise, or even eliminate, the agony.

The secret of success lies more in good preparation and fire management than in actual cookery. Get this right and you'll soon see that the barbecue is really quite fish friendly. Because heat travels quickly through fish, you have a sporting chance of avoiding the classic barbecue mishap of a burnt exterior and raw interior – as happens so often with chicken and sausages. With fish, this will happen only if your fire is far too hot, or still flaming, when the fish goes on. In theory, a whole fish represents a perfect package of grillable food, the tender, delicate flesh being nicely protected by its skin. On the other hand, fish fillets and portions are always likely to give you more grief – but we'll do our best to steer you through the pitfalls shortly.

Barbecuing whole fish

For everyday fish barbecues in the back garden or on the beach, small and medium-sized whole fish – anything from 100g up to about 1.5kg – are best. Whole trout, sardines or small bass, bream or red mullet will always stand you in very good stead. Oily fish barbecue particularly well – and spanking-fresh mackerel will *never* disappoint.

Scaly fish such as bass, bream and mullet will need to be descaled (see page 55) for the skin to be edible. Having said that, if you're cooking a whole fish over a very crude open fire (your desert island might not run to a built-in patio barbecue), you may want to consider leaving the scales on. They will help protect the fish flesh from high heat and naked flames. You won't get crisp, edible skin – you'll get charred, inedible scales with burnt skin welded inseparably on to them. But the flesh inside should be moist and sweet.

There's one other very cunning fish barbecuer's trick you can always fall back on, and that's wrapping your fish in a parcel of wet newspaper (see the recipe

on page 200). It actually amounts to a different cooking technique, as if you're steaming the fish over the coals. Again, the skin, which usually sticks to the paper and comes away when it's peeled off, is sacrificed in the interests of tender, moist flesh within.

Assuming you do want to eat the skin, under the more controlled conditions of a nicely managed charcoal-fired barbecue-with-grill, it will need generous seasoning with salt and pepper before cooking, and probably during as well. Herbs can play a role, too – either sprinkled over the fish to flavour that crispy skin directly, or burned on the fire itself to aromatise the fish more subtly, with scented smoke.

It's not just whole fish that are neatly packaged for open-fire cooking. Whole shellfish can work brilliantly too. This may sound like a specialised skill of the fish barbecue professional, yet it is often so easy you'd be embarrassed to take credit for it. The shells of bivalves are ready-made cooking vessels and, like fish scales but more so, offer ample protection from fierce heat for the sweet meat inside. Large mussels or oysters opening up over smoking coals, or scallops bubbling in their shells on the grill, can all be eaten straight from their finger-scalding shells – with lemon juice, pepper and olive oil on standby to perk them up a bit.

And barbecued lobster or langoustines? Just because they're precious (and, unless you've caught them yourself, expensive) doesn't mean they're too good for the barbecue. The charring of fresh crustacean shells, which are composed of a concentrated mass of proteins, sugars and pigment molecules, produces a flavour that is quite inimitable. It manages to inveigle itself not only into your nostrils, as the shells crackle over the fire, but also into the interior flesh of the shellfish. The taste, further enhanced by a trickle of oil or melted butter on the charred flesh, is utterly seductive.

Barbecuing fish portions

We've flagged a problem with barbecuing fillets, essentially that they are fragile, but this is not insurmountable. It does, however, require a little care and attention to detail. So if it starts to sound like too much trouble, you can skip this bit (except the last two paragraphs about squid).

Let's start by saying that we don't tend to barbecue fish steaks or cutlets – thick cross-sections of salmon, for instance – at all. Cooking these involves bringing two flesh surfaces into contact with the bars and, since flesh is even stickier than skin, we think the potential for disaster is a little too great. It's not that we don't enjoy these cuts of fish (we most certainly do), but we prefer to employ other methods for cooking them. Frying, baking or steam-braising (see page 255) are the routes we'd choose.

If you're going to get to grips with fillets on the barbecue, then chunky, squared-off fillet portions, at least 2cm thick, with the skin still on, are best. These should be from substantial, firm-fleshed, round fish such as large (1.5kg-plus) sea bass or bream, wild salmon or sea trout. Large turbot and brill (3kg-plus) can also provide similarly robust, skin-on fillet portions – and slightly smaller ones (2–3 kg) can be portioned into on-the-bone 'tranches' (see page 72). These can be quite barbecue-friendly, as the bone in the middle gives them added rigidity.

In contrast, more fragile white fish such as pollack, pouting, cod and coley can be relied on to give you grief on the barbecue, however large they are, and however you try to prepare them. Their skin is fine and somehow extra sticky, and their soft flesh tends to tear and flake at the slightest prod of a spatula or tongs. We keep them well clear of our barbecue sessions (they are much more at home in our cold smoker).

Meanwhile, our chunky, firm fish portions, in neat squares and oblongs, are just the right size to be managed by a sharp-edged metal spatula. If they do decide to stick to the bars of the grill, all need not be lost, as we'll see in a moment. Fillet portions should be barbecued skin side down on the bars until almost cooked through, then turned for just a minute or two on the flesh side to complete the cooking.

The flatfish tranches will have two skin sides of course, and should therefore be turned over halfway through cooking. If they're chunky enough, i.e. almost as thick as they are wide, and therefore almost square in cross-section, you can also sear the two flesh edges as well, for a minute or so each, to get those nice char stripes across the creamy white flesh. That's great when it works – but it does offer four separate opportunities for the portion to attach itself to the grill. We'll come to the steps you can take to avoid that in just a moment.

Incidentally, if you're beginning to lose faith with these dastardly fillets and tranches, then one 'fish portion' you needn't think twice about barbecuing is a piece of fresh squid: it's never better than when turned for a couple of minutes over searing-hot coals. A quick marinade of oil, paprika and garlic (see page 204) must put it in the barbecue top five.

Squid aside, it's back to the fish with fins and skins. Remember, whether you're cooking portions or whole fish, you're still aiming for barbecue perfection: crisp, edible skin and tender, juicy flesh. How do you maximise your chances of achieving this? You need to know…

The five golden rules of barbecuing fish

1. LIGHT THE FIRE WELL IN ADVANCE As with all open-fire cooking, you should light your fuel – whether charcoal, small logs or gathered wood – well in advance. Then wait until the flames have died down and the coals are glowing red under a layer of white ash before you start grilling. Depending on how much charcoal or wood you're using, and how well it burns (the faster and hotter, the better), this may take between half an hour (for quick-burning charcoal to turn into glowing coals) and a couple of hours (for a gathered-wood bonfire to burn down sufficiently). Only when your barbecue/fire is settled – the predictable 'cooker' you need it to be – should you think about cooking. You want to have ahead of you a dependable hour of steady, upward-rising high heat, subtly infused with wood smoke, but past the risk of sudden flare-ups.

2. PREHEAT THE BARS OF THE GRILL Next you must make sure that the bars of the barbecue grill are really, really hot. They need to be thoroughly preheated, so that they sear the skin and flesh almost immediately. A low, slow heat will only exacerbate the adhesive tendencies of the fish's skin. So the grill, if it is the removable kind, should go over the fire a good 10 minutes before the fish goes on to it.

3. OIL THE FISH Now it's time to cook. You'll need to lightly oil the fish, *not the grill*. Your fingertips are the best tool for this job. Dip them in a saucer of oil – olive, sunflower or groundnut – and massage it evenly all over the skin of the fish, which should be completely dry before the oil goes on. The fish should not be dripping with oil, as this will dribble into the fire and flames may flare up and engulf the fish. It should, however, be well oiled all over – as if it was about to go and bask in the sun with a good book.

4. DON'T TRY TO MOVE THE FISH TOO SOON The next vital point is that once you have laid your lightly oiled fish on the searing-hot bars of your barbecue, *leave it there*. It will take a good couple of minutes for the bars to sear the skin and flesh to the point where the fish can be lifted and turned over. So, even if you don't like the angle you've laid it at, or think you could have left more space for the next fish, don't be tempted to try and shift it just yet. Live with it, until it's properly ready to turn.

5. BE FIRM AND DECISIVE WHEN TURNING THE FISH The moment at which you turn your fish is always a little nerve-wracking. The best-laid, best-oiled fish can still be a bit grill-sticky. However, if you've followed our prescription, any adhesion is likely to be fairly superficial – and easily remedied, provided you don't panic.

The best way to flip over a fish or fish portion is to take a little 'run up' – sliding the sharp blade of a wide metal spatula (or paint stripper!) along the bars of the grill towards the fish, and giving it a short, sharp jab, or a series of them, to get between skin and bars. If there is some stickiness, identify the point of contact between fish and grill and give another well-aimed scrape to free the fish from the bars. This way, though you might leave the odd tiny shard of fish skin on the bars, you will largely keep fish and skin together.

Before you turn the fish over, another light film of oil on the upper, uncooked side might not be a bad idea. If it's not too hot, you can still use your fingers to do this (anyway, committed barbecue cooks don't really feel pain). Or use a pastry brush, but don't overdo it.

Now flip or roll the fish over, so the lightly oiled, uncooked side gains contact with the hot grill. Again, you can use those asbestos fingers to steady the uncooked side of the fish as you turn it. Remember, don't move it. Wait patiently.

If you've got the skin how you want it but the knife test (see pages 113–14) tells you your fish is still not quite cooked through to the middle, then removing the fish from the grill and leaving it to rest for a couple of minutes, ideally on a warmed plate close to the barbecue, may well be enough to complete the transfer of heat to the middle of the fish.

If the fish is well charred on the outside but still has some way to go in the middle, you're in a bit of a fix – but not a terminal one. You can try to move it to a cooler part of the barbecue to finish cooking a little more slowly. Or, if you have any foil handy, you can take a double thickness of it, lay it on the grill beside the fish, and use the spatula to roll the fish on to it. The fish will continue to cook through without further damage to the skin.

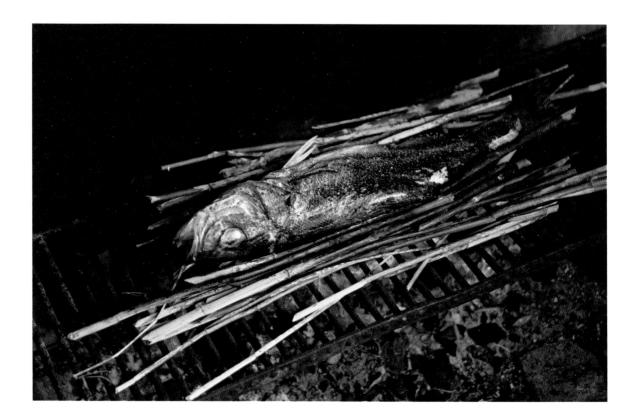

The grill

Your chances of consistent barbecue success depend not only on applying the rules outlined but also on the kit you're working with. The fuel and the fire may be laid and burned in any number of settings or vessels, temporary or permanent, from a ring of stones on the beach to a brick-built altar in your garden, from a portable, pot-bellied cast-iron cauldron to any of the hundreds of manufactured barbecues on sale in garden centres up and down the land. But more important than the bit that holds the fire is the grill itself – the metal frame on which the food is laid.

When it comes to fish, you'll always be much better off with fairly chunky bars, set nice and close together. Barbecuing on fine wire grill bars, or worse still a square wire mesh, is a bit of a nightmare, as it can rip the whole skin off a fish – there is so much wire in contact with the fish that the opportunities for sticking are too great. Improvising with grills and wire racks taken from old ovens or grill pans is therefore less than ideal.

The grill we use on our homemade feed trough barbecue, which you can see above and in several other pictures in this chapter, was picked up in a salvage yard almost ten years ago. It used to be the cover of an open drain in a dairy yard. The spacing and bar sizes are pretty much spot-on, and it has always done us proud, especially for fish. It can also be taken to the beach, field or woods, and propped up over any kind of wood fire. It is quite heavy, though, so tends not to travel too far from the boot of the car.

On the other hand, those special wire-framed, fish-shaped baskets that enclose a fish, and those folding, long-handled sandwich grills (see page 197) may look a bit gimmicky but they are quite useful bits of kit, especially for cooking over the hot embers of an open wood fire. They hold and contain the fish, and by turning the basket/grill over you turn the fish too. You can regulate the heat by propping them up closer to or further from the fire, and even if the fish does stick a bit, you can get it away from the coals before it burns to a crisp. If you're in the realms of campfire cooking, then picking crispy bits of fish skin off the basket, once it's cooled a bit, is quite an engaging task. Even so, apply the same anti-stick principles when using these: heat up the basket/grill over the coals, and lightly oil the fish before it goes into it.

Flavouring the fish, and the fire

The flavour of grilled fresh fish, especially when eaten in the open air, needs little help to please a hungry diner. But you can certainly enhance its deliciousness with some fresh herbs. Stuffing them into the fish will work well, of course, and we rarely barbecue a whole fish without slipping a couple of bay leaves into the belly cavity. But sometimes we like to push the boat out and use herbs to perfume the smoke that wreathes around the fish as it cooks.

The key to success is to be generous. No pussyfooting around with sprigs: use armfuls of fennel twigs, bushels of rosemary, in order to inform the flavour of your fish thoroughly. These can be laid on the hot coals, where they will crackle and smoke and release a heady fragrance before being consumed by the fire. But our preferred method is to lay the herbal offerings over the grill itself and place the fish directly on the smouldering leaves – for example, we often grill mackerel over branches of bay (see page 194).

Beyond barbecues

Finally, we would like to mention a couple of other ways of using raw fire to cook fish. Wood-fired ovens, the kind that are so good for baking pizzas or loaves of sourdough bread, are also great for fish. There is a particular dry, fierce quality to the heat generated in these clay or brick structures that will crisp the skin and cook the flesh in a trice. Moreover, because the heat comes from a fire built on the floor of the oven itself, there is an element of hot smoking involved in the cooking, too. Whether it's a tray of mackerel or sardines, or a whole big salmon, bass or brill, the flavour of wood-roasted fish is always distinctive and truly delightful.

You could also take a tip from the Scandinavians, who know a thing or two about cooking fish outdoors, and try their open-fire method. They simply nail a side of fresh salmon or a few spatchcocked trout to a plank of wood, season the fish with salt and pepper and lean the plank against a brick or stone just beside a crackling log fire, either indoors or out. The heat, not ferocious enough to burn the fish, cooks it gently, while once again the smoke adds its perfume. It is a very simple and elegant technique, and a neat illustration of the fact that there are a hundred and one ways to cook your catch without ever setting foot inside a kitchen.

Mackerel barbecued over bay

Our all-time favourite fish for barbecuing is mackerel. This is partly because its firm, slightly oily flesh responds beautifully to the searing, charring heat. But it's also because barbecued mackerel has a certain emotional significance. It's a fish that's plentiful and easy to catch, and we've lost count of the times we've cooked up a good haul of it in the open air, surrounded by family and friends.

Tucking bay leaves into the cavity of the fish can impart a subtle flavour but, being big fans of bay, we sometimes really go to town and grill the fish on top of whole branches of it. A word of warning: make sure you take them from a strong, established tree. We once had a young bay shrub that fell foul to an enthusiastic pruning prior to a mackerel barbecue... it never quite recovered.

Mackerel

Olive oil

Half a dozen branchlets of bay leaves
   (i.e. a few dozen leaves on the stalk)

A lemon

Salt and freshly ground black pepper

Gut your mackerel (see pages 58–9) and rinse with cold water. Pat dry with a clean cloth or kitchen paper, then massage each fish with a few drops of olive oil. Season the mackerel well, inside and out, with salt and pepper.

Make sure your barbecue is hot and ready to cook over (see page 189). Put the grill over the coals and give it a good few minutes to heat up, then lay a thin bed of bay leaves on the hot grill and lay your mackerel on top of that. Drizzle a little olive oil over the fish and add a squeeze or two of lemon juice. The bay will crackle and pop over the heat of the fire and release lots of perfumed smoke. It's quite normal to see a few shooting flames at this point, too. Don't be alarmed; this is all good and sends the flavour of the bay deep into the fish. Turn the fish after 5 minutes and cook for a few minutes longer, until the flesh is opaque all the way through.

Serve straight away, with salsa verde (see page 316) if you like, plus a green salad, and some new potatoes lightly bashed and tossed with oil or butter. Or, for a more simple approach, serve with a lemony mayonnaise and some good bread.

Also works with:
· Sea bass
   (small-medium)
· Black bream
· Red mullet
· Grey mullet
· Scad
· Garfish
· Trout
· Sea trout

Barbecued sardines *serves 4*

The scent of fresh sardines grilling in the open air on a warm evening need not be the preserve of a Mediterranean holiday if you tap into the seasonal supply of plump pilchards, caught off the Cornish coast (see page 420).

These fish are quick and easy to cook, but it is important to season them well and grill them over a really high heat. This gives them the crisp, salty skin that all sardines should have. As long as your barbecue is good and hot, you shouldn't have any problems, though we do recommend using a sandwich-style barbecue basket to avoid the problem of sticking as you turn the fish.

Also works with:
· Herring
· Mackerel
· Scad

12 large, fresh sardines or Cornish
  pilchards
1 tablespoon olive oil
2 teaspoons chopped marjoram
1 teaspoon chopped thyme

3 garlic cloves, finely chopped
Coarse or flaky salt and freshly ground
  black pepper
Lemon wedges, to serve

Sardines have delicate flesh that will bruise and tear quite readily, so be careful when preparing them. You can rub off their soft, overlapping scales with your thumbnail. Now use a stout pair of scissors to snip open the belly and trim off the fins. Pull out the guts and carefully tear out the gills (see page 60). Wash them gently under the tap, pat dry, and they're ready to go.

In a bowl, mix the olive oil with the herbs and garlic. Massage this mixture over the fish, rubbing a little inside the belly too. Sprinkle generously with coarse salt and pepper.

Lightly oil the sardines and pack them into a barbecue basket. Cook the fish over very hot, glowing embers for 2–3 minutes on each side, or until golden and crisp. Serve with lemon wedges, and accompany with bread and a tomato salad.

Barbecued red mullet with fennel *serves 4*

If you grow fennel in your garden, this recipe is one to cook in late summer, when the plants are overgrown and going to seed. Those leggy stalks may be too fibrous for eating but they're still full of aromatic oils, which can perfume fish as it cooks.

Also works with:
- Grey mullet
- Mackerel
- Scad
- Black bream
- Sea bass
- Gurnard
- Zander
- Trout

A bundle of overgrown fennel sticks, flower heads and all
4 red mullet, gutted
4 garlic cloves, lightly crushed

4 bay leaves
Olive oil
Salt and freshly ground black pepper

Take four 10cm lengths of the freshest fennel sticks and bash them with a rolling pin to release their flavour. Put a piece inside each red mullet, along with a crushed garlic clove, a bay leaf and some seasoning. Lightly brush the fish with oil and season the skin – do this generously, as the cooking will burn off a lot of the seasoning.

Spread the rest of the fennel sticks on the grill over a hot, ready-for-cooking barbecue. Lay the red mullet over the steaming fennel stems. As the fish cooks, the fennel will first steam and then burn, infusing the fish with its flavour. Cook for 6–7 minutes on each side, until the skin is crisp and the flesh opaque.

Serve steaming hot, with minted new potatoes and a salad – a dish of paper-thin slices of fennel bulb, dressed with orange juice and olive oil, will echo and enhance the fennel notes in the fish.

Trout newspaper parcels

This is a very nifty way of cooking over a fire or barbecue, and a great by-the-river-bank or on-the-beach improvisation for fish you've just caught. The fish steams inside its wet newspaper parcel, so stays nice and moist. You won't get crisp skin – in fact, the skin usually peels away with the burnt newspaper – but you will get lovely, tender flesh.

Also works with:
• Sea trout
• Mackerel
• Scad
• Perch
• Grayling
• Sea bass

A 400g trout per person (or an 800g trout for 2 people), gutted
A few bay leaves and/or sprigs of thyme

A knob of butter
Salt and freshly ground black pepper
A lemon

Lay the cleaned fish on some newspaper (three sheets if it's a tabloid, two for a broadsheet), with a bay leaf and/or a thyme sprig in the belly and another tucked underneath it. Put a few scraps of butter on top of the fish and inside it, then season it well, with salt, pepper and a squeeze of lemon. Wrap up the fish in the newspaper so you have a snug, secure parcel. Repeat with all the fish you have, then soak the parcels in water until the paper is completely wet through.

It's important that the barbecue coals or the embers of your fire are fiercely hot, with plenty of burn time left. Make sure the grill over the barbecue or fire has had time to heat up, then place the parcels on it and cook for about 15 minutes or until the newspaper is blackened, charred and starting to burst into flame (if the paper catches fire sooner than you'd like, sprinkle it with water so you can continue cooking).

Unwrap the parcels carefully, trying to prevent newspaper ash falling on the fish flesh. Serve straight away with whatever accompaniments you can muster. Steamed sorrel or spinach and new potatoes are particularly good.

Oysters, mussels or cockles on the fire

Barbecuing is a surprisingly good and effortless way to cook oysters, as well as really big mussels or cockles, or even large razor clams. If you're out foraging and you've had the foresight to bring a grill with you, then you can build a little fire and cook your molluscs as soon as you've gathered them. We've done it several times and it's a really fantastic way to enjoy them. However, since oysters and the like are at their best during winter, you might want to bear in mind that this technique can work just as well with an indoor fire.

Once your barbecue or fire is ready for cooking (see page 189), use a pair of tongs to place your oysters, mussels or cockles on the grill (if you're cooking oysters, make sure you place them flat side uppermost). Grill them until they just pop open, then remove them from the grill with the tongs. As soon as they're cool enough to handle, open up the shells, using an oyster knife if you're barbecuing oysters. You can then eat the meat, which will be nicely poached in its own juices, just as it is, absolutely plain. Alternatively, dress it with a little olive oil and lemon juice, or a dab of melted garlic butter. Heaven.

Barbecued scallops in their shells *serves 4*

This is a neat way of preparing scallops, using the shell as a miniature frying pan. These sweet, luscious shellfish will be rubbery if overcooked, but if you get the barbecue searingly hot and follow the little ritual described here, working your way down the line of scallops to add flavourings, and again to flip them over, they should be perfectly cooked by the time you've finished.

12 large, hand-dived scallops	3 garlic cloves, finely chopped
Olive oil	12 sprigs of thyme
1 small dried chilli, deseeded and finely chopped	1 lemon
	Salt and freshly ground black pepper

Open and prepare the scallops as described on pages 105–7. If the roes are bright and plump, leave them attached. Otherwise set them aside with the rest of the frills and trimmings and freeze for bait or stock. Keep the bowl-shaped half of each scallop shell – it might be necessary to rinse it to remove any traces of grit. Combine about 2 tablespoons of olive oil with the chilli and garlic and set aside.

Make sure your barbecue is really hot, then put the scallop shells on the grill, inside up, like bowls, so they heat up. Drizzle a little olive oil into each hot shell, let it heat up, then add a scallop (or 2 or 3 if you have more scallops than shells). If they don't pop and spit, the oil isn't hot enough. Once you've placed the last scallop in its shell, return to the first one and add a sprig of thyme and a splash of the garlic and chilli oil. Do the same to each scallop. Return to the first one again and flip it over in its shell. Season it with salt, pepper and a squeeze of lemon, then repeat with each scallop. By the time you've flipped the final one, the first should be ready to eat – golden on the outside and just firm to the touch. It should take about 4 minutes, from first scallop in the shell to last one off the grill. Enjoy the juices in the shell – as well as the succulent scallops themselves.

Nick's limpets in garlic butter *serves 4 as a starter*

Limpets are never likely to be the guests of honour at the high table of seafood but they are definitely worthwhile, and this simple procedure is an easy experiment at any beach barbecue. The only essentials are butter and garlic, though a few other little additions will help the dish along.

We (strictly speaking, Nick) devised this recipe on one of our fishing trips to the Channel Islands, inspired by the fact that limpet shells function as tiny cooking vessels. It's based on a dish he encountered in a harbourside restaurant in the Canary Islands, where the limpets arrived in a heavy-based pottery plate with dimple-like indentations to house each mollusc in its own pool of garlic butter, like escargot plates. We felt we'd much rather cook and serve them in their shells.

24 large limpets

FOR THE GARLIC BUTTER:
100g unsalted butter, softened
4 garlic cloves, crushed

1 heaped tablespoon finely chopped
   parsley (if available)
1 teaspoon lemon juice or a few drops of
   white wine (if available)
Freshly ground black pepper

Soak the limpets in a bucket of clean seawater for at least 30 minutes, rummaging occasionally to stir them around a bit. This purging process will encourage them to rid themselves of grit and sand.

To make the garlic butter, beat all the ingredients together and then set aside.

Remove each limpet from its shell by scraping a sharp knife around the inside rim of the shell, cutting underneath the rubbery 'foot'. Once the limpet is free, you have to make a decision: keep the black, bulbous stomach sac that rests beneath the foot or lose it? Some limpet lovers swear it's the best bit – others tell you to chuck it. It does taste very good, but it looks a bit intestinal, too – you've got to be in the mood. Whatever you decide, remove the limpet from the shell, put a dab of garlic butter inside, replace the limpet and spread some more garlic butter on top.

Put the buttered limpets on a hot barbecue grill for 5 minutes or until the butter bubbles merrily. And here's a useful finger-saving tip: use a gardening glove when you're removing the limpets from the grill. Tongs are tricky, and using bare fingers is downright dangerous.

Eat the limpets straight from the shell, or tip each one, with its garlicky juices, on to a chunk of crusty bread.

Seared squid *serves 4–5 as a starter*

This is a fabulously fast bit of cookery, which gives you a toothsome, piquant dish in next to no time. Don't attempt it with very large squid, though, or you'll end up with a tough result – monster cephalopods tend to respond best to long, slow cooking. Small (not tiny) and medium squid are what you want here, and the key to success is speed. If you can be identified as anything more than a blur with a pair of tongs, you're moving too slowly. And, whether you're using a griddle plate, barbecue or frying pan, high heat must be the order of the day.

For a change from paprika, try making this with sumac. A Middle Eastern spice of crushed, dried berries, it has a lovely, lemony tang that pairs beautifully with squid. You'll find it in larger supermarkets and delicatessens.

4–5 small-medium squid (about 750g–1kg in total)	1 tablespoon sweet or smoked paprika, or sumac (see above), plus 1 teaspoon to finish the dish
1 large garlic clove, very finely chopped	
1 tablespoon olive oil	Salt and freshly ground black pepper

Clean the squid (following the instructions on pages 97–100). Set aside the trimmed tentacles. Now cut open the squid pouches and 'butterfly' them (see page 100), making sure you don't cut right through the flesh. Cut each butterflied squid body into 2 or 3 smaller pieces.

Combine the squid pieces, along with the tentacles, in a bowl with the garlic, olive oil, paprika or sumac, and salt and pepper, tossing them together with your hands and making sure lots of the flavourings get trapped in the diamond cuts.

Heat a barbecue, cast-iron griddle or heavy-based ridged pan until really hot. Lay the pieces of squid on it, diamond side up, and the tentacles as they fall. Let them cook for just 1 minute, then turn them all over. Cook for a minute more. The butterflied squid pieces will want to curl up, so flip them over one more time to encourage them to do so, and allow the curled-up pieces to get a final minute of cooking. Total cooking time: 4 minutes max.

Serve immediately, with a few more pinches of paprika or sumac flicked over the squid. On the side: a few dressed, peppery salad leaves, such as rocket, mustard and baby kale. And, if you want to make a main course out of it, chips.

Squid with chilli, lemon zest and garlic

This is another simple preparation, in which the paprika is replaced with a mixture of chopped fresh chilli and lemon zest.

Zest a lemon, or finely pare the zest, removing any pith, and then finely chop the pithless rind. Split and deseed a medium-hot red or green chilli and chop it very finely (or use a generous pinch of dried chilli flakes). Mix the lemon zest and chilli with the garlic, olive oil and salt and pepper and toss with the butterflied squid. Make sure the garlic and chilli are well distributed, catching in all the diamond crevices of the squid. Leave for 10 minutes or so, then toss again.

Cook, exactly as described left, on a searing hot griddle or barbecue, and dress with a few drops squeezed from the lemon. Serve with salad and/or chips.

Barbecued lobster with lime and chilli butter

serves 2

Wood-roasting lobster shells release a unique and delicious aroma, which is just one good reason to try this recipe. The lightly charred sweetness of the lobster flesh is another – and then there's the fresh, piquant butter…

You can cook this using a hot grill or griddle rather than a barbecue, but fresh air and open coals will lend the whole meal an irresistible dimension.

1 live lobster, weighing about 1kg
Olive oil

FOR THE LIME AND CHILLI BUTTER:
125g unsalted butter, softened
¼ garlic clove, mashed with a few flakes
   of salt

½–1 medium red chilli (depending on its
   strength, and your taste), deseeded and
   finely chopped
Juice and finely grated zest of 1 large or
   2 small limes
Salt and freshly ground black pepper

Prepare your lobster for humane cooking by putting it in the freezer for about 2 hours (see page 93). Meanwhile, make the butter by simply mixing all the ingredients together thoroughly.

Remove the comatose lobster from the freezer. Now split it right down its length and clean it, following the instructions on pages 94–5. Make sure you leave the tomalley – the greeny-black sticky stuff – in place, as it sets firm and turns pink when cooked, and is quite delicious. Season the cut surfaces of the lobster and brush with a little olive oil.

Put the lobster halves, cut side down, on the bars of a searing-hot barbecue. After 2–3 minutes, turn the lobster over. Dot the flavoured butter all over the seared flesh, now facing upwards, and cook for a further minute or two so the butter melts and dribbles down into the shell. Serve straight away, with good bread and salad.

VARIATION
Grilled lobster with lime and chilli butter

You can follow the same procedure to cook the lobster on a ridged, cast-iron griddle pan. But if you want to cook this dish under an overhead grill, then it's slightly different: rub the cut sides of the lobster halves with a little olive oil and season well. Then cook, cut side up, under a very hot grill for about 2–3 minutes, until starting to brown. Turn over to grill and colour the shell side for a couple of minutes, then turn back over and dot the lime and chilli butter over the surface. Flash under the grill again, just until golden and bubbling.

Whelks cooked in a tin of seawater

Using seawater for cooking seafood is an obvious and natural choice, as long as you're sure that the water is really clean. Indeed, if you're cooking your catch on the seashore, what else would you use? Whelks respond to this treatment very well, and the salty cooking medium seasons them nicely. If you live inland, well-salted tap water is the next best option…

Whelks
A bucket of clean seawater
Pepper – black or white
Vinegar – cider or malt

<u>Also works with:</u>
• Winkles

Wash the whelks well. As you handle them, you may find that some of them release a certain amount of slime – don't worry about this, just rinse it away.

Put them in a stout large tin or metal bucket and cover them with clean seawater. Set the tin over a heat source, which could be a campfire, a barbecue or a kitchen hob, and bring to a gentle simmer. Cook for 12–15 minutes, then drain the whelks and leave them to cool.

Work them out of their shells with a pin and remove the coarse cap or foot from the front end and the digestive sac from the tail. Sprinkle with pepper and vinegar and eat. White pepper and malt vinegar is the seaside classic; black pepper and cider vinegar is the gentrified alternative.

Baked and grilled fish

In the mission to get fish hot, which we've established is the essence of most fish cookery, your oven is clearly going to prove useful. Just how far it can take you along the road of fish cookery may surprise you. Here are three simple approaches to get you started...

Put a whole large fish in your preheated oven and very soon it will be hot, and therefore cooked. A few slashes through the skin and flesh will speed up the transfer of heat to the thicker parts of the fish. They are also an irresistible opportunity to introduce some seasonings to the flesh – salt, pepper, a trickle of olive oil and maybe a sprig or two of thyme and some shards of chopped garlic; or perhaps some grated ginger and garlic, a little soy sauce and a pinch of sugar. With minimal time and effort, you'll have a crisp-skinned whole roast fish ready for the table. This kind of oven-bashing approach works for anything from whole cod to whole plaice, saddle of conger eel to the head of a large coley, ling or pollack. Our Roast pollack head with thyme, bay and garlic (page 380) has become something of a River Cottage 'house special'. Or...

Lightly oil a roasting tin and arrange half a dozen cleaned, gutted mackerel in it. Lay them out nose to tail, as if in a sardine tin. Sprinkle with garlic, salt and pepper, add a few torn bay leaves, a trickle of olive oil and a squeeze of lemon. Scrunch a foil lid over the tin and bung it into your hot oven. About 20 minutes later you've got yourself a fishy feast. It's a method that scales up well, if you use two big roasting tins, to what we call the mackerel 'triple 20' – feeding 20 people in 20 minutes for about 20 pence a head. (Yes, you really can buy twenty mackerel for £4, or maybe £5 if they are big ones, if you're buying them harbourside, straight from the boat, in the middle of summer. Though if you are reading this in the year 2020, those figures may well look absurd.) Or...

Imagine you have a magnificent fish of 3 or 4kg – a sea bass, or even a once-in-a-lifetime wild salmon you've caught yourself. Tear off a metre of foil, lay it on a baking tray and grease it with olive oil or butter. Put the fish in the foil and anoint it with some trusted flavourings: salt, pepper, parsley, a sliced onion, a squeeze of lemon. Wrap up the foil round the fish like the pastry of a giant Cornish pasty, adding a splash of wine before the final crinkle, then put it on a baking tray, and bake for an hour. When you open that parcel, prepare to be assaulted by a rush of aromatic steam. No need to knock up a sauce. It's there waiting for you, pooled around the fish at the bottom of the foil parcel. Just be careful not to lose a single precious drop.

This is how easy and joyous fish cookery can be when you turn to the oven. It's maximum payback for minimum effort. Not that you're shirking your responsibility to the fish. There's nothing remotely second best about any of the suggestions above. But the oven is a great friend to the weary cook, or indeed the weary fisherman. Imagine, for instance, that you've just come back from a day's fishing, you're tired, you're hungry and you want to eat some of that lovely fish you've caught with minimum further ado. Whatever you've caught, the oven can always see you right.

You'll see from our table on pages 116–17 that 200°C/Gas Mark 6 is our normal oven temperature for roasting fish. If in doubt, we would recommend defaulting to this. But there's no fixed rule: raising or lowering the temperature simply speeds up or slows down the cooking time, as you'd expect. We usually cook our foil-parcel fish at a slightly lower temperature – around 180–190°C/Gas Mark 4–5 – otherwise it can suddenly be boiling rather fiercely in its pool of liquid. Higher temperatures – as much as 230°C/Gas Mark 8 – are good for rapid

roasting of unwrapped fish where you want to get good crisping and blistering of the skin. If you're roasting in a wood-fired pizza oven, the temperature may be up to 250°C or more, and small fish such as sardines or mackerel will be cooked through and crisped up, like a good pizza, in just a few minutes.

The oven/grill partnership

Most ovens now have an overhead grill built into them, which is why we've also included a handful of grilled fish recipes in this chapter. The overhead grill is rather marginalised these days, if not stigmatised – its thunder has been stolen by the chargrill and the ridged griddle pan (a very useful tool, which we discuss on page 298). But thirty or forty years ago it was a mainstay of British cooking, and eye-level overhead grills were all the rage.

If you have one, either at eye level or, more likely these days, at thigh level, do use it – because it is a very handy bit of fish-cooking equipment indeed. It's particularly useful when you are cooking whole fish and looking for that blistered, salty skin that can be so irresistible. Although you can get a good, crisp finish by starting your fish in a hot frying pan, then finishing the cooking in the oven (see opposite), it will never be quite the same as a proper grilling.

Indeed, an excellent alternative to the pan-with-a-hint-of-oven method is the oven-with-a-hint-of-grill approach. In other words, if you are roasting a fish and it's more or less done, but you feel the skin could use a little help to crisp up, then give it an extra brush of oil, and/or a quick baste with any pan juices, and put it close beneath a hot grill for just a minute. Watch it like a heron, though – nice brown blisters can turn to black charcoal faster than you can say, 'What's that burning smell?'

Of course, you can cook fish wonderfully by grill and grill alone, as our Grilled devilled sprats (page 245) and Grilled lemon sole with lemons (page 246) demonstrate. And the grill is often as handy as the oven when time is short and the crew is looking mutinous. To cook a few plate-sized (300–500g) whole fish, such as mackerel, trout, red mullet or small bream, start your grill heating up to medium-high while you get your coat off. Then line the grill pan with foil, brush the foil with some oil, sprinkle it with salt and pepper, plus a bay leaf or two if they're handy, and put your fish on top. Brush them with oil too, season them well, then give them 5 minutes on each side under fairly ferocious bars and you'll have a delicious supper in no time at all.

Beyond basic oven work

We use these basic oven methods – sometimes in conjunction with that flash under the grill – all the time. And sometimes we customise them to a slightly more refined level. The mackerel-in-a-roasting-tin, for example, can be expanded to create an entire meal by adding potatoes and onions to the tin and baking the fish on top of them. The juices from the mackerel mingle with the potatoes and onions; the effect is greedy and delicious, yet somehow rather chic – see page 218 for the full story.

There are many riffs on the foil-parcel theme, too: it can be used to cook a sandwiched pair of fillets – sea bass and bream are our favourites – as well as cooking whole fish. We might go for a more intense package of flavours: shaved fennel bulbs and lemon zest, for example, or a heady oriental mix of ginger, soy sauce, garlic and spring onions.

Even handfuls of small shellfish can be foil parcelled. A double layer of foil is best to protect against piercing by sharp shells – because, of course, you want to keep in those aromatic juices. Mussels, clams or cockles, scrubbed clean, can be parcelled up with a splash of wine, some garlic, some herbs and a good knob of butter, then baked at 220°C/Gas Mark 7. Within 10 minutes, they will have opened in the heat, allowing their juices to mingle with the other flavours and make a lovely, chin-dripping sauce. These one-per-person parcels can be opened on the plates, so everybody gets the benefit of that aromatic whoosh up the nostrils.

It is also to the oven that we turn when we want to create one of our most spectacular fishy set pieces: a whole hefty sea bass or bream baked in a thick, crusty jacket of salt (see page 226), or a saltdough crust (see page 225). The cracking and lifting of the crust to reveal the tender, aromatic flesh within creates a sense of occasion right up there with a whole poached salmon or a towering seafood platter. It's gone down a storm at various anniversaries and family birthdays – and it certainly takes the pressure off the cook.

The oven in a supporting role

When you have a fish to cook, whatever it is, the oven is so often the best option for getting the job done from start to finish. But it can also back up other cooking methods. The most obvious example, touched on above, is the use of the oven to finish off fish – usually whole ones – that have been started in a frying pan. The pan gets the seasoned skin nice and crisp, then the oven completes the job of getting the heat to the middle of the fish, which the pan might struggle to do on its own with a thick fish. We'll come to this very neat pan/oven double act again in the chapter on frying.

However, the role of the oven in fixing and finishing dishes that have been started somewhere else goes beyond this 'rounding-off' of whole fish in frying pans. There's a whole genre of fish-in-the-oven cookery that provides some of the most homely dishes in this book. These are what you might think of as 'composed' recipes, where fish is combined with other ingredients to make pies, pasties, tarts, gratins and bakes.

The baking of a fish pie (see page 236), with its crisp, browned topping of forked-up mashed potato, is a classic example of oven magic at work; the raising of a rich, creamy, smoked fish soufflé (see page 177) is another. We've even, in experimental mode, rustled up a crab bread and butter pudding. It turned out surprisingly well (see page 239). Gratins of fish and shellfish, or béchamel- and cheese-topped seafood crêpes, will also need a spell in a hot oven to crisp up their crumbs or bubble their cheese. Without the oven they would all be unfinished works: edible, maybe even delicious, but lacking a certain something – the ability not merely to satisfy appetites but to warm cockles and win hearts.

This kind of home-baking-with-fish may be a little more time consuming than the pared-down oven procedures we discussed at the beginning, but it's still enormously satisfying. Having started with a simply seasoned baked whole fish, we seem to have fetched up in the realms of creamy, indulgent fishy comfort food. It's not such a bad place to be.

Roasted whole plaice with cherry tomatoes

serves 2–4, depending on the size of your plaice

This is one of the best and simplest treatments for this wonderful flatfish. The crisp, blistered skin of the plaice is almost as delicious as the white meat beneath, and the unrivalled sweetness of little tomatoes, which burst in the mouth, sets it off perfectly.

This is definitely a dish to cook with one large fish rather than several small ones. Large plaice are, sadly, not as easy to find as they once were, but they are still out there. The fish we cooked for this photograph weighed nearly 2kg. If you aren't fortunate enough to come across such a monster, use a large brill, flounder, megrim or witch.

Also works with:
• Brill
• Flounder
• Megrim
• Witch

Olive oil

1 large plaice, weighing at least 1kg, descaled and gutted, but skin on

A large knob of unsalted butter, cut into small pieces

500g sweet cherry tomatoes, such as Sungold

About 6 sprigs of thyme

About 6 bay leaves

Salt and freshly ground black pepper

Oil a baking tray large enough to accommodate your plaice. Season the surface of the baking tray and place the fish on it, pale side (underside) down. Drizzle the fish with olive oil and massage it in. Season all over with pepper and lots of salt and dot the little pieces of butter over it.

Scatter the cherry tomatoes around the fish, along with the thyme and bay leaves. Bake in an oven preheated to 220°C/Gas Mark 7 for 20–30 minutes, until the fish is just cooked and the tomatoes are blistered and soft.

Once roasted, the flesh of the plaice should lift easily from the bone in neat fillets. Remove the top two fillets using a fish knife and fork. Ease the skeleton away to reveal the remaining two fillets from the underside. Serve the fish with the tomatoes and all their buttery, salty-sweet roasting juices.

Mackerel on potatoes and bay

serves 4

This is a fantastic and very simple one-dish meal. The juices from the fish mingle with the olive oil and lemon juice to make a delicious, aromatic sauce that flavours the vegetables beautifully. Go for new potatoes if you can, but main-crop are fine too. Choose a waxy variety, such as Cara or Maris Peer, and parboil them for 5 minutes or so before you begin. Either way, keep all the veg nice and chunky – this should be a wonderfully rustic sort of dish.

For a more child-friendly version of this dish, use fillets from larger fish instead of whole fish.

Also works with:
- Sardines
- Red mullet
- Scad
- Garfish

Olive oil
1kg new potatoes, scrubbed and cut into
    rough chunks about 2cm thick
2 onions, thickly sliced
4 garlic cloves, very roughly chopped

2 lemons, halved and sliced into thickish
    pieces
4–6 bay leaves
2 sprigs of thyme
4 mackerel, gutted
Salt and freshly ground black pepper

Pour enough olive oil into a large, shallow roasting tin just to cover the base. Use your fingers to spread the oil all over the dish. Combine the potatoes, onions, garlic and lemons, season with plenty of salt and pepper and spread them out in the dish. Tuck the bay leaves and thyme in amongst the vegetables so they won't burn in the oven.

Put the roasting tin in an oven preheated to 180°C/Gas Mark 4 and bake for 30–45 minutes, until the potatoes are lightly browned and just about tender, taking the tin from the oven every 10 minutes and turning the vegetables over in their oily juices.

Meanwhile, season the mackerel well with salt and pepper. When the potatoes are ready, lay the mackerel on top, pour on another good splash of olive oil and return to the oven. Turn it up to 200°C/Gas Mark 6 and bake for a further 15–20 minutes (10 minutes if you're using fillets), until the mackerel is just cooked and the vegetables are beginning to catch and crisp up nicely. (If you like, take the fish out halfway through for a quick basting with the juices from the tin.)

Serve straight away. The dish doesn't really need any accompaniment but a green salad wouldn't go amiss.

Whole fish baked in a foil parcel *serves 2*

If you enjoy fish – and presumably you do, or you wouldn't be reading this now – this method should be part of your core repertoire. It is incredibly easy and very forgiving (even if you overcook the fish a little, it will still be delicious). Bream and bass work best, but you can extend and expand the technique to accommodate any whole fish for which your foil, and oven, are sufficiently capacious. You'll certainly need a double layer of foil for anything over 1.5kg. The biggest fish we've ever cooked this way was a salmon of about 3.5kg. It took just over an hour.

<u>Also works with:</u>
- Salmon (organic farmed or self-caught wild)
- Trout
- Mackerel
- Carp
- Pike
- Pollack
- John Dory
- Small whole flatfish

One 2-portion-size (or two 1-portion-size) black bream, sea bass or other whole fish, descaled and gutted
2 garlic cloves, peeled and lightly squashed with a knife
A few bay leaves

1 lemon
A few herb sprigs: fennel fronds, thyme and/or flat-leaf parsley (optional)
50g unsalted butter
A glass of white wine
Salt and freshly ground black pepper

Season the inside of the fish and put in the squashed garlic, along with a bay leaf or two and 1 or 2 slices of lemon. If you have other herbs to hand – some fennel tops, say, or a little thyme or parsley – you can pop some of those in too. (If you're using flatfish, sit them on top of these flavourings in the foil parcels.)

Take a sheet of foil for each fish, large enough to envelop it completely. Grease the inside (dull side) with a little of the butter. Put a fish in the centre and bring up the sides of the foil a little. Scatter a few more herbs over the fish and dot with the butter. Pour on the wine (you'll need a little less if you're cooking just one large fish) and add a good squeeze of lemon juice. Season again, bring the foil up around the fish and scrunch the edges together until the parcel(s) are completely sealed.

Put the foil parcel(s) on a baking tray and bake in an oven preheated to 190°C/Gas Mark 5 for 20–25 minutes (small fish) or 30–35 minutes (larger fish). Small flatfish may take less time.

Bring the parcel(s) straight to the table and open them up on the plate to release a cloud of fragrant steam. The fish will be sitting in a pool of deliciously rich and aromatic juice – your sauce. Choose very simple accompaniments – perhaps roasted fennel or steamed spinach, and maybe a small pile of mash or rice.

Mackerel baked with cider and apple *serves 2*

This is a quite unusual and delicious riff on the foil-parcel theme.

Also works with:
• Scad

2 large mackerel, gutted
4 bay leaves
1 small onion, very thinly sliced into rings
1 small apple, cored and thinly sliced

50g unsalted butter, diced, plus extra
  for greasing
200ml medium cider
Salt and freshly ground black pepper

Season the cavities of the fish and put a bay leaf inside each one. Mix the onion and apple slices together and divide them between two sheets of buttered foil, adding the remaining bay leaves. Put the mackerel on top and dot the butter over the fish. Scrunch up the parcels from the sides and ends, then pour half the cider over each before the final wrap-up.

Put the foil parcels on a baking tray and bake in an oven preheated to 190°C/Gas Mark 5 for 20–25 minutes. The apple, onion and cider will cook down to a sweet, fragrant mixture, which is delicious mingled with crushed, boiled waxy potatoes.

Brill tranches with chanterelles *serves 6*

'Tranching' a fish means to cut it into steaks, still on the bone; it's a great technique for dealing with larger flatfish such as brill, turbot or plaice. Once you've got your steaks, you can cook them any way you like. We like to roast tranches of brill and serve them with sautéed chanterelles; September and October are the best months to look for these delicate mushrooms. When they are not to be found, other mushrooms – including good organic cultivated ones – will happily stand in for them.

Also works with:
• Turbot
• Plaice

Olive oil
1 brill, weighing about 2kg, cleaned and cut
  into six 200–300g tranches (see page 72)
50g unsalted butter, diced
1 teaspoon chopped thyme

Chanterelle mushrooms – at least one good
  handful per person (or use other seasonal
  mushrooms), trimmed and halved if large
2 teaspoons chopped parsley
Salt and freshly ground black pepper

Lightly oil a large roasting tin and lay the tranches of brill in it. Dot the fish with the butter, scatter with the thyme and season with salt and pepper. Place in an oven preheated to 200°C/Gas Mark 6 and roast for 12–15 minutes, until the fish is just cooked.

Meanwhile, heat 1 tablespoon of olive oil in a frying pan over a medium-low heat. Add the mushrooms and fry gently for 3–4 minutes, until tender. Season with salt and pepper and add the parsley.

Put the fish on warmed plates, trickling over any buttery juices left in the roasting tin. Spoon the mushrooms and their juices over the fish, and serve at once, accompanied by a tomato and red onion salad and some crusty bread.

Chinese fish parcels *serves 4*

This was the first dish ever to be cooked at the original River Cottage HQ, served outdoors in the February cold as work began transforming the shabby old farm buildings into a kitchen, dining room and teaching space. We'd had a bumper catch of sea bass a couple of days before. As the light started to fail, we wrapped the fish up with lots of aromatic ingredients and cooked them in a split oil drum over glowing embers. We ate the steaming fish straight from the parcels as we huddled around the fire. We've cooked this dish countless times since and it remains a great favourite.

A 1.5–2kg, or two 750g–1kg black bream or sea bass, descaled and filleted

4 large carrots

2 large leeks, trimmed and very thinly sliced

A large knob of ginger, very thinly sliced

2 garlic cloves, very thinly sliced

2 medium-hot chillies, deseeded and finely sliced

About 4 tablespoons soy sauce

About 2 tablespoons sesame oil

Lay the bass fillets, skin side down, on a board. Run your finger down the centre of each one, from head end to tail end, and use tweezers to remove any pin bones you find. Slice each fillet in half – or in quarters if you've just got one really large fish. You need 8 equal portions.

Peel the carrots and cut them into matchstick-sized pieces. A mandolin is very useful for this, if you have one. Otherwise, you'll need a good sharp knife.

Tear off a large sheet of foil and place a rough eighth of the carrot in the centre. Pile an eighth of the sliced leek on top, then some sliced garlic, ginger and chilli. Splash with soy sauce to taste, then a little sesame oil. Put a piece of fish, skin side down, on the pile. Add another layer of carrot, then leek, then garlic, ginger and chilli, then another piece of fish, skin side up. Finish off with a little more soy and sesame oil. Bring up the edges of the foil to envelop the ingredients and fold or twist the edges to seal the parcel tightly.

Repeat with the remaining ingredients to make 4 parcels. Place the parcels on a large baking tray and put in an oven preheated to 220°C/Gas Mark 7 for about 15 minutes, depending on the size of the fish, until the flesh is opaque all the way through. It's important that the oven is very hot. This ensures that all the juices from the fish, along with the soy and sesame oil, produce lots of fragrant steam to cook and flavour the vegetables.

Eat the fish straight from the parcels, or transfer to plates and serve with noodles or plain steamed rice.

Also works with:
- Sea trout
- Salmon (organic farmed or self-caught wild)
- Mackerel
- Brill
- Gurnard
- Grey mullet
- Carp

Whole bass or bream in saltdough crust *serves 4*

In general, salt is used to draw water out of food but, if you mix it into a stiff dough, you can use it to seal moisture in. This is an elegant, theatrical cooking method – but rewarding too. If you're cooking one really big fish, bear in mind that you'll also require a really big oven tray, and plenty of oven space.

A 4-portion size (1.5–2kg) sea bass or
  bream, or 2 fish weighing 750g–1kg
  each, gutted but not descaled
4 bay leaves
50g unsalted butter
1 lemon, sliced
Salt and freshly ground black pepper

FOR THE SALTDOUGH CRUST:
1kg plain flour
600g fine sea salt
6 egg whites, lightly beaten
1 egg yolk, mixed with a splash of milk,
  to glaze

To make the saltdough crust, sift the flour into a large mixing bowl and mix in the salt. Make a well in the centre, add the egg whites and mix well. Gradually work in about 400ml water to bring the dough together. Knead the dough on a lightly floured surface for about 2 minutes, until smooth and pliable. Wrap in cling film and leave to rest for 20 minutes. Don't put it in the fridge or it will become too stiff to work with.

Dust a clean, dry work surface with flour. Cut the saltdough pastry into two equal pieces (four if you're cooking two fish). With a rolling pin, roll out one of the pieces into an oval 5cm larger all round than your fish. Lay the fish in the centre of the saltdough. Put the bay leaves, a pinch each of salt and pepper, the butter and a few slices of lemon inside the fish (or, if you're using two fish, divide these ingredients between them).

Roll out another piece of saltdough of a similar size to cover the fish. Use a pastry brush to brush a little cold water around the edge of the saltdough with the fish on it. Lay the second piece of dough over the fish and gently, using the side of your hand, mould and shape it until the contours of the fish are visible. Crimp the edges well to ensure the saltdough package is sealed and airtight. There should be a 1–2cm border of dough around the fish – trim away any excess. Brush the dough all over with the egg and milk glaze. Lay the dough-encased fish on a baking sheet and place in an oven preheated to 220°C/Gas Mark 7. Cook for 20–25 minutes for small fish, 30–35 minutes for a large one.

Bring the fish to the table and break open the saltdough crust. Lift off the crust and peel away the skin, then gently take the flesh off the bones, using a palette knife or small fish slice. Serve with very simple accompaniments, such as a green salad and sautéed potatoes. Don't eat the saltdough crust!

Also works with:
• Sea trout
• Salmon (organic farmed)
• Mackerel

Sea bass baked in raw salt *serves 4–6*

This is the cruder, speeded-up version of the previous dish. Instead of taking the trouble to make a salty dough, you just pack damp salt over and around the fish. It's rather more extravagant with the salt, but a good way of dealing with a couple of smaller fish of around 1kg or so.

Also works with:
- Sea trout
- Salmon (organic farmed or self-caught wild)
- Black bream
- Mackerel

1kg fine table salt
1kg coarse sea salt
8–12 bay leaves
1 garlic clove, finely chopped

2 sea bass, weighing about 1kg each, gutted but not descaled
Freshly ground black pepper

Put each type of salt in a separate bowl. Starting with 1–2 tablespoons, add enough water to each to dampen the salt and create a mouldable paste consistency, similar to damp sand. Then combine the two salts.

Lay out a thick bed of salt on a large baking tray (or use two smaller trays, one for each fish). Put a couple of bay leaves on the salt and sprinkle on the garlic and some black pepper. Lay the bass on the salt, put 2 bay leaves inside each fish and a couple more on top. Fold the bellies closed so no salt can make its way inside the fish. Top the fish with the rest of the salt, packing and moulding it closely around them and leaving only the heads exposed. Place in an oven preheated to 200°C/Gas Mark 6 and bake for 25 minutes.

Bring the salt-crusted bass to the table and break off the salt crust in chunks. Then peel back the skin to reveal the succulent, aromatic flesh.

Pot-roasted gurnard *serves 4*

Like poultry and meat, whole fish work well in a one-pot casserole brimming with winter veg. If the vegetables are sweated for a while first, they can finish cooking in the time it takes a couple of nice whole fish to cook through, and lend their delicious juices to the dish. Pat Carlin, our regular River Cottage skipper, reckons this is the best way he's ever tasted gurnard – and it's one of his favourite fish.

Also works with:
- Grey mullet
- Red mullet
- Black bream
- Zander

A large knob of unsalted butter
3 tablespoons olive oil
2 medium leeks, white part only, cut into 2cm thick slices
300g celeriac, peeled and cut into 2cm chunks
2 onions, thickly sliced
2 large potatoes, peeled and cut into 2cm chunks

2 large carrots, cut into 2cm chunks
1 large (about 1.5kg) or 2 medium (about 750g) or 4 small (about 400g) gurnard (or other whole fish), descaled and gutted
A glass of white wine
2 bay leaves
Salt and freshly ground black pepper

Put the butter and olive oil in a large flameproof casserole over a medium-low heat. Add all the vegetables, season well and toss them in the fat, then sweat gently for about 10 minutes, until they begin to soften. Don't let them colour.

Season the gurnard with salt and pepper, then add it to the pan, pushing it down so it is snuggled in among the aromatic vegetables. Sprinkle over the wine and a glass of water, tuck in the bay leaves and cover the dish. Bring to a gentle simmer on the hob.

Now transfer the casserole to an oven preheated to 180°C/Gas Mark 4 and bake for 30–40 minutes, depending on the size of fish. To check that the fish is ready, insert the tip of a knife at the thickest part to pull the flesh away from the bone. It should be opaque all the way through.

If you have one or two larger fish, take the flesh off the bones in big chunks. Otherwise, simply serve one fish per person, with plenty of the vegetables and juices alongside.

Stuffed conger *serves 4–6*

We only cook a conger once a year, if that (see page 500) – so when we do, we really push the boat out. This is our take on an old Cornish recipe from Dorothy Hartley's *Food in England* (Macdonald, 1954). It sounded so bizarre that we felt we had to give it a go – and the results were really good. In fact, this fishy roast could easily take pride of place at Sunday lunch. The flesh of the conger is moist and full of flavour, and the juices make a lovely rich gravy. You probably won't find the skin palatable but it helps to hold the slices together as you serve the fish.

1.5kg section of a medium conger eel (a 5–10kg fish is perfect), cut from the middle of the fish, skin on
10 smoked streaky bacon rashers
1 small dessert apple, such as Cox's or Russet
35g unsalted butter
250ml medium cider, plus a little extra for the gravy, if necessary
1–2 teaspoons plain flour
Salt and freshly ground black pepper

FOR THE SAUSAGE STUFFING:
250g coarsely minced organic or free-range pork shoulder
1 small onion, finely chopped
50g fresh white breadcrumbs
A good pinch of ground mace
A pinch of cayenne pepper
A small handful of sage leaves, finely chopped
A small handful of thyme leaves, finely chopped
Grated zest of ½ lemon
2 tablespoons brandy
1 dessert apple, peeled, cored and cut into small cubes
½ teaspoon salt
Freshly ground black pepper

By hand, thoroughly mix all the stuffing ingredients in a large bowl, squishing everything together with your fingers. Then put the mixture in the fridge so the flavours can mingle while you prepare the conger.

Wash and dry the piece of conger. Open up the belly cavity and remove the section of backbone, teasing the flesh away from the bone with a sharp filleting knife until it comes free. Use tweezers to remove any other bones you find. Conger has a lot of tiny pin bones, so you do need to take your time over this. Run your fingertips up and down the flesh to locate the bones before pulling them out.

Now bring the sides of the fish together and sew them with butcher's string to form a cavity for the stuffing. Pack the pork stuffing into the cavity and season the fish all over, then place the bacon rashers over the top. Cut the apple in half and use the halves to plug the ends of the stuffed joint.

Melt the butter in a roasting tin over a gentle heat. Place the stuffed conger in the tin and pour over the cider. This will be your basting liquid and the base of your gravy.

Roast the conger in an oven preheated to 220°C/Gas Mark 7 for 10 minutes, then reduce the temperature to 180°C/Gas Mark 4. Cook for a further hour, basting regularly, until the stuffing is cooked right through (the tip of a skewer pushed into the middle of the stuffing should come out hot – a probe thermometer should read 70°C).

(continued overleaf)

As you remove the roast conger from the oven, transfer it to a warm platter and leave it to rest in a warm place, while you make gravy – in just the same way you would after roasting a joint of meat. If there is a lot of liquid, simply pour it into a saucepan and boil it down until it reaches the level of intensity you require. Alternatively, if there's not so much to play with, place the roasting tin over a gentle heat and stir the flour into the juices to thicken them. Allow to bubble for a few minutes to cook out the flour and finish the thickening. If you feel you need extra liquid, add more cider, or some fish stock. Either way, simmer the gravy for a minute or two, then taste and adjust the seasoning.

Remove the bacon and apple halves (which you can serve with the fish), and the string. Slice the conger fairly thickly, then serve with boiled, buttered potatoes or mash, some greens, such as Savoy cabbage or Brussels sprouts, and a jug of the hot conger gravy.

Brill baked with leeks and potatoes *serves 6*

Brill responds very well to a one-pot treatment, but because of its flat shape, it needs a slightly different approach. Strictly, this is a two-pot treatment, but still very straightforward.

A large knob of unsalted butter
3 tablespoons olive oil
4 medium leeks, white part only, cut into 2cm thick slices
4 large potatoes, peeled and cut into 2cm chunks

A couple of bay leaves
1 brill, weighing 1–1.5kg, descaled and gutted
A glass of white wine
Salt and freshly ground black pepper

Also works with:
• Plaice
• Turbot
• Sole
• Lemon sole
• Megrim
• Witch
• Flounder

Heat the butter and olive oil in a large saucepan over a medium-low heat. Add the leeks and potatoes, cover and sweat, stirring frequently, for 10–15 minutes, until the potatoes are almost tender.

Transfer the vegetables to a large roasting tin, so they form a shallow layer, and tuck in the bay leaves. Season well. Place the brill on top of the veg, then nestle it down so there are vegetables under, around and on top of it.

Trickle the wine and a glass of water over everything and cover the tin with foil. Put in an oven preheated to 180°C/Gas Mark 4 and bake for about 30 minutes, until the fish is cooked.

Mussel, spinach and bacon gratin

serves 4 as a main course, 6 as a starter

Moules marinière meets creamed spinach and gets an irresistible gratin top. This is the kind of simple but unexpected dish that gets people very excited.

Also works with:
- Cockles
- Palourdes

2 tablespoons white wine
1 shallot, diced
1kg mussels, scrubbed and debearded (see page 103)
1 tablespoon olive oil, plus a little more to finish
150g smoked bacon or pancetta, diced fairly small
1 fat garlic clove, finely chopped
About 400ml whole milk

50g unsalted butter
50g plain flour
500g fresh spinach, thoroughly washed, tougher stalks removed
A squeeze of lemon juice
75g fresh white breadcrumbs
50g Cheddar or Parmesan cheese, grated (optional)
Freshly ground black pepper

Place a large pan over a high heat and add the wine, 2 tablespoons of water and the diced shallot. Bring to a simmer, then throw in the mussels and cover with the lid. Let them steam open in the pan for 3–4 minutes, shaking the pan once or twice. Remove the mussels from the pan with a slotted spoon (discarding any that have remained firmly shut) and set aside until they are cool enough to handle. Pick the mussels from their shells and set aside. Strain all the cooking liquor through a fine sieve, or a coarse sieve lined with a cloth.

Heat the olive oil in a frying pan, add the bacon and sauté gently until starting to crisp up. Add the garlic and cook for a further minute or so, being careful not to let the garlic burn. Remove from the heat and transfer to a bowl.

Now you need to make a béchamel sauce. First, combine the reserved mussel cooking liquor with enough milk to make 500ml and heat gently in a pan. Melt the butter in a separate pan. When it is foaming, add the flour and stir well to make a smooth roux. Gradually add the warmed milk, stirring well after each addition to prevent lumps. Bring to a simmer and cook gently for 4–5 minutes to give a smooth, creamy sauce.

Drop the spinach into a large pan of boiling water and cook for just a minute, until wilted. Drain, leave to cool a little, then squeeze out excess water with your hands. Chop the spinach roughly.

Fold the bacon, mussels and spinach into the béchamel sauce. Season with freshly ground black pepper and a squeeze of lemon juice. Divide the mixture between 4 buttered shallow ovenproof dishes (or 6 ramekins if you're serving it as a starter) or spread it evenly into one large buttered gratin dish.

Sprinkle over the breadcrumbs, plus the cheese if using, and trickle over a little olive oil. Bake in an oven preheated to 200°C/Gas Mark 6 for 10–12 minutes, until golden and bubbling. Serve piping hot, with crusty bread.

Devilled spider crab in the shell *serves 2*

You might think of crabmeat as a very delicate thing, not suited to the rough and tumble of vinegar, mustard, chilli and other devilling ingredients – but it has a robust depth that can easily hold its own in a dish like this.

Baking the crab in its shell gives you the bonus of an extra shot of flavour. Crustacean shells are formed from concentrated proteins and sugars, and the heat of the oven causes them to release a nutty, rich flavour.

About 50g unsalted butter, plus a little
  extra for dotting on the breadcrumbs
1 large onion, finely chopped
100ml sherry
2 tablespoons cider vinegar
1½ tablespoons Worcestershire sauce
1 heaped teaspoon English mustard
1 teaspoon cayenne pepper or a generous
  shake of Tabasco sauce

200ml double cream
2 cooked medium spider crabs (about
  1–1.5kg), brown and white meat picked
  out, shells cleaned (see pages 89–93)
A squeeze of lemon juice
50g fresh white breadcrumbs
Salt and freshly ground black pepper

Also works with:
- Brown crab
- Blue velvet swimmer crab

Put a large, heavy-based pan over a medium heat and add the butter. Toss in the chopped onion and sweat gently until softened but not coloured – about 10 minutes should do it. Pour in the sherry, let it boil for a few seconds, then add the vinegar and Worcestershire sauce and let them come to the boil too.

Stir in the mustard and cayenne pepper or Tabasco, then add the cream. Let the mixture come to a simmer, cook for 2 minutes or until it just starts to thicken slightly, then remove from the heat.

Fold the crabmeat into the sauce. Season well with salt and pepper and a little lemon juice, then spoon the mixture into the cleaned crab shells or individual gratin dishes. Don't try and fill the shells up, just make a good mound of the mixture in the middle. Sprinkle with the breadcrumbs and dot a little butter over the top.

Place the crabs on a baking tray and bake in an oven preheated to 190°C/Gas Mark 5 for 20–25 minutes, until the breadcrumbs are golden and the crab bubbling devilishly. Serve piping hot, with doorsteps of thickly buttered toast and a green salad.

VARIATION
Devilled crab on toast

To ring the changes and speed things up a bit, you can make a lovely version of this dish with the bread on the bottom, in the form of toast, rather than on top, as breadcrumbs. It cuts out the baking stage, too.

After folding the crabmeat into the sauce, simply pile it on to hot buttered toast. A scaled-down version of this makes an excellent canapé: put generous teaspoonfuls of the hot (or cold) saucy crab on small squares of toast or little crostini and serve with drinks.

Hugh's mum's fish pie *serves 6*

This is a classic, creamy, comforting fish pie, which should delight fish eaters of all ages. The basic principle is to have some smoked fish, some white fish, some oily fish and some prawns. But, of course, you can vary the species according to what's available – and good value – on the day.

FOR THE FILLING:
400g cooked, shell-on Atlantic prawns
500g smoked white fish fillets, such as
  pollack or haddock
300–400g fresh white fish fillets
300–400g organic salmon fillets
1 onion, roughly chopped
1 large carrot, roughly chopped
1 celery stick, chopped
1 bay leaf
A few peppercorns
A bunch of flat-leaf parsley, leaves
  chopped and stalks reserved

About 750ml milk
3 large eggs, at room temperature
50g unsalted butter
75g plain flour
2 tablespoons chopped chives
Salt and freshly ground black pepper

FOR THE MASH:
1kg floury potatoes, such as Maris Piper
  or Désirée, peeled and cut into chunks
50g unsalted butter, plus extra to dot on
  top of the pie
100ml whole milk, warmed

Shell the prawns and put the shells and heads in a saucepan: they will help to flavour the sauce for the pie. With a sharp filleting knife, skin the fish (see page 73). Add the skins to the saucepan, plus the onion, carrot, celery, bay leaf, peppercorns and parsley stalks. Pour in enough milk just to cover, bring to a simmer, then take off the heat and set aside to infuse for at least half an hour. Remove any pin bones from the fish with tweezers and cut up all the fish into roughly 2cm cubes. Combine with the shelled prawns and set aside.

While the milk for the sauce is infusing, make the mashed potato. Boil the spuds in salted water until tender. Drain and leave them in the colander to steam for a minute or two, then return to the pan and mash with the butter and milk. Season to taste with salt and pepper.

Bring a pan of water to the boil, add the eggs and boil for 7 minutes. Take off the heat and put the pan under cold running water to stop the cooking. When the eggs are cool enough to handle, peel them.

To make the béchamel sauce, strain the infused milk into a jug and place by the hob. Melt the butter in a pan over a medium heat, add the flour and stir well to make a smooth roux. Cook this gently for a couple of minutes, stirring, then gradually add the infused milk, beating well after each addition so you don't get any lumps. Allow the sauce to cook gently for a couple of minutes, stirring occasionally so it doesn't stick. Remove from the heat, season to taste and add the chopped parsley and chives. Stir in the fish and prawns.

Cut the eggs into quarters and arrange them in a pie dish (about 30 x 20cm). Spoon over the fish mixture, then top with spoonfuls of mashed potato, spreading it evenly over the fish and raking the top into wavy lines with a fork to maximise crispness. Dot the potato with a little butter and bake in an oven preheated to 200°C/Gas Mark 6 for about 25 minutes, until the top is starting to brown and the sauce is bubbling up the sides of the mash. Serve with buttered peas.

Seafood pancake gratin *serves 12 as starter, 6 as a main course*

This follows the same kind of comfort-food principles as a really good fish pie: a rich combination of smoked fish, white fish and prawns, bound in a creamy béchamel sauce and all held together with a satisfying bit of starch – in this case, pancakes. The addition of a little bubbling cheese only adds to the feel-good factor.

1 quantity of fish pie filling (see page
  236, but without the eggs)
2 tablespoons white wine
300–400g mussels, scrubbed and
  debearded (see page 103)
100g Gruyère or Cheddar cheese, grated

FOR THE PANCAKES:
250g plain flour
A pinch of salt
2 large eggs
250ml whole milk
Sunflower oil for frying

Make the filling according to the fish pie recipe but set aside 5–6 tablespoonfuls of the béchamel sauce before you add the fish. (You're saving it to pour over the pancakes, for a creamy, bubbling topping.)

Bring the wine and 2 tablespoons of water to the boil in a saucepan over a medium-high heat and add the mussels. Cover and cook, shaking the pan a couple of times, for 3–4 minutes, until the shells are open. Discard any that remain closed. When the mussels are cool enough to handle, remove them from their shells and add to the fish and béchamel filling.

For the pancakes, sift the flour and salt into a bowl, make a well in the centre and break in the eggs. Pour in half the milk and start to whisk, bringing the flour gradually into the egg and milk in the centre. Add the rest of the milk and 150ml water and keep on whisking until there are no more lumps. Stir in some more water (around 100ml) until the mixture is the consistency of thin cream.

Place a large frying pan over a medium-high heat and add 1 tablespoon of sunflower oil. Swirl it round the pan, then pour the excess out into a cup. Pour a small ladleful of batter into the pan and swirl it round quickly to form a crêpe. Cook for 1–2 minutes, until browned underneath, then flip over and cook the second side for a minute. Remove from the pan and set aside.

Repeat with the remaining batter, stacking the pancakes up between squares of greaseproof paper, then set them aside to cool. Add another swirl of oil to the pan after every 3 pancakes or so. You need 12 pancakes in all, and may have some batter left over.

Place a large spoonful of the fish and sauce mixture in the middle of one pancake. Roll up the pancake around the filling, fold in the ends to seal the filling in and continue rolling up the pancake. Place in a greased ovenproof dish in which the rolled pancakes will fit snugly (you might find it easier to use two dishes). Continue the filling and rolling with the remaining pancakes.

Gently reheat the reserved sauce, adding a little milk if it is very thick, then spoon it over the filled pancakes and scatter the grated cheese on top. Bake in an oven preheated to 200°C/Gas Mark 6 for 20–25 minutes, until bubbling hot and lightly browned.

Crab bread and butter pudding *serves 6*

This is a lovely comforting dish, based on a Jane Grigson recipe – ideal for the winter months, and cheap and cheerful too. It's not something you'd want to do from scratch with a couple of live crabs; they'd be better served really simply. It is more a way of spinning a clever crowd-pleaser from ready-picked brown and white meat.

125g softened unsalted butter	A day-old white baguette, cut into slices
300g white and brown crabmeat	1.5–2cm thick
A good pinch of cayenne pepper	4 eggs
2 tablespoons chopped mixed herbs, such	250ml milk
as parsley, chervil and chives	250ml single cream
A squeeze of lemon juice	Salt and freshly ground black pepper

Use some of the butter to grease a medium gratin dish generously. Combine the crabmeat with the cayenne, mixed herbs and lemon juice, and season well.

Generously butter the baguette slices. One good approach is to construct two giant, multi-decker, Scooby-snack style crab sandwiches, which will lie side-by-side in the gratin dish. Start with a buttered slice of baguette. Cover it with crab mixture. Add a second slice of bread, some more crab, then another piece of bread. Keep going till you have a sandwich long enough to fit the dish.

Place the sandwich in the dish on its side and then make a second one to lay beside the first. Use the remaining bread slices and filling to make smaller sandwiches to fit around the edge of the dish and fill any gaps.

Whisk together the eggs, milk and cream and season well to make a savoury custard. Pour this mixture all over the crab and bread and leave to soak for at least 10 minutes. Then bake in an oven preheated to 180°C/Gas Mark 4 for 25–30 minutes, until the custard is set and golden.

Serve warm, rather than hot, with something slightly bitter on the side, such as a salad of white chicory, radicchio, rocket or watercress with a citrus dressing – this helps cut the richness.

Also works with:
• Spider crab

Smoked pollack and spinach tart *serves 6*

This is one of the best savoury tarts we know. The balance of the lightly salty, slightly smoky fish, the sweetness of the onion, the greenness of the spinach and the just-set creaminess of the custard, all on crumbly pastry, is a kind of perfection. Is this the best recipe in the book? Arguably…

300–350g smoked pollack fillet

Up to 1 litre whole milk

A knob of unsalted butter

2 onions, finely sliced

400g fresh spinach, washed thoroughly, tough stalks removed

50g mature Cheddar cheese, grated

200ml double cream

2 eggs

2 egg yolks

Salt and freshly ground black pepper

FOR THE PASTRY:

200g plain flour

A pinch of salt

100g cold unsalted butter, cut into small cubes

1 egg, separated

About 50ml cold milk

Also works with:
- Smoked haddock and other smoked white fish
- Kippers
- Smoked salmon or trout

Start with the pastry. Put the flour, salt and butter in a food processor and pulse until the mixture has the consistency of breadcrumbs. Add the egg yolk and then, with the processor running, slowly add the milk, stopping as soon as the dough comes together. Tip out on to a lightly floured board, knead a couple of times to make a smooth ball of dough, then wrap in cling film and chill for half an hour.

Roll the pastry out thinly on a lightly floured surface and use it to line a 25cm loose-bottomed tart tin. Let the excess pastry hang over the edge of the tin. Prick the base in several places with a fork, line with a sheet of greaseproof paper and fill with baking beans or rice. Bake in an oven preheated to 160°C/Gas Mark 3 for 15 minutes, then remove the paper and beans and return the pastry case to the oven for 10 minutes, until it looks dry and cooked. Lightly beat the egg white and brush all over the pastry. Return the pastry case to the oven once more and bake for another 5 minutes, until golden. This helps to seal the pastry and prevent any filling leaking out. Trim off the excess pastry using a small, sharp knife.

Put the smoked fish in a pan, cutting it in two if necessary to make it fit neatly in a single layer. Pour in enough milk just to cover the fish, then cover the pan and bring to a simmer. Remove from the heat. The fish should be just cooked. If it isn't, turn it over and leave it in the hot milk for a minute or two more. Once it is done, remove the fish from the pan, strain the milk and set aside to cool.

Heat the butter in a pan, add the onions and fry gently until soft and golden brown – this takes a good 15 minutes. Drop the spinach into a large pan of boiling water and cook for just a minute, until wilted. Drain and leave until cool enough to handle, then squeeze out the water with your hands. Chop the spinach coarsely.

Flake the pollack into a bowl, discarding the skin and any bones, and add the cheese, onions and spinach. Mix well, then put the mixture into the tart case. Mix 200ml of the strained fish poaching milk with the cream, eggs and egg yolks. Season with salt and pepper and pour into the tart case. Bake at 160°C/Gas Mark 3 for about 40 minutes, until lightly set and browned. Serve warm or cold.

Crab tart *serves 8 as a starter*

With its creamy, soft-set filling, this tart is very rich and very gorgeous. You could use the recipe to make individual tarts, though a large one is less fiddly and avoids the potential pitfall of a too-high pastry-to-filling ratio.

1 cooked large brown crab or 2 spider
   crabs (or one of each), brown and white
   meat picked out (see pages 89–93), or
   300g fresh crabmeat
2 tablespoons olive oil
1 large onion, finely sliced
2 garlic cloves, finely chopped
½–1 fresh red chilli (depending on heat),
   deseeded and finely chopped
Juice of ½ lemon
2–3 tablespoons coarsely chopped
   coriander
50g Parmesan cheese, grated

2 eggs
2 egg yolks
200ml whole milk
200ml double cream
Salt and freshly ground black pepper

FOR THE SHORTCRUST PASTRY:
200g plain flour
A pinch of salt
100g cold unsalted butter, cut into
   small cubes
1 egg, separated
About 50ml cold milk

Start with the pastry. Put the flour, salt and butter in a food processor and pulse until the mixture has the consistency of breadcrumbs. Add the egg yolk and then, with the processor running, pour in the milk in a thin stream. Watch carefully and stop adding the milk as soon as the dough comes together. (You may not need it all.) Tip out on to a lightly floured board, knead a couple of times to make a smooth ball of dough, then wrap in cling film and chill for half an hour.

Roll the pastry out thinly on a lightly floured surface and use it to line a 25cm loose-bottomed tart tin. Let the excess pastry hang over the edge of the tin – don't trim it off. Prick the base in several places with a fork, line it with a sheet of greaseproof paper and fill with baking beans or rice.

Bake in an oven preheated to 160°C/Gas Mark 3 for 15 minutes, then remove the paper and beans and return the pastry case to the oven for 10 minutes, until it looks dry and cooked. Lightly beat the egg white and brush it all over the pastry. Return the pastry case to the oven once more and bake for another 5 minutes, until golden. This helps to seal the pastry and prevent any filling leaking out. Trim off the excess pastry using a small, sharp knife. Turn the oven up to 180°C/ Gas Mark 4.

Loosely combine the brown and white meat in a bowl, taking care not to break it up too much or reduce it to a paste.

Heat a large frying pan over a medium-high heat and add 1 tablespoon of olive oil. Add the onion, sauté for 5–10 minutes, until soft and light golden, then remove from the pan and set aside.

Add another dash of olive oil to the pan and throw in the garlic and chilli. Fry until the garlic just begins to colour and gives off a nutty aroma, then immediately toss in the crabmeat. Stir to combine it with the chilli and garlic, then take the pan off the heat. Stir in the onion, along with the lemon juice, coriander and Parmesan. Season with salt and pepper.

Spoon the crab mixture into the baked tart case. Don't press it down or pack it in, just arrange it carefully with a fork.

Combine the eggs, egg yolks, milk and cream, season well and pour the mixture over the crab. A poke and a nudge might be required at this point to encourage the custard to spread evenly through the crab filling.

Bake the tart in the oven for 30–35 minutes, until the custard is just set, then set aside to cool slightly, for about 15 minutes before serving.

Curried trout pasties *makes 4*

These are perfect for picnics, lunchboxes and other mobile meals. You could use leftover cooked fish, but the final texture will be a little more paste-like, a little less fresh and flaky. Using pastry that's been stained golden with turmeric is a nice touch but it's far from essential.

Also works with:
· Salmon (organic farmed or self-caught wild)
· Mackerel
· Scad
· Black bream
· Gurnard
· Grey mullet

2 tablespoons groundnut oil
A large knob of fresh ginger, finely chopped
2 garlic cloves, finely chopped
½ teaspoon ground coriander
½ teaspoon ground cumin
Seeds from 1 cardamom pod, ground with a pestle and mortar
½ teaspoon ground turmeric
1 large onion, finely sliced
2 teaspoons good curry powder – as mild or as hot as you like
100ml double cream or coconut milk
35g sultanas

6 dried apricots, cut into quarters
250g trout fillet (preferably wild), skinned, pin-boned and cut into chunky cubes
2 teaspoons chopped coriander leaves
Salt and freshly ground black pepper

FOR THE PASTRY:
200g plain flour
A pinch of salt
1 teaspoon ground turmeric (optional)
100g cold unsalted butter, cut into cubes
1 egg, beaten with 1 teaspoon milk, for glazing

Start with the pastry. Put the flour, salt and turmeric, if using, into a food processor, add the butter and pulse until the mixture looks like breadcrumbs. With the processor running, slowly add enough cold water (3–4 tablespoons) to make the mixture come together in big, damp crumbs. Tip out on to a lightly floured surface and gently knead into a ball. Then wrap in cling film and place in the fridge while you make the filling.

Heat the oil in a pan over a medium heat. Add the ginger, garlic, ground coriander, cumin, cardamom and turmeric and fry for 30 seconds. Add the sliced onion and stir it around so it absorbs the spices. Add the curry powder and continue to fry gently until the onion is soft. Pour in the cream or coconut milk, bring to a simmer and cook gently for a few minutes, until thick. Remove from the heat. Add the sultanas, apricots, trout, chopped coriander and some seasoning, and mix well. Cover and set aside.

Cut the pastry into 4 pieces and roll out each one into a round about 4mm thick. Using a bowl or saucer as a guide, cut out a circle about 18cm in diameter. Put a pile of the trout filling on one half of each pastry circle, brush the edges of the pastry with a little of the egg and milk glaze and bring the other half of the pastry over the filling. Crimp the edges together to seal them, using your fingers or a fork.

Transfer the pasties to a greased baking sheet and brush with more of the glaze. Bake in an oven preheated to 190°C/Gas Mark 5 for about 30 minutes, until golden brown. Eat hot or cold.

Grilled devilled sprats *serves 4 as a starter*

A single sprat makes one satisfying mouthful, so they need to be cooked in quantity. Luckily, however, that's generally how they're caught, and preparing and cooking them is quite speedy. Simply grilled with olive oil, salt and pepper, they make delicious finger food. Take a few minutes to devil them with a spicy sauce and you're on to a real winner.

Sprats are also very good barbecued. Thread them on to long skewers, pushing the spike up through each fish behind its head and cramming as many on to one skewer as you can. Brush the fish with oil and cook over a barbecue for 2–3 minutes on each side.

24–32 sprats
Salt and freshly ground black pepper

FOR THE DEVILLED SAUCE:
2 tablespoons cider vinegar
1 tablespoon Worcestershire sauce

2 tablespoons sherry
1 tablespoon English mustard
8 shakes of Tabasco sauce or a good
  pinch of cayenne pepper
2 teaspoons redcurrant or crab apple jelly

To prepare the devilled sauce, put all the ingredients in a very small pan and whisk to combine. Bring to the boil and boil for a minute or two, until the sauce has reduced by about half and is a light syrupy consistency. Remove from the heat and set aside.

Using sharp kitchen scissors, snip a thin strip of belly from each sprat, then rinse out the innards under the cold tap (see page 60). If you like the idea of eating the heads and all, then pulling out the gills at this point, with thumb and forefinger, will make the heads more tooth-friendly. Pat the sprats dry with kitchen paper.

Preheat the grill to high. Lay a piece of foil on the grill pan, oil it lightly and lay the sprats on top. Season them with salt and pepper and, using a pastry brush, brush with the sauce. Aim to use up about half of it here. Slide the pan under the hot grill and cook for about 3 minutes until the sprats are brown and blistered. Turn them over, brush with the remaining sauce and cook the second side for 2 minutes or so. That's it, they're done – serve them as quick as you can.

Grilled lemon sole with lemons *serves 2*

This is a great way to do justice to this lovely fish. You get the best of everything: a crisp, savoury top from the heat of the grill, a sweet, succulent middle from cooking on the bone, and a delicate lemon infusion from the base.

Also works with:
• Dab
• Flounder
• Witch
• Megrim
• Plaice

1 lemon sole, weighing about 750g,
  descaled and gutted, but skin on
1 lemon, plus extra wedges to serve

A few knobs of softened unsalted butter,
  plus extra for greasing
Sea salt

Preheat the grill to maximum. Trim the fins and tail from the fish. Cut the lemon into slices about 5mm thick – to make a bed to lay the whole fish on. Butter a grill tray and arrange the lemon slices on it, roughly forming a sole shape. Smear the butter all over the fish, season both sides with salt and lay it, dark side up, on the lemon slices. Score the top a few times, up to 5mm deep, with a very sharp knife – a herringbone pattern is nice, to mirror the shape of the head.

Now slide the tin under the fiercely hot grill. You need to keep an eye on it, and you may need to adjust your shelf height to achieve, after about 10 minutes' cooking, a deliciously browned and bubbled-up top skin and a just-cooked centre (test this by sliding a table knife in at the spine – the flesh should just pull away from the bone). Baste the fish with the buttery, lemony juices a couple of times during cooking.

Incidentally, if you're wondering, the heat conducted through the grill tray should have cooked the underside of the fish from underneath, but you can accelerate this by taking the tray out from under the grill about halfway through cooking and placing it on a hob over a high heat for just half a minute, then returning the pan to the grill.

When the sole is ready, slide it, sizzling hot, on to a serving platter – the lemon slices will probably come with it. Serve with nothing more than a few salad leaves and some plain boiled potatoes to squash into the juices, plus the lemon wedges to squeeze over the top.

Soups, stews and poaching

The title of this chapter may suggest an element of miscellany; that it's a keep net for a school of cooking methods that are only loosely related. But in fact the recipes here are in many ways a closer-knit bunch than those in the other chapters. What unites them is that they all involve cooking fish with, or in, a liquid. We are returning the fish, if you like, to the element from which they came, albeit with a few carefully chosen flavourings.

The liquid may be a well-worked combination of ingredients to produce a rich, multi-layered amalgam of spices, vegetables, stock and fresh fish. Or it might be little more than a scant splash of wine and a scrap of butter, perhaps with a pinch of garlic and/or herbs, as described in our simple steam-braising method for cooking hearty fillets, steaks and cutlets of fish such as ling, brill, turbot and John Dory (see page 255). There are a couple of common denominators. One is that the fish is immersed and cooked in the hot liquid – and since liquid conducts heat faster than air, that cooking is usually very rapid. Another is that, in most cases, once the fish is cooked, everything that's in the pot can be eaten – fish, liquid, vegetables and all. And therein lies the great charm of these dishes.

What you call these fish-in-liquor dishes – chowders, soups or stews – may depend on their final consistency, their heartiness or quite possibly their country of origin (or yours for that matter). You might argue that a real chowder, for example, should come from North America. I might disagree. But it isn't really worth our quibbling. What matters is that all these dishes are delicious – and somewhat saucy.

Yet this approach is often given scant consideration by British cooks, perhaps because soups and stews don't form a significant part of our fish-cooking heritage – Cullen skink (page 261) being a notable exception. It's about time we changed all that, because they are among the most exciting options for fish cooks. What's more, once you have embraced the simple methods advocated here, the possibilities are endless – it's no accident that there are more recipes in this chapter than any other.

The aim – as with any soup or stew – is to assemble a dish that's greater than the sum of its parts, one where a range of flavours and textures complement and support each other. Sometimes the flavours blend seamlessly together, sometimes they come in waves – sweet, then salty, then sour, then hot – with some tastes lingering longer than others.

This is as true for fish stews as it is for meat, though the means of construction and assembly may be slightly different, as we'll see. A single piece of fish might be the standout element, or a crowd of different marine species might mingle on the same plate, giving up their juices to a shared sauce. Some of these dishes can get quite busy and may seem, at first sight, a bit chaotic. But the best of them are composed from a set of well-chosen ingredients, each of which makes a distinctive contribution.

How fish behaves in a hot liquid

The alchemy of flavours in such dishes may be complex, but the way in which the fish element is cooked is straightforward. Immersing fish in a hot liquid to heat it through is a predictable, dependable method that gives the cook a high level of control – provided the speed of the heat transfer is fully appreciated. Think of boiling an egg – after just 3 minutes in boiling water, the middle of that egg is warm to hot. In the same amount of time, even a fairly thick fillet of fish (say, 2–3cm) will be hitting that 55°C mark, which (as discussed on page 112) is the critical point for the tenderisation, flaking and therefore 'doneness' of most fish.

Consider this and you'll realise that a liquid does not have to be boiling, or even simmering, for a piece of fish to cook through in it. Smaller pieces of fish can be dropped into soups and stews that are very hot but not boiling – at around 70–80°C, the kind of temperature at which you might wish to serve them. At this temperature, the fish can still be confidently expected to cook through in a few minutes. Incidentally, 70°C is a good working minimum for another reason: it is bug-killing temperature, so any microbes on the surface of the fish will be zapped after a couple of minutes.

The downside of the speed at which fish cooks in liquid is that the consequences of overcooking it in a stew, soup or sauce can be fairly dire, particularly where fragile white fish are concerned. The proteins that bind the cell structure are weak: cook fish in a liquid for too long or boil it too hard and, as the fibres separate, the fish will break up. The problem is exacerbated by boiling, because everything is in constant motion, so the fish fibres can literally drift apart. If you're not careful, you may end up with shreds and strands of overcooked, fibrous fish instead of nice curds and flakes of delicate, tender flesh.

For these reasons, cooking fish in liquid for a long time is generally a no-no, although there are, of course, exceptions. There is the lovely Japanese slow-cooked mackerel (page 286), simmered for 3 hours in order to transform its texture and impregnate the fish with all the marvellous flavours of the sauce. Why doesn't it dissolve into fish sludge? Well, if you prod and poke it at the wrong moment it probably will. But towards the end of this long, slow, gentle simmer, the mackerel flesh seems to come back together. It appears to be a characteristic of oily fish, because the same thing can be done with salmon, sardines and tuna. Tinned sardines are a good example: cooked at a high temperature inside the tin, even the bones become tender enough to eat, but the fish still hold their shape.

There are other, non-fishy sorts of seafood that are exceptions to the don't-slow-cook rule – squid and cuttlefish, for instance. Rather like liver or steak, these require either the briefest possible searing in a very hot pan or a really long, slow cook, bathed in liquid – hence the Braised squid stuffed with chorizo and rice (page 285), which needs at least 2 hours in the oven but then comes out meltingly tender – almost the texture of soft cheese. Nevertheless, such anomalies aside, brevity is generally the watchword when it comes to braising, poaching or stewing fish. Good judgement, speed of thought and decisive action are required on the part of the cook.

Building up flavours before the fish goes in

Because the fish element cooks so quickly, these dishes are robbed of the time it would take for the fish and cooking liquid to exchange flavours and marry together. So the business of building up a concoction of pleasing flavours is often undertaken in advance. For example, contrast a slow-braised shin of beef with a fish stew. In the braise, the blending of meat flavours with stock, tomatoes and herbs happens during 3 hours or more of gentle simmering. In the fish stew, you will need to complete the underlying alchemy – the mingling of liquid ingredients, vegetables, herbs and spices – before you add the fish. Your fillet of smoked pollack, or your fresh mussels, say, add the final touch to the delicious base you've already created. Our Fish (and chorizo) soup (page 260) is a good example of this: the greater part of the recipe is taken up with creating a rich, flavoursome base from onions, celery, fennel seeds, tomatoes, chorizo and fish stock (and maybe some potatoes or chickpeas if you want to make a hearty stew out of it). The fish element is added right at the end to complete the dish, giving texture and that little bit of fresh, sweet fishiness. It's not that it's an afterthought – far from it – but to get the best from fresh fish as an ingredient in a soup or stew, it's generally best to view it as the final flourish.

However, it would be misleading to suggest that most of these recipes do not see any fish at all until the end. Fish is often used early on in the proceedings to impart flavour to the brew – in the form of fish stock. Knowing how to make a good fish stock is useful – arguably essential – if you want to get the best from this chapter.

A good fish stock

Whenever you are left with a nice collection of fresh fish heads, skeletons and skins, it would be a crime to throw them away. Using them to make stock is economical (good ready-made fish stock is hard to find and never cheap) and also respectful of the fish itself. But above all, it's a great asset to your fish cooking. A fish stock on standby in your freezer means that when a bit of good fresh fish comes to hand you have access to a whole range of recipes beyond the simple fry/bake options.

Happily, good fish stock is even easier to make than good meat stock. And, in theory, every chance to buy good fresh fish is also a chance to pick up ingredients for stock. So whenever you visit the fishmonger's, it's worth asking for some fresh heads and frames – even if it's just to lay down some stock in the freezer.

A really good fish stock will bind together the elements of many of the dishes in this chapter and anchor them all with a base note of deep, savoury fresh fish flavour. Not that fish stocks need be 'fishy' in the negative sense. A good one, made with scrupulously fresh heads and frames from white fish, can be used as a base for non-fish soups, which won't taste fishy, just robust (we often make a nettle soup with fish stock, and nobody has ever guessed that it has fish in it). It goes without saying that fish stock is the liquid medium for fish risottos, too.

People often think that fish stocks are technical, the preserve of the experienced cook or even the professional chef. We know a few keen cooks who would never pass up the chance to make a chicken stock from the carcass of a roast bird, yet who remain hesitant about taking the plunge with a few fresh fish frames. It really shouldn't be like that. Fish stocks are easy – though you do, of course, need to understand what you're doing with your ingredients.

The key point is that a fish stock requires much less cooking time than a meat one. Because of the structure of the flesh and the fish's delicate bones, you can extract all the flavour and goodness in half an hour or so of gentle simmering. Vegetables used for flavouring should be chopped fairly finely or even shredded or grated, so they give up their flavour in a similarly short time. With chopped fish frames and shredded vegetables, plus a few fragrant herbs, a gentle sub-simmer is all that's required to turn tap water into great stock.

Overcooking fish stock, or boiling it too hard, will not only fail to extract further good flavours, it may start to generate some bad ones. A chalky flavour will arise as calcium salts in the bones start to dissolve into the stock. Next comes a strange, ammoniac taint – the sort of thing you'd associate with fish that's off – even if you're using spankingly fresh ingredients. Shellfish stock is the same: boil too long or too hard and, though it may still taste okay, you'll catch an offputting waft of ammonia. Bear all this in mind, and the simple recipe for fish stock on page 256 will stand you in good stead.

Simple poaching and court-bouillons

Not all poached fish is cooked in the liquid in which it will be served. It is sometimes better for whole fish and fish portions to be immersed in a relatively unseasoned liquid, such as lightly salted water or milk. A sauce to serve with such a simply poached fish – a salsa verde, perhaps, or a classic hollandaise – might be prepared separately, and bear no direct relation to the cooked fish until the two meet on the plate. There's nothing wrong with that. It's how fish is cooked and sauced in many respectable restaurants, but we think it's something of a missed opportunity.

Flavour your cooking liquor with a few herbs and vegetables, maybe a splash of wine, and not only will you enhance the flavour of the fish being cooked in it, you'll also be effectively making a fish stock as you go. This can then be strained and reduced to concentrate the flavours – enriched with cream or a bit of butter, and spiked with some fresh chopped herbs (chives or chervil are the most useful), so that you have a sauce. Or you can simply strain and freeze the cooking liquid and keep it as standby fish stock.

This kind of flavoured cooking liquid is called a court-bouillon – meaning 'briefly boiled'. The name refers to the fact that the flavouring ingredients and liquid (water and sometimes wine) are usually boiled for 10 minutes or so before the fish goes in to begin the exchange of flavours. It's the classic liquid medium for poaching a whole fish in a fish kettle. Sometimes, adding the fish to the liquid, taking it off the heat and placing a lid on it is all that's required to cook the fish through. Many whole fish respond well to this type of poaching, including sea bass, sea trout and salmon; see page 281 for our recipe.

A court-bouillon based on fish stock rather than plain water and wine is called, in the language of classic French gastronomy, a *fumet* – it will be even more intensely flavoured and will always lend itself to reduction for a sauce.

The fish kettle

If you are poaching a fairly large whole fish, weighing between 1.5kg and 5kg, you'll certainly need a fish kettle – an essential big gun in your fish cookery armoury. You can use it for cooking two, three or more smaller fish, or even a load of fish fillets, too.

The light stainless steel ones you can get in most decent kitchen shops are fine and relatively inexpensive, but it may be worth spending a little more on something fairly robust. Some cheap ones are simply too short, and won't accommodate a really good size fish unless you cut off its head or tail – which rather spoils the whole experience. Furthermore, they won't stretch properly across two rings on the hob, which is surely the entire point of the design. If you're shopping around, you'll generally find the choice is between a 45cm kettle and a 60cm one. Go for the larger one every time.

As well as poaching a fish in a kettle, you can also steam it. For either method, the fish sits on a trivet, or removable rack: for steaming it is suspended above the simmering water; for poaching it is fully immersed in a simmering, or very hot, court-bouillon (see above).

If you are poaching, the fish will continue to cook in the hot court-bouillon, provided you keep the lid on, even after you turn the heat off beneath it. And this, indeed, is the best way to poach a fish: lower it into the very hot (but not quite boiling) court-bouillon, bring it back up to a simmer, put the lid on, then turn the heat off. Leave the fish to cook through for 15–40 minutes, depending on its size (see page 281 for more details).

Incidentally, you can also use a fish kettle outdoors, on a barbecue or open fire. You'll just need a bit of careful fire management – arranging the hot embers in a lengthways configuration – to get an even heat through the length of the kettle.

Steam-braising

This is not a term widely known to chefs, at least none outside our acquaintance. We think we made it up, but it's based on a method we picked up from Hugh's French mother-in-law. It involves cooking fish – usually boneless fillets or chunky medallions of meaty white fish such as ling, brill or turbot – in a covered pan with a little oil or butter and a splash of water or wine, plus a few herbs and spices (see the recipes on page 289). Some versions use quite a few flavourings, but it also works well with just a bay leaf and a scrap of garlic.

We call it steam-braising for want of a better term, since it sits somewhere between those two methods. It's a lovely way to cook fish quickly and simply, and it's pretty much foolproof. The fish doesn't stick to the pan, stays beautifully moist and can – should – be served up with the spoonful or two of the juices that accumulate in the pan as it cooks. If you want to transform them into a scant but lovely sauce, you can whisk in a little butter, a teaspoon or two of cream and a few chopped fresh herbs.

Further improvisation

No recipe is ever set in stone, but the ones in this chapter are particularly open to adaptation and improvisation. And so they should be, given that you never know what the catch of the day (or the freshest fish on the slab) might be.

Once you have an understanding of the gentle touch needed to make a good base liquor for a fish soup or stew, and the similar restraint required when cooking fish in it, you have all you need to get the most from these recipes.

If you do go your own way with some of these recipes – and we hope you will – please spare a thought for your guests. You can make a lovely big chowder with whole unfilleted fish in it, which will look spectacular, but people will then have to fish them out and effectively fillet their own dinner before they can eat it. You might see this as part of the fun – but fellow diners may struggle to share that view. It really depends on how formal or informal the meal is, and how well you know your guests. We reckon it's generally best to do the hard work for them...

In which case, take the fillets off the fish before you start cooking, and use the bones and heads to make your stock. You can then add other ingredients to the stockpot – vegetables, herbs, spices, even meat and pulses – which might contribute enough structure to make a stew rather than a broth. For example, if you just throw in a little sieved, roasted tomato and a few herbs before adding the fish, you've got a lovely, soupy starter. But build up the dish with onions, fennel or shredded greens, potatoes, maybe chickpeas or white beans, perhaps pasta, and you'll create a warming, filling main-course dish. And if it can be relished to the last drop of liquor in the bottom of the bowl, then so much the better. What you choose to call your concoction – a bisque, bourride, braise, broth, chowder, curry, mouclade, nage, soup or stew – is, as we said a while back, entirely up to you.

Fish stock *makes about 1.5 litres*

This is our basic fish stock, a light, well-flavoured broth that we use as a base for all manner of soups, plus sauces and risottos. It's particularly good in 'green' soups – watercress, nettle or parsley, for example – even if no fish is being added to the soup.

Follow the general advice on preparing fish stock on pages 252–3. Get into the habit of freezing all your white fish trimmings and you can soon build up a good stash for making stock. You can use all of the fish frame: bones, skin, head, tail – anything that's not guts or gills. Not only is this good, thrifty cooking but making your own stock also gives you control over its flavour. Indeed, this recipe is only a guide. The more fish bits you pack into the pot, for instance, the more intense your stock will be. You can vary the vegetables too: trimmings of fennel bulbs, celeriac and shallots are all good candidates for inclusion.

The golden rule: *all* the fish trimmings must be scrupulously fresh (or fresh when they were frozen). A fish that only just passes the sniff test (see page 45) might have fillets that are just about worthy of the frying pan, but its bones will not be worthy of the stockpot.

2kg white fish trimmings, including at least 4 good heads	2 carrots, chopped
4 celery sticks, roughly chopped	2 bay leaves
2 garlic cloves, bruised but not peeled	5 thyme stalks
2 onions, peeled and halved	A handful of parsley stalks
	½ teaspoon black or white peppercorns

Rinse the fish trimmings in cold water and put them in a large stockpot with all the other ingredients. Pack them in fairly well and add just enough cold water to cover everything. Bring up to a very gentle simmer. Skim off any scum that rises to the surface, then cover the pan and simmer for half an hour, taking care that the stock doesn't boil fast at any point. A gentle, popping simmer is all that is necessary – overcooking or boiling can make the stock cloudy and chalky tasting.

Let the stock cool slightly before straining it into a container. You can use it straight away, or refrigerate it for up to 2 days, or freeze it.

Shellfish stock

A stock made with the shells of crabs, lobsters, prawns or any of their kin makes a particularly rich and delicious base for soups and stews. You can get quite cheffy about it, using uncooked shells chosen specially for the purpose, sautéing them, then adding a splash of brandy and flambéing the whole thing before you add the water and aromatics. The result is an incredibly rich and intense broth, and well worth the effort.

However, a simpler version, employing the trimmings from shellfish that have already been used in other recipes, is perhaps more useful and practical for the lay cook. What's more, it's a great way to use up those thin back legs of a crab, lobster or langoustine. Though they contain flavoursome meat, these can be the very devil to crack open and deal with. But crush them and cook them in the stockpot and you can feel satisfied that you're wasting nothing. In fact, where large edible crabs are concerned, these little meaty morsels, along with the finer parts of the body shell, are preferable to big, thick chunks of carapace and claw. Not only are these very hard and therefore difficult to break up, but they can make your stock taste chalky.

Replace the white fish trimmings in the fish stock recipe opposite with mixed crustacean shells, legs and heads (excluding the main carapaces and large claws of big crabs) from any prawns, lobsters or crabs that you have already cooked and picked – you can always stockpile such leftovers in the freezer until you have enough to make a good stock. Including the shells and heads of some prawns or langoustines will make for a richer, better-balanced stock than crab trimmings alone.

You really need a good kilo of such trimmings to make a decent stock, but you can always supplement, say, half a kilo of shellfish trimmings with some frames and heads of fresh white fish.

Crush the shells with a rolling pin or meat mallet so they can release their flavour. If you like, you can sauté the shells in a little butter and oil for 2–3 minutes to create an extra layer of flavour, before adding the other ingredients, but it's not essential. Either way, add the stock vegetables, herbs and water and cook as per the fish stock recipe, making sure you don't go over the 30-minute mark. You can then simply strain the stock through a large sieve, pressing the shells hard with a ladle to extract as much juice as possible, or blitz the whole lot in a heavy-duty blender before straining.

A shellfish stock, or a mixed shellfish and fish stock, makes a particularly good base for any fish soup, stew, risotto or chowder to which other shellfish or crustaceans are going to be added.

Nettle soup with smoked fish *serves 6*

A soup made with the bright green tips of early spring nettles is a delicious and velvety affair. We've discovered that it's very successful when made with fish stock, which seems to enhance the nettle flavour without making the soup taste fishy. Add a generous sprinkling of smoked fish to finish it and you have a substantial dish.

Half a carrier bag full of nettles – tops or
   young leaves only
50g unsalted butter
1 large or 2 medium onions, finely sliced
1 small head of celeriac, peeled and cut
   into cubes
1 large garlic clove, crushed

1 litre fish stock (see page 256)
300g smoked pollack or haddock fillet
3 tablespoons cooked rice, or 3 rice cakes
2 tablespoons thick cream or crème
   fraîche, plus extra to serve
Salt and freshly ground black pepper

Wash the nettles thoroughly, checking them for unwanted extras – vegetable or animal – and discarding any tough stalks.

Melt the butter in a large pan over a low heat. Add the onion, celeriac and garlic, cover the pan and sweat gently, stirring occasionally, for 8–10 minutes, until softened but not brown.

Meanwhile, pour the stock into a separate pan and bring it to a simmer. Add the smoked fish and poach gently until cooked – no longer than 5 minutes, just until the flesh flakes easily. Scoop out the fish with a slotted spoon and keep warm. Pour the hot stock over the softened vegetables in the pan and simmer for 5 minutes or so, until the celeriac is almost tender. Pile in the nettles. Return to the boil, reduce the heat and simmer for 2–3 minutes, until the nettles are wilted and tender. Season with salt and pepper.

To keep the colour nice and bright, you'll need to purée the soup immediately – in batches if necessary. Tip it into a blender, add the rice or rice cakes and whiz to a purée. Pour into a clean pan, stir in the cream and reheat but do not let it boil. Check the seasoning.

Ladle the soup into warmed bowls. Flake the fish flesh from the skin, discarding any pin bones. Heap some flakes of hot smoked fish in the middle of each bowlful and finish with a swirl of cream.

Fish (and chorizo) soup *serves 5–6*

This soup has become a classic at River Cottage. We make it with all sorts of fish, from black bream to pouting. Many things can be added but the three basic ingredients are always the same: fillets of very fresh fish, sometimes lightly salted, roast tomato sauce and fish stock. You can make it a bit more 'deluxe' by adding squid and/or various shellfish. Usually, but not always, we add some of our homemade chorizo for an extra kick of spice and texture. And you can turn it from a starter soup to a main-course stew by adding potatoes, chickpeas or shredded greens, as suggested below.

The tomato sauce is an old favourite of ours, and very versatile. It's a brilliant way to deal with a glut of tomatoes, if you have one, as it freezes beautifully.

4 small, hot chorizo sausages, about
   250g in total, sliced on the diagonal
   (optional), or a little olive oil
2 garlic cloves, sliced
2 onions, sliced
2 celery sticks, finely chopped
A pinch of fennel seeds
200ml white wine
500ml fish or shellfish stock (see pages
   256–7)
500g lightly salted white fish fillets (see
   page 124), such as pouting, whiting or
   pollack (or unsalted bream or sea bass)
1 tablespoon finely chopped parsley
   (optional)

FOR THE ROASTED TOMATO SAUCE:
1kg ripe, full-flavoured tomatoes, halved
2–3 garlic cloves, finely chopped
2 tablespoons olive oil

OPTIONAL 'LUXURY' EXTRAS:
Up to 200g small-medium squid or
   cuttlefish, cleaned and 'butterflied'
   (see pages 97–102)
1–2 scallops per person, shelled, cleaned
   and sliced in half (see page 104–7)
½ dozen mussels per person, steamed
   open in a little wine (see page 262)

OPTIONAL 'BULKING' EXTRAS:
Up to 750g potatoes, peeled and cut into
   chunky cubes
Up to 500g pre-cooked or tinned (rinsed)
   chickpeas
Up to 250g spinach, Swiss chard or other
   greens, finely shredded

First make the tomato sauce. Arrange the tomato halves in an ovenproof dish so they sit snugly side by side, rather than on top of each other. Mix the garlic and oil together and trickle them over the tomatoes. Season lightly, then roast in an oven preheated to 180°C/Gas Mark 4 for 35–45 minutes, until the tomatoes are soft, pulpy and slightly browned. Rub them through a sieve, discarding the pips and skin, and set aside.

Put the chorizo (if using) in a large, heavy saucepan and fry over a medium heat until lightly coloured. Otherwise heat a little olive oil in the pan. Add the garlic, onions, celery and fennel seeds. If using potatoes, add them at this stage. Fry gently for 10 minutes, to soften the vegetables without browning them, then pour in the wine and simmer until reduced by half.

Add 250ml of the tomato sauce (you might have a little more than this, but any extra will keep well in the fridge) and the stock, plus the chickpeas if you are using them, then bring to a simmer and cook, covered, for 20 minutes.

Meanwhile, skin the fish fillets (see page 73) and remove any pin bones by slicing down either side of the bone line. Cut the fish into fairly large chunks – small pouting or whiting fillets can be used whole.

When the tomato soup base has had its 20 minutes, add the fish, together with the squid or cuttlefish and scallops if using. Cook briefly in the gently simmering soup for 2–3 minutes, adding any mussels and shredded greens after a minute.

Season the soup with pepper, adding salt only if necessary (with chorizo, you really shouldn't need it). Ladle into warmed bowls, garnish with chopped parsley if you like, and serve with crusty bread.

Cullen skink *serves 4–5 as a starter, 2–3 as a hearty supper*

This is our version of a classic Scottish soup. We're not sure how it would go down in Cullen, the small village in the northeast of Scotland where the recipe originated, but we hope they'd find it passable.

Onions have always been a traditional part of this soup but our recipe uses more of them than is usual. We find cooking them down to a rich, sweet mass gives the soup a really wonderful depth of flavour.

50g unsalted butter

50ml olive oil

About 1kg onions, finely sliced

500g smoked pollack or other cold-
  smoked white fish

500ml whole milk

750ml fish stock (see page 256)

500g white potatoes, peeled and cubed

Salt and freshly ground black pepper

Heat the butter and oil in a large saucepan until the butter begins to foam. Add the onions and cook for 45–60 minutes, stirring regularly, until golden and buttery-soft. Don't let them catch on the pan.

Put the smoked fish fillet in a pan and pour over the milk. Cover the pan and bring to a gentle simmer. By the time the milk is simmering, the fish should be perfectly cooked and you should be able to remove it straight away. However, if you've got a particularly thick fillet from a monster fish, it might need to be left in the hot milk for a minute or two to finish cooking. Remove it when it's done.

Add the poaching milk, fish stock and potatoes to the onions, bring to a simmer and cook until the potatoes are tender. To thicken the soup slightly, crush some of the potatoes against the side of the pan with a wooden spoon and stir them back in.

Flake the pollack from its skin, discarding any bones. Add the fish to the soup, bring back to a gentle simmer and season to taste. Ladle into warmed bowls and serve with some good bread.

Smoked pollack and mussel chowder *serves 6*

Chowders can vary enormously, from tomato-based broths to flour-thickened, milky stews, but all should be soothing, rich and comforting. We favour the classic, creamy, New England-style chowder, based on potatoes – and the principle of balancing the sweetness of shellfish (mussels here, cockles in the recipe on page 264) with something salty (smoked pollack here, bacon there).

We've also specified different types of potato – the floury ones used in this recipe will crumble a little and help to thicken the soup, while the waxy ones called for overleaf will hold their shape much more and give a different, but just as delicious, texture. You can, of course, adapt either of these recipes, or mix and match between them. Cockles and mussels will work equally well in either, and the choice of potato is really up to you, too.

Also works with:
• Clams
• Cockles

1kg mussels, scrubbed and debearded (see page 103)

½ glass of white wine

1 tablespoon olive oil

2 leeks, white part only, quartered lengthways and thinly sliced

1 onion, finely diced

2 garlic cloves, finely chopped

30g unsalted butter

750ml fish or shellfish stock (see pages 256–7)

300g smoked pollack or haddock fillet

250g floury potatoes, such as King Edward, peeled and cut into 5mm dice

200ml double cream

A small handful of parsley, finely chopped

A small bunch of chives, finely chopped

Salt and freshly ground black pepper

Prepare the mussels first: heat a pan large enough to hold them all comfortably, add the wine and, when it's bubbling, tip the mussels in. Shake the pan well and cover. Steam the mussels over a medium-high heat for 3–4 minutes, until the shells are open. Remove them from the pan using a slotted spoon and discard any that haven't opened. Strain the cooking liquor through a fine sieve, or a coarse sieve lined with a clean tea towel, and reserve. Remove two-thirds of the mussels from their shells and set aside. Save the remainder for serving.

Place a large, heavy-based pan over a medium-high heat and add the olive oil, followed by the leeks, onion, garlic and butter. Reduce the heat and let the vegetables soften gently for 5 minutes. Pour in the stock and the mussel cooking liquid and bring to a gentle simmer.

Carefully lower the smoked fish into the pan. Poach for 4 minutes or until just cooked, then remove with a large fish slice. Add the potatoes to the simmering soup and cook until tender. Meanwhile, flake the fish off the skin, removing any bones you find along the way.

Add the cream to the soup, followed by the shelled mussels and the flaked smoked pollack. Stir gently, season with salt and pepper and add the chopped parsley and chives. Simmer gently for just a minute or two to reheat the fish – no more, or the potato will completely disintegrate.

Divide the shell-on mussels between warmed bowls and ladle over the hot chowder. Serve piping hot, with toasted sourdough bread.

Smoked pollack and sweetcorn chowder

If mussels are not to hand, you can make a really lovely smoked haddock chowder without them, using fresh sweetcorn kernels to complement the salty fish. Follow the recipe opposite, omitting the mussels. Slice the kernels from 2 corn cobs and add them to the soup just before the potatoes are cooked. Let them simmer for a couple of minutes before finishing the soup with the smoked fish and herbs.

Kipper, potato and spinach soup *serves 8*

This is simplicity itself, a kind of pared-down alternative to the more elaborate chowder opposite, but with the same soothing quality.

200g spinach, coarse stalks removed

1.5 litres fish stock (see page 256)
  or vegetable stock

250g kipper fillets

50g unsalted butter

1 onion, chopped

1 leek, white part only, finely sliced

1 large garlic clove, sliced

250g potatoes, peeled and diced

100ml double cream, plus extra to serve

Salt and freshly ground black pepper

Chopped chives, to finish

Also works with:
• Smoked pollack
• Smoked haddock

Bring a large pan of water to the boil, drop in the spinach and cook for 1 minute. Drain and allow it to cool a little. Squeeze all the excess liquid out of the spinach with your hands, then chop it finely and set aside.

Bring the stock to a gentle simmer in a large pan. Add the kipper fillets and poach for about 4 minutes, until the fish flakes easily. Take care not to overcook it. Remove the fish from the stock and flake the flesh away from the skin into a bowl, checking for bones as you go. Take your time over this, as kippers do have lots of little bones.

Melt the butter in a large pan over a medium-low heat. Add the onion, leek and garlic and sweat gently until soft. Add the fishy vegetable stock to the pan, along with the potatoes, bring to a simmer and cook for 20–30 minutes, until the potatoes are tender.

Purée the soup in a blender until smooth. Return to the pan and reheat gently. Add the flaked kipper flesh, spinach and cream and season well. Let the soup simmer very gently for 5 minutes, then divide between warmed bowls. Serve garnished with another swirl of cream and some chopped chives.

Cockle or palourde chowder *serves 4*

Like the recipes on the preceding pages, this chowder uses stock as the main cooking medium rather than the more traditional milk, but is finished off with a slosh of cream. The sweet shellfish component takes the form of cockles or palourdes (a nod to the classic clam chowders of New England) and the salty element is provided by the bacon.

Also works with:
• Other small clams
• Mussels
• Razor clams

1 tablespoon olive oil
2 knobs of unsalted butter
150g smoked bacon or pancetta, cut into
  small cubes or lardons
1 large leek, white part only, quartered
  lengthways and thinly sliced
1 onion, diced
2 small garlic cloves, finely chopped
1 large, waxy potato, such as Cara, peeled
  and cut into 5mm cubes

750ml fish or shellfish stock
  (see pages 256–7)
1kg cockles, palourdes or other small
  clams, purged if necessary (see page
  103)
A glass of white wine
50ml double cream
Salt and freshly ground black pepper

Heat a heavy-based pan over a medium heat and add the olive oil and a knob of butter. When the butter is foaming, add the bacon and sauté until it starts to release some of its fat. Add the leek, onion and garlic, then cover and sweat gently for around 5 minutes, without letting the vegetables colour. Add the potato and sweat for 5 minutes more, then pour in the stock and bring to a gentle simmer. Cook, covered, for about 10 minutes, until the potato is soft – keep an eye on it, though, as you don't want it to disintegrate completely.

Meanwhile, scrub the cockles or clams under cold water, discarding any that are damaged or open. Put a large, wide pan over a high heat and add the wine, a glass of water and a knob of butter. Bring to the boil and add the cockles or clams. Cover at once with the lid, shake or stir after a minute or so, and cover again. Cook for 2–4 minutes, until the shellfish are open (discard any that remain firmly closed), then tip the contents of the pan into a colander set over a bowl to catch the juices. Set aside a few cockles or clams and pick the remainder from their shells.

Strain the juices through a fine sieve, or a coarse sieve lined with a cotton cloth, and add them to the chowder, along with the shelled cockles/clams. Stir in the cream, season to taste and reheat gently if necessary. Serve piping hot, garnished with the shell-on cockles or clams and accompanied by some bread.

Crustacean soup *serves 6*

This is an old favourite, which deserves to be included because it is so good. It's an endlessly flexible recipe – more of a guide, in fact, which you should use to your own ends, depending on what shellfish you have to hand. You can use just about any species of crab, though we favour velvet crabs for their sweet flavour.

1 large or 2 medium brown crabs or
    spider crabs
About 8 blue velvet swimmer crabs
    (optional)
About 6 large Dublin Bay prawns, or
    125g ordinary prawns
1 whole white fish, such as a gurnard or
    wrasse, gutted and skinned (optional)
2 tablespoons olive oil
1 onion, chopped
1 carrot, chopped
2–3 large tomatoes, chopped (or 250g
    cherry tomatoes)
4 garlic cloves, crushed
A few sprigs each of fennel, chervil and
    parsley, as available
2–3 bay leaves

A few parsley stalks or leek tops (optional)
A pinch of cayenne pepper
Salt and freshly ground black pepper
Croûtons and grated Gruyère cheese,
    to serve

FOR THE CHEATY ROUILLE:
1 garlic clove, peeled
1 hot red chilli, very finely chopped
¼ teaspoon coarse salt
1 teaspoon Dijon mustard
1 egg yolk
100ml olive oil
150ml groundnut oil
A squeeze of lemon juice
Freshly ground black pepper

Make the rouille in advance to allow the flavour to develop. Crush the garlic, chilli and salt to a paste with a pestle and mortar, then transfer to a bowl. Stir in the mustard, then the egg yolk. Combine the two oils in a jug and trickle them on to the yolk mixture as thinly as possible, whisking all the time with a balloon whisk, to create an emulsion. Once the mixture has thickened, you can add the oils a little more quickly. You should end up with a thick, wobbly mayonnaise. Taste and add lemon juice, pepper and more salt if necessary. Chill until needed.

Kill and cook all the crabs as described on page 89. Cook the prawns as described on page 96. Leave everything until cool enough to handle. Now break open the crabs and discard the dead men's fingers and stomachs, then remove as much brown meat as you can from the carapaces and all the white meat from the larger claws (see pages 90–3). Set the meat aside. Peel the prawns (Dublin Bay or otherwise) and set them aside, separately from the crabmeat. Cut the fish into chunks, if including.

Discard the main carapaces of the brown crabs. Put all the other heads, legs and shells of the crabs and prawns in a large bowl or heavy saucepan and pound them to pieces with a hammer or rolling pin.

Heat the olive oil in a large pan. Add the onion, carrot, tomatoes, garlic and herbs and fry gently for a few minutes to soften. Add the hammered shellfish, and the fish if using. Pour over enough water just to cover everything and bring to the boil. Simmer gently for 20 minutes (no more), then take off the heat.

This shellfish stock can then be processed in a number of ways. Either strain it through a heavy-duty conical sieve, pressing hard with the back of a ladle to extract as much fishy juice as possible; or, put everything in a heavy-duty blender, whiz it up and then pass through the sieve; or, if you are feeling strong, you could press the stock through a heavy-duty mouli-légumes or potato ricer.

Put the stock back in a clean pan over a low heat and stir in all the white and brown meat you saved from the crabs. Heat through but do not let it boil. Season to taste with salt, pepper and cayenne, then divide between warmed bowls. Add the prawns and serve with croûtons, grated Gruyère and the rouille.

Thai crab and fish soup   *serves 4*

Here's an adaptable fish soup/stew. It begins life as a luscious crab soup but is easily adapted to take the fish and shellfish you have to hand. The idea is to create a creamy soup with just the right balance of salty, sweet, sour and hot flavours before adding the fish right at the end.

The crabmeat is literally a last-minute addition. The same would be true of just-steamed-open mussels or cockles. Raw additions, such as squid or white fish, will need a couple of minutes' simmering to cook them through.

1 tablespoon sunflower oil

1 onion, finely chopped

50g nugget of fresh ginger, cut into fine matchsticks or coarsely grated

3 fat garlic cloves, finely chopped

1 small, hot red chilli, deseeded and finely chopped

2 lemongrass stalks, tough outer layers removed, finely sliced

400ml well-flavoured fish or shellfish stock (see pages 256–7)

400ml tin of coconut milk

A dash or two of soy sauce

A dash of Thai fish sauce (optional)

Juice of 1–2 limes, plus lime wedges to serve

1 heaped tablespoon chopped coriander

FOR THE FISH:

Brown and white meat from 1 large brown crab (about 300–400g meat in total)

And/or 300–400g in total of raw prawns, squid rings, scallops, chunks of white fish fillet

And/or a dozen mussels or cockles, steamed open in a little water or wine (see page 262)

Heat the oil in a large saucepan over a medium heat. Add the onion, ginger, garlic, chilli and lemongrass and sweat gently, stirring from time to time, until the onion is soft and golden. Add the stock, bring to a simmer and cook gently for 10 minutes, allowing the stock to infuse with the lemongrass and garlic. Add the coconut milk, stir well and bring back to a simmer.

If you're adding any raw fish or shellfish, put it in now and cook at a gentle simmer for 2–3 minutes, until it's just done. Then add the crab, and the cooked mussels or cockles if using, and heat through gently for just 30 seconds or so. Taste the soup and season with the soy, fish sauce (if using) and lime juice. Serve straight away, scattered with the coriander and accompanied by lime wedges.

Leek, celeriac and oyster broth *serves 6*

This delicate broth is a great way to serve celeriac and oysters together – a pair that get on so well but meet so rarely. Well-flavoured fish stock is essential, so make some in advance. It's also important to cut the vegetables into small, neat, evenly sized pieces.

50g unsalted butter

1 tablespoon olive oil

About 400g celeriac, peeled and cut into
small dice (like square petits pois)

1 small potato (about 100g), peeled and
cut into small dice

2 tender inner sticks of celery, peeled and
cut into small dice

1 large leek, white part only, quartered
lengthways and finely sliced

1 small onion, finely diced

2 garlic cloves, very finely chopped

750ml fish or shellfish stock (see
pages 256–7)

½ glass of white wine

18 fresh oysters

100ml double cream

Salt and freshly ground black pepper

Set a large saucepan over a medium heat and add the butter and olive oil. When the butter is foaming, stir in all the chopped vegetables and garlic. Cook gently for 5–10 minutes, until softened but not coloured. Add the stock and white wine and bring to a gentle simmer. Cover and cook for 20–25 minutes, stirring once or twice, until all the vegetables are tender.

Meanwhile, place a large pan over a high heat and add half a glass of water. When it's boiling, place 6 oysters in the pan. Cover and allow them to steam for 2 minutes. This will open the shells and allow you to remove the meat: you will still need to shuck them (see page 104), but it will be a much easier task. Repeat with the remaining oysters. Each oyster will have a little juice in its shell – make sure you don't spill this.

Finish the broth by stirring in the cream and the juice from the oysters and seasoning to taste. Divide the warm poached oysters between warmed bowls and ladle over the hot broth, making sure each person gets a fair share of vegetables along with the liquor.

Ad hoc fish curry *serves 6*

As you can imagine, much of our travel is fish-related, and in warmer climes we have, between us, probably encountered dozens of versions of the fish curry. The recipes vary hugely, of course, but if they have one thing in common it is that they are versatile, accommodating whatever comes to hand from the day's catch.

This curry originates, vaguely, from a trip to the Seychelles, where it might be put together from any number of different fish and shellfish, including bonito, snapper, grouper, jobfish, needlefish, crab, squid and octopus. It can just as well be put together from an apparently motley collection of British fish, from a day's angling or a trip to the fishmonger's. The tip is to include some large-headed, firm-fleshed bony fish, such as gurnard, bream or even wrasse, and to use oily fish such as mackerel sparingly. White fish such as pollack are more than welcome to make up the numbers, but don't use only them.

Also works with:
- Pouting
- Pollack
- Whiting
- Coley
- Grey mullet
- John Dory
- Gurnard
- Black bream
- Dogfish
- Garfish
- Mackerel

About 2kg mixed whole fish, descaled and gutted
500g prepared scallops (see pages 105–7), or cleaned squid (see pages 97–100) or cuttlefish (see pages 101–2), or a mixture
Stock flavouring veg, such as 2 onions, 2 carrots, 2 celery sticks, ½ fennel bulb
A few parsley stalks
A couple of bay leaves
3 tablespoons vegetable oil
1 large onion, finely chopped
2–3 large garlic cloves, finely chopped

A walnut-sized piece of fresh ginger, finely chopped or grated
3–4 tablespoons medium-hot curry paste or powder
400ml tin of coconut milk
500g floury potatoes, peeled and cut into forkable chunks
Cayenne pepper
Juice of 2 limes (or lemons)
Salt and freshly ground black pepper
Fresh coriander leaves and lime wedges, to serve (optional)

Fillet the fish (see pages 63–7) and set aside with the prepared shellfish. Chop up the fish skeletons and place them in a large pan with the heads. Roughly chop the stock vegetables, add to the pan with the parsley and bay, then cover with water. Bring to the boil, skim, then reduce the heat and simmer for 30 minutes. Leave this stock to cool and infuse, then strain and set aside.

Heat the oil in a large, clean pan and gently fry the onion, garlic and ginger for a few minutes. Add your trusted blend of curry paste or powder in a quantity that conservatively reflects the amount of heat you like. Fry for a few minutes, then stir in about a litre of the fish stock, plus the coconut milk and a good pinch of salt. Add the potatoes, bring to the boil and simmer gently for 20–30 minutes, until the potatoes begin to break up and thicken the sauce a little. Taste the sauce and adjust the seasoning, including the heat level, using cayenne pepper.

Slice any larger fish fillets into thick strips or chunks and add to the gently simmering sauce, along with the scallops, squid or cuttlefish and any other fresh seafood you want to include. Simmer for only 3–5 minutes, so the fish is just cooked through, then stir in the lime juice to taste.

Serve at once, in bowls rather than plates, as this is practically a soup. If you like, sprinkle over fresh chopped coriander and squeeze over a little extra lime. Serve with plain boiled rice, spooned into the bowls at the end to mop up the sauce.

Juan's limpet stew *serves 4*

We met Juan Salado, a marine biologist who works for the Alderney Wildlife Trust, during a Channel Islands fishing trip, when he took us foraging on the stretch of beach known as Clonque Bay. It was a great opportunity for us to learn from an expert, as what he doesn't know about seaweed, shellfish and rock pools could be written on a limpet's winkle. Juan cooked this Spanish dish on the beach, with limpets freshly prised off the rocks, and it was utterly delicious. The limpets are chewy, but pleasant nonetheless, and the stew liquor is fantastic.

2 tablespoons olive oil
2 garlic cloves, finely chopped
2 large onions, finely chopped
1 large green pepper, deseeded and
　chopped
200g cooking chorizo sausage, coarsely
　chopped

1kg tomatoes, peeled, deseeded and
　roughly chopped (or two 400g tins of
　chopped tomatoes)
½ glass of white wine
4 dozen medium-large limpets in their
　shells, scrubbed well and purged (see
　page 108)
Salt and freshly ground black pepper

Heat the olive oil in a large, heavy-based pan, add the garlic and onions and sweat gently for 10 minutes or so. Add the green pepper and chorizo and cook for a few more minutes. Add the tomatoes and wine and bring to a simmer. Let the stew bubble away gently for about half an hour, stirring from time to time, so it reduces and thickens and the pepper softens.

Add the limpets and stir them into the stew. Keep the whole thing simmering, stirring now and then, for about 2 minutes, until the limpets start to come free of their shells. You now need to pick the limpets out with your fingers or a fork and then toss them back into the stew, along with any juices, discarding the shells. Give the stew a final stir, season to taste, then ladle it into warmed dishes and serve with chunks of bread for dipping.

Moules frites *serves 2*

Although this is quite a quick dish to make, it does require a little organisation, as the chips and mussels both need to be cooked at around the same time. It's also easier to cook in fairly small quantities, so this is a perfect two-person project, both in the cooking and the eating.

As with all the best chips, the *frites* are fried twice – once to cook the potato through, then again at a higher temperature to create the deliciously crisp, golden exterior every *frite* lover hankers after.

Also works with:
• Cockles
• Palourdes

1 tablespoon olive oil

A good knob of unsalted butter

1 garlic clove, finely chopped

4 small shallots, finely chopped

1kg mussels, scrubbed and debearded
   (see page 103)

½ glass of white wine

2 teaspoons double cream

1 tablespoon finely chopped parsley

Salt and freshly ground black pepper

FOR THE FRITES:

2 large, floury potatoes, such as
   Maris Piper, Désirée or King Edward

2 litres groundnut oil

Fine sea salt

Start with the *frites*. Peel the potatoes and cut them into matchsticks, about 5mm thick. Wash them in cold water to remove excess starch, then drain and blot dry with a clean tea towel.

Pour the groundnut oil into a deep-fat fryer or a deep saucepan and heat it to 130°C. Put the chips in the frying basket and lower it into the oil. Cook for 7–8 minutes, or until soft all the way through but not coloured. Remove the chips and drain on kitchen paper. If you wish, you can leave them at this stage and keep in the fridge for up to a day before their second frying. If you want to serve them straight away, increase the temperature of the oil to 190°C. Lower the chips in again and cook for 1–2 minutes, until light golden brown. Drain them again on kitchen paper to absorb any excess oil, then toss them in a little fine sea salt and put into a large bowl.

For the mussels, heat the olive oil and butter in a deep, wide pan over a medium heat. Add the garlic and shallots and cook for a few minutes, until softened. Add the mussels, increase the heat and add the wine and some salt and pepper. Cook, covered, for 3–4 minutes, shaking the pan a couple of times. Once all the mussels are open (discard any that remain steadfastly shut), stir in the cream and parsley and serve, juices and all, with your *frites*.

West Country cider mussels

serves 4 as a starter, 2 as a feast

Most ways of cooking mussels are variations of the recipe on page 272: steaming them open in a flavoured liquor, which becomes their sauce. And, of course, you don't have to serve them with chips – a hunk of bread, some pasta or rice can all be used to make a meal of them, or they can be served with just their broth, as a starter. This is our own locally inspired take on the classic *moules marinière*, using leeks, thyme and cider.

50g unsalted butter

1 or 2 leeks, white part only, finely shredded, or 1 onion, finely sliced

2 garlic cloves, finely sliced

1 teaspoon thyme leaves

1½ teaspoons cider vinegar (optional)

½ glass of real cider (medium is best; or use dry plus a splash of apple juice)

1kg mussels, scrubbed and debearded (see page 103)

2 tablespoons double cream (optional)

Sea salt and freshly ground black pepper

Also works with:
• Cockles
• Palourdes

Heat the butter in a deep, wide pan over a medium heat and add the leek or onion, plus the garlic. Cover and sweat for about 5 minutes, stirring occasionally, until soft but not coloured. Raise the heat and throw in the thyme. When its scent hits you, add the cider vinegar, if using, and cider, then the mussels and some salt and pepper. Give them a quick stir and a shake, then cook, covered, for 3–4 minutes, shaking the pan a couple of times. When all the mussels are open (discard any that remain closed), finish with the cream, if you like, and serve with some good bread and more cider (in a glass, this time).

VARIATION
West Country beer mussels

There's no reason to stop at cider. A good ale also makes a fantastic cooking medium for mussels. Avoid cheap, light lagers or very heavy stouts and instead go for a real ale with a bit of lightness and some floral, grassy, herbal notes. We would say this, but we have no hesitation in recommending our own organic Stinger beer, made with nettles (see the Directory, page 592). Proceed pretty much as above, but use beer in place of cider and leave out the cream. Serve with hunks of buttered bread.

Curried mussels *serves 4 as a starter, 2 as a main course*

Mussels can stand pretty robust spicing and, if you like your curry hot, feel free to play fast and loose with this recipe.

Also works with:
- Cockles
- Palourdes

A knob of unsalted butter
1 tablespoon olive oil
4 shallots or 2 onions, finely chopped
2 teaspoons mild curry powder
½ glass of white wine
750g–1kg mussels, scrubbed and
  debearded (see page 103)

3–4 sprigs of coriander, finely chopped
3–4 lovage leaves, finely chopped
  (optional)
2 tablespoons double cream
Salt and freshly ground black pepper

Heat the butter and olive oil in a large pan. Add the shallots or onions and sweat gently for 10 minutes, until soft. Add the curry powder and cook for a minute, then pour in the wine and half a glass of water and bring to a simmer.

Add the mussels to the pan, cover and let steam open over a medium-high heat for 3–4 minutes, until the shells are open. Remove them from the pan with a slotted spoon and discard any that stay resolutely shut. Pick all but a dozen mussels from their shells and put them into warmed bowls, reserving any liquid. Set aside the mussels in their shells.

Add the chopped coriander and the lovage, if using, to the liquor that remains in the pan, along with the cream and any liquid from shelling the mussels. Simmer for 2–3 minutes, then season to taste and ladle over the mussels in the bowls. Garnish with the shell-on mussels and serve straight away, with fresh bread.

Winkles in a court-bouillon *serves 6 as a snack or a canapé*

You can boil winkles in plain salted water or seawater, but if you add a few
aromatics and a splash of wine, the flavour improves considerably. The
following is just a guide – use as many of the court-bouillon ingredients as you
have available. An onion and a bay leaf would be better than nothing – quite
acceptable, in fact.

Winkles shouldn't need purging, unless they come from a particularly sandy
place. If you think grit may be a problem, soak them in cold fresh water overnight
before cooking.

3–4 dozen winkles, cleaned
  (see page 108)

FOR THE COURT-BOUILLON:
2 carrots, finely sliced
4 celery sticks, finely sliced
1 leek, finely sliced
2 onions, finely sliced

3 garlic cloves, bruised
2 bay leaves
A large sprig of thyme, if handy
A large sprig of tarragon, if handy
4 parsley stalks, if handy
2 teaspoons cracked black peppercorns
2 teaspoons salt
A glass of dry white wine

Start by making the court-bouillon. Put all the ingredients in a large pan and
add 1.5 litres of water or seawater. Bring to the boil and simmer for 20 minutes.
Add the winkles, bring back to the boil and simmer gently for about 5 minutes.
Drain the winkles, discarding the court-bouillon and its bits. You can eat them
hot or cold, but any you don't eat must be refrigerated and eaten within 24 hours.

Either way, to eat them you need some kind of winkle-picking device. The easiest
thing to use is a large pin, with which you can remove the fingernail-like 'door'
that seals the shell before skewering the little mollusc inside and hoicking it out.
Eat them just as they come, without vinegar or any other accompaniment.

Palourdes with chanterelles *serves 1 or 2*

This is a real favourite with Gill, the River Cottage chef. It's the result of a happy experiment when we happened to have palourdes and fresh chanterelles in the kitchen at the same time. It isn't a hard coincidence to arrange. Frilled, apricot-coloured chanterelle mushrooms can be found in the wild as early as July, and right up until December in a mild autumn, with September/October being the prime time. Look for them in beech woods, amid the leaf litter, or on mossy banks – though in Scotland, they often favour pine forests. Palourde clams (and cockles) can also be gathered, or bought, at this time.

A good handful of fresh chanterelles
2 knobs of unsalted butter
1 garlic clove, chopped
2 tablespoons white wine

2 dozen palourdes, purged if necessary
 (see page 103)
Salt and freshly ground black pepper

Also works with:
• Cockles and other clams

Prepare the chanterelles, trimming off the stalk bases and giving the mushrooms a gentle brushing to remove any dirt or soil. If they're really big, cut them in half.

Put a knob of butter and the garlic in a wide pan over a medium heat. When the butter has sizzled for a minute, add the wine. When the wine is bubbling, add the palourdes and cover the pan. Let them steam for 2–3 minutes, until the shells are open (discard any that stay shut). Remove the palourdes from the pan and pick them out of their shells, making sure you collect any juices from the shells as you go. Return them to the winey juices in the pan, place back on the heat and boil until the liquid has reduced to about a tablespoon.

Place a frying pan over a medium heat, add the second knob of butter and allow it to bubble, then throw in the chanterelles. Sauté gently for 2–3 minutes, just until they soften, then add the palourdes and toss them with the mushrooms. Add the clam liquor and season with pepper – and salt if necessary, though it may well not be. Serve straight away on a warmed plate, with bread and butter.

Razor clams with butter, garlic and parsley

serves 4 as a starter

Also known as razor fish, razor clams are wonderful, succulent shellfish. They are a rare treat, so you won't need a whole host of recipes – this trio should be enough. We love them best of all steamed open in white wine with lots of butter, garlic and parsley – a sort of razors *marinière*.

16 razor clams
75g unsalted butter
Olive oil
2 garlic cloves, finely chopped

1 fresh red chilli, finely chopped (optional)
1 glass of white wine
A handful of parsley, chopped
Salt and freshly ground black pepper

Also works with:
• Palourdes and other clams

Scrub the clams well in cold water. Heat a large, deep frying pan or wide, shallow saucepan over a high heat. Add the butter and a dash of olive oil. When it is hot and bubbling, add the garlic, the chilli, if using, and the clams. Toss the clams in the butter, then let them fry for a couple of minutes. They will start to open.

Pour in the wine and let it bubble for a further minute. Then add the parsley and season with salt and pepper. By this time, all the clams should be open (discard any that stay firmly shut) and the flesh perfectly cooked. Serve the clams in warmed dishes, with the delicious cooking liquor spooned over them. Some good bread for mopping juice is essential.

VARIATION
Razor clams with chorizo

You'll need the same ingredients as above, plus a chunk of chorizo (about 150g). Thickly slice or roughly chop the chorizo and fry in a little olive oil for about 5 minutes. Then chuck the butter, garlic, chilli and clams into the pan with the sizzling chorizo and continue as above.

VARIATION
Barbecued razor clams with lime butter

Razors also cook well over the barbecue, in a similar way to large mussels and cockles. Try barbecuing razors until they just open, then trickle them with a hot lime, garlic, chilli and parsley butter (made like the flavoured butter in the lobster recipe on page 206). Serve as tapas or a starter.

Whole fish poached in a court-bouillon

serves 8–10

You may have call for a fish kettle (see page 254) only a couple of times a year but you'll find it very useful for cooking a large fish for a big occasion – with minimum fuss and trouble.

Gentle poaching in a kettle is a fantastic treatment for species with firm, rich flesh that falls between what we conventionally describe as either 'white' or 'oily'. A large sea trout or small salmon is a case in point, but it works very well with sea bass, too. You can serve your fish hot, with a classic hollandaise sauce, as below, or cold, with mayonnaise (using the recipe on page 352, omitting the garlic and anchovies). You could even decorate a cold fish retro-style, with layers of cucumber 'scales'.

A court-bouillon is a light stock that usually contains some white wine, lemon juice or vinegar. This dash of acidity helps preserve the colour and texture of the fish as it cooks. To maximise the flavour, slice or chop everything quite finely. Once the fish is cooked, you will have a delicious fish stock that can be boiled down and made into a sauce or frozen and used later.

A 2.5–3kg sea bass, sea trout or organic farmed (or self-caught wild) salmon, descaled and gutted

FOR THE COURT-BOUILLON:
2–4 carrots, finely sliced
6–8 celery sticks, finely sliced
2–4 onions, finely sliced
1 teaspoon black peppercorns
4 teaspoons salt
400ml dry white wine

PLUS THE FOLLOWING, AS AVAILABLE:
1–2 leeks, finely sliced
4–6 garlic cloves, bruised
A couple of sprigs of thyme
A couple of sprigs of tarragon, or some
   fennel fronds
A few parsley stalks
Juice and pared zest (no pith) of 1 lemon

FOR THE CHEATY HOLLANDAISE:
1 egg yolk
150g unsalted butter
A squeeze of lemon juice
Salt and freshly ground black pepper

Also works with:
• Trout
• Carp
• Pike
• Zander

Start by making the court-bouillon. Put all the ingredients in a large saucepan or stockpot with 3 litres of water, bring to a simmer and bubble gently for 20 minutes. Strain through a fine-meshed sieve or conical strainer, preferably lined with muslin. If you're not using it straight away, the court-bouillon can be stored in the fridge for up to 3 days.

Pour the court-bouillon into a fish kettle and bring it to a simmer. Lay the fish on the kettle's trivet and carefully lower it into the court-bouillon, making sure the fish is covered by the liquid (add some more water if not). Bring back to a simmer and turn the heat right down. The liquid should just vibrate with the gentlest of simmers – anything more will damage the flavour and texture of the fish. You can even turn the heat off under the kettle and put the lid on. Reheat to simmering after about 10 minutes, then turn the heat off again.

Gently poached in this way, a fish of 2.5–3kg should be done in about 20 minutes, tops. Even a fish twice that size shouldn't take more than 30 minutes. Remember the principle that as soon as the heat reaches the middle of the fish, it is done

(continued overleaf)

(see page 112). You can use the knifepoint test (see pages 113–14), but another good test for doneness is to see if the dorsal fin (the one in the middle of the fish's back) pulls away from the fish without too much resistance.

Just before the fish is ready, make the hollandaise (which we refer to as 'cheaty' because it is a short-cut version that doesn't include the usual base of wine vinegar and herbs). Put the egg yolk in a bowl. Melt the butter in a small pan, then trickle it gently on to the yolk, whisking all the time to create an emulsion. Season with a squeeze of lemon juice and some salt and pepper and serve warm. This sauce isn't as stable as the classic version, so you need to serve it up quite quickly. If the sauce has to stand for a while, keep it warm by standing the bowl in a larger bowl of hot but not boiling water.

Lift the fish from the kettle on the trivet, allowing any liquid to drain from it as you do so. Carefully transfer it from the trivet to a serving plate, using two spatulas or fish slices. Remove the skin by making a shallow cut along the backbone and around the sides of the head down to the belly, then carefully peeling the skin back from backbone to belly. Turn the fish over and repeat the process. Gently ease portions of the fish away from the backbone with a spatula or fish slice. When you've done the first side, you can remove the whole backbone, head and tail, leaving a nice fillet with just a few bones in the belly flesh on the platter.

Serve the fish straight away, on warm plates, with the hollandaise, buttered new potatoes and a lightly dressed salad.

VARIATION
Pike and zander in a court-bouillon

Good-sized pike and zander, caught in sweet fresh water, then poached in a fish kettle and served hot or cold, can be outstanding. With a pike, though, you must be aware of the bones. There is a good case for serving the pike cold, as it gives you a chance to remove the bones as you serve up the fish. This is not such a tedious chore as many assume: once you realise that there is a pitchfork-shaped bone between each flake of flesh along the dorsal fin, they are really quite easy to identify and remove.

If you're serving poached pike warm, it's delicious with a sauce made by simply stirring lots of snipped chives and chopped chervil into some melted butter, along with a pinch of seasoning and a squeeze of lemon juice. Or you could rustle up the more hollandaise-like caper sauce we suggest serving with Pike fishcakes (page 330) – or omit the capers to make a chive sauce. Cold, your flaked pike will be ably supported by a dressing of half mayonnaise, half full-fat plain yoghurt, seasoned well, spiked with a dab of mustard, and again flavoured with chives.

Grey mullet braised with tomato and fennel

serves 5–6

The first stage of this recipe involves making the aromatic, Provençal-inspired sauce in which the fish will be cooked. It is well worth taking the time to get this right, not least because it's a delicious concoction which, once you've tasted it, you may well want to use in other dishes. It makes a great base for a fish soup, for instance, a good sauce for a seafood pasta dish, and is also wonderful as a straightforward accompaniment to grilled fish. Use ripe, fresh tomatoes if you can – although tinned ones will be fine as a substitute – and make sure you cook the mixture down to a rich, pulpy sauce. Season it well, and don't forget the all-important pinch of sugar.

A large grey mullet (about 1.5-2kg), descaled and gutted
2 tablespoons olive oil
2 onions, sliced
4 celery sticks, finely sliced
2 large fennel bulbs, trimmed, cored and cut into eighths
3 garlic cloves, finely sliced

1kg ripe, fresh tomatoes, skinned and chopped, or two 400g tins of chopped tomatoes
Zest of 1 lemon, pared into thin strips
½ teaspoon thyme leaves
4 bay leaves
1 glass of white wine
A pinch of sugar
Salt and freshly ground black pepper

Also works with:
• Sea bass
• Black bream
• Brill
• Turbot
• John Dory
• Gurnard
• Zander

Prepare the mullet by cutting it into 5 or 6 thick cutlets at right angles to the backbone (see page 71). Start just behind the head and make each cutlet a good 3–4cm thick, leaving a longer tail portion (8–10cm) to compensate for the tapering shape. Keep the head. It can be added to the pan for extra body and flavour, and offered to an enthusiast for picking over.

Heat the olive oil in a large, heavy-based casserole. Add the onions, celery, fennel and garlic and sauté over a medium heat until the onions are beginning to soften and colour slightly. Add the tomatoes, lemon zest, thyme, bay leaves, white wine and sugar. Bring to a gentle simmer, then turn the heat down and cook for 35–40 minutes, until you have a rich, thick sauce. Taste and adjust the seasoning.

Carefully place the mullet cutlets and the head in the pan, pushing them gently into the sauce so that it almost covers the fish. If you feel the sauce is too thick, add a few tablespoons of water or fish stock. Transfer the casserole to an oven preheated to 180°C/Gas Mark 4 and bake, uncovered, for 10–15 minutes.

Remove and leave to stand for 10 minutes before serving. It is delicious with ribbon pasta, which can be mixed with the rich, tomatoey sauce.

Slow-braised cuttlefish or squid

serves 5–6

This is one of our favourite ways of cooking larger squid and cuttlefish – for a good long time, until meltingly tender. These days we often bulk up the recipe into a hearty main course by adding potatoes (new potatoes in the summer, Pink Fir Apple in late summer and autumn) and seasonal vegetables – Florence fennel in summer and autumn, celery in autumn and winter.

2–3 large cuttlefish or squid, cleaned
   (see pages 97–102), about 1kg cleaned
   weight, ink reserved if possible
4 tablespoons olive oil
1 large red or white onion, finely sliced
2 large garlic cloves, crushed
1kg ripe, fresh tomatoes, skinned,
   deseeded and chopped, or two 400g
   tins of chopped tomatoes
A squeeze of lemon juice (optional)
A few sprigs of fennel
2 bay leaves

About 5 strips of thinly pared lemon zest
About 5 strips of thinly pared orange zest
A glass of red wine
Salt and freshly ground black pepper

OPTIONAL INGREDIENTS:
500g waxy potatoes, thickly sliced
2 large or 3 medium bulbs of Florence
   fennel, tough outer layers removed,
   thickly sliced
½ head of celery (or 5–6 good sticks),
   thickly sliced

Cut the prepared cuttlefish or squid pouches into 1cm-thick strips and set aside with the tentacles.

Heat half the olive oil in a large, heavy-based saucepan and sweat the onion gently in it until softened. Add the garlic and cook for a minute or two. Add the tomatoes and bring to a simmer. Cook, uncovered, for about 30 minutes, until you have a nice, pulpy sauce. Season to taste, adding a few drops of lemon juice if you like.

Heat the rest of the oil in a large frying pan. Add the cuttlefish or squid and stir-fry over a high heat for just a few minutes, until lightly browned. Then add it to the tomato sauce with all its juices and the oil. Add the fennel, bay leaves, lemon and orange zest, red wine and the ink from the fish, if you have it. Season with black pepper, plus just a little salt at this stage.

Bring to a very gentle simmer and cook, uncovered, until the fish is completely soft and tender, almost melting in the mouth: 1½–2 hours usually does it. Stir occasionally to make sure the sauce is not catching on the bottom of the pan, and add just a dribble of water if it seems to be getting too thick. Adjust the seasoning, adding more lemon juice if necessary. To add the extra ingredients, gently sweat the potatoes, fennel and/or celery in a little oil in a small frying pan for 5–10 minutes, then add to the cuttlefish or squid after it has been cooking for about 1¼ hours, so they have about half an hour to cook through in.

Serve with a mound of rice or rice-shaped pasta (risoni), or some good bread.

Braised squid stuffed with chorizo and rice

serves 4 a starter, 2 as main course

This is a rich and hearty dish – the spicy rice spills out of the squid and mingles with the robust tomato sauce in a satisfying way. It also works with cuttlefish, though it is best with small squid, as their tubular form is perfect for stuffing.

4 medium-small squid, 12–15cm body
    length (about 200g each, unprepared
    weight)
1 tablespoon olive oil
2 garlic cloves, finely sliced
500g ripe, fresh tomatoes, skinned,
    deseeded and chopped, or a 400g tin
    of tomatoes
200ml fish or shellfish stock (see
    pages 256–7)
Thinly pared zest of 1 lemon
2 bay leaves
100ml dry sherry
A small bunch of flat-leaf parsley,
    finely chopped
Salt and freshly ground black pepper

FOR THE STUFFING:
1 tablespoon olive oil
1 small onion, finely diced
4 garlic cloves, finely chopped
1 celery stick, finely diced
50g long grain white rice
1½ teaspoons finely chopped rosemary
1½ teaspoons finely chopped thyme
200g cooking chorizo sausage, rind
    removed, meat crumbled
A squeeze of lemon juice

Prepare the squid as described on pages 97–100, so that you are left with a clean, empty body cone, the tentacles and the trimmed wings.

To make the stuffing, heat the olive oil in a small pan, add the onion, garlic and celery and sauté gently for about 10 minutes, until soft. Leave to cool a little. Finely chop the tentacles and wings of the squid. Put them in a bowl with the cooked onion mixture, all the remaining stuffing ingredients and some salt and pepper and mix well – it's easiest just to use your hands. Stuff the mixture into the cleaned squid bodies, but don't pack it in too tightly as the rice will expand quite a lot during cooking. Each squid body should be about two-thirds full. Secure the open ends with wooden cocktail sticks. Any remaining stuffing can be stirred into the sauce.

Choose a heavy-based casserole in which your squid will sit snugly side by side. Place over a medium heat, add the olive oil and throw in the sliced garlic. When it's just beginning to colour, add the tomatoes, followed by the fish stock, lemon zest, bay leaves and sherry. Season with salt and pepper. Place the squid in the dish, carefully pushing them down into the sauce. Bring to a very gentle simmer.

Transfer the dish, uncovered, to an oven preheated to 120°C/Gas Mark ½ and cook for 2–2½ hours, until the squid is very tender. Don't worry if some of the stuffing has forced its way out. Serve scattered with the chopped parsley and accompanied by a crisp green salad.

Japanese slow-cooked mackerel *serves 6–8*

Long, slow cooking is an unusual technique for fresh fish and you certainly wouldn't normally think of simmering mackerel for around 3 hours. But by keeping the heat very gentle and ensuring the fish are covered with liquid, you prevent the drying out you might expect. The fish remain intact, the flesh is tender – the texture, almost, of tinned sardines – while the bones of smaller mackerel will be soft enough to eat. If you like intense, aromatic, oriental flavours, this is an outstanding recipe that we urge you to try.

Also works with:
- Scad
- Trout
- Salmon (organic farmed or self-caught wild)
- Sea bass

2 large, hot, dried red chillies
½ fist-sized piece of fresh ginger, very thinly sliced
3–4 large garlic cloves, thinly sliced
75ml soy sauce
40ml cider vinegar
20g soft brown sugar
About 400ml apple juice

6–8 small-medium mackerel, gutted, heads and tails removed (or fewer, larger fish, each cut into 2–3 chunky pieces)
Cayenne pepper

TO ACCOMPANY:
Cooked noodles or rice
Steamed spinach, pak choi or other greens

Put the chillies, ginger, garlic, soy sauce, cider vinegar, sugar and about half the apple juice into a small pan. Bring to a simmer, stirring occasionally to dissolve the sugar, but taking care not to break up the chillies.

Arrange the mackerel in a heavy-based saucepan. They should be packed in closely, with few or no gaps between them. Pour over the sauce. If it doesn't quite cover the fish, add some more apple juice until it does – but only just. Give the pan a little shake to re-blend the sauce and apple juice, if necessary, then place on the heat and bring to a simmer. As soon as you see the simmer beginning, turn the heat down so it doesn't boil.

Cook, covered, at a very gentle, popping simmer for 3 hours. You may need to top up the pan with a little more apple juice from time to time. Don't let it boil and don't be tempted to move the fish until the 3 hours are up. Then take them out of the cooking liquid, set aside and keep warm. Remove and discard the chillies.

Return the pan containing the cooking liquid to the hob, turn up the heat and boil until it is reduced by about a third to a half. Taste and adjust the seasoning. You are looking for a good balance of sweet, hot, salty and sour, so add more apple juice or a dash of vinegar or soy sauce, as appropriate. If you feel the sauce lacks heat, you can pep it up with a pinch or two of cayenne pepper. Arrange the fish on a pile of noodles or rice, and/or some steamed spinach or pak choi. Pour over the sauce and serve.

Steam-braised ling with thyme and lemon

serves 4

Here's a recipe that demonstrates the simplicity and effectiveness of a technique we've dubbed 'steam-braising', of which we are extremely fond. Cook this and you'll see how easy and adaptable it is. The fish sits in just a little bit of simmering, aromatic liquid in a covered pan and is half-poached, half-steamed, while being infused with lovely flavours. It'll be perfectly cooked in less than 10 minutes and will have created its own delicious little sauce. This particular recipe includes quite a few aromatic flavourings, but it also works with just a bay leaf and a scrap of garlic.

1 tablespoon olive oil	½ teaspoon fennel seeds (optional)	**Also works with:**
A knob of unsalted butter	1 small garlic clove, finely sliced	• Brill and most other
1 tablespoon white wine	(optional)	white fish
A squeeze of lemon juice	750g–1kg thick ling, pollack or whiting	• Grey mullet cutlets
2 strips of finely pared lemon zest	fillet, cut into 2–3cm thick medallions	• Small whole flatfish
A couple of sprigs of thyme	(see page 72)	
2–3 bay leaves	Salt and freshly ground black pepper	

Put the olive oil, butter and white wine in a large, wide saucepan or a deep frying pan along with a tablespoon of water, the lemon juice, zest, thyme and bay – and the fennel seeds and garlic, if you're using them. Bring to a simmer. Season the fish medallions lightly with salt and pepper, then arrange them in the pan in a single layer. Cover and cook for 4–6 minutes, depending on the thickness of the fish, turning them once, very carefully, so they don't break up. That's it.

All you need do now is transfer the fish to warmed plates and spoon over the juices. Boiled spuds or mash and something fresh and green – broccoli, perhaps, or spring greens – are the only accompaniments you need.

VARIATION
Steam-braised zander with juniper and bay

The simple steam-braising technique works just as well with freshwater zander – often described as being like a cross between a perch and a pike.

Bring the braising liquor and flavourings to a gentle simmer as above (adding 1 teaspoon juniper berries, lightly bruised, and omitting the garlic and fennel seeds). Very lightly season 4 zander fillets, 200–250g each, then lay them skin side down in the pan, giving the pan a little shake to make sure they're not sticking. Cover and cook for a couple of minutes before turning them over, covering again, and cooking for a further minute or two.

Also works with:
• Perch
• Grayling
• Pike
• Gurnard
• Sea bass
• Black bream
• John Dory
• Brill

Transfer the fish fillets to warm plates. You can either spoon over the pan juices as they are, or concoct a richer sauce as follows. Remove the bay leaves from the pan and add another 2 tablespoons of white wine. Simmer until the pan juices have reduced to about a tablespoon, then whisk in 50g butter or 2 tablespoons cream. Taste and season as necessary. Spoon the sauce over the fish and serve with creamy mash or buttered new potatoes and broccoli or peas.

Whole steam-baked brill *serves 6–8*

You may not have a turbotière – a giant, flatfish-shaped fish kettle – but you can still poach a whole large flatfish in a court-bouillon, or at least 'steam-bake' it, as described below. It's a lovely, simple way to cook the fish, and the sauce made from the cooking liquid is delicious. Obviously, the bigger the fish, the bigger the dish you'll need – something to bear in mind when you're sizing them up on the fishmonger's slab.

Also works with:
- Turbot
- Plaice
- Dover sole
- Megrim
- Witch
- Flounder

4 leeks, white part only, finely sliced
3 celery sticks, finely sliced
1 onion, finely sliced
2 sprigs of thyme
4 parsley stalks
2 bay leaves
A few strips of finely pared lemon zest

2–3 teaspoons black peppercorns
1 large brill, weighing 1–1.5kg, gutted
A glass of white wine
A large glass of water
100g unsalted butter, cut into small cubes
Salt and freshly ground black pepper

Place the vegetables, herbs, lemon zest and peppercorns in your chosen shallow baking dish. Put the fish on top, then pour over the wine and water. Don't expect it to cover the fish; it's just there to steam it through and give you a sauce at the end. Season with salt. Cover the dish with foil and place in an oven preheated to 160°C/Gas Mark 3. Cook for 45 minutes to 1 hour, until the flesh is just coming away from the bone.

Remove the fish from the dish using a couple of fish slices (have someone help you do this if the fish is big). Transfer it to a warmed serving plate. Strain the cooking liquid into a pan and boil until it has reduced by half. Remove from the heat and gradually whisk in the butter to make a sauce. Taste and adjust the seasoning. Pour into a warmed jug.

Serve the steam-baked fish with the sauce, steamed green vegetables and creamy mash.

Shallow and deep frying

Frying fish is rarely a bad idea. In fact, we can't think of a single species that doesn't respond well to this treatment, which is why reaching for the frying pan is, or should be, second nature to the keen fish cook. It is to us. In fact, when we've been out fishing, and finally got home with some nicely prepped fish (assuming we've been both lucky and conscientious), we can find ourselves placing the frying pan on the hob and trickling in a little oil even before switching on the kettle, or opening the fridge and reaching for a beer.

Basic shallow frying is such a simple, reliable and effortless way of cooking fish that it's worth mastering this technique before any other. Incidentally, we won't call it 'pan-frying', as some modern chefs do, because not only is this a tiresomely tautological term but it also rather smacks of bogus industry inside-knowledge, claiming credit for a level of expertise where none is due. You really don't need to be a trained chef to fry fish, any more than you need to be trained

in the use of a knife and fork to enjoy it. So for anyone who likes to eat fish but is (temporarily) stuck in the mindset that it's difficult to cook, this chapter is a good starting point.

The joy of frying lies not just in its simplicity but also in its results. There are few more pleasing sensations than biting into a crisp skin, crumb coating or batter to find tender, delicate, lightly steaming fish flesh within. The merest dab of a simple relish – a homemade tartare sauce (see page 324), for example – elevates it to the gastronomic heights. You find yourself asking, 'Could this be done better, and enjoyed more?' and the answer is usually, 'No'.

Simple shallow frying

All you need is a decent pan, a bottle of olive or groundnut oil, some salt and pepper – plus perhaps a scrunched bay leaf or two and a bit of garlic. Just heat a layer of oil a scant millimetre thick in your frying pan, season your fish, or fish fillets, and fry until crisp. Once you've got the knack, you won't need a cookbook, not even this one.

With the acquisition of that knack in mind, it's just as well to get the theory straight. One important thing is to banish the idea that every pan you put a bit of fish in should be searingly, smokingly hot. Certainly, it should be on the hotter side of medium but, if you put a very fresh fillet into a very hot pan, the heat will quite often shock it into curling up. This happens because the fibres on the outside of the fish contract rapidly on contact with the fierce heat, while those on the inside are unaffected. This curling can make it difficult to cook the fish evenly, and indeed to get a good, crisp exterior, as it's hard to achieve even contact between the curled fillet and the flat pan. The trick is to start the fish over a medium heat at a gentle sizzle, pressing it lightly with a spatula if it shows an inclination to curl. Then turn the heat up a couple of minutes into the cooking time to achieve that toothsome exterior.

You might have noticed that we've already made an assumption that it's fillets you're putting in the pan. Much as we love to cook whole fish, it's well-trimmed fillets that lend themselves best to shallow frying. They naturally lie flat in the pan, and cook quickly and evenly in a matter of minutes. You'll be wanting a crisp skin, of course, and most fish – including sea bass, bream, salmon and pollack – will require descaling to prepare the skin for this treatment. Mackerel is one of the very few that will not. Its scales are tiny, and by the time you've got it into the kitchen it's lost most of them anyway. The few that remain cook imperceptibly into the skin as it crisps up.

The classic way to fry a fillet of fish is to season the skin with salt and pepper first, then put the fillet skin side down on to that layer of hot oil, keeping it there at a nice sizzle. If at any point it buckles up, gentle pressure of the spatula should be applied. Only when the skin is crisp and the edges of the fillet on the upper side look opaque should you flip the fillet over – for just a minute or two to finish it off. This method guarantees a good crisp skin and, because the fish is skin side down most of the time, it stops the flesh absorbing too much oil.

Once you've achieved that irresistible crisp skin on your fillet, you obviously want to enjoy it – or have your guests enjoy it – at its best. Always serve the fillet crisp side on top. If it's served the other way up, the skin will quickly soften and become soggy.

Shallow frying whole fish

Shallow frying a whole fish – say, a plate-sized bream, bass, trout or mackerel, or a small flatfish such as dab or lemon sole – is a slightly different business from frying a fillet. For a start, you have that uneven, round-bodied shape to contend with (less so with flatfish, obviously). A whole round fish, such as mackerel or bass, does not have two obligingly flat sides, so the contact between fish and pan is limited. In other words, frying one is more like frying a sausage than a burger. Indeed, with really round-bodied fish – mackerel is the best example, but it applies to small grey mullet and gurnard too – the sausage comparison is useful. They can, like sausages, be turned in the pan several times rather than just once, and you can try to balance them on their bellies and backs as well as their flanks. Another way to address the issue is to use considerably more oil in the pan – a centimetre rather than a millimetre, to increase the amount of contact between hot oil and fish. You're on your way to what we call 'deep shallow frying', which we will come to later.

Incidentally, some species benefit from a neat procedure of trimming and de-finning that prepares them for shallow frying, making them a little more manageable in the pan and tidier to eat. It works particularly well with spiny and relatively two-sided fish, such as bream, bass, red mullet and, should you find yourself somewhere exotic, snappers and their ilk. It's described in detail on page 61. But however well trimmed, a whole fish is always likely to be thicker than a boneless fillet, and therefore take a little longer to heat through – and of course you are aiming to get the skin crisp on both sides of the fish. With an overheated pan, and an overzealous attempt to get that skin crisp, you may find that it's frazzled on the outside but, on applying the knife test (pages 113–14), still raw in the middle. Best to go for a steady sizzle over a medium heat, aiming to give the fish 3–5 minutes on each side, depending on size. A total cooking time of 6–10 minutes should see you right for most single-portion fish.

However, if you are frying a larger fish – a fat, 1kg-plus specimen that challenges the size of your pan, perhaps to the extent that you have decided to remove its head and/or tail (not to mention dignity) to help you fit it in – then you will have to slow things down a bit in the pan, as it may take as long as 15–20 minutes' total cooking time to be hot through to the bone.

Alternatively – and this is a trick you may come to rely on quite a bit if you're a regular shallow fryer – you can deploy the oven to finish the job of cooking the fish through (if you have an Aga, this makes perfect sense as you have always got the oven on anyway). Fry a whole fish for a couple of minutes on either side over a fairly high heat to get that seasoned skin nicely crisped, then lay it in a preheated ovenproof dish or roasting tray and put into the oven. If your frying pan has a heatproof handle, you can just transfer the whole thing to the oven. So: fish into pan, 2 or 3 minutes each side; pan into oven at 200°C/Gas Mark 6; 8–10 minutes later, fish out. This sequence works beautifully with flatties such as brill, plaice or Dover sole weighing around 1–1.5kg, as well as bass, bream and large red mullet.

A word of warning: if you go the pan-into-oven route, the chances are that, one minute after the pan comes out again, you'll pick it up by its burning-hot handle. So you should always wrap a folded tea towel several times around the handle as soon as it comes out of the oven – and leave it there until the empty frying pan is deposited safely in the sink, preferably under a cold running tap.

Shallow frying tranches and cutlets

Between the boneless fillets and the whole fish is the portion of cut fish often called a tranche. As described (and pictured) on page 72, this is a portion of fish cut from a larger specimen – usually a chunky flatfish – often (but not always) with some bone. It may be a whole middle section from a medium-sized brill or turbot, or a half or even a quarter of such a piece if taken from a really big fish – a 5kg-plus turbot or a huge halibut.

A good tranche is roughly square in cross-section – or at least more or less rectangular. It therefore has two skin-covered sides with a good surface area, and shallow sides of cut flesh, with a bit of backbone running down the length of the third, middle side that helps to hold the tranche together. Obviously tranches will vary in shape according to where they are taken from, but if you're cooking several, you'll want them to be more or less the same weight.

You can see immediately how such a fish portion would lend itself well to shallow frying: four fairly flat sides, each of which can have a turn in contact with the hot pan base. You will want to concentrate on the two skin sides, of course, getting them as crisp as possible. The two flesh sides, as with the flesh side of a fillet, will need just a brief searing to give them a little colour and a nice savoury surface.

The other kind of bone-in portion of fish is the cutlet: a sliced cross-section of a round-bodied fish, such as a sea bass, salmon or large grey mullet (see page 71). Cutlets can also be shallow-fried, but it's the flat flesh sides, rather than the rounded, skin-covered edges, that will come into contact with the pan (as shown above left). They're easy to cook, though, and hold their shape well in the pan, so should not be overlooked.

Ridged griddle pans

We should mention here another bit of kit, which, at least superficially, is related to the frying pan. A heavy ridged griddle pan is a very useful tool for the fish cook, helping to create a crisp skin and beautiful, seared stripes on your fish, which you would normally only achieve on a barbecue. In fact, food cooked in a griddle pan is really being subjected to a form of indoor barbecuing. It's not being shallow fried at all but, since there is a natural link between a flat pan and a ridged one, we're sure you'll forgive us for discussing it here.

We particularly like griddle pans for cooking squid or scallops because the charring created by the ridges gives a special flavour that you won't get from using an ordinary frying pan. But a really hot griddle pan is a good place for any piece of fish to find itself – flattish fillets or portions being the optimum choice because they will lie flush against those searing ridges.

The secrets of griddle cooking success are largely the same as those for barbecuing (see pages 189–91). The basic idea is to oil the fish (not the pan) lightly and get the pan fiercely hot before you introduce the fish to it. Once you've added the fish, resist the temptation to move it until it's ready to turn over – many griddled fish have shed their skin through impatience. These steps should ensure that you can griddle your fish successfully without any of it adhering to the pan... well, not much anyway.

Dustings and coatings for extra crispness

Let's return to shallow frying, and the pursuit of that crisp exterior, which can become mildly obsessional. If it's not part of your plan to achieve it then, frankly, the 'steam-braise' technique described on page 255 is more forgiving and reliable (and offers that nice little spoonful of juices as a by-product). But assuming you want to maximise crispness when shallow frying your fish, it's a simple matter to enhance the results by dusting it with a starchy flour or grain of one sort or another. The idea of such coatings is not merely to lead to the holy grail of crispness – though it should certainly help achieve that. They also provide a fine but significant protective layer for the fish beneath, keeping it moist and tender.

The first obvious option is a simple dusting of seasoned flour. This alone is enough to create the most delicate of crusts, and is particularly useful when you're dealing with thin-skinned white fish, such as pollack, whiting and coley. There are alternatives to flour, which all have their own charms – semolina works well, as does matzo meal. It's worth ringing the changes to explore the

subtly different textures created by these starchy granules. Go further and dip your floured fish in beaten egg and you'll get a lovely, slightly pancakey jacket over your fillet – the result is not so crisp but for some reason children seem to love it. The next step is to press your lightly egged fillets into a plate of breadcrumbs – only a few minutes' more work, but resulting in that crunchy exterior that is perhaps the apex of crispness (see page 324 for the ultimate in crisp-crumbed, shallow-fried fillets).

A crumb coating, being thicker and more absorbent than mere flour, will require you to add a little more oil to your frying pan – to about 5mm depth, say – but you're still in the realms of shallow frying. It's only when you start using thick batters that it becomes necessary to turn to the deep-fat fryer. But that does open the door to some particularly delicious recipes, so we'll be wheeling out our fryer shortly.

Battered or breadcrumbed fish dishes are usually the ones that people who are not out-and-out fish lovers (poor things) tend to go for. Or, to put it another way, plenty of people who say they don't like fish will happily eat fish fingers. And, with these recipes, you can use that natural liking for the crisp and crunchy, to branch out into slightly less familiar but nevertheless crowd-pleasing versions of fried fish. Fish fingers don't have to come from the freezer. They don't even have to be finger-shaped. The breadcrumbs don't have to be dayglo orange. The reinvented, homemade fish finger, or crumbed fillet, is almost invariably an improvement on the mass-produced big-brand version. By jingo, you can even call it a goujon.

So this is, if you like, the Trojan horse chapter; you can use it to wrong-foot the fish phobic. 'Don't worry,' you can say, 'it's only a bit of fried fish.' Just don't tell them that it's a pouting, a whelk or a piece of squid! The familiar crunch of batter or breadcrumbs will lull them into a false sense of security, which will have them conquering a whole new dish, or fish, before they know it.

Deep frying fish for ultimate crispness

We know and love deep-fried fish mainly, of course, through our experience of the Great British Fish and Chip Shop (300 million portions of fried fish are sold every year in the UK, so they must be doing something right). The deep-fat fryer will always be a delightful way of cooking fish fillets and other crumb- or batter-coated morsels of seafood, including prawns, squid, scallops and even oysters. And there is no reason why we can't reproduce the chip-shop effect at home, if we set our minds to it. Nor does it require a custom-built deep-fat fryer. A deep, wide, stainless steel pan will do the job. The great thing about doing it at home is that we may somehow feel less compelled to drown our lovingly made fish supper in a vat of vinegar and a kilo of ketchup.

However, successful deep frying does require a little more skill – or at least attention to detail – than shallow frying. To paraphrase the marriage service (not for the first time in a River Cottage book, according to our editor), to enter into it lightly or wantonly, without a little forethought, may well lead to disappointment or, far worse, outright danger. It is therefore understandable that many fish cooks, even experienced ones, make the decision that they will leave the whole business of deep frying to the professionals, and concentrate on exploring other areas of fish cookery. If you are inclined to put yourself in that category, and particularly if you have young, inquisitive children who like to be around and involved when you are cooking, then fair enough. On the other hand, if you consider yourself a responsible, well-organised cook, or at least one with a built-in sense of self-preservation, there is no reason why you can't explore the delights of deep-frying fish at home. In terms of kit, you will want to go one of two routes: you can either purchase a plug-in, domestic 'safety' deep-fat fryer or, if you're sure you know what you're doing, you can deep fry in a suitable large saucepan – something robust and solid (stainless steel is preferable to aluminium), and at least 25cm in diameter and 20cm high. And it should *never* be more than a third full of oil.

At home we both still use the large-saucepan-of-oil approach, with a selection of wire baskets and 'spider' spoons for removing the cooked food from the oil (the ones we like best have heatproof bamboo handles, and can be found in Chinese grocers). However, we know from fellow cooks that the plug-in domestic fryers are very useful, especially if you plan to deep fry more than once in a blue moon. Although they can be pricey, they give consistent results and are a particularly safe way to deep fry. If you're shopping for one, don't be tempted by a bargain or anything secondhand. Get something new that smacks of quality – and ideally comes with a clear set of instructions and an unambiguous warranty.

If you are planning to do as we do and use a saucepan, one small investment you should make is a fire blanket (domestic size). It's the only safe way to smother and put out a chip pan fire. Keep it close to the cooker, and know where it is. You'll never have to use it, of course, but its very presence will make you a safer fryer.

Such a belt and braces attitude to safety will stand you in good stead, because the secret of successful deep-fried fish is good preparation and a little bit of confidence. It's all about having everything ready – and especially having your batter right and your oil hot enough (but not too hot, as we'll see). All fish for deep frying should have some kind of coating, and usually that means breadcrumbs or a liquid batter into which the fish is dipped. Even more than with shallow frying, the function of the coating is not only to create that delectable crunchy crust but also to protect the delicate fish inside from the fiercely hot oil. By inflicting severe heat damage on the breadcrumbs or batter, it just so happens that you make them rather delicious. Do the same to a piece of unprotected fish fillet and you would dry it out and spoil it.

Battered and breadcrumbed fish fillets are the stock-in-trade of deep-fat frying, but occasionally it may be rewarding to deep fry a whole fish, with bones still in, that has simply been dusted in seasoned flour (see page 337). You'll need a fish of the right size (not too big for your pan of oil), with a skin that, after descaling, is robust and prone to very satisfactory crisping (small bream and gurnard spring to mind).

The effects of temperature and timing

When you place a piece of battered fish in a pan of hot oil, the heat causes the water in the batter to boil and evaporate (that's why you see that mass of tiny bubbles). Once all its moisture has vaporised, the batter becomes crisp. You can tell this is happening because the bubbles slow down and the batter changes colour to that appealing golden brown. But if you go on frying much beyond this

point, the batter will start to take in oil and become greasy – particularly if it's a batter made with wheat flour, as the gluten it contains is absorbent. So, since you don't want to leave your fish frying for too long, you need a high temperature that will cook it right through to the centre, before the batter on the outside starts soaking up lots of oil.

Fortunately, as we've discussed, fish conducts heat pretty well. And although the batter coating provides a protective and somewhat insulating layer, the surrounding heat will cook the fillet through fairly fast. If all goes well, the effect is almost as if the fish is steamed inside its batter crust – when it happens, that's chip-shop nirvana.

Things can go wrong, though. If the fillets are too thick and come straight from a very cold fridge, they may still be uncooked in the middle when the batter reaches perfection. If they're too thin, they may be soft and mushy. Success therefore depends on working within the right parameters of oil temperature, fillet size and frying time. As it happens, 2–3cm is about the right thickness for a fillet, and 3–4 minutes about the right cooking time. And the right oil temperature, most professional fish fryers would concur, is between 160°C and 180°C. Whole fillets in a thick batter need the lower temperature to give them time to cook through; smaller pieces, or those coated in only a thin dusting of flour or breadcrumbs, can happily take a higher heat.

Fortunately, it is not difficult to monitor your oil temperature. The best way, if you're using the big-pan-of-oil approach, is with a cook's thermometer. Most domestic deep-fat fryers have a thermostat that you can set to a desired temperature. But you can also make a good estimate of the temperature by using the old cook's trick of dropping a cube of white bread into the hot oil. If it turns light golden brown in about 90 seconds, your oil is at around 160°C; 50–60 seconds signifies a temperature of around 175–180°C. If it takes about 25–30 seconds, you've got very hot oil – about 190°C – appropriate for the final frying of chips and just about okay for flour-dusted squid rings, which will cook in barely a minute, but a bit too hot for a battered fish fillet. If it takes any less than that for the bread to colour, your oil is dangerously hot and you should cool it down before you think of cooking anything in it. Otherwise you might be reaching for that fire blanket.

If you've made a good batter that coats the fish well and you've got the temperature of the oil right, you'll have a lovely, deep golden crust around your moist white fillet. But you will still need to drain the fish well. Lift it from the hot oil with a wire basket or a spider spoon and give it a little shake. Prop the basket or spider over a drip tray or bowl and leave for half a minute. Give it another tap or a shake. Then lay it on several layers of absorbent kitchen paper for another half minute or so, turning once. It's now ready to serve – still crisp and piping hot.

There's no denying that, however well it's done, deep-fried crumbed or battered fish will always be a relatively fatty food. That, combined with the skill and care required to get a perfect result, means that it is best seen as something of a treat. However, fried at the right temperature for the right time, and well drained and blotted, your fish should never be oil-logged or greasy, and certainly no more calorie-laden than a blob of homemade mayonnaise or even a slab of cheese on toast – and who would ever quibble with everyday treats like those?

The all-important oil

What you fry your fish in is important, and some oils are quite unsuitable. Volatile oils, including seed or olive oils described as 'cold pressed' or 'extra virgin', are simply too fragile and unstable at high temperatures, and will smoke long before they reach the required 180°C. Smoking oil not only releases toxins into the air, it also taints the flavour of the food you're frying. We tend to use groundnut oil, though sunflower oil is also a good option. Both are very stable at high temperatures – in other words you can get them very hot before their molecular structure changes and they start to smoke.

Some sources will tell you that once you've deep-fried fish in oil, you should discard the oil straight away because the flavour will be tainted. We think that's unnecessarily extravagant and wasteful. In fact, if your fish was good and fresh to start with, and encased in a protective batter, you should be able to reuse that oil several times, as long as you filter it between frying sessions to remove any solids. At home, passing the oil through a funnel lined with a coffee filter is a good way to clean it. But, obviously, never pour it back into a plastic bottle until it's cooled right down.

You can't go on using the same deep-frying oil forever, though (and changing the oil regularly marks the difference between a good chip shop and a bad one). If you've reused some oil a few times, then left it sitting around in a jar or bottle for a month or two, and you want to see whether it's still good, then the best test is a taste test. Just heat a tablespoon of the oil in a small frying pan and shallow-fry a cube of bread in it until golden. Taste it. If it's fishy, or a bit musty, or unpleasant in any way, then discard the oil and start with fresh. If the fried bread tastes fine, then the oil is good for another go.

A middle path: deep shallow frying

If you feel nervous about deep frying, for whatever reason, bear in mind that there are very few dishes in this book, and even in this chapter, that absolutely have to be cooked that way. Only quite large pieces of fish, completely coated in batter, need total immersion in hot oil to give the right results. A viable alternative for many recipes, including anything coated in breadcrumbs, is what we like to call the deep shallow fry, where you need only about a 5mm depth of oil in your pan. You are still deep frying, really, but you're deep frying one side at a time.

The vast majority of recipes in this chapter are not about using great panfuls of oil at all. They're about using just a little bit – a tablespoon or so – to get very quick, very good results. Sometimes there will be something coming between the fish and the oil, a variation on the theme of flour, egg or breadcrumbs; and sometimes the fish will be cut into small pieces and mixed into a fritter batter or made into some kind of fishcake before being fried. But there are many recipes here in which the fish remains naked, or wears nothing but its own skin, and is just placed directly on to a thin film of hot fat and flipped over after a couple of minutes. These are among the fastest, most instantly gratifying fish recipes you'll find. So if in doubt, or a hurry, reach for the frying pan.

Quick-fried mackerel fillets with garlic and bay

This is perhaps the simplest way to enjoy a catch of fresh mackerel when you get home, tired but elated after a few good hours at sea. It's super-quick and very family friendly.

Also works with:
- Sardines (large)
- Herring
- Trout (small)

Fresh mackerel, 1 per person
Olive oil
A few garlic cloves, thickly sliced

A few bay leaves, roughly torn
½ lemon
Salt and freshly ground black pepper

Cut the fillets from either side of the mackerel, bait-cutter style (see pages 62–3). Season them with a little salt and pepper.

Put a large frying pan over a medium heat and add a thin film of olive oil. When the oil is fairly hot, scatter in the garlic and bay leaves, then lay the mackerel fillets over them, skin side down. You're looking for a gentle sizzle rather than a fierce flash-fry. As it cooks, the mackerel flesh will change from translucent pink to opaque white. When the fillets are almost completely white, turn them over for just a minute to finish cooking. The whole process won't take longer than 5 minutes. Let the garlic and bay just sizzle in the oil under and next to the fish, flavouring it gently.

Lift the mackerel fillets from the pan, leaving the bay and garlic behind (they're probably just starting to burn a bit). Give the fillets a squeeze of lemon juice and serve straight away, with salad (a sliced tomato salad is delicious with mackerel) and either new potatoes or buttered bread.

Black bream with herbs *serves 2*

This dish is really about the preparation of a whole fish of a certain size (a one-portion fish), especially for the frying pan. It's descaled, beheaded, de-spined and trimmed, so it's easy to cook, easy to get a nice crisp skin and deliciously easy to eat. The removal of the fin line along the spine and tail allows the oil, butter and herbs to penetrate deep into the centre of the flesh. It works best with bream and their near relatives.

2 black bream, weighing 500–750g each
A small bunch of thyme sprigs
2 small, tender sprigs of rosemary
25g unsalted butter
3 bay leaves

2 tablespoons olive oil
2 garlic cloves, skin left on, bruised with
 a knife
Salt and freshly ground black pepper

First you need to descale your fish (see pages 55–6) and then remove the bream's spiny fins (see page 61). Use sharp kitchen scissors to snip off the small pectoral fins on the underbelly and gut the fish (see pages 58–9). Decapitation is optional, but it will give you more room in the pan. If you're going to do it, cut the head off just behind the pectoral fin. Trim the tail, too, if you think you're tight for space.

Slash the fish two or three times on each side. Stuff a little thyme and rosemary into the slashes and cavity of each fish, along with the butter. Put a bay leaf into each cavity. Season the fish all over with salt and pepper.

Heat the olive oil in a large, non-stick frying pan over a medium heat, then add the other bay leaf and garlic so they can gently release their flavour as the fish cooks. Lay the fish in the pan and fry for 5–6 minutes on each side, until cooked through to the bone. You can turn the heat up towards the end of cooking, if necessary, to help crisp the skin. Serve at once, with a leafy salad and sautéed or boiled new potatoes.

Also works with:
• Red mullet
• Sea bass

Witch with lemon zest mash *serves 2*

Witch is a ghostly looking little flatfish that makes surprisingly good eating, fully deserving its place alongside its cousin megrim on our list of the top ten most underrated fish (see page 49). It's great simply flashed under a grill or gently fried. The goujon treatment – filleted, dipped in seasoned flour, egg and breadcrumbs, then fried – would also be a good option. A citrus-infused mash works beautifully as an accompaniment.

Also works with:
• Lemon sole
• Dab
• Flounder
• Megrim
• Plaice

1 tablespoon olive oil
2 witch, weighing about 500g each, gutted
25g unsalted butter
Juice of 1 lemon
1 tablespoon marjoram leaves (optional)
Salt and freshly ground black pepper

FOR THE LEMON ZEST MASH:
500g floury potatoes, such as Désirée, Pentland Javelin or Wilja
2 bay leaves
50ml whole milk
25g unsalted butter
2 tablespoons extra virgin olive oil
Finely grated zest of 1 lemon

First prepare the mash. Bring a large pan of salted water to the boil. Peel the potatoes and cut them into roughly equal pieces. Pour cold water over them, stir, then drain (this removes some of the starch). Add the potatoes and bay leaves to the pan of boiling water, bring back to a steady simmer and cook until they are completely tender. Tip them into a colander and leave for at least 3 minutes to 'steam off' (this helps to reduce the water content). Discard the bay leaves.

Put the milk, butter, olive oil, lemon zest and some black pepper into the warm pan and place over a low heat to melt the butter (but don't let it boil). Pile the potatoes into a potato ricer and rice them directly into the seasoned hot milk and butter mixture (or push them through a sieve if you don't have a ricer). Stir well with a wooden spoon to get a smooth, even texture, then taste to check the seasoning. Keep warm while you cook the fish.

Heat a large non-stick frying pan over a medium heat and add the olive oil. Season the fish on both sides, add to the pan and cook for 4–5 minutes on each side. Divide the mash between two warmed plates and put the fish next to it. Return the pan to the heat. Add the butter, lemon juice, and marjoram if using, and allow the butter to foam for a minute or so. Spoon over the witch and serve.

Sea trout fillet with sorrel sauce *serves 4*

Larger than brown or rainbow trout, sea trout is a relatively rare treat – a fish that's available only during spring and summer, when it returns from the sea to our rivers to spawn. Its oceanic journey seems to give it a fantastic extra depth of flavour.

You can cook sea trout whole, in many of the same ways you'd cook other trout, or salmon, but a big fish will yield lovely meaty fillets, which are quite delicious with a velvety sorrel sauce.

In fact, the sauce – which is extremely quick and easy to make – should be a mainstay in any fish cook's repertoire. Somewhere between a herb and a salad leaf, sorrel has a startlingly lemony flavour, which makes a perfect foil for everything from barbecued mackerel to steamed brill or fried pollack (or indeed a poached egg on toast). Be warned, though, that the leaf undergoes a dramatic change of colour when cooked, turning from vibrant green to a dull, army-fatigue khaki. Don't worry – the taste remains bright and fresh.

Also works with:
• Salmon (organic farmed or self-caught wild)
• Trout
• Sea bass
• Mackerel

4 thick, roughly square, fillet pieces
 (200–250g each), cut from large sea
 trout fillets, skin on but descaled
1 tablespoon olive oil
1 tablespoon groundnut or sunflower oil
4 bay leaves
2 garlic cloves, skin left on, bruised with
 a knife
Salt and freshly ground black pepper

FOR THE SORREL SAUCE:
50g unsalted butter
1 large bunch of washed sorrel
 (about 200g), stalks removed,
 leaves coarsely chopped
1 egg yolk
1 tablespoon double cream (optional)

Heat a large non-stick frying pan over a medium-high heat. Season the sea trout fillets all over. Add the two oils to the pan, along with the bay and garlic, which will subtly perfume the fish. Place the fish, skin side down, in the pan and cook for 5–7 minutes, by which time the skin should be crisp and the fish cooked at least three-quarters of the way through. Flip the fish over and cook for a further minute, until opaque, but only just, all the way through. Transfer to warmed plates (discarding the bay and garlic) while you make the sauce.

Sorrel cooks very fast, so this sauce can be whipped up in minutes. Put the butter in a small pan over a medium heat. When it is frothing, throw in the sorrel, which will quickly wilt and turn a dull greeny-brown. Give it a quick stir to make sure all the leaves are wilted. Remove the pan from the heat, let it cool for 30 seconds, then beat in the egg yolk, which will thicken the sauce. Season to taste with salt and pepper. If you like, enrich the sauce by stirring in the double cream. You can re-warm it, ever so gently, over a low heat, but be careful not to scramble the egg in it.

Serve the fish fillets with the warm sorrel sauce and some waxy new potatoes.

Sea trout with creamed spinach

If sea trout with sorrel sauce is a light, peck-on-the-cheek of a dish, then the same fish with wilted spinach in a creamy béchamel sauce is a comforting hug.

To serve four, blanch 500g trimmed fresh spinach in salted water. Refresh in cold water, then squeeze out as much liquid as you can. Roughly chop the spinach. Grate a small onion and $^1/_2$ carrot and put in a pan with 250ml whole milk, a bay leaf, some ground black pepper and a few gratings of nutmeg. Bring almost to boiling point, then leave to infuse for 10 minutes. Strain into a warmed jug, discarding the herbs and vegetables.

Melt 50g butter in a pan and stir in 25g plain flour to make a loose roux. Cook gently for a couple of minutes, then stir in half the milk. When the sauce is thick and smooth, stir in the rest of the milk. Simmer gently for just a minute, then stir in the chopped spinach. Heat through until thoroughly hot, but don't let it bubble for more than a minute. Taste and adjust the seasoning with salt, pepper and a touch more nutmeg if you like. Serve at once, with your fried sea trout fillets. Note that this creamed spinach is also a very good accompaniment to crumbed, fried fish fillets (see page 324).

Fried bream fillets with pea purée *serves 4*

Fillets from bream that you've just caught, served with a purée of peas that you've just picked... it must be July.

Also works with:
- Sea bass
- John Dory
- Red mullet
- Brill
- Lemon sole

Leaves from 1 large bunch of mint, chopped (keep the stalks)
400g freshly podded peas (or use frozen peas)
Olive oil
1½ garlic cloves – ½ finely chopped, the other clove skin left on and roughly bruised with a knife

75g unsalted butter
2 bay leaves
2 black bream, weighing about 450g each, descaled, filleted and pin-boned
Salt and freshly ground black pepper
Lemon wedges, to serve

Bring a pan of water to the boil and throw in the mint stalks. Add a pinch of salt and the peas and boil for 4–5 minutes, until the peas are tender (overgrown 'cannonball' peas may take a little longer). Drain and reserve the cooking water, but discard the mint stalks. Put the peas in a blender and set aside.

Set a small pan over a medium-high heat, then add 1 tablespoon of olive oil and the finely chopped garlic. Sizzle gently until the garlic just begins to colour, then quickly pour it into the blender with the peas. Add 50g of the butter, a pinch of salt and pepper and the chopped mint leaves. Add 2 tablespoons of the pea cooking water and blend the whole lot to a purée, adding a little more liquid if necessary, to give a consistency that is similar to coarse hummus. Taste and adjust the seasoning.

Put a large, non-stick frying pan over a medium-high heat. Add 1 tablespoon of olive oil and the remaining butter. Throw in the bay leaves and the bruised garlic clove to flavour the fat. Season the fish fillets all over and, when the fat is hot, lay them skin side down in the pan. Cook for about 3 minutes, until the flesh has turned opaque nearly all the way through, then flip them over and cook for a final 30 seconds.

Arrange the fish fillets skin side up on warmed plates, with a generous dollop of pea purée alongside. Serve with lemon wedges, plus a tomato salad.

Scallops with chorizo *serves 4 as a starter, 2 as a main course*

There are many ways to cook scallops, but few to beat this. It's one of the best possible expressions of the salty-spicy-pork meets sweet-succulent-shellfish concept so beloved of the Portuguese.

If you're cooking this dish in the summer when fresh broad beans are available, blanch some and toss them into the pan at the last moment. Sweet little fresh peas are another delicious addition.

To make this a more 'British' dish, you could substitute black pudding for the chorizo. Add 6 torn sage leaves to the pan with the scallops to bring out the flavour of the sausage.

12 large, hand-dived scallops
Olive oil
250g fairly hot cooking chorizo, cut into
  1–2cm thick slices
1 teaspoon fennel seeds (optional)
Few bay leaves (optional)
A squeeze of lemon juice
Salt and freshly ground black pepper

OPTIONAL EXTRAS:
Baby broad beans and/or garden peas,
  podded and blanched for 2 minutes

Open the scallops as described on pages 105–7 (reserve the frills for bream bait or to make fish stock). If the corals are plump and bright orange, leave them attached to the main muscle. Otherwise add them to the frills for stock. Pat the scallops dry with kitchen paper and set aside.

Heat a large, heavy-based frying pan over a high heat, add a little olive oil, then throw in the chorizo and, if you like, a sprinkling of fennel seeds and a few bay leaves. Fry for 3–4 minutes, stirring all the while, as the chorizo releases its salty, spicy fat.

Move the chorizo to one side of the pan. Check that the pan is still really hot, then add the scallops. Leave for about 45 seconds to 1 minute, then carefully turn them over. After another scant minute, using a sharp shake of the pan – or a light stir with a spatula – toss the chorizo and scallops together with all that lovely, flavoursome fat. (This is the moment to add the optional broad beans and/ or peas.) Cook for just another minute, tossing and shaking regularly.

Add a twist of pepper, a little bit of salt (the chorizo is already pretty salty) and a few drops of lemon juice, then divide the mixture between warmed plates and serve straight away, with bread and a green salad – for which the oil from the pan, with a few more drops of lemon juice, will make a sublime dressing.

Red mullet, woodcock-style *serves 2*

This recipe is loosely based on a traditional preparation for woodcock, where the bird is left ungutted during cooking, then the innards are removed and spread on a piece of toast, on which the bird is served. The flavour of the guts is creamy and mildly liverish, making it an excellent dish. Since the liver of the red mullet is also highly prized, it makes perfect sense to use the same approach. It works a treat. Indeed, it *is* a treat.

2 very fresh red mullet (350–500g), descaled and gutted, livers reserved
1 tablespoon olive oil
25g unsalted butter
1 small garlic clove, unpeeled
1 bay leaf
2 green olives, finely chopped
1 anchovy fillet, finely chopped
1 tablespoon white wine
Salt and freshly ground black pepper

Remove the livers from the fish and set aside. Season the fish. Place a large non-stick frying pan over a medium-low heat. Add the oil and butter, the garlic clove and the bay leaf, then add the whole fish. Sizzle gently for about 8–10 minutes, then turn them over and continue cooking for 6–7 minutes or so, until cooked right through (test the thickest part – see pages 113–14). Remove from the pan and keep warm.

Keeping the pan on the heat, remove the cooked garlic clove, then peel and chop it – it shouldn't be too burnt if you have cooked the fish gently. Combine it with the chopped olives and anchovy. Add this mixture to the hot pan, along with the fish livers and wine. Sauté for just half a minute to reduce the wine a little, then remove the pan from the heat and mash everything together with a fork.

Smear this paste over the skin of the mullet, and serve, accompanied by plain mash or sautéed potatoes and a tomato and chive salad.

Mackerel stuffed with salsa verde *serves 4*

This is a really impressive way of preparing mackerel. Fresh, vibrant salsa verde works beautifully as a stuffing and really complements the rich flesh of the fish. You can try the same technique with other stuffings, such as pesto or a piquant chilli salsa. The tail-on filleting technique suggested here gives you a very attractive little parcel. Remove the pin bones to create the all-important channel that holds the salsa verde, then simply sandwich two fillets together before tying with string.

Also works with:
• Trout (small)
• Sardines (large)

4 medium-sized mackerel, gutted
Olive oil
Salt and freshly ground black pepper

FOR THE SALSA VERDE:
A generous bunch of flat-leaf parsley,
  tough stalks removed
6–8 basil leaves

6–8 mint leaves
1 garlic clove, finely chopped
4 anchovy fillets
2 teaspoons capers, rinsed
1 teaspoon English mustard
Juice of ½ lemon, or to taste
Olive oil

Make the salsa verde first: put the herbs on a large board and chop them well. Combine the garlic with the anchovies and capers and chop/mash them together into a coarse paste. Bring the chopped herb and anchovy mixtures together and chop again. Pile the whole lot into a small mixing bowl and add the mustard, lemon juice and some black pepper to taste. Stir in just enough olive oil to make a thick green sauce (it shouldn't be runny or sloppy). Taste and adjust the seasoning, then set aside.

Now fillet the mackerel bait-cutter style, as described on pages 62–3, but leaving the fillets joined at the tail end. Make sure you remove all the pin bones. You should be left with a boneless, headless pair of fillets, still joined at the tail, and with one V-shaped channel in each fillet where the pin bones have been removed.

Run a good smear of the salsa verde down the V-shaped groove in each fillet of mackerel, then smear a little more over the flesh. Close up the fish and secure in a couple of places with kitchen string. You can do all this preparation several hours in advance and chill the fish until needed. In fact, the flavour will be better this way.

To cook, set a large, heavy frying pan over a medium heat. Brush the fish lightly with oil, season them and fry for 5–6 minutes on each side, until the flesh is cooked through. Alternatively, brush them with a splash of oil, season and roast in an oven preheated to 200–220°C/Gas Mark 6–7 for 12–15 minutes. They can also be barbecued.

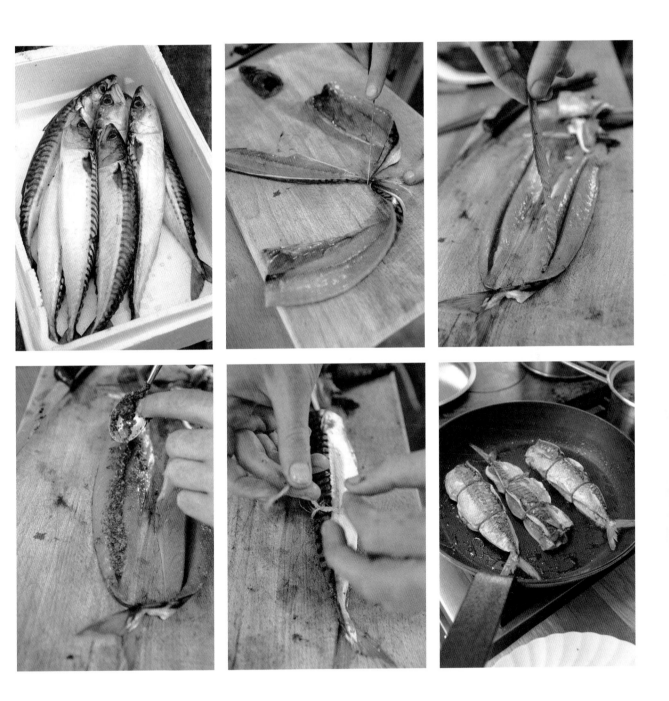

Brill with celeriac and crispy pork belly

serves 6 as a starter, 4 as a main course

This is further compelling evidence of the success of the pork/fish collaboration (see Scallops with chorizo, page 313). The first time we served this dish, it was a hit. Our friend and occasional fishing partner Paddy Rudd, who joined us for dinner that night, still talks about it.

Pork enthusiasts may notice that the procedure for the belly is really just an accelerated version of homemade bacon.

Also works with:
- Turbot
- Megrim
- Witch
- Flounder
- John Dory
- Black bream
- Sea bass

750g–1kg slab of organic or free-range boneless pork belly, cut from the thick end
1–1.5kg brill, skin on but descaled and filleted

FOR THE CURE:
100g fine sea salt
100g light brown sugar
6 juniper berries, bruised
4 bay leaves, finely shredded
1 teaspoon cracked black peppercorns

FOR COOKING THE BELLY:
½ head of garlic, lightly crushed with the back of a knife

2 celery sticks, roughly chopped
2 carrots, roughly chopped
2 onions, cut into quarters
2 bay leaves

FOR THE CELERIAC PURÉE:
1 small or ½ large head of celeriac
Up to 1 litre whole milk
50g unsalted butter
Salt and freshly ground black pepper

TO FINISH:
1 tablespoon lard or oil
2 garlic cloves, sliced
Leaves from 1 sprig of thyme
1 tablespoon olive oil

Mix all the cure ingredients together. Put the pork belly in a bowl and rub the cure mix all over it. Cover and place in the fridge for 12–15 hours. Revisit, and re-rub, once or twice during this time.

To cook the pork, wash it under gently running cold water to remove the cure, then pat dry. Place in a pan with the garlic, vegetables and bay leaves and cover completely with water. Bring to the boil, then cover and simmer very gently for at least 2, perhaps 3 hours, until the belly, including the skin, is very tender. Drain the meat and leave to steam off, so it dries a little as it cools. Discard the stock vegetables. If you're not serving the dish on the same day, you can cool and then refrigerate the pork at this point.

An hour before serving, peel the celeriac and cut it into cubes. Place it in a pan with enough milk to cover and bring to a gentle simmer. Cook until the celeriac is tender, then drain, reserving the hot milk. Purée the celeriac with the butter, adding enough of the hot milk to give a thick, but silky consistency. Season to taste and keep warm.

While the celeriac is cooking, finish the pork belly. Cut it into neat cubes about 2cm square. Heat the lard or oil in a large frying pan over a medium-high heat. Add the belly cubes and sizzle hard, turning them frequently, until browned and lightly crisp. Throw in the garlic and thyme for the last minute or two of cooking. Turn off the heat and leave the meat in the hot pan while you cook the fish.

Heat the olive oil in a large, non-stick frying pan over a high heat. Cut the brill fillets into neat pieces – enough to give each person 2 or 3 generous chunks. Season the brill, add to the pan, skin side down, and cook for 2–3 minutes, until the flesh has become opaque nearly all the way through. Turn the fish and cook for just a minute more.

Spoon some celeriac purée on to each warmed plate, then put 2 or 3 pieces of brill beside it. Scatter the browned pork belly over the fish and the celeriac, along with a trickle of its warm, aromatic cooking oil. Serve at once.

Fried mackerel in oatmeal with bacon   *serves 2*

An oatmeal coating is traditional for fried herring, where it provides a lovely, crunchy contrast to the fish's oily flesh, but it works just as well with other oily fish, such as mackerel. The bacon contributes its own, salty-sweet savour, making the whole combination surprisingly rich and substantial.

2 mackerel, filleted

100g medium oatmeal

1 tablespoon sunflower or groundnut oil

4 streaky bacon rashers, cut into lardons

Salt and freshly ground black pepper

Also works with:
• Herring
• Sardines
• Garfish

Season the mackerel fillets well. Spread the oatmeal out on a plate. Coat the mackerel in the oatmeal, pressing it on to the fish firmly.

Heat a large, heavy-based frying pan over a medium heat and add the oil, then the bacon. Cook until crisp and golden, then remove the bacon with a slotted spoon, leaving the fat in the pan.

Keeping the pan on a medium heat, add the coated mackerel fillets, flesh side down. Fry for 1 minute, then turn over and fry for 1–2 minutes, until the skin beneath the oatmeal is golden brown.

Serve the fried mackerel straight away, with the crisp bacon, some bread and butter and a salad. Or, if you want to make a breakfast of it, serve with a fried egg on the side.

The FLT *serves 1*

This is the ultimate fish sandwich: a fried fillet of plaice with lettuce and tomato in a bun. Make sure you use a decent bap – nothing too cotton-woolly – and good mayonnaise, and this becomes a delicious experience. You can make it for as many people as you like, of course, but somehow it's the kind of top-notch fast food that is particularly good cooked and eaten all by yourself, after a hard day, with a cold beer to hand.

Butter

A dash of olive oil

1 small plaice fillet (about 100g), skinned if you like

A little plain flour, seasoned with salt and pepper

1 large, white, floury bap

A few Little Gem lettuce leaves

1–2 ripe tomatoes, thickly sliced

1 tablespoon mayonnaise

Tomato ketchup (optional)

Salt and freshly ground black pepper

Also works with:
- Pollack
- Coley
- Whiting
- Pouting
- Megrim
- Witch
- Lemon sole
- Flounder
- Black bream

Heat a knob of butter and a dash of olive oil in a non-stick frying pan over a medium heat. Dust the fish fillet with seasoned flour and fry for about 2 minutes on each side. Alternatively, if you're a sucker for crisp skin, fry it skin side down for about 3$^1/_2$ minutes, then give it a quick 30 seconds on the other side to finish.

Slice and generously butter the bap. Lay the lettuce leaves on the base of the bun, followed by the sliced tomato, then the fish. Season well. Spread a generous amount of mayonnaise on the top half, add ketchup if you feel like it, then close up the bap and eat straight away, while the fish is still warm.

Fish tacos *makes 5–10, depending on size*

This is the classic street food of Baja California and the other coastal resorts of Mexico. There, the fish is often battered and deep fried. However, good fish can get a bit lost if enveloped in batter and a tortilla, so we prefer just to dust the fillets with a little seasoned flour – which also means they can be shallow rather than deep fried. Use boneless fillets of absolutely any fish, from whiting to dogfish, plaice to bass. There's no need to use extravagant fish, unless you've had some good fishing and happen to have a surfeit of it. You can mix up the fish with scallops and/or squid as well.

The soft tortillas do take a bit of work but they are fun to make, and really not at all difficult.

A handful of plain flour
Roughly 1kg boneless, skinless fish
  fillets, cut into 2-bite-sized pieces
Groundnut or sunflower oil for frying
Salt and freshly ground black pepper

FOR THE TORTILLAS:
500g plain flour
A generous pinch of salt

FOR THE TOMATO SALSA:
1 teaspoon sugar
1 tablespoon wine vinegar or cider vinegar
10 ripe tomatoes (about 500g), skinned,
  deseeded and diced
2 small red onions, finely diced

FOR THE GUACAMOLE:
2 ripe avocados
1 red chilli, as hot as you like, finely
  chopped
A small bunch of coriander, finely
  chopped
Lime juice, to taste

OPTIONAL ACCOMPANIMENTS:
Soured cream or crème fraîche
Chilli sauce or Tabasco

First make the tortillas: mix together the flour and salt and add enough water to make a soft but not sticky dough – probably 300–325ml. Knead for a few minutes, until silky and smooth. Take one small piece of dough at a time (a lime-sized lump is good, but you can make them any size you like), shape it into a ball (the rounder your ball, the rounder your tortilla), then use a rolling pin to roll it out into as thin a circle as you can.

Heat a heavy-based frying pan (a flat griddle or a pancake pan would be even better), without any oil, until hot but not smoking. Quickly but carefully lay a tortilla in the pan and cook on both sides until it is bubbly and ever so slightly charred, but still soft and floppy. Roll out the next one while the first one is cooking. Stack them on a plate as they are done, covering with a cloth.

To make the tomato salsa, simply toss all the ingredients together, leave for a few minutes, then toss again before serving.

To make the guacamole, halve, peel, stone and mash the avocados. Stir together with the chilli and coriander, plus as much lime juice as you like.

When you are ready to eat, reheat the tortillas, wrapped in foil, in a low oven at (120°C/Gas Mark ¹/₂). They will probably have gone a little hard on cooling, and this will soften them up again.

To cook the fish, season the flour generously with salt and pepper, toss the fish pieces in it, then shake off the excess. Heat a shallow layer of oil in as large a frying pan as you have and fry the fish over a medium to high heat for a minute or so on each side. The pieces should be lightly browned and just cooked through. Do this in batches if necessary – don't overcrowd the pan.

As soon as the fish is cooked, it's time to serve: simply load a warm tortilla with a bit (or a lot) of everything, including soured cream and chilli sauce if you like, then roll it up. Eat messily.

Garlic-sautéed Billy Winters *serves 4 as a starter*

'Billy Winters' is affectionate West Country parlance for the fat local prawns – the same kind you find in rock pools all around the coast, but bigger – fished with special prawn pots from around November until February. They make extremely good eating, especially when cooked in this simple but intensely flavoured way. It's all very quick and simple – the prawns go from hot water to hot fat in a matter of seconds, and are ready to eat about two minutes later.

25g unsalted butter

A dash of olive oil

500g live Billy Winters, or very fresh
 raw Atlantic prawns

2 fat garlic cloves, finely chopped

A pinch of cayenne pepper

1 tablespoon cider brandy (optional)

Salt and freshly ground black pepper

Lemon wedges, to serve

Bring a large pan of heavily salted water to the boil. When it's bubbling, heat a large frying pan over a medium heat next to it on the hob and add the butter and olive oil.

Throw the live prawns into the rapidly boiling water to kill them instantly. After no more than 30 seconds, fish them out with a large slotted spoon or a small sieve and tip them into a waiting tea towel. Shake them in the towel to dry them a bit (this helps stop them spitting madly in the frying pan), then transfer immediately to the pan of hot butter and oil, adding the garlic at the same time. Cook them for 2–3 minutes, stirring and shaking from time to time. Add a little salt, plenty of black pepper and a pinch of cayenne as they cook.

If you feel like it, you can add the cider brandy and set it alight at the end of the cooking time, tossing the prawns vigorously until the flame dies down. This gives another rich layer of flavour, but it's really not essential. Tip the hot prawns out on to a warmed plate and tuck in straight away, peeling them with your fingers. Have some brown bread and butter to eat with them, and more black pepper, cayenne and lemon wedges to hand.

Crumbed plaice fillets with tartare sauce

serves 4

Crisp, golden, breaded plaice fillets occupy the same kind of cherished niche in our fish-eating culture as battered cod. The crunchy crumb and soft, white fish make an incredibly successful marriage, especially when attended by a freshly made, creamy but piquant tartare sauce. Forget those awful plastic sachets of flavoured salad cream, which are an insult to the name; instead, take the time to make your own mayonnaise as a base and you'll find that proper tartare sauce is a thing of joy. Don't reserve it for this recipe alone – it will enhance almost any kind of battered, crumbed or fried fish.

Also works with:
- Pollack
- Whiting
- Pouting
- Megrim
- Witch
- Flounder

4 fillets of plaice, weighing about
  200g each
100g plain flour
2 large eggs, lightly beaten
150g fairly fine fresh white breadcrumbs
250ml groundnut oil
Salt and freshly ground black pepper

FOR THE TARTARE SAUCE:
2 generous tablespoons mayonnaise
  (preferably homemade, see page 332,
  omitting the garlic and anchovy)
1–2 hard-boiled eggs, finely chopped
1 tablespoon roughly chopped parsley
1 teaspoon chopped dill
2–3 gherkins, finely chopped
2 teaspoons capers, finely chopped
Juice of ½ lemon

Make the tartare sauce first by simply stirring everything together in a bowl. Set aside.

Put the plaice fillets on a board and skin them (see page 73), then give them a quick bone check with your fingertips.

Put the flour in a deep plate and season it with salt and pepper. Put the beaten eggs and the breadcrumbs in two separate deep dishes.

Lightly coat one fillet of fish in the flour, shaking off any excess. Dip the floured fish in the egg, making sure it's well coated, then roll it in the breadcrumbs so it's generously covered. Repeat with the remaining fillets.

Set a large, fairly deep, non-stick frying pan over a medium heat and add the oil – it should be about 1cm deep. When it's hot, fry the breaded fillets, in batches if necessary, for 2–3 minutes on each side, until golden brown and crisp. Serve with the tartare sauce, along with buttered peas or creamed spinach (see page 309) and sautéed potatoes, chips or mash.

Smoked mackerel fishcakes

serves 4 as a starter, 2 as a main course

These make a great starter or family supper and are really quick and easy
– though if you take the time to smoke your own mackerel (see page 158), they
will be even better.

Also works with:
• Smoked trout

500g medium-sized potatoes, peeled
  and halved
1 garlic clove, peeled
50g unsalted butter
1 tablespoon hot horseradish sauce
  (or 1 good teaspoon freshly grated
  horseradish root)

1 teaspoon wholegrain mustard
500g smoked mackerel fillets
1 tablespoon chopped chives
A little flour for dusting
Olive, groundnut or sunflower oil for
  shallow frying
Salt and freshly ground black pepper

Cook the potatoes and garlic in boiling salted water until tender. Drain,
discarding the garlic, and leave the potatoes to steam-dry for 10 minutes.
Mash them with the butter, horseradish and mustard.

Peel the skin from the mackerel fillets and discard. Flake the fish into the
mashed potato, watching out for any bones as you go. Add the chives and fold
the whole lot together, being careful not to break up the fish too much. Season
to taste with black pepper and some salt, if needed (the mackerel will be quite
salty). Dust your hands with flour and shape the mixture into little patties.

Heat a large, non-stick frying pan over a gentle heat and add a thin layer of
oil. Add the fishcakes and fry gently for 3–4 minutes on each side, until golden
brown. Serve with a substantial salad – shredded raw beetroot and chopped
apple, tossed in lemon juice and olive oil, is particularly good.

Spicy crab cakes with citrus salsa _serves 6 as a starter_

With their Thai flavourings, these crab cakes are quite peppy. The hot-sweet-sour salsa is also rather lovely with any simply fried or grilled fish (see also page 337).

500g fresh white crabmeat

100g fresh breadcrumbs (rye or
sourdough, if available)

1 hot red chilli, deseeded and finely
chopped

2 large garlic cloves, finely chopped

A thumb-sized piece of fresh ginger,
finely chopped

2 lemongrass stalks, tough outer layers
discarded, finely chopped

2 tablespoons finely chopped coriander

2 eggs, lightly beaten

100g sesame seeds (optional)

Groundnut oil for shallow frying

Salt

FOR THE SALSA:

1 grapefruit

1 orange

1 lemon (or ½ lime and ½ lemon)

½–1 red chilli, very finely chopped

½ red onion, very finely chopped

1 small bunch of coriander and/or mint
leaves, finely chopped

1 small garlic clove, very finely chopped

A pinch of salt

A good pinch of sugar

Freshly ground black pepper

Prepare the salsa first. Use a sharp knife to cut away the peel and pith from all the citrus fruits. Slice out the segments of fruit from between the membranes, so there is no pith or membrane left on them – work over a large bowl so you collect any juice that drips from the fruit. Now cut the segments crossways into little chunks and put them in the bowl with the collected juice. Add the chilli, onion, coriander and/or mint, garlic, salt, sugar and some black pepper. Mix well and set aside for at least half an hour for the flavours to infuse.

To make the cakes, put the crabmeat in a bowl and combine with the breadcrumbs, chilli, garlic, ginger, lemongrass and coriander. Season well with salt, then fold the eggs through the mixture. With wet hands, shape the mixture into 12 little cakes, about 1cm deep. Put them on a tray and chill for 1 hour.

If you're using the sesame seeds, scatter them over a large plate. Press the crab cakes on to the seeds, so they're coated on both sides.

Heat a thin layer of groundnut oil in a heavy-based frying pan over a medium heat. Fry the crab cakes, in batches, for 3–4 minutes on each side, until golden. Serve with the citrus salsa.

Whelk fritters *serves 8–10*

Not everyone is instantly enamoured of the whelk, but we love these chunky, humble sea snails. We therefore see it as our mission to lead a whelk revival. The following recipe has been known to convert even the most diehard whelk sceptic.

Also works with:
• Winkles

10–12 whelks

1 celery stick, roughly chopped

1 carrot, roughly chopped

1 bay leaf

3–4 rashers of fatty bacon, diced

1 onion, chopped

2 medium eggs, separated

2 garlic cloves, very finely chopped

1 tablespoon chopped parsley

½ teaspoon thyme leaves

A good pinch of curry powder

40g fresh breadcrumbs

Sunflower or olive oil for frying

Salt and freshly ground black pepper

Scrub the whelks under the cold tap. As you handle them, you may find that some of them release a certain amount of slime – don't worry about this, just rinse it away. Put the cleaned whelks in a large pan, cover with cold water and add the celery, carrot and bay leaf. Bring to boiling point and cook at a gentle simmer for 8–10 minutes. Drain, discard the vegetables and leave the whelks to cool.

Extract the cooked whelks from their shells, using a fork to twirl them out. Remove the coarse cap or 'trap door' (like a black fingernail) from the front end and the dark digestive sac from the tail end. Roughly chop the whelks.

Gently cook the bacon in a frying pan until it releases its fat and is lightly cooked. Add the onion to the pan and fry until soft, then set aside to cool.

Put the egg yolks into a bowl and lightly break them up with a fork. Stir in the chopped whelks, bacon and onion, garlic, parsley, thyme, curry powder, breadcrumbs and salt and pepper to taste.

In a separate bowl, whisk the egg whites until they form soft peaks. Gently fold them into the whelk mixture. Form the mixture into even-sized patties, around 5cm in diameter.

Pour a 1cm depth of oil into a large frying pan and set over a medium-high heat. When hot, add the patties (be careful, as they can spit ferociously) and fry for 3–4 minutes per side, until crisp and golden. Serve the fritters hot from the pan, with a little lemony mayonnaise dabbed on top if you like.

Pike fishcakes with caper sauce *serves 4*

This is more than just a thrifty way to use up leftover pike. So distinctive is the taste of the pike, and therefore the fishcakes, that this is a dish worth planning for. So when you have a decent-sized pike in your kitchen, think in terms of poaching or baking it for your first meal, but having enough left over to make these fishcakes the following day.

Lightened up with egg whites and enriched with cream, they're a cross between a traditional fishcake and a more cheffy quenelle. You can vary the quantities a bit, depending on how much pike you have, but make sure there's never more potato than fish.

Also works with:
- Perch
- Zander
- Grayling
- Sea bass
- Gurnard
- Black bream

250g floury potatoes, such as King
   Edward, peeled and cut into large
   chunks
500g cooked, boneless pike
1 tablespoon each chopped chervil, chives
   and parsley
2 egg whites
100ml double cream
A little flour for dusting
Groundnut oil for shallow frying
Salt and freshly ground black pepper

FOR THE CAPER SAUCE:
150g unsalted butter
1 egg yolk
1 teaspoon mild mustard
1 tablespoon finely chopped capers
1 tablespoon chopped chives
A squeeze of lemon juice

Cook the potatoes in boiling salted water until tender, then drain and leave to steam-dry for 10 minutes. Mash them and leave to cool.

Mash the cooked pike meat with a fork, double checking for any bones, then put in a bowl with the herbs and plenty of seasoning and combine well. Lightly whisk the egg whites – you just want them loose and foamy, not meringuey – then stir them into the cooled potato, along with the cream. Finally, combine the potato mixture with the pike. Leave in the fridge for at least 2 hours to firm up.

With lightly floured hands, shape the mixture into little cakes – it will be quite difficult to handle but this results in a lovely, light texture.

Heat a thin layer of groundnut oil in a large, non-stick frying pan over a medium heat. Fry the cakes, in batches, for 3–4 minutes per side, until golden brown. While they're cooking, make the sauce.

Melt the butter in a small pan until gently sizzling. Have the egg yolk ready in a small bowl. Gradually trickle the butter on to the egg yolk, whisking vigorously to form an emulsion. Whisk in the mustard and plenty of seasoning, then stir in the chopped capers and chives, plus a squeeze of lemon juice to taste.

Ideally serve the hot fishcakes straight away with the sauce. If it has to stand for a while, keep the sauce warm by placing the bowl in a larger bowl of hot but not boiling water.

Saltfish and parsnip rösti fishcakes

serves 4–6 as a starter, 2–3 as a main course

Saltfish and parsnips appear together in various medieval recipes, but they tend to be complicated. Charmed by the idea of the combination, we improvised this very simple recipe, which absolutely hits the spot. A fried egg (or two) per person, and a bit of salad, makes a good supper of them.

1 large or 2 medium parsnips (about 250–300g), coarsely grated
1 small onion, coarsely grated
100g hard-salted fish, such as ling, pollack, pouting, whiting or cod, rehydrated (see page 127), or 200g lightly salted fresh white fish fillets (see pages 124–5), cut into 1cm cubes

1 garlic clove, finely chopped
Leaves from 1 small sprig of rosemary, finely chopped (optional)
1 large egg, beaten
Groundnut or sunflower oil for frying
Freshly ground black pepper

Mix all the ingredients except the oil together in a bowl. Heat a thin layer of oil in a large frying pan over a medium heat and when it is hot, put a handful of the fish and parsnip mixture into the pan. Squash it into a cake roughly 8cm in diameter and 1cm thick. Repeat until you have 4 or 5 cakes in the pan.

Fry fairly gently, so the heat has time to penetrate into the centre of the cakes without the outside burning. Press each cake down with a spatula from time to time. After 5–7 minutes, when they are nicely browned on the underside, flip them over and continue until the second side is browned. Remove and drain on kitchen paper.

Serve the fishcakes piping hot, with a green salad on the side.

Fried squid rings with garlic mayonnaise

serves 4 as a starter

This is delicious and very easy. The mayonnaise is a doddle if you use a food processor and the squid takes seconds to cook, so you can get it all on the table very quickly. Served with a cold beer, there are few better summer meals.

Use medium-sized squid, about 15–25cm body length (i.e. not including head or tentacles). They tend to be less chewy than their larger fellow cephalopods and therefore more suited to quick cooking methods.

4 medium-sized squid, cleaned
  (see pages 97–100)
100g plain flour
About 1 litre groundnut or sunflower oil
  for deep frying
Salt and freshly ground black pepper

TO SERVE:
Coarse sea salt
Lemon wedges

FOR THE GARLIC MAYONNAISE:
2 very fresh egg yolks
2 small anchovy fillets or 1 salted
  sardine fillet
2 garlic cloves, roughly chopped
1 heaped teaspoon English mustard
A small pinch each of salt, sugar and
  black pepper
1 tablespoon cider vinegar or lemon juice
100ml olive oil
200ml groundnut oil

Start by making the mayonnaise. If you're a purist, you can do it by hand, crushing the garlic and anchovies and mixing them with the egg yolks and seasoning before slowly whisking in the oil. If not, put the egg yolks, anchovies, garlic, mustard, salt, sugar, pepper and vinegar or lemon juice into a food processor and process until smooth. Combine the two oils in a jug. With the processor running, start pouring in the oil in a very thin trickle. When the oil starts to emulsify with the yolks, you can add it a little faster. By the time you've added all the oil, you'll have a thick, glossy mayonnaise. Adjust the seasoning and, if it seems too thick, thin it slightly with a little warm water. Cover and chill until needed.

Prepare your squid into rings about 1cm thick (as described on page 100). Cut each ring of tentacles in half at the base. Put the flour in a bowl and season it well.

Heat the oil in a deep-fat fryer or a deep, heavy pan to a temperature of 180°C. To test this, drop a cube of white bread into the oil. It should turn golden brown in about a minute.

Toss a handful of squid, say 7 or 8 rings, into the seasoned flour. The best way to do this is to place the squid in a sieve with a few tablespoons of the flour. Shake the sieve until the flour has evenly coated the squid and any excess has dropped through.

Put the squid gently into the hot oil and fry for 1–1½ minutes, until golden. Transfer to a tray lined with a few sheets of kitchen paper. Continue in this way, flouring and frying a handful of squid at a time, until it's all cooked.

Serve straight away, sprinkled with coarse salt, with lemon wedges and a dish of the mayonnaise alongside.

Fish in beer batter *serves 4–6*

What makes a good batter? What creates that crisp, savoury, golden coating that seals in all the moisture of the fish it covers? The answer, or at least one answer, is beer. It not only contributes a wonderful lightness to the mixture but adds flavour, too: a nutty, wheaty edge to the crunch. But beer isn't the only important element. A good batter also needs to have the right consistency: too thick and floury and you'll end up with a pancakey, chewy result; too thin and it won't stick to the fish.

This recipe is one of the most useful in the book because you can use it when you're deep frying almost any fish or shellfish. As well as the obvious fillets of white fish, such as plaice, pollack, coley, cod, haddock and whiting, we've had great success with beer-battered dogfish goujons, squid rings, even scallops.

We've included our tried and tested recipe for homemade tomato ketchup here too, as it never fails to please with battered fish. The recipe is based on one by Lindsey Bareham in *The Big Red Book of Tomatoes* (Michael Joseph, 1999).

200g plain flour

Groundnut oil, including plenty for
  deep frying

About 250ml good beer – anything really,
  including stout, but preferably not cheap
  lager

Mixed fish of your choice

Salt and freshly ground black pepper

FOR THE TOMATO KETCHUP:

3kg ripe tomatoes, roughly chopped

4 onions, sliced

1 large red pepper, seeds and white
  membrane removed, chopped

100g soft brown sugar

200ml cider vinegar

¼ teaspoon dry mustard

A piece of cinnamon stick

1½ teaspoons allspice berries

1½ teaspoons cloves

1½ teaspoons ground mace

1½ teaspoons celery seeds

1½ teaspoons black peppercorns

1 bay leaf

1 garlic clove, peeled and bruised with
  a knife

Paprika to taste (optional)

Salt

For the ketchup, combine the tomatoes, onions and red pepper in a large, heavy pan over a medium heat. Bring to the boil, then simmer, stirring occasionally, until very soft. Push the lot through a coarse-meshed sieve and return the purée to the pan with the sugar, vinegar and mustard. Tie the spices, peppercorns, bay leaf and garlic in a square of muslin and drop it into the pan. Bring to the boil, then reduce to a slow simmer. Allow to bubble gently, for at least an hour, stirring often. The time will depend on how juicy your tomatoes are, but you should cook the sauce until it is really thick and pulpy. Taste it a couple of times during cooking and remove the spice bag if you feel the flavour is getting too strong.

Once cooked, season to taste with salt and paprika, if you're using it, then leave to cool. Pour the ketchup through a funnel into suitable bottles and seal. Stored in the fridge, it will keep for a month.

To make the batter, sift the flour into a bowl, or put it in a bowl and whisk it (which is almost as effective a way to aerate the flour and remove lumps). Add 2 tablespoons of groundnut oil, then gradually whisk in the beer, stopping when you have a batter with the consistency of thick emulsion paint. Beat it well to get rid of any lumps, season generously, then leave to rest for 30 minutes or so.

Heat the oil in a large, deep, heavy-based pan until it reaches 160°C, or until a cube of bread dropped into it turns golden brown in 1½–2 minutes.

Dip your chosen piece of fish into the batter so it is thoroughly immersed, then lift it out and hold it over the bowl for a few seconds so any excess batter drops back in. Now lower the battered fish into the hot oil. Do this one piece at a time, if using large portions, or in small batches for smaller pieces, so as not to crowd the pan. Fry large pieces of fish for 4–5 minutes, and smaller items, such as squid rings, for 2 minutes or so, until golden brown and crisp. Scoop them out with a wire basket, or 'spider', and transfer to a warm dish lined with kitchen paper. Keep them warm while you fry the remaining fish, then serve straight away, with your ketchup or perhaps some tartare sauce (see page 324).

Deep-fried whole fish with citrus salsa *serves 2*

A deep-fried whole fish (such as the one shown on pages 292–3) may seem a bit of a curiosity but it works very well, as you get lovely, crisp skin and tender flesh through to the bone. When you or your fishmonger are preparing the fish, leave the fins on. They become deliciously crunchy when cooked.

It's worth pointing out that you do need a large cooking vessel to make this dish successfully. A proper deep-fat fryer with a lid is ideal but, failing that, you'll need a pan long and deep enough to accommodate a whole fish submerged in oil, bearing in mind that for safety's sake the oil should come no more than a third of the way up the sides of the pan.

Groundnut or sunflower oil for deep frying
2 single-portion-size red gurnard, black bream, red mullet, grey mullet or sea bass (500–750g each), descaled and gutted

2 tablespoons plain flour
Salt and freshly ground black pepper
Citrus salsa (see page 327), to serve

Heat the oil in a deep-fat fryer or a very large, deep heavy-based saucepan until it reaches 190°C. You can test this by dropping in a cube of white bread. It should turn golden brown in about 25–30 seconds.

Dry the fish well inside and out, using kitchen paper. Use a sharp knife to slash the sides of the fish, going almost down to the bone, 5 or 6 slashes on each side. This helps the heat penetrate the flesh and speeds up the cooking. Season the flour well with salt and pepper and use it to dust the fish all over. Lower the fish into the hot oil and cook for 5 minutes, until the skin is puffed up and crisp and the slashes have opened up a little. Remove and drain on kitchen paper.

Take a little of the salsa and spoon it on to the fish, so the flavours penetrate via the slashes in the flesh. Serve straight away, with the remaining salsa on the side. The flour-dusted, deep-fried skin will be lovely and crisp. Dab a little salsa on each forkful and eat everything but the bones.

Smoked pollack croquetas *makes about 20*

This is a dish for those who don't mind a little bit of a fiddle, and are not afraid of the deep-fat fryer. Crispy on the outside, creamy and lightly smoky in the middle, they're worth every ounce of the effort spent in preparing them.

75g unsalted butter, plus a little extra for frying

25g smoked bacon, finely chopped

250g smoked pollack (or haddock) fillet

About 500ml milk

½ onion, sliced

1 bay leaf

75g plain flour

25g mature Cheddar cheese, grated

1 heaped teaspoon chopped parsley

1 egg, lightly beaten

75g fresh white breadcrumbs

Groundnut or sunflower oil for deep frying

Freshly ground black pepper

Heat a little butter in a frying pan over a medium heat and fry the bacon in it until crisp. Set aside.

Put the smoked pollack fillet in a saucepan just large enough to hold it (cut the fillet in half if necessary). Pour over enough milk to cover the fish and add the onion, bay leaf and a few twists of black pepper. Cover the pan and bring the milk to a gentle simmer. By the time the milk is simmering, the fish should be perfectly cooked and you should be able to remove it straight away. However, if you've got a particularly thick fillet from a monster fish, you might need to leave it in the hot milk for a minute or two longer.

Flake the flesh off the skin of the fish into a bowl, checking for bones as you do so. Strain the milk and reserve it, but discard the flavourings.

Heat the 75g butter in a saucepan over a medium heat. Stir in the flour to make a roux and cook gently for a couple of minutes. Gradually stir in about 300ml of the reserved fish poaching milk and cook, stirring, until it becomes very thick – it needs to bind the croquetas together, so it must be robust. Bring this fishy paste to a simmer and cook very gently for 5 minutes, stirring constantly. This ensures there's no taste of raw flour in the finished sauce. Remove from the heat and stir in the grated Cheddar, flaked fish, chopped parsley and cooked bacon, being careful not to break up the fish too much. Leave the mixture to go cold, then chill until firm.

Put the lightly beaten egg in one shallow bowl and the breadcrumbs in another. Take dessertspoonfuls of the chilled fish mixture and, with lightly floured hands, roll them into short, fat, thumb-sized sausages. Roll each one in the beaten egg, then the breadcrumbs. Cover and return to the fridge for another hour.

When you're ready to fry, heat the oil in a deep, heavy pan or a deep-fat fryer until it reaches 180°C. To test this, drop in a cube of white bread. It should turn golden brown in about 1 minute. Fry the croquetas in small batches for about 3–4 minutes, until deep golden brown and crisp. Alternatively, you can shallow fry them in a 1cm depth of oil, turning regularly. Either way, drain them on kitchen paper and serve straight away.

Deep-fried fish calzone *serves 2 as a hearty snack or light supper*

Deep-frying fish within a thin wrap of pizza dough is an excellent way to cook fillets from more robust, well-flavoured species. Unlike the usual batter, pizza dough absorbs very little oil, so comes out satisfyingly crispy – like a spring roll, but with more substance. The fish inside cooks delicately in its own steam. We serve it with a spicy tomato sauce.

Once you have the cooking method down pat, the variations are endless. You could flavour the dough (finely chopped rosemary would be good), or add a smear of salsa verde (see page 316) to the fish fillet before wrapping it.

You can also ring the changes by baking the dough-wrapped fish instead of deep frying. About 10 minutes at 230°C/Gas Mark 8 should do very nicely.

Also works with:
• Brill
• Red mullet
• Grey mullet
• John Dory
• Gurnard
• Sea trout

2 fillets of salmon, sea bass or bream, weighing about 200g each, descaled if necessary (or four 100g mackerel fillets)
Groundnut or sunflower oil for deep frying
Salt and freshly ground black pepper

FOR THE DOUGH:
7g dried yeast
160ml warm water
125g plain flour
125g strong white bread flour
5g salt
1 tablespoon olive oil

FOR THE CHILLI-SPIKED TOMATO SAUCE:
1 onion, finely chopped
1 garlic clove, finely chopped
1 tablespoon olive oil
5–6 large tomatoes (about 600g), skinned, deseeded and chopped (or a 400g tin of tomatoes in their own juice)
½–1 fresh red chilli (or a pinch of dried chilli flakes)
A squeeze of lemon juice
A good pinch of sugar (optional)

First make the dough: dilute the yeast in a little of the water, then mix all the dry ingredients together in a bowl and stir in the yeast mixture, the olive oil and the remaining water. Mix until evenly combined.

Turn the dough out on to a lightly floured work surface and knead until smooth, silky and stretchy. This combination of plain and strong flour with a dash of olive oil produces a good, soft, elastic dough that is easy to roll.

Return it to the bowl, cover and leave to rise in a warm place until doubled in size – or longer, if you want. It will happily ferment all day – just knock it back every now and then to stop it getting too big. It will even keep in the fridge for a couple of days.

You can make the sauce while the dough is rising. Sweat the chopped onion and garlic in the olive oil for 5–10 minutes, until soft but not coloured. Add the tomatoes and chilli and cook gently until thick and pulpy. Season with salt and pepper, a little lemon juice, and a pinch of sugar if it needs it, then set aside.

Take a lemon-sized ball of dough, or slightly bigger, dust it lightly with flour, then roll it out to about 2mm thick. Cut a rectangle long enough to wrap around a single fish fillet (or a sandwich of two fillets, in the case of mackerel) and wide enough to overlap by a centimetre or two, so you can seal it. (You can either make a 'jacket', with just half a centimetre of fish poking out at each end, as in the pictures opposite, or a sealed parcel, which will protect a more fragile fish.) Roll out a second piece of dough and cut a rectangle in the same way.

Season the fish on both sides, lay a fillet (or two, for mackerel) on each rectangle and fold the dough around it. Seal the lip along the length of the fillet by pressing it to the dough underneath – and the overlapping ends too, if you're going for the sealed parcel. Leave to prove for 5 minutes – time for a few small but significant air pockets to form in the dough.

Heat the oil for deep frying in a deep-fat fryer or a large, deep, heavy-based saucepan to 180°C or until a cube of white bread dropped into it turns golden brown in 50–60 seconds. Now lower one of the wrapped fish into the oil and cook for about 5 minutes. The parcel will puff up and float to the top pretty quickly, after which you will need to turn it every now and then to ensure even cooking.

When it is done, drain the calzone on a few layers of kitchen paper, then keep warm while you cook the second one.

Serve with a good spoonful of chilli-spiked tomato sauce on the side. As soon as the calzone are cool enough to touch, pick them up and eat with your hands, dabbing the fish into the sauce as you go.

Cold fish and salads

'Cold fish' isn't perhaps the most inspiring phrase in the English language – you wouldn't want to be seated next to one at dinner. But having one in front of you on a plate wouldn't be quite so bad. Because cold fish can be absolutely delicious.

Just to be clear, we're not talking about raw or marinated fish – though sushi, ceviche and a good rollmop are examples of just how appealing cold fish can be. We've already shone the spotlight on them, however. Nor are we dealing with leftover fish. We'll tackle that rich topic with great glee later on. No, our focus here, believe it or not, is on fish that you cook with the *deliberate intention of letting it go cold before you eat it*. It's not really such an eccentric thing to do. Think of a quick snack of potted shrimps on toast, or a full-on feast of cold poached sea trout with homemade mayonnaise, and perhaps you'll realise you're already quite at home with the idea of cooked fish served cold.

The tastes and textures offered by cold fish are quite different from those you get when eating it hot – and that's part of its charm. When fish is potted or made into a pâté, the different flavours will merge as it ripens and, if it's a good recipe, the combination will have a subtle harmony that often eludes warm, sauced fish. When cold poached (or even tinned) fish is tossed in a salad of fresh vegetables, leaves and herbs, the ingredients remain separate, yet together. Every mouthful offers a different combination – Salade niçoise (page 360) is the apotheosis of this phenomenon. But even when fish or shellfish is simply cooked and left to cool, then eaten at room (or garden) temperature with minimal adornment – a dressing of good oil and lemon juice, perhaps – there is a clarity of flavour about it that can be very satisfying.

The chef at any half-decent pub knows that there is no more sure-fire winner on a summer menu than half a pint of cold, shell-on cooked prawns served with a blob of mayo. Even with a relatively indifferent salad on the side and mayonnaise from a jar, it's still something of a treat. But if the pub chef goes the extra yard – whips up a homemade mayonnaise, offers leaves from a freshly torn lettuce, some buttered brown bread and half a lemon, he or she will have the customers in clover. And why stop there? How about a freshly boiled lobster or cracked crab with homemade garlic mayonnaise? Consider other shellfish – langoustines, winkles, whelks – and you'll see why 'cold fish' needn't be a term of derision. In fact, serving these delightful shellfish cold, with some kind of simple dressing or mayonnaise, is the obvious default setting for enjoying them at their best.

The two ends of the spectrum are the *grande assiette de fruits de mer* at a *fin de siècle* Parisian brasserie, and the cup of whelks from a seafront stall in one of Britain's bucket-and-spade holiday resorts. One may be gilt-edged and glamorous, the other plebeian and packed in polystyrene, but affection for both runs deep – and so it should.

It's not just shellfish that tastes good cooked and served cold with a light dressing. Many fish are fabulous this way too, though you should opt for those with a reasonably robust flavour. The oilier varieties – mackerel, salmon and trout, for instance – are the most obvious examples. In fact, when they've been smoked – either hot or cold smoked – then eating these species cold is the norm. But they certainly don't need to be smoked to shine in or around a salad. Baked, poached or even barbecued, then left to cool and served with a suitable dressing – lemony or garlicky, or perhaps both – they are outstanding. The same is true of a whole bunch of other less obvious, yet still robust, full-flavoured fish: sea bass, bream, gurnard, red mullet and scad, to name but five. They may rarely be given the chance to display their charms at room temperature, but they will certainly not disappoint when they do.

This cannot be said of all fish. There are some species that definitely don't float the boat as cold cuts. White fish such as pollack, pouting, haddock and cod, and the more delicate flatfish such as plaice, tend to be better in hot dishes. Since the flavour of any food is a little muted when eaten cold, a very delicate bit of fish flesh can become insipid when the warmth has left it. There's a fine line between subtle and dull, and with fragile white fish it's often crossed when the fish goes from warm to cold.

How cold is cold?

Coldness is, of course, relative, but we know roughly what it means in the context of food. No doubt somebody somewhere has served an anchovy ice cream (and if it was Heston Blumenthal, it was no doubt delicious). But on the whole, we are talking about serving fish somewhere between fridge temperature (4–6°C) and room temperature (20–25°C). Even this 20° window offers quite a range of sensations for the palate to explore.

Food at 4–6°C is *really cold* – a full 30°C colder than the temperature inside our mouths. Any food served at that temperature, or at anywhere up to about 10°C, is going to taste distinctly chilly. Generally speaking, this is not the temperature range to which we are referring when we suggest a dish can or should be served cold. In fact, the word to use for food served at this temperature is 'chilled' – and you would only choose to serve food, including fish, this way if you wanted the distinct effect of putting something cold in a warm mouth. That might be because it is simply intended to cool or refresh the palate; or because, like a set mousse or jelly, it is meant to melt in the mouth, releasing new and perhaps surprising flavours as it does so.

The traditional fish cookery canon does include such dishes: fish jellies, aspics and mousses abound in the works of Mrs Beeton, Mrs Marshall and Escoffier – not to mention their latter-day champion, Fanny Cradock – and they still have their followers amongst the starry-eyed chefs of today. But we don't have much time for such concoctions, not least because more often than not they involve a great deal of fuss: the puréeing and sieving of fish flesh, the mixing with egg yolks, the whipping of cream, the creaming of butter, the whisking and folding in of egg whites, the reducing of fish stock and/or the dissolving of gelatine. Frankly, who needs it? It shouldn't take an army of sous-chefs and a truckload of gizmos to extract the joy from a fish. So our soufflé on page 177 is as far as we're prepared to go along this route. It's half the fuss of any fish mousse recipe and, we would say, twice the pleasure of most. It is meant to be eaten hot from the oven, of course, though we've found the leftovers quite passable straight from the fridge.

Generally, the recipes in this chapter are best served at, or perhaps a little below, room temperature – say, 12–20°C. This is easy enough if they are created at room temperature, or cooled to it immediately after cooking, and then served without delay. But sometimes – the Potted mackerel on page 357 springs to mind – refrigeration is part of the preparation of a dish. In this case they will benefit from an hour or two out of the fridge before serving, to take the chill off them. In dishes where no refrigeration is prescribed, however – i.e. where a fish is simply cooked and left to cool – common sense should prevail. If it's a baking-hot day, or just baking in the kitchen, then a short spell in the fridge is in order.

What we're trying to avoid here is wedding-salmon syndrome. The point is that the temperature at which we propose you serve most of the dishes in this chapter is not one at which they should be allowed to hang around for long. Room temperature is also bug-breeding temperature (and so is garden/marquee temperature in the summer months). So if you need to store a cold fish dish before serving it, the best place is in the fridge (or, for al fresco feasts some distance from the kitchen, a properly chilled cold box).

The window for serving such dishes should be kept to an hour or two at most, and any leftovers should be refrigerated without delay and consumed within a day or two, max. If in doubt, use leftovers to make fishcakes or kedgeree and make sure in both cases that they are thoroughly heated through – beyond the magic 70°C for 2 minutes, which kills those bugs.

Tinned fish

One often unsung 'family' of fish that offers a useful set of ingredients for the cold-fish enthusiast is the kind we like to buy in tins. Everyone should have a shoal of well-chosen tinned fish in their larders. They are invaluable stand-bys for any keen composer of what Tom Norrington-Davies, a food writer we both enjoy, calls 'larder salads'. They're quite handy for larder sarnies, too.

Most notable by far – because they are the most delicious, and also the most versatile – are the mighty tuna and the diminutive sardine. One is so huge that a single fish might find its way into a thousand tins; the other so small that it might require half a dozen bedfellows to occupy just one.

Both may be eaten hot or cold, but on balance we prefer cold. Good sardines in good oil, forked straight from the tin on to buttered toast, with a couple of sticks of celery or maybe a raw carrot, make a classic stand-up lunch. It's the kind of meal you eat hovering in the kitchen while waiting for the kettle to boil (and very much the kind that has fuelled the writing of this book).

Tinned tuna offers similarly instant gratification – all the more so when it's tinned in oil rather than brine. The pleasure, though, comes increasingly at a price to the conscience, as discussed on pages 447–51. So, whether you're bashing out tuna sandwiches for the kids' lunchboxes or putting together a well-balanced classic Salade niçoise (page 360) for an outdoor summer lunch, always think beyond the tin, to the finned blue torpedo that travels the oceans of the world – increasingly in flight from our technology-laden boats (and even helicopters). We're sure you wouldn't want any fish to be hounded and harried to extinction, but especially not one that tastes so good. Please, only buy sustainably sourced tinned tuna – the Fish4Ever brand is the one we recommend (see the Directory, page 591).

There are other fish in tins, of course, and among them we particularly enjoy mackerel fillets and whole pilchards (which are really just big sardines and can be used in many of the same recipes). The tinned mackerel in oil will readily stand in for any recipe that calls for tuna – and so can certainly help in any bid to keep one's fish shopping sustainable.

Anchovies

We certainly mustn't leave the subject of tinned fish without mentioning one fabulous little contender. All hail the anchovy, without whose intense piquancy – sheer essence of fish – some of the recipes in this book would fail to reach the dizzy heights we expect of them.

Anchovies come preserved in various forms, including salt, vinegar and oil. Some cooks, and many restaurant chefs, like to buy them in bulk – packed and pressed in a tub of salt, headless but otherwise whole, with the backbone still in. These need to be lifted carefully from their crusty salt bed and split open with a small knife (or, if you've got the knack, a fingernail), so the fragile backbone can be removed and discarded. They then need gentle rinsing to remove the excess salt. After that they can be used straight away – or transferred to a smaller jar or plastic box and covered in oil.

Most of us, though, buy anchovies in small jars or tins of oil. These have already been salted, rinsed and filleted before being packed in oil. They are ready to use in any recipe that calls for anchovies, as several of ours do. (If you only ever cook one of them, we'd recommend it's the Anchovy and chilli dressing on page 398. Here we suggest it as an accompaniment to purple sprouting broccoli or curly kale, but you'll soon find it has a million and one uses.)

In many ways the greatest charm of the anchovy is its ability to lend its potent fishiness at short notice to some impromptu culinary experiment. A salad of new lettuces and hard-boiled eggs makes a simple and charming summer supper. But crack open a tin of anchovies (and a bottle of rosé while you're at it) and suddenly you're dining like kings. With anchovies added, a gratin dauphinois becomes less a greedy, creamy side dish, more a meal in its own right. It's on its way to what the Scandinavians call Jansson's temptation. Similarly, a pile of Puy lentils – simmered until just tender, left to go cold, then dressed with olive oil and lemon juice – make a lovely accompaniment to a cold fish dish (see page 355). But with some leftover cooked mackerel and a tin of anchovies roughly chopped and mixed through, they *are* a cold fish dish (see page 400).

Anchovy fillets come in various oils and vessels under a bewildering range of brands, mostly Italian or Portuguese. They vary slightly, and aficionados can exhibit fierce brand loyalty. We're a bit more happy-go-lucky, taking what comes our way. We've rarely, if ever, felt seriously let down by an anchovy, except the ones that come in vinegar. The Spanish call these *boquerones*, and they are emphatically not what is called for when a recipe asks for anchovies. They taste only of vinegar and are rarely as good as a decent rollmop. Unless you're sitting in a bar in Spain, with a glass of chilled Manzanilla to hand, they are bordering on pointless.

Fresh anchovies, on the other hand, should be snapped up at every opportunity. Tossed in seasoned flour and rapidly shallow or deep fried in olive oil, they can be munched head, guts, tail and all. You'll sometimes find them in fishmongers during the winter months, as boats out fishing for sprats occasionally get amongst huge shoals of anchovies (which are related to the sprat, as it happens). Sam and Sam Clark, who run the lovely Spanish/Moorish restaurant Moro in London, are always on the lookout for fresh anchovies. And when they get them, they cook them quite beautifully, coated in a coarse Spanish flour called *harina de trigo*, then deep fried.

Cooking fish for serving cold

When your cold fish doesn't come from a tin, you'll need to cook it yourself first. To do this, you won't need much in the way of special techniques – the various methods described in previous chapters will serve you in good stead. It's worth making a bit of a fuss over the fish as you cook it, just as you would if it were to be served steaming hot, because you still want to get as much flavour into it, and then out of it, as you possibly can.

The cold salmon, sea trout or sea bass on page 355, for instance, is poached in an aromatic court-bouillon before cooling, while Potted mackerel (page 357) is first baked in foil with garlic and bay leaves. These recipes illustrate the two main ways of cooking fish for serving cold – poaching and baking – both of which give you plenty of opportunity to infuse that fish with lots of flavour.

It's worth noting that a slightly shorter cooking time is usually in order if you're going to let the fish cool completely after baking or poaching. This is because, even after you've taken the fish away from the heat source, the heat will continue to travel to the middle of it.

Cooking shellfish for serving cold

When it comes to serving shellfish cold, the various species each have their own cooking processes. These are described either in specific recipes or in the relevant sections of the chapter on Shellfish skills (page 86). It's often easy enough to buy them ready cooked but we'd urge you to buy them live and boil them up yourself whenever possible. It's the best way to ensure the job's done well – not least because some fishmongers err on the side of over-boiling their crabs and lobsters.

Once you've got the cooked, cooled crustaceans in front of you, don't be daunted by the cracking and picking part of the deal. The way we look at it, the bashing of shells and wrenching of claws and legs is all part of the sense of occasion that befits the arrival of these armoured marine aliens at the table. It's also the best possible way to appreciate them in all their glory. You'd be cheating yourself, and your guests, if you didn't take the opportunity to marvel at their otherworldly bodies. The process of dismantling them and removing their flesh is both a ritual and an education.

You'll need the right equipment, of course, and the toolbox may be as useful a place to look as the kitchen drawer. Nutcrackers and rolling pins, small screwdrivers and tweezers will all come in handy. Even if you've never done it before, you'll soon be at it, almost literally, hammer and tongs.

River Cottage dressed crab *serves 2*

This is our favourite way to eat a really fresh crab – usually one that we've caught, cooked and picked ourselves. It can be served up in the main shell of the crab or on a plate. Or it can be made into lovely open sandwiches, as described in the variation below.

Brown and white meat from 1 medium-
large brown crab (see pages 89–93 for
cooking and picking instructions)
The crab's main shell, scrubbed under a
hot tap and left to dry (optional)
1 large hard-boiled egg, peeled and
coarsely chopped
2 teaspoons mayonnaise

½–1 teaspoon English mustard
Freshly ground black pepper

TO ACCOMPANY:
Buttered brown bread
1 small red onion, very finely chopped
A few lemon wedges

Lightly flake the white crabmeat, doing a final check for any slivers of shell, then pile it up in the middle of the carapace shell or on a medium serving plate. Put the soft brown meat in a bowl and combine with the chopped hard-boiled egg, mayonnaise, English mustard to taste and some black pepper. Make two mounds of the brown meat mixture on either side of the white meat.

Serve the crab with the brown bread, red onion and lemon wedges. The idea is to put some white meat on your bread, top with a little of the brown meat mixture – use it almost like a sauce – then sprinkle with a little chopped onion and a squeeze of lemon juice.

VARIATION
Dressed crab open sandwich

Use the same ingredients as above, minus the onion, plus a few crisp leaves of butterhead lettuce. Prepare the white and brown meat as above. Generously butter 2 large, thick slices of brown or granary bread. Spread thickly with the brown meat mixture. Scatter over a few leaves of lettuce. Arrange the white meat over the lettuce, then season with black pepper and a few drops of lemon juice.

Crack your own crabs

It's not always necessary to fuss around preparing dressed crab for your guests. If you think they're even half-competent shellfish enthusiasts, it's much nicer to put the cooked whole crab on the table and let them dig in for themselves.

Arm them with appropriate tools for shell cracking (rolling pins, small mallets, nutcrackers) and for winkling out (tweezers, chopsticks, small knives), provide a couple of dishes for the disposal of dead man's fingers, then sit back and watch as everyone sets to. It's a fantastically sociable way of doing things.

It's worth doing this with crabs alone – perhaps 3 nice big ones for 6 people – but there's no need to stop there. Cook some langoustines or prawns too, some lobster if possible, and perhaps some whelks or winkles. Make sure that your table is laden with the right sort of accompaniments. There are no fixed rules but a good mayonnaise, ideally homemade, is pretty much essential. You can customise it, if you like, by adding a little scrap of crushed garlic, some chopped chives and a squeeze of lemon. We'd also recommend good bread and butter, a green salad, a new potato salad, some English mustard, Tabasco sauce and lots of lemons. A copious supply of napkins is advisable.

And if you want your guests to feel really pampered, you might even provide them with finger bowls of warm water and a slice of lemon.

Lobster with herb mayonnaise *serves 4*

Generally speaking, the less you do to the sweet, pearly flesh of a lobster, the more impressive it will be. But anointing your freshly cooked crustacean with a little homemade mayonnaise laced with fresh herbs is one of the best treatments imaginable – simple, luxurious and somehow the epitome of summer.

2 live lobsters, weighing about 750g each

FOR THE HERB MAYONNAISE:
2 very fresh egg yolks
1 anchovy fillet, chopped
1 small garlic clove, chopped
1 teaspoon English mustard
A small pinch each of salt, sugar and
  freshly ground black pepper

Juice of ½ lemon
100ml olive oil
200ml groundnut or sunflower oil
1 tablespoon small capers, rinsed and
  finely chopped
2 tablespoons mixed very finely chopped
  parsley, chives and basil

Begin by putting the live lobsters into the freezer for around 2 hours. This is the RSPCA-sanctioned method of reducing them to a state of unconsciousness, which means they will know nothing about it when you then drop them into a large pan of well-salted boiling water. Cook according to the instructions on page 93. Allow them to cool completely but don't try and speed this up by dunking them in cold water – they'll get waterlogged. Just let them steam off naturally.

While the lobsters are cooling, make the mayonnaise. Put the egg yolks, anchovy, garlic, mustard, salt, sugar, pepper and a squeeze of lemon in a food processor or blender and blitz until smooth – 30 seconds or so will do it. (Alternatively, whisk the ingredients together in a bowl.) Combine the two oils and start adding them, trickling them in a thin stream through the hole in the lid of the processor (or by hand into your bowl). Keep whizzing (or whisking) all the time, to emulsify the oil with the egg yolks. When you have a thick, smooth mixture, you can add the oil a little faster. Keep going until all the oil has been added and you have a thick, glossy mayonnaise. If it's too thick, add a tablespoon of warm water to 'let it down' slightly.

When you're happy with the consistency of the mayonnaise, fold in the capers and chopped herbs. Taste and adjust the seasoning with salt, pepper and lemon juice, then cover and put in the fridge until you're ready to serve.

Split the cooked lobsters in half (see page 94), then give each person half a lobster with a good dollop of the mayonnaise. A new potato and marsh samphire salad goes well with this. When everyone's finished eating, don't forget to save the lobster shells for stock (see page 257).

Cold fish with salsa verde mayonnaise *serves 8–10*

This recipe is a fond tribute to Hugh's days as a sous-chef at London's River Café, where one of the many dishes he served was cold poached sea bass with a piquant salsa verde. We've just taken the idea and mellowed it a little by folding the salsa into a homemade mayonnaise. As a celebratory summer feast, you'd be hard-pressed to do better than this.

Don't poach your fish a day ahead and refrigerate it, as some would suggest, as the fish will dry out too much, and anyway, it's better eaten at room/air temperature rather than chilled. Ideally, cook it about 4 hours before serving and leave it to settle in a draughty kitchen or cool larder.

1 quantity of court-bouillon (see page 281)

1 sea bass, black bream, sea trout, or organic farmed or self-caught wild salmon, weighing about 2.5kg, descaled and gutted

FOR THE SALSA VERDE MAYONNAISE:
2 very fresh egg yolks
A small pinch each of salt, sugar and black pepper

1 teaspoon mustard
1 tablespoon lemon juice
200ml olive oil
300ml groundnut oil
2 anchovy fillets
1 large garlic clove, very finely chopped
1 tablespoon capers, rinsed
A good handful of flat-leaf parsley leaves

Put the court-bouillon in a fish kettle and add the fish, placing it on the kettle's trivet. Bring to a simmer, put the lid on, then turn the heat off underneath the fish and leave for about 40 minutes, until the fish is cooked through and the kettle is only hand hot. Remove the fish and transfer it to a platter. Don't skin it until it has cooled, or it will lose precious moisture.

To make the mayonnaise, put the egg yolks, salt, sugar, pepper, mustard and lemon juice into a food processor or blender and process until smooth. (Alternatively, whisk by hand in a bowl.) Combine the two oils in a jug. With the processor running (or with your whisk arm working), start pouring in the oil in a very thin trickle. When the oil starts to emulsify with the yolks, you can add it a little faster. By the time you've added all the oil, you should have a thick, glossy mayonnaise.

Combine the anchovies, pre-chopped garlic, capers and parsley on a board and chop them all together as finely as you can, then stir them into the mayonnaise. Taste and adjust the seasoning with more salt, pepper or lemon juice as needed. Chill until ready to serve.

To serve the fish, peel off the skin from the upper side and bring the whole fish to the table. Gently ease portions of the fish away from the backbone with a spatula or fish slice and place on serving plates. When you've done the first side, lift off the backbone, head and tail, and gently break the remaining side into portions. Accompany the fish with the salsa verde mayonnaise, plus some cold, cooked Puy lentils that have been tossed with olive oil and plenty of seasoning. Buttered new potatoes or a potato salad, and a leaf salad or a salad of shaved fennel, also make fantastic accompaniments.

Potted mackerel *makes about 500g*

Potting is another of those preserving techniques borne of necessity that have survived into the age of fridges and freezers because the results are so delicious. This is our much-used recipe for potted mackerel, which is perfect served on hot brown toast.

4–5 medium mackerel (about
  300g each), gutted
4–5 garlic cloves
4–5 bay leaves
1 teaspoon ground mace
½ teaspoon cayenne pepper

1 tablespoon chopped parsley
1 teaspoon chopped thyme
250g unsalted butter
Juice of 1 lemon
Salt and freshly ground black pepper

Put the mackerel side by side in an oiled roasting tin. Crush the garlic cloves roughly and put one inside each fish cavity, along with a bay leaf. Season the fish well with salt and pepper. Bake in an oven preheated to 180°C/Gas Mark 4 for 12–15 minutes, turning the fish over halfway through, until they are just cooked. You can check this by gently lifting the flesh from the bone; it should come away without any resistance.

When the fish are cool enough to handle, flake the flesh into a large bowl, carefully checking for bones as you go. Discard the skin, heads, bay leaves and all but one clove of garlic. Add the mace, cayenne, parsley and thyme to the flaked mackerel.

Melt the butter in a pan over a gentle heat. Finely chop the reserved garlic clove and add it to the butter. Leave the butter to settle (it will separate into a clear, golden layer on top and a whitish layer on the bottom). Pour two-thirds of the clear butter over the mackerel mixture. Add the lemon juice and season well with salt and pepper. Toss together gently, so as not to over-process the mixture.

If you're going to serve the potted mackerel within a day or two, you can pot it in individual ramekins. However, we make large batches to keep for several days, so we like to use sealable glass jars such as Le Parfait. Either way, make sure your pots/jars are spotlessly clean and pack the mixture in so there are no air spaces. Leave a little room at the top of each. Top the mackerel mixture with a layer of the clear, golden butter (discard the milky white solids left in the pan). This butter seals off the mackerel from the air and will help it keep a little longer. When cold, seal the jars (if you're using them).

Store your potted mackerel in the fridge and use open ramekins within a day or two, sealed jars within a week.

Also works with:
• Herring
• Scad
• Sardines (large)
• Trout

Kipper, orange and carrot salad *serves 4 as a starter*

This is a lovely recipe. It's cheap and cheerful, yet it poshes up nicely for a dinner party. You can get all the main ingredients from your average corner shop (yes, in desperate circumstances, frozen boil-in-the-bag kipper fillets can be used).

4 double kipper fillets (about 400g)

2 large oranges

1 tablespoon good wine vinegar or cider
vinegar

Juice of ½ lemon

2 large donkey carrots (about 500g)

2 tablespoons good olive oil

Freshly ground black pepper

The kippers and oranges need to macerate together, so prepare them a good couple of hours in advance. Peel the oranges with a sharp knife, slicing off the rind and all the pith. Cut between the membranes to release each segment – do this over a bowl so you catch all the juice, dropping the segments into the bowl as you go. When you've finished, add the wine vinegar and lemon juice to the bowl.

Skin the kipper fillets, removing any bones you come across, and cut them at a slight angle into slices 1–2cm thick. Add them to the orange segments and toss gently but well. Leave to macerate for an hour or so, tossing once or twice.

Peel the carrots and cut them into fine matchsticks, using a food processor or mandolin if you have the right blade, or by hand if you don't (grated carrots are not what you want here – they're too soggy). Toss the carrots with the kippers, oranges and olive oil and season with black pepper. Leave for another half-hour or so, gently turning once or twice. Serve with buttered brown bread.

Tuna, white bean and red onion salad
serves 4 as a starter or light lunch

This shows why it's always a good idea to have a couple of tins of tuna and a tin of white beans in the cupboard. It takes all of 10 minutes to knock together and makes a delicious, sustaining and very healthy light lunch.

Two 120g tins of sustainably caught
tuna in oil

1½ tablespoons olive oil

2 tablespoons lemon juice

1 teaspoon English mustard

A pinch of sugar

400g tin of white beans, such as butter or
cannellini beans, drained and rinsed

1 small red onion, finely sliced

1 heaped tablespoon chopped flat-leaf
parsley

Salt and freshly ground black pepper

Drain the tuna, keeping 1½ tablespoons of the oil. Mix this oil with the olive oil, lemon juice and mustard. Season with salt, pepper and a pinch of sugar and whisk or shake together to make a creamy dressing.

Break the tuna into large flakes and put into a bowl. Add the rinsed beans, the onion and parsley and toss together. Re-whisk or shake the dressing, add to the salad and toss together again. Serve straight away, with crusty white bread.

Salade niçoise *serves 4*

At its best, this classic dish is a sheer delight but in the wrong hands it can become a bit of a mess. Anyone who's eaten a few different *salades niçoises* will have come across an ingredient that has no business being there – fennel, cucumber, green peppers, capers, *pine nuts*? We wouldn't be so arrogant as to claim ours as the ultimate version, and there's no accounting for taste, but we reckon we're in the zone here, both in terms of authenticity and flavour. In our view, tinned tuna is better and more authentic than fresh. (And, on that basis, this recipe would be equally at home in the chapter on Fish thrift and standbys.) Choose a brand that's line-caught sustainably.

As with any simple dish, it's important to get every ingredient absolutely right. The tuna must be tinned in oil, not brine, while the lettuce should be a butterhead type, not Cos or, God forbid, iceberg – and only the crisper, inner leaves at that. The eggs should be boiled until the yolk is set but still just soft in the middle, the French beans must be really young and fresh, and the olives should be baby niçoise ones, if you can get them. Once you have gathered these beautiful ingredients, putting the salad together is a simple matter.

200g small new potatoes
200g French beans, topped, tailed and
  halved
4 eggs, at room temperature
Two 120g tins of sustainably caught
  tuna in oil
2 butterhead lettuces, floppier outer
  leaves discarded
A handful of small black olives, preferably
  baby niçoise
8–12 anchovy fillets in oil, cut in half
  lengthways if large

FOR THE DRESSING:
1½ tablespoons olive oil
1½ tablespoons sunflower oil (ideally
  from the tuna tin)
1 tablespoon white wine vinegar
½ teaspoon Dijon mustard
A pinch of sugar
Salt and freshly ground black pepper

Cook the potatoes in boiling salted water until tender, adding the French beans to the pan about 5 minutes before the potatoes are done. Drain and leave to cool.

Meanwhile, bring a small pan of water to the boil, add the eggs and simmer for 5–7 minutes (5 minutes for small eggs, 7 minutes for large). Drain and rinse under cold running water to stop them cooking further. Peel and halve the eggs.

Drain the tuna (reserving a little of the oil for the dressing) and break it into chunks. Make the dressing by whisking all the ingredients together.

Rather than tossing everything together with the dressing, which can result in all the fish falling to the bottom of the dish, it's best to build up the salad in layers. Begin by arranging the lettuce leaves over a large, shallow serving dish (or use individual dishes, if you prefer), then distribute the potatoes over them. Strew the beans on next, and trickle some dressing over the whole lot. Next come the eggs and the olives, with a little more dressing, and finally the tuna and the anchovies, with a spoonful of dressing to finish it all off. Eat straight away, preferably in the sunshine, with a well-chilled rosé.

Rollmop, apple and potato salad *serves 4 as a starter*

Should you ever find yourself wondering what to do with a jar of rollmops, other than eating them straight from the jar with your fingers, then give this a go. It's lovely.

2 tablespoons crème fraîche

1 good teaspoon English mustard

6 rollmops, or other good-quality marinated herrings, plus a little of their pickling liquid

A pinch of sugar

300g waxy salad potatoes, such as Anya or Pink Fir Apple, cooked, cooled and thickly sliced

1 smallish red onion, finely sliced

2 hard green apples, such as new season Cox's or Granny Smith's, cored and thinly sliced

2 tablespoons chopped dill or flat-leaf parsley

Salt and freshly ground black pepper

Start by making the dressing. Combine the crème fraîche and mustard in a bowl with 3–4 teaspoons of the rollmop pickling liquid. Season to taste with salt, pepper and sugar (bearing in mind that the pickling liquid will already be pretty salty). Set aside while you prepare the salad.

Cut the rollmops into thickish strips and place in a large bowl. Add the potatoes, onion and apples and toss together lightly. Add the dressing and chopped herbs and toss together again. Taste and adjust the seasoning if you think it's necessary. Serve straight away, with rye bread on the side.

Thai whelk salad *serves 4 as a starter*

Experience has taught us that this is another fine way (in addition to the Whelk fritters on page 328) to win round a whelkophobe. We first made this dish several years ago to sell at the Lyme Regis regatta and it was a roaring success. To get the most from it, make sure you chop the ingredients for the salsa really finely.

2 dozen large or 3–4 dozen smaller
   whelks, plus a couple extra for the cook

FOR THE STOCK:
Large knob of fresh ginger, sliced
3–4 garlic cloves, crushed
1 tablespoon salt
Stalks from a bunch of coriander
  (used for the salsa)

PLUS, IF THEY ARE TO HAND:
3–4 lemongrass stalks, sliced
2 onions, sliced
A few bay leaves

FOR THE SALSA:
1 small red onion, very thinly sliced
3 medium-hot fresh red chillies, deseeded
  and very finely chopped
½ small garlic clove, very finely chopped
1 small or ½ medium cucumber, peeled,
  deseeded and cut into pea-sized dice
Leaves from a large bunch of coriander,
  chopped
2 tablespoons sunflower, groundnut or
  light olive oil
Juice of 1 orange
Juice of 1–2 limes
A few drops of Thai fish sauce (optional)
Salt

To make the stock, put all the ingredients into a large pan (plus any extras you have to hand) with 3 litres of water and bring to the boil.

Meanwhile, scrub the whelks under cold running water. As you handle them, you may find that some of them release a certain amount of slime – don't worry about this, just rinse it away.

Drop the whelks into the boiling stock and cook at a cheerful simmer for 8–10 minutes, then drain and leave to cool.

To make the salsa, combine all the ingredients in a bowl, adding the lime juice, fish sauce and salt to taste. Stir together thoroughly, then set aside to infuse for at least 1 hour.

Remove the cooked whelks from their shells with a fork, discarding the coarse cap from the front end and the dark digestive sac from the tail end. If any are still a little slimy, give them a wipe with a tea towel.

Toss the whelks thoroughly with the salsa. Leave to infuse for an hour or so, then toss again. Taste one whelk, adjust the seasoning with more lime juice or salt, if you like, taste another, then serve.

Fish thrift
and standbys

Fish, like meat, is a particularly precious food – not least because a creature has been killed to provide it for us. Throwing away any of the edible parts of a carcass is quite an insult to that animal. So it's the duty of conscientious fish cooks to use their raw materials wisely and thriftily – which is where the last of our cookery chapters comes in.

However, this isn't just a 'branch' of fish cookery. The principle of maximising ingredients and minimising waste is very close to our hearts and, we hope, underpins this whole book. When we're cooking fish, we really try *never* to throw anything edible away – by which we mean anything except the scales, bones and guts (and even the guts, in the case of the red mullet, can be a bit of a treat – see page 315). The fact that we catch our own fish is significant here. It is particularly painful – almost shaming – to waste fish you've caught yourself (as you'll understand if you've ever done it). When it comes to ecological living, we're far from paragons, but when it comes to food generally, and fish in particular, we try to shop, cook and eat in the most sustainable way we can.

Duty aside for a moment, being thrifty with fish can and should be tremendous fun and very satisfying, presenting just as good an opportunity to express your creativity as cooking 'expansively' with unlimited fresh fish (although of course, in a wider sense, fish resources are *always* limited). Cunning and delicious recipes made with leftovers are one part of the thrift challenge, but the way you approach a fresh fish is important too. It may be the fillets you're really after, but could you not also eke out an extra – and surprisingly wonderful – meal from the heads, tails, even skin and bones?

You'll find recipes here that go beyond leftovers into really thorough-going thrift-with-fresh-fish – recipes where you are, essentially, stealing 'scraps' from the cat. Because, as with meat, it's at the thrifty margins of necessity that some of the most inventive and appealing fish dishes have been devised.

Fresh fish thrift

Your thrift radar must be allowed free rein from the moment you start thinking about acquiring some fresh fish. If you're going to the fishmonger's, might they have some lovely fresh heads and skeletons that could make a stock – the beginnings of some future fish soup or sauce? It's a far easier thing to prepare successfully (see pages 252–3) than a meat stock. But that is only the most obvious of many possibilities. Might one or two of those heads be substantial enough to stand up to a good roasting? If so, see page 380. (Or, in the case of salmon heads, a souping? If so, see page 378.)

Cultivate a good, discursive relationship with your fishmonger (or, more importantly, spend a bit of money in the shop) and you might find all sorts of treats coming your way. If you're splashing out on a princely sea bass or great slab of brill, then a couple of fistfuls of cockles or whelks might find their way into your bag, gratis, in the same spirit as your butcher will often let you have a pair of pig's trotters on the house when you're buying a Sunday roast.

Such casual generosity is often to be found when you buy fish straight from the boat, harbourside, as we love to do. The friendly fishermen at West Bay will make you a keen price, but not a silly one, when they sell you their sole. But it's hardly a Faustian pact when they also start offering you some of their bycatch – a couple of dabs or mackerel, or even a live crab 'for your tea'.

If you're catching your own fish, thrift should soon become second nature. As you're gutting the fish on the way back in, by all means throw the contents of your catch's stomachs to the gulls that mob and dive above the boat's wake. It's a time-honoured ritual. But if you get as far as filleting, then don't give in to their persuasive chatter, begging you to throw more. Stash the heads and neatly folded frames in the cold box, along with the fillets. They are all meals in waiting.

A tale of fishy thrift

Arguably our 'personal best' fishing-trip thrift (aside from regularly taking leftover fresh squid bait home to add to a stew of the day's catch) came on a spectacularly good bass fishing day out of Weymouth. The bass had been hitting the sprats – and our shiny lures designed to imitate them – hard. And from the jaws and stomachs of the bass we killed we managed to recover a number of the little silver fish in surprisingly good nick. They must have been snapped up only moments before our rubber imitations. So we took them home (the least digested half dozen or so) and fried them up as chef's perks.

Besides providing welcome sustenance (while we took our time in doing justice to the bass), it also felt like a good thing to do – almost as if the sprats hadn't died in vain. Not that it's a sprat's ambition to be gobbled by a bass – or indeed a human. But a bass would never waste a morsel of its prey fish; every scrap of it would go to nourish its powerful, predatory body. And so a dead sprat coughed up on the deck would somehow have failed to do its job, for the bass. Of course, we could have lobbed it to a passing gull. But somehow, by eating it ourselves, we were honouring the sea bass's own thrifty intentions. We kept the sprat on track, in line with the food chain that had already claimed it – the one that ended up on our plates.

Fish with rice and pasta

Of course, fish thrift is not only about what you do with the fish but also what else you put with it on the plate. Because everything you eat that isn't fish makes the fish go a bit further. To this end, the most obvious and versatile companion commodities are rice and pasta: the great bulkers, permanently on standby in the larders of every sane cook.

They are infinitely versatile with leftovers, as we'll see, but also, once in a while, brilliant with fresh fish that have been specially chosen to accompany them. Indeed, one or two of the recipes in this chapter depart somewhat from thrifty principles in that they call for fresh fish that may be far from cheap. But those dishes still don't use extravagant amounts of fish. Scallops with fennel risotto (page 397) springs to mind. It makes six juicy scallops feed four, and the frills from the scallops go into the stock for the risotto. The point about combining fish with rice or pasta is that, more often than not, it inverts the norm: the meat of the meal, so to speak, is the starch component. The fish is really the spice or, to recklessly mix metaphors (not to mention split infinitives), the icing on the cake. The point is that a little fish is made to go a long way.

In this context, it is perhaps worth remembering just how closely rice and pasta are related historically. Rice can also make noodles, of course, and in the rice noodles of China and Southeast Asia lie the origins of Italian pasta. The use of a small amount of highly seasoned fish (or meat) as a seasoning or topping for a plate of belly-filling starch is a daily act of thrift – not merely in Asia but also in Africa and other food cultures less extravagant than ours the world over. It may be borne of necessity, but it's really not a bad way to foster respect for a precious ingredient.

There are, of course, some highly sophisticated, even indulgent, fish dishes that use rice and pasta. In the 1990s you could barely avoid little mousselines of lobster encased in ravioli and floating in some kind of fish soup. These days the trend is for fishy fusion fantasies – like deep-fried maki rolls with a soft-shell crab filling, scattered with wind-dried tuna flakes. Once in a while such concoctions may be rather amazing, but they are best left to chefs with brigades of underlings. Here we're more interested in recipes that involve flinging some fresh, briny things together with a few choice companions – a smattering of garlic, a little bit of tomato, a dash of cream – plus a nice pile of comforting starch. If that happens to be fresh pasta you've taken the trouble to make yourself, then so much the better.

The obvious choice for rice and pasta dishes is fish that is either strongly flavoured in itself or highly seasoned, which is why many of the recipes coming up call for oily fish, smoked fish and shellfish. Delicate white fish can very easily get lost in a bowlful of carbohydrate. Whiting risotto anyone? We don't think so. But try substituting slivers of kipper fillet for the ham in a classic spaghetti carbonara (see page 390) and you are absolutely on the money. Although the quality of the fish is, as ever, of paramount importance, quantity often is not. If you're shovelling in a whole forkful of spaghetti, you only need one juicy cockle tangled up in it to make it special.

This is what we mean when we say the fish can be the spice. Take kedgeree, for instance. Essentially it's a dish of curried, oniony rice with eggs, further seasoned with a smattering of smoked fish (quite a generous smattering in our case, see page 393). Take the fish out of it (but leave the eggs in, please) and it would still be a worthwhile supper. Include the fish and it's unbeatable.

Cooking pasta for fish

The whole point of cooking pasta is to put food on the table fast. For the most part, you want to be able to pull together the saucy, fishy element of the dish in the time the pasta takes to cook, so a larder bristling with dried pasta in the usual range of shapes and sizes – spaghetti, linguine, tagliatelle, penne, risoni – is always going to be handy for the fish cook. However, if you make or buy fresh egg pasta, its softness and rich flavour will certainly bring a new and delicious dimension to many fish dishes – Creamy cockles with tagliatelle (page 386) springs to mind.

The normal cooking rules for dried pasta apply. Here's a quick recap. Bring a really big pan of water (at least 4 litres) to a rolling boil and salt it generously (allow 20g salt for 4 litres). The pasta absorbs the water as it cooks, which is why the salt is so important. Underseasoned cooking water means underseasoned pasta, which can really undermine the finished dish. Throw your pasta into the pan and keep it at a good rolling boil (not a feeble simmer), stirring occasionally so the pasta moves about freely. Cooking times can vary from brand to brand, so be guided by the instructions on the packet. Keep testing, however, and stop cooking as soon as your pasta has reached the *al dente* stage, and before it becomes soft.

Once your pasta is cooked and drained, it's important to combine it quickly with the hot sauce and get it into warmed dishes and on the table pronto. Unsauced pasta that sits around for any time at all will quickly turn itself into a sticky mass. If you need to hold it for a few minutes, toss it with a trickle of oil, a knob of butter, or both. Come to think of it, do that anyway.

Just cooked (*perfectly* cooked) oiled or buttered pasta often needs nothing but some flaked leftover fish, and any pan juices or sauce that might have been saved with it, to make a meal of it. But obvious 'zingers' that can lift such an improvisation include a clove or two of garlic, finely sliced and gently sweated for a minute or two – in the butter or oil you were going to toss the pasta in anyway; a teaspoon of capers (whole if small, roughly chopped if large); a few anchovies – just enough to season and intensify rather than drown out the main fish leftovers; and some finely chopped fresh parsley. Should you happen to have all four of the above, they'll all go together rather well.

Fish and rice

Fish risottos may take a few more minutes than pasta but they are still great standby dishes. If you've got some fish stock in the freezer (not inconceivable if you've taken our advice to heart), some risotto rice in the cupboard and an onion in the larder, you're laughing. If not, you can use a stock cube (preferably organic) or, better still, make an 'instant' fresh vegetable stock. Just coarsely grate a large carrot, a large onion, and a couple of sticks of celery if you have them. Put in a pan with a bay leaf or two and pour over a litre or so of boiling water from the kettle. Bring back to the boil and simmer for at least 10 minutes – up to 20 minutes if you have that long to spare. Strain and use straight away.

We've included only two risotto recipes here but both are ripe for customisation into infinite variations. Cooking a fish risotto is a lot like cooking a fish soup and the principles of building up flavours (outlined on pages 251–2) apply here too. What you're doing is creating a really good, flavoursome base into which some fresh fish can be dropped just before serving. The ingredients you use to make that base (onions, celery, garlic, wine, vermouth, tomatoes, fish ink…) and the fish you add at the end (strips of squid, slices of scallop, steamed mussels, a handful of leftover barbecued mackerel…) are up to you.

Many other cultures have their risotto equivalents, their fish-with-rice favourites. In the UK, we've co-opted the kedgeree – originally of Anglo-Indian origin – as a kind of national dish. And throughout Asia, such dishes as the pilaf, or pilau, still rule. Spain has its paellas – though some will argue that seafood versions are recent bastardisations of what was originally a very earthy dish featuring rabbit and snails.

Nomenclature aside, whether you think you're making a kedgeree, a paella, a pilaf, or are even still in risotto territory, it is rarely a bad idea to combine some seasoned, perhaps quite highly spiced, rice with some well-flavoured fish or shellfish, lightly sizzled onions and maybe a few peas or beans. You could go so far as to call it a gumbo and, even if you weren't from New Orleans, if it was delicious enough we'd forgive you.

The cheese issue

One thing we can't ignore in the context of pasta and rice recipes that include fish is the knotty question of whether cheese is allowed to feature in the proceedings. Some people balk at the very idea of cheese with fish but we are not among them (the Smoked pollack soufflé, page 177, and Smoked pollack and spinach tart, page 241, would both be diminished without their Cheddar). We are, however, firmly in the Italian camp when it comes to rejecting Parmesan on fish pasta dishes or fish risottos. It just doesn't work.

The fact is that in most cases, even with a tomato-based sauce, you are looking for the taste of the fish to stand out as clear and true, and so a grating of Parmesan is generally a flavour too far. (Note that the cheese element has been removed from the Kipper carbonara on page 390 – it would be an overkill of savoury elements.) A twist of black pepper and a swirl of grassy, extra virgin olive oil in some cases, a knob of butter in others, will make a better finish.

Managing fish leftovers

Everyone knows, surely, that all the best dishes are made with leftovers. That may seem an odd thing to say in a cookbook full of recipes that demand spanking-new, super-fresh ingredients, and we don't mean to malign any of the dishes we've introduced you to so far. But you know what we mean, don't you? We think leftovers generally, and fish leftovers in particular, are worth getting excited about. There's something about a meal cobbled together from last night's this, yesterday's that and a tin of whatnot from the back of the cupboard which, when you get it right, is so astronomically satisfying as to rank up there with your finest culinary achievements.

Still, even if you concur with us about the winning nature of leftover meals in principle, you may feel that there's something not quite right about eating leftover fish. It's not exactly the same as cold roast chicken, is it? Well, actually, we'd say it can be every bit as good. Indeed, a clandestine session picking fish bones, wheedling little morsels of cold fish off the half-eaten frame of a big sea bass or sea trout, is just as joyous as working over a chicken carcass that's sitting in the larder. If that fish was lovely and fresh before it was cooked, if it was cooked well, and if it's been properly stored, there's no reason why it shouldn't be delicious on its second outing – even if that's two days later. In fact, if you find yourself with a good, fresh piece of fish that you can't eat straight away, it's far better to cook it immediately and then use it cold the next day than to leave it, uncooked and turning stale, for another 24 hours.

This might sound strange, but so convinced are we of the virtues of leftover fish that we actively go out of our way to create it. We'll often deliberately cook more fish than we know we can eat for one meal, so that a second meal is already half-made. Picking over the surplus mackerel, bream or bass has become one of the rituals at the end of a good fish supper, resulting in a pile of skin on one side for the cat and a pile of clean fish meat on the other, to be kept in the fridge for tomorrow's improvised supper.

There's more to this end-of-meal fish-picking ritual than greedy anticipation of the next meal. It's actually much easier to do it while the fish is still warm. Put a messy pile of remains in the fridge and try picking over it the next day:

skin, flesh and bones are all stuck together with fishy superglue. Do it soon after cooking, however, and not only does the flesh flake nicely from the bones but any juices or poaching liquid can be collected too, before they congeal, to lubricate whatever new dish is rustled up the following day.

However disciplined you are at picking over your fish, cooking with leftovers is often an unpredictable affair. You may not know exactly what and how much you're going to have to work with ahead of time. For that reason, almost all of these recipes are guides, not prescriptions – spontaneity is the order of the day. If you don't have as much fish as we suggest, don't abandon the recipe, try it anyway, maybe adding a little more of something else instead. Even a small amount of fish can spice a salad or a pile of pasta.

You'll notice that tinned fish (already discussed on pages 346–7) gets a regular outing in these recipes too. This is because it has a similar status to yesterday's fresh fish – a kind of perpetually available leftover. Keep a couple of tins of good (sustainably sourced) tuna and sardines in the cupboard and, even if you don't have any cold mackerel, salmon or brill, you can still cook most of these recipes.

Other friends of leftover fish

Useful though they are, pasta and rice do not have to monopolise your leftover fish cooking. All sorts of other ingredients, including some storecupboard staples, can get in on the act. Here are a few suggestions to get you going:

Potatoes
If you have a couple of potatoes to accompany a modest pile of fish leftovers, you're in business. If those spuds are also leftover – mash, maybe, or boiled new potatoes – then you're only minutes away. Fishcakes are an obvious option, and Fish bubble and squeak (page 405) is a lovely variation on the same theme. Another way to go is what we call 'leftover fish and chips' – where you fry up some previously cooked potatoes until crisp (maybe with some chopped garlic and thyme), then throw in some fish leftovers for the last few minutes.

Pulses
Versatile and often interchangeable, dried and tinned pulses get some of their most worthwhile outings when there's leftover fish around. Puy lentils and other varieties that hold their shape are delicious with fish, hot or cold. All you need to do is cook the lentils, toss them with the leftover fish, dress with oil and lemon, and maybe fling in a bit of chopped parsley and/or a few capers. See page 400 for a fractionally more prescriptive approach.

Creamy tinned beans such as cannellini, borlotti and butter beans are crying out to be combined with leftover, or even tinned, fish. Along with a few slivers of onion and a little vinaigrette, they absolutely do the business. It may be only a whisker away from that classic student stand-by – a tin of tuna mixed with a tin of kidney beans – but at least it was always one of the better ones.

Chickpeas are extremely useful for transforming a soup such as the Fish (and chorizo) soup on page 260 into a more substantial proposition. They can also be deployed like tinned beans in salady cold fish improvisations – in which case, lots of chopped fresh parsley, a slug of olive oil and a little freshly squeezed lemon juice are always in order.

Eggs

Fish omelettes are always a delight (a sardine omelette being a great favourite in the Fearnley household), but if you have potatoes too, then a Fish frittata (page 403) may well be in order. Hard-boiled eggs with leftover fish, lettuce and any other good salad leaves are a very sound combination. You may not have everything necessary to pull together an authentic salade niçoise, but cold leftover mackerel with lettuce, hard-boiled eggs and a few anchovies and/or capers and/or spring onions still makes a fine summer supper.

Salad leaves

Lose the eggs but hold on to the salad – lettuces mainly, but other sweet, good-natured leaves like baby spinach, mâche or winter purslane – and you still have a great opportunity to put together a winning 'chef's salad'. Think Caesar rather than niçoise, if it helps. Some anchovies and croûtons will add piquancy and a certain substance respectively.

Bread

Talking of croûtons, if the bread is fresh and yielding, it probably seems a waste to fry it. Nor is there any need to, when you can put together a really cracking cold fish sandwich (page 409). And just as we have pointed out how rewardingly tinned sardines may double for leftover fish, the opposite also holds true. Leftover mackerel, dressed with olive oil, black pepper and just a squeeze of lemon, may be squashed on to hot buttered toast with complete confidence.

Another tale of fishy thrift

The crowning glory of dishes made from fish leftovers must be one we had in the Channel Islands, on board Pat Carlin's fabulous boat, *Channel Chieftain*. We'd just devoured a garfish version of the mackerel-with-potatoes described on page 218, and all we had left on our plates were the luminous green backbones of these much-underrated fish. Nick took the empties through to the *Chieftain*'s galley, where the rest of us thought he was uncharacteristically proposing to do the washing up. But a few minutes later he popped out again, bearing a plate.

Sitting on a paper towel were some crispy slivers that had clearly just been frazzled in hot oil. They looked jagged and slightly dangerous but, after an initial crackly crunch, they crumbled in a most pleasant and yielding way. They were beautifully seasoned too – salty and peppery with just a hint of garlic. 'Fried garfish bones,' Nick announced. 'Apparently they're mad for them in Japan.' He had rubbed a clove of garlic along each of the bones, then tossed them in seasoned flour and shallow fried them in very hot oil for barely a minute. They were absolutely lovely.

Herring roes on toast *serves 4 as a starter, 2 for tea*

One should always feel a little uneasy about eating roe. Try to source your herrings with care – choose MSC-certified fish where possible. If you catch or buy herrings that are full of roe (which can happen at various times of the year, see page 419), it would be a waste not to put it to good use.

You can, of course, buy the roes separately, though they will usually have been frozen, and you are unlikely to get any sourcing or sustainability information with them. Ideally, this dish uses both the firm roes of female herring and the softer roes (technically called milts) from males.

8 herring roes, or 4 roes and 4 milts	Unsalted butter
2 tablespoons plain flour, seasoned with salt and freshly ground black pepper	4 slices of granary bread
	1 tablespoon chopped parsley
1 tablespoon olive or sunflower oil	2 lemons, halved

Lightly dust the roes in the seasoned flour. Heat the oil and a knob of butter in a large frying pan over a medium heat. Add the roes and let them sizzle gently for 5–6 minutes, until they develop a golden brown crust. Meanwhile, toast and butter your bread.

Serve one roe and one milt, piping hot from the pan, on each piece of toast. Sprinkle with chopped parsley and serve a lemon half on the side for squeezing to taste.

Salmon frame soup *serves 3–4*

Industrial-scale fishing involves the waste of hundreds of tonnes of fish frames – dumped off the back of the boat after the fish have been filleted, along with all the undersized and mangled fish from the day's trawl. There may be little we can do about this, but using up every scrap of fish that makes it into your kitchen feels like a gesture, at least, towards redressing the balance.

Moreover, creating something delicious out of what someone else might have thrown away – in this case, the head, tail and skeleton of a filleted salmon – is enormously satisfying. A decent-sized salmon carries a surprising amount of meat in and around its head, and if you combine it with a few inexpensive ingredients, it can be transformed into something hearty and filling. When you're filleting a salmon, if you know that you'll be making this soup, leave some flesh on the tail end section.

Also works with:
- Sea trout
- Trout
- Sea bass

The frame (head, tail and bones) of 1 large organic farmed (or self-caught wild) salmon (about 1kg total weight)
50g unsalted butter
1 tablespoon sunflower oil
1 large onion, sliced
1 leek, halved and finely sliced

200g new potatoes, scrubbed and quartered
6–8 dill stalks, plus 1 tablespoon chopped dill
6–8 parsley stalks
2 fresh bay leaves
100ml double cream
Salt and freshly ground black pepper

Place the salmon frame on a board and wipe it well with kitchen paper to remove any blood. Use a heavy knife to cut the head and tail from the skeleton, then chop the skeleton into 4–6 pieces.

Set a good-sized pan over a medium heat and add the butter and oil. Throw in the onion, leek and potatoes and let them soften for 5 minutes or so, without colouring. Add the salmon head, tail and bones to the pan, nestling them in among the vegetables. Add the dill and parsley stalks and the bay leaves and pour over a scant litre of cold water – just enough to cover the ingredients. Season with salt and bring up to the gentlest of simmers. Skim off any scum that rises to the top, then cook gently, scarcely simmering, for about 20 minutes, until the potatoes are tender. Remove from the heat.

Take the fish head and bones out of the pan and leave to cool for a couple of minutes. Remove and discard the herb stalks. Carefully pick the meat from the head of the fish, as well as any that is still clinging to the bones. You should really pull the head of the salmon apart, teasing out the various strangely textured bits around the eyes, cheeks and mouth. Anything that isn't a bone is meant to be eaten.

Return this 'meat' to the pan. Stir in the cream and chopped dill and adjust the seasoning with salt and black pepper. Serve straight away, in warmed bowls, with buttered bread.

Roast pollack head with thyme, bay and garlic

serves 2–3

This thrifty treatment has been a favourite of ours for several years and a version of it was published in *The River Cottage Year*. It's an absolute must if you ever catch a good-sized pollack.

If you're getting a head from the fishmonger, you may have to take it as it comes. But if you're preparing it from a fish you've caught yourself, then you want the head cut 'long' – i.e. with a generous amount of 'shoulder' still attached (see pages 63–4). Roughly speaking, allow one small head (from a 1.5–2kg fish) per person; one medium head (from a 3–4kg fish) for two; one monster head (from a 5kg-plus fish) for three or four.

Also works with:
- Ling
- Coley
- Cod

1–3 pollack heads (about 4–5kg total weight) – no need to remove the eyes, gills or pectoral fins
Olive oil
A few garlic cloves, thinly sliced

Several small sprigs of thyme or rosemary, or both
A few bay leaves
Sea salt and freshly ground black pepper

Give the pollack head(s) a thorough rinse under the cold tap, then pat as dry as you can with paper towel or a clean cloth. Rub a tablespoon or two of olive oil all over the head(s). Using the tip of a small, sharp knife, make little incisions in the meatier parts, then stuff the slices of garlic and sprigs of thyme and/or

rosemary into them. Tear the bay leaves roughly and tuck pieces under each fin, in the mouth, and any other obvious crevices. Scatter a little more garlic and thyme, and plenty of salt and pepper, over the head(s) and trickle over a bit more olive oil.

Put the anointed pollack head(s) into a dish and bake in an oven preheated to 220°C/Gas Mark 7 for 25–40 minutes, depending on size. The fish is done when the flesh is flaky and opaque and the skin blistered and crisp.

Dig in! We generally start by using a knife and fork to wheedle away chunks of succulent flesh wherever we find them, but usually it's impossible to resist attacking the head with our bare hands as soon as it's cooled a little. It is delicious accompanied by small pasta, such as risoni or small macaroni, which should be sauced with the delicious juices from the oven dish.

VARIATION
Roast pollack head with ginger and soy

Replace the olive oil with groundnut, tuck thin slices of root ginger instead of thyme into the incisions along with the garlic, and ditch the bay leaves. Before the head(s) go into the oven, sprinkle with a couple of tablespoons of soy sauce and a couple of pinches of sugar. You'll get very different, but equally delicious, results. Serve with noodles and wilted greens.

VARIATION
Roasted skeletons with garlic and rosemary

This is the 'full-length' version of the dish, and the one shown in the photograph on pages 366–7. As with the heads, if you're filleting fish and you know you want to make this dish with the 'spares', it helps to deliberately leave some flesh at both ends.

Wash and dry 3 or 4 good-sized whole fish skeletons with heads and tails (black bream, brill, pollack, gurnard or plaice, for example) and place them in a large roasting tin. Break 1/2–1 head of garlic into individual cloves and squash them a bit with the flat side of a heavy knife, but don't peel. Wedge and tuck the garlic and a generous handful of small rosemary sprigs in amongst the skeletons. Trickle over 3 tablespoons of olive oil and season well with salt and pepper. Roast in an oven preheated to 200°C/Gas Mark 6 for 12–15 minutes, until the heads and tails are golden and crisp around the edges.

Serve with lemon wedges. Dispense with cutlery and allow all your nibbling and gnawing instincts to take over. Buttered bread is also useful for clutching and dabbing at the fish flakes and pan juices.

Deep-fried fish skins *serves 4–6 as a snack*

There are many recipes in this book that ask you to skin your fish. If that skin is free of scales and in good condition then it will be, we have discovered, rather delicious lightly floured and deep fried. (Although we tend not to fry the skins of very oily fish such as mackerel.)

This simple snack, prepared in a truly holistic spirit and affectionately known as 'pollack scratchings', has proved a hit at River Cottage. Deeply savoury, crispy and salty, the little fried morsels are perfect for dipping. We like them with the citrus salsa that goes with the crab cakes on page 327, but they would also be good with tartare sauce (see page 324), a chilli-spiked tomato sauce (see page 340) or just some simple garlic mayonnaise (see page 332).

Also works with:
- Black bream
- Sea bass
- Salmon (organic farmed or self-caught wild)

Groundnut oil for frying
Skins from 2 large or 4 medium pollack
   fillets, scales removed

1 garlic clove, peeled
2 tablespoons plain flour
Flaky sea salt

Pour a 3–4cm depth of oil into a deep, heavy-based pan and place over a medium-high heat. Bring it up to 180°C, or until a cube of white bread dropped into the oil turns golden brown in about a minute.

Check your fish skins for scales and any bones that are still attached. The skins don't need to be completely devoid of flesh – in fact, it's good to have a very thin layer clinging to them. Bash the garlic clove with your palm to crush slightly and release its oils, then carefully rub it over the skins. Take care not to tear them.

Use a sharp knife to slice the skins widthways into strips, 1–2cm wide. Dip the pieces in the flour, shake off the excess, then drop them into the hot oil. Fry for 2–3 minutes, until golden and crisp. Remove from the oil and drain on kitchen paper. Sprinkle with flaky salt and serve immediately, with your preferred dip.

Spaghetti with cockles *serves 2*

This is our take on *spaghetti alle vongole* – *vongole* being the Italian name for various species of clam. Cockles, which are very similar bivalves, work just as well in this classic seafood pasta dish.

Also works with:
• Palourdes and other small clams

4 tablespoons good olive oil
2 tablespoons white wine
500g cockles, scrubbed (and purged if you think they may be very gritty – see page 580)
2 garlic cloves, sliced into paper-thin slivers
400g tin of chopped tomatoes, or 500g fresh tomatoes, skinned and chopped

A pinch of sugar
1 bay leaf
200g spaghetti or linguine
2 knobs of unsalted butter and a trickle of olive oil
1 tablespoon chopped flat-leaf parsley (optional)
Salt and freshly ground black pepper

Set a large saucepan over a medium heat and add 1 tablespoon of olive oil and the white wine. Throw in the cockles, cover the pan and give it a shake, then cook for 2–3 minutes, until all the cockles are open (discard any that steadfastly refuse to do so).

Tip the contents of the pan into a colander set over a bowl to collect the juices. Strain the juices through a fine sieve, or even a cloth, to get rid of any grit or shell fragments. Pick two-thirds of the cockles out of their shells, then set all the cockles, shell-on and shell-off, aside.

Heat the remaining olive oil in a large frying pan, add the garlic and fry until just beginning to colour. Quickly throw in the tomatoes, followed by the cockle cooking liquid, the sugar, bay leaf and some salt and pepper. Cook over a gentle heat, stirring from time to time, for 25–30 minutes, until you have a thick, pulpy sauce.

When the sauce is nearly done, bring a large pan of water to the boil. Salt it generously, then add the spaghetti or linguine and cook until *al dente*.

Add all the cockles to the tomato sauce with a small knob of butter and the parsley, if using, and toss over a medium heat for a minute, until they are piping hot. Drain the pasta and toss with the second knob of butter and a trickle of olive oil. Divide between two warmed dishes and ladle the cockle and tomato sauce over the top. Serve straight away – without Parmesan!

Creamy cockles with tagliatelle *serves 2*

This is a creamy, *marinière*-style cockle dish, a comforting, wintry alternative to the fresh, tomatoey one on page 384.

Also works with:
- Palourdes
- Mussels

1 tablespoon olive oil
A good knob of unsalted butter
1 garlic clove, finely chopped
1 onion or 4 small shallots, finely
    chopped
500g cockles, scrubbed (and purged if
    you think they may be very gritty – see
    page 103)

½ glass of white wine
50ml double cream
200g tagliatelle or linguine
1 tablespoon finely chopped parsley
Salt and freshly ground black pepper

Heat the olive oil and butter in a deep, wide pan over a medium heat. Add the garlic and onion or shallots and cook for a few minutes, until softened. Add the cockles (discarding any open ones that won't close after a sharp tap), increase the heat and add the wine and some salt and pepper. Cover and cook for 2–3 minutes, shaking the pan a couple of times. When all the cockles are open, remove from the heat. Scoop the cockles out of the pan and set aside in a warm dish.

Pour the pan juices through a sieve lined with muslin or a thin tea towel to get rid of any grit. Return the juices to a clean pan, add the cream and let bubble for a few minutes, until thick and glossy. Taste and adjust the seasoning.

Remove about two-thirds of the cockles from their shells, leaving the rest shell-on.

Cook the pasta in a large pan of boiling salted water until *al dente*, then drain and return it to the hot pan. Toss in the hot, creamy sauce and shelled cockles, and scatter over the chopped parsley. Transfer to two warmed dishes, top with the shell-on cockles and serve.

Spaghetti with samphire and salmon *serves 4*

Marsh samphire is a seasonal treat, a luscious, sweet, salty plant that looks like a miniature spineless cactus, and whose succulent flesh tastes of the sea. It's a wild food, gathered on the coast between June and August, particularly in East Anglia. Any good fishmonger will be able to get it during this time. Before cooking, it needs a thorough wash and a ruthless trimming – you need to remove any vestige of its tough, whiskery roots. Unless you've got particularly young, delicate stems, don't be surprised if you find yourself discarding around a third of the samphire you started with. Once that process is done, however, this is a simple, elegant dish.

500g fresh marsh samphire

350g spaghetti or linguine

Olive oil

500g organic farmed (or self-caught wild)
    salmon fillets

A good knob of unsalted butter

Juice of ½ lemon

Sea salt and freshly ground black pepper

Also works with:
- Sea trout
- Trout (large)
- Mackerel
- Sea bass

Carefully pick over the samphire, removing all the root and any tough stems. Wash and rinse it thoroughly to get rid of any grit, then break up larger, multi-branched pieces into smaller pieces.

Bring a large pan of water to a rolling boil, salt it generously and add the pasta. Cook until *al dente*, adding the samphire to the pan for the last minute of the cooking time.

Meanwhile, heat a little olive oil in a frying pan over a medium heat. Season the salmon fillets, add to the pan and fry for 2–3 minutes on each side, until just cooked through. Flake the cooked salmon off its skin, removing any bones that you find as you do so.

Drain the spaghetti and samphire and return them to the hot pan. Add the butter, plus a dash of olive oil and plenty of black pepper, and toss together. Transfer to warm plates and scatter over the flaked salmon, finishing off each portion with a squeeze of lemon juice, more black pepper and a scattering of flaky sea salt.

Crab linguine *serves 5–6*

This recipe is an old favourite (you may remember it from *The River Cottage Cookbook*) and a truly wonderful way to enjoy the luscious meat of the crab. It works brilliantly with spider crab, but brown crabs are very fine too.

White meat from 2 large spider crabs
  or brown crabs (see pages 89–93 for
  cooking and picking instructions)
500g linguine or other pasta
2 tablespoons olive oil
3 garlic cloves, chopped

1–2 small red chillies (according to heat),
  deseeded and finely sliced
1kg ripe tomatoes, skinned, deseeded and
  roughly chopped
1 tablespoon chopped chives
Salt and freshly ground black pepper

Make sure you retrieve all the white meat from the crabs, including the claws and legs. (Collect the brown meat too, to use for a fish soup or crab sandwiches.)

Bring a large pan of water to the boil, salt it well, then add the linguine and cook until *al dente*. Meanwhile, heat the olive oil in a pan, add the garlic and sweat until softened. Throw in the red chilli (check for heat and use sparingly). Before the garlic takes any colour, add the chopped tomatoes. Simmer for 5–6 minutes, until soft and pulpy, then add the white crabmeat and heat through. Season to taste, adding more chilli if you like, then add the chives.

Drain the pasta, return it to the pan and add the crab mixture. Toss lightly and serve straight away.

Crab pasta salad *serves 4 as a starter*

This salad is based on the same deliciously sweet set of flavours as our beloved Crab linguine (above).

150g shell-like pasta shapes, such as
  conchiglie or orecchiette
2 tablespoons olive oil
300–500g white meat from 2 large spider
  crabs or brown crabs (see pages 89–93
  for cooking and picking instructions)

½ hot red chilli, deseeded and finely
  chopped
250g sweet cherry tomatoes, such as
  Sungold, quartered
Juice of ½ lemon
A large handful of basil leaves
Salt and freshly ground black pepper

Cook the pasta in a large pan of boiling salted water until *al dente*, then drain, toss with the olive oil and leave to cool.

Meanwhile, put the white crab meat into a bowl. Add the chilli and cherry tomatoes, season well and toss together.

When the pasta is cool, toss it with the crab mixture and some lemon juice to taste. Shred the basil leaves finely, then toss them with the salad and serve straight away.

Kipper carbonara   *serves 5–6*

A classic carbonara is made with ham or bacon, which is salty and sweet. So, we thought, why shouldn't it work with salty, sweet kipper flesh?

500g spaghetti or linguine	4 egg yolks
400g kipper fillets	200ml double cream
A small knob of unsalted butter	Salt and freshly ground black pepper

Bring a large pan of water to a rolling boil, salt it well and add the pasta. Cook until *al dente*.

Meanwhile, cut the kipper flesh off the skin and remove any pin bones. Slice the flesh into small strips, about 0.5 x 3cm (a bit like bacon lardons). Fry gently in the butter in a small pan for a couple of minutes, until cooked through.

Put the egg yolks and cream into a bowl, season (going easy on the salt because of the kippers) and whisk together.

As soon as the pasta is cooked, drain it well, then return it to the still-hot pan. Add the egg and cream mixture and the kipper lardons and quickly toss everything together using two forks. The eggy cream should be cooked – and slightly thickened – by the heat of the pasta and the pan. If it looks a bit runny, you can put it back on the hob for just a minute, but don't overdo it. The finished sauce should coat the pasta strands like silky custard – not scrambled egg.

Serve straight away and pass the pepper mill round.

Quickest-ever fish pasta supper   *serves 2*

This is so simple that it almost doesn't qualify as a recipe, but next time you get home late on a cold, wet night – tired, hungry and in no mood for cooking – try it. You will be comforted and sustained – and there's very little washing up.

200g spaghetti or linguine	1 garlic clove, finely chopped
120g tin of sustainably caught tuna in oil	Salt and freshly ground black pepper
1 tin or jar of anchovies in oil	

Bring a large pan of water to a rolling boil, salt it well and add the pasta. Cook until *al dente*.

Meanwhile, pour the oil from the tuna and anchovies into a pan, set it over a medium-low heat and add the garlic. Let it cook very gently for just a minute or two, so it releases its fragrance but doesn't colour, then remove from the heat.

Chop the anchovies, flake the tuna and stir both into the garlicky oil. As soon as the pasta is cooked, drain it, return it to the pan and tip in the fish mixture. Add a good grinding of black pepper, toss together, then tuck in immediately.

'Risoniotto' *serves 4*

In the Fearnley household, this is a much-loved teatime standby, devoured by young and old with equal enthusiasm. Basically 'leftovers with risoni pasta', it's never the same from one outing to the next – the spinach doesn't always get a look-in, for instance. But the principles don't change: garlicky, buttery onions meet flakes of leftover fish before joining a big pot of steaming pasta.

We favour risoni, which is pasta shaped like rice (or white mouse droppings, as Oscar has been known to point out). It gives the dish a particularly pleasing texture, not unlike a risotto. However, you could use other types of pasta, such as small macaroni, but nothing too big or too fancifully shaped. You want to keep that comforting texture, with everything mixed snugly together.

A small knob of unsalted butter
1 tablespoon olive oil
1 large onion (or a small bunch of spring onions), finely chopped
1 fat garlic clove, chopped
½ small red chilli, deseeded and finely chopped (optional)
100–200g blanched spinach or greens (optional), roughly chopped

250–400g cold cooked fish, broken into small flakes – e.g. tinned sardines, flakes of mackerel, chunks of white fish
Lemon juice
350g risoni pasta
Salt and freshly ground black pepper
Extra virgin olive oil, to serve

Heat the butter and olive oil in a frying pan over a medium heat and add the onion and garlic (and chilli, if you like). Cook gently for 10–15 minutes, until the onion is soft and translucent. Throw in the chopped spinach or greens, if using, and mix thoroughly with the buttery onions, then stir in the fish and a squeeze of lemon juice.

Cook the pasta in a large pan of boiling salted water until *al dente*, then drain and return it to the hot pan. Throw in the fish and onion mixture, add some seasoning and toss together well. Serve in warmed bowls, with a little extra virgin olive oil trickled over.

VARIATION
Risoni salad

Cold pasta is very often a terrible idea. However, this is simply a cooled-down version of the dish above, and works very well.

Cook the chopped garlic and chilli (no onions) in olive oil (no butter), before tossing them with the fish and the cooked pasta. Leave to cool. Throw in 1 small, finely sliced red onion, 1 tablespoon chopped flat-leaf parsley, some cooled, cooked petits pois (instead of greens), 1–2 tablespoons of crème fraîche or ricotta cheese and a good squeeze of lemon juice. Season well and serve.

Kedgeree *serves 4*

There are many variations on this classic Anglo-Indian dish. Some are complex, involving a plethora of different spices, a creamy sauce made separately and the addition of vegetables, while others are too baldly simple: fish, rice, eggs. We think this version is just about perfect, combining soft flakes of fish, lightly spiced oniony rice, a few herbs and the all-important hard (but not too hard) boiled eggs. The result is a soothing, perfectly complete dish.

300ml whole milk
300ml water
1 bay leaf
400g smoked pollack or haddock fillet
1 tablespoon olive oil
2 good knobs of unsalted butter
1 large onion, finely sliced

2 teaspoons mild curry powder
175g basmati rice, rinsed and drained
4 large eggs
2 tablespoons coarsely chopped coriander
1 tablespoon chopped lovage (optional)
Lemon wedges
Freshly ground black pepper

Put the milk and water in a pan with the bay leaf and smoked fish, cover and bring to a gentle simmer. By the time the liquid is simmering, the fish should be cooked through. If not, turn it over in the hot liquid and leave, off the heat, for 2–3 minutes to finish cooking. Remove the fish from the pan and set aside. Discard the bay leaf and reserve the poaching liquid. When the fish is cool enough to handle, break it into flakes, discarding the skin and picking out any bones.

Heat the olive oil and a large knob of butter in a pan over a medium heat. Add the onion and sweat for 5–10 minutes, until soft. Stir in the curry powder, then the rinsed rice. Stir the rice gently for a minute or two, then add 300ml of the fish poaching liquid. Bring to the boil, cover with a tight-fitting lid, turn the heat down as low as it will go and cook for 15 minutes. Turn off the heat, fluff up the rice with a fork, then put the lid back on until you are ready to assemble the dish.

Add the eggs to a pan of boiling water and simmer for 7 minutes. Drain, rinse under cold water to stop the cooking, then peel. Fold the smoked fish into the rice, along with half the chopped coriander and the second knob of butter. Cut the hard-boiled eggs in half – they should still be just a bit soft in the middle.

Spoon the spicy, fishy rice on to warmed plates or wide bowls, top with the egg halves and sprinkle with the remaining coriander – and the lovage, if using. Add a wedge of lemon and a good twist of black pepper, then serve.

VARIATION
Kedge-overs

Giving leftover cooked fish the kedgeree treatment – whether it be smoked haddock, mackerel, bream, bass, gurnard or even salmon – creates a tasty supper.

Fry the onion, then add the curry powder, a pinch of salt and the rinsed rice. Pour in 300ml water and cook as above. Meanwhile, flake the leftover fish – as little as 200g will do. When the rice is cooked, stir in a knob of butter, the fish and a handful of chopped herbs – coriander and lovage, or parsley or chives. Serve straight away, adding a couple of quartered hard-boiled eggs.

Squid and tomato risotto *serves 4*

Fish and tomato is nearly always a winning combination and, since the squid here is added right at the end, this recipe could very easily be adapted to suit other fish or shellfish – scallops, for example. As you'll see in the pictures on pages 394–5, the difference that squid ink makes to the colour of the risotto is like switching from day to night.

Also works with:
• Cuttlefish

2 large or 4 small squid, cleaned
    (see pages 97–100), ink reserved
    if possible
2 knobs of unsalted butter
1 tablespoon olive oil
2 onions, finely chopped
1 garlic clove, finely chopped
700ml fish or shellfish stock (see
    pages 256–7)

About 600ml roasted tomato sauce (see
    page 260), made with 2kg tomatoes
350g Arborio or other risotto rice
Salt and freshly ground black pepper
1 heaped tablespoon chopped flat-leaf
    parsley, to finish
Extra virgin olive oil, to serve

Slice the cleaned squid bodies and wings into thin strips; roughly chop the tentacles. Set aside.

Heat a knob of butter and the olive oil in a large saucepan, add the onions and garlic, and sweat for 10 minutes, stirring from time to time, until soft and translucent. Don't let them brown.

Meanwhile, heat the fish stock and roasted tomato sauce together in a pan over a low heat. You need to keep it hot – just below simmering – as you will be adding it to the risotto.

Add the rice to the onions in the pan, stirring well for a minute or two to coat the grains in the butter. Add a ladleful of the hot fish and tomato stock and let the rice simmer gently away, stirring constantly, until the stock has almost all been absorbed. Add another ladleful and continue cooking in this way until all the stock has gone in (if you have any squid ink, that can be added about halfway through the cooking time). You should find that it takes you about 20 minutes of ladling and simmering to incorporate all the liquid into the risotto, and that the rice at that point will be tender, with just the merest suggestion of bite still in it. Stir the squid into the simmering risotto about 5 minutes before the end of the cooking time – probably with the penultimate ladleful of stock.

When the rice is cooked, season with salt and plenty of black pepper and turn off the heat. Scatter a few little scraps of butter over the surface of the rice and cover the pan for 2 minutes. Then remove the lid, stir in the melted butter and spoon the risotto into warm dishes. Finish with the chopped parsley and a trickle of very good extra virgin olive oil.

Scallops with fennel risotto

serves 4 as a starter, 2 as a main course

This is one of a few favourite recipes we've included, updated a little, from *The River Cottage Cookbook*. It's a pleasingly thrifty sort of dish using the bits of the scallop that normally get thrown away, plus the fennel trimmings, to make a delicious stock that forms the basis of the risotto. If you can't get your scallops in the shell, it's still worth making – just use a good white fish stock instead.

6 large scallops in the shell

2–3 fennel bulbs (about 500g before trimming)

2 small onions – 1 sliced for the stock, 1 finely chopped for the risotto

1 bay leaf

1 small glass of white wine

3–4 tablespoons olive oil

1 garlic clove, finely chopped

150g Arborio or other risotto rice

A dash of Pernod (optional)

Salt and freshly ground black pepper

Prepare the scallops as described on pages 105–7, putting the corals, the fleshy fringe around the edges, the juices, plus any meat left clinging to the shells (i.e. everything bar the black sac, which should be thrown away, and the main muscle meat) into a pan. Cut the scallops horizontally in half and set aside.

Prepare the fennel by cutting off the finger-like tops and the coarse outer layer or two (depending on size and freshness). Roughly chop these trimmings, reserving a few of the frondy leaves for later, and add to the pan of scallop trimmings with the sliced onion, the bay leaf and white wine. Pour over about 500ml water – the contents of the pan should be generously covered. Bring to the boil and simmer gently for no more than 20 minutes, then strain through a fine sieve. If you think the scallops may have been harbouring any sand or grit, strain the stock through cotton or muslin. Return to a clean pan and keep warm over a very low heat.

While the stock is simmering, quarter the clean, firm hearts of the fennel bulbs. Place a medium frying pan over a low heat and add 1 tablespoon of olive oil. Season the fennel and add to the pan. Fry gently on all sides until soft and caramelised, then transfer to a low oven to keep warm while you cook the risotto.

To make the risotto, heat 1–2 tablespoons of olive oil in a heavy-based saucepan over a medium-low heat. Add the chopped onion and garlic and sweat gently for a few minutes, until softened. Add the rice and stir to coat the grains in the oil, then add a third of the warm scallop stock and bring to a gentle simmer. Cook, stirring constantly, adding more stock as the liquid in the pan is almost absorbed. If you run out of stock before the rice is done, use boiling water instead. The final result should be smooth and creamy, with the rice still a little *al dente*.

When the risotto is almost done, heat a heavy, non-stick frying pan, cast-iron skillet or griddle pan until very hot. Brush both sides of each scallop disc with olive oil and place in the pan. They will need no more than 30 seconds on each side, so as soon as you have laid the last one down you should turn over the first one. When they have a lovely, golden exterior, remove them from the pan.

Finely chop the reserved fennel fronds and stir them into the risotto, along with the Pernod, if using. Check the seasoning. Divide the risotto between warmed plates, arrange the scallops and fennel on top, and serve.

Anchovy and chilli dressing *makes about 200ml*

This is a truly fantastic way of putting a tin of anchovies to use, producing a piquant dressing of great versatility that can be served warm or cold. We love it with lightly cooked earthy greens, such as kale or broccoli, but it makes a great dip for crudités, or you can use it as a dressing for almost any other vegetable. Or, trickle it over any leftover fish tossed with pasta or Puy lentils, hot or cold.

50g tinned anchovy fillets with their oil
150ml olive oil
2 garlic cloves, roughly chopped
Leaves from 2 good sprigs of thyme
A few basil leaves (optional)
½ small red chilli, roughly chopped
 (or a pinch of dried chilli flakes)
1 teaspoon Dijon or English mustard

2 teaspoons wine vinegar or cider vinegar
A few twists of black pepper

TO SERVE:
500g curly kale or purple sprouting
 broccoli
A knob of unsalted butter

Put all the ingredients for the dressing in a blender and whiz until completely smooth and creamy. Pour into a jar or pot, for which you have the lid.

Bring a pan of lightly salted water to the boil, add the kale or broccoli and cook for 3–5 minutes, until just tender. Drain thoroughly and toss with the butter. Arrange the kale or broccoli on warmed plates and trickle or spoon over a generous amount of the dressing from the jar. Serve at once, with soft brown bread for mopping.

The leftover dressing will keep in the jar in the fridge for a couple of weeks. It can go a bit sludgy, as the olive oil partially solidifies when chilled. Take it out of the fridge an hour or two before using and, when the oil has liquefied again, shake the dressing vigorously in the sealed jar.

VARIATION
Warm bagna cauda dressing with crudités

You will need a selection of vegetables, such as fennel, carrots, baby lettuces, asparagus, courgettes, French beans and celery (tender stalks from near the heart). Lightly blanch the asparagus (unless very fresh) and the French beans. Cut the vegetables into thick sticks or other dippable portions.

Put the dressing in a small pan and warm it over a low heat, whisking in a knob of soft butter as it heats up. This should give you a nice, smooth emulsion but don't worry if it separates a bit. If it splits completely – into big lumps and a pool of oil – whiz it in a blender with a teaspoon of warm water and it should soon right itself.

Serve the sauce in a warmed bowl in the middle of a large plate, with the crudités arranged around it.

Puy lentil and mackerel salad *serves 4*

We cook a lot of mackerel and urge others to do likewise. Inevitably, we are sometimes faced with leftovers – the last few fish on the barbecue that no one could quite make room for. But mackerel's high oil content means that, even when cold, it retains its punchy flavour and moist texture, so any leftovers can be quickly transformed into a zesty and delicious standby meal. Almost all fish work well in this salad, though it is less good with delicate, soft white fish flesh.

Puy lentils are an essential storecupboard staple for anyone interested in thrifty cooking. They add protein, flavour and texture to a whole range of thrown-together, leftover-based dishes.

200g Puy lentils
Stock vegetables – e.g. 1 celery stick, cut into 2–3 pieces, 2 carrots, cut into 2–3 pieces, 2 garlic cloves, unpeeled but roughly bruised, and ¼ onion (all optional)
A few parsley stalks (optional)
2–3 leftover cooked mackerel (baked or barbecued are perfect for this dish)

1 small onion, preferably red, or a few spring onions, finely sliced
3–4 anchovy fillets, finely chopped
1 tablespoon baby capers, rinsed and chopped
2 tablespoons chopped parsley
A glug of extra virgin olive oil
Juice of ½–1 lemon
Salt and freshly ground black pepper

Rinse the lentils under cold running water, then put them in a large saucepan – with the stock vegetables and parsley stalks, if you want to flavour them up a bit. Cover with fresh water, bring to a gentle simmer and skim off any scum that rises to the surface. Simmer for about 20 minutes, until the lentils are *al dente*, topping up the pan with fresh water if necessary. Strain the lentils, discarding the water and any flavouring vegetables you've used.

While the lentils are cooking, pick all the flesh from the mackerel, flake it and place in a bowl, making sure you discard any bones.

Toss the warm lentils with the mackerel. Add the red onion or spring onions, along with the chopped anchovies, capers and parsley. Stir in the olive oil, then season to taste with lemon juice, salt and pepper. Toss gently together and serve straight away.

Chloe's sardine and onion omelette *serves 2*

We're not saying she was the first person ever to make one, but there's no doubt that in our book at least, the sardine and onion omelette was invented by Hugh's oldest, Chloe, aged ten. And it's become something of a Sunday supper favourite, being one of the fastest and tastiest storecupboard standbys we know.

1 tin (about 120g) of sardines in oil
1 small onion, preferably red, finely sliced
5 eggs

A small knob of butter
Salt and freshly ground black pepper

Drain the sardines of their oil and break them up into large flakes, removing the bones only if you feel the need to. Put them beside the hob, along with your sliced onion. Break the eggs into a bowl, add a little seasoning and beat them lightly.

Heat the butter in a large frying pan over a medium heat. There are now two ways to proceed. You can pour in the eggs and let them cook for a couple of minutes, giving them the odd prod/stir to allow uncooked egg to meet the bottom of the pan, until the omelette is pretty much cooked but still a bit wet on top. Scatter the flakes of sardine and the red onion all over the top, add a final twist of pepper, flip one half of the omelette over on the other and slide it out of the pan. In this version, the sardines and onion are very much a filling – warm, but only just, in the middle of the folded omelette (which can, if this is to your taste, be quite runny in the middle).

Alternatively – this is Chloe's original method and our preferred way – mix the sardine flakes, onion and seasoning into the raw eggs before pouring the whole lot into the buttered pan, then cook it, with a little bit of stirring, until barely set. Flip it over like a pancake to finish cooking for just half a minute. In this version the bits of onion and sardine are set in and scattered through the whole omelette, which is relatively 'well done'.

Either way, serve immediately. If you have a little green salad, or some ripe tomatoes to slice, or some good bread and butter to hand – or all of these – then you'll have a very decent supper.

Fish frittata *serves 4*

A frittata (or tortilla, or Spanish omelette, whatever you like to call it) is a kitchen rescue remedy – a vehicle for anything from leftover sausages to sardines, not to mention yesterday's rice, that last bit of Cheddar and almost any vegetable you can think of.

This recipe is only a guide, not a prescription. As long as you don't forego the three essential ingredients – eggs, lightly fried onions and cubes of cooked potato – you can add almost any other savoury ingredient you like. The golden rule is not to go crazy and literally clear out the fridge. A frittata made with just a few ingredients will always be more successful than one into which a dozen different elements have been squeezed. The other crucial thing about a frittata is not to serve it too hot. Room temperature is best, though slightly warm will be fine.

2 tablespoons olive oil

1 large onion, sliced

6 large eggs

300g cold cooked potatoes, cut into cubes

200g cold cooked spinach, chopped (or other green vegetables, such as peas, broad beans, asparagus or broccoli)

1 tablespoon chopped parsley

300g leftover cooked fish, broken into large flakes – tuna, salmon, mackerel, trout, tinned sardines, smoked fish, cod or its brethren – almost anything except shellfish and cephalopods, which may be rubbery if you reheat them

75g Cheddar cheese, grated (optional)

Salt and freshly ground black pepper

Heat the olive oil in a medium-large, non-stick frying pan and add the onion. Cook gently for 10 minutes or so, until soft and golden. Meanwhile, break the eggs into a jug, beat lightly and season well.

Add the potatoes to the onion and cook gently for a few minutes to heat them through, then stir in the spinach, parsley and flaked fish. Add some seasoning, make sure the ingredients are well combined and evenly distributed around the pan right up to the edges, then pour in the beaten eggs. Keep the heat under the pan low and don't move the ingredients around; just let the egg solidify slowly from the base up. After around 7 minutes, give the pan a little shake. You should be able to see that the bottom half of the frittata is set but there is still a good layer of wet egg on top.

Now sprinkle the cheese on top, if using, and place the pan under a hot grill. Again, you want the frittata to finish cooking slowly, so keep the grill heat moderate or, if the grill is part of your main oven, place the pan some distance below the heat source. Leave the frittata to finish cooking gently, until the top is set and golden brown – 10 minutes or so.

Leave the frittata to cool in the pan for at least 10 minutes. You can then either cut it in the pan or use a spatula to ease it out in one piece on to a board or plate. Either way, slice into wedges and serve with a salad or two (tomato and chives or sliced onions, say, and/or some good salad leaves tossed in a simple vinaigrette).

Fish bubble and squeak *serves 2*

The pairing of fish and potatoes is nearly always a roaring success, and this dish is no exception. A fantastic way to use up leftovers, it's good enough to eat on its own – possibly straight from the pan. If that seems uncouth, then serve it on a warmed plate with a fried egg on top.

The fish takes the place of the greens to form the 'squeak' (or is it the bubble?) here, but you could always add some leftover shredded cabbage as well, if you have any. In the spring, chopped blanched nettle tops are a good alternative. Almost any leftover fish will do, including smoked fish, but very oily fish such as sardines and herrings are perhaps not ideal.

About 500g leftover cooked floury
  potatoes or mash
A little butter and milk, if needed
250–300g cooked fish, broken into
  large flakes

2 tablespoons groundnut oil
10–15 spring onions, trimmed and cut
  into 5mm thick slices
Salt and freshly ground black pepper

If the leftover potato isn't already mashed and seasoned, mash it with a knob of butter melted in a little warm milk and season it well. Roughly mix with the fish.

Heat the groundnut oil in a large frying pan over a medium heat and add the spring onions. Fry gently for a couple of minutes, until soft but not brown. Add the potato and fish and pat into a cake in the pan with a spatula. Sizzle gently until the underside is a crisp golden brown.

Turn the mixture over, either with a flip of the pan or by using a wide spatula and turning it in several tranches – don't worry if it breaks up a bit. Just squish it back together again in the pan. Keep going, squishing, turning, then leaving to brown for a couple of minutes, until you have a well-formed, piping-hot cake with a golden brown crust on the top and bottom. Serve at once.

Fish-topped pizza bianca *serves 4*

Pizza bianca is just a simple pizza without tomato sauce. Topped with sweet, soft onions and a few herbs, it's the perfect vehicle for whatever standby or leftover fish you feel like using. Tinned sardines or tuna, or flakes of cooked mackerel or trout are particularly good options, especially if topped with an anchovy or two.

3 tablespoons olive oil
750g onions, very thinly sliced
1 quantity of pizza dough (see page 340)
A little flour or cornmeal, for dusting
About 200g tinned sardines or tuna, or
  other cooked oily or rich fish, broken
  into chunks

6–8 anchovy fillets, cut in half
A few tablespoons crème fraîche
Extra virgin olive oil
Salt and freshly ground black pepper
Chopped parsley or chives, to serve

Heat the olive oil in a large frying pan, add the onions and a good pinch of salt and cook gently over a low heat, stirring occasionally, for about half an hour, until soft and golden.

Preheat the oven to 250°C/Gas Mark 10 and put a baking sheet in it to heat.

Knock back the risen dough and cut it in half. Use a rolling pin or your hands, or both, to roll and stretch one half into a very thin piece that will cover your baking sheet. Take the hot baking sheet from the oven, scatter it with a little flour or, even better, some cornmeal, and lay the dough on it.

Spread half the soft onions over the dough, scatter over half the fish, including the anchovies, then add a few dollops of crème fraîche. Season with some salt and pepper, trickle on some extra virgin olive oil and place in the oven. Bake for 10–12 minutes, until the base is crisp and golden brown at the edges.

While it's cooking, roll out the second piece of dough, so it is ready to go in as soon as the first pizza is cooked. Serve hot, in big slices, sprinkled with the herbs.

Bloody Mary sardines on toast *serves 1*

There are few things more satisfying than hot buttered toast smothered with a generous chunk of soft, oily sardine. It's as simple and wholesome a snack as you're likely to come across. We did feel, however, that the toast/sardine partnership wouldn't suffer if given a boost. Sardines and tomatoes are classic bedfellows, and we thought the classic flavourings of a Bloody Mary cocktail might be the perfect way to spice things up. We weren't wrong.

Like any good Bloody Mary, you'll want to customise the seasonings to your taste, but here are the basic ingredients.

1 tin (about 120g) of sardines in oil, drained
1–2 teaspoons tomato ketchup
2–3 shakes of Tabasco sauce
4–5 shakes of Worcestershire sauce
Lemon juice

A pinch of celery salt
1 slice of toast
Butter
A dash of vodka (optional)
Freshly ground black pepper

Mix the sardines with the ketchup, Tabasco and Worcestershire sauce, roughly mashing them all together. Season with lemon juice, celery salt and black pepper to taste. Spread your hot toast with butter, then pile on the sardine mixture. Finish off with a light sprinkling of vodka, if you like, and serve straight away.

The cold fish sandwich *serves 1*

Even if you have only a couple of spoonfuls of leftover fish (or perhaps a tiny fillet of fresh fish that needs cooking), you can still make a meal of it. It's a bit silly to call this a recipe, really, since what you put in it will obviously depend on what you have to hand – a little green salad wouldn't go amiss and some hard-boiled egg wouldn't hurt – but we thought it was worth sharing the general principles here, in case the idea of a cold fish sandwich had never occurred to you before.

Butter
2 thickish slices of very fresh brown
  or rye bread
Mayonnaise (homemade, if possible)

1 teaspoon chopped chives or dill
100–200g cold cooked fish
A bit of lemon
Salt and freshly ground black pepper

Butter your bread and spread one slice with a generous slick of mayonnaise. Sprinkle the herbs over this. Break the fish into smallish chunks and arrange over the mayo. Season with lemon juice, a little salt and plenty of black pepper. Slap on the top slice of bread, cut the sandwich in half and eat.

3. British fish

Now here's a part of the book you might not have been expecting: our personal guide to the edible fish and shellfish resident in British coastal waters. Most of these we reckon to have handled (dead or alive) and eaten (raw or cooked) at some time in our rather fish-geeky lives. And those we haven't, we're very keen to hook up with…

We think of these species almost as a cast of characters in the great, sprawling story of our seas and rivers. Here are, if you like, their 'profiles', taking in a bit of history (natural or otherwise), several fishermen's tales (some taller than others), a fair few cooking tips – and, crucially, their current ecological status. They are biographies, not obituaries – though sadly one or two might be heading that way.

Why have we invested so many pages of a cookbook on such inedible (though not, we hope, indigestible) matters? Because we are convinced that the more you know and understand about your fish, the better equipped you will be to enjoy them at every level: the catching, the handling, the prep, the shopping, not to mention the cooking and eating. The list is by no means taxonomically complete, but we believe it covers all the mainstream food fish that are landed here in the British Isles and find their way on to the fishmonger's slab.

Of course there are anomalies, such as fish we don't eat much but should eat more of (garfish, pouting, velvet crabs and the like), and some freshwater fish that anglers might want to think about eating (perch, carp and zander spring to mind). There are also a couple of 'foreign' interlopers – several species of tuna

and also of tropical prawn – that we have included not only because they form such a significant part of our seafood culture but also because as consumers we are all heavily implicated in the ecological repercussions of their consumption. Incidentally, we've omitted all other foreign contenders, including the chef's favourites, swordfish and red snapper – they're tasty enough, but ecologically about as dodgy as they come.

We've worked closely with the Marine Conservation Society (see page 34) to make sure the most up-to-date information on the ecological status of each fish has been included. To give a simple, at-a-glance indication of this, we have borrowed the MCS's rating system: '1' is the 'best' rating, indicating sustainably harvested fish and shellfish that you can eat with a clear conscience, while '5' is the worst, given to fish that should currently be avoided altogether due to their being over-exploited, endangered or caught using destructive methods. Those awarded 2, 3 and 4 are grey areas… reading the profiles will fill you in on the problems and ambiguities with the species in question and help you decide what stance to take as a consumer. If a range of ratings is included – such as 3 (2–4) – it indicates that fish from different waters or those caught by different methods have been awarded varying scores. The initial figure is the MCS's overall rating.

Except for those species that you should avoid, along with its MCS rating you'll also find a recommended minimum size. This is the length at which the species will have reached sexual maturity and so is likely to have reproduced – at least once. If we want to safeguard their future, killing fish before they've had a chance to breed does not make sense. But minimum landing sizes are not always enforced by law, and not always observed by fishermen or retailers. Paradoxical as it sometimes seems to 'waste' fish that are already dead, a consumer stand on undersized fish (along with a boycott of fish caught by unsustainable means) does send a clear message back to the industry. We have also given an indication of times to avoid fishing individual species, primarily during their spawning season. As far as freshwater fish are concerned, you should always check local regulations regarding specific closed seasons.

Finally, a word on the photographs in this section. They are not in any technical sense 'identification' pictures of consistent scale and setting. They were taken all over the place – on board boats (ours and others), at the fish market, on the kitchen table. They have all been chosen to give you a clear view of a typical member of the species in the best possible nick. And so they are, at the very least, an aid to identification. Some fish in the pictures were recently deceased. Others were very much alive. In fact, quite a few of those, having been returned to the water, may well *still* be alive. Which raises the not inconceivable possibility (however mathematically remote) that you might, some day, get to meet one of them in the flesh.

Sea fish

Herring family

Herring *Clupea harengus*

If ever a fish punched above its weight, it was the herring. For a small, rather insignificant-looking fish of barely half a pound, herring has had a major influence on our economic history. Two centuries ago it delivered unparalleled prosperity to a whole swathe of coastal Britain, at the same time underpinning the Scandinavian and Baltic economies to an even greater extent.

Like the cod – its only rival as a truly nation-shaping fish – the stocks of herring were once thought to be inexhaustible. In its heyday, the herring's potential to deliver prosperity to the communities well placed to exploit it was limited only by the fishermen's resourcefulness in removing it from the sea. In its way, the herring rush of the early nineteenth century was almost as sensational as the Californian gold rush. Remote Scottish settlements such as Wick and Peterhead became boomtowns on the back of herring fishing, and were said to harbour (as it were) some very wealthy individuals indeed.

One of the most notorious episodes in Scottish history contributed to this success story. The Highland clearances of the eighteenth century were a consequence of the booming wool trade – a mini gold rush in itself. Absentee English landlords and powerful Highland chiefs set about maximising the land available to farm sheep. Their henchmen 'encouraged' the resident tenants to move off the land (1792 became known, with bitter understatement, as the Year of the Sheep). Many of the displaced emigrated to North America (where they founded, among other places, Nova Scotia). Those who remained were accommodated in poor crofts in coastal areas where farming could barely sustain them. They had little choice but to take up fishing.

The lucky ones discovered huge summer shoals of herring. At first these merely provided vital subsistence. But as fishing techniques developed, the catches far exceeded what could be consumed locally. Herring, salted and stored in barrels, became an important commodity that could be traded. Some of the crofters were soon successful businessmen, building huge open-boat fleets to net the 'silver darlings', and trading their salted catch with brokers in the south. Here the salted fish were rinsed and dried, then smoked for several days to make a form of kipper – the original 'red herring'.

Salted and red herrings were all very well, but Londoners and other southern city folk also had a taste for fresh herrings from the short seasonal catches around the southeast coast. Clearly anyone who could feed this demand at other times of year would be on to a good thing. But fresh herring do not keep well. They are, like mackerel, very rich in oils – a plus for flavour but definitely a minus for shelf life. So shifting fresh herring from the ports to the cities had better be done quickly, or not at all.

And so the herring trade financed the infrastructure that was built in order to carry the fish from the ports that landed them to the cities that consumed

MCS RATING: 3 (2–5)

REC MINIMUM SIZE: 25cm

SEASON: N/A as spawning can occur throughout the year

RECIPES: pages 146, 147, 196, 304, 319, 357, 376, 400, 407

them. The uncompromisingly thorough reach of the British railway network in Scotland is directly attributable to the herring trade. By the end of the nineteenth century the network had penetrated to the furthest shores: Oban, Mallaig, Kyle of Lochalsh, Ullapool and Scourie in the west; Thurso, Wick, Helmsdale, Dornoch and Peterhead in the east. This engineering feat was undertaken not so much with the intent that men could reach these distant outposts, but so that fish could be transported to the great urban centres where they were in such demand.

Herring live in huge pelagic shoals, always on the move (herring means 'army' in Old Norse), following the clouds of zooplankton on which they feed. Mrs Beeton, in her *Book of Household Management* of 1859, pithily summarised the annual migration thus:

The herring tribe are found in the greatest abundance in the highest northern latitudes, where they find a quiet retreat, and security from their numerous enemies. Here they multiply beyond expression and, in shoals, come forth from their icy region to visit other portions of the great deep. In June they are found about Shetland, whence they proceed down to the Orkneys, where they divide, and surround the islands of Great Britain and Ireland.

In the north, herring were pursued for most of the year, while more southerly ports enjoyed them only as a brief seasonal catch. But even here in Dorset the summer catch was once economically significant enough to give its name to villages such as Langport Herring and Chaldon Herring.

It took two world wars to put a dent in the seemingly limitless herring stocks. The relationship between the national fishing fleet and the navy has always been symbiotic. In times of war, the skilled seamen and their vessels become vital to the navy. In times of peace, technology developed in the interests of national security – radar, echo-location and the like – is constructively redeployed within the fishing fleet. Yet while many commercial fishing boats were commandeered for service, the Scottish herring fleets continued to fish throughout both wars, as their contribution to the national diet was considered vital.

Throughout the first half of the twentieth century, the British government was particularly supportive of the herring industry, and awarded various grants to help build up the fleets. One key innovation was the introduction of 'herring buses'. These were huge motherships, into which the 'smacks' – smaller local herring boats – could transfer their catch. By the early 1950s, our herring fleet was huge and ruthlessly efficient. The Scandinavians and Dutch had made similar progress, in pursuit of what each regarded as *their* national fish. The unthinkable became the inevitable and between the early 1950s and mid-1960s the North Sea stocks fell by over 50 per cent.

The human greed that halved the herring stocks went beyond rampant culinary enthusiasm for the fish. It had become an industrial – and agricultural – commodity. By the mid-1960s, more herrings were being fed to animals and used as fertiliser than were being consumed by humans. After centuries of providing our nation (and others) with so much, our golden goose was cooked. From 1970, measures began to be taken, both internationally and locally, voluntarily and legislatively, to address the crashing population. Throughout Scotland, over 70 per cent of the fleet was either laid off by decree or simply gave up, because the fish just weren't there to be caught.

During the last twenty years, the fishery has shown a slow but encouraging recovery. There are now some recognised sustainable sources of herring in our waters, including the driftnet fisheries in the Thames, Blackwater and the eastern English Channel, as well as the North Sea and eastern English Channel autumn-spawning stock. Herring stocks in the Norwegian Sea (spring spawners), eastern Baltic and the Gulf of Riga are also assessed as being healthy and harvested sustainably. (Our own encounters with the herring hardly amount to scientific proof, but each summer we seem to see a few more of them – bigger shoals, staying for longer – in Lyme Bay; we even catch a few when feathering for mackerel.)

More than the decimated cod, the herring has shown signs that it may be capable of coming back from the brink. If it does, we can't take much credit. But we can endeavour not to make the same mistake twice. We must rely on our good judgement, not our good luck, to ensure a future for the herring, and the many irresistible forms in which we love to eat it.

Foremost of these are fillets of herring in some sort of cure or pickle. The Danish rollmop is a classic form – double herring fillets rolled up around sliced onions and pickled in vinegar. The quality varies hugely: at the cheaper end the 'vinegar' is industrially distilled acetic acid, a by-product of the brewing industry, which is so harsh as to obliterate the herrings' rich oily character. There are endless variations on the Scandinavian pickled herring but some of the best commercially produced examples we have come across are not from the fjords but from the Scottish islands. The Orkney Herring Company (see the Directory, page 591) has an excellent range that includes cures of sweet dill, juniper and sherry. Perhaps the only way to match these – or even improve on them – is to cure some herring fillets yourself. See page 146 for our own favoured procedure.

Kippers are the other great manifestation of the cured herring. These can range from the divine to the iniquitous. Those from Craster in Northumberland vie with Manx and Loch Fyne kippers for the title of most exalted. At the unforgivable end of the spectrum are any number of oversalted shoe-leather specimens and those unfeasibly red fillets that some fishmongers seem to get from God knows where. This unnatural colour is painted on to make them look more smoked than they really are.

Purists would advise favouring whole kippers, though we have noted that on occasion fillets can be excellent. The pale and interesting specimens from Isle of Skye Seafood's smokehouse (see the Directory, page 591) are exceptionally sweet and rewarding – and blissfully easy to eat (though Nick would argue quite vociferously that part of the joy of eating a whole kipper is to wrestle the flesh off the bone on your plate and nibble tasty morsels off the skeleton). Whether on or off the bone, a good kipper needs only to be grilled as it is, fried in a little butter or poached in a little milk. The only necessary accompaniments are toast (brown) and eggs (poached or scrambled).

There are other great regional riffs on the smoked herring, such as bloaters (which are big in Norfolk and Suffolk). These are not split like kippers but lightly smoked whole, traditionally with the guts still in, to give a lightly gamey tang. They may be eaten raw or grilled, or made into bloater paste. The buckling, of Baltic origin, is a subtle variation on the same theme. Also usually cured whole, sometimes guts in, sometimes out, and ideally with roes intact inside, they are hot smoked and traditionally eaten without further cooking.

Pickled and smoked herrings are endlessly diverting, but one shouldn't overlook the possibilities offered by a fresh specimen. For these, there is a Scottish recipe that is very hard to beat: herring rolled in oatmeal and fried gently in butter and/ or bacon fat, rested for a few minutes and served warm (you can easily adapt the recipe for Fried mackerel in oatmeal with bacon on page 319). A fat lemon wedge is in order, and a dollop of homemade creamed horseradish never goes amiss.

Occasionally we've had the great good luck to prepare this dish with a herring we've caught ourselves – usually while looking for the early summer mackerel off Portland Bill. To eat a herring within hours of taking it from the sea feels very special indeed, and helps us understand just what a great fish this is.

The other unmissable treat from the herring is its tender, inimitably creamy roe. But how guilty should one feel about making a meal of a few hundred thousand unborn herrings? To be honest, not quite as wracked as one might about eating the eggs of other popular roe-yielding fish – cod, for example. Herring are fast-maturing fish that can often spawn within two or three years of their birth – and the timing of their spawning is, as we have said, unpredictable. So, in the management of herring stocks, the issue is less about avoiding the spawning season, more about not taking out too high a proportion of the fish in any given fishery. If your herrings come from a sustainable fishery, and they happen to contain roe, you should consider that a happy bonus, not a stick with which to beat yourself. Enjoy.

Sardine and pilchard *Sardina pilchardus*

What's the difference between a sardine and a pilchard? Answer: about one centimetre. From a biological perspective, sardines and pilchards are exactly the same fish. At 15cm they are still sardines, but by the time they have grown to 16cm they are officially pilchards. That's how the UK industry has traditionally made the distinction, though as we shall see, some are re-thinking the branding of this fish for the modern market.

From a British consumer's perspective, these fish have always been different. A pilchard is a fish that is only ever sold in a tin, made by companies like good old Glenryck, often preserved, headless but otherwise whole, in a thick, gloopy tomato sauce. They were traditionally served for tea on a Saturday (ideally circa 1972, just before *Dr Who*). Like the good Doctor himself, even as we were growing up, pilchards already felt somehow anachronistic.

Sardines, on the other hand, are sexy. Sure, they too are crammed into tins – rectangular ones with 'keys' taped to the side – but, compared to the pilchard, they have just a hint of added suburban chic. Take them out of their tins, though, and get them on the wet fish slab and they begin to drip with Mediterranean glamour. The tempting waft of sardines grilling over olivewood charcoal smacks of balmy summer evenings on a Greek island or in a Spanish fishing village.

Both these fish – the pre-Dalek snack and the Mediterranean appetiser – could well have been caught in exactly the same place: Cornwall. Around the Cornish coast there is a healthy, well-managed fishery that has been exporting *Sardina pilchardus* (yes, that really is its Latin name), packed and salted, to Italy since the middle of the sixteenth century. These fish have always been known as pilchards to the fishermen who caught and landed them, and sardines to the Italians who imported and ate them.

Sardines are a pelagic shoaling fish like herring and mackerel (see pages 416 and 444). They are nomadic wanderers who come and go with frustrating irregularity (if you're a fisherman), and feed on zooplankton as it rises and falls from a depth of 40 metres to the surface, depending on the light levels and time of day. The sardines caught around Cornwall mark the northern edge of the sardine range, and these fish, perhaps because food availability and water temperatures differ from those enjoyed by their more southerly cousins, grow slower but end up living longer and growing bigger. They can grow to 25cm and live to fifteen years of age.

Whatever you want to call it (and we'll always have a soft spot for pilchard), this is a lovely British fish, and one we'd encourage you to eat more of. Like mackerel, it's enormously rich in omega-3 fatty acids, known to be vital for maintaining coronary health, amongst other things. And currently, in a rare reversal of the modern trend, these Cornish sardines are not being overfished.

It's an unusual and cheering fishy success story, because in the past they were seriously over-exploited. Pilchards once underpinned a whole community in the Southwest with a modest export trade and a diverse range of products: oil for lamps, skimmings for soap makers, and dyes and lubricants for the leather-tanning trade. Then came the 'fishy gold rush' and, through greed, mismanagement and the forces of nature, the industry went into free-fall.

The problem was progress, specifically the completion of the Great Western Railway in the 1860s. The railway provided access to a previously untapped urban domestic market. In just a couple of decades, the number of pilchard

MCS RATING: 2 (2–3)

REC MINIMUM SIZE: 20cm

SEASON: best July–November

RECIPES: pages 146, 147, 148–9, 196, 218, 304, 316, 319, 357, 392, 400, 402, 403, 407, 408

fishing boats in the fleet rose from a couple of dozen to nearly 300. This extra pressure, combined with a natural change in pilchard migration habits, meant the fishery was practically exhausted by the time of the First World War.

Happily, the story isn't quite over: today, Cornwall is experiencing something of a sardine renaissance. Between the Wars, most pilchards were caught and canned in South Africa. All that was left of the Cornish fishery was the Pilchard Works in Newlyn, a business that exported a tiny quantity of barrel-salted whole fish to Italy, where they were known as *salacche inglesi* – the salted Englishman.

In the last few years, with some help from Marks & Spencer and Waitrose, the Pilchard Works has now re-branded its product as 'Cornish sardines'. And they can be bought fresh or tinned (though, sadly, no longer salted). The good news is that this time around, the fishing techniques are relatively gentle. The sardines are caught by small day boats, mostly skipper-owned and run, using old-fashioned ring-netting techniques that help prevent the accidental catching of other species. This is important not only to minimise the bycatch but also to prevent damage to the catch itself – a few dogfish, sharks or big bass thrashing around in the nets would wreak serious havoc on these delicate fish.

We always like to get our hands on a few boxes of fresh Cornish sardines (sorry, pilchards) at the height of the season (late summer and autumn) to grill on the barbecue or roast on a tray in the River Cottage pizza oven. About the only time we attempt anything more elaborate is when we make our favourite Sardine escabeche (pages 148–9). It may sound like a bit of a culture clash – but it's our culture clash and we love it.

Sprat *Sprattus sprattus*

Who'd want to be a sprat? Everywhere you look there's something – with wings, fins or a socking great net – that wants to eat you. Such is the heavy burden of being small, delicious and nutritious.

Understandably, being on everyone's menu makes sprats nervous. Standing out from the crowd is not their aim in life. In fact, losing themselves in the middle of it is the closest they get to feeling at ease. And so they travel around in massive shoals. Yet even when they're surrounded by their peers, packed tight into a protective school, sprats still show the jittery signs of being aware that they're someone's favourite lunch. Sprats are not hunters. Their 'prey', if you can call it that, is mere plankton. They're the hunted, and they know it.

Consequently a shoal of sprats is never still. They weave, twist and twitch with fraught anxiety. When they're not darting about trying to find their lunch, they're darting about trying to avoid being someone else's. And millions of them fail because when they migrate into our inshore waters, a sprat-killing frenzy begins.

Sprats are a seasonal migratory fish. When they arrive in late summer it's as if someone's flicked a switch and sent 5,000 volts zapping through the sea. Everything gets charged up, and the inshore waters start to boil and bubble. The mackerel, which may have been absent for a few weeks, are suddenly everywhere again, chasing shoals of sprats with ruthless abandon. Gulls, meanwhile, attack from the air. Harried from all sides, along the coast and into the surf, the shoals break up, exposing more individuals to snapping mouths and stabbing beaks.

MCS RATING: 3

REC MINIMUM SIZE: 8cm

SEASON: Western Channel, avoid January–July (spawning); North Sea, avoid March–August (spawning)

RECIPE: page 245

Sometimes the assailants force splinter groups of sprats right on to the beach, leaving them flapping and flipping on the shingle, gasping their silvery last.

Near us, along Eype Beach, West Bay and Chesil Beach, these sprat beachings usually occur several times each autumn. It's not something you can plan for but, if you happen to be there when it occurs, it's tremendous fun. The dog walkers and sea gazers start running up and down the shingle, filling their wellies and pockets with the silver-sided freebies. In these days of mobile phones, friends are called in to share the loot, and it can turn into quite a party.

Like humans, gulls' eyes may be bigger than their stomachs. Swooping and plunging the surf, emerging from each dive with a silver snack across their beaks, they keep going, up and down, up and down, on auto-gorge. They can't go on forever, though, and eventually you'll see seagulls resting on the surface of the water, bloated and bobbing, looking as if they may never get airborne again.

These freebies are not only to be had from the beach. One year, over autumn half term, West Bay Harbour filled up with scared sprats taking shelter from the slaughter. This may have temporarily saved them from the jaws of some sea predators but it placed them within easy reach of hungry holidaymakers. Buckets were filled. Nets bulged. The revellers were walking back and forth to their cars, carrying plastic shopping bags that flipped and flapped as they went.

Being plankton eaters, these diminutive members of the herring family are hard to catch on rod and line. You might take the odd one or two on tiny micro-feathers but you'd struggle to muster enough for lunch. The only really effective way to catch them is with a net. We favour an American-style cast net. This circular throwing net is surrounded by weights, which can be dropped from the harbour wall over a shoal of fish.

All kinds of nets can be used – and some are almost too effective. Last year we watched a man dragging a small draft net behind a tiny rowing boat. He caught so many sprats that he couldn't pull the net out of the water. It was a biblical moment as he struggled to heave it on to the stone steps of the harbour. But he saw sense and let most of his huge haul escape back into the water.

Further out to sea, big boats are doing the same thing with bigger nets, working long hours to cash in on a seasonal bonanza that lasts just a few weeks. Sprats don't yield high profits but they are easy to sell – who can resist these juicy little shards of silver? The good news is that, as a short-lived, fast-growing species, they have what's known as 'a high resilience to fishing'. That means that the sprats we catch are quickly and easily replaced by next season's youngsters. Their stocks are currently healthy. To help them remain so, avoid fish caught using the pair-trawling technique, where two boats sling a huge net between them and scoop up whole shoals. It's better to buy fish caught with seine or trawl nets because some will be left behind to perform their function as one of the crucial links in the marine food chain.

Sprats are easy to cook as well as to catch. When they're super-fresh, you don't even have to bother removing the guts. Frazzle them in a hot pan, or under a fierce grill, then all they need is salt, pepper and a squeeze of lemon. You can munch them up, heads and all. But if you're feeling (a bit) more dainty, you can nibble or suck the flesh off the bones. Either way, knives and forks aren't needed.

During the sprat rush, we gorge ourselves on them. We grill or fry them, obviously. Then we devil them, mush them on toast, salt them to make phony anchovies, and smoke them in their dozens. If they continue to make themselves available, we even freeze some in small bags as pike bait. And then, one day, it's over. The sprats are gone. We'll just have to wait again till next year.

Whitebait

The Italians enjoy a famous dish called *fritto misto*, which is a cunning ruse to make a lot of undersized fish edible. They deep fry a random collection of small whole fish – little red mullet, tiny soles, juvenile bream – in batter or lightly dusted with flour, and serve them piping hot with garlic mayonnaise and salad. The Spanish and French also have a long tradition of eating all manner of small fish whole, including heads, fins, bones and tails. Ecologically, as we'll see, it's a highly questionable practice – but gastronomically it's hard to resist.

In Britain, we rarely eat whole small fish, except for whitebait. In a country where most diners go all wobbly and weird if you so much as serve a fish with its head still attached, it seems strange that whitebait have managed to remain so popular. But you'll often find them served as a starter, even on an otherwise uninspired pub menu (though they're almost certain to have been

MCS RATING: N/A as whitebait is not a specific species, but the advice is to avoid eating them

frozen and imported). The critical point is that whitebait are so tiny they're
hardly recognisable as whole fish at all. Their bones, fins, heads and tails barely
register – so they bypass British squeamishness altogether.

The first record of whitebait appearing on an English menu dates back to
1612, but it wasn't until the 1780s that they became the smart thing to eat in
London's riverside taverns. Back then, the fishermen and chefs who championed
whitebait believed – with some support from contemporary biologists – that it
was a separate and distinct kind of fish. The French naturalist Valenciennes
even instituted a new genus, *Rogenia*, to accommodate the new 'species'. The
truth, though, is that whitebait is simply a collective term for the fry of Clupeoid
fish – members of the herring and sprat family. This is why whitebait doesn't
have a Latin name – although you could call it *Clupeas varias*.

So when you sit down to a plate of 'whitebait', you're actually eating a plate of
immature herrings and sprats – and probably quite a few more species besides.
In 1903, Dr James Murie, in his 'Report on the Sea Fisheries and Fishing
Industries of the Thames Estuary', conducted studies on the contents of boxes
of whitebait being sold from Billingsgate to the Thames-side pub market. He
discovered that some boxes of whitebait contained up to twenty-three species of
immature fish, including the fry of eel, plaice, whiting, herring, sprat and bass.
For good measure, there were also shrimps, crabs, octopus and even jellyfish.

It seems the whitebait craze of the late eighteenth century was started by an
entrepreneurial fisherman, Richard Cannon of Blackwall. In 1780 he persuaded
local tavern keepers to serve this crispy, salty, fish fry-up to their thirsty punters.

The season ran from February to August and at its height there were daily races between Thames water taxis to see who could carry MPs from the Houses of Parliament to Greenwich, the centre of whitebait consumption, the quickest. Like schoolboys racing to the tuck shop at the playtime bell, politicians would pour out of Parliament, grab their favourite water taxi and see who could be first to sup a pint and crunch a whopping great basket of crispy whitebait.

The unfettered consumption of whitebait, which was caught in purse nets all around the Thames estuary, caused the river authorities to attempt a ban on whitebait fishing. Surprisingly conservation minded for the time, they rightly believed that whitebait were immature herrings and sprats. But Cannon and a few tame scientists kept on claiming that whitebait were a separate and distinct species and so no harm would come to the precious herring stocks. They had the Lord Mayor of London on their side, and the fishing continued unchecked.

By the 1890s, whitebait was still the toast of the Thames, but the famous Greenwich taverns, such as the Trafalgar and the Crown and Sceptre, were now serving whitebait that had been caught way downstream in the Thames estuary, beyond Gravesend, or else in the River Medway. At Greenwich, whitebait fishing was completely spent. The huge shoals of whitebait that had annually turned the river silver from Tower Bridge to Greenwich Docks had vanished.

Overfishing wasn't the sole cause of the destruction. Much of the damage was done by toxic pollution pouring downstream, as a result of all the new industrial development along the river. Old tanneries and new factories pumped industrial effluent into the Thames, which, along with the sewage of London, combined to turn the river into a kind of noxious liquor.

We've cleaned up our act considerably since those dark days. Now the Thames is one of the cleanest major rivers in Europe, and vast shoals of whitebait are returning to the capital. There's even been talk of starting up the fishery again and persuading some of the Thames-side publicans to spark up their deep-fat fryers (at least for something other than breaded scampi – see page 544). Who knows, we might once again see politicians scuttling down Parliament steps to launch themselves into a high-speed race to an early lunch of whitebait.

It's a tempting and romantic idea – but surely a mad one. Given that whitebait consists of the immature fry of herrings, sprats, sardines, mackerel, bass, plaice and many others, it simply makes no sense to harvest from this valuable fish nursery. By removing these fish at a juvenile stage, before they've had a chance to grow much bigger than a stickleback, we'd be decimating future stock – adult fish that could be either eaten or left to breed.

There is still plenty of imported frozen whitebait for sale in fishmongers and supermarkets. Those bags you see nestling in the bottom of the freezer cabinets may seem insignificant – a fishy surplus that might as well be enjoyed. In reality they are much more insidious than that. They come from various far-flung parts of the world, and may consist of all kinds of rare and threatened species. Once they're smeared in batter, it's impossible to tell. Ignorance is bliss – there's no regulation, because the contents, be they from home or abroad, are unknown.

This is one of those occasions when the conscience wrestles with temptation. Because properly prepared, freshly fried, lightly floured whitebait – crunchy and sweet, with a wedge of lemon of course – is absolutely delicious. We could never bring ourselves to order it. But should some wickedly mischievous publican place a bowl of it in front of us, could we honestly say that we'd push it back at him? It might be a struggle, but we like to think we'd make the right choice.

Cod family

Cod *Gadus morhua*

For a fish that has changed the world, the cod is a little unremarkable. It's greedy and rather dim, and certainly no athlete. On the contrary, it will seek out the least taxing location in which to exist – along with a few thousand of its brethren. Somewhere out of the strong currents, where it won't have to put in much effort to hold position and where the food will mostly come to it. Usually it'll dine on shoaling baitfish, such as sand eels and sprats – provided it doesn't have to work too hard. But it'll happily scavenge too, with the widest possible interpretation of what constitutes a meal. All manner of debris, from boots to bottles, has been recovered from the bellies of cod.

Perhaps the only predators hunting at sea who are greedier than the cod are humans. And it's cod's misfortune to be our favourite fish supper. This is the fish that the whole world wants to eat, for no better or worse reason than that it's easy to catch, and people like it. Not love it – their passions are reserved for soles and mullets, and even eels. But cod will always do. It has 'done' so well that in the thirty years from the 1960s to the 1990s, we managed to reduce the cod population of the North Sea by over 90 per cent. We also managed to drive a fish that was so plentiful as to defy calculation, and vital to the economies of several nations, to the brink of extinction.

In our 'codmania', we made and destroyed communities and collapsed entire ecosystems. In fisheries such as the Grand Banks, off the coast of Nova Scotia, where there once massed biblical shoals of cod, there are now only crabs, shrimps and a few small sharks. In towns that were built on the backs of the cod, towns like Fortune, Grand Bank, Trepassey and Marystown, communities are decimated.

MCS RATING: 5 (2–5)

REC MINIMUM SIZE: 50cm

SEASON: avoid February–April (spawning)

RECIPES: pages 150–1, 178–9, 179, 180, 331, 380–1, 403

Despite the cod crash, we're still fishing for them, squabbling over the few that are left. It continues because, for commercial fishermen, catching cod, where they are still to be found, is not hard. Only the weather stands in their way. The fish themselves do everything to make things easy, shoaling where there is little current, relying on their ample swim bladders to keep them weightless in the water. Trawling in such seas, where there is little current to drag on the net and the fish are reluctant to abandon their easy holding pattern, is a relative cinch.

Its torpor is in many ways the cod's undoing. Besides making it an easy catch, it also enhances our desire to eat it. Because basically, the lazier a fish is, the whiter its flesh will be (see page 21). And we all love white fish, don't we? Yes please, the whiter the better... If we haven't obsessed to the same degree over the cod's cousins, the coley and the pollack, it's surely not because of how they taste. They taste great. But it may be because there is a subtle greyish tinge to their flesh. The fillets don't scrub up quite so shiny white on the slab. What lethal prejudice.

It's clear that a series of social upheavals in the UK have also played their part in the cod's fatal story. The two World Wars had far-reaching effects on the nation's choice of food, and changed forever the technology we used to produce or provide it. During both wars, fishing boats were requisitioned by the Royal Navy and fishermen were conscripted, so many of the traditional fishing grounds went unmolested for the duration. After the Second World War, fish stocks were in better shape than they had been for decades. Inevitably there was a rush to plunder them; pure white cod flesh was just the kind of treat with which to loosen the belt of wartime rationing.

In the UK, and other maritime nations, huge resources were directed at reviving the fishing fleet. It wasn't just about claiming our share of those plentiful cod; it was also about the defence of the realm. Governments had been reminded – all too forcefully – of the benefits of an experienced navy in time of war. Our Second World War fleet had been built upon the backs of our fishermen – so it made perfect sense to develop a big fishing fleet that could form the backbone of another navy in the event of future conflict.

In this era of new technology, the rules of engagement with the cod were changing fast. During the war, naval engineers worked feverishly on sonar equipment, radar, navigation aids, echo depth sounders, and faster, more efficient marine engines. All of these were incorporated into the fishermen's armoury after the war was over. (In the US and Canada even spotter planes were handed over to fishing fleets to help track down the biggest shoals.)

Food fashion was changing too, and people wanted a bright new diet to go with their bright new kitchen appliances. The fish that had continued to feed people during wartime were those that could be caught relatively easily in the inshore fishery – such as herring, pilchards, sprats and mackerel. But these fiddly, bony, oily species were suddenly old hat. They had become not only overfamiliar but overfished – whereas the cod, with its big, white, boneless curds of flaky flesh, seemed somehow new and exciting. Amongst the modern appliances that housewives welcomed into their brave new kitchens were fridges with ice compartments that could conserve frozen food for months. These piled greater pressure on the cod stocks, as innovative frozen food companies such as Birds Eye and Findus created irresistible new lines, including the redoubtable fish finger, launched in 1955. With the benefit of hindsight, it's easy to see that from that moment, the cod was in serious trouble.

Almost half a millennium earlier, in 1497 when John Cabot first 'discovered' Newfoundland, he reported that the cod were so plentiful that all his men needed to do was lower a basket over the side of a boat and it would be filled with fish. A hundred years later, fleets from Bristol were regularly making the passage to the other side of the Atlantic to fish for cod. Some of those they netted stood taller than a man. These huge, brood stock fish were at least fifty years old. Among the most fecund creatures on the planet, each was capable of producing up to nine million eggs at a single spawning.

The catch was filleted and then salted to preserve it. Salt cod became one of the staples for feeding navies, merchant fleets and the slaves that were transported to work in the British colonies. The Spanish and Portuguese used it in just the same way. You could say that cod was being not so much fished as mined; it was a vital fuel for the discovery and exploitation of the new world.

As Europe's great nations continued to build their empires over the ensuing centuries, their fishermen sailed thousands of miles in order to raid a seemingly endless supply of cod. They barely put a dent in the overall stock. In 1883, at the International Fisheries Exhibition in London, the naturalist Professor Thomas Henry Huxley made the following statement: 'Any tendency to over-fishing will meet with its natural check in the diminution of supply. This check will always come into operation long before things like permanent exhaustion has occurred.' His judgement, in other words, was that overfishing these stocks was a scientific impossibility. They were quite simply inexhaustible. Yet a century later, after a sudden collapse on top of a slow decline, the cod were all but gone. In 1992 the Canadian government finally declared a moratorium on cod fishing on the Grand Banks: there was to be none at all until the now almost-invisible stock had recovered. Fifteen years later, the ban still stands. There has been no discernible recovery of cod numbers, and there may never be one.

However, astonishingly, cod are still being caught, even in the most depleted fisheries, such as the North Sea. Much of this fishing is legal, even though it targets fisheries that are known to be unsustainable. The EU has been pathetically weak at protecting the cod. 'Governments are not listening to their own scientists,' says Dr Cat Dorey, Oceans Campaign Researcher for Greenpeace. 'For the past seven years, scientists have said that we should not be taking cod from the North Sea at all, and yet every year the EU continues to set a cod quota – fishermen are told they can quite legitimately bring these fish in.'

According to the Marine Conservation Society, the recommended minimum limit for cod stocks in the North Sea is 150,000 tonnes, but the current estimates of stock size are between 30,000 and 40,000 tonnes, meaning stocks could be as low as 20 per cent of the recommended minimum.

There is widespread law-breaking too, with unregistered boats using unlicensed methods and then transshipping (unloading their catch at sea) to registered boats that are allowed to land in the UK. According to Harry Koster, former head of the European Commission Fisheries Inspectorate in Brussels, around half the cod being landed in Britain today is technically illegal.

Even massively depleted populations have their 'ups and downs'. As it happens, the catches of cod right here on our doorstep in Dorset have increased in the last couple of years. Many skippers choose to take this as a positive sign, and some chartered angling boats will target cod on the wrecks or over the sandbanks. 'You don't want to believe everything you read about cod,' said one Weymouth skipper last season. 'There's plenty around if you just know where to look.' We fear this is opportunistic ignorance masquerading as inside knowledge. In truth we should take no encouragement from these catches; cod *are* in crisis.

Such misplaced optimism wouldn't be the first false dawn in the cod's history. A very worrying event occurs when fish stocks are at a critical level, known as hyper-aggregation. This is when fish whose wider population is in crisis gather together in ever greater densities. The highest ever catches of the Grand Banks trawler fleet were recorded in 1992, months before the total collapse of the fishery.

It's clear that the state of cod stocks is little short of desperate. So what is the consumer to do? Stop buying it, that's what. If it's flaky white fish you're after, choose one of the excellent alternatives, such as pollack (page 430), pouting (page 442) or coley (page 432). Or, if you absolutely must have some, then choose fish that has been clearly labelled stating exactly where it was caught and indicating that it is the product of a properly managed fishery. The Marine Stewardship Council certifies some Pacific cod (very similar to Atlantic cod) from the Bering Sea, for example, which you can find in several UK supermarkets (see msc.org.uk or fishonline.org for further details). Atlantic cod stocks from the Icelandic fishery are also healthier than elsewhere. The Icelanders have fought, and won, several 'cod wars' over who's allowed to fish where. These international political battles, chiefly with the British, but also the Spanish and Canadians, have occasionally tipped over into violence. At times of the highest tension, foreign trawlers had their nets cut by the Icelandic coastguard, and British gunships were deployed to offer protection to our fishing fleet. In 1976 the Icelanders finally succeeded in achieving a 200-mile exclusion zone around their coasts. They have since managed their cod stocks with considerable skill and a view to the needs of future generations – which is more than we've achieved.

It is an irony, though perhaps not an unjust one, that almost the only Atlantic cod we can currently recommend as ecologically acceptable is Icelandic line-caught cod. It's expensive – but so it should be. It's time we all acquired a new mindset about this fish – almost to think of it as a newly discovered species and a very precious one. We have no right whatsoever to be affronted that cod is no longer cheap.

There is now another type of cod on the market – farmed cod from Scotland and Scandinavia. The question of whether such aqua-cultural enterprises really take the pressure off wild stocks is a thorny one (see page 35). The fact is that most farmed fish are fed on processed wild fish – industrially caught species such as the sand eel (page 503). Removing these species from the food chain puts more pressure on wild stocks as they lose out on an essential food source.

There is one organic cod farm, Johnson's, in Shetland, where the cod is raised less intensively and with fewer chemicals. Moreover, the feed is produced from offcuts of herring and mackerel already caught for human consumption – a far more sustainable option than taking fish directly from the sea to feed the farm. Johnson's sell their cod under the No-Catch brand (see the Directory, page 591). If you have a hankering for cod that just won't go away, this is one option we would recommend.

Cod has a fascinating history. But is history what we want this fish to become? To be honest, rather than trying to pick a path through the ethical minefield of farmed cod, or seeking out the meagre portions of 'sustainable' specimens, we think that, for now, you should find other fish to nurture and excite your children with. Pollack fingers all round! Then maybe their children will get to enjoy cod again. Once in a while.

Pollack *Pollachius pollachius*

'Oi wouldn't give pollack to me cat,' said Padraig, a salmon ghillie we fished with in County Mayo. 'Pollack is rubbish. Not fit for human consumption. Any man in Ireland who could even be bothered to bring pollack back home would only be after using it to fertilise their veg patch.'

Sadly this is not merely the ranting of an obsessive riverman who has made salmon his life's work. Badmouthing pollack as an eating fish is practically a national sport among anglers – even those who like to catch these handsome, green-gold lovelies. These days, cod stocks are crippled and haddock's taken a serious knocking too; yet few cooks and anglers stop to reassess the potential of the other members of the cod family – coley and pouting, as well as pollack. They take the rotten reputation on trust, and pass it on as a 'well-known fact'.

The anti-pollack brigade are the fishy equivalent of flat earthists, and it's time they were stopped. We eat a lot of pollack (more, perhaps, in the last couple of years than any other fish with the exception of mackerel), and we think it is delicious. We fillet and flour them for the frying pan, batter them for that chip-shop experience, smoke them, salt them, put them in pies, even eat them raw as pollack carpaccio or sashimi.

The simple fact is that anything you can do with a cod, you can do with a pollack. It may be a touch less pearly white in colour and, if not stored well, prone to becoming a bit soft, but in terms of taste and texture, fresh, well-iced pollack is very hard to distinguish from fresh, well-iced cod. We'd go further, and say that if history and habits were reversed and the cod was the pollack and vice versa, we are utterly convinced that it would be the cod that would be disparaged as cat food, and the pollack worshipped as the great white fish that changed the world. Do we make ourselves clear?

We have a theory about how this terrible reputation, so at odds with the plain facts, has come about. Because of its habits and lifestyle (of which more shortly) the pollack just happens to be a rather hard fish to target commercially. But it's a relatively easy one to catch on rod and line – one of the mainstays, in fact, of British coastal wreck and reef fishing trips for angling clubs and happy amateurs up and down the land. Now, at the risk of offending a lot of people, we say this: sea anglers have generally been more concerned with sport than food, and for the most part have been rubbish at looking after the fish they catch with a view to its end use in the kitchen. Okay, okay, things *are* improving. But until recently, hardly any charter boats bothered to take ice chests out with them, even in the summer. When it came to protecting their catch from the glare of the summer sun, a stinky old fish box with a wet rag draped over it was as far as most went. No wonder the poor pollack and pouting were barely fit for pot bait by the end of the afternoon.

When pollack is treated with the same respect that a cod gets when it hits the deck of an Icelandic trawler (i.e. gutted, washed, wiped and packed in ice within minutes) it actually stands some comparison with that revered fish. And that, of course, is what we do when we go pollack fishing. We stun the fish as they come on board, cut their gills to bleed them for a few minutes in a holding box, give them a wash and a wipe, then put them in the ice chest. On the way back into port, we gut and descale them and remove the gills, maybe fillet a few of the biggest fish, and then put this lovingly prepped fish back on ice until we get it home – where it goes straight into the fridge.

MCS RATING: **2 EAT MORE!**

REC MINIMUM SIZE: **50cm**

SEASON: avoid January–April (spawning)

RECIPES: pages 130–2, 133, 134–5, 150–1, 170, 176, 177, 178–9, 179, 180, 182–3, 236, 238, 258, 260–1, 261, 262, 331, 338, 380–1, 382, 393 et al.

Happily, pollack is common all around the coast of Britain and Ireland. It looks superficially similar to cod, with a large head and big eyes. But it's really far more handsome. Its back is a darker, greeny-brown colour and its flanks are often bright bronze or gold. It doesn't have the cod's green measles or pot belly either, which can only be a plus. Like cod, however, it does have a very distinctive lateral line. This runs the length of its body, like a cod's, but just behind the head it curves sharply downwards in a very stylish-looking 'hip' – just like the rear end of a 1950s Italian sports car.

Pollack can be caught from beaches, boats, rocky headlands and even piers, but most are caught by anglers on charter boats on offshore wreck marks. We catch them on wrecks between 30 and 75 metres deep, where they've often become resident and territorial. They make a living by hunting small fish, worms and crustaceans that use the wreck for shelter. They have big eyes and big mouths, and they're not too fussy what they wrap their laughing gear around. A pollack bite is powerful, especially in a strong tide. They nail a bait firmly, and once they realise they're hooked, they fight with impressive runs and reel-straining dives.

The best pollack fishing around Dorset is among the copious collection of First and Second World War wrecks that litter the Channel from Weymouth to Cherbourg. Our favourite way to fish these wrecks is by drifting over them using rubber jelly worms, red gill lures, storm lures, or even a string of baited mackerel feathers. We drift, preferably during a strong tide, with the lures bumping across the seabed and then we reel up a few turns to bring our tackle clear of the wreck structure. Depending on the force and direction of the tide, the fish will have taken up residence either in front, behind or on top of the wreck. They'll be facing into the current, waiting for prey fish (or preferably our baits) to be swept past on the tide.

Rod and line wrecking trips are a great way to catch pollack and have much less of an impact than trawling or wreck netting. Nonetheless, it is still important to keep stock conservation in mind. Pollack that have been reeled up from a depth of over 50 metres rarely survive being released. Their gas-filled swim bladders expand as they ascend and they're unable to deflate them to descend again, so if they're released at the surface these fish will perish. That means that pollack caught at this depth are destined for the fish box from the moment they're hooked. As a consequence, any charter skipper or commercial rod and line fisherman needs to self-regulate how many fish they take from a wreck. They also need to be aware of the spawning season (January to April), and if female fish are caught full of ripening eggs, then it makes long-term sense to take very few fish during this period.

Although we love, *absolutely* love, pollack roe (salted, smoked and made into taramasalata or squished on squares of wholemeal toast with lemon juice), to take too many breeding fish before they've had the chance to spawn is madness. If we kill a fish that turns out to be full of roe, we'll use it. But once we've landed a couple of roe-laden females, we'll move on elsewhere and fish for another species.

Most commercially caught pollack are netted from wrecks using tangle nets, or taken as bycatch by conventional cod and haddock trawlers. Trawled pollack suffers the fate of most trawled fish, in that it gets unduly crushed in the net. It's unlikely to get much attention until after the more valuable fish have been stacked and stowed, so the best pollack to buy is rod and line caught (Cornwall is a good place to find it), or caught by static inshore nets.

There are encouraging signs that pollack is finally beginning to shrug off its image as cod's poor relation, and it does now appear on the menus of enlightened chefs and the slabs of more forward-thinking fishmongers. It's used more and more in commercially produced ready meals too, such as fish pies and fish fingers, as an alternative to cod.

That's exactly how we should all regard pollack: not as a poor substitute for cod but as a genuine and worthwhile alternative. And also, perhaps, as the fish that might just do its cousin, the cod, with whom it's been so insultingly compared, a massive favour – by giving it a break.

Coley *Pollachius virens*

This is one of those fish that has somehow, over time, slipped from our consciousness. Only a couple of hundred years ago, it was so important to the British diet that we had over fifty different regional names for it, including blockan, coalfish, cuithe, gilpin, greylord, piltock, saithe, sillack and sillock. Now, most of us wouldn't recognise a coley if it moved in next door.

Coley looks very similar to pollack (if that helps you) – its closest relation in the cod family. Perhaps the easiest way to tell them apart is by looking at their tails: a pollack's is shovel-shaped, a coley's forked. Coley also have dark,

MCS RATING: 2 (1–4)

REC MINIMUM SIZE: 60cm

SEASON: avoid January–March (spawning)

RECIPES: pages 144, 270, 321, 380–1

blue-brown, almost black colouring along their backs, as opposed to the green-gold of the pollack, and a salmon-like silver to their flanks. And if pollack is underrated as an eating fish, then coley is doubly so.

Like pollack, coley can be caught on wrecks, but large specimens are usually only found on deep wrecks, over 50 metres. We don't see much of them here in the Southwest, as they don't come into the inshore rocky headlands or kelp beds in the way that pollack do. But in northern England and Scotland they congregate closer to the coast, particularly when young, and half-pounders (cuddies, as they're known) are a not uncommon catch when you're out mackerel fishing.

In many areas, including the waters around the British Isles, stocks of coley are very healthy and look likely to remain so, thanks to sustainable fishing methods. Indeed, several fisheries in the North Sea and off Norway are currently being assessed for MSC certification (see pages 33–4). There are areas where overfishing of this species is a danger – notably Iceland and the Faeroes – so avoid fish from there. As with any species, line-caught fish are the most sustainable option.

Like most cod family members, coley will eat just about anything. But they're hunters rather than scavengers – opportunistic fish with big eyes and big mouths. They'll hide in the lee of a wreck or rock and gobble up smaller fish that swim by. Generally they live in dark, deep sea where little light penetrates. At 60 metres down, visibility is minimal, so they have to rely on vibrations, smell and instinct to find their food.

It's in Scotland that the economic contribution of coley (or saithe, as they're best known there) has been most critical in times past. For the rugged island dwellers of Orkney, they provided not only essential protein but also, by way of a bonus, illumination. The traditional way to prepare coley was to split them, salt them and slowly smoke them over a smouldering peat hearth for a few days. As the coley dried out, they began to emit a phosphorescent glow. Orkney folk claim that when the catch had been good, the abundance of hanging coleys would produce enough light to read by.

However, if coley was once a beacon of mild prosperity in the dark Scottish crofts, it shines no longer. Its value as an eating fish was largely forgotten, even in Scotland, as modern trawling techniques began to bring copious amounts of cod and haddock to the market. Part of the issue is undoubtedly to do with the appearance of their flesh: cod and haddock have noticeably whiter flesh than coley – something that no doubt helped them establish a reputation for somehow being superior. Once they'd been sold on the gleaming, creamy curds of the new pretenders, consumers barely gave coley a backward glance. It became confined to the cat bin, or was occasionally used for fish pies or minced fish products.

There's no question that coley does have a slightly grey-blue tinge to its flesh, which makes it less obviously appealing on the slab. But it's short-sighted to judge it by its appearance: the grey colouring doesn't for one instant reflect its flavour and texture, which are every bit as good as cod. Sadly, the coley's tarnished image is proving hard to rehabilitate. 'Now it's mainly the ethnic communities who regularly buy coley,' says Billingsgate veteran Charlie Caisey. 'It's a great fish and they realise that. They use it very intelligently. They're more than happy to buy it with the head on, too, which they use in their recipes. They've shown us better ways of using and appreciating our own fish.'

We learned to love the coley on a never-to-be-forgotten wrecking trip out of Weymouth with Pat Carlin. We fished over the wreck of the *Admiral Stamp*, a huge naval tug that was accidentally shelled during a Second World War bombing exercise. Now, 60 metres beneath the Channel, she offers a safe haven for pouting, pollack, conger eels and a fair few sizeable coley.

Pat warned us in advance about handling a coley: 'A pollack will bite hard and swim downwards with the bait, taking ten or twelve feet of line,' he explained. 'But a coalfish fights harder. He'll take twenty or thirty feet and then keep going. Anglers often panic and start thumbing the spool to stop the fish running. That's a big mistake, the line breaks and then they say, "God what was *that*?" And I tell them it was a ten-pound coalfish – *was*. We lose a lot more than we catch.'

It was Hugh who then experienced the tug-and-run antics of a big, angry coley. After a rod-bending battle, he heaved a fourteen-pounder on board (see the picture on page 433), which we took back home to the kitchen. After taking two fat fillets, nearly four pounds each, from either side of the fish, we decided to roast the huge, staring head. Studded with garlic and rosemary, seasoned and splashed with olive oil, it went into a fiercely hot oven to roast for 45 minutes. It came out crisp and spitting, and we ate it with creamy mashed potato. We pulled gobbets of meat out of its cheeks and lips, probed hidden crevices of its skull and picked off the salty, crisp skin where we could find it. It may have been the best fish supper we've ever shared.

Haddock *Melanogrammus aeglefinus*

Like its chip-shop rival the cod, haddock is a much-celebrated fish that has paid a heavy price for its fame. Until recently it seemed to be competing with cod not only for the affections of the public but also in the race to extinction.

However, while no one is saying this fine fish is out of the woods, there is some positive news on the state of haddock populations. At the time of writing,

North Sea stocks are currently at a twenty-year high. It should be said that this is mainly due to one very good breeding year in 2001, but fish conservationists are more optimistic about haddock than they used to be.

However, that doesn't mean we can throw caution to the wind and eat this fish every day. Haddock remain under intense fishing pressure and it will only take a couple of bad years to send their population into free-fall again. Another ecological problem with commercial haddock trawling is that it also brings in cod, including undersized fish – and there's no doubt about the trouble they're in.

Haddock are also markedly less fecund than cod. A female haddock can carry up to 1.8 million eggs – which sounds a lot, but a cod can produce a tear-inducing 9 million. Haddocks' limited breeding capacity is a function of their size and slow growth, which in turn follows from their choice of deeper, colder (and more northerly) waters. A very large haddock would weigh in at around 5 kilos, whereas a big cod would spin the scales to 20 kilos or more.

This is a fish we should continue to eat with caution. According to the Marine Conservation Society, haddock that are caught from the fisheries around Rockall, Faeroes, Iceland and the North and Irish Seas are increasingly unsustainable, and should be avoided unless they're clearly labelled as being line caught. It might sound illogical – or unconstructive – to shun fish that are already dead on the slab. But the reason for buying line-caught fish (even from fisheries that are ecologically depleted) is the vital message it sends back to the retailers and the industry: source/catch your fish sustainably and we'll buy it. Don't, and we won't.

Just like cod, haddock are demersal: bottom-feeders that have a nerve-filled barbule (a goatee-like wibble of skin) jutting out from their chins to help locate food at murky depths. They look like cod too, only smaller, paler, with a black-etched lateral line and a grey-black blotch (known as the 'fingerprint of St Peter') beneath their pectoral fin. And they are similarly greedy and catholic in their tastes, making them a popular fish among anglers – those who can get to their northerly feeding grounds, that is.

We'd love to tell you our own fishermen's tales of haddock derring-do, along with top tips for catching them. But sadly neither of us has ever caught one. If we wanted to, we'd probably go to Scandinavia, where they are pursued enthusiastically by local anglers. Apparently they will obligingly devour both natural baits and lures, and can be caught, like mackerel, on a string of hooks, several at a time.

MCS RATING: 3 (2–5)

REC MINIMUM SIZE: 35cm

SEASON: avoid February–June (spawning)

RECIPES: pages 150–1, 170, 176, 177, 182–3, 236, 238, 241, 258, 262, 263, 338, 393

One thing we *can* tell you about haddock, however, is that they are noisy lovers (that's not first-hand information, by the way). Both male and female haddock emit a variety of grunt-like noises that change according to whether they are feeding, travelling or resting. The male in particular has a range of courtship noises that increase in rapidity and intensity according to his mounting state of sexual arousal. At the height of his passion, the frequency of his excited grunts blurs into a loud, continuous humming.

In Britain, there is a clearly defined north–south divide that has evolved around haddock and cod. In Scotland and the north of England, haddock is king. Fish and chip shops there sell more portions of haddock than they do cod. And up north, fresh haddock fillets are a common sight on fish counters. Down south, we only regularly see smoked or frozen haddock. This is largely due to geography. The fact that most haddock is landed in northern ports has earned it a fierce local loyalty down the years.

The Icelanders and Danish, too, would take haddock over cod any day. Haddock flesh is softer and breaks into smaller flakes than cod, and because it is more delicate it isn't so suitable for salting. As a result, haddock was traditionally preserved by drying and smoking. Smoked haddock is a wonderful base for so many dishes because of its lovely pervasive 'oaky-smoky' flavour. Chowders, kedgeree, soups, tarts and soufflés succeed or fail on the quality of the smoked fish, so it's worth learning how to spot the good stuff.

There are a few different styles of smoked haddock commonly found on the fishmonger's slab – dyed and undyed, Finnan and Arbroath smokies – and they are described in more detail in the chapter on smoking (pages 152–83). The sustainability question mark hangs over all of them, but the ones we would urge you to avoid on the grounds of taste – and also, arguably, health and safety – are those that have been dyed.

For reasons known only to the Secret Guild of Haddock Dyers, the chemical most commonly used to give dyed haddock its bilious yellow scream of colour is E104 – quinoline yellow – which is added during the brining process. A synthetic coal tar dye that is also found in ice cream and Scotch eggs, it is one of the colours that the Hyperactive Children's Support Group recommends should not be consumed by children. It is commonly used in the UK but has been banned in the US, Australia, Japan and Norway.

Dyes have been used to doctor smoked fish since the mid-nineteenth century. In America in 1884, complaints were lodged against manufacturers who used dyes derived from pyroligneous acid (produced from rotting wood, and now known to be a serious health hazard). This was fraud, pure and simple. Salting, storing and smoking all takes time: days, sometimes weeks. Time is money. Space is money. Great savings could be made by an unscrupulous fish smoker if he could make a fillet *look* as if it had been smoked for days, by simply brushing on a 'smoke coat.' It's a fraud that's also perpetrated on the palate – this stuff will always be inferior to the real thing.

If you share our enthusiasm for smoked haddock, but also our concern for the haddock's still uncertain ecological state, then the best thing you can do is to buy smoked pollack for your chowders and kedgeree instead (see the Directory, pages 590–1 for suppliers). It really is every bit as good.

And if it's fresh haddock that really tempts you, go for line-caught every time, or seek out and enjoy some very palatable relatives: pollack again, but also coley (page 432) and pouting (page 442).

Hake *Merluccius merluccius*

We all have our weaknesses, certain things – like roulette, scrumpy or chocolate – we can't quite trust ourselves to be around. The Spanish tend to lose their heads over fish, and none more so than hake. *Merluza*, as they call it, is their fish of choice, bordering on a national obsession – and now bordering on an international ecological disaster.

Hake is closely related to cod – both belong to the same family of Gadiformes. Hake lack the cod's goatee-like barbel and pot belly; instead they have an impressive array of vicious-looking pointy teeth and an almost snake-like body. When caught, they are a wet-slate grey and very quickly turn soft if not properly chilled, adopting a slack, evil grin that seems to get more malevolent as the jaw shrivels. Nobody would describe hake as a pretty fish. But the texture and flavour are far, far superior to cod. Or so any Spanish cook will tell you.

Practically all of the hake caught worldwide now ends up in Spain. Madrid's ultra-modern Mercamadrid fish market is the biggest in Europe, which is not bad considering it's around 300 kilometres from the sea. Sprawling over a 332-hectare site, it is the world's most powerful hake magnet, attracting hauls of specimen hake from the North Sea to the southern Atlantic. Much of it is caught by Spain's extensive deepwater fleet, the biggest and most heavily subsidised in the European Union. Few species, apart from cod (page 426) and bluefin tuna (page 447) are under more pressure.

European hake from southern stocks is now rated by the Marine Conservation Society as a '5' and listed as a species to avoid, on account of the depleted state of stocks – described as 'desperate' around Spain and Portugal. Moreover, although a recovery plan has started to see some hake returning to the northern European fishery, stocks there are still reckoned to be below the 'critical biomass'. If anyone is listening to these warnings, it's certainly not Spanish fishermen, the Spanish government or Spanish consumers. Here are a couple of stats: in 2006 over half the hake consumed in the whole of Europe was eaten by the Spanish. And hake made up a staggering third of all the fish the Spanish ate.

Hake is not a fish we often see in the UK these days. It was once a regular catch for trawlers fishing out of Brixham and the other Southwest ports. Indeed, Britain had its own little love affair with hake in the late nineteenth century (though we never quite matched the Latin passion for it). Fresh hauls were rushed from Brixham to Portsmouth by fast-sailing cutter, before being loaded on to horse-drawn 'refrigerated' fish wagons – essentially just blocks of ice on wheels – and galloped to the London fish markets. The fish was traditionally stuffed with milk-soaked breadcrumbs, onions and herbs, and served curled round with its tail in its teeth.

The odd British-landed hake still turns up on the fishmonger's slab. But not often. Because, guess what, the Spanish have eaten them all. Some might say *stolen* them all. Sorry, but there's no point in ducking this issue. In Charles Clover's excellent book *The End of the Line* (Ebury Press, 2004), which traces the wanton decimation of so many global fish stocks, he cites examples of how the Spanish have systematically bent and broken fisheries rules set by the European Commission, effectively rendering their hake catches illegal. An example: in 2003 a Spanish fishing company using British-registered boats was fined £1.1 million for fraud. Swansea Crown Court heard how successive skippers of the *Whitesands*, fishing off the west coast of Scotland but landing

MCS RATING: 4 (3–5)
REC MINIMUM SIZE: 50cm
SEASON: avoid February–July
(spawning)

their catch in Spain, cooked the logbooks and declared only 4 per cent of their total catch. By falsely recording catches over nearly fifty separate trips, they effectively 'stole' 508 tonnes of fish – hake that wasn't theirs to take. This is not an isolated case. The sums at stake are so huge that big Spanish and Portuguese fish traders are ready to take such fines on the chin.

According to Harry Koster, former head of the European Commission Fisheries Inspectorate in Brussels, some 60 per cent of all hake landed in Spain still goes unrecorded. When fishing logs are pure fiction, any hope of using them to help estimate overall stock levels and plan for the future is destroyed. But before we begin hurling rotten fish heads at the Spanish, Koster also points out that roughly half of the cod for sale in the UK is technically illegal (see page 428).

Not everyone who tries hake loves it. It is soft and tender, yet dense and flavourful. You have to embrace its borderline mushiness in order to appreciate how the surprisingly meaty taste melts over the tongue. The Spanish passion for hake has spawned some lovely dishes, and some pretty strange ones too. For *merluzas rellenas*, whole hake are boned and stuffed with ham, eggs and herbs, then poached; the classic Andalusian hake dish is a *caldillo de perro*, or 'dog soup', a taste-bud shocker made from bitter Seville oranges and tiny (illegally landed) hake, known as *pescadillas*. An undoubtedly winning combination is to braise cutlets of hake in a rich, garlicky tomato sauce, to which you might add olives, potatoes and sliced fennel bulbs.

A ray of hope for hake comes from the South African Hake Trawl Fishery, which was certified by the Marine Stewardship Council in 2004. It targets Cape hake, which are now being harvested in a sustainable way, due to a conservative TAC (total allowable catch), a strict limit on the number of licensed vessels, and an increased net mesh size of 110mm to allow juveniles to escape. The main export market for Cape hake fillets is, of course, the Iberian peninsula. Spanish consumers make no distinction between Cape hake and European hake, and continue to consume all the hake they can lay their hands on, regardless of the provenance or the consequences. So, while the certified southern hemisphere stock seems secure, its presence in the market does little to alleviate the pressure on northern stocks, which continue to crash towards extinction.

If you've never tasted hake, then perhaps you should – just the once, to see what the Hispanic fuss is about. But we're betting you'll find that, for all its qualities, hake is a fish you can live without. Let's hope so.

Whiting *Merlangius merlangus*

MCS RATING: 4 (2–4)

REC MINIMUM SIZE: 30cm

SEASON: avoid March–April (spawning)

RECIPES: pages 144, 148–9, 260–1, 270, 321, 324, 331

If a whiting were a man, he'd live in Surbiton, drive a reasonably priced hatchback, wear sensible shoes and like to talk at length about his personal pension plan. In keeping with his beige image, the whiting's gastronomic reputation is similarly insipid. It could be worse, in that he doesn't quite suffer the indignity of the pouting, which is widely (and wrongly – see page 442) thought of as little better than cat food. The whiting's traditional role has perhaps been to feed the carers of those cats. Somehow it has shouldered the reputation of being a fish most suitable for the elderly and infirm. The highest praise it is likely to receive is 'very digestible'.

This does the flesh of the whiting a terrible disservice. Instead of striving for bland, we'd recommend giving whiting something to shout about: like a crackling beer batter (see pages 336–7), a chorizo-laced stew (see pages 260–1), a smear of pungent salsa verde (see page 316), or even, for a whole fish, a foil-wrapped inferno of chillies, ginger, soy and garlic.

Fresh whiting fillets are a blank canvas, an excellent opportunity for any confident cook to show their mettle. They're not exactly a frenzy of natural flavour but, like other demersal (bottom-dwelling) fish, they have dependable white flesh that works well in a whole range of dishes (you'll see it in the 'also works with' section in a number of our recipes). A good, firm, fresh fillet, floured, egged, crumbed and fried (see page 324), then served with a homemade tartare sauce or even a dab of ketchup, should please fish fans of all ages.

Most fishmongers sell whiting in fillets. It's unusual to see them on sale whole, and for this reason they're rarely cooked on the bone. In fact, they're a very good fish to cook whole – roasted in foil with a few fresh herbs, a trickle of olive oil and a squeeze of lemon. A decent-sized fish (700–800g) makes a lovely supper for two, with a good dollop of creamy mash to mop up the juices from the parcel.

In Scotland they've traditionally been cured, but in a different way from herring or haddock. They are split open like kippers, with the bone left in, and then wind dried ('blawn', as the Scots say). The whiting are hung up by their eye sockets and repeatedly re-wetted with seawater, then re-dried by the wind. It's an ingenious and parsimonious process that wouldn't work with much larger fish, as you'd need extra salt to penetrate the thick flesh. These are called 'speldings', and are traditionally grilled, buttered and served with oatcakes. Very nice, too.

Nevertheless, it's hard to get *too* excited about fishing for whiting. There are no whiting appreciation clubs. Whiting tend to travel in large, indiscriminate shoals. They crave the security of numbers (a plate-sized one-pounder offers an appealing opportunity to any large marine predator, especially sharks, dolphins and seals), and if you come across a shoal, they're not hard to catch since they're always hungry and obliging.

Yet for all the whiting's damp reputation, it is still a highly effective predator, with very catholic tastes in food. Peep inside a sheepish-looking whiting's mouth and you'll get a shock. They may be meek in manner, but they carry around a set of hard, sharp teeth that can rip, gnaw or chomp through anything from a soft rag-worm to a hard-shelled, pincer-protected shore crab. Even cuttlefish, which carry their own armoury of secret weapons, can fall foul to the well-appointed dentistry of the bashful whiting.

Interestingly, the shoals are themselves distinctly territorial. Research and tagging programmes have shown that although populations are scattered right across the Atlantic, from Iceland to Portugal, they don't tend to mingle. They set up separate local populations and then stay on their patch. They prefer a very middle-of-the-road stretch of sea – not too deep, shallow or rocky, but a nice, sandy patch where they can ferret around for crabs, shrimps and worms. And they're not too fussy about what they eat; place just about any bait in their feeding zone and they'll happily hang themselves on your hook.

Perhaps the best thing about whiting, from the point of view of both anglers and commercial fishermen (who can trawl good hauls when they locate a shoal), is their sense of timing. They turn up in our inshore waters at the most boring time of year: November to March, just when all the A-list fish like bass and bream have moved offshore to find deeper, warmer water.

In fact, it's probably the whiting's sense of timing that sets it apart from its cousin, the pouting. Whiting isn't really that much better than pouting as an eating fish. They're very similar – both junior members of the cod family, with pleasant, tender white flesh – but whiting are seasonal. They have a tad more cachet because they're around for only a few months, and so haven't bred the contempt amongst anglers that the perennial pout seems to have earned.

Fishmongers, too, are grateful to have something new on the slab at a time of year when their displays can look a bit lacklustre. The chilly weather also works in the whiting's favour as, like pouting, whiting need to be killed and chilled immediately on catching, or their delicate flesh will deteriorate all too rapidly.

We are happy to eat as much whiting as we can lay our hands on because, in our part of the world, stocks are considered healthy and well managed. Sadly, this isn't true everywhere. Unlike cod, it doesn't suffer because everyone wants to eat it; on the contrary, it suffers because not enough people want to eat it. A huge amount of whiting is hauled in as bycatch (particularly in the North Sea) and then either discarded or turned into fishmeal. In other words, it's treated as dross. If the whiting were accorded more respect, if it were seen as desirable, perhaps we'd all be motivated to manage its stocks properly. Then, and only then, will it have the chance to fulfil its potential as an alternative to cod.

So, show whiting some respect, we say. It may not be glamorous but it is still a great white fish to catch or buy, and a perfect foil for strong flavours – anything from chorizo to cheese, curry to coconut. It's also ripe for light salting and/or smoking. Once you get your whiting home, let him change out of his sensible shoes and express himself. He may just surprise you.

Ling *Molva molva*

If Dr Frankenstein had practised on fish, he might well have created the ling. It's such an obvious composite: the head of a cod grafted on to the body of a conger eel. Taxonomically though, it's all cod.

In fact, the ling is the largest member of that tribe (the Gadidae), with the potential to grow up to 30 kilos in weight and live to a ripe old age of twenty-five. It shares much the same lifestyle as cod, moving into shallower water during the warmer months to spawn. It has a big mouth, and a big appetite for just about any fish or crustacean of manageable size that crosses its path.

Discernment is not the ling's forte. In common with big cod, big ling will eat just about anything that even vaguely resembles food. One snack found not infrequently in the bellies of these bigger fish are white plastic cups. These discarded pieces of marine litter are often sucked up by lazy big fish, who think they look like a dead squid and are therefore worth a speculative munch.

Like its cousins cod and haddock, ling are 'white fish'. This means they're demersal or bottom-dwelling fish, with clean, clear, non-oily flesh (see page 21). Unlike mackerel and other pelagics, they don't move around at different depths. They prefer a deep, sheltered refuge in amongst shipwrecks or craggy ledges – places where the current is slack and life can be lived without too much effort.

We catch most of our ling around the wartime wrecks that litter the Channel between Weymouth and Cherbourg, usually at a depth of 50–100 metres. Early

MCS RATINGS: 5 (4–5)

REC MINIMUM SIZE: 90cm

SEASON: avoid March–July (spawning)

RECIPES: pages 144, 150–1, 178–9, 179, 180, 289, 331, 380–1

in the year, fish that move from deeper water to these comparatively shallow wrecks could well be about to spawn. The spawning female may be heavy with ripe eggs that she's just about to deposit amongst the sheltered parts of the wreck. Ling are slow growing, taking five or six years to reach sexual maturity, but when they do spawn, a big female may lay up to 60 million eggs.

Ling roe is delicious stuff, either fresh or salted and smoked (see pages 178–9). Blanched roe fried in butter with a squirt of lemon juice makes a spectacular meal. However, eating the next generation of little lings before they've even had time to hatch is obviously something we try to do only occasionally.

Nor is targeting ling for their flesh something that should be done without question. The ling population doesn't get the environmental or scientific attention of its cousin the cod, and currently there are no measures to control its capture. But the MCS has beam-trawled ling from deep water on its 'Fish To Avoid' list because these stocks are overfished, and the deepwater terrain is particularly vulnerable to the damaging effects of trawling. As far as the cod family goes, faster-growing pollack and pouting are considered more sustainable alternatives. A couple of environmentally aware supermarket chains have stopped selling ling altogether. However, a ling that has been line caught from inshore waters outside the spawning period is more acceptable to eat. It will have already deposited its eggs and had some feeding time to regain its physical condition.

On the culinary front, ling has always been the poor – or at least cheap – relation to cod. In the nineteenth century, it was associated with the Irish immigrant community in the more impoverished parts of London. Salted and dried ling was a staple of New Cut Market in Lambeth, where it was popular with the area's poor, for whom cod was prohibitively expensive.

The ling's liver was also put to good use by the Victorians. A huge organ, it can easily represent 10 per cent of the fish's overall body weight – i.e. anything up to 3 kilos. It is full of oil, which was once used as fuel for lamps. It wasn't ignored by cooks either, and could be sliced, fried and served as an accompaniment to ling steaks and fillets (eaten, perhaps, by the light of a ling oil lamp).

If you can buy a soundly sourced ling or, better still, if you manage to catch one yourself, inshore and outside of the breeding season, treat it exactly as you would cod – and expect it to be just a little firmer and chewier. It's a versatile fish that can be used to bulk out a fish pie, or roasted with capers, fried in batter, salted, smoked, made into fishcakes, or braised with fresh peas and bacon. Thick fillets of ling, lightly salted and cold smoked for a good twelve hours or more, make a robust and satisfying alternative to smoked haddock, and can be the making of many a fine chowder (see page 262), tart (see page 241) or kedgeree (see page 393). Despite the ling's rich culinary potential, however, the current uncertain management of this fish should make it an occasional, seasonal treat.

Pouting *Trisopterus luscus*

Nobody likes pouting. Fishmongers don't stock it. Restaurants won't serve it. And even anglers moan when they catch it.

Sea anglers are generally rude about pouting because it turns up in the wrong place at the wrong time. It's classed as a 'nuisance' fish, a fish that will all too eagerly take bait intended for other, more prestigious, species. So, while out wreck-fishing for A-list fish such as bass or bream, anglers get annoyed that fat pout swallow their carefully prepared hook-baits long before the more cautious target species have even noticed that lunch is served. They feel a good, rattling bite, strike with enthusiasm, reel in with anticipation, only to be greeted by a bronze-backed, goggle-eyed pouting floating to the surface instead of the longed-for bass or bream. And then, in the fug of their disappointment, they say some very unpleasant things. You'd have to sympathise with a pout if it turned out to be suffering from self-esteem issues. Here's a fish that needs a PR makeover.

And we're the men to do it, because we *love* pouting. Treated with care and respect, its glorious white, clean, tender, flaky flesh is ripe with potential for soups, stews, escabeche, fishcakes and even fried fillets. Larger fish will salt and smoke beautifully too.

We shouldn't feel *too* sorry for pouting. Although they don't score highly in the popularity stakes (and may die an undignified death in the hands of an unenlightened angler), they generally have a good life. They grow very fast, becoming sexually mature within their first year. They then go on enjoying an active, fecund life through a seven- or eight-year life span. Pouting live fast, die middle-aged, and breed like rabbits. If their PR was in order, we'd think of them as the swinging party animals of the wrecks and reefs.

MCS RATING: **2 EAT MORE!**

REC MINIMUM SIZE: 20cm

SEASON: avoid March–April (spawning)

RECIPES: pages 148–9, 260–1, 270, 321, 324, 331

Part of the pouting's predicament is, in fact, its pedigree. It is a member of the great and mighty cod family, and carries the noble emblems of its cod lineage: three dorsal fins and a pronounced barbel hanging from its chin. Unfortunately, in this country pout has none of the cod's culinary cachet. It's like the embarrassing relative that no one ever mentions. Pouting caught commercially in the UK is generally destined for fishmeal or fertiliser. It's not even that popular among crab fishermen for pot bait. They reckon it's too soft, and will get washed away before it's had time to attract enough crustaceans.

The pouting's popularity problems are purely a British prejudice, though. The marble slabs of the fish markets in Spain always display a few neat piles of pouting (*faneca*) fillets – and they're a housewife's favourite. Even tiny fillets are prized, served dipped in beaten egg and fried.

A pouting's only crime is that its flesh is very delicate. It needs to be kept cool after death or else it will very quickly go into, and through, rigor mortis. It takes only a couple of hours on a warm day for the corpse to stiffen and then relax, leaving the flesh mushy. But treat the fish with respect from the moment it's caught and this problem can be easily avoided. Despatch it quickly with a crack on the head, and snip the gills to allow the fish to bleed out (see page 54). Then gut the fish, give it a rinse, and pack it in ice or slush immediately. Even a cool bag with a freezer block is enough to keep it fresh. Killed and chilled quickly and efficiently, the flesh will stay firm and fresh for a good couple of days.

Finding pout on a fishmonger's slab is still a rare occurrence in the UK, so when it happens it's something to be celebrated and encouraged – with a purchase. The Marine Conservation Society, whose campaigns are directly designed to protect the future of our fish stocks, recommends we eat more pouting.

Also, remember – just because a fish isn't fashionable doesn't mean it's not tasty. Thirty years ago monkfish was barely considered fit for human consumption. Now, kilo for kilo, monkfish is more expensive than fillet steak. Pouting might not be quite in the meaty monkfish league but for recipes involving white, flaky fish, it's cheap, versatile and very palatable.

We'd love to see pouting catch on in the chip shop (a good-sized fillet responds well to battering and deep frying – see pages 336–7). Perhaps a bit of sponsorship might help it hit the big time – a trendy beer would be the perfect PR partner. We can see the campaign now: 'Pouting. It's Always Posh with Beck's!'

Mackerel family

Mackerel *Scomber scombrus*

For a fish that is often barely given a second glance, the mackerel is stunningly beautiful, and a just-caught specimen is always worth a long, appreciative appraisal. In France, they may consider his sartorial style a little *de trop*: the French name, *maquereau*, also means pimp. But to us, the mackerel's blue-black-green tiger-striped back and flanks and disco-shimmering silver belly are always an inspiring, and indeed mouthwatering, sight.

Here in Dorset, you know winter has finally been kicked into touch when the first mackerel are caught from Chesil Beach, often in early April. It's best to avoid them so early in the year as they may still be spawning, but as the water hots up, so will the fishing. Mackerel are the harbingers of plenty, running ahead of the summer migration of bass, black bream, sole, garfish and smoothhound.

They are full of promise and full of fight and, truth be told, empty of sense. A shoal of mackerel will snap at anything. You can catch them on a simple strip of foil wrapped round a hook, and sometimes even bare hooks are enough. But the classic tackle that has been luring these kamikaze fish to their doom for generations is a string of 'mackerel feathers' – six hooks, each with a coloured feather tied to its shank. When a mackerel shoal is passing, it's not unusual to catch a 'full house' of six wriggling specimens.

Mackerel are so co-operative with even the most inexperienced angler, that many people remember them fondly as the first fish they ever caught – usually on a round-the-bay mackerel trip at some seaside resort. And for many once-a-year holiday anglers, mackerel will remain the only fish they ever catch.

Because of its obliging nature, you could say that, economically speaking, the mackerel works harder than any other fish in the sea – twice as hard, really. It provides both a steady catch of quality food fish for inshore commercial fishermen and a very welcome boost to the tourist economy in small harbour towns all over Britain. The mackerel provides a great example of how the economic value of fish should not be measured purely in terms of the cash generated at the fish market. It's a lesson that could and should be applied to a number of other popular sporting species: notably bass, bream and pollack.

Related as they are to the mighty tuna, mackerel are designed for speed and distance. Being true pelagic fish (see page 21), they roam the seas searching for food, burning up calories and maintaining a permanently taut muscle tone. They have a classic streamlined torpedo profile: deeply forked tails, fins that fold back into recessed slots like the wings on an F-16 jet fighter, a mouth that hermetically seals, and eye sockets flush to the head – all of which minimise water resistance and maximise speed. They are tireless hunters who feed at any depth from the seabed to the surface, on anything from ragworms to sprats, sand eels to plankton.

Their healthy lifestyle makes them a great source of nutrients – much appreciated by seabirds, seals and all kinds of predatory fish (our beloved bass

MCS RATING: 3 (2–3)

REC MINIMUM SIZE: 30cm

SEASON: avoid March–July (spawning)

RECIPES: pages 130–2, 133, 134–5, 137, 142–3, 147, 148–9, 175, 182, 194, 218, 222, 286, 304, 316, 319, 326, 357, 392, 393, 400, 403 et al.

and pollack prevalent amongst them), as well as hungry humans. Sadly, though, not enough serious sea anglers eat mackerel. On many charter boats, mackerel are regarded purely as bait. They get chopped up to make rubby-dubby (a giant mashed-fish teabag, hung over the side of the boat to attract bigger fish, especially sharks). Or else they get made into 'flappers' (filleted with the head on, to flap enticingly in the current) to catch conger, tope, turbot and big bass. They are rarely the target species; to these fishermen they're just a means to an end.

There's no denying mackerel make fabulous bait. Like the ubiquitous squid, they will catch fish in any sea. And even in fresh water, too, they are excellent for catching pike, crayfish, zander and eels. But, for all their value as bait, it would be insane to overlook mackerel as table fish.

Fresh mackerel are an outstanding food fish – and one you can enjoy in good conscience, as stocks are doing pretty well almost everywhere except the North Sea. There's no doubt that the best you'll ever eat is one you've caught yourself. If you want to make it absolutely unforgettable, then cook your mackerel over a smoky driftwood fire, sipping Dorset cider while watching the fat summer sun set over Lyme Bay. (Feel free to relocate fantasy to beach and tipple of your choice.)

A sprinkling of salt is the only seasoning a wood-grilled mackerel requires, though some branches of bay wouldn't go amiss (see page 194). And that's just a start. There are so many ways to prepare this delicious fish, including raw, baked, soused, smoked, cured and potted. We love this underrated overachiever. And for that reason we've devoted more recipes to it than any other fish.

But – and it's a big but – you can only extract the full joy from a mackerel if it's nice and fresh when you eat it. And this means treating it with respect from the moment it's caught. So, whenever we go sea fishing in the summer, we take a couple of blocks of ice in an old cool box to keep the mackerel in top condition. We diligently despatch every mackerel as it comes on board, by knocking its head or breaking its neck and then cutting the gills to bleed out the fish (see pages 53–4). Then we give it a rinse in fresh seawater and pop it in the ice box.

Delicious as it is, fresh mackerel isn't easy to retail. It doesn't last long on the slab unless it's been very well iced, and any blood left in the flesh causes it to deteriorate even quicker, as the blood attracts bacteria. As soon as it's more than a couple of days old, it begins to look very sorry for itself, with sunken eyes and a slimy residue around the gills and belly flap. By this point a sourness is creeping in and it will taste as disappointing as it looks. (In the seventeenth century, mackerel was the only fish that was allowed to be sold openly on Sundays. Even the Archbishop of Canterbury realised that if a good mackerel wasn't shown a cooking pot quickly, it would spoil beyond repair.)

Fishmongers traditionally like to display mackerel whole, and often ungutted, no doubt because it's such a handsome fish. But, for the reasons outlined above, it does in fact keep much better if it has been gutted and beheaded. Some supermarkets have taken to selling trimmed, headless, gutless mackerel, and indeed fresh mackerel fillets, in film-covered trays. These can be a good buy because the supermarkets need to start with extremely fresh fish if they are to achieve the three- or four-day shelf life they prefer. If you buy supermarket mackerel that still has three or four days to go before its use-by date, it's likely to be not long off the boat. It seems odd to think, and perhaps painful to admit, that fish wrapped in plastic on a supermarket shelf may be fresher than a whole fish presented on a fishmonger's slab. But we've done our research on this, and with mackerel it is often the case.

Tuna

Bluefin *Thunnus thynnus* **Bigeye** *Thunnus obesus* **Albacore** *Thunnus alalunga*
Yellowfin *Thunnus albacares* **Skipjack** *Euthynnus* or *Katsuwonus pelamis*

Tuna is a worry. It's now the world's most popular eating fish. Everyone loves tuna because it has lean, healthy meat and plenty of omega oils (see page 19). It somehow promises to make us fit. And it's delicious. What is there not to like?

Here's what: the fact that we may be devouring a spectacular species – several, in fact – into extinction.

Until recently this family of fish was not widely known in the UK. But its near-global distribution means that subsistence fishermen all around the Pacific, Atlantic and Indian Oceans have long been catching it, whenever and wherever they could. The Japanese have, for several centuries, prized it for sushi (though it would have been made with salted tuna, not fresh, until the beginning of the nineteenth century). But it is around the Med that it has been a staple the longest – for a few millennia, in fact. All the great Mediterranean civilisations – the Greeks and Romans, the Egyptians and Carthaginians – prized tuna, pursuing it voraciously with traps, nets, baited hooks and spears. In fact, tuna fishing and processing – specifically salting and drying – was one of the first 'food industries' of the Roman Empire.

The British, however, had no appetite for eating tuna, and nor did the Americans until the second half of the twentieth century. Prior to 1960, the only tuna on sale in the USA was canned – and not for people but for their pets. Since then, though, a global appetite for tuna has exploded. The 1960s and 1970s were the decades in which we discovered tinned tuna – culminating in the dizzy heights of the tuna and sweetcorn sandwich. In the 1980s and 1990s, we grew up and learned to love it fresh, seared and served rare, or even raw. These days tuna seems to have a place in every home and restaurant, and crops up in everything from kids' lunchbox sandwiches to executive expense-account dinners. And we're *still* feeding it to our pets, too. The problem is, however we buy it (as fresh steaks or in oil-filled tins) or wherever we order it (in the sushi bar or sandwich bar), most of us haven't a clue what sort of tuna we're actually eating.

There are, in fact, seven different species of tuna that are regularly caught for food: there are three types of bluefin, then there's yellowfin, bigeye, skipjack and albacore. All these tuna are hunted, sold and eaten with scant regard for the future of their stock. All three species of bluefin – the Northern, Southern and Pacific – are critically endangered, according to the World Conservation Union (IUCN), and feature on the Marine Conservation Society's list of 'Fish to Avoid'. The bigeye tuna is currently rated as 'vulnerable', while most yellowfin stocks are being fished at full capacity. Overall, stocks of albacore and skipjack are considered to be in a reasonable state, though in certain areas even they are badly affected by overfishing.

Such is the culture of selling tuna that when we buy it we almost never know which species we are getting. Sometimes it's written on the tin – but do we really take that in? And when it comes to fresh, we rarely ask, and are rarely told. It's true that many consumers have begun to engage their consciences in their choice of tuna – but not generally on behalf of the species they are eating. It's a fellow mammal that's tugging at the heartstrings, and people will go to great lengths to make sure that their tin of tuna is 'dolphin friendly'. Which is not to say that

MCS RATINGS: bluefin and bigeye 5 DON'T EAT!; yellowfin 3 (3–4); albacore 3 (2–5); skipjack 3 (2–5)

REC MINIMUM SIZE: N/A as buying a whole tuna is unlikely!

SEASON: N/A as skipjack and bigeye spawn all year round. Most others spawn in summer but, since they inhabit both hemispheres, this can mean any time of the year.

RECIPES: pages 359, 360, 390, 400, 403, 407

this is an ethical irrelevance – of course fishing methods should not put other, untargeted species at risk. But buying dolphin-friendly tuna is a completely irrelevant gesture *from the tuna's point of view.*

Is the tuna really less worthy of conserving than the dolphin? Does its demise matter? Well, at the risk of stating the obvious, it does if you want to keep putting it in your sandwiches. But, we'd also ask, is the tuna really less awe-inspiring, less worthy of our respect than the other species we seek so energetically to save? It may lack the brainpower of a dolphin, and consequently it may struggle to perform back flips to order in a seawater swimming pool to a coach load of kids. In other words, it may be only a fish. But what a fish!

The three species of bluefin tuna represent the absolute pinnacle of marine evolution, the ultimate in fish design and performance – and their cousins are not far behind. A bluefin is capable of growing up to 700kg in weight, living for thirty years or more, and migrating over two million miles in a lifetime. Tagging programmes have shown that Brazil to Norway is quite an average commute for a bluefin – they regularly cross the Atlantic in as little as sixty days. But it's not its stamina that really makes the jaw drop – it's the speed and acceleration. A bluefin can out-torque a Porsche 911, clocking 0–50 mph in three seconds – and that's underwater, where the resistance is far greater than on land.

They achieve this by a phenomenal combination of power and hydro-dynamics. All fish are cold blooded, but bluefin have evolved a unique thermal exchange system that allows them to retain 95 per cent of the heat generated by their muscles. By keeping the muscle tissues warm, they work more efficiently, allowing the tuna to swim further and faster. They are streamlined to perfection, with pectoral fins that fit into foldaway slots, ensuring zero drag. The purpose of such speed and power is not merely to travel but to hunt, and at this they are supreme. It helps that they have the most acute eyesight of any fish (except some sharks). Oh, and they can dive a kilometre deep in about a minute to find their prey. If there was a Top Trumps deck for fish, the bluefin tuna is the card that every awestruck child would want.

But there's one Top Trump stat that is not doing the bluefin any favours. It is officially the most expensive fish in the world, with individual ones selling for as much as $180,000 in Tokyo's Tsukiji Fish Market; the equivalent of around $300 per kilo. More than 90 per cent of all European-caught bluefin goes directly to the Japanese market. Last year Japan imported 23,000 tonnes of it – a trade worth $354 million.

Bizarrely, the price of bluefin, though still staggering, has been dropping over the last couple of years, not that we can take encouragement from this. What's been happening is that the technology of catching tuna has become so ruthlessly efficient that catches have soared. Snatching the tuna is now as fast and furious as a *Miami Vice* offshore drugs bust (except you could say it's the bad guys in hot pursuit). Shoals are searched out by helicopters, which then radio their GPS position to super-fast tuna boats that can be among them in just a few hours. The fish may be netted, or caught on heavy hand lines with lures. Sometimes they are killed, iced and taken straight to the nearest freezer-boat to be blast frozen, then air-freighted to market. But increasing numbers of bluefin are now transferred alive, in cages dragged slowly behind the boats, to the nearest tuna holding pen. Here, in anchored nets as much as a kilometre in diameter, they await their fate. They will be fattened up before being selected and killed according to the daily fluctuations of the international tuna market.

The sushi and sashimi market in Japan, now being drip-fed from these
'farms', is no longer a slave to the fluctuations of wild tuna catches. The price
has fallen because there are now more places where a trader can buy tuna more
consistently – in effect, there's more competition. As it has become cheaper and
more affordable, consumer demand has increased – so the fishermen now have to
catch more fish to make the same money.

The bluefin tuna is fast becoming one of the rarest pelagic fishes in the
world. The western Atlantic stock has been reduced by around 90 per cent since
the 1970s, as dealers clamour to get a piece of the ravenous Japanese market.
It's entirely possible that our generation will be responsible for eating the
last bluefin in the sea. Is this really what we want? Things are so desperate,
according to some campaigners, that it is time to take the matter out of the
hands of consumers.

The Marine Conservation Society is calling for a complete worldwide ban on
catching bluefin. But it looks unlikely to happen. Not with the fish at that price.
For the time being, a consumer boycott is the only meaningful action that can be
taken. If you are offered tuna for sale and you think that there's even a chance

that it is a bluefin, you should leave it well alone. As Dr Bryce Beukers-Stewart, Fisheries Policy Officer of the MCS, succinctly puts it, 'Would you eat a panda?'

One of the problems for the bluefin is that the Japanese sashimi culture insists that no other member of the tuna family is an adequate substitute. Top sashimi chefs and their followers would no doubt claim that this is down to the inimitable qualities of bluefin flesh: its density, texture, flavour, etc. Of course, these aspects will differ subtly from species to species, but in the end it's a matter of tradition, and the increasing rarity and prestige of the target species. No doubt if it was albacore or skipjack that had been hunted almost to extinction, the Japanese would now be insisting that bluefin, prolific and vulgar in our parallel universe, could simply never come up to the mark.

Meanwhile, choosing tinned tuna may also be a bit of an ethical minefield but it does have one big thing going for it: it's never going to be bluefin, which is far too valuable to be put in tins. The tinned stuff is normally either albacore or skipjack, and occasionally yellowfin. It's reassuring to know that these three species are in much better shape than the big bluefin.

Of all the tuna, skipjack and albacore have the most robust stocks, and should therefore be the choice of the conservation-minded tinned tuna shopper. Of the seven commercial species, skipjack is the smallest and quickest to mature. It spawns younger, and more often in its lifetime, which makes it a more efficient breeder and much more resistant to fishing pressure than its cousins – especially the mighty bluefin.

So how should we pick a clean path through the ethically booby-trapped tuna aisles? For a start, the whole 'dolphin friendly' business is fraught with ambiguity. The claims of some brands can be misleading or inconsistent. 'Line caught' means caught by long-lining methods, which are often branded as 'dolphin friendly'. It looks good on the tin. But in practice it often involves lines of 50 miles or more, with thousands of baited hooks, set adrift in the open ocean. And though they won't accidentally catch dolphins, they may well catch, or tangle, endangered turtles, sharks, swordfish and even seabirds. Dolphin safe they may be, but plenty of other species that should concern us just as much are taking a hammering as a result of their use.

We think the tuna you should choose is the one that favours the continued survival of the fish that's in the tin. This means you should be looking for skipjack, albacore or yellowfin that has been 'pole and line caught' (in other words, with a form of manhandled fishing rod). Or 'troll caught', which means they've been caught on individual lures dragged (or 'trolled') behind a small fishing boat. (Wouldn't it be great if this meant that those ugly, stumpy oafs had finally given up hanging around under bridges and harassing goats and run away to sea?) 'Hand line caught' is good too – unlike line caught, it means fish have been caught and landed individually. All these methods target tuna very accurately (and will not catch dolphins). And they are the sustainable option not merely because of a lack of collateral damage, but also because they allow the monitoring and management of the tuna themselves.

Given the bewildering range of tinned tuna available to the consumer, we thought it might be worth mentioning a couple of brands that we know use sensitive fishing methods within well-managed fisheries. The Glenryck Eco-Friendly brand of pole-caught skipjack comes from a sustainable fishery in the Indian Ocean and is available in most supermarkets, while the Fish4Ever brand of albacore is sustainably fished nearer to home in the northeast Atlantic.

As for fresh tuna – sorry, but right now we reckon it is best avoided altogether. If you're in a sushi bar, treat yourself to another plate of shimi saba (Sushi mackerel, see page 137) instead. Or give the hugely underrated scad a whirl (see page 481). If the prospect of life without seared tuna steaks fills you with desperation and despair, then make it a very rare treat indeed, possibly in both senses – if you're going to eat a species into oblivion you might as well enjoy it. Seriously, please make sure it *definitely* isn't bluefin. If you are intent on eating fresh tuna, yellowfin is the least worst option (albacore and skipjack being almost impossible to source fresh).

We'll stick to tinned tuna, and do you know what? We actually think of it as rather a treat. In fact, we genuinely prefer it to fresh (when it's tinned in oil, not brine). Salade niçoise, for example, is a dish of real genius – the squeaky beans, the salty olives, the lovely egg (see page 360 to complete the scene). But when, in fancy restaurants, they insist on making it with grilled tuna fillet, served rare, we can't help feeling they've wasted their time and ours. And, of course, another slab of endangered fish flesh.

Small sharks and rays

Bull huss (or rock salmon) *Scyliorhinus stellaris*

'Prairie oysters' are not shellfish, they are bull's testicles. 'Chicken of the woods' is not a form of feral poultry, it's a fungus. And 'rock salmon', far from being some shy, reef-dwelling member of the salmonid family, is a chunk of bull huss or some other minor member of the shark family. The catering trade has always had a way with words, inventing culinary euphemisms for ingredients, or body parts, that otherwise might not instantly stimulate the appetite. And not just in Britain. *Andouillette* is how the French charcuterie trade manages to persuade millions of people to eat what would better be described as *saucisse de cul* – or arse sausage. And the huss itself they call *veau de mer*, or veal of the sea.

Huss (shown in the photograph, left) and its small, sharky relatives, the spurdog (*Squalus acanthias*), smoothhound (*Mustelus mustelus*) and Starry smoothhound (*Mustelus asterias*), are all close cousins to the lesser spotted dogfish (see page 454), and all are regularly found among the bycatch of beam trawlers, long lines and inshore gill nets. No doubt they were always appreciated by a few coastal dwellers in the know. But it wasn't until the early part of the twentieth century that these species began to gain widespread respectability, albeit under an assumed name, by appearing on chip-shop menus alluringly described as rock salmon. Nobody seems to know where or by whom the name was coined but it rapidly caught on. It was a cunning commercial alliance between fishermen, who were landing large quantities of fish that were not easy to shift, and chippies, who were pleased to be able to offer a cheaper alternative to cod and haddock.

The choice of 'salmon' as part of its name gave this pretender a lot to live up to. Its success is as much a tribute to the eating quality of these species as the nous of the marketing ruse that reinvented them. Their flesh is very palatable: their tightly packed, muscled bodies produce firm meat with a good depth of flavour. The other great appeal of these mini sharks is that they don't have a conventional skeleton – no fiddly bones, just one cartilaginous spine that is easy to remove. Once beheaded, skinned and trimmed, they present benignly on the slab – any trace of their sharky origins consigned to the fish offal bin. With a coating of crisp batter, the disguise is complete.

Which would all be good news, except for one vital hitch: the rock salmon concept has been too successful. It simply isn't sustainable. If you were looking to rock salmon to ease the conscience and plug the cod gap, think again. Frustrating though it may be (we're the first to say there's many a fine meal to be made from this family of fish), we have to urge you not to buy fish that is labelled huss on the fishmonger's slab, or rock salmon on the chip-shop menu.

MCS RATING: 5 DON'T EAT!
REC MINIMUM SIZE: N/A
SEASON: N/A

The problem with these mini sharks (and bigger sharks too, come to that) is that they're not equipped to stand any amount of heavy predation – least of all, sustained commercial fishing pressure. This is due to their unique reproductive biology. Species such as cod and pollack, which inhabit the same ground as many types of huss, are egg-laying fish (oviparous). They are able to produce millions of eggs in one season. It's a large-scale, chaotic gamble, but one that does offer the potential for millions of young. And these species have evolved to expect and survive heavy losses – from seals, sharks and the like (though not, as we are now discovering, on the scale meted out by humanity).

The huss approach to breeding is much more refined. The female keeps her eggs safely inside her body; the male huss provides her with a 'package' of sperm, which she uses to fertilise her eggs. These eggs continue to develop internally until eventually, after several months, they are laid and attach themselves to the seabed. These egg parcels are known as 'mermaids' purses' and resemble transparent ravioli parcels with frizzy tendrils tied at each corner. You can find hatched empty egg parcels washed up on beaches all around the coast during the summer.

Inside each purse are all the essential nutrients for the growing huss 'pup', so that by the time they hatch out (two months after being laid) they're miniature versions of their parents, already strong enough to feed and fend for themselves.

Some members of the clan go to even greater lengths to ensure a good start for their offspring. The smoothhound and the spurdog are 'viviparous': they actually give birth to live young. The average litter of pups is a mere ten, and they will have taken a year to gestate.

These breeding techniques are very effective for maintaining a high survival rate among a relatively small population, but they do mean that future stocks of these species are dependent on a high survival rate among the adult population. They are able to achieve this, under natural circumstances, because they have few predators – only a bigger shark would attempt to eat an adult huss. And so their ability to maintain a healthy population takes only light losses through predation into account. They are therefore hugely sensitive to fishing pressure.

Tope (shown right) is another shark that should be left well alone. A much-prized sporting fish among anglers, as well as being good eating, it can grow up to 2 metres long and may appear on fishmongers' counters simply labelled as shark or even huss. It is viviparous and slow-growing, just like its smaller relatives, and the global population has declined significantly in recent years. Some UK fisheries have recently proposed a total ban on the landing or killing of tope – something we heartily support. Eating one, we feel, is an absolute no-no.

The one exception to the shark family rule seems to be the lesser spotted dogfish. As the huss's next of kin, they breed in the same way. But they are by far the most successful and adaptable of the family (see overleaf). The smallest of the tribe, they reproduce a little younger, and more frequently. Skilled at hunting small prey and scavenging fish debris on the sea floor, they can scratch a living almost anywhere. If we wanted to, we could catch dogfish all day long in Lyme Bay. But with bull huss and smoothhound, we'd be lucky to see one a month. We'll happily kill, skin and take home a few good-sized doggies, but we'll always do our best to unhook a huss with care and return it to live and breed another day.

When it comes to distinguishing between these species on the fishmonger's slab, things can get confusing. All the mini sharks tend to be generically labelled 'huss' (rock salmon is mostly just a chippie's term). How can you tell if you're buying plentiful dogfish or endangered huss or hound? Basically, if any part of the skinned, tapering body is thicker than your wrist, or if the whole thing is longer than your forearm, then it's definitely not a lesser spotted dogfish. Ideally, though, if your fishmonger can't guarantee it's doggie, then don't buy it.

It may seem a little contrary to keep mentioning all manner of fabulous British fish, then in the same breath be telling you not to eat them. At least with the rock salmon family we can steer you firmly in the direction of the dogfish. We must admit, as fishermen, that we do get to eat the occasional huss – when it's swallowed the hook deep and we've had to kill it. Under such circumstances, we feel it would be wrong not to eat it. When it comes to cooking it, we'll go chip shop all the way: our beer batter (page 336) and tartare sauce (page 324) will always do the huss justice. But a dogfish done the same way will be no lesser treat.

Dogfish *Scyliorhinus canicula*

When humankind has finally finished meddling with this planet and has managed to render itself and most other evolved species extinct, all that'll be left on Earth are rats and cockroaches. And all that'll be left in the sea are dogfish. When the underwater lights finally go off, only a pair of dogfish eyes will be left glowing in the dark.

Lesser spotted dogfish are members of the shark family and sport the requisite regalia: tough, sandpapery skin, rows of sharp teeth, a cartilaginous (as opposed to bony) skeleton and spooky, slitty, sad, dark eyes. They behave like scavenging pack animals: they will eat just about anything, roam just about anywhere and have the bulletproof constitution of those types who get themselves into the *Guinness Book of Records* by eating aeroplanes.

Their thick shark-family hide is part of their defence armour. They have no scales to damage or lose; just rough, tough, abrasive skin. In the past, this skin was dried out for use as sandpaper. Fishermen would use it to scour the varnish and paint on their boats, while sculptors favoured it for sanding down alabaster, and milliners for raising the hair on a beaver hat. It was even used to make non-slip grips for sabre handles.

Most sea anglers hate dogfish most of the time – or at least they pretend to. Yet all sea anglers have experienced those long, uneventful days of angling, when the arrival of a few doggies is a welcome distraction from the tedium of an unbent rod and an untugged line. Sometimes hooking dog after dog when you're trying to catch another species can be a morale-sapping angling experience. But to ward off repetitive dog syndrome, skippers and seasoned anglers like to think of oblique and mildly disparaging ways to refer to these persistent offenders. 'The kennels are open then,' is one favourite rejoinder for the first dog of the day. Or, 'Keep him off the grass,' as another one comes on board. 'I'm afraid my boat's on heat' was a good recent addition to the dictionary of dog-dissing quotations. It's done with some affection, and all adds to the camaraderie of a fishing trip. Actually most anglers believe, even if they wouldn't admit it, that the world would be a far sorrier place without these over-friendly pups.

MCS RATING: 3

REC MINIMUM SIZE: 60cm

SEASON: avoid late summer–November (spawning)

RECIPE: page 270

They're really not hard to catch. A dogfish will take big bait, small bait, fresh bait, old bait – in fact *any* bait. They will sneak into nets, traps, crab pots and lobster creels to eat the bait, and when that's all finished they might even have a go at a crab or lobster that is caught in the trap (though a really big lobster might equally have a go at them). Dogfish are adaptable, omnivorous and, as far as one can tell, fairly immune to disease and pollution. They are, in short, survivors.

Many species of sea fish can't survive the process of being hauled up from depth, either by rod and line or by a trawled net. Their swim bladders expand with the change in pressure, they have no way of releasing the gas fast enough and become fatally buoyant. Fish that are then put back over the side of the boat will just flounder at the surface and end up as seagull food. But not the doggie. Having been thrown back, dogfish are able to descend right back down to the seabed with little effort or consternation. Like all sharks and cartilaginous fish (including skates and rays), they don't have swim bladders; instead they use their oil-filled livers as ballast to sink themselves.

At sea, dogfish have little to fear. Their only real predators are larger members of their own family – sharks and very big skate. But now the skate population, especially around the south of England and Wales, is all but extinct (see page 456) and the number of larger sharks is in steady and tragic decline. As their numbers tumble, the wily dogfish seem ever on hand to fill the gaps. In places where there was once a huge diversity of species, now you'll often find only a few stragglers – and endless dogfish.

Around January and February, before the sea has started to warm up and grow the algae and plankton that kickstart the food chain, most species migrate to deeper, more southerly waters. But the dogfish sticks around to pick up the pieces. In the absence of others, whatever food is around is theirs for the taking. So in tough times these fish don't just survive, they thrive.

Sadly, this isn't the case for the dogfish's larger cousins, such as the bull huss, spurdog and smoothhound. They are less hardy, and far more sensitive to overfishing and the changing ecology of the sea (see page 452). But while we do everything to give these vulnerable species a break, we feel free to tax the local population of lesser spotted dogfish on a regular basis. Taking a few dogfish out of the local food chain can only improve the chances of a huss (or greater spotted dogfish, as they are also known) surviving long enough to breed.

We highly recommend eating LSD (the lesser spotted dogfish, that is, not the drug). It may not be the subtlest fish on the slab, and can have a faintly acidic tang to it, but it has firm, succulent meat that holds together well, and combines excellently with well-flavoured sauces. If you've caught a dogfish yourself, the only impediment to a very good meal is that fiendish skin – but removing it is actually very easy (see pages 74–5). When you're buying from a fishmonger, they are usually pre-skinned anyway.

One of the delights of cooking dogfish is the fact that it's boneless. It's easy to cut or nibble the cooked flesh from the central cartilage – and easy to take fillets from a skinned, raw body too. This makes it very child-friendly eating.

We often turn our dogfish fillets into crisp, beer-battered goujons and serve them with homemade tartare sauce, or even a dollop of salsa verde (see page 316). And sometimes we drop them into a fish soup, stew or curry. A chunk of dogfish needs a scant five minutes to cook through, so put it in the pot just before you serve up and by the time you've laid the table it'll be done.

Skates and rays Rajidae family

The bold claim made by the French gastronome Louis Lemery in his much-respected *Treatise of All Sorts of Foods* of 1702, was that Parisians ate skate in much better condition than those who lived by the sea. The implication was that the long journey from the fishing ports of Normandy or Brittany to the French capital somehow did the fish good. In other words, that this is a fish that is actually better to eat when less than absolutely fresh. Unlikely, you would have thought. But true.

The fishing industry has evolved around the notion that the passing of time is detrimental to the product. Ancient British trading laws had already been modified to allow fishmongers to sell herring and mackerel on Sundays – otherwise they'd be rank by Monday. But with industrialisation came refrigeration and faster transport: the fish business was a prime motivation for the development of the railway network in the nineteenth century, so fresh fish could get from harbour to city in double-quick time, fetching better prices and shifting bigger catches, and consequently stimulating the whole coastal economy.

There's no doubting the general rule that fresh fish is better than stale: all dead fish get progressively worse for wear as every day passes. And in most cases the effect on the eating quality of their flesh is a negative one. But skates and rays are a curious exception; turbot and Dover sole are others, but for slightly different physiological reasons (see pages 461 and 471). The consensus is that a freshly caught skate or ray is best stored in the fridge for a couple of days *before* you cook and eat it – for reasons we'll explore shortly, this enforced period of fridge purgatory will render it far more tender and sweet.

But first, let's clear up some confusion about names. When you buy or order a 'skate wing', it doesn't actually come from a skate but a ray (it isn't really a wing either – we'll come to that in a moment). The 'skate' we eat is in fact any of ten or so different species of ray found in British waters, including the thornback, blonde, homelyn, starry, spotted, cuckoo and undulate rays. The word 'skate' correctly applies only to four other species: the common, long-nose, black and white skates. These are far bigger species than the rays we see on the fishmonger's slab and can also be distinguished by their pointy noses – hence their other collective name, long-nosed rays. Common skate are found in deep water, mostly around the north of England and Scotland, often weighing well in excess of 90 kilos, and currently they are far from 'common'. In fact all four have become very rare (the common, long-nose and white skates have completely disappeared from the Irish Sea) and no one now should even consider killing one. The grim irony is that the skate, which lent its name to a great delicacy of fish cookery, has been overfished – but not generally in the cause of gastronomy. The larger specimens, being too coarse to bear preparation for the table, have usually been processed for fishmeal and fertiliser.

Rays are members of the same family as skate (Chondrichthyes, sub-class elasmobranchi) and their names have always overlapped. In the British culinary context, despite being correct, it's pretty much impossible to impose the word 'ray' over 'skate'. But in other European countries it's rightly known, to chefs as well as naturalists, as *raie* (France), *raya* (Spain) and *raja* (Poland).

Both skates and rays are cartilaginous fish. This means that, like their cousin the shark, they have a different internal structure from bony fish such as cod or mackerel. Instead of a bony skeleton, they have a central cartilaginous spinal

MCS RATINGS: all 5 DON'T EAT!, except spotted, cuckoo and starry rays 3 (3–4); thornback 4 (4–5)

REC MINIMUM SIZE: N/A except spotted and cuckoo rays 60cm; starry ray 45cm; thornback 75cm

SEASON: N/A except spotted ray, avoid April–July (spawning); cuckoo ray, avoid December–May (peak spawning); starry ray, avoid summer and early autumn (spawning)

column with a fan-like collection of 'fingers' spreading into their 'wings'. As for those wings: the word is really just a description of the tapering, flattened sides of the kite-like bodies that are the defining characteristic of all skates and rays. Some species (for example, the tropical eagle ray and huge manta ray) actually flap them in a bird-like manner to propel them through the water. Others, mainly bottom dwellers, ripple the edges as they hover over the seabed.

The word 'wings' has passed into the lingo because of the way that rays are prepared for market. The wings are cut away from the head, backbone and tail of the fish and then skinned, leaving the characteristic tapering, triangular portions of pink-tinged flesh, through which is spread a radiating fan of fine, finger-like 'bones' (technically cartilage). This cutting is usually done on board by the fishermen who catch them. The remaining head and body is a substantial piece, and will often be kept for processing as fishmeal.

Dealing in pre-cut 'wings' is obviously convenient for fishmongers: it would be wasteful of space to present whole rays on the slab, and time-consuming to wing and skin them to order. But there is also an old tradition among fishmongers that to show these fish fully intact would be 'inappropriate'. All species of skate and rays have very obvious external sexual apparatus. The male has a pronounced pair of elongated, testicle-like 'claspers' hanging from his belly. In Victorian times it was deemed unseemly to display a fish with such obvious tackle. They were sure to be seen by ladies.

Another thing that might have caused the ladies to reach for the smelling salts is the faint but unmistakable whiff of urine that emanates from this fish. It's no olfactory illusion: urea is present within the flesh of skates and rays, an integral part of their biology and a defence against the salinity of the seawater in which they live.

All sea fish have evolved to deal with the constant presence of salt: if they didn't have some chemical defence against it, it would dehydrate them, like brine curing a ham. Bony fish solve the problem with their gills, which have special cells to filter away excess salt. Cartilaginous fish don't have the same gill structure, so instead they maintain a supply of urea within their bloodstream. The urea is rich in other dissolved minerals, which prevent the fish losing their bodily fluids to the saline water by osmosis.

When they die, though, the urea starts to break down and is released as ammonia. You could hardly say that this is a more pleasant smell than urea – but from the would-be diner's point of view it's a good sign as it indicates the flesh is purging itself. At the same time, its texture changes from hard, chewy and rubbery to a yielding tenderness. After two to three days the process is complete, and the fish pot-worthy. And happily, the honk of ammonia largely disappears with cooking. All of which explains the astute observation made by Lemery three centuries ago: that it's better to eat a skate that's travelled inland to Paris for a couple of days than one that's just flopped off the boat at Boulogne.

The four true skate (as opposed to the numerous rays sold as skate) that are present in UK waters – the common, the long-nose, the black and the white – are *all* assessed as critically endangered. So no one should be going anywhere near them with a fishing net, let alone a knife and fork. As for the ten or so species of rays that are caught around our shores and comprise the 'skate' we eat, most are now deemed to be already endangered or at least near-threatened species. It's the larger ones that are suffering the most from fishing pressure: the blonde, sandy, small-eyed, thornback, undulate and shagreen rays. Part of the problem is that rays breed like their cousins the sharks (see page 452), and depend on a high survival rate and few problems from predators to maintain a steady population. The smaller species, such as the spotted, starry and cuckoo rays, aren't in such bad shape because they grow faster and reach sexual maturity younger than the larger rays.

The tradition of cutting and skinning skate wings on board the boats that catch them presents an increasing dilemma for the ethical fish shopper. It makes it impossible to accurately identify the species of origin. Even wholesalers and supermarket fish buyers cannot always tell which species they're buying and then offering for sale. This has been the case for decades, but is only just being addressed by the major players in the food industry. In 2006 Sainsbury's, the biggest retailer of fresh fish in the UK, made a bold and laudable decision, based on consultations with the Marine Conservation Society, to stop selling skate wings altogether. (Subsequently, Marks & Spencer, Waitrose, Tesco, Asda and Morrisons have also restricted their range to just a few of the smaller ray species.)

However, even when wholesalers can identify the species they're dealing in, it doesn't necessarily solve the problem. Rays don't hang around in species-specific groups. If a trawler is dragging for flatfish (which tend to inhabit the same kind of ground), it could easily catch several different species of skates and rays in the same haul. On the other hand, skates and rays are some of the few species able to survive relatively well after being trawled, so there is an opportunity to return the more vulnerable species alive. The key is to educate fishermen in order to ensure they can identify the most threatened skates and rays, so they can be released to breed another day. Just recently, real progress has been made in this area. A joint partnership between the Sea Fish Industry Authority, the Shark Trust and MCS has produced skate and ray identification guides for fishermen and an online database so they can check what they land.

As sea anglers, we catch the occasional ray, usually when bottom fishing for bream, gurnard and plaice on the shingly banks off Portland Bill. This allows us to identify the species – usually with a little help from our skipper – so the 'wrong' rays can always be returned unharmed and the 'right' ones theoretically kept for the pot. A few years ago we might indeed have killed and eaten a cuckoo or a spotted ray, whereas a thornback, undulate or blonde ray would always be released to fight another day. Now they all go back. They are such intriguing fish to encounter that returning one, and watching it flap those aptly named wings as it heads back to the bottom, is no great hardship.

We must admit that we still buy the occasional pair of wings directly from one of the day boats in Weymouth or West Bay. They're usually cut but not yet skinned, so we can see what type we're buying. But we acknowledge that it's a flawed ecological gesture to choose a pair of cuckoo ray wings when those of a good-sized blonde ray, taken in the same net, are clearly visible in the fish box.

It's the sheer joy of eating this fish that has made occasional hypocrites of us. A skate wing gently fried in foaming *beurre noir* (perhaps the only dish for which the cook is actively encouraged to burn the butter), then finished with a scattering of capers and a squeeze of lemon, is and always will be one of the best fish suppers there is. The flesh is easily pulled from the cartilage in immensely satisfying long, flaky strips. Like piscatorial tagliatelle, they curl neatly around the capers, and soak up just the right amount of buttery juice. All that remains of those alarming odours is the merest hint of gaminess.

It is, very sadly, a pleasure we are now resolving to forego. If only some enlightened fishery could get together with a credible conservation body, do whatever it takes to manage and certify the right species of ray, and restore it to our menus with the promise of a clean conscience... but, if there's to be such a ray of hope in our lifetime, they'll have to get their skates on.

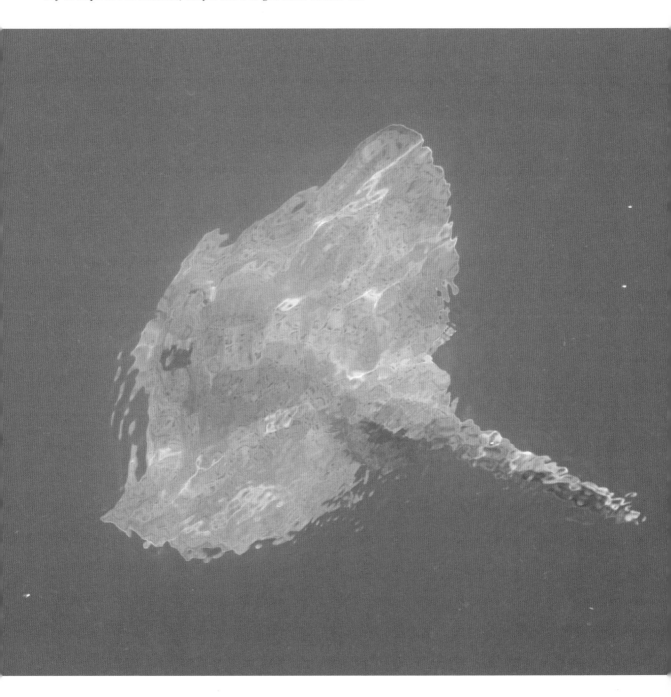

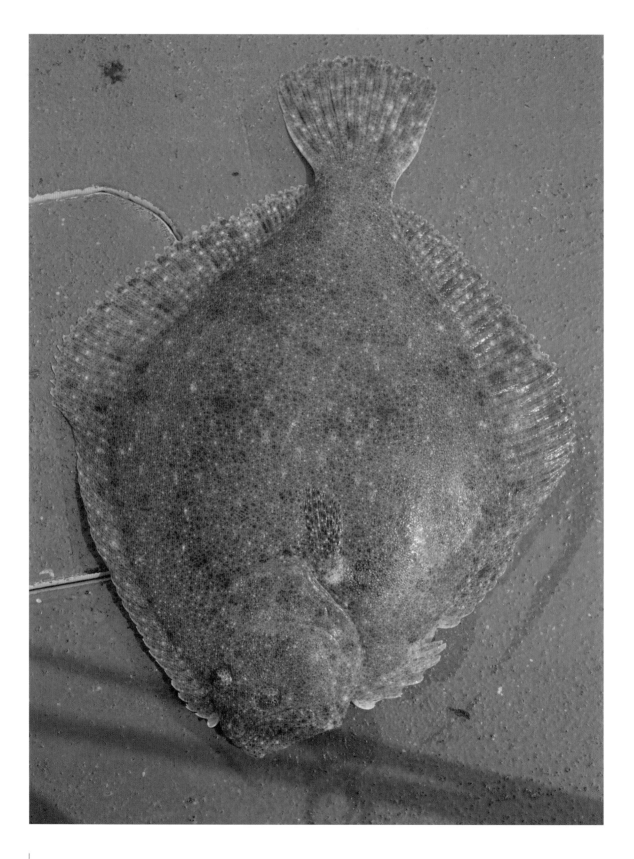

Flatfish

Turbot *Psetta maxima*

The French Revolution was a bloody affair: a violent uprising of the masses, ending with a flurry of decapitations of the rich and famous. Heads rolled. Hearts stopped. The streets ran red with blue blood.

None of this had much impact on the great chef Grimod de la Reynière, however, whose only diary entry relating to the entire Revolution stated: 'Disaster. Not a single turbot for sale in the market for weeks.'

Amongst the gourmets and gourmands of Europe, turbot has always been held in high esteem. Turbot is fish royalty. The Victorians were particularly enamoured of the thick curds of flesh and the rich, almost gamey flavour, which gained it the reputation of being the 'pheasant of the sea'. It was luxurious food for grand occasions. Served out of a turbot-shaped fish kettle (a *turbotière,* no less), steamed with its white underside upwards, it was often slathered in a pink lobster sauce.

Turbot are the largest of the most important flatfish family – important because it also includes plaice, brill and flounder. And, like their cousins, they have a remarkable natural history. Turbot eggs have a droplet of oil attached to their egg sac, which makes them buoyant. As a result, instead of the eggs lying on the seabed, where a catalogue of scavenging bottom-feeders would eat them, they float to the upper layers of the water column and comparative safety.

Like all flatfish, turbot don't start life flat. After the eggs hatch, the young fry swim around for their first six months or so in a conventional 'upright' manner, eyes on top of their heads and belly below. They feed on plankton, and as they grow they tip over sideways and gradually metamorphose into flatfish. They develop their characteristic 'squashed head' appearance as their right eye slowly migrates around their head towards the left. The wandering eye ends up cheek by jowl (so to speak) with the left eye, giving the turbot its typical cross-eyed visage. This eye migration happens as the juvenile fish itself is leaving its mid-water nursery and migrating downwards to the seabed. When it gets there, it'll give up plankton sucking and start to earn its keep amongst the other bottom-feeding crew.

Turbot are highly successful predators who grow to be big, powerful fish. This is perhaps largely due to their economy of energy. They might actively hunt at the start and end of each tide run, but mostly they like to lie buried in the sand and wait until something dumb or dead just happens to drift by on the tide. Like most flatfish, their chief weapons are stealth and camouflage.

Being flat makes hiding in plain sight easy. A flatfish only has to worry about the top elevation of its body, because its belly is always going to be hidden snug against the seabed – which is why all flatfish have white bellies and seabed-imitating backs. Instead of scales, turbot have a thickish skin covering their backs with a few bumpy, bony lumps called tubercles. These give the fish a

MCS RATING: 4 (2–5)

REC MINIMUM SIZE: 30cm

SEASON: avoid April–August (spawning)

RECIPES: pages 141, 222, 231, 283, 290, 318–19

degree of protection, as well as adding a bit of texture to their camouflage. A few flicks of their fins half-buries them in the sand, and the whole 'I'm-just-a-patch-of-seabed' deal is complete.

Turbot have enormous, gaping, articulated mouths, which can open to suck in a vast array of food – and the generous baits offered to them by keen turbot anglers. They are enthusiastic omnivores. Biggish fish like them will hunt the slower, bottom-dwelling fish such as poor cod and pout, they'll crunch up crabs, mussels and all manner of crustaceans, and they'll eat their share of any carrion drifting about on the seabed. However what they really love is sand eels, which at dusk need to dig themselves into the sand to hide from predators. It's while the eels are digging their holes for the night that they're at their most vulnerable: too busy working on their overnight quarters to notice the large turbot creeping up on them.

Most turbot are caught from boats and are rarely targeted from the shore. But Chesil Beach is famous for producing some stunning shore-caught specimens, especially when fished with big mackerel and squid baits close behind the surf after a gale. Bass anglers who lob out big, hopeful bait occasionally hook turbot by accident – a very happy accident.

When we're in search of turbot from a boat, we normally drag fresh bait (a mackerel fillet, lightly hooked through the end of the tail) along the sandy undulations of the Shambles Bank. The boat drifts broadside across the bank, and fishing's best at the quieter ends of the ebb or flood tides. Even slack water can be productive. Lazy turbot don't feed when the tide is racing. They'll move away from big currents to find somewhere calmer to hide out.

Such is the premium price for this fish that it is inevitably targeted by commercial fishermen as well as anglers. Heavy bottom-trawling gear is what will find turbot and other flatfish, and such equipment is no friend to the sea floor. It's not that it couldn't recover from it – given time. But it can't take a beating week after week, year after year. So the conservation issues here are not merely to do with turbot numbers, but also the preservation of a fragile ecosystem that supports a vast range of interdependent species. As with scallop dredging, the common-sense answer to this problem is the zoning of the fishery, with zones left to 'rest' in rotation for ecologically meaningful periods of time.

Until such conservation measures are in place, it is perhaps best to uphold the tradition of turbot as a special-occasion fish – an annual treat, perhaps. Turbot from the North Sea fishery should certainly be avoided, as these stocks have already taken a hammering and, in all cases, line caught or static net caught is far preferable to trawled.

Catch a good one yourself (anything over 2 kilos is a keeper in our book), however, and you should feel more than entitled to take it back to the kitchen. Not only have you pulled off a mean feat of angling, you've picked that fish cleanly off the sea floor with your baited hook, barely troubling the fauna – micro and macro – with which it shares its habitat. Putting a smaller one back is hard, but when your hunger pangs have been assuaged by the cheese sandwich in your lunchbox you'll realise it was the right thing to do.

The quality, firmness and succulence of the turbot's flesh is such that it will stand up to most cooking techniques: frying, grilling, baking, steaming, poaching and even barbecuing – though in all cases, it would be a heinous crime to overcook it. Turbot is so tasty that minimal accompaniments are required – a trickle of butter and a squeeze of lemon or lime will do the job. At the same time, it's robust enough to withstand more elaborate saucing – hollandaise is the classic accompaniment (see our cheaty version on pages 281–2), salsa verde (see page 316) makes a pleasingly piquant modern alternative, especially to a barbecued tranche (see page 72). Traditionally, one should never remove the fins of a turbot before cooking – they're meant to be saved as a tasty treat for the most honoured guest. Pulled gently from the cooked fish, they come away with some shards of particularly juicy flesh attached.

A final tip: if you are ever lucky enough to catch a turbot yourself, or happen to buy a just-caught fish direct from a boat, it would be a mistake to eat it on the day it was caught. Curious as this may sound, a turbot can actually be too fresh to eat (a characteristic it shares with skates, rays and Dover sole, among others). It requires at least 24, ideally 48 hours – on ice of course – for the flesh to settle and become tender and palatable. Prior to that, you might find your turbot rubbery and curiously bland, and may well end up wondering what all the fuss is about.

Halibut *Hippoglossus hippoglossus*

Our friend Dave Holt, with whom we fish on the west coast of Scotland, was once birdwatching high on the cliffs at Duncansby Head near John O'Groats, where the fulmar colony was in the full hue and cry of nesting.

Looking down from the birds to the water below, he saw a massive, green-brown shape just below the surface, which at first he took to be a huge raft of floating kelp. 'But I could see it was a bit too tidy for that,' says Dave, 'and it was moving. I saw it heading for a dead fulmar chick that was floating in the water. It came up and sucked it off the surface, like a trout taking a dry fly. I watched it for a couple of minutes, and it took two or three more chicks. It must have been 12 feet long, and at least 4 feet wide, and well over 400lb. I knew exactly what it was, but I still couldn't quite believe it. It was simply one of the most awe-inspiring things I've ever seen.' As the shape slipped back down into the slate-blue water and disappeared, Dave was sure he had seen not a shark or a seal, or even a dolphin. He had just seen a halibut.

Fish witnesses don't come much more credible than Dave Holt. Apart from birdwatching, fishing is his great passion and, for over ten years now, he has been catching giant skate in the Sound of Mull, tagging and releasing them as part of a programme run by the Glasgow Museum's Science Department. He knows how to estimate the size and weight of a huge fish.

Nor is he the first man to have been profoundly moved by an encounter with a halibut. On 26 April 1784 William Cowper wrote his heartfelt ode, 'To the Immortal Memory of the Halibut on which I Dined This Day'. It wasn't the quality of its flesh that inspired him. Rather, not unlike Dave, he was full of admiration for the fish as a physical specimen, and a totem of maritime adventure:

> *Indebted to no magnet and no chart,*
> *Nor under guidance of the polar fire,*
> *Thou wast a warrior on many coasts,*
> *Grazing at large in meadows submarine.*

MCS RATINGS: wild 5 DON'T EAT!;
farmed 2
REC MINIMUM SIZE: N/A
SEASON: N/A

At the time halibut was a reasonably common eating fish but by no means a fashionable one. It was reckoned to be rather coarse and dry – a big, cheap, chewy fish that poor people were forced to eat. Some disdainfully called it 'workhouse turbot'. And, for all the passion of his ode, Cowper does not at any point seek to redress popular culinary opinion of the fish.

By the late nineteenth century, halibut had garnered a few fans, but its 'workhouse' reputation was always going to be a hard one to shake off. *Cassell's Dictionary* of 1880 put it in a nutshell: 'This excellent fish is not as prized as it ought to be, probably on account of its cheapness.' Well, it's not cheap any more. Today even farmed halibut costs at least £20 per kilo, while a wild-caught Alaskan halibut can fetch double that, putting it right up there in the UK's 'Top Ten Most Expensive Fish'.

Halibut went through the transformation from food zero to culinary hero within a generation. Post-war, it gained ground as the price of other 'smart' fish, such as turbot and Dover sole, went up. In the 1950s it was a regular on the menu at Wheeler's restaurant in Old Compton Street, Soho. The artist Francis Bacon, who dined there regularly, was said to be a fan. As Wheelers expanded into a chain in the 1960s and 1970s, halibut caught on as a restaurant-menu kind of fish that was chef-friendly – it made a lovely square fillet portion in the centre of a big round plate, and took a sauce well. The consensus among chefs was that halibut was no longer a fish to be denigrated but one to serve up with buttered spinach, hollandaise sauce and a hefty price tag.

However, being so slow growing, halibut offer very little resistance to commercial fishing pressure. By 1983, wild stocks of Atlantic halibut had been so overfished that the Seafish Industry Authority's Marine Farming Unit in Argyll began attempting to farm them. There were many teething problems, principally the high mortality rate of the tiny, larval fish in the first year of life. These have now been overcome, and the farming of halibut is a growing area of aquaculture, both in northern British waters and in the fjords of Scandinavia.

One would hesitate, however, to call halibut farming a success story: it is subject to many of the same environmental criticisms as the farming of salmon (see page 508). Particularly problematic are the huge amounts of food – usually meal made from wild-caught 'industrial' species, such as sand eel and blue whiting (see page 504) – required to fatten these slow-growing fish. Progress is being made on more sustainable halibut farming in Scotland but there is still some way to go.

Halibut is a true flatfish, and the unrivalled giant of the family. It prefers colder, deeper water than most of its relatives and, as a result, grows slower but much, much bigger. The largest recorded halibut ever caught in a net was landed in Norway and tipped the scales at a massive 282kg. Fishing for wild halibut, by trawl and also with deep long lines carrying baited hooks, has always been at the tough end of a tough business, not only because of cold waters and rough seas but also because this huge fish has something of an attitude. Halibut seem to deeply resent being caught. If you drag a 25–50kg halibut on to the deck of your boat, the chances are it is going to use every steel-hard muscle in its powerful body to try to smash nine kinds of crap out of you and your vessel.

Broken bones and seriously damaged boats used to be commonplace, until fishermen decided to swing the odds somewhat back in their favour. Most hand-lining commercial halibut boats (and even, in Canada, some halibut angling boats) now carry a handgun or captive bolt gun (the kind used for slaughtering cattle) in the wheelhouse, in order to shoot the hooked halibut in the head when it comes alongside the boat. (There is hardly any recreational halibut angling in British waters. Apart from the distances and dangerous seas involved, our strict gun laws continue to stack the odds in favour of the fish.)

We almost never eat halibut. We'd hesitate to malign it as an eating fish – it's good, but not *that* good. Having a tendency to dryness, it needs careful cooking and a good sauce to help it slip down. We couldn't square choosing a portion of wild halibut, from either the fishmonger's slab or a restaurant menu, with the very serious concerns about its stocks (wild halibut scores a 5 in the MCS list and is considered endangered by the World Conservation Union). As to farmed – not only, for the reasons mentioned above, is halibut a questionable choice of fish for aquaculture in the first place but the end product is another rung or two down the ladder of eating quality. So halibut, in any form, is currently too expensive, too unsustainable and, frankly, too replaceable to justify a purchase. There are many better options, farmed and wild, for both the palate and the conscience (check out our lists on page 49).

But to see one in the wild, as Dave did – now that we'd pay good money for. Is anyone out there offering halibut safaris?

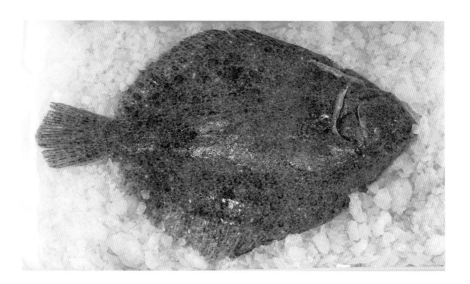

Brill *Scophthalmus rhombus*

Poor brill. Being the rather plain sister of the more glamorous turbot can't have been easy. For centuries much extravagant praise and culinary pampering were lavished on the turbot, while the beleaguered brill skulked unnoticed in its shadow, sweeping the ocean floor and scrubbing the used scallop shells. The Victorian natural historian Frank Buckland summarised the lot of the brill when he wrote, 'The brill is considered inferior to the sole, but much superior to the plaice. It is, in short, a poor people's fish.' Not any more it's not. Brill is catching on, and deservedly so.

Although brill still doesn't have quite the same culinary cachet as the turbot, it now costs almost as much; if turbot retails for £X per kilo (X being anything between £12 and £30, depending on the season and weather), then it's likely that a few brill will be alongside it on the slab, priced at about £X minus £2 per kilo.

The chef-led cult of turbot worship ruled for most of the twentieth century. The turbot became popular simply for being popular. But take a good look at it (and a taste, of course) and you'll see that brill is just as good – arguably better, if it happens to be to your taste. The two are by no means indistinguishable. Brill is the lighter, less meaty of the two, splitting the difference between, say, the turbot and the cod. Another way of describing it would be to say it's like chunky Dover sole – an appealing idea in anyone's book (particularly ours).

In truth, though, brill and turbot are so closely related, and so similar in terms of their habitat, behaviour and diet, that the two have been known to interbreed, and brill-turbot hybrids are quite common (we should probably call it a trill, because there's already a fish called a burbot). Turbot have the potential to grow larger than brill, but middle-ranking fish (from 2–4kg) of both species are commonly encountered on the same territory. So, when we fish the mussel beds and sand banks near Portland, with a long, thin strip of mackerel dragged along the bottom behind a drifting boat, we are fishing for turbot and brill. And, on balance, being the kind of guys who cheer for the underdog, we'd both probably rather catch a brill.

MCS RATING: 4 (3–5)

REC MINIMUM SIZE: 40cm

SEASON: avoid spring and summer (spawning)

RECIPES: pages 140, 141, 216, 222, 223, 231, 283, 289, 290, 310, 318–19, 340–1, 381

Other than size, the obvious differences between them is in their markings. A turbot has tubercules (hard, horn-like lumps) sprinkled across its back, whereas a brill is smooth. In fact, the Turkish name for brill translates as 'nail-less turbot'. Like turbot, brill is usually a left-hand flatfish. This means that when the fry, who start life upright as normal 'round' fish, keel over to one side and move to the seabed to become committed bottom-feeders, their eyes migrate round to the left side of their face.

Brill's mounting price is a reflection not merely of its increasing popularity but of the fact that stocks are by no means inexhaustible. This is a fish that will need some management if it is to continue to delight its growing band of fans on a regular basis. Brill are mainly taken as bycatch in beam-trawl fisheries in the North Sea, and a considerable proportion of the catch is immature. Avoid these fish if you can. A better choice is otter-trawl-caught fish – from pretty much anywhere else – preferably over 40cm in length. (An otter-trawl net is held open by heavy wooden 'otter boards' and is often used to catch shoals of herring or mackerel mid-water. But they can also be fished to 'bounce' the bottom – and are much less destructive than the heavy chains of the beam trawler.)

Over the years, the brill has suffered from some pretty insulting treatment in the kitchen – such as brill Mornay, which is fillets served in a cheesy sauce to supposedly give them flavour. This is madness. Brill can be cooked like turbot. It's versatile – and robust enough in texture and flavour to be fried with capers and black butter (as if it was skate wing), or served with a sorrel sauce (as if it were a piece of sea trout, see page 308). But it doesn't disappoint when dusted with seasoned flour and sizzled in a pan like a modest piece of pollack or pouting.

Big brill, like turbot, are sometimes sold in 'tranches' – cross-sections cut across the whole body (see page 72). A generous tranche can be fried, grilled or even barbecued, in each case turned several times to cook all four sides (two skin sides, that is, and two flesh sides). But what we really like to cook is a whole, family-sized brill of around 1.5–2kg, steam-baked in a suitably capacious tin with some good seasonal vegetables, then brought ceremoniously to the table to be carved off the bone (see page 290). There's only one word to describe that.

Plaice *Pleuronectes platessa*

'Men get weird about plaice,' says Pat Carlin, our favourite Weymouth charter skipper. 'Don't really know what it is about the fish. But there's something. Anglers get all obsessed and serious about them. They come on our boat to fish with crazy homemade rigs – stuff with beads and bells and spoons. I can have ten blokes on board fishing a drift and no one says a word. All their brows are furrowed from concentrating so hard.'

It's hard to define what it is about plaice that tickles the fancy of so many sea anglers. There's nothing better about them than any of the other flatfish. On the contrary, brill and turbot grow bigger and taste much better. Sole are smaller but their flesh is finer. Dabs are more plentiful. Flounder are more fun. Yet plaice seem to refresh the parts of sea anglers that other flatties cannot reach.

Sandbanks like the Shambles, near us off Portland, and Dogger Bank, off the northeastern fishing ports, are traditional plaice-trawling grounds. Like most

flatfish, plaice love sand, mud and gravel because they can hide in it, or stir it up with their wing-like fins and snouty mouths to expose crabs and other goodies. They migrate to the huge seed mussel beds to the west of Portland Bill in spring and early summer. Their tough, bony mouths allow them to tear off these tiny mussels and swallow them whole, digesting their sweet orange flesh. Often they are so fixated by the mussels that they won't eat anything else – certainly nothing as mundane as a regular angler's bait. Hence the plaice-obsessive's fancy rigs, a desperate bid to distract their quarry from the business of gorging mussels. The culture of rig and tackle adornment began with the humble plaice spoon: a dessertspoon with the handle chopped off and a hole drilled in one end. A ring was clipped to the spoon and attached to the line a few inches behind the hook bait. The purpose of the spoon was to kick up sand and sediment during the boat's drift, suggesting a lively alternative to the mussel menu for the plaice to come and investigate. Over the years, the spoons have become more elaborate, and are now fully accessorised with coloured beads and rattling balls.

The bait and its presentation generate almost as much discussion as the rigs on which it is presented. 'Plaice like a long bait,' says Pat. 'Long, fat, with lots of movement. Two hooks, one above the other and then alternate ragworm and squid strips until the whole bait's about eight inches long.' But big baits don't mean big bites. Plaice bites are tender, twitchy, teasing little affairs that leave anglers unsure and insecure. They don't know whether to lift slowly, to strike hard or just wait and hope – hence the furrowed brows.

A plaice's brow is a curious thing too. Like most flatfish, they start life as normal upright, side-on fish. But as they grow, they tip over to one side and one eye migrates around the head, to sit squashed up against the other. Plaice are pleuronectidae, or right-eyed flatfish (most are left), with both eyes ending up together on the right side of the 'face'.

What makes them stand out most obviously from the flatfish crowd are the bright orange spots and splodges sprinkled across their greeny-brown backs. No other flatfish sports spots like these. Underneath, the bottom-hugging side of the plaice is, like most other flatfish, pure milky white.

Plaice skin is thick and tough and relatively easy to peel off in whole, unbroken sides. This makes it one of the few species suitable for tanning into leather. In the Second World War, when the Nazis invaded Denmark, they requisitioned all 'leather' (as conventionally made from mammal hides) for military use. The resilient Danes responded by making their leather from cod, salmon and plaice skin. In its heyday, it was known as 'Neptune's suede'. Even Queen Ingrid of Denmark put her best foot forward in a pair of evening sandals made from purple-dyed plaice skin. (If you want to see a pair of fish leather slingbacks in the flesh, or rather skin, then make your way to Northampton, where you will find a pair on permanent display in the Central Museum.)

Plaice have always been a popular eating fish and are easy to find on fishmongers' slabs all over Britain. But, sadly, they are victims of their own success. They have been subject to intense fishing pressure in many areas, and the Irish Sea is the only definite sustainable European source at the time of writing. Ask your fishmonger exactly where his or her plaice comes from and, if it's not Irish, it's best not to buy it. Choose otter-trawl-caught fish, if available: most plaice are caught by the beam-trawl method, which damages the seabed and also results in a very high bycatch of juvenile fish. The speed at which plaice grow, and the age at which they breed, varies hugely according to the depth and

MCS RATING: 4 (3–5)

REC MINIMUM SIZE: 30cm

SEASON: avoid spring (spawning)

RECIPES: pages 216, 222, 231, 246, 290, 306, 321, 324, 381

temperature of the water where they live and the availability of food. But they are generally slow maturing, and it takes between three and six years for a female to grow to spawning size.

The flesh of plaice is exceptionally fine and delicate. At its best, it's as white as a Hollywood Christmas and melts to velvet on the tongue. But this unusual tenderness and fragility may translate to 'mushy and watery' if a fish is out of condition, a day older than perhaps it should be, or has been cooked for a few minutes too long. Rather surprisingly, given its subtlety, plaice has survived for many years as a chip-shop fish. It's not the ideal fish flesh to batter, because the fillet is never that thick, so the batter–fish ratio will always be high. No doubt that appeals to some. But the delicate meat won't stand much squirting with industrial-strength malt vinegar.

Plaice are relatively easy and satisfying to fillet (see pages 68–9), and plaice fillets rolled up and stuffed (for example, with orange zest and breadcrumbs) were rather a popular conceit in the 1980s. But it all seems a bit fussy for a fish of such simple charms. Our favourite way to eat plaice is whole and on the bone. The skin, though substantial, is a definite asset and, if treated right, should end up nice and crispy (so not like shoe leather at all). If you've got a big pan, plaice can be fried in oil and butter or, better still, grilled under a hot, even, overhead grill. Bigger fish can be baked whole in a piping-hot oven (page 216). When you get it right, it's rather dreamy: the skin crispy-but-sticky and the melting, moist flesh gently clinging to the bone frame. Eat one side, flip it over and eat the other. Pick any cheeks or shoulder flesh from the head end and nibble the crispy tail. Then, when all the obvious bits have gone, just pick up that frame and suck every shard and flake of flesh out of the skeleton.

Oddly enough, the really obsessive plaice anglers, those who like to dream up new rigs with beads and rattling balls, rarely cook or consume their catch. They mostly want to photograph them, record their weight, the weather, water temperature and climatic conditions. Bizarre as it may seem, the true plaice fanatic may *only* be interested in catching them. In which case, nutty or not, he might be a good friend to cultivate.

Flounder *Platichthys flesus*

Dab *Limanda limanda*

If turbot and sole are the aristocrats of the flatfish dynasty, and plaice and brill the respectable middle classes, then dabs and flounders are, in the eyes of the trade at least, little more than snot-nosed street urchins. But we feel they are worthy of higher regard.

Although both dabs and flounders can be easily caught close inshore around most of the British Isles, there's no targeted fishery for them. Any flounder or dab that finds its way into a fish market gets there by accident – a casualty of bycatch from a vessel targeting top-end flatfish. (It's better, by the way, to buy fish caught by seine-netting rather than the more damaging demersal trawl method.)

There's no doubt that these two are hiding their light under a bushel. They're drab-looking fish with plain, rough skin and no elaborate markings or exotic

MCS RATINGS: both 2 EAT MORE!

REC MINIMUM SIZE: flounder, 25cm; dab, 20cm

SEASON: flounder, avoid January–April (spawning); dab, avoid April–June (spawning)

RECIPES: pages 216, 231, 246, 290, 306, 318, 321, 324

dab

flounder

coloration. They're also much smaller than the fancier flatfish, with the average dab weighing in at about 250g. Flounders can grow bigger, but it's unusual to see one much over 500g. And when it comes to preparation, small means fiddly. None of these characteristics exactly endears dabs and flounders to the British fish consumer – but they do ensure that they are usually offered at a very keen price.

The further good news is that dabs and flounders are plentiful around the British Isles and easy to catch on rod and line: from beach, estuary, pier, harbourside or breakwater. Summer is the best time to catch them – and harbour dabs are popular with fair-weather holiday anglers. They have small mouths, so small hooks are essential, but they will eat just about any bait, including lug worms, rag worms, mussels, crabs, fish strips or shrimp. It doesn't have to be fresh bait, either, since dabs and flounders won't turn their noses up at bait that has grown a bit old and stinky.

Most serious sea anglers tend to target these species in estuaries. Neither shows any aversion to living and feeding in brackish water (where fresh river water mixes with the sea). Flounders particularly seem to revel in the reduced salination. Although they're sea fish, they can often be caught many miles upstream in a river where there is almost zero salinity. In Holland flounders have even been successfully fattened up in freshwater pools.

The flounder's love of shallow, muddy estuaries led to an unusual style of fishing, which evolved long before the invention of static nets or rod and line. This is known as 'flounder tramping' and involves locating flounders at low tide as they hide just beneath the wet mud, using your bare feet. Once a flounder is felt, one foot is kept on top of it to pin it down, until it can be hand-speared or grabbed and placed in a wet sack.

This method of fishing was revived in the nineteenth century in Dumfriesshire, and has now become an annual sporting event – the Palnackie Flounder Tramping Championships – held on the estuary of Urr Water. Every

August, over 300 contestants compete to see who can tramp and hand catch the most – and biggest – flounders. In some ways, the indignity of this fate speaks volumes, but we are assured by those involved that all the flounders end up being put to good use in local kitchens. So, to put a positive spin on it, you could say it goes to show that there is, somewhere, some affection and appreciation for the flounder – and so there should be.

Disparaging comments about their texture and flavour – they've variously been accused of being 'watery', 'poor eating' and a 'wet flannel' – are wholly unfounded. We believe this short-sighted, uneducated propaganda is being circulated by a vicious gang of turbot-supremacists. They must be stopped!

Because flounder is lovely. A whole one simply grilled and served with a generous trickle of melted butter, flaky sea salt and chopped fresh parsley can make a grown man cry fat tears of joy. And dab meat is some of the sweetest, softest fish flesh ever to grace a fork. A pair of dab fillets served in a crusty bun, smeared with homemade tartare sauce, is almost a religious experience.

As is so often the case, our national prejudice against dabs and flounders is not shared by the rest of Europe. In Galicia, on the Atlantic coast of Spain, the flounder is considered a great delicacy and is served fried, steamed or filleted, often with a light, creamy saffron sauce. In Belgium, flounder is smoked and served with lemon and soured cream. In Denmark, dabs are salted and dried; they are the celebrated regional speciality of the Jutland peninsula.

So, we'd like to invite you to join our new group, SPUDF (Society for the Promotion and Understanding of Dabs and Flounders). There's no subscription, and no monthly newsletter. All you have to do is shop positively. Whenever you see dabs and flounders on the fishmonger's slab – and you certainly will from time to time – snap them up quick, and tell him you'll be back for more.

Dover sole *Solea solea*

Dover sole doesn't actually come from Dover – but you probably didn't think it did. It acquired the name because Dover was the most reliable port from which to source sole for the thriving London market. These days, most Dover sole for the British table is bought and sold at Brixham market in Devon, though it's caught all around the British coast, and its wider distribution stretches right across the North Atlantic, from the fjords of Norway to Senegal. However, the plump soles that are landed in British ports are considered the best, and are in demand all over Europe. They have been for a couple of centuries.

Throughout the nineteenth and early twentieth centuries, sole was the most prized of all sea fish, rivalled only by turbot. The size of the sole you served reflected your level of success on the social ladder. The upper echelons, and those aspiring to buy their way into them, ate the bigger soles, while the next social tier had to make do with smaller soles called 'slips' or 'tongues'. So revered was the flesh of the Dover sole that it sent classical chefs into a frenzy of fiddly excess. Chef Louis Saulnier's massive tome of 1914, *Le Répertoire de la Cuisine*, listed no fewer than 340 different ways of presenting sole fillets. Maybe he was cocking a snook at his former master, Auguste Escoffier, who could only manage to muster a paltry 180 sole recipes in *Le Guide Culinaire* of 1903.

MCS RATING: 3 (2–5)

REC MINIMUM SIZE: 28cm

SEASON: avoid April–June (spawning)

RECIPES: pages 231, 290

It's questionable whether the gastronomic attentions lavished on this fish have really been to its greater glory. It was a culinary arms race. Chefs competed to pile on the most extravagant sauces and accompaniments to serve with their beloved sole. Truffles, Muscat grapes, foie gras, ceps, champagne-flavoured custards and screaming pink sauces were all requisitioned in the cause. The poor sole fillets never stood a chance. Happily, today's more skilled chefs have learned gentler ways of getting the best from the sole.

Dover sole is rightly loved (if sometimes wrongly smothered) for its velvety texture and natural flavour. Surprisingly, these improve with a little ageing – a phenomenon that has been the making of the Dover, as it can store well, or travel long distances, and still remain delicious. It may seem counter-intuitive that a fish could ever be *too* fresh. But the prevailing wisdom with Dover sole is that it needs at least 24 hours, ideally 48, to reach its mellow best. We can corroborate that this is no fishy marketing ploy, used to excuse less than super-fresh sole. We have tried eating spanking-fresh Dovers, bought straight from the boat in West Bay harbour, still flapping, and cooked within hours. We won't be doing it again. They were rubbery and curiously tasteless.

The sole benefits from the fishy equivalent of hanging game. In order to release its exceptional, well-rounded flavour and become tender enough to be palatable, it needs to experience the beginnings of the bacteriological action that would eventually rot it. The same is true, to a less obvious degree, of several

other flatties: the turbot, the halibut and most rays (usually sold as 'skate wings'). All are best after two or three days' 'ripening' (though they need to be chilled during this period). Properly iced and sensitively handled, a decent-sized Dover sole is good for a week – some would say ten days (but we're not inclined to test that theory). It's unlikely that you'll find a Dover sole in a British fishmonger's that's 'too fresh', but if ever you buy a just-landed fish direct from a boat, or from a wholesaler who tells you it was caught within the day, then give it 48 hours in your fridge, covered in a wet cloth, before honouring it with your full attention at the stove.

Dover soles are predominantly night feeders. They creep around sandy or muddy areas of the seabed, using the rippling edge of their 360° fin like the legs on a millipede. To help them hunt for crabs, worms and mussels hiding under the mud, Dover soles have a well-developed sensory organ located on the underside of their heads. They also possess a concertina mouth, which dislocates and protrudes to enable them to pick up objects from the seabed.

Their nocturnal habits mean that Dover sole are rarely caught on rod and line by anglers (at least that's our excuse). Even though they're an inshore fish for much of the year, they're normally only caught in fixed trammel nets, by baited long lines or by beam trawlers.

The sole is not a fish to eat with abandon, and it's important to try to ascertain where it comes from and how it was caught (for our views on beam trawling, see page 29). Some stocks are in relatively good shape, with the best-managed British fisheries being located within the North Sea and the eastern end of the English Channel. Particularly recommended as a sustainable source is the Hastings-based trammel-net fishery, which has been certified by the Marine Stewardship Council as an environmentally responsible source (see pages 33–4). Stocks of sole off Devon were badly overfished until recently. The European Commission has recently adopted a 'Sole Recovery Plan', which should bring the flatties back to this area, but they still have a way to go.

The Dover sole's posh reputation may make you feel intimidated about cooking it at home. Don't be. It's an easy fish to get the best out of. It can be cooked whole, filleted, skinned or unskinned, and it has remarkably resilient and forgiving flesh. It really doesn't need fancy sauces. Normally, the coarse dark skin from the upper side is removed before cooking. It is extremely thick, and its fine but tough scales do not respond much to the descaler. Have a go at removing it yourself (see page 74); it's not as hard as you might think, and is really rather satisfying. Or, of course, you can ask your fishmonger to do it. But if you do get him or her to skin, or fillet, your Dover, make sure you watch very carefully. Maybe you can do it yourself next time. And do take the skin, skeleton and head of a filleted fish back home to make a nice little stock (see page 256).

You won't always see Dover soles on the fishmonger's slab. The market for them is chef-driven and largely wholesale, both for the domestic and continental market. However, when you do find Dovers in Britain, they can be a surprisingly good buy – maybe twice the price of plaice, but often only half the price of turbot.

Our favourite way to cook Dover sole is simply grilled or fried on the bone, top skin off, bottom skin on, served whole with parsley and lemon butter. We like to serve vegetables or salad separately (if at all), so we can concentrate entirely on savouring every last mouthful of velvety flesh. Once we've whittled off the prime flesh with a knife and fork, it's time to lift up the skeleton and suck those bones clean. For us, it's fingers rather than fish knives all the way.

Lemon sole *Microstomus kitt*

The lemon sole is something of an impostor. It isn't a sole and it doesn't taste of lemon. In fact, it's a member of the plaice family, much more closely related to dab or flounder than to Dover sole. The 'lemon' is commonly assumed to refer to its coloration. But, let's be honest, it's nothing like a lemon's. It does have a smattering of tiny yellow flecks among its otherwise red-brown, seabed-camouflaged skin on the upper side. But it would hardly make anyone do a double take and shout, 'Oh my *God*, it looks *just* like a lemon!'

We prefer the notion that its shape, almost a perfect oval, is uncannily similar in profile to that of a lengthways cross-section of a lemon: even to the extent of the nose and tail of the fish being the bumpy nipples at either end of the lemon.

The lemon sole is widely distributed around the Atlantic, from the Bay of Biscay to Iceland, and is an important food fish, if not one that is voraciously sought after. It's caught consistently by the French and British fleets in the Channel, using seine and trawl nets. They'll be after more valuable bottom fish, such as turbot, brill and monkfish. But they won't pucker up at a lemon, as it's a good market fish that they'll never struggle to shift.

Since it is largely a bycatch, the lemon sole fishery is practically unregulated in the EU, with few size or quota restrictions currently in place. It isn't considered to be under pressure at the moment but it's an undeniably tasty fish, which may easily catch on and start to fetch a higher price, so any nonchalance about its sustainability could prove regrettable. It is heartening to see that the Cornish fishery has imposed a self-regulated minimum size of 25cm in length. If you can source fish landed under this scheme, so much the better – you could start by

MCS RATING: 2 (2–3)

REC MINIMUM SIZE: 25cm

SEASON: avoid April–August (spawning)

RECIPES: pages 141, 231, 246, 306, 310, 321

innocently asking your fishmonger where his lemon sole is landed. Being ready to ask questions like that is the beginning of your career as an ecologically aware fish shopper. And being ready to answer them is the sign of a good fishmonger who is also engaged with these issues.

If there isn't any reliable information on this score, impose a 25cm minimum size on your own shopping. By choosing fish of this size and bigger, you will avoid immature fish that haven't had an opportunity to breed. And steer clear of lemon sole from April to August, when the fish are breeding – not only for ecological reasons but also because the fish will be out of condition. If you can, avoid sole caught by beam trawling, which is a particularly destructive method.

Lemon sole is hardly ever caught by anglers on rod and line. Certainly neither of us has ever caught one. It generally inhabits seas from 40 metres up to 200 metres deep, and is a night-feeder. It is no doubt this combination of depth and darkness that puts it out of reach of most regular sea anglers – that, and perhaps its rather tiny mouth. Designed for chewing barnacles, it doesn't make the lemon sole a natural bait-gobbler.

Lemon sole is a really great little eating fish, which can be cooked exactly like plaice or Dover sole. You could say that the character of its flesh lies somewhere between the two – firmer than plaice, not as rich and meaty as a Dover. You can fillet larger specimens and then dust them in seasoned flour and/or breadcrumb them for frying. Or – and this is very much our preference – you can fry, grill or bake a whole one, then eat it off the bone. Cooked simply like this, it is very good with the lemon-zest mashed potato that we also serve with witch (page 306).

The most notable departure from these fairly standard approaches to pan-friendly flatfish is the Belgian penchant for salting and drying it. Once they've dried it, the Belgians then rename the fish with an equally inaccurate and inappropriate moniker: they call it a 'Scottish' sole. This is, of course, just another disguise. To be clear: the Scottish sole doesn't come from Scotland, look Scottish or have any connection with Scotland whatsoever.

Let's put one more thing beyond confusion: if you visit the fishmonger with an open mind and a view to what's best on the day, and you are sufficiently charmed by a fresh, plump lemon sole to part with your money and take it home, you are exceedingly unlikely to be disappointed.

Megrim _Lepidorhombus whiffiagonis/Pleuronectes megastoma_

Witch _Glyptocephalus cynoglossus_

It's not just because 'Megrim & Witch' sounds like a comedy duo that we've given them joint billing. They are closely related, and not easy to tell apart (see page 477). These members of the prestigious sole family have been caught by west coast trawlers for generations, yet you rarely seem them for sale in this country. This is mainly because a staggering 90 per cent of our megrim and witch haul is diverted to Spain and Italy. We suspect it's also because the British fish shopper just doesn't really like the _sound_ of them. Nor, indeed, the look of them. It's a shame, because they are great to eat – and could, as we'll see, be at the forefront of an exciting initiative to make the West Country fishery more sustainable.

MCS RATING: megrim 3 (3–4); witch 4

REC MINIMUM SIZE: megrim, 25cm; witch, 28cm

SEASON: megrim, avoid January–April (spawning); witch, avoid March–September (spawning)

RECIPES: pages 216, 231, 246, 290, 306, 318–19, 321, 324

Historically we have been spoiled by the ready availability of the most distinguished sole – the Dover (see page 471). This flatfish has always enjoyed the limelight, and consequently the lion's share of the UK sole market. While the flavour and texture of its flesh are indisputably fine, its tidy shape and dapper good looks certainly help make it popular (and increasingly unsustainable).

Beauty may be in the eye of the beholder, but it's doubtful that anyone would describe either witch or megrim as much of a looker. Compared to the Dover, with its rich, nut-brown top skin, both are rather anaemic-looking soles, almost transparent in fact – as you'll see if you hold one up to the light. But aside from their strange appearance and spooky names, witch and megrim are excellent eating fish. Pale, maybe, but definitely interesting. They really are a canny choice. Just consider the price difference: in today's market, a kilo of Dover sole costs anywhere from £15 to £20, while megrim and witch usually sell for between £4 and £5 a kilo.

All three of these soles share a similar lifestyle. They like to inhabit a muddy/sandy/shingly seabed, where they efficiently prey on crustaceans, worms and small fish. Their habitats overlap but megrim and witch tend to be caught in deeper water and further out to sea than Dovers.

Current stocks of megrim and witch are generally in better shape than those of Dover sole. So, is this a fish to eat with a clear conscience? Almost – but there's a catch. Most British hauls of these species are currently taken by beam trawlers targeting cod, haddock, plaice, monkfish and other deep-dwelling demersals. Several of these species are under grievous threat – even if the megrim/witch bycatch is not. Furthermore, beam trawling can cause deep structural damage to the seabed (see page 29). 'Otter-trawled' soles are a better choice, if you can find them, because the way in which they are fished has less impact. There is currently much constructive discussion amongst the West Country fisheries and the many trade outlets they serve about improving both the environmental impact of the beam trawl fishery generally (see pages 41–2) and the public image of the megrim in particular.

It's a tough call, but on balance we'd say choosing megrim and witch is a positive move, even if you don't know how they've been caught. It helps establish a market for species that *could* be targeted more sustainably in the very near future. No authority will bother to regulate or certify these fish for the UK market if no one wants to buy them.

So what can be done to stimulate demand for these very worthwhile species? Those in fish retail are convinced that what's required is 'rebranding'. And if that's what it takes, let's get on board. It's not exactly a makeover – nothing can be done to change the appearance of these insipid-looking soles. But the prevailing feeling seems to be that, from a retail perspective, they'd both benefit from a name change. We think megrim is a rather charming name but, according to the branding gurus, it has too many negative connotations. First of all there's the 'grim' bit. Secondly, the whole word sounds a bit like a 'migraine'. Ouch. Fair enough, megrim is a rubbish name.

A few years ago, Waitrose decided to market megrim as... megrim. They didn't shift. No matter how chunky and fresh the fillets on the slab, shoppers just couldn't see past the unappetising name. The latest plan, supported by Waitrose and other retailers, is to relaunch megrim as 'Cornish sole'. The model for this exercise was the successful relaunch of passé 'pilchards' as sexy 'Cornish sardines'. Maybe the same will work for megrim. We'd buy a Cornish sole.

megrim witch

Unsurprisingly, the 'witch' moniker is also up for a rethink. With the help of food marketing consultants, the Irish Sea Fisheries Board came up with the name 'Rockall sole' – after the famous fishing grounds. But there's competition, as Marks & Spencer has recently agreed with the Trading Standards Agency to sell witch under the name of 'Torbay sole', after the Devon fishery where many are caught. Surely only one brand can prevail. Our vote goes to Rockall sole – it's just more catchy. Not everyone wants to see witch rebranded, however. The readers of *Pentacle*, the 'UK's leading independent Pagan magazine', regard the ditching of 'witch' as proof of a widespread prejudice against weavers of spells.

In the kitchen, you'd cook megrim and witch in exactly the same way as any sole or plaice. The flesh of both species is slightly more delicate than Dover sole, slightly more robust than plaice, and they will happily stand in for either. A whole fish, well seasoned, started in a frying pan and finished in an oven (see page 296) is an excellent default treatment. A trickle of herb or garlic butter over the finished fish is all you need to make these soles soar.

Other sea fish

Sea bass *Dicentrarchus labrax*

In the kitchen, bass have class. Fried bass fillets served with just about anything from Puy lentils to purple sprouting broccoli are the stock-in-trade of many very reputable restaurants – and with good reason.

Its firm, creamy-white, slightly oily flesh is like a cross between cod and mackerel – the best of both worlds, if you like. It's distinctive enough to enjoy simply cooked, with a minimum of seasoning, but robust enough to stand up to an onslaught of oriental flavours. It makes great sushi. No wonder that, for a couple of decades now, it's been top of the chef's hit parade.

It's easy to cook whole, too, and flakes nicely off its big, easy-to-spot bones, so it's a great choice for home cooks who want luxury seafood made simple. The only drawback – as you might expect for a fish in such high demand – is that it's always at the pricy end of what's on the fishmonger's slab.

And yet for all its classy reputation, and its undeniable contribution to the lifestyles of the rich and famous, on its own patch the wild sea bass is actually a bit of a thug. It's a violent, bullying hooligan of a fish that exists primarily to make the lives of other lesser fish a nerve-shredding misery.

The French call bass *loup de mer*, 'the wolf of the sea', because they are lethal predators who will hunt and kill in constant service of their voracious appetites. Young bass ('schoolies', as they are known) will hunt in huge shoals, working together to corral even huger shoals of finger-sized sprats or sand eels into tight bunches, which are rammed and plundered by their huge articulated mouths. Sexually mature bass of over 2 kilos patrol in smaller packs but with undiminished appetites. And big old bass of 5 kilos or more become lone hunters, leaving behind the shoal for a solitary life stalking larger individual prey.

In fast currents and stormy seas, the bass's hunter eyesight and streamlined profile give it the advantage over every other fish. It's well tooled up for this rough and tumble lifestyle. Razor-sharp gill covers reinforced with thick cartilage armour, along with stiletto-pointed spines fanned through all of its fins, serve for both attack and defence.

The head armour helps a big bass to hit its prey mouth-first. It will head-butt a bunch of feeble sprats and then scoop them up with its enormous mouth as they struggle to come to their senses. If a larger predator should attempt to pick a fight, the bass can fan out its sharp spines to become a jagged mouthful of pain. By the time it's reached a couple of kilos, there's little left to worry about, except perhaps the occasional very determined shark. Even the seals and dolphins would rather chase mackerel or pout.

We are lucky to live within a few miles of one of Britain's most powerful bass magnets – the Isle of Portland. This historic chunk of rock, which has been quarried continuously for hundreds of years to produce Portland stone, juts out into the Channel for 4 miles. Its effect is to funnel the flow of the incoming tide,

MCS RATING: wild 3 (2–5); farmed 4

REC MINIMUM SIZE: 40cm

SEASON: avoid March–June (spawning)

RECIPES: pages 130–2, 133, 134–5, 141, 144–5, 194, 198, 200, 220, 223, 225, 226, 260–1, 281–2, 283, 286, 289, 305, 308–9, 310, 318–19, 330, 337, 340–1, 355, 378, 382, 387, 393

which runs west to east along the Channel, increasing the tide speed around the Bill to as much as five times the mean rate for the rest of Lyme Bay. This tidal race, flowing over craggy, snaggy ledges, with plenty of ambush potential, is the perfect habitat for fit, hungry bass. And the back eddies created by the Bill in the lee of those fierce tides are an irresistible holding force for shoaling baitfish – a combination that makes for one of the best bass fisheries in the British Isles.

Having a fabulous bass fishery on your doorstep is a blessing but also a big responsibility. With too much fishing pressure and too many greedy fishermen we could quickly and easily destroy it. Managing the stock is the key. There are legal size limits in place – currently 36cm (about 750g) is the legal minimum keeping size, although an increase to 40cm is the topic of much current debate (and something we'd like to see ourselves). Either way, the idea is to prevent people taking too many immature fish and wiping out the next generation. Yet, and here's the dilemma, in many ways it's the bigger fish that need protecting, because they're the only ones capable of breeding and boosting bass numbers.

Bass need to be at least five years old to become sexually mature. Five years equates to roughly 2.5 kilos in weight, so it's the large fish that are most precious in terms of future fish. Which begs the question, why protect undersized fish when it's the big ones that matter?

The argument is that the small fish are future big fish. If they're preserved and protected, they might one day reach maturity. But by allowing a fisherman to kill bigger ones, it means that fish that have taken five years to mature could be slaughtered in the very week they're about to spawn the next generation. A bass fat with roe can be despatched legally, although its demise is much more serious to the future of the bass population than that of a protected one-pounder, still three years away from parenthood. We're not suggesting the minimum size be lowered; we'd rather see a minimum and a maximum size introduced to protect the spawning adults from being targeted and taken. If we ruled the waves, fish smaller than 40cm and larger than 55cm would all be returned alive.

Believe it or not, bass used to be regarded as a cheap alternative to cod. In the UK it didn't command much respect (or fetch much money) until the 1980s, when eating it became fashionable in London restaurants. (Marco Pierre White had a famous dish that symbolically charts the gastronomic rise of the bass – he served a fillet of it slathered with caviar.) But amongst the UK's Chinese community, bass have long been highly rated, even though they aren't native to any Chinese seas. The most popular way to serve bass in a Chinese restaurant is as a whole, individual, plate-sized fish, steamed with ginger and spring onions.

When the current minimum landing size was introduced in 1989, it officially put a stop to the Chinatown tradition of serving one fish per portion. No longer were plate-sized fish legal fare. This provided one of the prime motivations for solving the problem of farming bass – which initially proved hard to crack around our Atlantic coast, turning out to be easier in the warmer waters of the Mediterranean. They are now farmed in their thousands of tonnes each year, using sea-located fish cages all around the eastern Mediterranean, from Greece to Turkey and Cyprus to Malta; they're even being farmed off the coast of Wales.

You could argue that farmed bass have saved the lives of many wild bass. Every time someone tucks into a farmed bass, they're not eating an immature wild one. But bass farming is subject to the same environmental concerns as most other fish farming endeavours (see page 35). The sheer quantity of wild fish that is caught and turned into fish meal to feed the farmed bass, along with the amount of pollution that these concentrated populations excrete out on to the seabed, are undeniably having an impact on the marine environment.

As for the wild bass, which have to be among the most handsome and picture-perfect of all fish species, they are a prime example of how fish get short shrift in the public conscience, no matter how beloved they are on the plate. What would it take to stir the public conscience? A fur coat instead of scales?

From the mid-1980s onwards, as the bass became more and more fêted on our plates, the wholesale slaughter of breeding bass by the French and Spanish fleets continued unchecked and unhindered. But back in those days the drastic population crash of a favourite fish was just not headline news. Then it was reported that dolphins were dying in the bass pair trawlers' nets. The nation's love of cetaceans brought about legislation, which may have saved the bass from terminal decline – at least for the time being. But only by accident.

So when it comes to choosing bass for your own plate, how do you engage, and clear, your conscience? Stocks of bass all around the UK look pretty good, but that doesn't mean we'd suggest throwing caution to the wind when you buy them. The way bass is caught, even more than where it's caught, has a huge impact on how sustainable it can be said to be. If you can establish that your fish is 'line-caught' (like almost all of the Portland-caught bass that are landed at Weymouth) then we would say you're good to go. Unfortunately, the labelling of fish as line caught (or otherwise) is not yet mandatory – though it's practically universal in France now. But it is catching on among enlightened fishmongers and supermarkets. Organisations such as the South West Handline Fishermen's Association are also blazing a trail by tagging all their fish, so you can trace it back to the very hook that caught it – linecaught.org.uk will tell you more. If you don't know how a bass has been caught, at least look for the telltale signs of a trawled fish, such as missing scales, net marks and general damage.

Keep tabs on the MCS website too (see the Directory, page 592). It does not yet certify any bass fisheries, but it is assessing one off the northeast of England as we write. Hopefully, more will follow.

As to the farmed bass – well, they don't float our boat. These fish are not the predatory athletes their genes would like them to be, and it shows in their flabby and disappointingly insipid flesh. But if they can satisfy the appetites of those who would otherwise dine on wild fish caught by unsustainable means, then perhaps they'll have served their purpose. We've heard that organically certified farmed bass is in the offing. Maybe that will provide some viable solutions – or at least a creditable compromise.

The bass we would never begrudge you, though, is the one you catch yourself. Enjoy it. You've earned it.

Scad (or horse mackerel) *Trachurus trachurus*

The list of fish that we catch in British waters but don't much care to eat is long. Pouting, pollack, witch, megrim, grey mullet, hake, gurnard, ling, even sardine – all these are fish from our waters that we don't properly value. But the French, Spanish and Portuguese embrace them all, and are always happy to pay good money to take them off our hands.

Among the ranks of the under-appreciated is one British fish you may never even have heard of – the scad, or horse mackerel. We treat it as a trash fish in this country; it's mainly used as an industrial species (see page 504) and thought to be fit only for pot-bait, cat food, fertiliser, and making into fish pellets to feed farmed fish. It is almost never sold for human consumption – at least, not in the UK. Scad stocks carry no quota, no size limits, and there are no regulations on how they are to be caught. There are no restrictions on catching them, because nobody gives a damn. Yet the Japanese, who know a thing or two about fish, adore scad. It is one of the most popular species in Japan, and is used in all manner of traditional dishes, including sushi and sashimi. But the height of the scad's fame is in *namban zuke* – an escabeche-style dish in which the fish is first deep fried, then steeped in a piquant rice vinegar marinade.

One night in London, eating in a favourite family-run Japanese restaurant in King's Cross, we were presented with a 'special treat' by the sushi chef: a tiny dish of sliced raw fish that had been lightly pickled in vinegar and ginger. Firm and meaty, with a strong but clean flavour, it was stunning. The chef called the fish *aji*, and told us it had been bought at Billingsgate market that morning by his nephew. He tried describing it but we still couldn't guess what he was talking about. Eventually he disappeared back into the kitchen and emerged with the head and skeletal remains of his precious *aji*. It was, of course, a scad, identical to hundreds that we'd thrown back in the sea or chopped up for bait. We resolved never to be so wasteful again.

MCS RATING: **3**

REC MINIMUM SIZE: **25cm**

SEASON: **avoid June–August (spawning)**

RECIPES: pages 138, 141, 148–9, 194, 196, 198, 218, 222, 244, 286, 357, 400, 407

There is one region of Japan, Numazu, that is celebrated for its *aji himono* (dried scad). A reliably fresh, dry autumn wind makes for perfect fish-drying conditions. Before it is hung out in the breeze, the *aji* is first soaked in a brine of green tea, soy sauce and water from Mount Fuji. It is such a popular delicacy all over Japan that it's celebrated by a special Himono Day.

While the Japanese pay such homage to a fish, we feed it to farmed salmon – an end product arguably inferior to the scad it's getting fat on. How ignorant is that? And we're missing not just a gastronomic treat but a healthy one. The pelagic scad is right up there with the regular mackerel for omega oils (see page 19) and taurine – an amino acid that reduces human cholesterol levels.

Although this is a fish that appears regularly in British trawl nets and on anglers' lines, we know very little about it. And some of the things we think we know about it are wrong. We call it 'mackerel' and yet it's not closely related to mackerel at all. It is actually from the family of warmwater western Atlantic fish known collectively as jacks, which includes the blue runner, Jack Crevalle, kingfish, yellowtail and amberjack. It's rather an odd misnomer, as the scad doesn't even look much like our Atlantic mackerel. It doesn't have any of the green-blue tiger-stripe markings. Instead it is predominantly silver, with one black splodge on its gill cover and a very distinctive tail feature: a clearly defined row of thorn-like spines at the wrist of its tail. These spines can make handling the scad quite tricky.

One reason the scad has been called a mackerel may be that the two species like to hang out together. It's quite common to catch a string of mackerel on feathers and find that one of them is a scad. The shoals obviously intermingle from time to time but roam separately at others. On a recent trip to the Channel Islands, we found the scad fishing particularly good at night inside Alderney Harbour. They were falling to small spinners, feathers and even saltwater flies. The scad seemed to enjoy the shallow, dark water to feed in, whereas Atlantic mackerel tend to retreat to deeper water overnight.

At the time of writing, the scad population seems to be buoyant: its habitat range stretches from Iceland to Senegal, with a healthy concentration to be found inshore around the West Country. This is the modern fish crisis back to front. There's no shortage of scad to be caught – just a shortage of people who are ready to prepare, cook and appreciate what could and should be a delicious and rewarding addition to any fish enthusiast's repertoire. Isn't cultural subjectivity a weird thing?

Such is the Japanese nation's love and respect for scad that it's getting the attention we're only just starting to talk about for cod. Boxes of just-landed scad are electronically tagged with barcodes containing full details of when, where and how the fish was caught and landed. When these fish are cooked in a restaurant, the barcode is presented to diners so that they can scan it into a camera phone and read the profile of its source and capture. The same system will soon exist in supermarkets. For the Japanese, such hi-tech traceability systems are part of a branding enterprise that fosters customer trust and loyalty. The Japanese are not exactly paragons of environmental responsibility when it comes to commercial fishing but you have to hand it to them on this one.

Scad rates on our list of fish to eat more of (see page 49). If you apply the vital principle of reassessing fish on their merits rather than on their reputation, scad is an out-and-out winner. If you do manage to get your hands on some (line-caught is best), try preparing and cooking it as you would mackerel – either whole or in fillets. Unlike mackerel, though, it does need to be descaled (see page 55). And even before you do this, you should slice off those bony thorns by the tail with scissors or a sharp knife.

Scad flesh is not the same as mackerel flesh. It is less obviously oily, and more meaty (or even, as is sometimes said of other members of the jack family, chickeny). But the same treatments will serve it well. That's why we've included it in our 'also works with' list for almost every mackerel recipe in the book. The three we would most heartily recommend for scad, as they cover a good spectrum of techniques and tastes, are the escabeche (pages 148–9), the Japanese slow-cooked mackerel (page 286) and the Mackerel on potatoes and bay (page 218). Any of these recipes should rapidly convince you of the merits of the scad – and provide you with the means and the motive to give other, more vulnerable species a break.

Black bream *Spondyliosoma cantharus*

Black bream is Britain's most underrated sea fish – a bold claim in a book whose purpose is to shine some light on the kitchen potential of our lesser known species. But if the underrating ratings are based on the difference between quality of eating and recognition of such, then we're happy to give bream the top slot. Hotly contested by gurnard (see page 496)…

In our view, black bream are more fun to catch and lovelier to eat than many other fish we pursue – even the much-fêted bass. A good reason, we felt, to put one on the cover of this book. Their stocks are also at healthy levels. Those from Cornwall or the Northwest or North Wales fisheries are a particularly good choice because local by-laws prohibit the landing of undersized fish.

So why do these superb creatures have an image problem? Or, more precisely, a lack-of-image problem, since most people have never even heard of them. Those who have often make the mistake of confusing them with freshwater bream, which is unfortunate, as coarse anglers know freshwater bream simply as 'snotties', on account of the prodigious amount of slime that clings to their drab, grey skin.

Black bream are much more beautiful, both to behold and to consume, and yet only recently have they begun to find their way on to menus. As one London

MCS RATING: 2 EAT MORE!

REC MINIMUM SIZE: 23cm

SEASON: avoid April–May (spawning)

RECIPES: pages 130–2, 133, 134–5, 140, 141, 144, 220, 225, 260–1, 305, 310, 337, 340–1, 381, 393 et al.

restaurateur told us, black bream often gets overlooked because it doesn't sound appealing, which is why it is often described as 'sea bream'. But this approach can also confuse, because farmed gilt-head bream are also billed as 'sea bream' on menus. If you're unsure what you're getting when you're ordering bream at a restaurant or a fishmonger's stall, ask if the fish is farmed. If it is, then it's definitely not black bream. (By the same token, if you can ascertain that it definitely *is* a black bream, you can feel reassured that it is wild, not farmed.)

The underlying irony here is that black bream aren't black at all. During early summer, when they migrate inshore and we start to catch them, the males are sporting their full mating colours: steel-blue head, silver-purple sheen down both flanks, and an adder-like pattern of black slash-stripes along each side. It's only when they've been dead for an hour or two that black bream take on a charcoal-grey tinge along the top of their backs. But their flanks remain shiny silver and retain a hint of that violet gleam, especially when they're fresh and wet.

Here off the Dorset and Devon coast we catch most of our black bream from boats, either drifting over the mussel beds or anchored over rocky reefs or near a wreck. A few are caught from the shore, but not yet by us... this is partly because bream prefer deeper water, but also because they're just so tricky to hook! With their small mouths and rows of sharp, backward-slanting teeth, they are fiendish nibblers and bait thieves. They rarely grab and gobble. Instead, they'll 'worry' bait, pecking away at it like some demented sea bantam.

Because of this, black bream are nicknamed 'bastard fish'. This unfortunate sobriquet falls from the mouths of frustrated anglers who, on striking a lively nibble and starting to reel in, find they've missed another bite and lost another bait. When this has happened half a dozen times, hissing the word 'Bastard!' under your breath is practically involuntary...

The trick to hooking bream is to use small hooks and tidy baits: 'cocktails' of small squid or fresh mackerel strips, coupled with an inch or two of fresh rag worm (rather than whole wriggling worm). If you're a fan of eating fresh scallops (who isn't?), and a budding bream angler to boot, you must save and freeze the 'frills' from inside the shells (see pages 106–7). These make brilliant bream bait: not only will they stay on the hook but they come steeped in shellfish pheromone – which supposedly make bream behave as if they're in a Lynx commercial, throwing themselves at you with wild abandon. That may be pushing it a bit, but there's certainly a sense of heightened anticipation when scallop frills are available for bait – and it's often rewarded.

Catching black bream on light tackle makes for rod-bending action (as they say in the angling press). A black bream's fighting technique is distinctive. You'll soon begin to recognise the style: short, aggressive runs with rod-rattling head shakes. This means that you'll usually know when you've hooked a bream, long before you see it break the surface.

If you have access to a boat but don't know where to find black bream, here's a tip from John Gay, one of Poole Harbour's most famous bream and bass skippers: 'Look for the potters,' he says. 'Black bream like the same rough ground as crabs and lobsters, and they're attracted by the smell of pot-bait. Watch for when a potter is pulling his pots, because that's a great time to be fishing close by. The fish are attracted by the disturbance in the water and the algae released from pot ropes. Bream will swoop on the crustaceans unsettled by the hauling of the pots, and even eat the particles of pot-bait that get washed away with the tide. It's a lively time to have bait in the water.'

However, the main reason black bream arrive inshore in early summer is not to do with pots but with the spawning of cuttlefish. A female cuttlefish mates only once. After laying her eggs, she waves a fond farewell to her potential progeny and dies. So from May onwards, the rocky seabed is littered with the spent corpses of female cuttles. According to John Gay, 'The main diet of early-season black bream is dead cuttlefish. That's why we use squid as bait. Chunked up, squid and cuttlefish flesh is identical.'

When you do catch one, handle with care – a jab from its finger-piercing spines can be very painful. Kill it swiftly, bleed it, then gut it and put it on ice. Before you cook it, it'll need its scales removed, too. This is another opportunity to impale a finger or two – so snip off the spines with a stout pair of scissors before you start. There's a whole procedure we'd recommend to render a plate-sized bream easier to handle, cook and eat – see page 61.

So, all in all, the bream is pretty much an exemplar of all you could possibly want from an eating fish: firm and dense, fully flavoured, holding its moisture without getting soft or wet (as the cod family can sometimes be), and offering just a hint of meaty oiliness to make it rich and moreish. You can do just about anything with it, including making sushi and sashimi (pages 130–6) or baking a whole large one in a saltdough crust (page 225). But doing very little often produces the best results of all, and fried, baked or barbecued whole bream, with just a few herbs and a little garlic for some contact flavouring, is very hard to beat.

Catching black bream might be maddeningly frustrating at times. But eating them is utterly predictable, and never less than a delight.

Red mullet *Mullus surmuletus*

This small, shocking-red fish has earned a heady culinary reputation over the centuries, and that may be because it isn't really a mullet at all. It is, in fact, a member of the goatfish family – a tropical species that strayed into the temperate waters of the Mediterranean and the European Atlantic and decided to stay.

Mullet are often referred to as the 'woodcock of the sea', because of the French penchant for eating them whole, guts and all. As with woodcock of the air, the retention of the mullet innards – or sometimes just its liver – imparts a lightly gamey taste to the flesh, especially around the belly of the fish. Once the fish is cooked, the mashed guts are either incorporated into a sauce or spread on toast, then served with the fish. For our own easy-to-stomach version of this grand tradition, see page 315.

Whether they excite your palate or not, those insides are also notable for biological reasons: they are much longer than those of any other fish of a comparable size (except, as it happens, the unrelated grey mullet). This is because goatfish (and mullet) are mud-sucking bottom-feeders. They forage around muddy sand and silt, hoovering up everything in sight, and teasing out crustaceans and other organic material that can be digested. The generous length of their intestines maximises the conversion of organic material into usable energy.

Around the south coast inshore fishery where we mostly fish, it's quite unusual to catch red mullet on rod and line. We know of only a couple of local anglers – trainspotter types who are trying to tick off every species in the book – who have targeted them specifically, and both of them are still waiting to land their first one. Perhaps when they do we'll have a go ourselves.

Traditionally, red mullet are considered to be a Mediterranean fish. Yet as a result of global warming and rising sea temperatures, which have caused the northern migration of protein-rich zooplankton, these colourful fish are now being caught more frequently by trawlers on our side of the English Channel, and even up as far as the coasts of Scotland. So the would-be red mullet anglers may yet have their day. And there is more good news: the red mullet grows

MCS RATING: 3 (2–4)

REC MINIMUM SIZE: 22cm

SEASON: avoid May–July (spawning)

RECIPES: pages 148–9, 194, 198, 218, 226–7, 305, 310, 315, 337, 340–1, 400, 407

quickly and matures young so, if caught in UK waters, it's a sustainable choice too, whereas in the Mediterranean, red mullet are overfished.

The first people to get really excited by red mullet were the Romans. They loved their firm, generous flesh, but most of all they loved their redness. Red mullet glint and glisten like a pot of stolen rubies when they're alive, but as soon as they're dead they start to fade. In order to keep them bright and fiery, fishermen traditionally descale them as they come on board. By removing the scales, the pigments of the skin expand and become even redder. However, fish that die when they're still immersed in seawater will quickly lose their colour. Because of this, line-caught red mullet will always fetch more at market than those that died in a net.

With a zeal bordering on perversity, the Romans liked to keep their red mullet alive until the last possible moment, in order to enjoy every last glimmer of redness. They stored them in large, salty reservoirs and brought them to the table alive in decorative glass bowls. Once they'd had enough of this crimson visual apéritif, they would ask the cook to kill a fish for them, before taking it down to the kitchen to prepare. 'There is nothing more beautiful than a dying mullet,' wrote the Roman philosopher Seneca the Younger. 'In the very struggle of its failing breath of life, first a red, then a pale tint suffuses it. And between life and death there is a gradation of colour into more subtle shades.'

By the reign of Caligula in the first century AD, the mania for mullet had got truly out of hand. Individual fish were selling for outrageous sums, as powerful citizens tried to outbid each other for the biggest specimens. The satirist Juvenal records a mullet that weighed six pounds selling for 6,000 sesterces, and also notes that to buy the fisherman himself as a slave would cost less than half the price of the fish.

At River Cottage, we're exceedingly lucky to have access to red mullet at an unusually competitive price. In late summer and early autumn the Weymouth fishery sees reliably good catches being landed for two or three months, usually by inshore day boats using gill nets. We always try to buy a few from our favourite wholesalers, Weyfish (see the Directory, page 591), for the best possible price. They're never cheap – but they're certainly less than half what they'd go for in London.

With whole red mullet costing more per kilo than filleted cod loin, this will always be a luxury fish. So is the fuss justified? Well… yes. It really does have an exceptional flavour: a deep, savoury taste that no other fish can quite match. The texture is special, too – its rich, curdy flakes inhabiting pretty much the perfect halfway house between white and oily fish.

As far as we're concerned, it's essential to cook and serve a red mullet whole (that is to say, on the bone, even if you wish to take the guts out). This way, not a morsel need be wasted – and you get to relish those extra-special flavours that come only when fish flesh and bones are cooked contiguously. In fact, we'd say that filleting red mullet (as so many chefs seem to feel the need to do) is a heinous crime. It's not a fish for steaming or poaching either. Some of that fine flavour is in the skin, which, once freed of the large, loose scales, begs to be crisped up.

And so, to get the best from this lovely fish, we like to cook whole specimens, seasoned lightly with salt and pepper and a few sprigs of thyme, if possible with the liver still in the cavity, either in the frying pan or on the barbecue. That's quite Bacchanalian enough for us.

Grey mullet *Chelon labrosus*

Grey mullet are very Zen. They've come to terms with who they are and what their role is in the huge, swirling, fishy cosmos. Mostly the ocean is populated by thugs and bullies, making their way by voraciously hunting and eating other fish and crustaceans. The grey mullet is an exception. A non-aggressive being, it is happy to derive its nourishment from algae, seaweed, worms, maggots and mud.

A grey mullet's lifestyle is unusually transparent and open to scrutiny. Just about everyone has enjoyed eating a portion of cod, yet very few have ever seen a cod alive, going about its underwater business. The opposite is true with mullet – hardly anybody has ever eaten one, but nearly everyone has seen one swimming about, even if they didn't know what it was. You think you haven't? If you've ever strolled around a harbour or fishing port, at home or abroad, and seen a small shoal of fish nudging the surface as they harry a piece of discarded bread, or even litter – those fish are grey mullet.

Mullet may be among the most visible of sea fish; but even if they are never shy of putting in an appearance, they are exceedingly wary of a fisherman's baited hook. It's almost as if their boldness in going about their harbour business comes from an awareness of just how hard they are to catch. Most fish are fairly easily tempted by the usual range of live or dead bait: mussels, worms, prawns, crab and squid or fish chunks. Mullet will eat none of these – at least, not until they are reduced to practically particle form (fish soup almost). They can, however, be tempted by bread, but they suck and nibble this with their abnormally thick lips in such tiny morsels that to present a small enough bait, on a hook small enough to deceive them, is a feat of wily cunning beyond most anglers – including us.

Only the most dedicated light-tackle anglers regularly succeed. The members of the National Mullet Club are really freshwater anglers who've heard the call of the sea – or at the least the harbour or estuary. The tackle they use isn't the heavy-duty stuff of the boat or beach fanatic, it's freshwater gear: twelve-foot float rods, two-pound breaking strain line and minute hooks. These guys use onion sacks full of stale bread and mashed fish bits as a ground-baiting technique. (Channel Islanders, who know about mullet fishing, call this 'chervy'; elsewhere it's known as 'chum'.) The bags slowly release flakes and crumbs of bread and fish, which lure in the mullet. Then, over this chum slick, the mullet maestros waft minute bread flakes on tiny hooks under ultra-sensitive waggler floats.

When a big mullet is hooked, the ensuing battle is truly spectacular. Pound for pound, the grey mullet is one of the strongest fighters of them all. When it's hooked in shallow water, it has no choice but to run away; it can't dive deep or take refuge in a wreck, it can only sprint as far and as fast as its fins will carry it. These spectacular runs make for heart-pumping, rod-bending action.

Like carp anglers, mullet aficionados spend infinite time and patience in pursuit of their beloved fish. And, just like carp anglers, they hardly ever eat their catch. 'You're never going to put a mullet recipe in your book?' asked Leon Roskilly, famed mullet angler, when we pumped him for mullet knowledge. We certainly are, we told him (see page 283). And why not? Mullet are not in short supply, and they're naturally protected by their wily ways. If you ever manage to catch one, you more than deserve the reward of eating it.

Though underappreciated in this country, the flesh of the grey mullet makes indisputably good eating. It has tender but robust, lightly oily flesh – perhaps not quite up there with bass or bream, but not far short. It's versatile, too, and

MCS RATING: 4 (3–4)

REC MINIMUM SIZE: 35cm

SEASON: avoid June–August (spawning)

RECIPES: pages 144, 148–9, 194, 198, 223, 226–7, 244, 270, 283, 289, 340–1

works as a substitute for plenty of other oily and white fish (you'll see it listed as an alternative in quite a few of our recipes). There are a few troublesome bones, which make the mullet a little hard to fillet – on balance, it's easier to leave the bones in during cooking and remove them on the plate. However, the thick, round body of the mullet lends itself to another portioning technique: larger fish are often cut into cross-section chunks, a few centimetres thick, sometimes referred to as cutlets (see page 71).

Grey mullet are caught commercially in British waters but only in relatively modest numbers, usually by day-boat fishermen using inshore gill nets – often when targeting bass. They'll turn up occasionally on a fishmonger's slab – more regularly in the south than the north and perhaps most reliably in the Southwest. Among the few places you'll consistently find them is in the fishmongers of London's Chinatown. The Chinese have a special affection for mullet and use it in all sorts of ways – among the most popular being steamed with garlic, spring onions, ginger and soy.

However, it's around the Iberian peninsula and the Mediterranean that grey mullet is given full rein to express its culinary potential: it's grilled, poached, stewed, baked and fried with all manner of accompaniments. The Greeks like to stew it with tomatoes and olives, while in Portugal it's stuffed with breadcrumbs and spring onions and served in a caper and tomato sauce.

Around the island of Sardinia, mullet are vigorously pursued not merely for their flesh but also for their eggs (both female roe and male milt, in fact). Piles of roe are heavily salted, then compressed and sun-dried into dark, red-brown blocks, like fishy hashish (not that we'd ever inhale). This pungent delicacy, called bottarga, sells for £10 per 100g, and is probably the nearest thing the fish world has to a truffle: grated on to pasta dishes, eggs and risotto it moves its fans to sighs of ecstasy. But to be honest, we wouldn't pick a quarrel with anyone who whispered that it might be a touch overrated.

So, grey mullet is unquestionably a fish to explore and, if it needed any further sell, recent studies appear to corroborate the idea of fish as a good food for the brain. Mullet, it seems, is an amazing source of dietary iodine – a lack of which is thought to be the number-one reason for intellectual underachievement in children. So, if you want a slogan to help spread the good news about this fish, might we suggest: 'Grey Mullet for Grey Matter – You Know It Makes Sense!'

cuckoo wrasse

Cuckoo wrasse *Labrus mixtus*

Ballan wrasse *Labrus bergylta*

These are the most common of our five species of wrasse, which inhabit some of the rockiest and weediest inshore grounds around the British coastline. They have a fascinating natural history, not least in their approach to gender, which is somewhat fluid. Wrasse are all born female, but all very large wrasse, aged six years or more, are male. Female wrasse can simply choose to become male wrasse – it's not (so far as we can tell) because they always felt trapped in a man's body. It's simply for the good of their local wrasse community.

Male wrasse are few and far between. Some sections of coastline will be dominated by one big, fiercely territorial male, who is attended by a harem of sexually mature females. However, should anything untoward occur, and the alpha male wrasse get eaten by a predator or caught by a fisherman, then the dominant female in the harem will take over. She will give up her life as a wife and mother and metamorphose into a scary male. She will develop male sex organs, male behaviour, and dress herself in the colourful garb of the 'big daddy'. From that day forth, as Lou Reed put it, 'she was a he'.

From now on (s)he performs all the sexual and paternal duties associated with the job. But the life of a harem-minding male isn't quite the lazy, skinless-grape-eating business that you'd think it might be. Maybe it's because males are outnumbered by females to such an extent that, although he's the only fertile male in the neighbourhood, he still has to work hard for his women. Wrasse are nest-building fish, and it's the male who has the job of constructing the perfect place for a fecund female to lay her precious eggs. In fact, the quality of the build is everything; if she doesn't like his nest, she won't lay her eggs in it.

Nest building is part of the courtship ritual. The male cleans an area of rock or a crevice with his teeth, then binds together a bed of seaweed and gravel using his own mucus as cement. If a female is impressed enough with his 'design', she will deign to lay her eggs in his nest and allow him to fertilise them.

Building a nest and fertilising the eggs is just the start of a male wrasse's paternal duties. Maybe it's because he used to be a she that he takes his family responsibilities very seriously. Post-ejaculation, it's not the male who does a

ballan wrasse

runner, it's the female. She leaves to return to a normal life, while the male hovers over the nest of eggs, fanning them gently with his tail to keep them clean and oxygenated. He'll continue to guard them until they hatch and disperse into the upper layers of the sea, where they start life on a diet of plankton.

The cuckoo wrasse rarely reaches much more than half a kilo, while the ballan wrasse is regularly encountered at two to three kilos. Both move inshore during the warmer months and will eat just about anything that even remotely resembles food. Equipped with strong jaws, rubbery lips and bulletproof teeth, they're happy to nibble algae off rocks, wrecks and breakwaters, and crunch up anything from starfish to barnacles, shore crabs to squat lobsters. This means that wrasse are often quite easy to catch. Scuba divers know just how inquisitive and curious they can be; often they follow divers for long periods of time, looking for a free feed disturbed by the divers' flippers.

Apart from their peculiar gender issues, the most remarkable thing about wrasse is their exotic coloration. The cuckoo wrasse, in particular, wouldn't look out of place on a Caribbean coral reef.

Wrasse aren't generally regarded as being much of an eating fish – their bony flesh and thick skin make them unpopular with cooks. Most British anglers enjoy catching them, though – they fight well when they're hooked – but they generally return them to the sea. They do have their uses in continental fish cookery – the most common being to make stock for a classic *bouillabaisse*. It's a job they do well, since they have plenty of 'body' to give to the dish.

Since wrasse are reef-dwelling, territorial creatures, there isn't an endless supply of them. They came under some pressure in the 1970s and 1980s, when competitive spear fishing became increasingly popular. Large ballan wrasse, with their broad flanks, were an easy target and in some areas the numbers of big fish declined drastically. Thankfully this sport is no longer pursued in such a cavalier manner. (In our view, spear fishing, though undeniably exciting, is acceptable only when coupled with a responsible 'one or two for the pot' mentality.)

If you catch a wrasse and can't return it to the sea alive (usually because its swim bladder has blown from coming up too quickly from some depth – see page 432 – or because it's too badly hooked to survive), then do take it home and make it part of a fine fish stock. Otherwise, we'd always recommend putting them back – a living wrasse has much more entertainment value than a dead one.

Monkfish (or anglerfish) *Lophius piscatorius*

There is no such fish as a 'monkfish'. In the same way that 'rock salmon' is just a creative chippie's way to describe bull huss and other small sharks (see page 452), so monkfish was the name adopted to retail the anglerfish – a creature with looks that only a mother could love, which for a long time languished on the bycatch pile, destined only for the cat-food cannery.

And yet, with a bit of rebranding and some careful presentation, it overcame the odds and ascended to the heights of culinary chic. The great Keith Floyd had a hand in its rise up the fish charts. In his excellent television series *Floyd on Fish* (first broadcast in 1984), he cooked it a couple of times, most memorably while being tossed about in the galley of a Brixham trawler. Filmed Scorsese-style, in a single take, it's one of the best television cooking sequences of all time. And, like Delia and the cranberries, it can't have done monkfish sales any harm.

Before Keith came along and saved it, the anglerfish was scratching a living as a kind of 'mock lobster' in restaurant fish stews and even, when portioned, crumbed and deep fried, doing a passable imitation of scampi. But what he and other enterprising chefs realised was that this fish's fat tail yielded a great hunk of succulent, snow-white flesh that deserved much more than a supporting role.

By the end of the 1980s, monkfish had become hugely popular with chefs and, increasingly, with home cooks. It's obvious why. Its uncomplicated bone structure makes it a doddle to prepare and its meat is firm and relatively forgiving of the chef. As a result, it's fantastically easy and versatile. You can fry, barbecue, poach, steam, stew or roast a tail, and even overcook it by a factor of 50 per cent without fear of it dissolving to a flaky mush. (It might end up a bit dry but it will still look right.) Consequently, aspiring gastropubs and dinner-party hosts have staked their fish-course reputation on its user-friendly flesh. Roasted monkfish tail wrapped in Parma ham was the chicken Kiev of the 1990s (or at least one of them).

Monkfish is sold only in 'tails' (usually skinned, but just occasionally with its pinky-purple mottled skin still attached). There's a reason for that, besides convenience. An anglerfish's head is not a pretty sight. In fact it's a nightmare: piggy, serial-killer eyes, black, blotchy skin and a huge gin-trap mouth, full of pointed teeth. Basically, it's a monster, which looks scarier than any shark and about as edible as a muddy tractor tyre. The trade's view, understandably, is that simply seeing a head would scare shoppers off eating the tail. (Heads would also take up a lot of prime space on the fish counter.) As a result anglerfish are invariably beheaded on board ship – which is a pity, as the heads would no doubt make a wonderful stock. The only part of them that is saved, on larger specimens, is the cheeks. These juicy scallops of meat are the muscles that work that enormous jaw, and you'll sometimes see them on the fishmonger's slab.

It's a shame we never get to see an anglerfish's head, as it's absolutely fascinating. It is grotesquely disproportionate, several times wider than the thickest part of its body and squashed flat, like underwater road kill. Growing out from the middle of its forehead are a couple of flexible spines and on the end of each hangs a bobble of tattered skin that flutters in the current. These protuberances – apart from presenting one of those evolutionary posers with which creationists attempt to have a field day – are the angler's 'fishing rods', and the blobs on the end of them its bait. They look like a tasty, aquatic morsel, and are also spookily luminous, so they glow in the dark at any depth. Fish feeding

MCS RATING: 4 (3–5)

REC MINIMUM SIZE: 70cm

SEASON: avoid spring and early summer (spawning)

in poor light on the seabed will see the phosphorescent 'bait' and quite possibly 'smell' it too, as it is also primed with chemical attractants. What they don't see is the anglerfish's head. It is brilliantly camouflaged by warty, tattered skin that looks like seaweed on a rock, and swively, protruding eye sockets that could easily be barnacles clinging to it. The first thing an unlucky prey fish knows about the anglerfish is the moment when a rock opens up beneath it – and turns out to have a huge tooth-ringed mouth. It's also the last thing he'll know about it.

In the path of a trawler, however, the anglerfish's disguise does it no good. It's an easy prey. By the end of the 1990s it was in dire straits, with all the main fisheries in a downward spiral. Many remain in a critical condition – you certainly shouldn't eat monkfish caught off Spain or Portugal, for instance, where stocks are in serious trouble.

There is a glimmer of hope, though. Since fisheries managers are actually biting the bullet with catch restrictions, monkfish is now staging something of a recovery in some areas. According to the Marine Conservation Society, there is one British fishery in which monkfish numbers are at a sustainable level: the Southwest. A few years of responsible management have also resulted in the beginnings of a fight-back for some Scottish and Shetland Island stocks. However, this fish is certainly not out of the woods yet.

Another problem is that, even in the Southwest, most monkfish are caught by beam trawling, which is among the most destructive of fishing methods (see page 29). Some monkfish are caught on long lines, and a few in static nets, but that information is hard to come by at the point of sale, though it never hurts to ask. For these reasons, we still see monkfish as a fish to avoid. Neither of us has ever caught one, but it's not inconceivable that we will one day, as a few are landed every year on rod and line around Weymouth. If we did catch one, we'd release it. (At least that's our plan, but we know what the road to hell is paved with…)

You'll find no recipes that specify monkfish in this book, though plenty could be adapted to its easy meat. We'd rather you chose something else, though. Something operating under its real name, for a start. Anyone for gurnard?

John Dory *Zeus faber*

The John Dory is an optical illusion with fins. Now you see it. Now you don't. That's if you're another fish. If, on the other hand, it's lying on a bed of crushed ice and you're a human looking for dinner, then it's quite hard to miss. It's the ugliest fish on the slab.

Let's adopt that fish-eye view to try to understand how it does this. From the side, as it swims right past you, a John Dory looks much like any other fish: roughly oval, head at one end, tail at the other. But from the front, looking at it straight in the face, it just sort of... disappears. The silvery, almost mirrored, planes of its head reflect and refract the light, making it appear invisible – or rather, not appear at all. Confused? That's the whole point.

This vanishing trick is its greatest weapon (and, when it's little, its greatest defence). 'John Dory are total ambush-merchants,' says charter skipper Pat Carlin. 'They sneak up on something, or lie in wait for a fish – they won't even notice him – then, bosh! He grabs them with his big tube mouth.'

A John Dory's mouth is its other great asset – a sucker punch, almost literally. In naturalist-speak it's 'highly protrusible', which means it can dislocate, unfold and extend, like a telescope crossed with a concertina, and all at the speed of a Mike Tyson jab. It can effortlessly swallow large bait fish in one swift gulp. 'We sometimes catch them on the Channel wrecks when we're fishing for big bass,' says Pat. 'Even a small Dory can fit a whole live mackerel in its mouth, no problem.'

Though you'll find John Dory from the Canary Islands to Scotland, by far the most likely place to catch one, whether you're an angler or a commercial trawler skipper, is in the English Channel – particularly off Devon or Cornwall. Known to some West Country fishermen as 'Plymouth's proudest', most Dory are caught as bycatch, in trawl nets targeting other pelagic species such as mackerel and bass. Because catches are sporadic and unpredictable, there is no dedicated

MCS RATING: 3

REC MINIMUM SIZE: 30cm

SEASON: avoid June–August (spawning)

RECIPES: pages 220, 270, 283, 289, 310, 318–19, 340–1, 407

UK fishery for John Dory, and no fixed quota restrictions. It's an unprotected species – which is not to say it has no value. A commercial fisherman will always be delighted to see some good-sized Dory in his trawl. Due to its outstanding culinary reputation (of which more below), it's right up there, price-wise, with top-end fish such as turbot, brill, bass and red mullet.

Although it's important not to get cavalier about eating John Dory, it does do quite well in the sustainability stakes. It grows fast and matures fairly young, which means its stocks can withstand a reasonable amount of fishing. Add to this the fact that it's a bycatch species and never taken in large numbers, and you can see why it's not likely to become threatened in the near future. If you want to help ensure this remains the case, make certain your JD is big enough to have spawned at least once.

Quite how John Dory acquired its straight-from-the-phone-book name is a matter of speculation. Attempts to unmask the John in question have floundered. Some insist that there is no John, and that the name is a corruption of the French *jaune doré*, which you could translate as 'yellow and gold' (though the fish more often appears silvery grey in colour). Others (including Richard Parnell in his book *Fishes of the Firth of Forth*, published in 1838) have credited the eighteenth-century actor and epicure John Quin with championing the fish – hence it became John's Dory. Far more likely (we think) is that John was just a friendly nickname thought up by fishermen – perhaps to make its ugly face seem less bothersome. The habit of bestowing Christian names on God's creatures, like Jenny Wren, Tom Tit or Robin Redbreast, was common in the early nineteenth century; another example of one that stuck, and passed into the field guides, was Jack Daw. As late as the 1880s, the celebrated naturalist Frank Buckland still insisted on referring to this fish simply as 'Dory' – the implication being that the 'John' was a familiarity for fishmongers and hobbyists only.

The John Dory is also widely known, in various languages, as 'Saint Peter's fish' (in Portuguese it's *peixe sao pedro*, in Swedish *sankt pers fisk* and in French, simply *Saint-Pierre*), on account of the two dark splodges in the centre of its body. These are said to be the thumb and forefinger prints of Saint Peter himself, who plucked one from the Sea of Galilee at Christ's command. In fact the John Dory doesn't exist in the Sea of Galilee but there is a local species, with similar 'fingerprints', that carries the saint's name. The naturalist's interpretation is that the marks are part of the John Dory's cunning display – false eyes that flash a warning to potential predators. They can glint with malice as the fish turns, making believe, at the very moment that it sheds its cloak of invisibility, that it's no tasty morsel but a big, bad fish that you wouldn't want to mess with. (Sometimes it seems there's no end to this fish's tricks, or indeed its aliases. Check out the Latin name. *Zeus faber*! How cool is that?)

The John Dory may be hard to catch deliberately, but it's increasingly easy to sell. Such is the high regard for this fish among chefs (and 'afishionados') that there is a worrying trend for offering it in ever-smaller sizes. Recently we've seen Dorys of barely 250g on the slabs of fishmongers who, frankly, should know better. We'd like to see a minimum landing size brought in, and (if its price doesn't do the job for us) we certainly wouldn't encourage you to think of it as an everyday fish.

When you buy a whole Dory, bear in mind that the enormous head and capacious belly cavity constitute about 60 per cent of its entire body weight. If you haven't tackled one before, you may feel a mite diddled. But don't be put off.

You can cook one whole (baked in foil, for example – see page 220) and simply pick every succulent scrap off the head and bones. Or you (or your fishmonger) can fillet it – in which case, be sure to put that massive head and frame to good use. It makes stunning stock (page 256) for a fine fish soup, stew or risotto.

The two fillets, which scallop out nicely from each side of the fish, may look diminutive compared to the frame, but they are of outstanding flavour and texture – right up there with turbot, no less. They are ready for anything, unsauced or sauced, as straight or as fancy as you like. We like them pretty straight, seasoned but not floured, gently fried in butter with a dash of olive oil and a sprinkling of fresh thyme leaves and chopped garlic – served with just a squeeze of lemon and a small amount of creamy mash.

For the reasons discussed above, we don't expect to be buying and eating a lot of John Dory. But one day, perhaps when out bass fishing with Pat, we hope we might catch a good one. It would be great to hold such a redoubtable and intriguing fish in our hands and look it in the eye. And, provided it didn't vanish on us, very satisfying to welcome it into our kitchen, and on to our plate.

Red gurnard *Aspitrigla cuculus*

MCS RATING: **2 EAT MORE!**

REC MINIMUM SIZE: **20cm**

SEASON: avoid spring and early summer (spawning)

RECIPES: pages 226–7, 266–7, 337, 381, 393 et al.

Nothing can really prepare you for the shock of catching your first red gurnard. You cast your bait in the grey-green English Channel and reel in a fish that looks as if it comes from the Great Barrier Reef. It may have the blunt forehead of a Portsmouth pub brawler but it also sports the dazzling colouring of a tropical sunset. For all its finery, there's no doubt it's dressed for battle, with spines, barbs and a bulletproof helmet.

In British waters we have three types of gurnard: the red, the grey and the tub (which is very similar to the red, only bigger and rarer). The one you're most likely to find (or catch) is the red. It very rarely grows above 1.5kg and is most commonly caught at around 500g, or less.

Most gurnard are caught by accident – anglers rarely target them. They can be caught quite easily, though, especially on mackerel fishing trips. The best method is to use a set of traditional mackerel feathers but to put a chunk of bait (a strip of mackerel or squid) on the bottom two hooks. They will take a bare feather but are attracted more effectively with the scent of a little fresh bait, too. They also crop up on plaice and flatfish fishing trips when you're drifting sand banks, dragging baits with silvery plaice spoons or beads attached. Gurnard love a bit of flash and sparkle.

There's a lot to be said for going out of your way to catch gurnard, as we'll see, and the best time to catch them is late summer and autumn. The English Channel is a hotspot, but they rarely migrate further up the east coast than Norfolk. The west coasts of England, Scotland and Ireland do contain plenty of gurnard, probably because the sea temperature is higher due to the Gulf Stream.

There is functionality in the gurnard's arresting physique. In particular, its unique, fan-like pectoral fins perform three distinct roles. As with most fish, they provide paddle-like propulsion through the water; they are used as 'feet' for crawling along the seabed; and, most unusually, the lower three rays of the fin are separated to create finger-like fronds, which are loaded with sensory organs. These feeler-feet are used for detecting the movement of crustaceans hiding beneath the sediment. Once it has found its prey, a gurnard makes short work of consuming it.

However, gurnard don't limit themselves to defenceless crustaceans. They'll hunt for live fish, too – such as young whiting, plaice and sand eels. And they'll leave the sea floor for a hunting foray higher up the water column, if that's where the food is to be found. A gurnard is nomadic and omnivorous – in other words, it'll travel anywhere to eat anything.

Over the centuries, gurnard have garnered a range of odd colloquial names. These include sea robin, feeler fish, red fish, soldier, elleck, rotchet and croaker. In Scotland they are also known as crooners, on account of the snoring/croaking noise they emit when they're being unhooked. The noise – a low, repetitive grunt – is made by special muscles that vibrate rapidly, using the swim bladder as a resonating chamber. Gurnard are very gregarious and the grunting is thought by some to be a basic means of communication with their own kind.

If nothing prepares you for the shock of catching your first red gurnard, then eating it may be an even bigger surprise. And an extremely pleasant one. The robust flavour of the flesh, its firm texture, and the way the meat so completely peels off the skeleton without releasing any annoying bones makes the whole experience a sheer delight. We seriously rate this fish, and would argue that it's right up there with bass and bream.

Yet, astonishingly, the gurnard has never been very popular as a table fish. It was most commonly used as crab pot-bait and, until recently, rarely sold in fishmongers at all. Charlie Caisey, a fishmonger in the East End of London for over fifty years, remembers buying red gurnard for his market stall – but not for his customers to eat. 'We'd hang them up over the fish display,' he says, 'because they'd look like bright-red flying fish, and kids would drag their mums over to have a closer look. Next thing you know, they ask you what sort of fish it is, then you've got a dialogue going… and that's how you sell fish.'

It's ironic that this cunning marketing wheeze was probably being used to shift fish that, from a gastronomic point of view, are not even in the gurnard's class. Perhaps this fish has simply seemed too weird and 'foreign' to the British fish buyer. Yet even in France and Spain, where most of our B-list species are more appreciated, the gurnard has never quite received the acclaim it deserves.

One possible reason for the continental cold shoulder is that, due to its colour and triangular head, the gurnard has inevitably been compared to the more desirable (and more expensive) red mullet. Oddly enough, the one member of the gurnard family that is better rated in France is the only one that isn't red, and so doesn't tempt comparison with the mullet. It's the grey gurnard – which the French call *la tombe*, on account of its coffin-like shape. It also has a following in Bulgaria, where by tradition it's served with a walnut sauce.

The upshot is that gurnard remains a bargain compared to the A-list species, not because of any deficiency in flavour or texture but simply because few people know about it. And for now, that's part of its charm.

However, a fish this good can't stay hidden for long. Our guess is that you'll increasingly see red gurnard for sale at your local fishmonger's and maybe even in the supermarket. And that seems fair enough: the red gurnard is rated by the MCS as a fast-growing and currently sustainable fish. So you can eat it with a clear conscience and a voracious appetite.

But perhaps we should be a little wary of the possible consequences of a 'red-rush' for this lovely fish. Only a generation ago monkfish was the proverbial pot-bait. Then it became a superstar fish, beloved of top chefs. Soon after, it became a serious conservation concern. Let's hope red gurnard stocks can be managed with some vision and care. With this in mind, you should never choose immature fish less than 20cm in length, as these haven't yet had a chance to breed.

When you do buy your first red gurnard, you might feel a bit miffed that you have to pay for such a large head in proportion to the compact, tapered body. But you really shouldn't worry – this fish is packed with more flesh than is obvious from the exterior. When you're picking the meat off a cooked gurnard, you'll discover plenty of thick chunks of creamy-white flesh in some unexpected places, including right up into its 'shoulders'.

Another wonderful characteristic of red gurnard is that the tight, meaty flesh holds together perfectly during cooking, unlike that of many white fish. Gurnard work particularly well in soups and stews, as the flesh won't disintegrate even if it's simmered for a little too long.

So that's the gurnard for you: beautiful, delicious, cheap, sustainable and idiot-proof in the kitchen. Could there be a higher recommendation for a fish?

Garfish *Belone belone*

MCS RATING: not rated but they grow fast and mature young, so considered a safe choice

REC MINIMUM SIZE: 40cm

SEASON: avoid May–June (spawning)

RECIPES: pages 194, 218, 270, 319

The garfish is a design classic. From its beak-like nose to its deeply forked tail, it's an example of hydrodynamic perfection – and one of the fastest fish in British waters. It uses its super speed for two purposes: to hunt small fish and to escape large fish. It's agile too: it can leap out of the water, not only to elude a pursuing predator but also, among rocks in the shallows, to gain access to hunting grounds other fish cannot reach.

In the sea, garfish live alongside mackerel. They can be caught and cooked in the same way as mackerel, because they too are oily pelagic fish. Most mackerel recipes will apply perfectly to garfish. Like mackerel, garfish are summer visitors to the coastline of Britain. In fact, garfish are known as the 'mackerel guide' because they migrate from deep water into the sun-warmed coastal shallows just ahead of, or in convoy with, the mackerel shoals.

The name 'garfish' is derived from the ancient Anglo-Saxon *gar*, meaning spear. The French call it *aiguille* (needle) but also, affectionately, *bécassine de mer* (snipe of the sea). In the Channel Islands, one of the few places where garfish is considered to be a delicacy, it's known simply as longnose. The Danish, meanwhile, call it *hornfisk*. Even if you've never seen one, you might be starting to pick up some clues about its appearance. It has a very striking long, pointed 'nose' – its beak-like toothed jaws, in fact, with which it snaps at its prey with impressive accuracy.

This is by no means its only distinctive feature. Another regional name is greenbones, due to its shockingly bright green – almost luminous – skeleton. This bizarre physical attribute has given rise to much suspicion about eating garfish. Some cookbooks claim they are poisonous, but in fact the green colouring in its bones is caused by a perfectly harmless phosphate of iron, called vivianite. And there's more: garfish also have tiny turquoise scales that detach very easily when they are handled. You can spot a keen garfish angler by his shiny, green-speckled hands, looking like the victim of some horrific radioactive disaster.

Unsurprisingly then, anglers seem a tad reluctant to eat the garfish they catch. More fool them. They're quite delicious. Should you get the chance to catch or buy one, grab it (as you always must with a garfish) with both hands. Underneath the pointy exterior, and clinging to those slightly scary bones, is flesh that when cooked is robust, moist and right up there with mackerel or even bass.

You're most likely to catch a garfish around piers, breakwaters and rocky headlands. The trusted technique is to fish with a fairly small hook under a sea float, using little finger-sized strips of mackerel (or other garfish!) as bait. In the Channel Islands, garfishermen will often take along a bucket of 'chervy' to entice

the fish to feed. This is basically a sloppy mix of bread, fish guts and fish oils, which is spooned into the water little and often. It creates an underwater scent trail to lure the garfish to the bait (and their fate). Many anglers have their own secret ingredients with which they customise their chervy. These may include Thai fish sauce, anchovy oil, malt extract and even ox or pig's blood. Obviously they're not *that* secret – that's fishermen for you.

Hooking a garfish on light tackle is a thrilling experience. They are often described as 'miniature marlin', on account of the aerial acrobatics they can perform in their attempt to escape. A hooked garfish will leap right out of the water, 'walk' on its tail, or dive deep in a vigorous attempt to shake the hook.

The perfect garfish to cook is over 40cm long and around 500g in weight. This size is easy to gut and can even be filleted (if you want to remove the green bones). It'll feed two people as a hearty main course or four as a starter. From an ecological perspective, at 40cm long a garfish has reached sexual maturity and will have already had the opportunity to spawn. In fish-boffin speak, garfish are said to have 'medium resilience to fishing'. In other words, they grow fast and mature early, so the population can fairly readily replace the fish it loses. Nevertheless, it's still best to opt for garfish caught by the least intensive methods – i.e. fish you've landed yourself or those taken as a bycatch.

Once you've come to terms with the visual oddities of this fish (which are mere tricks to stop you eating it), you can set about enjoying its excellent flesh. The classic French method for cooking garfish is to poach or fry bite-sized chunks and serve them with a sorrel sauce. The Channel Islanders prefer to grill them and serve them up with mushy peas and mashed potato. The Danes like their *hornfisk* fillets pickled, smoked or lightly cured. All of which is testament to the surprising versatility of this fish.

The Japanese go one better – they like to eat the bones as well as the flesh. Once the cooked flesh has been taken from the bones, they dust the skeleton in spicy flour and deep fry it in hot oil. Needless to say we had to try this – with some we caught during a fishing trip to Guernsey. See page 374 for the verdict…

Conger eel *Conger conger*

MCS RATING: 5 DON'T EAT!
REC MINIMUM SIZE: N/A
SEASON: N/A
RECIPE: pages 229–31

Every sea fisherman has a conger story to tell; some twisty tale of a huge, snapping eel with a head the size of a boiled ham, teeth so sharp they could fell a pylon, and the attitude of a Jack Russell with a wasp up its nose.

We love the story of the Dorset crab potter who found a five-footer curled up in one of his hauled pots. He shook the felon on to the deck, only to have the conger respond with a tantrum so malevolent and violent that the fisherman dived into the wheelhouse for safety and locked the door. According to local legend, he stayed there, peering out of the window, for the next six hours, while the conger ran amok on the deck. It smashed everything of value while thrashing round the boat, until eventually escaping out of one of the scuppers.

Another favourite conger-revenge tale is of an angler who lost control of a big, fat wriggler he'd just hauled out of the sea on to a low pier wall. He put his foot on the conger's neck to 'pacify' him and in the next blink the conger twisted around and bit through his welly boot, top and bottom, sinking his fangs

simultaneously through the sole and upper. The howling fisherman kicked so hard he broke two of the eel's lower teeth. The tips of them are still buried in the arch of his foot to this day.

Congers are great fable fodder because, let's face it, there aren't many British fish likely to give you a serious fright. No one's going to be traumatised by a surprise encounter with a roach. Nobody ever went to A and E after a mauling from a whiting. Congers have been called 'legless pit bulls with scales' – which is apt except not only do they lack legs, they also lack scales. They are quite uncannily smooth skinned. Even freshwater eels have scales on their skin – practically undetectable by the naked eye, but they're there nonetheless. A conger, on the other hand, has not a speck of a scale on it from fang to tail. It does have a thick layer of slime, though, that helps to ease it in and out of tight hidey-holes.

Conger eels love to hang out among deep shadows. They slither around undersea wrecks and reefs, lurking in holes and caves, from where they ambush

their prey with surprising speed and agility, given their size. During the rush of tide, congers like to keep themselves tucked away from the current in the sanctuary of wreck or reef. But when the tide slackens, small- to medium-sized eels (up to 10kg) will venture on to open ground, ranging the bottom in search of a feed. They're not fussy – almost any fish or crustacean will do, dead or alive.

Anglers who target conger eels tend to position themselves near reefs and wrecks, and to sit at anchor on slack water, when there's little or no tide. They use big baits, such as half a mackerel or a chunky fish head, on large, strong hooks. These are attached to the reel line by either a steel wire trace or an extra-thick (60kg) nylon leader, to offer resistance against the conger's teeth.

The sensible way to tame a big eel is to steer it straight from the landing net into a coarse hessian sack, cutting the line so the hook stays in the conger's mouth until it has calmed down somewhat. Then it is a two-person job: let only the head out of the sack, one person gripping it firmly through the hessian just behind the gills, while the other goes for the hook with a pair of pliers held in heavily gloved hands. Unhooking should *never* be attempted solo by a conger novice. It would be better to cut the line and return the conger with the hook still in. The facial piercing may or may not impress its friends but it will rust away soon enough.

Bagging a conger for the pot is something we do only once in a blue moon – this is not a species we should be yanking out of the sea at every opportunity. Congers only breed once in their lifetime (and they swim to the waters off Portugal to do it), so there's every chance that the conger you haul in will not yet have had a chance to reproduce. They also take a long time to reach sexual maturity – up to fifteen years. They are not under serious commercial fishing pressure but 'specimen-hunting' anglers have taken their toll on certain heavily fished wrecks and reefs over the years. Since the conger is primarily an angler's fish, we think those who do battle with them should return them to the sea unharmed – and this is increasingly the practice among conger enthusiasts. The only conger you kill and eat, we feel, should be the one you've had to kill because it has swallowed your hook deep, and cannot be unhooked without causing serious damage.

If you do choose to kill a deeply hooked conger, prepare for something of an ordeal. Again, the hessian sack comes in handy. When the conger is fairly still and steady, you should deliver several very hard blows just behind the eyes with a very heavy priest. If this seems to make things worse rather than better, back off for a moment and then try again. Once the conger is stunned and subdued, you need to finish the job by stabbing it between the eyes with a stout knife and/ or severing the spinal column with a deep cut behind the head. Don't be alarmed if some twisting and writhing goes on after this operation has been carried out – the conger's nervous system continues to operate, sometimes for an hour or more, even after the fish is dead.

And what should you do with this reluctantly acquired carcass? Take some trouble over turning it into dinner, surely. In Britain generally, conger has a reputation for being bony, rubbery, grey and unpalatable. But that judgement is unduly harsh. Cornish fishing communities used to eat a lot of conger eel, stewed and served up with a garnish of fresh marigold petals (we like to imagine the sheer chagrin of the mighty conger thus prettified). And among Cornwall's cultural kin in Brittany, the conger is still highly rated – so esteemed in fact that it's been nicknamed *boeuf bellilois*, to celebrate its meaty prime-rib qualities. On the coast of Morocco the conger eel thrives in the harsh rocky crevices and reefs that are pounded by the Atlantic, and in the fishing port of Essaouira, *tagine de congre* is a speciality, served with couscous. The vital elements of the recipe are hotly debated by local chefs and fishwives – rather like the bouillabaisse of Marseille.

We've enjoyed experimenting with the occasional conger we've killed in the last few years. We've beer-battered and deep-fried trimmed fillets, chip-shop style. We've road-tested the British Conger Club's classic of conger poached in cider. We've smoked a whole 'side' of conger and used it to make kedgeree. We've dropped little scallops of conger 'loin fillet' into our Fish and chorizo soup (pages 260–1). We've even stuffed and roasted a thick hunk of conger 'saddle' as if it was a meat joint (see pages 229–31). All these dishes have been successful. They work because conger meat is white, firm and ready to take on any number of flavours.

The tail section – final third, if you like – is the only piece that doesn't yield good meat. It's just too tough, bony and fibrous. But it does make a fine addition, along with the head, to a good fish stock.

In Britain the conger is unlikely to become the fish cook's favourite – and nor should it, when you take its biology into account. But if you find yourself in possession of one, it's well worth investing some time in getting to grips with its substantial carcass. Otherwise, once you've had your adrenalin rush, return your conger alive to the sea so it can give another angler an even bigger fright.

Sand eel *Ammodytes tobianus*

A sand eel doesn't command much public attention or affection because, at least in the UK, as a food fish, it's considered worthless. However, as an intermediary in the fish-to-human food chain, it plays a crucial role. You may never have eaten sand eel but you are sure to have eaten a fish that has. We love them, because they are by far the most effective bait to catch sea bass, one of the fish we most love to eat. But they also play a major part in the economics of commercial fishing – as a much-abused 'industrial' species, caught in vast numbers to be processed into fishmeal.

To anglers, the best sand eel is a live one – freshly scooped from an aerated bait bucket, ready for a size 3/0 long-shank hook to be inserted through its top lip. Live sand eels are a deadly bait, and we have to admit we have skewered hundreds of them over the years, then dropped them on a weighted line to the seabed, in the hope of hooking a sea bass. As bass anglers, we require our sand eels to be full of vim and vigour. The more lively they are on the hook, the more likely they are to tempt a passing bass (or pollack or ling) to suck them in and gulp them down in an underwater dine-and-dash. Then we will have our sport and, with a bit of luck, a fine dinner to show for it.

However, sand eels are often reluctant to play ball. Frail creatures, they like nothing better than to curl up and die. Once they've been caught, either with a small trawl net dragged behind a boat, or by fishing a string of tiny feathered hooks (like mackerel feathers, only smaller), keeping them alive and wriggling is a tricky business. Good charter angling boats will have a live bait 'well' – some kind of tank in which freshly drawn seawater is aerated by a pump, in order

MCS RATING: not rated
SIZE AT MATURITY: 8cm
SEASON: avoid February–April and September–November (spawning)

to keep the moody sand eels hanging on in there. Charter skippers know the value of keeping a catch of sand eels lively all day, because to some extent their reputation depends on it. On his amazing new boat, *Channel Chieftain*, our friend Pat Carlin has installed a rather ancient blue plastic barrel for a bait well, which is connected to a pump circulating seawater. 'You've got to keep sand eels in something *round*,' says Pat. 'If you do that, they'll swim in circles, which keeps them happier, so they stay alive. I've known boats with smart purpose-built tanks that are rectangular. They look great, but all the sand eels just huddle up in one corner and die.'

Few anglers have the patience to catch their own sand eels. Instead they buy them. Through the bass season (summer and autumn) in busy sea-angling ports, sand eels are gold dust. The charter skippers in Weymouth, for example, collectively employ a local fisherman to trawl for sand eels and provide a constant supply for visiting anglers. But, even so, the supply can still be erratic. Certain stages of the tide cycle make it impossible to trawl for sand eels and as soon as the cold weather starts, the eels move out into deeper water. Frozen dead sand eels can be bought all year round. On a good day when the bass are on a voracious feed, dead eels will work just as well. But on a tough day, when the fish need to be enticed, only a live eel will do the business.

You may or may not approve of using live fish as bait for other fish. We do it regularly, so it would be hypocritical to suggest it troubles us greatly. Perhaps it should trouble us more, and perhaps, as we get older, it will. But it's hard to argue against the economics of this enterprise. On a local level, trawling for sand eels, to sell live or frozen as bass bait, makes perfect sense. It's often said, if not economically proved, that the Weymouth bass are worth more alive, to visiting anglers and the tourist economy that they support, than they are dead to the local fish trade. Sand eels play a vital role in that, and the relatively modest harvest required to supply the charter boats is perfectly sustainable.

What isn't sustainable, though – nothing like it – is the way sand eels are plundered further offshore. In parts of the North Sea and northeast Atlantic, vast shoals of sand eels are removed by 'industrial fishing'. They congregate so tightly, and can be targeted so clinically, that 'removed' really is the correct word. Sometimes sand eel trawlers fill their massive holds on just a single trawl, and have to head back to port at top speed before returning for their next enormous scoop of the shoal. At the end of the 1990s, sand eels accounted for around half of all the fish taken from the North Sea, with up to a million tonnes a year being hauled in. Catches have dropped significantly in recent years but are still in the hundreds of thousands of tonnes.

Sand eels – along with capelin, blue whiting and scad (page 481) – are classed as an 'industrial' species. This grim epithet describes fish destined not for direct human consumption but for processing – into fishmeal and fish oil – and thence into pellet food for farmed fish and poultry, and even into fertiliser. The wisdom of taking vast quantities of fish for such purposes is highly questionable, since we are effectively stealing from the mouths of valued eating species, such as cod, salmon and bass, all of whom thrive on wild sand eels. It's inefficient, too – 3 kilos of wild fish, for example, are required to make the pellets to produce 1 kilo of farmed salmon flesh. But one particular use of sand eels seems to us sheer ecological insanity: in the 1980s and early 1990s the Danish government found themselves with so much surplus sand eel oil that they used to burn it in their power stations.

It seems almost self-evidently wrong to use fish to fuel a furnace. But it wasn't until 1996 that public outrage, harnessed by environmental campaigning groups including Greenpeace, brought an end to the practice of turning fish into electricity.

The long-term implications of taking such vast quantities of bait fish out of the food chain are impossible to measure. When assessing falling cod stocks, for example, how do you distinguish between the effect of catching fish by the thousands of tonnes and the effect of catching their lunch in even greater masses? You can't – but clearly there will be an effect.

Until recently, there was scant public awareness about the plight of sand eels and its ecological significance. The PR breakthrough came not from concerns about fish (a familiar tale this – see dolphins and tuna, page 451) but from concerns about another group of animals. Around 1995 the plummeting sand eel numbers were believed to be affecting the seabird population, especially around the east coast of Scotland. Certain colonies of kittiwakes and puffins seemed to be struggling to find food to raise their young; the RSPB, one of the most powerful charities in the world, was on the case in a flash. Questions were asked in the House of Lords, which subsequently led to significant areas of the sand eel fishery being closed altogether in 2000. It would be nice to think that the local cod population drew some benefit. But if they did, it was never intended. We're all for the conservation of seabirds – watching them fish more successfully than us is one of the pleasures of sea angling. But we absolutely do not see why their protection counts for more than the management of our fish stocks. Surely the conservation of species we like to eat is at least as important as the conservation of those we like to look at?

We say 'like to eat' but, as we have implied above, sand eel cuisine is not, in our view, the gastronomic heights. In French fish markets you'll often see a modest pile of dead sand eels offered alongside other small species as *fritures*, to be fried up like whitebait. Having tried this on sand eels, big and small – tossed in seasoned flour and fried in hot fat – we cannot get evangelical about them. They are soft and mushy, and surprisingly bony for their size. Getting them to crisp up, whitebait-style, is something of a struggle. In our view the best final resting place for a sand eel is not a human stomach, and certainly not the belching belly of a power station, but rather that of a cod, bass, pollack or salmon.

Freshwater fish

Salmon family

Salmon *Salmo salar*

The extraordinary and complex life cycle of the wild Atlantic salmon makes it an immensely impressive fish – but also a vulnerable one. Even as we have admired its greatness, we have inadvertently plotted its downfall. In fact, if we'd openly declared war on the fish, we could hardly have done a more thorough job – first almost annihilating wild stocks, then corralling fish into huge concentration camps – or fish farms, as they are known.

This may sound a tad melodramatic – but the history of salmon evokes passion. Here in northern Europe, the war against this fish has been waged for a century and a half. The industrial pollution of its river habitat and systematic harvesting of wild fish from the sea, estuary and river have taken a massive toll. Salmon stocks are now thought to be at a quarter of their pre-industrial abundance.

A new front opened up in the latter part of the twentieth century, as the farming of salmon became a major economic enterprise. At the time, it was vehemently argued that this could only benefit wild stocks of fish. It hasn't. Fish farming has led directly to the spread of sea lice, and to fungal infections that have killed wild fish in their tens of thousands. The farmed fish are inoculated against such problems (through additives in their feed); wild stocks, obviously, are not. And the pollution of sea lochs, by rotting fish food, fish excrement and fish-farming chemicals, has had a devastating effect on local ecosystems.

To cap it all, escaped farmed fish (up to half a million a year in Scotland alone) have crossbred with wild fish, leading to the dilution of 'river specific' stocks of salmon. Ever since the retreat of the ice sheets, wild salmon have been subtly adapting to the individual rivers in which they are born, and to which they return. Adding farmed-fish DNA to the mix is messing with 10,000 years of fish evolution. It's still not clear what the effect of these maladapted, crossbred fish will be on the future of salmon stocks.

The natural life cycle of the wild salmon places enough obstacles in the path of its survival. Faced with such man-made meddling on top, you might think it's a wonder there's a salmon left anywhere on the planet. But salmon are epic survivors, and their future doesn't look entirely gloom-laden. Their resilience comes from the extraordinary journey that is the story of every salmon's life.

The curse of the wild salmon is that it can successfully spawn only right up in the tiny, clean, bubbling, oxygen-rich streams at the head of their river, where shallow gravel beds provide the cool, aerated environment essential for eggs to grow. They'll hatch from eggs laid in these tiny tributaries, move down into larger tributaries that feed into fatter rivers, such as the Blackwater in Ireland, the Tweed in Scotland, the Wye in Wales and the Exe down here in the West Country. They hatch from their eggs in spring and live off their nutritious egg sac for a few weeks before starting to forage on their own. It takes this tiny newborn (called

MCS RATINGS: wild 5 DON'T EAT!; conventionally farmed 3; organically farmed 2 EAT MORE!

REC MINIMUM SIZE: 70cm

CLOSED SEASON: generally November–January in England and Northern Ireland, mid-October to mid-March in Wales, and December in Scotland

RECIPES: pages 133, 134–5, 138, 143, 281–2, 340–1, 355, 378, 387, 393, 403 et al.

an 'alevin') about three years of feeding on tiny aquatic insects to develop into a 'smolt': a hand-sized silver fish with black spots on its back and sides.

They grow so slowly because food is limited in British rivers, especially through the winter months when aquatic insect life is in short supply. In order to pack on the pounds and become hefty great fish, these puny smolts have to undergo a life-threatening transformation – because the food that will make real salmon of them is out at sea. Sand eels, herring, capelin, prawns, squid and crabs are the high-protein foods that can transform 20cm runts into fish that weigh up to 30 kilos and stand as tall as a man. So the smolts will swim downstream, in the river that has been their home since birth, into the estuary – the threshold to their impending greatness. But before the would-be salmon can reach the seafood banquet, it has to make the transition from fresh, sweet river water to harsh, salty seawater. It is one of an elite group of fish that are 'anadramous' – able to pass from one aquatic atmosphere to another. The change is severe: the salts in seawater attack the tissues, eyesight and gills, leaving the tiny fish weak and disorientated at the most crucial moment of its life. The mortality rate is correspondingly massive: from every 5,000 eggs laid, only fifty smolts will make it to the sea.

The lucky ones – or perhaps the brilliant ones – will have survived the journey downriver, past pike, eels, otters, mink, herons, cormorants and everything else keen to dine on fresh smolt. It will have resisted the trauma of salt water. And it will be ready to attempt the journey of several hundred miles to the salmon feeding grounds just west of Greenland or in the North Norwegian Sea.

After one to three (or even sometimes four) years of dining on sand eels, squid and prawns, fully-fledged adult salmon may weigh anything from 3 to 30 kilos. They'd better be fully fit, because they now have to embark upon an even more strenuous journey, from the deep northern sea all the way back to the same tiny tributary in which they were born. And this time they're travelling upstream.

The miracle – or madness – of a salmon's life cycle is that this fish, having experienced the death-defying danger of escaping its river environment to take its chances at sea, now has to make precisely the same journey – in reverse. Only now it's not 20cm long, running downstream with the flow, it's 60–120cm long, struggling over rocks, against the current, up rapids and even waterfalls. But it *has* to go back, or it will never reproduce.

How a salmon manages to navigate across an open ocean to the same estuary mouth that it left several years before is still a mystery. It's widely believed that they possess some incredibly accurate receptors that can sense tiny differences in the earth's magnetic field, and perhaps also in water quality, and that they use these as a homing device. But the honest truth is, nobody really knows.

Its size gives it the strength and stamina it needs but makes it no less vulnerable to predators. On the contrary, it's now the king of edible fish, the best pack of protein in the sea, and it's worth the most strenuous efforts of the sea's finest predators – seals, sharks, whales, dolphins, otters and even eagles – to try to catch one. But the most vigorous and deadly efforts come from humankind, to whom a fresh wild salmon is currently worth around £30 per kilo – or maybe five times that, served up in a fancy restaurant.

Trawl nets, drift nets, gill nets, haaf nets, ring nets and poacher's fish traps… these are just some of the death-dealing obstacles that have been put in the path of the salmon as they home in on the mouths of the rivers of their birth. At best, only five of the fifty smolts that originally survived (from the 5,000 eggs laid) will ever return to the river – which is where their problems *really* begin. They return in the spring and summer when river levels are often at their lowest. But these huge fish require a reasonable depth of water to swim in. Often they are kept waiting for weeks, stuck in shallow, stagnating pools, for rain to come and fill the river before they can continue on their way. Dams, weirs, lock gates and pumping stations will also obstruct their passage. As a result of continued pressure by salmon preservation groups, salmon 'ladders' and even cage-like lift devices have been installed to transport them upstream. But such 'luxuries' merely transform their journey from the impossible to the miraculous.

Like all great missions, there's a deadline. Salmon have to get all the way up to these streams before autumn turns to winter. To make matters worse, they stop eating as soon as they enter fresh water. Even if it takes months of waiting for rains to swell the river to make it navigable, they won't eat a morsel for sustenance. Their quest requires total focus; hunting or feeding would simply waste time and energy. The salmon will even begin to digest its own muscle tissue and bones; every nutrient is directed towards the development of the all-important eggs or sperm. As they ripen, the salmon withers. And yet still it's capable of leaping waterfalls, climbing rapids and scurrying through stony shallows no more than a couple of inches deep – just to reach the very same spot where its mother laid the egg from which it hatched. Then it has to find a mate.

By the time they arrive they are wasted, covered in fungus and scars, and very weak. Once they have laid their eggs or delivered their sperm, most will die. Only an average of 5 per cent will ever make it back to the sea, for a slim chance of healing themselves and growing strong again. An infinitesimally small elite may even breed again. The rest will do so only once, before succumbing to predators, disease or exhaustion.

Now for the promised good news: our unwitting war on the salmon is finally abating – it seems we may be capable of calling a truce. In Britain, a century and a half of industrial poisoning of our river courses is gradually being reversed. Those who for generations have set coastal salmon nets in the North Atlantic have finally responded to the radical new policy of 'buying out' (or perhaps 'selling off'?) their rights to fish. Through the actions of various fishery boards and international bodies such as the North Atlantic Salmon Conservation Organisation, they are now being paid not to catch salmon – giving migrating fish a better chance of re-entering the rivers and breeding.

The last three years on the Tweed have been the best on record, with rod catches around the 14,000 mark, of which over half are now returned as part of the conservation effort. The Tyne is currently the most productive salmon river in England – whereas in the 1970s its salmon stock was almost extinct. Salmon stocks are recovering in the Clyde, the Severn and the Thames, and in many previously industrialised streams all over Britain. Given a chance, they will recover and perform.

Yet despite these signs of hope, the wild salmon population is, at best, fragile in most European rivers. Eating wild salmon is a contentious act. Even the most fanatical salmon anglers – in fact, especially the most fanatical anglers – return almost all the fish they catch to the river alive. Their prize may be the occasional cock fish – the logic being that any gravid hen (pregnant female ready to spawn) who gets as far as a viable redd (spawning place) is unlikely to be short of male companions ready to offer their sperm. As with many threatened species, conservation of breeding females takes precedence.

You could argue (and we would) that the only people entitled to eat a wild salmon are those who are actively engaged in their conservation. If you want to join their ranks, either as an angler or simply as a concerned conservationist, you should contact the Association of Rivers Trusts (ART) in England and Wales or the Rivers and Fisheries Trusts of Scotland (RAFTS) – see the Directory, page 592. Then, once in a while, you may feel entitled, through the knowledge you've acquired and the commitment you've made, to kill, buy or eat a wild salmon.

Dare we put ourselves in this category? Perhaps writing this book has earned us a portion or two. We love to fish for salmon, and grab any chance we get. But success is rare. Through the sheer enthusiasm with which we regularly fail to catch them, I think we're entitled to call ourselves salmon conservationists.

The obvious alternative is farmed salmon, of course. It's a whole different subject and, as we've touched on above, a controversial one. It's also a whole different – and lesser – eating experience. Since it is such a key part of the fish economy, and such a critical issue in the environmental impact of fish production, we've already said plenty about it in our discussions on fish farming (see pages 35–9). But we'll summarise here, for reasons outlined there: if you're going to buy farmed salmon, make it organic.

In the kitchen, you'd be ill advised to do anything too elaborate with a wild (or organically farmed) salmon. A fillet with the scaled skin on, fried until that seasoned skin is crispy, then turned to the flesh side for just a minute (so verging on rare in the middle), is perhaps the best way to enjoy the flesh cooked. Poached and then served cold (page 355), with mayonnaise, appeals to traditionalists. If you've managed to build a cold smoker at home (see pages 161–6) and you rate its performance, then at least once in your smoking lifetime you'll want to put it to the ultimate test: smoking a whole side from a fresh wild salmon, just in from the sea. And, if your smoker comes up trumps, you may well enjoy one of the most exquisite treats of your fish-eating career.

Sea trout *Salmo trutta*

Here's an enigma. Sea trout look just like salmon; even experienced anglers find it hard to distinguish between the two. And they behave like salmon, migrating between fresh water and the sea. Yet sea trout are a quite distinct species – distant cousins only of the salmon (with which they are incapable, for example, of interbreeding).

Here's another enigma. Sea trout look nothing like the river-dwelling brown trout, which are bronze rather than silver, covered with a sprinkling of ruby-red spots, and usually much smaller. Yet a sea trout, taxonomically, actually *is* a brown trout. In fact, all sea trout and all brown trout start their lives as the same thing: *Salmo trutta* eggs. After hatching, some will remain in fresh water as brown trout, while others head out to sea and a quite different destiny – which is why we have two entries for the same species (see also pages 515–18).

You'd think it might be timing or geography that determines the future life story of any given *Salmo trutta*, but it's subtler than that. Two trout eggs laid side by side from the same mother at the same moment, in the spawning beds of the same river, may be destined for totally different futures. The eggs hatch, they mature into fry, and become 'parr', all at exactly the same time. But then, within a year or two of birth, one parr might be behaving brown troutishly, living and feeding inland, in fresh water, while its sibling, though it still looks like a brown trout, begins to change into a sea trout. There are many factors that determine which direction a little *Salmo trutta* will take – environment, the amount of food available, and an element of genetic predisposition. But to the casual observer, it's an unpredictable and mysterious toss-up.

Before it even leaves the river and heads to the ocean, the soon-to-be sea trout will start to 'silver up' – an ingot of bronze dashed with rubies becoming a bar of polished platinum subtly speckled with black. Then, when it enters the estuary and meets salt water for the first time, the trout has to perform the complicated biological somersault of all anadromous fish (those born in fresh water who migrate to sea to feed and then return to fresh water to spawn). It grows salt glands in its gills to cope with the increased salinity that would otherwise quickly kill it. And it starts to hanker after seafood.

Two or three years later, those two siblings are living very different lives. The brown trout, having not moved more than a mile from where it was born, weighs anywhere from 100–600g. The sea trout, which by now tips the scales

MCS RATINGS: line-caught 4; organically farmed 2

REC MINIMUM SIZE: 40cm (but check local regulations)

CLOSED SEASON: generally November–March

RECIPES: pages 172, 220, 281–2, 308–9, 355 et al.

at anywhere up to 9kg, is meanwhile many miles away, searching the wide ocean for protein-packed prawns, crabs, small fish and squid. The sea trout will continue to grow at a rate of one or two kilos a year, while the stay-at-home brownie, who has a more frugal diet of tiny aquatic insects, may remain a stunted sprat all his life.

One thing we do know about these two siblings is that the adventurous sea-faring one is much more likely to be female. The seafood diet is good for growth and fecundity, and the most successful females eventually grow into magnificent sleek silver torpedoes of anything up to 10kg. Meanwhile the males, waiting for another drowned fly and reluctant to move even as far as the next downstream pool, are lucky to put on 50g a year. But oddly enough, female sea trout and male brownies may yet come together to breed. Since a disproportionate amount of sea trout are female, they inevitably accept as their mates small brown trout who have never gone to sea – in other words, the fit female supermodels are content to be served by the runty little males. Which is somehow consoling.

Generally, sea trout don't venture nearly so far as salmon in their maritime mission to gain weight and become healthy breeders. British-born salmon will range several hundred miles to the seas off Greenland (see page 508), whereas the latest research suggests that most sea trout stay within a radius of fifty or so miles from the estuary of their river of birth. All but a tiny fraction of the salmon who migrate to Greenland only ever do the journey and the re-entry to fresh water once. Most of them die after spawning. Sea trout, on the other hand, by staying local are able to shuttle back and forth from river to sea quite regularly. And so they can spawn several times – in some cases over a dozen.

In many ways, sea trout should be the more plentiful of the two species. They don't submit themselves to the same levels of stress and danger and they are, in theory, more adaptable to anadromous change, simply because they 'practise' it more often. Yet in recent years the sea trout populations around our coast have been falling at an alarming rate.

One of the identified causes of sea trout decline is the salmon. Not wild, but farmed. One drawback to farming salmon (there are quite a few – see page 508) is the vast number of sea lice a concentration of caged salmon will attract. Migrating sea trout increasingly have to run the gauntlet of nearby salmon farms, and the resident lice love to hitch a ride on a passing sea trout. These parasites do rapid damage to their host fish, sucking nutrients through its skin, leaving it weakened and covered in sores. Already weak from the stress of moving from salt to fresh water, sea trout succumb easily. Fatalities in some areas are reckoned to be in the thousands – and most, of course, are females who were looking to get back to the river and breed.

When not under pressure from sea lice and the like, sea/brown trout can breed and spread extremely successfully. In Argentina, Chile and New Zealand, where British brown trout eggs were seeded in the late nineteenth century (see page 516), they have flourished and, by virtue of their double life as sea trout, successfully populated other rivers adjacent to the ones into which they were introduced. Unlike salmon, sea trout are quite broadminded about the fresh water they return to in order to breed in. Since they have several chances at spawning, tactically it makes sense to ring the changes, spreading their genes through different rivers in the same area. Southern hemisphere sea trout have grown huge – the record in Argentina stands at over 15 kilos – and even the landlocked brownies, whose food supply tends to be far richer than that of their European cousins, can reach 10 kilos and more (in Britain, only farmed and ferox brownies ever get close to this kind of size).

One thing that can be said of all sea trout is that they are truly delicious. They are not as rich and oily as a salmon fresh in from the sea; they have lighter, paler flesh with a more delicate flavour and finer texture. They are more 'sea fresh', though, than brown or rainbow trout, without a trace of muddiness. When we have a plump sea trout of over a kilo in our hands, there aren't many fish we'd swap it for. Whether fried (pages 308–9) or baked (page 220), very lightly cured (page 172) or even completely raw (page 134), it will be a matchless treat.

You could argue that a species under pressure should not be caught and eaten at all. At the same time, as with salmon, those who love to catch and cook these wild fish are often those working hardest to protect them. It seems harsh to begrudge them the occasional fish for the table. We have a good relationship with the Axe Valley Fly Fishers' Association, which is working hard to improve spawning conditions in the lower reaches of the Axe, Yarty and other local rivers. They are looking at the streams on our land at River Cottage HQ to see if they might make a suitable site for hatching boxes (artificial shelters that improve the survival rate of the newly hatched fish). In return, we get the odd evening's fishing – though neither of us has yet managed to land an Axe sea trout.

Fresh wild sea trout isn't easy to buy and, given current anxieties about stocks, nor should it be. In the West Country we see them occasionally in fishmongers during the summer months. The returning fish are usually caught in gill nets as they enter the estuaries. They are often outstanding value: a fraction of the price of wild salmon and every bit as good. We'd sympathise if you felt unable to resist buying the odd one. Line-caught fish, if you can find them, would be preferable. Should you feel the need to appease your conscience after such a treat, you could always make a donation to the Atlantic Salmon Trust (atlanticsalmontrust.org), since their conservation work encompasses sea trout as well as wild salmon.

Farmed sea trout are increasingly coming on to the market. Some argue that they are better suited to life in a sea cage than salmon are. Others who champion the wild sea trout emphatically disagree. As with any type of fish farming, it's the source and content of the feed, the location of the farm and the quality of the water that determines how environmentally friendly (and indeed how tasty) that fish will be. With farmed fish, you really should find out what you are buying before you hand over your money (see page 38).

But the best sea trout you'll ever eat – and arguably the only one you *should* eat – is the fish you have caught yourself. Most sea trout are caught in rivers by fly-fishing. They're not easy to catch (although often easier than sulky salmon) and it's best to fish for them at and after nightfall, as they're easily spooked during the day. Casting a fly rod at night in a river surrounded by trees is often fraught with pain, grief and fairly profane swearing. But should you actually manage to catch, cook and eat a sea trout, you'll remember all that misery and suffering as some of the best fun you've ever had fishing.

Brown trout *Salmo trutta*

While Queen Victoria sat on the throne, her armed forces were on the march, painting the map of the world pink. For good or ill, they carried with them the values of colonialism – and some big boxes of brown trout eggs.

Back home in Britain, the noble sport of fly-fishing for trout was in its infancy. Hitherto, catching trout and other freshwater fish by rod and line had involved the use of natural bait. A worm, a maggot, a slug or a grasshopper threaded on to a hook would, of course, tempt a fish, because these are the things a fish likes to eat. But in the mind of a gentleman, this was so obvious and easy as to be unsporting. Surely a fairer challenge would be to fashion something by hand that *looked* like a trout's lunch. For example, to tie together scraps of fur and feather to imitate a daddy longlegs with such accuracy that a brown trout was duped into swallowing it – now *that* would require skill and intellect.

To master this new art, the budding fly fisherman would need a grasp of entomology and an understanding of trout feeding habits, as well as some insight into light levels and water quality. He would need to study books, to keep journals and to have enough expendable income to afford state-of-the-art fly tackle, which was at that time in limited supply and very labour-intensive to manufacture. Using the latest rods made of bamboo canes that had been split, whittled and reassembled, fly lines made out of pure woven silk and clear tippet lines made from catgut, the aspiring fly-angler would present his hand-tied artificial lure to the fish.

Naturally many such gentlemen were serving officers in Her Majesty's Army, charged with the vital work of defending and extending the Empire. But the prospect of being posted to some far-off land where their beloved trout didn't exist filled them with dismay. So why not take the brown trout with them?

MCS RATINGS: line-caught 4; organically farmed 2

REC MINIMUM SIZE: 25cm (but check local regulations)

CLOSED SEASON: generally 1 October to 14 March

RECIPES: pages 134–5, 200, 244, 403 et al.

The plan was to introduce them to likely looking rivers and lakes around the colonies. But it soon became clear that the fragile fish would not travel well; their eggs, on the other hand, were a different matter. Refrigerated transport and electric circulation pumps – vital tools of modern fish farming and live egg transportation – were as yet uninvented. But what this madcap scheme had on its side was the full logistical resources of the British Civil Service, coupled to the determination of some deeply competitive individuals. The race – to find a method that would keep the eggs alive during sea voyages of several months – was on.

Scottish trout from Loch Leven were chosen because they were known to be a hardy breed that could survive cold winters and scant food. Their fertilised eggs, gathered from the spawning burns that fed the loch, were gently packed between layers of damp, living moss for the long journey. The moss was stacked in custom-built wooden crates with drainage holes top and bottom, into which fresh water, filtered through charcoal, was poured daily. The living eggs were developing into tiny trout even as they crossed the world.

The first successful acclimatisation took place in India in 1863, followed by Tasmania in 1864, elsewhere in Australia and New Zealand in 1867. South Africa and Canada, Chile and Argentina were soon colonised too. Within twenty years, the small, ruby-spotted Scottish strain of wild brown trout had spread to every continent of the world bar Antarctica. And the European sea trout had hitched a ride too – being, genetically, the same species, how could it not?

In truth, some of these trout actually preferred their new homes. They thrived in waters that, though similarly cool and clear, were far more abundant in food than the dour Scottish lakes and rivers from whence they came. They also often benefited from an absence of predators and disease. In the Southern hemisphere there were no salmonid competitors – just a variety of rather placid bottom-feeders that posed little threat to the arrivistes. In Scotland, to catch a brown trout of even 5lb was (and still is) exceptional. But in New Zealand, within a dozen years of introduction, fish of 20lb and more were being recorded. In British waters, until recently, only the ferox strain of brown trout ever attained anything like that kind of size – a 10 to 15lb fish being the catch of a lifetime. These ferox trout are wild fish that have grown large enough to take on other small fish as prey, and so achieve the potential to grow much larger. Mostly they cannibalise their own kin – smaller brown trout, which are sometimes the only other fish in the water they inhabit. Today, farmed brownies can also be reared to this kind of size, simply by fattening them up on pelleted fish food. They are released into commercial fisheries, often along with similarly bloated rainbows, where anglers will pay for the chance to catch a double-figure fish. But it's not what a Victorian gentleman would have called sport.

As brown trout thrived around the world, they started to struggle at home. The Industrial Revolution brought terrible pollution to our inland waterways – and brown trout are particularly sensitive. They need clean, well-oxygenated water in order to survive. In many ways they are the canary in the watery coal mine – if brown trout turn belly up, then other species will soon follow suit.

The good news is that, after suffering over a century of pollution, our native wild brown trout are on the up again. De-industrialisation and strict legislative action against polluters mean that our waterways are now the cleanest they have been for over 150 years. Once again, brown trout are populating rivers where they hadn't been caught in over a century. They can do this because of their double life as sea trout – fish that leave one river to feed at sea may return to spawn in another (see page 514). Some of the resulting progeny will become the river's resident brownies, and may never go out to sea. Sea trout have recently been caught in the Thames in central London – and wild brownies found a hundred or more miles upstream in places like Lechlade.

It is the larger, female sea trout, returning to the river systems, that will be the most successful breeders, and their eggs may well be fertilised by 'local' male brownies who have never left the river (of the resulting progeny, only a few, mostly females, will go out to sea). However, amongst landlocked populations of brown trout, such as those in Scottish hill lochs, even fairly tiny females (of no more than half a pound) will develop and lay eggs.

Those brown trout that have settled for the freshwater life are pretty fiercely territorial. In rivers, they compete to take possession of a specific 'lie' – a strategic position in the current, in the lee of a rock or bend perhaps, to provide them with maximum security and maximum feeding potential. Once a fish has found a good 'lie', it will hold it for days, or even weeks, until it is forced away by a bigger fish or a predator. It will position itself with its head facing upstream, gills flaring to extract oxygen from the running water. Trout don't so much 'hunt' for their food as station themselves in the spot where an insect lunch is most likely to be served up on the passing current. They'd rather not move more than a few feet to grab it (and their eye sockets can swivel upwards to spot any food being carried past in the current). This all adds to the art of catching them. First you need to spot your fish. You may need to stalk it, to get within casting range. You then have to choose a convincing-looking fly and cast it to land in a natural manner within the feeding zone of your chosen fish. You can perhaps sense the thrill of this kind of fishing – it is, after all, the reason that brown trout have spread all over the world.

We love catching wild brown trout and we love eating them. But in many truly wild fisheries, particularly among the chalk streams here in the Southwest (such as the Piddle, the Puddle and the Stour), most fish are returned to the water alive in the interests of conservation. Taking one or two good fish for the pot per season is an honoured convention in many club-run fisheries. The mayfly hatch is the most exciting time to fish. For several weeks in late May and early June, these ephemeral insects, with their errant wings and fat, long bodies, emerge in such numbers that the trout lose all sense of caution and are moved to a feeding frenzy. The trout can still be heart-stoppingly hard to hook, though. Such is the generosity of the natural banquet that the artificial imitations have to look, and land, just right if they're going to persuade.

We probably get to catch more brownies on Scottish holidays than in Dorset downtime. It's particularly good fun fishing with imitation daddy longlegs on wild Scottish hill lochs. Here the fish are often small but plentiful – they breed successfully, but lack the food supply to maintain a weight much over half a pound. There is generally quite a relaxed take on killing these fish for the kitchen.

The brown trout that you find on sale (at fishmongers, supermarkets and by mail order) will invariably have been farmed. Truly wild brown trout are generally too small (and too difficult to catch) to find their way on to a wet fish counter; even at 3 to 5 years old, a wild brown trout will often weigh well under a pound. But farmed brownies can be delicious, especially if they've been reared in a location where they can feed on some natural aquatic insect life as well as their processed pellets (which is much more likely to be the scenario in an organic trout farm). There is no real difference in eating quality between a farmed brown and a farmed rainbow trout – in both cases it's the quality of the farming practice that counts (see below).

A genuinely wild brown trout is an even better prospect in the kitchen. Its taste will reflect the quality of the water from which it has been taken – clean as flint if it comes from a Dorset chalk stream; lightly peaty if it comes from a Highland burn or hill loch. Those that have been feeding on freshwater shrimps (mainly summer fish caught in the south of England) have a distinctive pink-orange flesh and are the tastiest of all.

They're easy to cook – by pan, barbecue, or wrapped in foil and baked in the oven. Bigger isn't always better either. If you're lucky enough to get a chance to fish on one of those Scottish hill lochs we mentioned, then treat yourself to a pair of little brownies. Rolled in oatmeal, then fried in butter or bacon fat, there's no better angler's breakfast.

The only trout that'll top a wild brownie for taste is a wild sea trout. As it happens to be exactly the same species, biologically speaking, perhaps that's no surprise. See pages 512–15 for more on what happens when a brown trout embarks on this extraordinary biological adventure.

Rainbow trout *Oncorhynchus mykiss*

While brown trout are seen as a noble, honourable member of the salmonid family – a fabulous British colonial gift to the world (see pages 515–16) – rainbow trout are not always spoken of with such admiration, either by anglers or by chefs. To many they are flashy, garish American invaders who give trout a bad name: they're oversexed, oversized and over here. And the fact that they often taste muddy doesn't help their cause.

But in truth, any problems we have with them are largely of our own making. They are only here because of the trout angler's lack of patience with our native brown trout, which, for all their pedigree, can be moody, awkward little buggers. When conditions don't suit them, they will sulk in deep water, eating nothing and avoiding eye contact with even the most artfully tied fly. In contrast, rainbow trout are usually enthusiastic and obliging, ready to snap at almost anything.

Consequently, almost all commercial trout fisheries – where fly fishermen pay to come and fish for stocked, rather than wild, trout – will keep some rainbows as well as browns. So when it's too hot, too cold or too something-you-can't-quite-put-your-finger-on for the brownies to bite, the rainbows, with a bit of luck, will still come out to play.

This mix-and-match approach to stocking our lakes and rivers began in the mid-nineteenth century. At the same time as Britain was exporting brown trout to the far corners of the Empire, it was also importing rainbow trout from their native west coast of America. In 1854 the first boxes of rainbow trout eggs were brought to Britain by steamships and seeded in lakes and rivers. They survived, but never really thrived. It soon became apparent that rainbow trout would struggle to breed naturally in Britain, mainly because our average water temperatures are too cold. Whilst rainbows will feed, grow and stay healthy in relatively cold water, for breeding they like it a bit warmer than we can

MCS RATINGS: organically farmed 1; farmed 3

REC MINIMUM SIZE: 25cm (only relevant for wild fish)

CLOSED SEASON: no compulsory UK closed season (but check local regulations); avoid October–December (spawning)

RECIPES: pages 134–5, 200, 220, 244, 403 et al.

generally muster. And so, apart from a few rare resident breeding populations (for example, in the Derbyshire Wye and the Erfon in Wales), every single rainbow trout in Britain has been artificially bred.

Initially rainbows were bred purely for sporting purposes. The first commercial fish farm in the UK, breeding plate-sized rainbows for the 'table market', was started in 1950. Now there are over 350 trout farms nationwide, producing rainbows for food as well as for stocking and restocking our sporting fisheries.

The market for farmed rainbow trout for eating has seen a steady increase over the decades. But the quality of such fish varies hugely, depending, as you might expect, on the way in which they are farmed. Freshwater fish will always taste of the water in which they live. So when rainbows are crammed into small, muddy ponds, which soon become polluted with their own excrement and uneaten food that sinks to the bottom, it's no great surprise that they'll end up tasting mucky. In contrast, spring-fed, gravel-bottomed ponds, where the water is constantly changed and naturally filtered, will produce far sweeter-tasting fish, provided they are not overstocked.

The Soil Association now certifies organically farmed rainbows. It stipulates strict limits on stocking densities and the use of chemicals and insists on additive-free, sustainably sourced fish feed. One excellent trout farm in Wiltshire, Purely Organic (see the Directory, page 591), from which we regularly buy fish, has holding ponds downstream from an organic watercress farm. So, apart from the pellet feed they receive, the trout also have freshwater shrimps, snails and insects washed downstream to them from the watercress beds. The farm's owner, Tony Free, reckons that well over half their feed comes from this natural source. This kind of mutual back-scratching, fish-and-food-farming relationship is exactly the kind of aquaculture that makes sense to us. More power to you, Mr Free.

If you're going to dine on rainbow trout (and we'd recommend you do), we think you should find out where your fish was farmed and what it was fed on. Unfortunately, farmed fish provenance is generally invisible. It requires good labelling, or a knowledgeable fishmonger, to tell you the story of the fish you're thinking of buying. Such guidance is not always easy to come by – particularly in a supermarket. You should always press for it, but if you can't get it you can at least look hard at your trout…

There are some visible clues that will tell you what sort of a farm life your trout lived. Check the fins and tail. If the fins are worn and split, or bloody, then the fish have been cramped and badly handled. Tails should have sharp edges. If the tail or fins are rounded and stubby, they've been worn away by frequent rubbing against net mesh – in other words, the fish have been kept in a very confined space. Any lumps or fungus in the gills or sores on the head or flanks are also a sign of poor water quality and/or overstocking.

Meanwhile, the fly fisherman's appetite for the feisty rainbow is now on the decline and so, correspondingly, are stocking rates in our fisheries. This is due to a sort of sporting snobbery, borne of a desire to turn the clock back to a time when only pure, native trout roamed our rivers. It's a bit like the current trend for chopping down all the Norwegian pine forests that were planted in the 1970s and replacing them with broad-leaf, indigenous trees. One can understand these purist sentiments. And perhaps it's right to phase out the stocking of these American-spawned salmonid in some of our more historic rivers, such as the Test and the Itchen. But a shift in conservation sensibilities doesn't make a spruce a 'bad' tree, or a rainbow trout a 'bad' fish.

On the contrary, rainbows are a great fish. We should be producing them to the highest possible quality, enjoying the sport they offer in our lakes and reservoirs and eating them with pleasure. They could hardly be more kitchen-friendly. Plate-sized rainbows are easy to cook by any of the obvious methods: baked in foil with butter, a splash of wine and a few herbs (page 220); fried to get the skin crispy (page 296); or barbecued. Bigger rainbows smoke and cure beautifully too: gravad trout and cold-smoked rainbows are two of our favourite ways of honouring any fish we catch that tip the scales at over 2 kilos.

So, let's call a truce and stop the rainbow bashing. On the end of our lines or in our kitchens, a well-fed rainbow from good, sweet water is always welcome – no matter which side of the Atlantic its forefathers came from.

Grayling *Thymallus thymallus*

There's a saying amongst purist, old-school trout anglers and river keepers: 'The only good grayling is a dead grayling.' There was a time, a couple of decades ago, when any grayling caught in the chalk-stream rivers of southern England was unceremoniously knocked on the head and, quite probably, tossed over the hedge. What a senseless waste of a fine sporting fish and its surprisingly palatable flesh.

From a trout-centric point of view, it's easy to see why grayling might have been unloved. For starters, they were aliens – at least to our southern chalk streams – having been introduced from northern English rivers. The Ouse system of East Yorkshire originally acquired its grayling via the Danube basin, courtesy of the last Ice Age. These grayling have been present in our northern rivers for many thousands of years; those in the south for just a couple of hundred.

Grayling breed like aquatic rabbits and lay up to three times as many eggs as trout. They also compete with trout for food but, being better equipped, they win. Grayling have a down-slung mouth and downward-swivelling eyes, so they can feed from the river bed as easily as from the surface. Trout have beady eyes too, and lightning reactions, but they aren't made to feed from the river bed. So, in a harsh winter, grayling will survive whilst trout go hungry or die. And among the things grayling will eat during lean times are trout eggs. To the fly fishermen, a fish that snacks upon the unborn progeny of the hallowed trout is just too evil. Because of this, the closed season for trout was traditionally open season for grayling. River keepers would net them and electro-fish for them (along with the equally loathed pike), in the hope of giving the trout an easier ride, come spring.

However, this wasn't just river management, this was snobbery, fuelled by the fact that, as well as being alien to southern rivers, grayling were also classified (erroneously, as it later turned out) as a 'coarse' fish in the 1878 Freshwater Act. Technically, coarse fish are generally non-migratory fish such as perch, roach, pike or carp that spawn in the spring, whereas game fish are the salmonid species – trout, salmon and the char of the Lake District – that spawn in the autumn and, given the opportunity, migrate to the sea. But in truth, the distinction is a human one. In practical terms, coarse fish are freshwater fish that ordinary rod-and-line anglers like to catch, using simple, natural baits, such as live worms or maggots. Game fish, on the other hand, can – or rather should – be caught on a 'fly', which is a man-made confection of fur and feather that

MCS RATING: not rated
REC MINIMUM SIZE: 30cm
CLOSED SEASON: generally
15 March to 15 June
RECIPES: pages 200, 289, 330

imitates an aquatic creature. Once fly-fishing had been invented, coarse fishing was deemed crude and unsporting – suitable only for the working classes.

Grayling drew the wrath of the fly-fishing elite simply because it swam so happily in the same rivers as the trout. The fact that it would take a fly as readily as any trout did not seem to let it off the hook (so to speak) at least for a couple of centuries. It was the plebeian impostor, and was duly punished.

As if a class divide was not enough, the grayling also reflected the geographical one between north and south. Up north on the rivers of Yorkshire, Lancashire and Derbyshire, grayling enjoyed a more honourable reputation, even among the gentry. This was no doubt partly because they are meant to be there. Northern coarse and fly anglers on rivers such as the Wharfe, Ure and Swale were content to catch them, each by their own methods, and they loved and respected grayling, calling it 'the lady of the stream'. They still do to this day.

In the last twenty years or so, the southern attitude towards grayling has softened. The bad habit of culling them by all available means has been reassessed. Indeed, grayling has been reclassified since the original Freshwater Act, and now enjoys the distinction of being 'the fourth game fish' (after salmon, sea trout and trout). Apart from being ready to take a fly, all game fish have to display an adipose fin – a small, nub-like bump, located between the dorsal fin and the tail. Happily the grayling does. It is now officially a member of the sacred Salmonidae family. And it's been welcomed into polite society.

It's certainly dressed for social elevation. The outstanding feature of the grayling is its stunning sail-like, rainbow-speckled dorsal fin. It's not just for show, though, it's highly functional. It helps a fish hold station in a fast-flowing stream; it can 'bristle' an alarm to the rest of the shoal; and it can tenderly wrap over the back of a mate during spawning, to maximise fertilisation potential.

Whenever we fish for grayling, simply seeing one in the water, sail flaring as you try to bring it to the bank, is a great part of the pleasure of the day. And so is taking one or two home for supper. They can be cooked as you'd cook trout. We've smoked them, both hot and cold; we've baked, grilled and poached them too. We've had them hot topped with butter and toasted almonds, and cold with herby mayonnaise (see page 355). But perhaps the best grayling we ever shared was an early-spring fish from the River Wylie in Wiltshire. We sizzled it on the riverbank in a pan still greasy with sausage and bacon fat from our breakfast fry-up, then ate it scattered with just-picked, roughly chopped wild garlic leaves.

Other freshwater fish

Perch *Perca fluviatilis*

Perch are cheeky and gregarious fish, ducking and diving, bobbing and weaving, scheming and teaming up with their mates to traumatise the neighbourhood minnows. We're rather fond of perch – but not half as fond of them as they seem to be of themselves.

In their freshwater habitat of rivers, lakes and reservoirs, they are pretty much top dog. They know it, and have the uniform to show it: bright scarlet fins, black, warrior-like stripes down both flanks and an array of flesh-piercing spikes fanned through their fins. Only a pike, or a bigger perch, is likely to see them off (or have them for lunch).

If you watch the surface of a lake on a balmy summer's evening, you'll often see a frantic scattering of tiny, fry-sized fish leaping out of the water. These are juveniles (of any number of different species) being hunted by packs of omnivorous perch. These bullies corral the jittery juniors into cowering bunches and take it in turns to charge them with their gaping jaws and bristling spikes. Perch are, in their spiky, strutting way, very much the freshwater equivalent of their sea bass cousins. And they love doing to minnows exactly what bass do to sprats. So it should be no great surprise that, like bass, perch are really rather good to eat.

The Victorians loved to eat perch, which they ranked as high as any other freshwater fish. Favourite recipes of the day included Mrs Beeton's perch stewed with wine, and boiled perch with Dutch sauce. This fondness for perch may in part have been due to a perceived glut of salmon. Before the Industrial Revolution polluted our major rivers, salmon – hulking and plentiful – was considered a poor man's meal. Perch – small and colourful, with firm, pearly white flesh – was posh.

In fact, the Victorians held the perch in such esteem that it was the only fish, apart from their beloved brown trout, chosen to colonise the fresh waters of the expanding Empire (see pages 515–16). Cleverly transported as unhatched eggs in barrels of living wet moss, trout and perch were transplanted to the furthest corners of the globe.

The perch weren't always welcome. For example, in Australia, where they were introduced in 1860 as a sport and table fish, they ran amok. Within ten years the Inland Fisheries Service had declared them a 'noxious fish pest', because they had depleted, and in some cases eradicated, indigenous species. To this day, *Perca fluviatilis* is still near the top of Australia's most-hated-pest list. Huge populations of perch, stunted through overbreeding, now dominate waters that were once home to a diverse range of species.

Perch's gradual demise as an eating fish – in the face of ever-increasing competition from sea fish – was sealed by the Second World War. The best-known perch fishery, on Lake Windermere, had been trapping tons of fish each year,

MCS RATING: not rated
REC MINIMUM SIZE: 25cm
SEASON: avoid April–July (spawning)
RECIPES: pages 200, 289, 330

both for food and fertiliser. As the wartime scarcity of protein took hold, perch meat became commonplace. It was even tinned and re-branded as 'Windermere perchines', an austerity substitute for tinned sardines. But, as with so many of these make-do-and-pretend wartime foods, people came to resent them. Perch never recovered its former posh image – while our enthusiasm for cod was becoming a blinkered obsession. To cap it all, in the 1950s perch went on to suffer from a terrible plague that left the big Lake District populations reduced to a fraction of their previous size.

Perch today are in fine fettle again, with huge numbers in rivers, lakes and reservoirs all around Britain. Yet, like so many 'Great British Fish', actually buying a fresh perch to eat in this country is not easy. Markets such as Billingsgate do sell perch that has been netted from the Lake District or Ireland, but nearly all of it is exported to Europe. In Britain it's easier to buy a Nile perch, imported from Egypt, than it is to buy one of our own natives. By contrast, in northern European countries such as Finland and Sweden, native wild perch are still at the top of the locals' fish wish-list, prized even above trout and salmon. In Scandinavia, perch farming is a thriving form of aquaculture. It's worth noting that we have just the right conditions to do it here. Where are you, perch entrepreneurs?

Until we get a response to that rhetorical question, if you want to eat a perch, you'll just have to go and fish one out yourself. Patrolling their waters, as they do, in an ever-hungry rabble, they're not difficult to catch – at least until they grow big, solitary and wary. Three-quarter pounders, which make fabulous eating, can often be caught in good numbers, one after the other, if you find a good shoal and have the right bait.

Nearly every freshwater angler has caught a perch at some stage. Like mackerel, they are often the first fish a novice will catch. They're a classic 'bamboo-and-string-with-bent-pin-and-garden-worm' fish. They will eagerly attack a worm or maggot bait, and always put up a good fight, often coming reluctantly to the landing net with colours blazing and spikes flared indignantly. The best perch bait of all is minnow, either dead or alive. Minnows can be caught in simple traps made out of empty bottles that have been baited with bread. Fish them with a small treble hook under a float, or simply lying dead on the bottom, and await the attention of a hungry perch.

To cook your catch bankside, collect some wood and make a fire. As it burns down to hot embers, wrap each fish in a couple of pages of newspaper (two broadsheet, three tabloid) and dip them in the stream till the paper is thoroughly soaked. Place them on a grill and steam-bake over the fire (see page 200). When the paper is all but burned away, remove from the heat and cool for a minute or two. Then peel off the perch skin with the paper and season with a spot or two of butter, plus some salt and pepper. Get to it with fork or fingers and you'll soon see what the Victorians were excited about. And please call us when you've started your own perch farm.

Pike *Esox lucius*

Like so many predators that hang around at the top of the food chain, pike are bone idle. They may be hunters, but they're thrifty with their fuel. They want to avoid the vicious circle of constant hunting to replace the calories they just burned in the last hunt. And so, with their tiger-like green and gold camouflage, they are lurk-and-pounce merchants. They hang out among weeds and underwater obstacles, waiting for lunch to practically deliver itself.

The biggest and baddest pike are female. They live longer than males (to over thirty years, as opposed to the males' fifteen to twenty) and they grow much larger too. There's another reason male pike may well be cut off in their prime: mating. It's a risky business for him because when his job of fertilising the female's eggs is done, he stops looking like a potential father to her children and starts looking like a very tempting post-coital snack. From her point of view, it would be foolish to waste him.

Pike inhabit most forms of fresh water: rivers, gravel pits, lakes, reservoirs and ponds. They aren't fussy – they don't care if the water is clear or murky. Anglers like to say of pike that they 'thrive on neglect'. Before he saw the light and moved to Dorset, Nick regularly fished the ancient network of London canals and pulled out some deeply impressive pike (well in excess of 9 kilos) from amongst the shopping trolleys and joy-ridden scooters.

The biggest pike are the ones with easy access to the best food. In the last twenty years, increasing numbers of huge pike (13 kilos-plus) have been caught from large reservoirs that have been stocked with trout for angling. Providing a hungry pike with a constant diet of pellet-fed trout is a bit like feeding a sumo wrestler with fresh piglets on demand.

The angler's relationship with pike has changed over the centuries. Up until Victorian times the pike was regarded as a formidable sporting fish, being hard fighting yet co-operative: ready to attack a bait or lure in almost all weathers. Real fish baits – from small live roach to dead sprats or herrings – have always tempted pike. But the increasing sophistication of artificial lures, such as spinners, spoons and plugs, extended the culture of pike fishing into a wily art. It was also a culinary endeavour, since the flesh of the pike was highly rated as food. Pike was a noble fish pursued by both gentleman and yeoman.

MCS RATING: not rated

REC MINIMUM SIZE: N/A

CLOSED SEASON: generally 15 March to 15 June

RECIPES: pages 220, 281–2, 289, 330

Then the Victorians – at least the upper echelons – were seduced by a new development in angling: the art of dry fly-fishing for trout (for more, see page 515). The gentry turned its focus to managing rivers and chalk streams so that the wild brown trout could breed and grow with maximum mollycoddling and minimal molestation. As the principal trout killers, pike became *persona non grata*. In the hallowed fly-fishing rivers, such as the Test, Frome and Itchen, the pike culling began.

For most of the next century, trout fishermen were at war with the pike. They (or their river keepers) would net, gaffe, trap and catch them on night lines baited with minnows and the like. And instead of eating or selling them, they would usually throw them away with disdain. In any case, with the boom time in commercial fishing for species such as cod, herring and Dover sole, the public appetite was now for sea fish.

By the mid-twentieth century, even coarse anglers (who theoretically welcome all comers) had begun to persecute pike because they were known to devour roach, bream and all other freshwater fish. Coarse fishing was booming as a leisure activity. Gravel pits and reservoirs all over the country were increasingly run as coarse fisheries – a nice little earner, as they could charge anglers for day and season tickets. By the 1970s, up to four million people in Britain were regular anglers – more went coarse fishing on a Saturday than went to watch the football. But a rampant pike or two could easily ruin a fishery (or so it was widely believed at the time). Consequently, most anglers would kill any pike they caught by chance. Some fisheries turned to the relatively new techniques of electric fishing, by which all fish in a given strip of water are stunned with an electric current, so the less desirable species can be netted and removed. Soon some waters were even able to declare themselves completely pike-free.

The seeds of its rehabilitation were sown in the 1970s and 1980s, when 'specimen hunting' became increasingly popular. More and more fishermen began to pursue a single species. Size, of course, mattered. Carp was the obvious target, and soon became the focus of a deeply obsessed fraternity – some would say cult (see page 532). But pike, which could grow similarly huge, also got a look in. Pike-only anglers began hunting for ever-larger specimens, which they would weigh, photograph and return to the water alive.

At the same time as the offer of pike hunting became a potential source of income for fisheries, the effectiveness of culling pike was being challenged. It just didn't seem to work. Wherever big pike were being systematically slaughtered a pattern was emerging: within a year or two the same water would be riddled with small pike (pickerel). These were in fact much more destructive than a few big pike. Small pike eat fish eggs, fry and fingerling trout by the bucket load, whereas big pike can't be bothered. What a big pike really loves to eat, however, is little pike. And so fisheries learned to leave the big pike alone. The best way of managing the pike population, it turned out, was by leaving it to manage itself.

Pike and anglers get along much better now. In many well-stocked trout reservoirs, bailiffs recognise the benefits of having a pike population alongside their trout. Big pike keep the little pike numbers down, and also tidy up any dead or dying trout that might otherwise rot and contaminate the water. For all its hunting prowess and ambush tactics, the lazy pike is also a happy scavenger.

These days, as anglers take a broader view of the ecology of their sport, the pike is no longer a pariah. In fact, fly-fishing for pike, with big tinselly lures, is catching on. It provides welcome winter and early-spring sport when the trout are off limits. Yet pike is still not very welcome in the kitchen. Of the freshwater species, only trout, salmon and eels have kept their culinary cachet in the face of the ever-increasing supply of sea-caught fish – despite the fact that many freshwater species make excellent eating. Pike is undoubtedly among them; perch, carp, grayling and zander are, in our view, the other contenders.

On the continent, meanwhile, the culture of eating freshwater fish still thrives. Pike rates highly. *Quenelles de brochet* – light and moussey poached pike dumplings – is among the classics of French *haute cuisine*, and is often served with a crayfish sauce. The Germans like to stuff a whole pike with breadcrumbs, onions, herbs and spices and bake it. In fact, the continental appetite for pike has created some problems in international angling relations. Ireland has long been a mecca for British pike anglers. But in the 1990s the 'locals' were unsettled by an influx of German anglers coming to fish for 'their' pike. The 'invaders' arrived in their VW camper vans with battery-operated freezers so the pike they caught could be killed and taken home to eat. This drove the British pike guys mad. They like to catch, photograph, weigh (and even kiss) their fish before tearily releasing it back into the sweet Irish water, to be caught and kissed another day; and once a pike has been frozen by a German, this is hard to do. Now most Irish pike waters operate on a catch-and-release policy. Though some, mindful of alienating the Europeans, operate a very limited 'bag' system of, say, one pike of not more than 3 kilos per angler per week.

Pike do occasionally turn up dead at Billingsgate market, where they sell for £5–6 per kilo. A very few restaurateurs, keen to make more of our river fish, put them on their menus from time to time. Invariably they are either caught by the chefs or offered to them (perhaps in the hope of a meal) by local anglers. We've eaten pike cooked by Raymond Blanc at Le Manoir aux Quat' Saisons outside

Oxford. The fish came from the River Windrush, and he served them as *quenelles de brochet*. There's no doubt that river-caught pike taste better than lake or gravel pit fish, which can be muddy – the cleaner and sweeter the river, the cleaner and sweeter the flesh.

Once in a while we'll catch a pike from one of our Dorset chalk streams, such as the Piddle or the Puddle (whose crystal waters belie their ancient names). The best pike to kill for the pot is 2–4kg. This is primarily because it's a manageable size – neither too big to grapple with, nor too small and fiddly to fuss over. But also, from a conservation standpoint, it's unlikely to be top dog on its patch – so removing the odd one shouldn't upset the balance of the local habitat too much.

The first time you catch a pike ear-marked for the kitchen, do make sure you despatch it quickly and efficiently. Pike have an uncanny habit of 'waking up' in the kitchen sink several hours after they've been lightly flailed with a landing net handle. If you are going to kill one, make sure you use a proper heavy 'priest' or club (see page 53). And, for good measure, remove the guts at the riverbank, too. That should take care of it. Dealing with a sore, angry pike that has just woken up and is now breakdancing across your draining board is not a task for the fainthearted.

The one drawback of the pike as a table fish is its slightly fiddly bones. Forewarned is forearmed, though, so don't be put off. What you need to remember is that all along the prime meat of the pike's back is a series of two-pronged, pitchfork-like little bones – you'll find one between each distinct flake of meat. They are really not that hard to deal with, one at a time, even as you tackle the flesh on your plate.

Over the years we have honed a simple procedure for cooking a pike and getting several good meals out of it. We usually poach it in a fish kettle in a court-bouillon (pretty much as for a salmon or sea trout, see pages 281–2) – or, in the absence of a kettle, we'll bake it in foil with herbs, like a large bass (see page 220). The poaching liquid is then reduced by boiling, or the parcel juices simply collected and finished with a little cream to make a sauce. The next day, the remaining fish is flaked, boned and served cold, with a mustardy vinaigrette to which we'll add plenty of chopped parsley or chervil, or both. Any further leftovers will be used up in fishcakes (see page 330).

The pike's taste is quite distinctive – we'd say it has an edge of cucumbers and runner beans – which means it will never be in the 'also ran' or 'could-be-any-white-fish' category. It will taste of pike. We think every angler-cook should know that taste. And we think they'll like it.

Eel *Anguilla anguilla*

On moonless autumn nights, in streams, ponds and ditches throughout the land, an almighty slithering begins. In the Fenland drains and the Somerset Levels, in Highland burns and Welsh ditches, the shortening days are the trigger for big, dirty-yellow eels, with black eyes and nicotine-stained bellies, to up sticks. They leave their home water, slithering across wet grass if necessary, and slide into the nearest rain-swollen river, to embark upon a journey that seems implausible – even impossible.

All over Europe, the eels are mobilising. From the Rhine, the Loire, the Ebro and the Danube they are heading, at the same time, to the same place: a fabled body of water to the east of Bermuda, known as the Sargasso Sea.

The Sargasso is a sea within a sea, bounded by ocean currents: to the west by the Gulf Stream, to the north by the North Atlantic drift, to the east by the Canary current, and to the south by the North Atlantic equatorial current. It has its own counter-clockwise vortex, known as the Central Gyre, which can hold millions of tons of floating seaweed called sargassum, and other marine debris. Boats have often fallen foul of its strange forces. Spanish sailors travelling to and from the New World called these the 'Horse Latitudes', as those who got the worst of them were trapped in the vortex for weeks on end, and would slaughter their horses to conserve water and extend their rations. And it is to this place that every European eel heads, on a journey of thousands of miles, to find a mate and to perpetuate a species that is now in desperate decline.

What we know about eel spawning in the western Atlantic has only been understood for a matter of decades. Before then, our understanding of the sex life of the eel was largely conjecture (and fantasy) until the 1920s, when final proof, in the shape of minute, new-born eel larvae, was extracted from the depths of the Sargasso Sea. It's a complex tale and, if you fancy unravelling it some time, it's compellingly told in *The Book of Eels* by Tom Fort (HarperCollins, 2003).

Before the 'Sargasso proof', some bizarre theories about the origins of eels had circulated over the centuries: they were produced from the entrails of the earth; they grew from a mixture of horse's hair and river water; they condensed from dew drops; they sprung spontaneously from decaying mud; they even grew from the hair of dead sailors lost at sea.

The truth – only marginally less mysterious – is that an eel's life cycle is an epic round trip, from mighty ocean to muddy ditch and back, like that of a salmon in reverse (see page 508). A salmon is anadromous – it's born in fresh water and migrates to the sea, only to return to the river where it was born, as a mature, spawning adult. Whereas eels are catadromous – they are hatched out at sea, move to fresh water to feed and mature, then migrate back to sea in order to spawn.

As these fat, greeny-yellow river eels prepare to slither back towards the sea, a transformation begins. They turn silver and their eyes grow big and develop blue-sensitive eye pigments, required to see in salt water. Migrating silver eels, in their single-minded journey downstream, in the company of hundreds if not thousands of their fellows, also become easier to trap – and, according to those who trade in them, tastier to eat.

Once they reach the estuary mouth, it's believed (though not proved) that the eels then use the Earth's magnetic field as a navigational aid to guide them to the Sargasso Sea. Their mating – which is assumed to take place at great depth

MCS RATING: 5 DON'T EAT!
REC MINIMUM SIZE: N/A
SEASON: N/A
RECIPE: page 175

– has never been observed, though it seems certain that once they've spawned the adult eels die. The eel eggs then hatch into flat, leaf-shaped larvae no bigger than your smallest fingernail. Within a few months they will have grown to about an inch in length, but retaining their larval form. These larvae have no fins, tail, wings or method of propulsion. They are effectively little underwater 'sails', relying totally on the transatlantic currents to carry them away from the churning Sargasso, back towards Europe. This journey will take about a year.

As the swarms of larvae approach the European coastline, they change shape, transforming into tiny, transparent baby eels, about the thickness of a matchstick and the length of two. These are known as glass eels, or elvers. They seek fresh water and swim up tidal rivers en masse, moving with the high incoming tides, mostly under the cloak of darkness to avoid predators. These little elvers have an adhesive quality that allows them to climb weirs and waterfalls against the flow. They wriggle upstream in their tens of thousands, seeking new, safe waters to inhabit.

They might choose to stay in a mighty river, or settle in some drab little ditch, drain or pond. Here they'll feed, first on small aquatic invertebrates, later on frogs and fish, until they too grow to sexual maturity, which will usually take between eight and fifteen years. Then the Sargasso pilgrimage begins again.

This heroic life cycle makes the eel a natural wonder – but it may also prove its undoing, now that consumers have exerted such pressure on stocks. Eels are in great demand in all parts of the world, especially in Japan, where thousands

of tons of eels are eaten every year. One of the favourite lunches of the Tokyo salaryman is the *unagi* (eel) takeaway bento box: a plastic box of rice topped with fillets of roasted eel, glazed with a sweet-salty-sticky sauce. Hundreds of thousands of these are sold in Japan every day: that's a scary amount of eels.

To satisfy this demand, eels are being farmed – mainly in the Netherlands and the Far East – but not in the same way as other fish. Their unique reproductive cycle is extremely difficult to replicate or assist. Unlike salmon, there are no females packed with eggs to be manually stripped and fertilised, no males bursting with potent sperm, because this stage of sexual readiness doesn't normally happen until the eels are deep in the mid Atlantic on their long journey to the Sargasso Sea. And so these 'farms' have to be stocked with wild elvers, which are caught as they arrive at the major eel rivers of Europe in the spring. They are then taken to stew ponds, where they are fattened up on fishmeal for the next two or three years. So every eel we eat, whether farmed or otherwise, was once a wild eel spawned in the Sargasso Sea.

A huge percentage of these 'seed' elvers are currently caught in British rivers. The biggest elver fishery in the UK is based in Gloucestershire on the River Severn and its tributaries. Licensed elvermen fish the river with handheld nets on incoming tides in the dark of the night (the best bankside fishing spots, known as tumps, are handed down within families). Elver catches, live and wriggling, are packed in tanks of aerated fresh water and air-freighted around the world. Over the last decade, the price that elver fishermen have been paid per kilo for live elvers has rollercoasted, rising and falling according to the size of the European catch and the stocking needs of the eel farmers. In 1997 the average price was £145 per kilo, in 2005 it had shot to over £400, and at the time of writing it is back down to around £220 a kilo.

Until they became so valuable as seed stock, elvers were sold to be eaten. As recently as the late 1980s, in Severn-side pubs during March and April, you could order them by the half pint. They'd be fried in bacon fat and served with the rashers, perhaps even with a fried egg on top. The Spanish have always loved them, too – fried with chilli and garlic, then served up with flaky sea salt.

Eating elvers has never been a sound idea from a conservation point of view. But it's the sheer value of elvers for stocking farms, rather than any good sustainable practice, that has now priced them out of reach of most enthusiasts, both at home and abroad. They are still on the menus of a few restaurants in Madrid and Barcelona, where one imagines they are consumed by footballers and fashionistas. Lesser Spanish mortals can still feed on elvers, but not real ones. They have to put up with *anguilas falsas*, which have been extruded, like 'ocean sticks', from much cheaper fish into tiny 5cm-long elver copies, with black 'backs' and white 'bellies'. Sometimes they even sport a pair of fake 'eyes' to complete the illusion.

So, right now there are many millions of eels fattening up in stew ponds for this ever-growing market. But that doesn't mean we can afford to be complacent about the health of the eel population. Many authorities believe it is on the verge of a major collapse. The problem is the rapidly diminishing numbers of elvers returning to the European coastline from the Sargasso Sea. Since the turn of the millennium, it has hit an all-time low, and is still continuing to decline. Recent estimates by the International Council for the Exploration of the Sea (see page 31) say that the number of elvers coming to European shores is no more than 5 per cent of what it once was, and could be as low as 1 per cent.

It is unlikely that this is due to a lack of eels leaving European shores. Catches of wild silver eels, travelling downstream, have gone down in recent years but to nowhere near the same extent as for elvers. Perhaps the most persuasive current theory is also the most alarming. Climate change may be causing a shift in the direction of the Gulf Stream, pushing the larvae off course. Many millions of elvers may simply be lost at sea. Whatever the case, unless things change within years rather than decades, the dramatic decline in elver numbers will surely affect the stocks of wild adult eels in our waters – and we will be in the grip of a downward spiral in both adult departures and elver arrivals.

There's some hope to be had from the fact that the European Commission has just launched an international 'recovery plan' for eels, which, in theory, should greatly increase the number of silver eels allowed to return to their spawning grounds. However, it's far too early to know if this will succeed. Another faint glimmer of light is offered by the modern technology of fish farming (but given the track record of the industry in 'helping' solve problems with wild fish stocks perhaps we shouldn't hold our breath).

It's hard to be quite sure where we are headed, because of the intense secrecy of the companies operating in this area (due to the simply *huge* amounts of money at stake). Only a few years ago, achieving the captive spawning of eels, followed by successful fertilisation and hatching, was seen by those involved in the endeavour as the aquaculture equivalent of cold nuclear fusion. Now it seems they have cracked it – almost. Using methods as yet not revealed, eggs have been grown, harvested, fertilised and hatched. The remaining problem is how to nurture the larvae through the first year or two of life and into the elver stage. It simply hasn't happened yet.

If this breakthrough is achieved, the commercial pressure on wild stocks might be relieved. It's theoretically possible that captive-bred eels could be used to restock our lakes and rivers all over Europe. But could such fish ever find the Sargasso Sea and breed naturally? Or would they become a species entirely dependent on aquaculture? We could end up with a bizarre reversal of the current eel farming system, so that all 'wild' eels in our natural water courses will in fact be the progeny of captive-bred parents. There are still many more questions than answers about the future of the eel.

One thing's for sure. As we write this, every eel that you eat, whether wild or farmed, will have come from wild stock – which means it was born in the Sargasso Sea and could have made it back there to breed. But since it's now in your belly, that isn't going to happen. Currently, therefore, eel abstinence is your only sure-fire contribution to solving the problem.

We must admit that to us, that option looks pretty appalling. We love eating eel. We love it Chinese-style: filleted, fried with garlic, chilli and ginger, and dipped into a sauce of soy and spring onions. And we love it the French way: filleted and fried, then served with a *sauce verte* made from a handful of sorrel, parsley and spinach that has been wilted in the pan juices and finished with a few drops of wine, a knob of butter and an egg yolk to bring the sauce together. And Nick is quite partial to it cold and jellied, East End-style (whereas Hugh would much rather have the pie and mash).

Most of all, though, we both love it smoked – home smoked, if at all possible. For a while we mainly smoked and ate the eels we caught ourselves – from our favourite eely lake, not far from the original River Cottage. We could, of an evening, reliably hook half a dozen or so (using worms for bait). We'd keep the best two or three, salt them with their skin on, then cold smoke them for a few hours before finally cooking them through with a blast of hot smoke (see page 158). We'd eat them hot from the smoker, with buttered brown bread and homemade horseradish. Happy days.

Today the case of the slippery eel offers an apt example of the kind of grappling-with-guilt that we, as fish lovers, can hardly avoid. In truth, we are now wavering about the ecological soundness of our only-eat-what-we-catch approach to the eel. Of course, if everyone ate only eels that they'd caught themselves, the wild eel population would be in a lot less trouble. At the same time, by catching and killing even just a few eels, we are clearly adding to, not subtracting from, the problem. Should we settle instead for buying the odd one that's been commercially caught, or a delicious whole smoked eel from our friends at Brown and Forrest (see the Directory, page 590)? Or should we, if climate change is going to take the matter out of our hands, simply gorge ourselves on as much eel as we can, while we still can? Or perhaps – barely thinkable, this – simply never eat an eel again?

Such are the battles currently raging between our consciences and our appetites. And sometimes, but rarely these days, our appetites still win.

Carp *Cyprinus carpio*

Not everyone is grateful for what the Romans brought to Britain. We both have small boys who deeply resent the introduction of the bath. But neither of them – nor anyone else we know – has a problem with another Roman introduction: the carp. Indeed, *Cyprinus carpio* has been so wholeheartedly adopted in Britain that it is assumed by most to be a native of our waters. Mrs Beeton refers to it as the 'queen of the river' – a slight misnomer, since most British carp have been settled in still waters.

Originally from around Turkestan and the Black and Caspian Seas, for centuries carp were cultivated by the Romans as an eating fish in man-made ponds – these were early fish farms. For its generous contribution to the Roman table, carp was honoured by association with Venus, the goddess of fertility (a female carp is so fecund that she can produce up to a third of her body weight in eggs). As their Empire expanded through Europe, Roman armies took with them supplies of live carp, stored in bundles of wet moss. By the time of their retreat, carp was a valued food fish throughout northern Europe.

The Britons particularly took to carp. They are easy to breed, can be kept alive for years – even in fairly stagnant 'stew' ponds – and will eat practically anything. For many households, they came to serve almost as aquatic pigs – mooching around in a pond out the back, ready to grow fat on any scraps that came their way. They were (and still are) good eating – the flesh rich and robust, and easily removed from the uncomplicated skeleton. The only downside might have been a distinct earthy flavour – derived from the often rather grubby water they lived in and their mud-sifting feeding habits. But unless you lived near the coast and were spoilt with fresh sea fish with which to compare them, carp's silty tang would be unlikely to bother you.

MCS RATING: not rated

REC MINIMUM SIZE: 25cm

CLOSED SEASON: generally 15 March to 15 June

RECIPES: pages 175, 220, 223, 281–2

In medieval times, carp served the Church and its ecclesiastical communities exceedingly well. Monasteries kept carp ponds, where the fish would be fed on corn and potatoes. Every Friday, a day of abstinence from meat, one of the monks would hoick out a couple of fat ones to feed the brothers. At various times over the centuries, during periods of heightened fervour, such 'fish days' were extended to two and even three times a week. This inevitably led to the digging of further ponds and the stocking of yet more carp. Hence the fish's remarkably thorough distribution throughout the British Isles.

However, the carp's ancient and traditional pond life, settled for almost two millennia, has changed massively in the last few decades. It has ceased to be a food fish and has been claimed almost aggressively by modern anglers, who never eat them. In fact, the British carp angler would rather swallow his maggots, or shave off his beard, than harm a carp. There are hundreds of thousands of carp anglers who are all, in varying degrees, obsessed with this fish (some save their passion for the weekends; others think about carp more than most men think about sex). And as there is no longer a compulsory closed season on stillwater carp lakes or canals, most can pursue their 'hobby' 365 days a year. But though they might well stop for a portion of cod and chips on their way home from yet another 48-hour marathon carpathon bivouak, most would blow a fuse at the thought of one of their beloved fish in a crisp beer batter.

To people who have recently arrived from Eastern Europe, where carp is still valued as a food fish, this is all very confusing. Over the last couple of years there have been a number of incidents of carp club members reporting Polish carp anglers to the police for having the temerity to take a fish home to cook. Admittedly, their 'angling' methods are not always conventional. Just last summer, police in Hertfordshire questioned four Eastern Europeans about an incident at the local carp lake involving snorkels and a spear gun. You can see why this might have been inflammatory, but you have to admire their determination. Or their appetite.

Maybe this is our problem, however, not the Poles'. Maybe we should be a little less uptight over a fish that was brought here to feed us in the first place, is in plentiful supply, and could take pressure off other threatened species. We'd like to see coarse anglers adopt a more 'holistic' approach to their fishing. By all means enjoy a day's sport, and take all the photos you want to impress your friends. But if you want to impress your family – which is not a bad plan, given that you are in the habit of deserting them for days at a time – why not take 'one for the pot' and bake them a carp when you get home?

At the same time, let's be even-handed. We understand how an angler would feel if a thirty-pound fish he'd known by name (yes, carp anglers recognise and name individual fish) was plucked from his local gravel pit and turned into Christmas lunch for a bunch of foreigners. But how about a bit of give and take? We'd like to see Polish anglers invited to carp clubs to learn a little British fishing etiquette – perhaps in exchange for revealing the secrets of a good stuffed carp.

So what happened in this country to turn carp from dinner into deity? Progress? Certainly, from the late nineteenth century, with the development of bigger and better trawlers and the rapid expansion of the rail and road network, fresh sea fish became much more readily available. Coarse freshwater fish, including carp, roach and perch, simply faded from the cook's consciousness as herrings, haddock and the mighty cod took over the kitchen.

In 1952 the fishing writer Richard Walker captured a mirror carp on Redmire Pool, near Hereford, weighing 44lb. He smashed the British rod-caught record and his catch became a national news story. From that moment, serious carp fishing took off in Britain. The fish was christened Clarissa and she took up residence in the aquarium at London Zoo. Clarissa became the inspiration for a new generation of carp anglers, many of whom made a pilgrimage to visit their living goddess. Carp became big business: angling clubs bought specimen fish to lure carp hunters to their waters. Ultra-modern tackle – brand new carbon-fibre rods and invisible monofilament lines – were developed to aid carpists in their quest for behemoth fish. The mother of all British carp had spawned a new brotherhood of British carp anglers (it wasn't until 1981 that Clarissa lost top billing to 'the Bishop', a 51lb 8oz monster, again bagged at Redmire).

The carp's large eyes and sensitive hearing make it a wily prey. And the older and larger it grows, the more canny it becomes. For British anglers, these huge, hard-fighting carp, previously considered almost uncatchable, presented a brand new sporting challenge. And they still do: a fish of over 20lb gives you unofficial entry into the brotherhood – you can dare to speak to your fellows. Catch a 'Thirty' and you will be invited to pass the pictures round, and may even get a slap on the back. Land a fish of over 40lb and you can reasonably expect other carp anglers to genuflect as you pass. But the obsession to catch such a specimen can grow so strong that it can rule an angler's life – even ruin it. True 'carpoholics' hunt their prey for days and nights on end, 'bivvying up' by the waterside, boiling up strong coffee and Pot Noodles to stave off sleep and hunger, lest they miss a bite. We've heard it said that in Essex, carp fishing is the number-two reason cited by wives in divorce cases. (In legal terms, we imagine it covers both 'unreasonable behaviour' and 'desertion'.)

Carp have a good memory – all that 'goldfish have a memory span of four seconds' stuff is nonsense – and they are savvy enough to avoid eating the bait that caught them out last time. So anglers have to dream up novel foods to tempt the suspicious specimen fish. Luckily carp seem to have adventurous appetites: bread, cheese, curry paste, custard powder, dog food, honey, luncheon meat, Marmite, pasta, pepperoni, pilchards, potatoes, strawberries and sweetcorn are just a tiny selection of the ingredients with which people have persuaded carp to take their hook.

If only they would apply such culinary creativity to the carp itself. There's undoubtedly tremendous potential for reviving the culture of eating carp in this country. A couple of millennia's worth of British and European cooks are not wrong about this fish. We've both eaten and enjoyed it: the rich, meaty flesh is not unlike salmon in its texture. Yes, it can taste a little muddy – but, as with trout, this is a reflection of the water it has taken in, not an intrinsic quality of the flesh itself.

So, we are delighted to hear of one Jimmie Hepburn, who has just started the country's first organic carp farm, not far from us in Somerset. Quite apart from the thrill of seeing this great fish back on our menus, there is another reason to be excited about this venture. Carp farming is potentially more sustainable than any other kind of freshwater aquaculture. Carp will thrive on an entirely vegetarian diet, so there is no need to bring in food made from processed wild fish (see page 37). The combination of organic standards and sweet Somerset water could prove a winner, and we can hardly wait to sample the first fish from Jimmie's spring-fed ponds – due to be ready in late 2008.

When it arrives, we will honour it with a classic recipe from Hannah Glasse's *The Art of Cookery*, published in 1747. We'll stuff it with onions, herbs and anchovies, spiced with mace, cloves and nutmeg, and bake it with half a bottle of white wine. And we'll rustle the cooking liquor into a sauce by whisking in butter and a little flour. It may be 260 years old, but that recipe looks very sound to us.

And after that initiation, we may well turn to carp to see how it holds up in various recipes in this book. With that in mind, and in anticipation of the great carp revival, we've already sprinkled the fish around the 'also works with' lists alongside the recipes. For the time being, that may seem eccentric. Ten years from now, we hope it'll just look like good sense.

Zander *Stizostedion lucioperca*

The zander is the dangerous stranger of our inland waterways – hunting mostly in the dark, peering out of spooky, killer eyes and then biting its unsuspecting victims on the neck with its stiletto-sharp fangs. Everything about this Eastern European infiltrator is murky and mysterious. And how it first arrived in England is a tale cloaked in intrigue.

Francis Russell, the ninth Duke of Bedford, was a naturalist, animal collector and all-round eccentric nobleman. On his travels to Germany he became so enamoured of the local freshwater predator, the zander, that he decided he just had to have one – or rather a couple of dozen. So in 1878 a deal was struck with the German Fisheries Association of Schleswig-Holstein and, after a hazardous

MCS RATING: not rated

REC MINIMUM SIZE: 30cm

CLOSED SEASON: generally 15 March to 15 June

RECIPES: pages 198, 226–7, 281–2, 283, 289, 330

journey involving a stormy Channel crossing and a dash from London by horse and cart, twenty-three fish arrived at Woburn Park. They were released into the lake by lantern light, in the dead of night.

The Duke was President of the Royal Agricultural Society, whose motto, 'Practise with Science', he interpreted in a rather gung-ho manner. Introducing alien species was his somewhat reckless hobby and many of them, having slipped beyond the walls of Woburn, are still with us today. The Chinese water deer and the muntjac are notable among them. They shouldn't really be here, but at least they have in their favour the fact that they are singularly good eating. And exactly the same is true of the zander.

For eighty-five years, like a time bomb slowly ticking, the zander stayed put, doing little harm at Woburn except eating the local roach and producing numerous little zander. Then, in 1963, ninety-seven of these were scooped from the lake and released into the wide, open waters of the Great Ouse Relief Channel in East Anglia. The Fenland River Board, having observed their apparent good behaviour over the years, introduced them in a well-meaning attempt to increase the variety of fish available to local anglers. Guess what? It went horribly wrong. Cut loose from the confines of a small still water, the zander went on a killing spree, wreaking havoc amongst the huge shoals of bleak and dace that swarmed through the Fens. The zander's perfect night vision meant the slaughter was relentless. They could hunt all day and all night. Within three years the local populations of shoal fish had been decimated.

The angling press went wild. 'Kill them all!' screamed the headlines. Throughout the 1970s, fishery managers and environmental agencies did just that. The zander were netted, electro-fished and persecuted wherever they cropped up. And they were cropping up in all sorts of places, with a little help from a few human allies – mainly misguided zander anglers. Whether out of curiosity, overenthusiasm or malice, they caught zander in the Fens and hoicked them off to different parts of the country. The most successful populations have been established in the canals of Birmingham and Coventry, and in the River Severn and its Gloucestershire tributaries. (These zander anglers, like the fish they pursued, became pariahs of the fishing fraternity. They would not be welcome in the bars of many fishing clubs.)

The spread of the zander struck fear into the heart of dedicated coarse and match anglers – the kind whose stock in trade is catching roach and bream by the hundredweight every Saturday and Sunday of their lives. Until this point they'd reserved their worst expletives for the pike. But, being a native, it at least earned some grudging respect. The foreign zander tapped into a different level of anxiety and bigotry, and some truly wild accusations were made. Anglers spoke of the zander's psychotic habit of killing purely for killing's sake. They insisted that, like a fox, zander would kill and kill again, taking out whole shoals of fish without even bothering to eat their prey.

It was all nonsense, of course. Their piercing vision makes zander at home in murky water but, as predators go, they're actually quite finicky feeders. They may have impressive fangs but they don't like too big a mouthful. They prey on small shoal fish, rarely taking on the kind of adult breeding fish that a big pike would relish. For all the talk of their thuggery, a hooked zander actually puts up a very limp fight. Some of the best zander we've caught, of 2.5–3.5kg, have come to the net displaying all the savage indignation of a damp rag. Nor have zander, as a species, fulfilled the paranoid predictions of the piscatorial doomsayers.

They have a sporadic distribution and, like other predators, survive or thrive only in proportion to the available bait fish. In the middle of the Fens, where all the turmoil began, you'd now struggle to catch a zander even if you set out specifically to get one. Nature is a powerful leveller. This imposter, having taken the locals by surprise, may have briefly held sway at the top of the food chain but order and balance have been restored. It scratches a predatory living, along with the resident perch and pike, but dominates no longer.

If you've never eaten zander, you really should. In parts of Eastern Europe, where zander are native, they are the top-selling freshwater fish, more popular even than trout. Mostly this table zander is farmed, although wild zander are available too. As in any comparison between wild and farmed fish of the same species, the wild ones are firmer of flesh (they work harder for a living) and sweeter of taste (they eat a more natural diet).

Here in the UK, zander does appear on some adventurous restaurant menus from time to time. And farmed zander, mainly imported from Holland, are just starting to appear on wet fish slabs too. We're betting that, sooner or later, one of the supermarkets will champion it.

If you do get hold of some, you'll be impressed. Its flesh looks like cod: nice big curds of milk-white flakes interspersed by easily removable bones. If anything, it's even firmer than cod. It fillets easily and, once scaled, its thick skin fries up satisfyingly crisply in the pan. It's one of those versatile fish, ready for baking and battering, frying and grilling and even cold smoking – after which you could happily use it in any recipe that called for smoked haddock or pollack.

A fresh wild zander is worth making a fuss of in the kitchen – particularly as acquiring one is no mean feat. Realistically, you'll need to befriend a zander angler. Or become one.

Shellfish

Crustaceans

Brown shrimp *Crangon crangon*

Afternoon tea. Cucumber sandwiches, scones with jam, coffee and walnut cake if you're lucky, Dundee cake if you're not. All washed down with a pot of Earl Grey. And, if you're striving for out-and-out perfection, something salty and fishy on toast – bloater paste, perhaps, or the Gentleman's Relish. But if you really want the best, you should make it potted shrimps.

The finest potted shrimps are still made from brown shrimps caught on the vast tidal sands of places such as north Norfolk and Morecambe Bay (where James Baxter became the first shrimp processor in 1799). They're still unbelievably good. If you think of shrimps as somehow inferior to prawns, then perhaps you haven't tasted them for a while. Or you may have fallen victim to the curious modern phenomenon of 'crustacean inflation', whereby the sheer size of prawns is peddled as a mark of quality. It's not. And we'd rather have a solitary Morecambe Bay shrimp on our plate than a swollen half-pound tiger prawn from some dodgy Malaysian prawn farm (see pages 542–3 for more on the shortcomings of prawn farming).

In the wild, the modest brown shrimp spends most of the daylight hours buried in sand or mud, with only its eyes and antennae poking out. Being such a scrumptious morsel makes life precarious. Most things in the sea would love to eat a shrimp. So a wise shrimp only comes out at night, when it'll go hunting for its own menu of even more minute invertebrates or juvenile fish.

Wide, silty estuary mouths are the habitat brown shrimps love best: the Severn and the Wash have had their boom times, but Morecambe Bay remains the mother lode of the British brown shrimp. Harvesting Morecambe Bay shrimps began centuries ago with simple hand nets, progressed through horse-drawn nets and those pulled by small sailing tubs called nobbies, and was eventually mechanised in the early twentieth century with the use of beach-going tractors and motor boats. Whether pushed by hand or pulled by a boat or tractor, all shrimp nets operate on the same principle: a pole, bar or board is dragged through the sand, forcing the shrimps out of it so they can be scooped up by the net that comes behind. Traditionally the shrimps are then boiled in seawater – sometimes in special shrimp kettles on board the boats.

Shelling or 'picking' Morecambe brown shrimps was until quite recently literally a cottage industry, with hundreds of local women processing them at their kitchen tables and then taking them on to the potting plant. Predictably, after two hundred years of providing locals with a good living, the practice has been outlawed by European health and safety regulations. Shrimps are now picked and packed mechanically in a new, state-of-the-art processing plant.

If you want to eat brown shrimps, the ones to buy are those taken from offshore trawl fisheries that use 'veils' (bycatch reduction devices) on their nets. Or you can support the traditional tractor shrimp fisheries of Lancashire and

MCS RATING: 3

REC MINIMUM SIZE: 3cm

SEASON: N/A as spawning period is protracted, so hard to avoid

Norfolk, who sell their catch through local fishmongers. Potted shrimps freeze well, and many fishmongers keep frozen stock – often from one of the old family firms, such as Baxter's, still fishing and potting in Morecambe Bay today. They are also available by mail order (see the Directory, page 590).

Best of all, go and catch your own. Get yourself a proper shrimping net – with a solid wooden bar across the front to push through the wet sand and send the shrimps into the sweeping net that follows – and tap into local knowledge about their whereabouts. To deal with your self-caught shrimps it's best to boil them in seawater (or add 30g salt per litre of fresh tap water) for just 3 minutes, then drain well and leave to cool. You can then peel them and pot them in spicy butter (all the commercial recipes are secret, of course – but we're betting that cayenne pepper, a little crushed garlic and a pinch of mace will get you close). Or just eat them one by one – in which case peeling them is by no means compulsory. You can just remove the heads and crunch up bodies and tails, shell and all. Or don't remove the heads and eat the lot. Or mix and match – it's really up to you.

Prawn

Common *Palaemon serratus* **Deepwater** *Pandalus borealis*
Tiger *Penaeus monodon*

Do you remember tasting your first ever prawn? We both remember ours. The first Fearnley prawn came from a rocky beach on the Welsh coast near the seaside town of Aberdovy. It fell to the rock-pool net of the five-year-old Hugh. Boiled in seawater, peeled while still warm, it was like eating a fishy sweet (in a good way). The first Fisher prawn came in a warm, wet brown paper bag from a shellfish stall in Cromer. It was actually a substitute for brown shrimps, which they'd run out of. Prawns seemed huge, exotic and so much easier to peel!

Sadly, not many people have poignant prawn memories any more because, like so many things that were once a rare treat, the prawn has become just something else we take for granted – a bog-standard sandwich filler. In the UK alone, we eat £175 million-worth of prawn sandwiches every year.

The EU is the largest importer of prawns in the world, receiving around 400,000 tonnes annually. In the UK we import 78,000 tonnes of foreign trawled and farmed prawns – on top of the 2,500 tonnes that our own fishing fleets catch. A high proportion of those prawns carry distinctly dubious ecological credentials. The prawns we slather in mayo and pack into sarnies are either fished from the sea by trawlers or grown in shallow tropical prawn farms. Sadly, both means of production are desperately damaging to the environment.

Globally, three million tonnes of 'wild' prawns are caught by trawlers every year, at a variety of prawn grounds all over the world: Mozambique, Sri Lanka, the Philippines, Venezuela, Greenland. One big problem with prawn trawl nets is that the necessarily small mesh size used to catch pinky-sized prawns will trap all manner of other creatures and fish. These unwanted species, or bycatch, die in the process of being hauled on board and are then dumped back into the sea. Some bycatch ratios in tropical prawn grounds can be as high as 20:1 – which means that for every kilo of prawns taken, 20 kilos of bycatch have been dumped.

MCS RATINGS: deepwater 3 (2–4); tiger 5 DON'T EAT! (except organic farmed); others not rated

REC MINIMUM SIZE: common, 6cm; deepwater, generally 8–12cm; farmed N/A

SEASON: common, avoid November–June (spawning); deepwater, avoid summer and autumn (spawning); release egg-carrying (berried) females at any time; farmed N/A

RECIPES: pages 236, 238, 257, 266–7, 267, 323

In total, prawn fisheries account for nearly a third of the global bycatch from all fisheries. In terms of direct impact on surrounding species, this is one of the most destructive forms of fishing there is.

There are three main types of prawn that we eat: the common prawn, the deepwater prawn and various members of the warmwater prawn family. All share similar features: they're decapods (ten-legged), with two pairs of front legs with pincers and another three pairs of legs for crawling or swimming. They all have a rostrum (a jagged, unicorn-like spike) in the middle of their forehead, which is used as a defence against predators.

The common prawn lives all around our coastline and can even be caught in rock pools with a dip net. It has a thickish transparent shell with visible stripy markings along its flanks. These prawns are still caught on a small scale with baited prawn pots, especially in the Southwest, and so occasionally appear in local fishmongers, on seafood stalls and in pubs and restaurants. Our own native prawns, self-caught or locally sourced, are among the few prawns whose consumption we would countenance. We see no reason whatsoever why you shouldn't enjoy them once in a while. We catch some ourselves, by putting out a few pots, baited with very ripe, stinky mackerel heads. September to November is the best time to catch the nice fat ones, affectionately known as 'Billy Winters' round these parts.

If boats and pots are too faffy, you can still get your share by buying a 'drop net' from a seaside tackle shop. Lowered off a harbour wall or off the edge of a rocky reef, baited with any old fish bits, it should soon attract a small ministry of busybody prawns ('ministry' isn't strictly the collective term for prawns – but we feel it should be).

The deepwater prawn (or the northern prawn, coldwater prawn or Atlantic prawn) is an inhabitant of the chilly Atlantic ocean, and the one that, if you are roughly our age, was most likely an ingredient in the first prawn cocktail you ever ate. They are still trawled in vast quantities, and almost always boiled, packed and frozen at sea. When you buy a 'pint of shell-on prawns' at the fishmonger's or seaside pub, it's likely to be these you'll get. They'll have been defrosted from a big catering pack and then served up in the shell. They're none the worse for it – provided they haven't been refrozen and defrosted (a not uncommon practice among our less conscientious fishmongers and, according to a recent BBC documentary, the fish counters of some supermarkets).

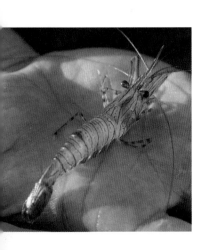

A pint of shell-on prawns, with a blob of good mayo, some brown bread and a few lettuce leaves to give the illusion of virtue, is an honourable custom for picnics and pub lunches and one we'd hate to put a dampener on. So if you want to buy prawns and can't get locally caught ones, deepwater trawled prawns are the least ecologically damaging. The MCS rating of 3 suggests they can be eaten, but with a degree of caution. The best choice is prawns that have been caught from an MSC-certified fishery or one that uses sorting grids to reduce the amount of bycatch (these are now compulsory in Norwegian, Canadian and US prawn fisheries).

Warmwater prawns come in many shapes and sizes but tend to be much larger than deepwater ones. They include tiger prawns as well as varieties labelled king, jumbo and fantail. Many wild stocks of these prawns are in desperate decline and almost all large prawns sold in the UK – either raw and frozen or cooked and frozen – have been farmed. This is absolutely not in their favour. Tropical prawn farming is a pretty unpleasant business, and its grievous

shortcomings are, we would say, reflected in the dubious quality of its products. Huge areas of mangrove swamps are being transformed into prawn farms – in some parts of the world this is seen as an aquaculture gold rush, and thousands of impoverished coastal dwellers are jostling to get involved. The mangroves are chopped down and large areas flooded and seeded with juvenile prawns. These are artificially fed until large enough to harvest and sell. After two or three years the water is so polluted with prawn waste – and the toxic chemicals used to neutralise it and prevent fungal diseases – that it becomes too toxic for prawn farming. Even when the water is drained, the remaining soil is so polluted that crops can't be grown for years.

On ecological grounds, we steer well clear of all farmed prawns. In our opinion, farmed prawns are not pleasant – and monster tiger prawns are the worst of the lot. They look impressive but it's a definite case of style over substance. The flesh is soft and mushy, since the prawns have grown fat fast. Farmed prawns often have a background taste of chlorine – which is scary. Or else they are faintly redolent of the crap they've been raised in – which is even scarier. When they are smothered in cocktail sauce, in a supermarket sandwich or takeaway salad, you might just miss the tang of tropical pollution.

As you can imagine, we don't eat prawns very often. Served cold with homemade mayonnaise is good enough. Sautéed in very garlicky butter is lovely too. A pinch of chilli flakes makes for a nice kick once in a while, for a treat. Which is what prawns should be.

Prawns *are* special, they *should* be expensive, and *should* be a luxury. But the random slaughter of bycatch species and the toxic destruction of huge swathes of previously untouched and carbon-friendly mangrove swamp is, in our opinion, far too high a price to pay. So, please, stick something else in your sandwich.

Dublin Bay prawn (or langoustine) *Nephrops norvegicus*

The Dublin Bay prawn is a much bigger and more impressive animal than your average prawn. The French name, *langoustine* (which could be translated as 'lobsterette'), does it more justice. It has a hard carapace that is orange, not translucent, and two proper claws, a cutter and a crusher, just like a small lobster – which is what it really is.

The 'Dublin Bay' label, in the same vein as the 'Dover' in Dover sole, came about because it was in Dublin that they were first regularly landed. Caught as unsolicited bycatch by trawlers fishing the northern edge of the Irish Sea, they were regarded as a perk for the crew. To make extra cash, the crew would sell the bite-sized lobsters to street vendors (one hopes Molly Malone sold a fair few from her famous wheelbarrow). Being not strictly 'above board', they were offloaded at sea, in Dublin Bay, before the ship landed its official catch in the harbour.

This unofficial market gave the prawn some commercial value – but not much. Unless the prawn haul was particularly good, or the commercial haul (of cod, plaice and other flatfish) was particularly poor, the prawns might just as easily be dumped over the side. But that all changed in the 1950s, when the Dublin Bay prawn was reborn in Britain – coated in breadcrumbs and deep fried, then served up with tartare sauce.

It was not a British innovation, but one copied from the Italians, who have been eating *Nephrops norvegicus* for generations, exploiting fisheries around the Atlantic coast of Spain and Portugal. They call them *scampi* (singular, *scampo*). And they have traditionally prepared them in dozens of different ways – in garlic butter, tomato sauce, on the barbecue, with spaghetti, or in a risotto. But it was the way they crumb-coated the prawns, after dipping them in egg, and fried them to a crisp crust that captured the imagination – or lack of imagination, perhaps – of the British.

Back then, in post-War austerity Britain, scampi was posh nosh. It was originally developed for the Ritz Hotel in 1946 by Young's Seafood. But in the following decades, as the scampi craze caught on, it gravitated from silver platter in the Ritz to mock-wicker basket down the pub. Production became increasingly industrialised: the prawn tails were removed, the rest discarded. Boiled, peeled, dipped, crumbed and frozen, then stacked by the palette load, 'prefab scampi' was then shipped out to pubs, hotels and restaurants all over Britain. It was served up, with chips of course, under the illusion that it had been rustled up only minutes before by an Italian chef. In reality the scampi made no more demands on the chef than the chips. The 1960s and 1970s were as much the 'scampi and chips years' as they ever were the 'prawn cocktail years'.

Demand for scampi tails has inevitably squeezed the supply, and pushed up prices. The tails of cheaper prawns, including farmed imports from the tropics, have been used to make imitation scampi. This industrial improvisation even extended to the use of extruded, artificially flavoured fish products – the crumbed equivalents of the dreaded 'ocean sticks'– that may have no real prawn (let alone real scampi) in them at all. British food labelling laws now insist that any product called scampi is made only from *Nephrops norvegicus*. So in theory at least, any ersatz versions should be clearly labelled for what they are. But sales of frozen breaded scampi are still massive, with 900 tonnes a year being consumed in the UK alone. Are they *really* all made with langoustines? We have our doubts.

MCS RATING: 3 (2–5)

REC MINIMUM SIZE: 3cm (from nose to end of main body shell, not including tail)

SEASON: avoid during autumn (spawning); release egg-carrying (berried) females at any time

RECIPES: pages 257, 266–7

Another strange twist to the scampi tale has recently come to light. Young's, still the largest seafood producer in the UK, now ships 600 tonnes of frozen langoustines to Thailand every year to be hand-peeled. Mechanical peeling damages the tails – and British labour wages are too high to get the job done by hand here. So the scampi are landed in Scotland but then travel 13,000 miles around the world, stopping for a few weeks somewhere near Bangkok, before they return home, crumbed and cosy, to nestle in a basket in a pub near you.

However, there's more to the Dublin Bay prawn than a breadcrumb jacket and cheap tartare sauce. Since the gastronomic revolution of the late 1980s, it has been living something of a double life. Whilst scampi continues to trade steadily, the langoustine – as chefs prefer to call it – has begun to receive the recognition it deserves. The River Café, for example, was one of the first restaurants to order live specimens by overnight train delivery from Scotland. For twenty years now it's been serving them more or less the same two ways: straight from the chargrill, with a dressing of garlic, chilli, parsley, lemon and olive oil, or atop a fantastic seafood risotto. Either way, they're served whole, so you not only get the tail but can pick every last morsel from the head and claws. The light brown meat inside the head is particularly sweet. (If it was us we'd collect up the shells from diners' plates to make a great crustacean stock for the next risotto.)

Like scallops and oysters, langoustines have become one of those seafood ingredients that all ambitious chefs are expected to conjure with. But the idea of mashing them up to use as a filling for a giant pasta parcel (a *scampo raviolo*?) frankly leaves us cold. Like all crustaceans – most shellfish in fact – it is so much more enjoyable to see them in their entirety, and to have a chance to admire their distinctive physiology before devouring them.

This double life of the Dublin Bay prawn, as 'Dr Langoustine' and 'Mr Scampi', is reflected in the two main fishing methods used to catch them – one considerably more industrial than the other. *Nephrops norvegicus* lives on soft and silty sea floors, where it is able to burrow into the ground and hide from predators during the day. It emerges at night to hunt its own prey – smaller crustaceans – and graze on the odd bit of carrion. One way to remove it from this habitat is beam trawling – a destructive method that disrupts the fragile ecology of the seabed and kills a lot of unlandable bycatch (see page 29). Inevitably the scampi trade is generally supplied by prawns that have been caught this way.

But there is a far more selective, less destructive, way to catch langoustines – in baited creels, just like lobster and crab pots, only with a smaller mesh and entry funnel. These target them quite specifically and do little damage to the environment. Chefs' insistence on cooking creel-caught langoustines may or may not be motivated by ecological concerns, but it certainly guarantees a quality product. And if you want a share of that catch, with a clean conscience, you too should insist on creel-caught langoustines. At present, we are losing out in this market to the continental competition. It's yet another story of foreign seafood buyers recognising the quality of a British product before we do.

One Scottish firm, the Loch Torridon creel fishery, has received certification by the Marine Stewardship Council for its zero-impact fishing methods using traditional hand-hauled creel pots. The only problem is that its langoustines are so fine, so conscientiously handled and carefully packed (each langoustine travels in an individual padded box, to avoid damage through fighting), that French and Spanish importers have recently guaranteed to buy every last one. We think that's a shame. In the end it's down to us – to you – to shop discerningly for British, creel-caught langoustines, so that those who catch them and trade in them can have the confidence to offer them up to more local markets.

As with lobsters, the way to deal with live langoustines humanely is to chill them enough to render them unconscious, then kill them by dropping them into well-salted boiling water and cooking for 5 minutes (see page 96). Eat them either warm with garlic butter or cold with good mayonnaise. Barbecuing langoustines over wood embers or charcoal is wonderful too – the charring of their shells creates a distinctive flavour that is picked up by the flesh inside. Kill them first (see page 97), but remove them from the boiling water as soon as they are dead – barely a minute. Let them steam off for a couple of minutes before laying them on the barbecue, which should be all fired up and ready. Then 3 or 4 minutes on each side should do it. Again, they need only the simplest of dressings – our lime and chilli butter, as per Barbecued lobster (page 206), is hard to beat, but a River Café-style dressing of olive oil and lemon juice spiked with finely chopped garlic, parsley and chilli is another way to give them zing.

Signal crayfish *Pacifastacus leniusculus*

One of the worst eco-blunders of the 1970s was the accidental introduction of the North American signal crayfish to the freshwater habitats of Britain. The distinctively red-clawed American signals were first brought over here to be farmed for the catering trade. Our own indigenous version, the native white-clawed crayfish, was never really considered viable for commercial use because it was too small, too picky in its habitats and too hard to catch.

The American signal had been introduced, and successfully farmed, in Sweden during the 1960s as a replacement for their native, the noble crayfish, which had been wiped out by a plague. It seemed to make sense to try to bring them to Britain, where crayfish already had some cachet as a luxury food item, and where farmers were always looking to diversify their activities.

So the British Crayfish Marketing Board was set up, and began encouraging farmers to dig ponds and stock them with American signals. But – as has

MCS RATING: not rated
REC MINIMUM SIZE: N/A
SEASON: N/A

happened time and again throughout the world with the introduction of alien species – it all went horribly wrong. Not enough research or piloting was carried out and, of course, no one took the time to explain to the incomers precisely what was expected of them. Failing to grasp the essential British characteristics of fair play, the signals refused to stay in their allotted, newly dug (and often government-subsidised) ponds. Instead they went on the rampage.

An American signal crayfish can survive out of water for up to three months. It can burrow, climb, swim and even run – or at least scuttle – at a surprisingly fast pace. So its spread, particularly around the south of England where it was originally introduced, was rapid and devastating. And the principal victim was our very own home-grown white-clawed crayfish.

The outcome of the crayfish wars was swift and inevitable. Our natives are smaller than the signals. They are much less aggressive and less well armed, and they are much more sensitive to pollution and disease. Certainly, they were no match for the swaggering American bullies, who not only ate the native crayfish and their eggs (an effective way of dealing with the enemy) but, for good measure, also infected them with a deadly fungal plague to which they are themselves immune.

'Does my noble Lord agree that the signal crayfish is the aquatic equivalent of the grey squirrel?' asked Lord Campbell of Croy in the House of Lords in 1996, seeking reassurance that the infestation was about to be tackled by new regulations. 'Will the government encourage as wide a consumption as possible, in the interests of preserving some ecological balance?'

He was saying, in other words, let's eat ourselves out of this mess! This may seem eccentric to some, but to us it was an intelligent response to the crisis. A serious incentive to catch and eat more signals would help redress the balance, and take the pressure off the natives in the few areas where they still survive. However, this common-sense solution is being badly hampered by bureaucracy.

Although alien species of crayfish now exist in an estimated 87 per cent of British river catchments and are expected to bring about the extinction of our native variety within the next thirty years, it's ludicrously difficult to get

permission to trap them. Even if it's for your own personal consumption, and on your own land, you will need to obtain from the Environment Agency, and fill in, Form FR2 – an Application to Use Fishing Instruments (other than Rod and Line) and/or to Remove Fish from Inland Waters. Whether permission to trap is granted will depend on local situations, in particular the presence of native crayfish. The EA will also take into account the possible detrimental effects that trapping could have on other species, notably protected animals like otters and water voles. You'll need to supply details of the location you intend to trap, including grid references. You'll also need to specify the equipment or trap you intend to use, give detailed measurements of the size of the water, and show separate written permission from the landowner (even if it's you). And you'll have to give the date you intend to set your trap, as the licence is valid for one day only.

As the Agency ties itself in knots of red tape, the red-clawed invaders roam unchecked. They've made it to the very seat of power – even the Serpentine in London's Hyde Park is now crammed with signals.

Crayfish trapping advice packs are available from the National Fisheries Laboratory (tel: 01480 483968), and further information on by-laws to do with trapping signal crayfish can be found on the EA website. A simple crayfish trap costs less than £15 and, baited with a lump of mackerel or a tin of cat food that's been punctured with a few holes, could easily attract enough crayfish for an exotic feed. They would need to be thoroughly rinsed in fresh water for a day before cooking. Of course, by catching, cooking and eating them without all the form filling, you would be breaking the rules. But as long as you don't harm other animals, you would be doing your bit for the conservation of our poor beleaguered native crayfish... and experiencing some of the most delicious freshwater crustaceans. This is the kind of civil disobedience we feel entitled to recommend!

In the kitchen you can think of signal crayfish as mini lobsters or large prawns. Like langoustines and lobsters, they should get the freezer treatment, rendering them inert for humane despatch. Put them on a tray in the freezer for 45 minutes to an hour – but don't let them actually freeze. Then drop them in a large pan of fast-boiling, well-salted water, bring back to the boil and give them just 5 minutes. Drain, then peel their tails as soon as they are cool enough to handle. Eat them with a garlic and chive mayonnaise or a prawn cocktail sauce. And don't forget to make a stock with the leftover shells and heads.

Legally trapped and farmed signal crayfish can be bought, alive or pre-cooked, from some fishmongers, supermarkets and larger wholesale fish markets such as Billingsgate. They can also be bought by mail order, delivered alive, from Continental Crayfish (see the Directory, page 590). Remember – every crayfish you eat means there's one less marauding through our British waterways causing mayhem amongst our native fauna.

Lobster *Homarus gammarus*

Lobsters don't like each other very much. Leave two of them in a tank overnight, and the chances are in the morning only one will be left alive. Any two lobsters – two males, two females, one of each – will fight (unless, that is, they decide to mate). And the winner will usually eat the loser.

The lobster's penchant for pugilism and cannibalism is one reason why attempts to farm this crustacean have rarely been very successful: as soon as a mother lobster's eggs have hatched and her babies have grown to the size of a fingernail, she'll eat them.

The males are particularly belligerent. Even in tanks big enough for them to have their own territory, they'll still do battle. Backing down isn't their style. In one holding tank, a male lobster, who had already lost both claws and most of his legs in a fight, was seen dragging himself around the tank like the dismembered knight in *Monty Python and the Holy Grail*, challenging other lobsters to bring it on. No doubt he was saying, 'Come back here and I'll bite your claw off.'

Researchers have concluded that this machismo is an important part of everyday lobster life, and restaurants who keep live lobsters in a vivarium have long since learned to keep their claws held shut with rubber bands. But not all conflicts are resolved by violent means. Bizarrely, the lobster's urine plays a vital part. Both sexes have their bladder located in their heads, and its contents are not just a waste product. A male lobster's physical assault is accompanied by an intense squirt of his urine. It's deployed like a squid's ink or even a skunk's spray – as a tactical device in both fighting and mating. In time, lesser lobsters will know to fear him, simply by the scent of his urine. They'll surrender without too many blows being exchanged, saving both sides the risk of serious injury – and improving the chances of both becoming successful breeders at some future date.

This same scent is also used to impress females. When she is ready to mate, a lady lobster will move to a shelter close to the dominant male and start regularly parading past his territory. If he's impressed, he squirts a jet of urine in her direction. If she is ready, she will return the gesture. Scientists now believe that the female's urine also contains a secreted hormone that intensifies as she gets nearer to breeding time. The effect of this secretion is to tone down the male's aggressive urges and turn his (very tiny) brain from thoughts of crushing and killing to ones of sex and procreation.

Besides squirting her urine when ready to mate, the female lobster will also shed her shell. When she has done so, the male will then mount her soft, shell-less body and impregnate her with his sperm. She will generally remain in his lair for a week or two, until her new shell has grown hard. Then she'll be on her way. The next female in line starts her seduction tactics almost as soon as the last one has left. It's pretty much a dream scenario for the male: he gets to laze around at home while a succession of willing females comes to call.

Once the female has got the sperm she wants, she can then choose at what time to use it to fertilise her eggs. She may even carry her eggs for the best part of a year before deciding the time for fertilisation is right. There's no strict seasonality to lobster procreation, and females carrying eggs (berried females, as they are known) can be found all year round. Generally, though, they'll decide to fertilise and hatch their eggs during the warmer months.

The careful treatment of breeding females is critical for the sustainable management of lobster fisheries. With a mass of little black eggs underneath her abdomen, a berried female is easy to identify. By law in some parts of the world (including parts of Britain), or by voluntary agreement in others, berried females should be returned to the water unharmed. In particularly well-managed fisheries, they are marked with a V-notch cut into their tails, to identify them as sexually mature. So if they're caught again, even if they're not carrying eggs, they can still be returned.

MCS RATING: 3

REC MINIMUM SIZE: 9cm (from nose to end of main body shell, not including tail)

SEASON: lobsters can spawn at any time; avoid egg-carrying (berried) females

RECIPES: pages 206, 257, 266–7, 352

Lobsters live at a range of depths, temperatures and light levels. They don't have very good eyesight but they do have a phenomenal sense of smell. Their 'nose' is actually a pair of twitching mini-antennae, covered in minute chemo-receptors that decipher the undersea odours. Many professional potters believe that if you're after lobsters specifically, as opposed to crabs and lobsters, it pays to use the most stinking bait you can find. Some lobstermen leave mushed-up dead fish pieces in a plastic bag in direct sunlight for a couple of days or more, until they're nearly putrefied. Practically nothing is too dead, too old or too rotten to become a lobster's lunch. Yet, miraculously, they transform all the filth they consume into some of the sweetest meat you'll ever eat.

Catching lobsters is, relative to other forms of fishing, unusually ecologically friendly. Lobster pots do little damage to the seabed, as they are lifted and dropped, and they target lobsters and crabs quite specifically, so that any bycatch (mainly dogfish and conger eels) can be released unharmed. More importantly, the target stock itself can be responsibly managed: mature females, as discussed, can be returned alive, along with undersized specimens of both sexes.

Nonetheless, lobsters are primitive creatures: slow growers and, compared to crabs, relatively inefficient breeders. Relentless heavy potting can significantly reduce a local lobster population in just a few seasons – indeed, many traditional lobster grounds around our coast are currently quite depleted. But there is an element of self-regulation built into the economics of lobster fishing: when catches become scarce, the potters will move on and, since the habitat has not been damaged, eventually a recovery in stocks can be expected. This is not a species we are likely to drive to extinction, but our desire to eat it, and the high price it fetches, means the pressure on it is fairly unrelenting. Lobsters are also important predators and scavengers, so if their numbers are kept down by fishing for too long, all sorts of other changes can occur in marine communities. Careful future management will be essential. Thankfully, in some areas, conservation measures are already being put in place. For instance, a lobster pot fishery off the Yorkshire coast between Staithes and Spurn Point is currently undergoing assessment by the Marine Stewardship Council.

In the UK, anyone can legally have a go at lobster potting – provided the catch is retained for personal consumption and not sold. On a practical level, you'll need to buy or make yourself a pot or two, and unless you're prepared to slog down to the end of a reef or rocky promontory at low tide, you'll want a boat to drop and haul them from. To minimise the risk of upsetting local fishermen trying to make a living at the same game, it's best to mention your intentions to the local harbour master. It might be considered provocative to throw your pots too close to existing ones. And never put out more than three or four pots, or you may look as if you mean business rather than pleasure. Finally, always observe the same rules of conservation as are expected of the professionals, returning all undersized specimens and breeding females.

Lobsters are expensive and, in restaurants, extortionate. If you fancy one, and catching your own is not an option, then buying a live one to cook and eat at home is the next best thing. Good fishmongers sell live lobsters, but if you're close to the coast you may save a few quid by buying them wholesale, harbourside, or even direct from a potting boat.

The correct procedure for killing and cooking live lobsters is described on page 93. When it comes to eating them, they're such a treat that you don't need to smother them in heavy disguises. But if you really can't resist the urge to get cheffy with your lobster, then thermidor is a retro classic that's hard to beat (there's a recipe in *The River Cottage Cookbook*). The whiff of charcoal on lobster flesh is also something special (see page 206). But when all's said and done, and the Michelin pretenders have hung up their aprons, a fresh lobster, simply boiled and served cold with homemade mayonnaise, will never disappoint.

Brown crab (common crab) *Cancer pagurus*

Apparently crab is the latest 'super-food'. According to the Sea Fish Industry Authority, sales of crabmeat in the UK more than doubled in 2006. This, we're told, is due to 'health-conscious diners who want to take advantage of crabmeat's low levels of fat and cholesterol'. And yes, it's true that crabmeat does contain high levels of essential minerals such as zinc and selenium (said to be good for, amongst other things, boosting a low sperm count). But to us, brown crab has always been a food that is super. It's just *delicious*.

The British crab-fishing industry is ancient. The most famous crab fishery is in Cromer, on the north Norfolk coast, where Nick spent a large portion of his

MCS RATING: 3 (1–4)

REC MINIMUM SIZE: 14cm across the carapace

SEASON: avoid January–March (spawning)

RECIPES: pages 234, 239, 242–3, 266–7, 267, 327, 350, 389

teenage years fishing. As a consequence, he developed a bottomless appetite for crab and a healthy respect for the local crab fishermen, whom he accompanied on numerous occasions to help them haul their pots.

In his *Guide To Cromer*, published in 1800, Edmond Burtell noted 'crabs in the finest perfection'. The reputation of Cromer crabs continued to grow, until by 1875 the marine scientist Frank Buckland decided to make a study of the fishery. The famous Cromer crab fishery was at that time in steep decline, with catches falling off rapidly. Buckland blamed the overfishing of immature crabs, known locally as 'toggs', which were caught, crushed and used for whelk bait. He calculated that up to three-quarters of a million undersized crabs were being removed from the fishery each month, with disastrous consequences. As a result of his findings, Parliament passed the 1876 Crab and Lobster Fisheries (Norfolk) Act, introducing a minimum size for crabs (4½ inches – about 11cm) and forbidding the sale of 'berried' (egg-laden) females. The next year this law was extended to the whole of England and Wales. It has stood the brown crab in fantastically good stead. With the exception of a few notable areas, there are no grave concerns about the future of our national crab fisheries.

Buckland had noted that the steep decline in crab stocks seemed to date from the introduction, some twelve years earlier, of a new type of crab pot – the 'ink well' – to the fishery. These were devastatingly effective, and rapidly replaced the labour-intensive, hand-fished hoop nets. The 'ink well' style of pot is still being used today. They are, in modern parlance, design classics. Originally made of hazel basketwork or hemp twine, now of heavy-duty nylon mesh, they are a simple, steep-sided chamber with a single funnel entrance in the top. Crabs, scenting bait inside, crawl over the pot, drop down through the entrance, and can't (usually) solve the conundrum of how to climb out again. A later modification, the 'parlour' pot, has since become more popular.

Parlour pots are slightly more complex than ink wells, because they consist of two 'rooms' – a bait room and a holding parlour. After feeding in the bait room, the crab climbs a mesh ramp, assuming it's the easy route out of the pot. But the ramp leads only to the parlour, from which there is no exit. Parlour pots are better at keeping crabs, which will eventually find their way out of the traditional ink well. If stormy weather prevents a crabber checking his or her pots for a few days, the ink wells will usually be stripped clean of bait and empty, whereas parlour pots will hold their catch more or less indefinitely.

Catching crabs in pots is, theoretically at least, one of the most fair-minded forms of fishing, because the creature is trapped alive and unharmed. So a crab in a pot is by no means doomed. Spend time on a professional crab boat and you might be surprised to see the vast number of crabs that are hauled from the deep, only to be eased carefully out of the parlour and then dropped back into the sea, unharmed. On some days, in the early summer especially, it's not unusual for a crab boat to return as much as 80 per cent of its 'catch'. Crabs may be returned to the sea alive for any of three reasons: if they're below the minimum landing size; if they're 'berried'; or if they're 'soft'. A 'soft' crab is one that has recently moulted – i.e. cast off its shell and started to grow a new one. These are also known as casters, white crabs, whitefoot crabs and glass crabs.

Soft crabs do *look* fantastic, with their pristine, shiny shells, but inside they're full of water, with deceptively little meat content. When a crab moults its shell, once or occasionally twice a year, to grow a bigger new one, its overall size increases by as much as 30 per cent. When the crab discards its old shell,

it pumps itself up with water to its new size, then waits until its soft skin gradually calcifies into new shell. Hardening takes up to two months, during which time the crab will hide in a secure place, owing to its vulnerable condition. So when the crab crawls back out into the big wide underwater world to show off its new shell, inside is just a lot of water and a very hungry, out-of-condition little crab. John Davies, a third-generation Cromer crab fisherman, puts it quite simply: 'The best crabs are the dirty ones,' he says. 'The ones covered in barnacles with old, battered shells – they're the ones you want to eat. They're the ones that have been feeding hard all year and are full of prime meat.'

John and his fellow crabbers are fiercely proud of the Cromer fishery and the informal code of conduct that helps it thrive. If you stand on Cromer prom at dawn and watch the crab boats preparing to launch, you'll see that the first thing to be loaded on board is baskets of empty crab shells and claws – leftovers from the crab-dressing workshops. These are dumped back into the sea around the crabbing grounds, to be picked clean by other crustaceans, including prawns and lobsters, who will use the extra calcium boost to help grow their own shells.

The second thing to be loaded on to the boat is the bait. With each boat regularly working up to 700 pots, in strings or 'shanks' of twenty-five, over a 20-mile radius, the Cromer fleet gets through an awful lot of bait. In the past, bait was caught locally, in the form of 'lesser' fish such as gurnard and scad. This no longer stacks up ecologically (it probably never did). These days, crab potters will buy in tonnes of frozen crab bait in the form of waste (heads and skeletons) from fish processing plants. This recycled fish makes a significant contribution to the diet of the local crabs. 'With the amount of bait we buy and put down day after day,' says John Davies, 'if you think about it, we're practically *farming* them. We don't mind rejecting as many as we do, because we know we'll get them again later, when they've grown bigger – on our bait!'

If you're choosing a crab at the fishmonger's, live or dead (and we'd say go for live every time), you may be offered the choice of a cock or a hen. One of each is the way to go! As a rule of thumb, cocks have slightly more white meat (mainly in their larger claws) and slightly stronger-flavoured brown meat; the hens, because of their bigger, more humped shell, normally contain a larger ration of brown meat. The one other consideration that should inform your choice is the season. The crab spawning cycle is complicated. Females move inshore to breed in late spring but they store the sperm after mating and don't fertilise the eggs until late winter, then carry them for about six weeks before hatching. So, all in all, this process takes up most of the year. Our advice is to avoid females between May and July, when they're preparing to breed, and to make sure you don't buy egg-carrying females – which you're likely to find between January and March.

The sex of a crab can be determined by looking at its 'tail' – a little flap of shell curled up under its body. The female's is wide and somewhat rounded – and, when she is berried, clasps the cluster of eggs to her body. The male tail is narrower and pointier.

A few warning bells have been rung of late, as reduced crab catches are being reported in some areas, including off Cromer, where catches were the lowest on record recently. Some blame overfishing elsewhere off the east coast, while others say it's all down to climate change. No one is suggesting we stop eating crab but it is important to shop with care: never buy small crabs but go for mature specimens that have had a chance to reproduce. Minimum landing sizes vary regionally from around 12 to 14cm, measured across the carapace. But it's easy to find much bigger crabs than that, and they are the ones to go for. Crabs caught off the South Devon coast are a particularly good choice. Subject to a policy called the Inshore Potting Agreement, crab fishermen here operate with a large minimum size and there are many sensible conservation measures in place, including some completely protected areas where crabs can breed in peace.

Of all the crustaceans in all the world, Nick would contend that British brown crab is the tastiest, Hugh would say a spider crab, see page 557, is *even* better. This is partly because brown crab has not one uniform kind of meat but several, of varying flavour and texture. There's the rich, nutty, creamy brown meat that lurks deep inside the carapace. There's the strands of sweet, tangy white meat that can be dug out of the leg sockets and body. Then there's a rich seam of short-grained white meat from inside the claws. And there's also the compressed pâté-like meat, tinged with pink and brown and tipped with black, that curls right up inside the 'toe' of each claw.

A freshly boiled brown crab is a wonderful thing to behold and to eat – best of all when you have chosen a live one and boiled it yourself. Cracking and picking your way through a whole crab, with the appropriate (or approximate) tools, and a bowl of homemade mayonnaise to hand, is one of the greatest pleasures to be taken from the sea (for the uninitiated, full instructions are on pages 90–2). Even if you cheat – by getting your crab ready dressed from the fishmonger's or some seaside eatery – it's never less than a pleasure. And the crab sandwich is certainly not to be sniffed at.

But although crab served cold is never dull, it would be a shame not to explore the hotter possibilities, in the sense of both temperature and spice. The sweet, robustly flavoured meat of crab can take a lot of strong flavours and still shine through. A curried crab soup (pages 266–7) and a piquant crab tart (pages 242–3) show the versatility of this armour-plated kitchen trouper. And, theologically controversial as it may sound, devilled crab (page 234) is sheer heaven.

Blue velvet swimmer crab *Necora puber*

Once, while fishing off the coast of Northern Ireland, we met a man who worked for Guinness Breweries as a draught beer pump fitter. He travelled around the province keeping the dark, velvety stout flowing. For many men, this would be a dream job, yet he was about to jack it all in and spend his savings on a boat, a winch and a collection of crab pots. His plan was to become a blue velvet swimmer crab fisherman. Needless to say, most of his friends thought he was insane.

Like many people in the British Isles, they'd never seen or heard of a blue velvet swimmer crab. Yet crab fishermen are plagued by them, particularly in the summer months. Commercial lobster and brown crab potters generally dislike blue velvet swimmers because they eat the bait intended for the other crabs, and have no commercial value in the UK.

In this country, it seems we like our crabs big. A blue velvet swimmer crab is tiny in comparison to the crabs we favour. The minimum landing size for a brown crab is 12–14cm across the carapace, yet your average velvet swimmer is no more than 8cm. They may be small in size but they're big on personality. Pay them some attention and they can become quite beguiling.

MCS RATING: not rated

REC MINIMUM SIZE: 6.5cm across the carapace

SEASON: avoid late winter and early spring (spawning); avoid egg-carrying (berried) females at any time

RECIPES: pages 234, 266–7, 327

The blue velvet swimmer gets its name from the covering of soft, thick hairs across its blue shell – and of course the fact that, for a crab, it's a surprisingly adept swimmer. Most crabs barely swim at all. They rely on crawling to get from A to B, and trust in their shell to provide protection in the case of an attack. But the two back legs of the velvet swimmer have evolved into distinct flat paddles. These allow it to travel at far greater speeds along and just above the sea floor, in a sort of swim-jump-crawl motion. So when faced with a hungry predator, the blue velvet swimmers don't just hunker down and hope their shell is a deterrent. They can scarper, and elude their tormentors with an impressive turn of speed.

Not that they're afraid to stand their ground. The velvet swimmer may be small, but it knows no fear. It will attack anything, of any size, and fight until the bitter end. A nip from one of these little crustaceans is no laughing matter. It hurts. The blue velvet swimmer crab is also known as the devil crab, or witch crab – names inspired by its wicked temper and fiery bright red eyes. They are devilish hunters, too. Their speed in the water makes them more efficient killers than other crabs – they can chase down prawns and ambush small fish, making them less reliant on carrion.

But the blue velvet swimmer – for all its attitude – has a tender side. When two velvet swimmers mate, the female needs to be in a soft-shell state in order for her to be receptive to a male's advances. It seems that a clash of hard shells simply wouldn't get a result. Having mated, the soft-shelled female remains vulnerable, so the male will clasp himself to her body and act as her shield and protector until her new shell has hardened sufficiently. During this phase, she will carry thousands of orange-coloured eggs (known as 'berries') under her body, until they hatch into tiny, shrimp-like larvae in the early spring.

Given their size, there's not a huge amount of meat in a velvet swimmer, but what you do get is very sweet and tasty. Of course, here in the UK we don't know that. But the Spanish do. They love our blue velvet swimmers, which they call *nécoras*, and they'll happily pay good money for them. Consequently there are now many crab potters who target velvet swimmers for export to Spain. All the crabs are transported live in seawater tanks. The trade seems to be booming, though it's hard to put figures on it. Currently, velvets simply get lumped together with all the other crab exports, including spiders and brown crabs. But according to the Spanish Fisheries Office, by far the greatest number of velvet swimmer crabs imported by Spain is coming from the UK.

In Spanish restaurants blue velvets are most often eaten in soupy stews. The crabs are served up whole, or halved, in the liquor, to be pulled apart with much cracking, sucking and licking of lips. A Galician favourite is *nécoras rellenas* – stuffed blue velvets. Meat is picked from the shell and claws of a few crabs and mixed with a seasoned béchamel sauce, then stuffed back into the upturned shell, topped with breadcrumbs and baked until golden brown. We have our own version of this – for which you can use any edible crab species – on page 234.

So why don't we eat blue velvet swimmer crabs? Why is it that something we deem a worthless nuisance sells for a pretty penny in Spain? Why is it impossible to buy velvets in this country, even though our crab fishermen are catching gazillions of them? Is it because they are too small? Too fiddly? Too scary? Too blue? We can't answer these questions, but we can encourage you to buck the trend. You'll need a little determination to track some down. You may even have to accost a fisherman, harbourside, and brandish some ready cash at him.

If you can organise some casual holiday potting, you may well catch a number of blue velvets. Even without a boat or pots, they can be caught off piers and breakwaters, with a simple drop net and a chunk of mackerel for bait. Summer and early autumn are most productive. After killing them with a spike (see page 89), boil for just 5 minutes in well-salted water. Let cool, then get cracking, with a bowl of mayonnaise to hand. You'll soon see what you've been missing... and why our Irish friend has turned his attention from Black Velvet to Blue.

Spider crab *Maia squinado*

There is something undeniably alien about spider crabs. With their mechanical legs and spiky, armoured bodies they look like *War of the Worlds* invaders. Their sheer redness adds to their 'Martian' aura – most shellfish only look that way *after* they've been cooked.

Every year they make further inroads, in numbers and range. Fifty years ago their northern expeditionary force, heading from their mothership in the Mediterranean, had only reached the Channel Islands and the tip of Cornwall. Now they've colonised crabbing grounds as far north as Anglesey. The odd one even turns up off Scotland. No one's exactly sure why they are doing so well, though global warming is an obvious possible explanation. They may be the beneficiaries of the same subtle rise in water temperatures that is encouraging red mullet, gilt-head bream and even trigger fish to establish breeding populations around our shores.

MCS RATING: 2 (2–3)

REC MINIMUM SIZE: 12cm across the carapace

SEASON: avoid April–July (spawning); avoid egg-carrying (berried) females at any time

RECIPES: pages 234, 239, 242–3, 327, 389

Their presence is becoming quite a zoological phenomenon. Every spring, in inshore waters from Sussex to Cornwall, there are huge migrations of *Maia squinado* tramping across the seabed. They appear as if from nowhere (though actually from further offshore) each May (hence *Maia*), tangling themselves up in fishermen's nets or clambering into crab pots where, according to more than one commercial potter, 'they scare the lobsters away'.

These migrations culminate in huge, orgiastic underwater mounds of crabs, appearing at intervals all along the submerged south coast. Divers and snorkellers regularly witness these heaving piles of spider crabs, yet marine biologists aren't really sure what the crabs are up to. One theory is that the males construct a castle of 'spiky shelled manhood' around the fecund females in order to protect their precious brood stock.

The sex life of the spider crab is certainly unusual. Most female crabs must moult from their shells, and so be in a soft state, in order to mate. Not so spiders. They'll mate with gusto even when both the male and female are hard-shelled and bristling with spikes. More astonishingly, the female spider crab can, if push comes to shove, dispense not only with the moulting but even with the male. In aquaria, female spider crabs that have been kept totally separated from males have been able to give birth to as many as five consecutive broods. This apparent gift for immaculate conception suggests that females can store sperm somewhere inside their bodies, if necessary for years, for use when good men are thin on the ground. (Or possibly even produce it themselves.) But no one has yet been able to locate their secret sperm stash. (Or gonads.)

It's no surprise that a creature as weird as a spider crab might want to take steps to camouflage itself. They may be big and spiky, but predators such as bull huss and big skate still think of them as lunch. To try to blend in, spider crabs have developed a technique that seems spookily intelligent (especially for a creature that, theoretically, is on the same intellectual plane as a woodlouse). They have been observed sticking seaweed 'cuttings' dipped in gummy saliva on top of their spiny shells. This kind of sub-aqua gardening-cum-hairdressing actually works. The more cutting-edge of these green-fingered crustaceans can be seen sporting growing fringes and comb-overs of self-planted seaweed, sometimes of several different species. (Apparently bladder wrack with sea lettuce highlights is very 'in' right now.)

Make no mistake – for all their other-worldliness, spider crabs are great eating (of which more shortly). Yet for years in the UK there was no recognition of their worth at all. (Is this sounding familiar?) Many potters, blaming them for the absence of other crustaceans, used to kill them as vermin. At best they'd be 'recycled' – smashed up and used for prawn pot-bait; at worst, simply thrown back into the sea, either dead or dying. What a waste.

This changed in the late 1980s, when British crab potters caught on to the lucrative continental market. Such is the Spanish love affair with the succulent *centolla* that they value it (and price it) even more highly than lobster. Nowadays, practically every spider crab landed in Britain is transported alive to Spain in specially designed lorries carrying oxygenated seawater tanks. No Spanish fish cook would ever contemplate buying a dead crab.

Thousands of tonnes of spider crabs are landed every year in Britain, many in nets but some, more sustainably, in pots. Pot-caught spider crab is on the MCS's 'Fish to Eat' list. However, actually buying one remains something of a challenge. You have to intercept the journey from Cornish crab pot to Catalan restaurant

somehow (preferably nearer to Cornwall than Catalonia). Unless you buy direct from a boat in the harbour (we get them fairly regularly from the netsmen in West Bay), or shop at wholesale fish markets such as Billingsgate and Brixham, you'll find this hard to do. Meanwhile, in Spain even the supermarkets sell spider crabs – most of which are no doubt caught in British waters.

It's madness. This is seriously fine eating – and there isn't even the excuse that they are too fiddly to be worth bothering with. The Fearnley view is that spider crab is better and sweeter than any brown crab. The Fisher perspective (biased in favour of anything from Norfolk) puts it second only to a Cromer crab.

We both love eating it, whenever we can get it. The bigger the better. The claws may look long and spindly, but they're deceptively meaty, and the body is loaded with sweet white meat. You can prepare it as for any brown crab recipe – including cold and dressed with good mayonnaise and lettuce. However, we reckon that spiced, stuffed back in the shell, crumbed and baked in a hot oven, it is unforgettably good.

At last, here in the West Country, there is some recognition of its true class. Several local restaurants, such as the Riverside in West Bay, are serving spider crab in season (late summer and autumn) and we hear rumours of others in Cornwall doing the same. A few London chefs are catching on, too, and the National Trust has just started taking them from Welsh fishermen to use in their restaurants around the UK. We think we might just be on the cusp of a spider crab breakthrough.

You could help this happen. Keep nagging your fishmonger; enquire at your supermarket fish counter (at least then they'll have heard of it); and be ready to board any crab boats you see pulling up to a quay near you, with cash at the ready. Then serve up the spiders, evangelically, to your friends. Let's embrace these charming aliens and make them our own.

Molluscs

Limpet *Patella vulgata*

Limpets are simple, unassuming gastropods that expect little more from life than a rock to cling to and some seawater to suck. They don't demand a lot of attention – and they don't get it.

They are always easy to locate. Amongst the seaweed and algae on rocks, iron pilings or breakwaters, their upturned cone-shaped shells stick out like miniature volcanoes. In fact they can be found practically everywhere the sea meets the land, as long as there's something solid and grippable to broker the encounter. So whether you're picking your way through a rock pool near Rhyll or inspecting the rusty legs of a Victorian pier in Brighton, you'll find a cluster of limpets welded in place, anchored by the epic suction of their wide, flat bottoms – or feet, as they are technically known.

These days, the only people who ever pay limpets much attention are shore anglers – and even they are rather reluctant. They may occasionally prise a limpet off a rock to put on their hooks for bait, but usually only when they've run out of superior baits, such as squid and rag-worm, and things are getting desperate. But you don't have to be desperate to want to remove a limpet. You could be hungry – or at least curious.

Limpets are not the most challenging quarry – they are hardly going to outrun you. However, they do have the power of suction on their side. Even so, they can be removed from a rock fairly easily, using a flat-bladed knife or a paint scraper, so long as you are quick. The trick is to make your first attempt the serious one. Don't dither, and don't fluff it. Strike hard and fast, sliding the blade between the lip of the limpet's shell and the rock in one speedy action. If you don't surprise your limpet with the first slice, it will suck down so tight that you'll never get it free – except perhaps by smashing it with a small boulder, which would be a little disproportionate.

Inside a limpet's shell you'll find a soft, mussel-like, mushy blob containing its internal organs, balanced on top of the thick, rubbery circular foot (or hidden underneath it if, as is likely, you're holding the limpet upside down – in other words inside up). The muscular foot is what anchors the limpet to rock. It has the consistency of a whelk foot or very tough squid, which makes for spectacularly durable hook bait. A piece of limpet foot will stay firmly on a hook through rough weather, umpteen casts, and even a few fish attacks. It works well for any rock-grazing fish, such as black bream. Fussier shoreline feeders, such as bass and smoothhound, might not be quite so easily impressed – but they'll certainly give it a chew if it happens to bump them on the nose.

In the Shetland Islands, limpet baits were traditionally used as a form of chum to attract coley. A fisherman would row out to sea with a good supply of boiled limpets, which he'd chew into an oily pulp and spit out on to the surface of the sea. As the oily limpet chum (or 'vam', as it was known locally) spread,

MCS RATING: not rated

REC MINIMUM SIZE: always take a mixture of sizes

SEASON: avoid September–January (spawning)

RECIPES: pages 203, 271

hungry coley would be drawn to the area, attracted by the pheromones exuded from the limpet flesh. They could then be caught on mackerel feathers or lures.

Poor limpets, sitting around doing nothing until someone decides to bash or chomp and chew them. But if they seem like passive victims, that isn't quite the whole story. They have a dark side. In fact they are, collectively, capable of wreaking mass destruction. They stand accused of undermining the very fabric of the nation: the white cliffs of Dover, no less.

A Victorian scientist by the name of Hawkshore was the first to suggest that limpets were responsible for eroding the foreshore at Dover but no one believed him. Now scientists have measured the amount of calcium present in limpet excrement and can confirm that he was, indeed, correct. As they creep around, nibbling algae, the limpets are eroding the chalk cliff footings to the tune of 1.5mm every year. It's a fact: the lowly limpet is slowly eating the nation, from the Southeast up.

So maybe it's time we began to eat them back? Or at least revive the tradition of doing so. Back in the eighteenth century, limpet harvests were so important to the inhabitants of northern Scotland that when they failed, there were violent protests and riots. The problem was the development of the kelp-cutting industry, which harvested the seaweed to burn and turn into potash for gardens in the south. This ruined the habitat for limpets, and so threatened the livelihood and diet of the islanders.

Besides being an important source of nourishment in times past, they also had medicinal uses. Limpet extract was used in the treatment of poor eyesight, rheumatism and 'lameness'. Even today, there's a health tonic popular in Australia created from extract of limpet shells. Limpets are also currently being studied in research for a skin cancer treatment, amongst other things.

Unlike us, the Spanish never gave up on eating limpets. Seaside restaurants in Spain and the Canaries present their *lapas* in huge, round, dimpled plates, like those used to dish up snails. The limpets are lightly boiled, removed from their shells and then swamped in puddles of rich parsley and garlic butter. They are perfectly pleasant, too – like rubbery *escargots*. 'Like rubbery rubber, then,' a cynic might say, and it's true that they wouldn't amount to much if they weren't

steeped in that pungent, chin-dribbling butter. But, if you are armed with a cocktail stick, a glass of chilled *rosado* and a hunk of crusty bread for dabbing at the juices on the plate, there are many worse ways to pass the time.

Limpets are still eaten in the Channel Islands, too – and that's where our own favourite limpet recipe comes from (see page 203). It's all about the quality of the liquor – to which the limpets contribute a very agreeable, slightly kelpy, flavour. The limpets themselves are really just there to keep the teeth busy.

However, before you rush out with your limpet picker, there is something else you should know. Limpets may be eating the cliffs but in other ways they are a force for ecological stability. The UK's foremost expert on limpets, Professor Stephen Hawkins of the Marine Biological Association, explains: 'Limpets turn from male to female as they mature, so picking all of the large ones in any given area could lead to a serious sexual imbalance, something that has led to limpet population crashes in the Azores with virtual extinction on some islands.'

Limpets are also important in maintaining the balance of the seashore, by helping to keep marine vegetation in check. So a population crash would change the whole ecology of the shoreline, and beaches stripped of limpets would become totally overrun with seaweeds.

We'd have to concede that limpets aren't likely to become the new fish finger. They're a wild food that will probably remain the preserve of the curious beachcomber – and, given environmental concerns, that's just as well. Clearly the occasional limpet feast enjoyed by the odd intrepid forager isn't going to wreak havoc on our beaches. But, if you do feel like giving these tenacious shellfish a go, bear in mind their unique biology and their crucial role in the food chain: take only a few, from a wide area, and go for a range of sizes. Remember that the little guys may be the only guys, and the big old girls can be a bit tough anyway.

Winkle *Littorina littorea*

In Victorian London, winkles were a staple food for the poor and a dirty little secret for the rich. Certainly, no gentleman would freely admit to eating them, because they were (according to *Cassell's Dictionary of Food*, published in 1880) 'a considerable article of food among the poorer classes'. Even the relentlessly thorough Mrs Beeton wouldn't stoop so low as to document the cooking of the plebeian periwinkle.

Winkles may well have been working class, but in reality toffs, particularly chaps, loved them too – on the quiet. In Edwardian times they became an essential part of the fashion for 'slumming it'. In the dead of night, down some dark alley in the grubby underbelly of the city, gentlemen of means were out among sailors and whores, scoffing the mollusc of the common folk with guilt-ridden glee. P. G. Wodehouse wrote of spying upon 'Marmaduke de Courcy, in the lower slums, hunched over a barrow in the street, eating winkles with a pin'.

Today the tables have turned full circle. Most winkles are sold in smart, francophile restaurants, either as a novelty *amuse-bouche* or to exhibit a commitment to thoroughness by providing an extra item on the *grand plateau de fruits de mer*. The days of their being peddled by the pint in some back alley or seaside promenade are largely gone.

MCS RATING: 4 (3–4)

REC MINIMUM SIZE: 2cm

SEASON: avoid February–June (peak spawning period)

RECIPES: pages 209, 277, 328

It shouldn't surprise us that the winkle is beloved of the French. It is basically a small *escargot* – one that doesn't mind getting wet and salty. Like its land-based cousins, the winkle moves around on a muscular, fleshy foot. But instead of munching through baby lettuces in your garden, the winkle makes its way in life by scraping algae off rocks with its surprisingly rough, serrated tongue.

Here is a sea creature that we can safely say is not on anyone's critical list. Winkles are plentiful, and tend to be gathered by hand, which is about as selective and sustainable as fishing gets. They are joyfully easy to collect, and a winkle hunt is not a complex affair. Almost every rock-strewn beach in Britain hosts a healthy population of winkles, which is revealed twice daily by the lowering tide. Some are an industrial grey-black in colour, some almost white, while others sport a variety of muted colours and stripes. All are edible. And all you have to do is pick them up and put them in a bucket.

Free seafood feasts don't come any simpler, and the boil-in-a-bucket approach makes for a great impromptu picnic. Simply rinse your winkles in clean seawater and boil in same for 5 or 6 minutes. Then start ransacking your beach bag for a safety pin – or go snorkelling for sea urchins.

For a more formal session at home, you can boost the flavour of the winkles by cooking them in a simple court-bouillon (see page 277). Drain them when they are done and then consider the only decision you have to make: do I want to eat these one by one from the shell, or delay gratification by shelling them all first and then gorging on several at a time? There's only one right answer, of course.

You can (and most do) eat them *au naturel*. Or you can dip them in a sweet, mustardy vinaigrette or good old garlic butter. Or there is always the end of the pier thing – dip them in malt vinegar and sprinkle with white pepper.

There are not many 'recipes' for winkles, but if you've had a really good haul and want to make something special out of them, you can cook and shell a good pile and use them instead of chopped whelk meat in the recipe for Whelk fritters on page 328.

Whatever you do with your winkles, you'll want a pin to get them out of the shell. It's done with a prick and a twist. Getting each winkle out whole, unbroken in any of its tight little spiral turns, takes concentration and dexterity – like peeling an apple without breaking the peel. Total success calls for a small celebration – the most obvious option being another sip of wine.

The flavour of this sea-going snail is a pleasant surprise. It provides a nutty/chewy/kelpy oral sensation, and once you've got the hang of the winkle-picking ritual it quickly becomes quite addictive. You can eat everything that comes out of the shell, including the not unbogey-like twist of innards that comes out last. It may look iffy but it tastes sweet and slightly livery. We think those who discard it are missing out.

The one thing you will definitely want to remove, though, is the scab-like sole to their single foot, which has the unmistakable texture of toenail. This is the operculum – a hard cover that winkles use like a small trapdoor to seal their shell from predators and prevent it drying out. Operculum removal presents another dilemma: do you nip it off with your fingernails and deposit it neatly in a saucer? Or bite it off, flip it once around your tongue to make sure there's no flesh sticking to it and then spit it in the general direction of the fireplace or bin? We guess that depends on the extent to which you are slumming it.

Whelk *Buccinum undatum*

Whelks were dragging their curly shells across the seabed 50 million years before the dawn of mankind, and they'll probably still be here long after we're gone. They are built to last – not just in an evolutionary sense but as individuals. Their armour-plated mobile home is made with layered deposits from their calcium-rich blood, and it gets thicker and more impregnable as they get older. It's virtually impenetrable to any predator – except humans.

As long ago as the Stone Age, whelks were a useful subsistence food for primitive coastal communities. And no doubt stones were the weapons used to smash open their shells and release their meat. But the whelks would have been mainly shoreline and rockpool inhabitants – dog whelks and the like – not the meaty molluscs that can be fished from deeper waters. It was the Romans who brought the kind of basket fish traps to Britain that could catch fat whelks in big numbers. Yet another thing to add to that list of things 'the Romans did for us'.

As a marketable commodity, whelks came into their own in the late medieval period. The Church's imposition of meatless fast days – as often as three times a week – meant almost any kind of fish got a look in. Whelk flesh is nothing if not meaty, so they were particularly welcome, and eaten enthusiastically by both rich and poor. Big households would order many hundreds of them to eat over Lent. They were also smart enough to mark a special occasion: for the enthronement feast of the Archbishop of Canterbury in 1504, 4,000 whelks were served – and that was just as a garnish (for a centrepiece of salted sturgeon).

MCS RATING: 4
REC MINIMUM SIZE: 4.5cm
SEASON: avoid November–January (spawning)
RECIPES: pages 209, 328, 364

Although they will dine on marine carrion, whelks are themselves predators. Their favourite food is live mussel, slurped straight from the shell. A whelk will position itself in front of a mussel and wait until it opens its shell to suck in water and food. Then, the moment the shell parts, the whelk shoves in its prehensile mouthparts, like a bailiff jamming his boot in a debtor's front door. Its tiny, razor-sharp teeth nibble furiously at the mussel's soft, exposed flesh. Anchored tight to a rock, with its door wedged open, the mussel is unable to move or defend itself – and within a minute or two, there's nobody home.

Amongst themselves, whelks are not the most sociable of creatures either. Like sulky teenagers, they hang out on the silty sea floor in small, single-sex groups. Male and female whelks only get together when they intend to mate. In the spring, as water temperatures begin to rise, female whelks start the courtship ritual by releasing potent pheromones, which will attract a gang of horny – and indeed horned – males. Fertilised eggs are laid by several different females in loose, cellular clumps, like balls of slimy bubble-wrap. These are often washed up on the beach in spring and summer, and are known by fishermen as 'wash balls', because they foam up like bubble bath when rubbed between the hands.

Modern commercial whelk fishing didn't kick off until the 1960s, stimulated by the increasing popularity of the whelk stalls in Britain's coastal resort towns. For holidaymakers and day-trippers, these shellfish shacks became an essential part of the seaside experience. You could choose from whelks, cockles and prawns.

In the 1980s whelk fishing cranked up a gear. The Koreans and Japanese took a liking to their flesh and a lucrative export market was born. Koreans especially love our whelks – boiled, sliced and served with pickled vegetables and a dressing of soy sauce and rice wine vinegar. They are invariably washed down with plenty of cold beer. (Some Korean men swear by them as a performance-enhancing 'love food' – but we reckon it's just the beer talking.)

For a while, the Far East market for whelks boomed, and many British crab and lobster fishermen switched to laying whelk pots, in order to ride the gravy train. But like so many fish market bubbles, it soon burst. First foreign buyers found cheaper sources, squeezing the British fishermen ever harder on price. Then, in the late 1990s, the South Korean economy took a dive. The whelk price halved in a matter of months and orders for British whelks rapidly shrivelled up.

Even in the boom times, whelk fishing was never a glamorous occupation. The 'pots' are usually just recycled plastic containers – jerry cans and the like – half filled with concrete and fitted with an inner lip of coarse nylon netting to stop the whelks getting out, once they've crawled in to investigate the smell. Whelk baits are as stinky as possible: putrefying fish guts or skeletons so ancient and manky that other bottom-dwellers would barely consider them food.

In the mid-winter months, when crab fishing slows down as the bigger crustaceans become semi-dormant, crab fishermen often switch to whelk potting instead. But it's not a seasonal shift they – or their loved ones – relish. 'After a week or two on the whelks, I'll lose all my mates,' says Steve, a Lyme Regis fisherman. 'I walk in the front door of the pub, and they all walk out the back. Even my wife won't let me in the house until I've stripped off on the doorstep.' Occasionally, whelks are dredged rather than pot caught. As with all dredging, this is a far less sustainable option, so avoid these if you can.

In Britain today, whelks are still mainly savoured as a rubbery seaside snack, served boiled and cold, then drenched in malt vinegar and white pepper. This tried and trusted combination certainly has its appeal – and some whelk fanciers would consider any deviation heretical. But we think it would be a mistake to imagine there is no room for improvement.

To get the best from whelks, buy them alive and cook them yourself at home. Scrub them well, then immerse them in a pan of cold water perked up with a splash of wine, a few twists of pepper, and maybe a sprinkling of fennel seeds. Bring them from cold to boiling on the hob. This helps to keep them tender, whereas plunging them straight into hot water toughens the meat. Simmer for about 10 minutes (a bit longer for really big ones, but don't overdo it or they'll toughen up), then serve them warm with garlic mayonnaise (page 332), or homemade tartare sauce (page 324). Or, if you want to mess only mildly with tradition, upgrade the vinegar to cider or red wine, to which you can add some finely chopped onions or shallots, and try paprika instead of white pepper.

However you're planning to enjoy them, first you need to get them out of the shell – a prod and a twist with a small fork will do it (pins are strictly for winkles). Opinion is divided as to how much of the contents you should eat. The big, curled, rubbery 'foot' is clearly the main meal – and the toenail-like trapdoor, or operculum, must be discarded. After the foot, from deep inside the shell, comes a trail of grey-brown innards. Many people discard these, but they actually taste quite sweet – liverish, rather like the brown meat of the crab. They can get a bit rich though, so we tend to eat a few and chuck a few.

Don't despair if you can only buy whelks pre-boiled and shelled (or even frozen – whelks freeze well, and are actually more tender, though a mite less juicy, when defrosted). It's still possible to transform the workaday whelk into something special. The exotic salsa on page 364 will whisk you straight from the drizzly seafront of a northern resort town to a palm-fringed hideaway. And should paradise ever become mundane, you can always reach for the malt vinegar and head home to Blighty.

Bivalves

Mussel *Mytilus edulis*

'Location, location, location' is the mussel's maxim. Get it right and life will be sweet. Get it wrong and the mussel will either starve, get munched by a fish, or cling forlornly to a rock near the low tide mark, wondering where its next meal is coming from.

Not that it's got much choice where it fetches up, buffeted as it is in its planktonic infancy by tides and currents way beyond its control. But if it, and a few thousand of its friends, should get lucky, and seed and settle themselves on a firm foundation in a moderate tidal current well stocked with nutrients, then they can hang out for a few years. They'll be going nowhere, just holding fast to see what the tide will bring to their doors. Their single-hinged, double-sided, hermetically sealed doors.

Mussels suck. All day long. A 5cm mussel will suck its way through 50 litres of seawater in a single day, extracting microscopic nutrition by using its flesh as a filter. Successful filter feeders need to live in water that is swirling with nutrients and deep enough to keep them wet, and feeding, most of the time. Some mussels spend their whole lives submerged, many metres beneath the surface of the sea. For others, life's a beach, as they end up living between the high and low tide marks.

Estuaries and shallow, muddy bays strewn with rocks and weed are good for mussels because they're normally silty, due to soil run-off brought down by the river and/or sediment stirred up by the tides. The only downside of living in the tidal zone is that you're left high and dry twice a day as the tide goes out. No water means no food. It also means exposure to hungry birds and mammals, who recognise the contents of a mussel shell to be an excellent feed. In the end it's a trade-off between good feeding opportunities and the risks of becoming someone else's dinner.

Whether a mussel is gripping the seabed, living in a rock pool, hanging from a mooring rope or clinging to a breakwater, it anchors itself with its 'beard', or byssal threads. If you've ever cooked mussels, you'll have first ripped out the cluster of fibres that protrude from the join between the two halves of the shell. Made from iron deposits that the mussel extracts from seawater, this 'beard' is remarkable stuff. Byssal threads collected from large mussels and other bivalves used to be dried and spun into cloth known as 'sea silk'. The resulting fabric was so light, so strong and so fine that a pair of gloves would fit into a walnut shell and a pair of stockings into a snuffbox. King Tutankhamen and many Roman emperors wore cloaks made of sea silk.

Mussels have been eaten for centuries all around the coastal regions of Europe and other parts of the world. But they fell out of favour in Britain in the second half of the nineteenth century, due to increasing industrial pollution. Being a bivalve filter feeder makes mussels prone to taking toxins on board. Like oysters,

MCS RATING: 2 (1–2) EAT MORE!

REC MINIMUM SIZE: 5cm

SEASON: avoid May–August (spawning)

RECIPES: pages 202, 232, 238, 262, 264, 267, 272, 275, 276, 386 they are at their most vulnerable during the breeding season: not only are their immune systems weaker as they lose condition but the seas are warmer, and bio-toxins more likely to thrive and multiply. This is why mussels and oysters are traditionally shunned when there isn't an 'r' in the month – from May to August. By the turn of the century, trust in the safety of the mussel supply was on the wane; food writers of the time devote very little space to mussel recipes.

Most of the mussels we now eat are farmed, their location chosen for them not by the vagaries of tides but by human planning. Of all forms of aquaculture, mussel farming is perhaps the most benign, and the least environmentally disruptive (see page 37). This is largely because the business of feeding – so fraught with the potential for irresponsible choices – is taken out of human hands and left to nature. In fact, the word 'farming' implies a higher level of intervention than is generally required to cultivate mussels. Choose a location where wild mussels are already thriving and all you need to do is provide some

suitable structures, easy to harvest from, for the future generations to grow on. The wild 'spat' – tiny, free-floating planktonic seed mussels – will find the structures, fix themselves to them and start to grow. No feed, no fertilisers and no chemicals required.

The first farmed mussels were grown on poles, especially in France, where the technique of erecting wooden *bouchots* – poles driven into the estuary mud – has been credited to a shipwrecked Irishman called Patrick Walton. According to French gastronomic legend, Walton found himself washed up in the Bay of Aiguillon in the early thirteenth century. The story goes that he erected crude nets between wooden poles hammered into the mud flats to catch migrating seabirds. He soon observed that tiny seed mussels were gathering on the poles. They fattened up beautifully, and so more and more poles were erected, as mussel cultivation took over from seabird trapping. *Bouchots* are still widely used, especially on the vast tidal mudflats of the Charente-Maritime.

However, most of today's farmed mussels are grown on lengths of heavy rope, studded with plastic spikes to increase the surface area available to the clustering bivalves. Suspended beneath huge floating rafts, the ropes are situated where mussels abound, currents are gentle and the seawater is full of nutrients. The mussels usually reach market size (5–7cm in length) within three years. They may have been 'farmed', but to all intents and purposes they are wild – a fact reflected in their quality and flavour. Farmed mussels, and the waters they come from, are regularly bug-tested, and those destined for supermarkets and the catering trade are often routinely treated with ultraviolet light in order to neutralise harmful bacteria. This does no harm to the mussel or its meat.

The suspended rope technique was a Spanish invention, and the rocky inlets around Galicia are still home to hundreds of mussel farms. Most British mussel farms are situated in the sheltered sea lochs of Scotland and Ireland, but bays, estuaries and harbours all around the coast have been tried with varying degrees of success. We get lovely local rope-grown mussels from Portland Harbour. (The huge, green-lipped mussels from New Zealand that you come across in supermarkets are not a patch on the best home-grown mussels.)

Unlike most other forms of aquaculture, a mussel farm can actually boost local biodiversity. The network of mussel-clad ropes attracts seaweeds, anemones and the like, providing a haven and nursery for various species of fish and marine invertebrates. So, what's the environmental downside? Well, the only serious accusation that has been levelled at mussel farms – usually by tourists – is their visual impact on a wild coastal landscape. And it's true that the floating rafts do not exactly adorn the remote sea lochs where they are often situated. But locals we have spoken to, in Skye and other Hebridean islands, are very supportive of their local mussel farms, which boost the islands' economies at little cost to the environment. A visitor's most constructive contribution is to order a big plate of these delicious mussels in one of the islands' many hostelries.

Mussels grow wild all around our coastline and can easily be collected at low tide. Given that you're unlikely to have an ultraviolet mussel zapping kit at home, how wary should you be about the safety of foraged shellfish? Well, we have gathered them regularly for years in the far north of Scotland, on the breakwaters of north Norfolk, and in and among the rock pools of Cornwall. Touch wood, neither of us has ever been caught out with a dose of poisoning.

We usually purge the wild mussels we collect, though, leaving them for at least eight hours in plenty of clear seawater laced with a little oatmeal. But this is not about making them safer, only nicer to eat. It encourages them to lose any sand or grit. Our own view is that paranoia about the safety of gathered wild shellfish is largely unjustified. However, you should always take local advice – and steer clear, for obvious reasons, of shellfish growing near sewage outlets.

In the end, the most important safety advice is simply this: only cook with live mussels. So, whether you've collected or bought mussels, reject any that don't close when you're cleaning them – they're dead, or as good as. Once they're cooked, reject any that have not opened in the pan.

Fresh, live mussels will keep for three or four days in the fridge and should take no more than 3 or 4 minutes to cook. As soon as they are open they are done, and should be removed from the pan. Cooked for just 2 minutes too long, they'll shrivel up and halve in size. This caveat aside, mussels are a doddle to prepare, perfect for those who yearn for some quick, intense sea flesh.

There are really only two ways we ever cook mussels, though the first, our default setting, has infinite variations on the theme. This is the classic *moules marinière*: the mussels are simply steamed open in a liquor of wine, butter and garlic, then perhaps finished with a dash of cream and a handful of chopped parsley. But wine can become cider, beer, a little fish stock or plain water. And aromatics can go in all kinds of directions: sake, soy, chilli and ginger; saffron; lemongrass and coriander, with or without coconut milk; Thai green curry paste.

Large mussels (like the lovely fat, wild ones we gathered on the Isle of Mull, shown on page 568) can also be barbecued in their shells until they pop open and then eaten as they are, or with a dab of butter or a few drops of olive oil and a squeeze of lemon juice. If you have complete confidence in the quality of the water from which they were taken, they can be eaten raw, like oysters. You may even prefer them this way – they are less substantial, but sweeter by far.

Oyster

Native *Ostrea edulis* **Pacific** *Crassostrea gigas* **Rock** *Crassostrea angulata*

To most people, oysters are the seafood that has come to stand for luxury and wealth. But it hasn't always been the case. In the mid-nineteenth century, Dickens wrote that 'poverty and oysters always seem to go together. The poorer the place, the greater the call there is.' So the status of this hefty bivalve has fluctuated over the centuries.

The Ancient Britons regarded most shellfish as subsistence food, to be scavenged when meat or fish wasn't available. But the invading Romans loved their oysters, and ours, and made prodigious efforts to cultivate and nurture them. They corralled the young seed oysters and grew them on in readily accessible beds in estuaries and sheltered bays. The most famous of these were clustered around Camulodunum (Colchester).

Once collected, the oysters were transported alive, in barrels of wet seaweed, to be enjoyed by wealthy Romans living far from the sea. In one 'shell midden' excavated at Silchester, Berkshire, more than a million oyster shells were found. British native oysters were deemed of such quality that they were even exported back to Rome.

MCS RATINGS: wild native 3–4; farmed native and Pacific both 1 EAT MORE!

REC MINIMUM SIZE: wild native 5cm; farmed oysters should be harvested at appropriate size

SEASON: wild native, avoid May–August (spawning); farmed oysters N/A

RECIPES: pages 202, 268

After the Romans departed, oysters fell back out of favour and it wasn't until after the Norman invasion in the eleventh century that the practice of farming, harvesting and transporting them around the country was revived. During the Middle Ages, the Church inadvertently boosted the oyster trade by its imposition of twice- or even thrice-weekly 'fish days', during which the eating of animal flesh was forbidden. Nowadays we credit oysters with being able to inflame the passions, but back then it was red meat that was considered to be the wicked fuel of lascivious desire. Oysters found favour almost as an anti-aphrodisiac. But the trade in oysters was stimulated, and swelled accordingly.

By the seventeenth century, Poole oysters, pickled in salt and vinegar, were being exported to Holland, Italy, Spain and even the West Indies. And for the next two centuries, most oysters continued to be either preserved or cooked, as a bulker of other ingredients in stews and pies, or baked into loaves of bread. The fashion for eating oysters raw in the half-shell didn't emerge until the late nineteenth century, when over-harvesting and harsh winters caused a collapse of the inshore beds. As they became scarcer, so they began to be treated with greater respect.

Today in the UK, nearly all our oysters are eaten raw. It's the naked, frilled, fleshy, wet rawness that makes slurping one such a sensual experience. Let's face it, a boiled whelk isn't a come-on. A vinegary cockle never got anyone in the mood (at least, no one we know). But a slippery, salty oyster, recumbent and ready inside its glistening, pearl-lined cavity, is undeniably arousing.

Any scientific evidence supporting the oyster's aphrodisiac reputation normally revolves around zinc. But it's a bit tenuous. Oysters, like many shellfish, contain high quantities of zinc compared to meat or fish. A deficiency in zinc can cause human sperm to become sluggish, so an oyster-derived zinc boost might, just, put a little more lead in your pencil.

Oysters hardly need science to make them sexy, however. They just need to be shared with the right companion. We'll leave it to the great Jonathan Swift to express the sheer rumpypumpiness of the oyster, in these lines from his poem 'Oysters':

So plump and so fresh,   *Of a lass or a lad;*
So sweet in their flesh,   *And Madam your wife*
No Colchester oyster   *They'll please to the Life;*
Is sweeter and moister: *Be she barren, be she old,*
Your stomach they settle,   *Be she slut, or be she scold,*
And rouse up your mettle: *Eat my oysters and lie near her,*
They'll make you a dad   *She'll be fruitful, never fear her.*

Three types of oyster are cultivated and eaten in Britain and Ireland: the native or European oyster, the Portuguese or rock oyster, and the Pacific oyster. The waters chosen to nurture them are sometimes salty and sometimes brackish, but always nutrient-rich and fairly shallow, estuaries and inlets along the coastal zone.

Native oysters are, as the name implies, our indigenous species. They're the smallest and slowest growing of the three types, with the roundest and least jagged shells. They breed naturally in British waters, tend to be the most expensive and are generally considered the best: sweet, dense and clean, with an almost minerally aftertaste.

Portuguese or rock oysters were artificially introduced from Iberian stocks in the nineteenth century to replenish our overfished stock. They are more robust and disease-resistant than our gentle natives, and grow faster and larger. They don't have quite the same cachet amongst connoisseurs as the native, and aren't able to spawn naturally in our colder waters. Their shells are much more ridged and spectacular than those of natives – and all too easy to cut your hands on when you're opening them.

The Pacific oyster, sometimes also called the Japanese oyster, is the most recently introduced (from the Far East), and the fattest and fastest growing of them all. Again, they can't breed here without human intervention. In their native Asia they are allowed to grow to a huge size, in order to be processed into oyster sauce, that sticky, savoury staple of oriental cooking.

Oysters are graded by size before they're sold, with Grade 1 being the biggest and 4 the smallest. Grade 2 is probably the best value for money. There's some confusion, not to say disagreement, about when you should eat oysters – though you will certainly find rock oysters offered for sale all year round. The adage about not eating oysters unless there's an 'r' in the month is based upon the native oyster's breeding season. From May to August, while it's spawning, the native oyster's flesh becomes 'milky'. It appears opaque and has a creamy texture, which can be off-putting. Since rock and Pacific oysters can't breed in our water temperatures, they can be eaten all year round. They may, however, go slightly milky in the summer months, a seasonal variation that some enthusiasts are happy to embrace, others less so.

The Portuguese and Pacific oysters are encouraged to spawn in temperature-controlled tanks in commercial hatcheries and nurseries. The hermaphrodite bivalves produce tiny, free-floating larvae – essentially planktonic – called 'spat'. After two to four weeks, they will begin to attach themselves to firm surfaces (some nurseries provide them with bricks and tiles, others with recycled scallop shells). Here they take the form of tiny oysters and begin to grow. These tiny 'seed oysters' will be harvested at around a centimetre (up to 3,000 individuals per kilo), then sold to growers, who will use them to seed their sites. In calm, predictable waters, with a mud, sand and shingle bottom, they may be left to grow loose on the sea floor. More often, they are contained within plastic mesh bags, which are raised when the oysters reach marketable size at around three years old.

Pollution, harsh winters and over-exploitation have historically posed the biggest threat to our oyster stocks. However, most manufacturing industry has disappeared from the UK and our coastal waters are far cleaner than they were only decades ago. Furthermore, global warming has taken the sting out of winter, and private oyster farms have regulated the exploitation of stock. So the biggest remaining threat to our oysters is now from parasites. The old guard of resident oyster predators, the slipper limpet, the starfish and the dog whelk, continue to take their toll on native and farmed stocks without ever reaching plague proportions. But two recent invaders – the stink winkle and the American oyster drill – are more worrying. Their *modus operandi* is to drill holes in the oysters and suck out their flesh. The long-term effects of these aliens is unclear.

If you're lucky, or persistent, you'll find native oysters growing wild, especially along the craggy island west coast of Scotland. The ones in the pictures on page 571 were hand-gathered by the Fearnley family on holiday on the Isle of Mull. The temptation to pick these in any serious quantities should be resisted: wild colonies need all the help they can get. But certainly sample a few, as the fine flavour of these lovely natives sets a benchmark, we think, for oyster excellence.

When you want an oyster feast, however, it's to the cultivated stock you should turn. Unlike so much modern aquaculture, oyster farming is to be encouraged, even celebrated. Well managed, it needn't negatively affect the environment at all. Oyster farms don't produce tons of waste material and don't require tons of processed wild fish as fodder. All an oyster needs is enough good clean seawater to suck and it'll grow fat and happy.

If you're buying oysters alive to eat at home, the only hurdle between you and your pleasure is the sharp, tightly sealed shell. Getting into it takes some skill – or, at least, a knack. In our experience, most relationships have a designated oyster-opener, even if both parties are enthusiastic consumers. One of us, as it happens, doesn't shuck oysters at all. He's ashamed to admit it, and the other has agreed to cover for him. The shucker tells you how to do it on page 104.

Raw may seem the connoisseur's choice but there's no shame in cooking an oyster. Not everyone likes them raw. And those who think they don't like oysters at all may well turn out to enjoy them cooked. We like them barbecued in their shells, round side down, bubbling in their own juices until they pop open. Or you can achieve the same effect by placing them in the embers of a fire. And then there's our much-loved Leek, celeriac and oyster broth (page 268).

We'll always come back to raw, though. And we'll always buy them by the dozen, not the measly half-dozen, per person. The full set of condiments allows you and your friends to ring the changes through the feast: half a lemon, a bottle of Tabasco, black pepper and, if time has allowed, some homemade shallot vinegar. Nick's an out-and-out Tabasco fiend. And the one who can't open them is a shallot merchant.

Scallop *Pecten maximus*

If all the bivalves held a bodybuilding competition (not that likely, we admit), the scallop would win the Mr Universe title every time. To work the hinges on their big, heavy shells they have evolved a meaty portion of pure muscle – the white adductor – and when we eat a scallop, it is this we consume. For all its strength, it is amazingly tender and sweet.

The great or king scallop, which is the species native to our shores, is one of the mightiest and meatiest of them all. Even in Latin – *Pecten maximus* – it sounds like a gladiator with a six-pack. Yet the scallop shell is an ancient icon of femininity. In Botticelli's *The Birth of Venus*, the newly born goddess of love is imagined rising up from beneath the waves, gently cradled in a giant scallop shell. The scallop shape has early Christian connotations, too, and is often incorporated into the baptismal font of medieval churches as a symbol of fertility and birth.

MCS RATING: 3 (2–3) EAT MORE diver-caught scallops!

REC MINIMUM SIZE: 10cm across the shell

SEASON: avoid May–August (spawning)

RECIPES: pages 141, 202, 267, 270, 313, 397

Whichever side you lean on, biologically speaking all scallops are both masculine and feminine: they're true hermaphrodites. Nestling up to the muscly white adductor is the pinkish-orange and cream, tongue-like coral. This is the scallop's impressive genital paraphernalia. The orange segment contains the eggs – up to 100 million of them – and the creamy-coloured tip contains the

sperm. Spawning normally takes place between May and August, when the scallop will release sperm and eggs into the sea – at different times and in different places, to avoid fertilising its own emissions. So, depending on the time of year and the point in the scallop's breeding cycle, the coral will be either plump and swollen or shrivelled and insubstantial.

Like all bivalves, scallops are filter feeders that suck in and squirt out water all day long, removing nutrients in the process. They like to lodge themselves into ledges and crevices. Once parked, they will then lie flat side up, covered with a thin layer of sand to camouflage their shell. But unlike their cousins, the oyster and the mussel, scallops don't need to anchor themselves on to rocks, reefs or piers. They prefer mobility, and can be surprisingly fast, using their adductor muscle to open and close their shell rapidly, squirting out water to produce a jet-propulsion effect. They're really not bad swimmers, and may change locations several times in a day, depending on tides or current. If you're a scuba diver, you'll never forget the first time you see a 'flock' of scallops taking off from the seabed.

There are two main methods of fishing for wild scallops and one of them is, indeed, scuba diving. The scallops are hand-picked from the seabed and collected in a simple rope bag. The amount that can be taken by an individual is regulated by his or her skill at spotting and picking the scallops, and the rules of safe diving. Size restrictions are easily observed – any scallops that are under the minimum landing size (currently 10–11cm across the widest part, depending on local laws) are simply left where they are.

The other method of fishing is by dragging several tons of steel link and chain along the seabed. The scallops are either prised out by a row of steel teeth or are spooked into swimming up off the bottom and into the trawl net that follows behind the dredge. Scallop dredging is about as thoughtful as strip mining or forest burning. It can inflict vast amounts of damage on the seabed, and on the populations of fish and crustaceans that rely on reefs and ledges for food and shelter. The longer it is allowed to continue in inshore waters, the longer the seabed will take to recover.

In our view, what makes scallop dredging so heinous – apart from the incalculable damage it causes – is the sheer obviousness of the less damaging alternative. As fishing methods go, scallop diving could hardly be more low impact. Diving is to dredging what hand-picking apples is to grubbing up the whole orchard with a JCB. We always avoid dredged scallops, and we would only ever buy or cook diver-caught scallops. And sometimes, just to remind ourselves what a special and sensitive habitat it is down there, we actually dive for them ourselves. Incidentally, restaurants that serve only diver-caught scallops are usually proud to say so on the menu.

A great scallop can live for over twenty years, but most are harvested at between three and five years old. This growth rate means that farming or 'ranching' scallops is a viable option. Like mussel farming, it need not impact heavily on the local ecosystem – mainly because the shellfish feed naturally in a largely unmolested habitat. The first stage of scallop life is difficult to replicate in the aquarium and so the spat (seeds) are collected from naturally breeding wild scallops. The spat is grown on in fine mesh net 'pockets' until they are around two years old and an inch or so wide. In European farms, they are then released to roam the seabed and feed and fend for themselves (in some other countries, the scallops are left in the nets until they are ready for harvesting). They won't go far – particularly if conditions in the chosen bay or fjord are

favourable – and are easy to collect by diving when they reach market size.
There are a few successful scallop farms, or 'ranches', around the British Isles
and Scandinavia – and, of different scallop species, around the world.

Because ranched scallops are gathered by divers, they may simply be called
'hand-dived' or 'diver-caught' and you will have no way of knowing if they're
wild or not. But in a way, this doesn't really matter. In sustainability terms,
a ranched, diver-caught scallop from a well-managed fishery is awfully similar
to a wild one.

British diver-caught scallops are a great product, in high demand in Europe
and the Far East, but still good value in this country – especially if you buy
direct from a commercial diver. If you can, spoil yourself and buy loads. They will
be cheaper to buy alive, in the shell, than shelled and cleaned. Preparing them
yourself is easy, and more than a little satisfying (see pages 105–7). It also gives
you the benefit of keeping the trimmings, which make a delicious, sweet addition
to any fish stock. Otherwise they can be saved and frozen – they are deadly bait
for bream (see page 484).

When it comes to cooking scallops, keep it simple, and keep it fast. Simplest
of all is raw – and they are quite sweet enough to enjoy without so much as a
squeeze of lemon. Though if you have it handy, a smear of wasabi or mustard,
and a dash of soy, is pretty damn good. If they're big ones, though, you might
want to slice them horizontally into three or four thin discs. We also love to
include scallops in our Ceviche (page 141), where they're 'cooked' in lime juice
and spiked with a little chilli.

For *actually* cooking scallops (in the sense of applying heat to them), the
frying pan is the tool of choice (the barbecue a more labour-intensive, but
delightful, option). You can 'sear' scallops by dry-heating the pan (or barbecue,
or ridged griddle), then very lightly oiling each surface of the muscle with your
fingertips. Season them with a tiny pinch of salt and pepper and give each side a
scant minute – just enough to caramelise the surface with speckles of brown. (It's
fine – desirable, some would say – for them to be raw in the middle.) You can also
fry scallops more conventionally in an oiled pan, in which case you should give
some thought to a few supporting flavours – garlic is a must. You could also add
chilli, fennel seeds and ginger – one, two or all three of them. A favourite trick of
ours is to fry up some slices of our homemade chorizo, then throw scallops into
the pan to take on the flavours of the highly spiced oil (see page 313).

Some cooks don't use the coral at all, and serve only the white scallop muscle.
This is madness – except when the coral is withered. Plump and orange and in
rude health, the coral is delicious – in fact, with its lightly granular, roe-like
texture, it is complementary to the white muscle meat. The two should be cooked
together, still attached, if possible – though on really big scallops it may be a
good idea to separate them, otherwise the coral can 'hang' from the middle of the
muscle without ever quite making contact with the pan.

There's certainly no need to think of scallops, as some seem to, as restaurant
fodder. If chefs love them, it's for the same reasons you should: they are blissfully
easy to cook, and even easier to eat, with no bones, skin or cartilage – nothing to
hamper your pleasure. The only thing you could possibly do wrong is to overcook
one – which isn't hard to do. So, whenever you cook them, just keep reminding
yourself how great they taste raw, and aim to serve them at least rare. Three
minutes is the most you will ever need to cook a scallop – and about three
seconds to eat it.

Cockle *Cerastoderma edule*

If you've ever wondered what the difference is between a clam and a cockle, the answer is, not much. Both are bivalve molluscs that live in muddy sand and feed by sucking seawater from which they filter minute planktonic organisms. Both clams and cockles belong to the same genus, and both are found in similar habitats, often living side by side. The only clear difference between them is the shape, size and direction of the ridges on their shells – i.e. from side to side on most species of clam but from edges to hinge on the cockle.

However, once you take them away from the beach and into the kitchen, a gulf opens between them – and it's largely social. Clams are posh. Cockles are common. Clams are used in classy continental dishes such as *spaghetti alle vongole* (Italy) or *palourdes à la commodore* (France). Meanwhile, here in Blighty, cockles get hard-boiled, drowned in industrial-strength vinegar and sold on the pier in polystyrene cups. Why? Hard to say really, except for the force of history and habit – neither of which is entirely to be trusted when it comes to assessing our native seafood.

You could play up the class distinction by arguing that a posh clam such as a palourde is a shade more tender and a touch sweeter than its close cousin, the cockle – but in most countries other than Britain you'd be wasting your breath. Everything you can do with a fancy clam you can do just as well with the humble cockle. Yet we continue to pay top whack for clams that have been imported from abroad (and often farmed) while our native, fresh, wild, hand-picked cockles (at least those we haven't pickled to death) are sent in the other direction – to the discerning seafood markets of France, Spain and Holland. Here they are deployed in all sorts of tasty dishes – the kind for which British chefs would generally insist on palourdes and other clams. It's all back to front.

MCS RATING: 3 (2–3)

REC MINIMUM SIZE: 2cm

SEASON: avoid May–August (spawning)

RECIPES: pages 202, 232, 262, 264, 267, 272, 275, 276, 278, 384, 386

Make no mistake, to foreign seafood buyers British cockles are known to be the best in the world. Amongst the most highly prized specimens are those from the famous cockle beds of Stiffkey (pronounced 'stookey') in Norfolk, known as Stiffkey Blues because of their blue-tinged shells – a result of the unique anaerobic mud they inhabit. In Wales, the Burry Inlet cockle fishery near Swansea has been renowned for the quality of its harvest ever since the Romans first discovered it.

The entire British cockle harvest is currently worth around £20 million a year, making it one of the UK's most valuable fisheries, but over three-quarters of that harvest is being exported. Much of the business is now in the hands of Dutch, German and Spanish companies who bought up many British cockle firms in the 1970s and 1980s. European companies now effectively control the market for UK cockles, including those exported to Spain and France. Sadly, most of our cockles are no longer ours.

There are two main methods of harvesting cockles: a modern industrial one and an old-fashioned labour-intensive one. Cockles in the Wash and the Thames Estuary are dredged or vacuumed up by large, fuel-guzzling vessels, while cockles in the Burry Inlet and Morecambe Bay are still raked by hand using converted gardening equipment, then hand-riddled or graded to ensure the immature seed cockles – or spat, as they are called – are returned safely to the mud and left to grow on. Dredging is obviously cheaper than hand-picking, but its impact on the cockle population is much greater. Dredged cockles sell for less than hand-picked ones because the final quality isn't as good – they often get cracked in the machinery. But the real downside of dredging is that it disturbs and even displaces entire cockle beds, and can damage or destroy the all-important spat.

Dredging has never been allowed in the Burry Inlet and methods haven't changed much since the 1800s, when harvesting was done by women with donkeys in attendance to carry the load. Throughout the entire history of the fishery, only hand-raking has been allowed, although donkeys and carts have been replaced by tractors (and women largely by men). Licences to pick are strictly controlled and there is a daily maximum quota of 250 kilos per picker. No night collection or Sunday picking is allowed.

As a result of this commitment to low-impact methods, the Burry Inlet cockle fishery has been awarded Marine Stewardship Council certification – the only British cockle fishery to be so distinguished. Even though the fishery restrictions are devised with conservation in mind, it still manages to yield well over 7,000 tonnes of top-quality, market-leading cockles every year.

It seems a great shame that these world-renowned cockles are being gleefully appreciated on the Continent – but not at home. So we think it's about time for a Great British Cockle Revolution. We'd like to get the misunderstood mollusc out of the vinegar vat and in amongst the garlic, cream and parsley. With that in mind, we've a couple of fine cockle recipes for you (pages 384 and 386). But we'd also urge you not to be shy of using them in recipes where palourdes or other clams are called for. And if you've got a favourite mussel recipe, try it with cockles for a change – it won't be the same, but it will be delicious.

To join the Cockle Resistance, press your local fishmonger for cockles that are fresh (i.e. alive, in their shells) rather than pickled, and if they can be sourced from a well-managed fishery, such as the certified Burry Inlet one (see the Directory, page 590), then so much the better.

Or, of course, you could have a go at collecting some of your own. Sandy mudflats at a low spring tide are where you'll find them – and it's always worth seeking out a little local knowledge. A garden rake, a bucket and bare feet are all the kit you'll need. The cockles live a couple of inches beneath the muddy sand. Rinse them off in a bucket of clean seawater as you find them. They should then be purged in a fresh bucket of seawater (or salted cold tap water) to which you've added a handful of oatmeal or breadcrumbs, and left for at least a few hours, or overnight.

After that, all they will need is a quick scrub under the cold tap and they're ready for cooking. If you've only ever had them pickled in vinegar before, you're in for a serious treat. We recommend you simply sweat a little garlic in a lot of butter and, just before it starts to brown, add a small glass of wine and another of water. When this liquor comes to the boil, tumble in the cockles, put a lid on the pan and give them a couple of minutes to pop open. It may be years before you cook them any other way again, and a lifetime before you even think about having them in vinegar.

Palourde (or carpet shell clam)

Tapes decussatus / Venerupis decussata

The carpet shell clam is one of your posher bivalves. Francophile chefs – almost all chefs, come to think of it – like to give them their French name, *palourdes*. We are rather charmed by the carpet shell tag – but somehow have got caught up in the whole palourde thing (one of us, at least, has the excuse of being married to a shellfish-loving Frenchwoman).

We have made a case for ranking the cockle alongside the palourde (see page 578). For those who've never tasted palourdes it is, we can see, a rather pointless comparison. But should you happen to be familiar with both, we're sure you'll understand that our position on this stems from our sense that the cockle is underappreciated – and not that the palourde is overrated. Let's be clear: palourdes really are delicious. They're a bit bigger than cockles and their meat is exceptionally plump and sweet. They are held in huge esteem in France, Spain, Portugal and Italy, where they're eaten raw in the half shell, like oysters, or cooked in all sorts of delicious ways, almost invariably including garlic.

Unfamiliar as they are to many, palourdes are native to Britain. They like more or less the same kind of rich, organic, silty, muddy sand as cockles, with a preference for the more gravelly end of the spectrum. When the two species are found together, cockles tend to dominate, and clams will be in the minority. But when you find a colony of palourdes on their own, they can be thick on the ground – or, more accurately, just under it. Compared to cockles and mussels, however, clams barely seem to have registered with the British shellfish forager. Apart from a few canny commercial clam collectors, most people don't have the foggiest idea what they are or where to find them.

They haven't always been so neglected. In his 1884 masterpiece *The Edible Mollusca of Great Britain and Ireland, with Recipes for Cooking Them*, the Victorian naturalist M. S. Lovell wrote admiringly of the palourde, noting that a popular term for it along the Solent, where it was gathered eagerly by locals

MCS RATING: not rated

REC MINIMUM SIZE: 4cm

SEASON: avoid April–June (main spawning period)

RECIPES: pages 232, 264, 272, 275, 276, 278, 279, 384, 386

(and still thrives) was 'butter fish'. This term has been applied to different fish and shellfish by various cultures (the Gambians use it for a type of puffer fish, the Sri Lankans for pompano). It's always intended as a compliment, of course, implying a rich sweetness and melt-in-the-mouth texture. Lovell also stated that connoisseurs preferred the palourde to the more humble cockle. Personally we're reluctant to concede clam superiority, but it's interesting to note that this whole 'clams are better than cockles' malarkey has been around for a while.

Palourdes appear inconsistently on the fishmonger's slab. They may be home grown and gathered but are also quite likely to be imported from the Continent – mainly France (the coast of Brittany and the Charente-Maritime region around La Rochelle are productive). If ever you see them, be ready to pounce. But before you part with your cash (of which you'll need quite a bit), you should really find out how they were caught. Those that have been dredged are best avoided; this method causes unnecessary damage to many other forms of marine life and may fill these tasty morsels with sand (see page 579 for information on cockle dredging). Hand-gathered palourdes are the ones to buy.

Near us in Dorset, there are a few commercial fishermen who turn their attention to palourde collecting in the early spring, hunting for them at low tide, digging and raking them out from beneath the sand, mud and gravel. These currently fetch around £6–8 a kilo wholesale (expect to pay at least double that at the fishmonger's). One of our fishermen, Kelvin (a regular guest host of our River Cottage foraging days), has been collecting local palourdes for the Spanish market for over twenty years. He admits that he hardly ever gets to taste one: 'They're much too valuable. At that price, we can't afford to eat them. Or rather, we can't afford not to sell them.'

As palourdes are always hard to come by in British fishmongers, and always pricy when you do, collecting them yourself can be an exciting experience – like panning for gold. If ever, on family holidays or fishing adventures, we find we are in striking distance of muddy, gravelly tidal flats, we'll try to check them out. If we don't find palourdes, we may well turn up cockles, or even razor clams. Should you be tempted to do likewise, set out at low water with rakes, spoons, boots (or bare feet) and buckets (maybe take some salt too, in the case of razor clams – see page 584). The palourde's giveaway sign is two air holes, side by side in the wet mud (cockles leave only one). Dig, rake and scavenge around the low-water mark or any 'tracks' you find, and you could get lucky.

Scrub the palourdes well, in clean seawater or fresh water. They don't usually need purging, and you may want to sample a few of them raw, right there on the beach. If you get a decent haul and take some back to the kitchen, the simplest *marinière* treatment serves them well (see page 272). But if you want an even bigger hit of garlic and butter, then steam them open in just a little water, drain them well, remove one half of the shell and arrange the flesh-filled other halves on a plate. Trickle a little hot garlic and parsley butter (or, realistically, a lot) over each clam and into the half shell. Slurp away.

We have also included a rather lovely recipe, Palourdes with chanterelles (page 278), which was devised as the culmination of a particularly gratifying day's foraging last October. To recreate it, you'll probably have to do some foraging yourself, or at least prostrate yourself before your bank manager. It'll be either one of the most luxurious free meals you've ever had or one of the most extravagant you've ever shopped for.

Razor clam *Ensis ensis*

MCS RATING: 3
REC MINIMUM SIZE: 10cm
SEASON: avoid May–September (spawning)
RECIPES: pages 262, 264, 278, 279

Collecting wild shellfish is always fun, but normally it's a rather one-sided affair. You might have to do a spot of digging or mud raking to expose cockles, or scramble over a few rocks to find a sprinkling of mussels, winkles or limpets. Once located, however, most molluscs haven't got much to offer in the way of fight or flight. A forager of native shellfish is therefore generally very much a 'gatherer'. Not so the razor clam collector, who is most definitely a 'hunter'.

The razor clam is a bivalve that, like most of its kin, sucks sandy, silty seawater for a living, extracting the minute creatures that are its food. To do this efficiently, it has to keep its water-sucking siphon above the sea floor, while its tasty body is enclosed within its shell, deep in the wet sand and out of danger. Most of the time, the razor clam's patch of sand is covered by the sea, beneath shallow inshore waves. Only on certain big spring low tides, particularly around the two equinoxes, will this habitat be exposed. And when it is, the razor clam must stay hidden beneath the sand, biding its time until the tide rolls back in. This is the window of opportunity in the razor clam hunter's diary.

He or she will walk these rarely exposed expanses of sand, searching for clues. But they are not obvious. Least subtle, but rarest, is a little spout of water, ejaculated from the siphon as the clam either dives from, or climbs to, the sand's surface. The eagle-eyed may also detect figure-of-eight 'prints' in the wet sand. These curious marks are caused by razor clams that have been caught out by the rapidly receding tide and left lying stranded on the sand. They don't stay there for long – and you hardly ever see them like this. They'll rapidly right themselves from horizontal to vertical before burrowing downwards, leaving these shallow scrapes in the sand. But the merest ripple of water will wash them away. Finally, there's the little pinprick of a breathing hole. Look closely and you'll see it isn't quite round, but elongated like the eye of a needle. (Fail to look closely, and you probably won't see it at all.)

Razor clams have excellent 'hearing', detecting vibrations above ground. They will dive at the merest footstep, even if it's several yards away. With the streamlined design of its shell and powerful thrust of its muscular 'foot', the razor clam can propel itself down through wet sand like a rocket launching in

reverse. The speed of its retreat is remarkable; it can easily plunge through the sand quicker than someone with a spade can dig after it. This makes gathering these shellfish one of the great free-food challenges for the amateur enthusiast.

Clever hunters make no attempt to beat the clam at the digging game but instead endeavour to persuade it that danger has passed and the tide is coming back in. They achieve this deception by putting neat salt or, better still, a strong saltwater solution, down the clam's escape hole, to imitate the approach of the incoming tide. The clam will pop its siphon up out of the sand at the taste of a new tide, and it's this moment the hunter must seize. You need to pinch the shell or siphon firmly between your fingers and apply an even, upward pressure. Don't try to lift them straight out or pull hard on the siphon; it's like a lizard's tail – designed to break off and re-grow – and works as a defence to stop birds hauling them out. The trick is to pull steadily and gently, then loosen a little and then pull again. Vary your rhythm and at some point, as the clam flexes its foot muscle, you'll feel it give, and it should slip out of its hole easily enough.

Razor clams can be found on tidal flats all around the British coast but the biggest and fattest are generally collected in Scotland. In Orkney, razor clams are called 'spoots' (we imagine that's 'spouts' with a Scottish accent) and spoot hunting is a favourite local sport. It can be a surprisingly tense and exciting activity – if somewhat bemusing to behold. George Henry Lewes captured it very nicely in his *Seaside Studies* of 1856:

There is something irresistibly ludicrous in grave men stooping over a hole, their coat tails pendant in the water, their breath suspended, one hand holding salt, the other alert to clutch the victims – watching the perturbations of the sand, like hungry cats beside the holes of mice...

A modest restaurant market for razor clams at home and, more vigorously, on the Continent, has spawned a few small commercial fisheries in Britain. In Scotland, divers wear scuba gear so they can collect the clams in shallow water at any state of the tide. In Ireland there are fisheries that use hydraulic dredgers to extract the clams; these tend to be of an inferior quality, with a high proportion of cracked and broken shells. As with the dredging of scallops, cockles and palourdes, hydraulic dredging of clams also causes damage to a sensitive habitat that supports a very complex food chain. We recommend you avoid them.

Commercially collected razor clams are sold live, usually in bunches of ten or twelve, depending on their size. Most razor clams collected in Britain are exported to Europe, and the Spanish, who call them *navajas*, and the French, to whom they are *couteaux courbes*, love them. Only a few are sold in the UK, mostly to enthusiastic restaurateurs. There's absolutely no reason, though, why a decent fishmonger should not be able to order some for you. Or you can always cut out the middleman and buy some direct from a fish wholesaler (see the Directory, pages 590–1). You'll be expected to order a decent quantity – but they're not that pricy. So why not have a spoot party?

The best way to cook razor clams is briefly, or not at all. Overcooked, they'll quickly develop the texture of a garden hose. If you've never tried them before, have a couple raw first – with a sprinkling of shallot vinegar, or sashimi-style with soy and wasabi. For shellfish sweetness, they're up there with scallops. Steam the rest open with garlic, butter and wine as for *moules marinière*, or grill them on a barbecue – adding a dash of lemon and olive oil as you serve them. They may well leave you marvelling at what you've been missing, and at the sheer madness of allowing so many of them to leave our shores.

Cephalopods

Cuttlefish *Sepia officinalis*

Most of us meet our first cuttlefish in the pet shop rather than the fishmonger's. Poking out between the bars of any well-kept budgie's cage is a rigid, white, ovoid disc of cuttlefish 'bone'. Though hard, it has the weight, look and feel of a piece of polystyrene. The budgies gnaw at it to keep their curved beaks from in-growing. How do they know to do that? In the wild, you don't see many budgies scouring the beach or dive-bombing the deep in search of cuttlefish.

Escaped budgies – or whoever collects these things for pet shops – should come to Dorset. Walking along Chesil Beach in the spring or early summer, you'll find hundreds of these buoyant 'bones' peppered across the shingle. They're not bones really, but the dried-out cartilage that gives rigidity to the cuttle's otherwise soft, fleshy body. These are the remains of female cuttlefish who have recently reproduced – an act that, as it creates new life, brings about their own death.

A seabed littered with dead female cuttlefish might seem like a grisly cephalopodic tragedy but to the rest of the locals it's a bonanza – and in some cases a vital part of their life cycle. Black bream, wasted from their own breeding exertions, restore themselves by feeding greedily on dead cuttles. Once a carcass has been picked clean by crabs, prawns and lobsters, its buoyant endoskeleton floats to the surface, where it bobs around, a plaything for curious young seagulls, until it washes up on the beach, ready for the pet-shop boys.

So, all we generally see of our Channel cuttlefish is either an odd piece of white jetsam (or is it flotsam?) on the beach, or a clean white cone of thick flesh on the

MCS RATING: 3

REC MINIMUM SIZE: 17cm

SEASON: avoid spring and early summer (spawning)

RECIPES: pages 260–1, 270, 284, 285, 396

fishmonger's slab. What we *don't* see, though, is truly amazing. For example, a cuttlefish has three hearts with which it pumps different types of blood around its veins in different directions. It moves about, often at some considerable speed, courtesy of two water-siphoning jet-propulsion systems. It has binocular vision and it also possesses the largest of all cephalopod brains, making it more intelligent than any other fish, and possibly even as smart as a rat.

To top it all, a cuttlefish can change colour faster than a chameleon. It's a true master of camouflage, and even at birth an infant cuttlefish has a repertoire of thirteen different disguises. If this doesn't work, a cuttlefish can protect itself by creating a 'smokescreen' with its ink. Even the ink itself is thought to be 'smart ink'. Apart from obscuring the direction in which the cuttle fled, it contains a scent-decoying element that interferes with the predator's sense of smell, giving the cuttle more time to escape. That it has evolved such an array of defences is quite understandable, given how thick, tender and delicious its soft flesh is.

But cuttlefish are themselves predators, and highly effective ones. We get mugged by them often, or at least our lines do, when we're fishing for bass with sand eels for bait. We know the cuttles are about when our sand eels come back to the boat bitten clean off just behind the head. More grisly still, some eels that first appear to be intact prove on inspection to have a mysterious semicircular crater in the flesh of their necks, as if clipped out by a cigar cutter. This macabre insignia of death is the mark of the cuttle's razor-sharp beak. It likes to begin by disabling its prey with a vertebra-severing bite behind the head. In the case of our baits, we can only imagine that, having performed its ruthless despatch, the cuttle detects the hook, mistrusts the meal, and moves on. Sometimes, it's not so smart and hangs on to the bait, or gets a tentacle caught on the hook, and we can reel it in, scoop it with a landing net, and get excited about sashimi for supper.

Besides these accidental catches by anglers, there is also a modest commercial fishery for cuttlefish around the south coast. A couple of boats that fish from our local harbours, West Bay and Lyme Regis, target them in April, May and early June when they come inshore to breed. These mature adults are, at up to a couple of kilos, impressive slabs of seafood.

The problem with this tactic, of course, is that there's a danger the cuttlefish will be scooped up before they've had a chance to spawn. Another risk is that they will actually lay their eggs on the traps and the eggs will then be destroyed as the traps are hauled in. There's some evidence to suggest that our cuttlefish populations are currently in trouble and we do need to be careful. Our advice would be to eat cuttlefish, if possible, outside their early-summer spawning season. We'd also love to see some innovations in the cuttlefish-catching techniques used in our waters – like the very clever traps devised by fishermen in Brittany. These have a removable outer layer so any eggs found on them can be returned to the sea.

Almost all of the British cuttlefish catch is currently exported direct to Spain. There's barely a viable market in Britain. Why not? We eat squid, for heaven's sake. Britain imports thousands of tonnes of frozen squid every year, yet a fresh cuttlefish knocks a frozen squid into a cocked hat any day of the week.

The cuttlefish traps that local fishermen use are like giant circular crab pots. Instead of being baited with food, these are fitted with an imitation cuttlefish, which lures more cuttlefish into the trap. Spawning time is a frantic period when the males are busy wooing the females, or trying to fight off other males. So it's hard to be sure, when a cuttlefish is enticed into the trap by the lure, whether

it actually wants to fuck it or fight it. And, since the decoy cuttlefish is nothing more stimulating than a plain piece of white plastic, about the size of an office envelope, flapping limply in the current, we can only conclude that the average cuttlefish is either extremely aggressive, extremely horny, or both.

Just like a squid, the cuttle uses its ink as a last line of defence, and being dropped on the deck of a boat is by no means too late to deploy it. We both have stains on our favourite fishing jackets that testify to this. A cuttle generally has a lot more ink than a squid, and a good dose usually remains, even if several shots of it have been fired. (Ink extracted from cuttlefish was used in early sepia print photographic processes – hence its Latin name, *Sepia officinalis*.) These days the ink is more likely to be saved for the kitchen than the darkroom (see page 102). It lends sweetness and a deep, seaweedy flavour, as well as a thickening texture, to a pasta sauce, fish stew or risotto.

Cuttlefish flesh is very similar to squid, a little sweeter and a little thicker, with a bit more bite to it. And, like squid, it needs to be cooked very quickly (in a wok or on a grill or barbecue, for just a couple of minutes) or very slowly (stewed long and gently, ideally with tomatoes and garlic, plus that ink if you've managed to save it, for a good hour). In the case of a very fresh specimen, zero minutes is also effective: cuttlefish makes excellent sushi, sashimi and ceviche.

As stocks of prime fish in our waters dwindle, it makes sense to explore some less obvious alternatives. And they don't come less obvious than the triple-hearted, ink-squirting marine chameleon.

Squid *Loligo forbesi*

If the squid didn't exist, Hollywood would have had to invent him. He is the Ethan Hunt of the sea, tooled up with gadgets, gizmos and secret weapons. He is capable of clever disguise, deceit and jet propulsion. He can swim backwards or forwards, in deep or shallow water. He has night vision, an armoury of hydraulic, sucker-covered arms, and a hidden, parrot-like beak that can slice right through a fat prawn like a laser. He is so well equipped that his mission – to eat, grow and reproduce – is far from impossible. And our mission is to eat him as often as we possibly can.

Like its close relative, the cuttlefish, the squid has a short and frenetic life. It is sexually mature within a year, and dead within three. The female squid spawns in her second year and dies soon after she has laid her eggs. Because squid live fast and die young, a squid fishery can fluctuate wildly from year to year, as numbers depend largely on the success or failure of each individual breeding season.

We're lucky to have a reliable seasonal opportunity to catch squid ourselves on rod and line. It's a winter-afternoon affair, kick-started by the drop in water temperature and shortening days some time around mid-November. This is when the squid migrate close inshore, around Weymouth and Portland harbours, in search of easy food. We often catch them in no more than 4–6 metres of water, just as the day fades and the night sucks up the light. In the encroaching darkness, the squid become bolder. They are less worried by predators, and their huge, bulbous eyes give them a strong advantage over their prey of small fish, prawns and crabs.

The hunting squid uses its enhanced night vision to locate prey, then grabs them with two extra-long extendable tentacles that shoot out like a Rocky Balboa jab. Once the victim's suckered, it's dragged into a lethal embrace, and the squid will start chewing its ear.

But it isn't hard to turn the tables on such a hungry and relentless predator. To catch squid, we use prawn-shaped lures called squid jigs, which have a cluster of tiny, barbless hooks around their tails, like a bizarre but deadly upturned grass skirt. The jigs, fished from a rod and line, are raised and lowered within the bottom metre or so of the seabed. The squid wrap their hunting tentacles around a jig, becoming entangled with the hook skirt. A smooth, steady retrieve is required to get them to the surface, where they can be scooped up with a small-meshed landing net.

In the absence of jigs, or sometimes as an extra enticement, we often use a small dead pouting as bait. No hooks are needed. The squid simply grabs the fish, holding on until you get it to the top. But if you fluff it with the landing net, beware, because a squid can open up its water-jet propulsion valve and rocket back and down at an impressive speed.

If you do manage to net it, a squid has one last secret weapon in the briefcase: its ink. Of course, once it's on board, the ink is hardly going to save it from capture. But it can give the squid the last laugh. An angry spray of fresh squid ink is practically impossible to wash out of clothes, and leaves the deck black, sticky and, a few days later, pretty stinky too.

Back in the squid's underwater world, the ink is used to evade predators, of which, as a soft-fleshed, protein-rich cephalopod, it has many. And so, if a hungry tope or marauding bass is closing in on it, it'll use its opaque ink ejaculation

MCS RATING: 3

REC MINIMUM SIZE: 15cm (body length, from tip of nose to end of body)

SEASON: avoid December–May (spawning)

RECIPES: pages 204–5, 267, 270, 284, 285, 332, 396

system as a smokescreen, to blind the enemy temporarily. The ink cloud of the squid (and cuttlefish) works on a number of levels. For a start, it is thought to contain a substance that will dull the predator's sense of smell. There are also theories that the squid's ink spurt isn't merely a random cloud but a rough and ready replication of its body shape. It's a squid silhouette, in other words, squirted to deceive the predator and leave it attacking a ghostly shape while the real squid beats a retreat. (It's a device uncannily like Arnie's handy hologram in *Total Recall*.)

If you ever have an opportunity to go squid jigging, grab it. It doesn't have to be a complicated boat trip. Many exceptional squid and cuttlefish are caught from piers and harbour walls using exactly the same basic methods. Even if you don't intend to kill and cook your catch, it is a revelation just to see one of these creatures alive. Angry at being caught, it will have shimmering ripples of light and colour pulsing over its body like a high-speed chameleon. It's really quite a show.

Around Britain, most squid are caught incidentally as bycatch in trawl nets, but they are also pursued intentionally by hand-fished jigs and baits. This locally caught squid is most likely to turn up on the fishmonger's slab in the autumn and winter months. However, the majority of squid sold in the UK comes from the Pacific coasts of North America and the Asiatic seas. It's fished by commercial jiggers that use banks of fluorescent deck lights to attract the squid to hundreds of automated jig-lines. The big ships working out of the Far East are capable of landing up to 50 tonnes of squid a night, processing and freezing them all on board.

Given that these squid occupy an important position at the base of the marine food chain, and few of the females will have yet reproduced, it would be questionable to apply the word 'sustainable' to this kind of fishing. Some well-managed squid fisheries (such as that around the Falkland Islands) take into account their effect on the ecosystem and limit catches accordingly. However, it's still better to buy British squid if you can, as it is the product of far less intensive fishing and hasn't travelled thousands of miles to end up on your plate.

Most imported squid is sold deep frozen, or previously frozen and defrosted, (which means that it shouldn't really be frozen again). It can vary in size from tiny whole squid no bigger than your little finger ('Japonica' squid), via hand-sized all-rounders, to a monster squid the size and shape of an ironing board, which will be cut and packed in 1cm-thick strips. Frozen squid makes reasonable eating but it never quite has the bite, tenderness or sweetness of fresh locally caught squid.

When you get some of that, the simplest cooking methods are the most rewarding. The skill (and a certain amount of fun) is all in the preparation (see pages 97–100). Larger squid make excellent fried squid rings (page 332) or portions for butterflying, marinating and barbecuing (pages 204–5). The really tiny ones can be stir-fried whole in less time than it takes to boil a kettle. In fact, never cook fresh squid for more than a few minutes – unless you are going to simmer it gently (in a rich tomatoey stew, for example) for around an hour and a half, until it is meltingly tender.

Cooked in any of these ways, super-fresh squid is a sheer delight. So don't just order it in restaurants, tackle it at home. Or, if you want the freshest possible squid, and the thrill of the hunt, try to catch some yourself. It's an experience you'll never forget.

Directory

This is a selection of some of the many seafood suppliers in the UK that sell the kind of fish we like to eat. All offer a mail-order service unless otherwise stated. We've also included sources of some speciality ingredients, as well as a list of conservation organisations, charities and fishing groups.

Seafood wholesalers, producers and suppliers

James Baxter and Sons
Thornton Road, Morecambe, Lancashire
LA4 5PB
Tel: 01524 410910;
www.baxterspottedshrimps.co.uk
Sells potted Morecambe Bay shrimps.

Billingsgate Fish Market
Trafalgar Way, London E14 5ST
Tel: 020 7987 1118; Seafood Training
School tel: 020 7517 3548;
www.billingsgate-market.org.uk
The UK's biggest fish market, open to both trade and public (children are not allowed on the market floor). Opening hours are Tuesday–Saturday 5am–8.30am; Sunday (shellfish only) 6am–8am. Fish cookery courses are held at the market's Seafood Training School.

The Blue Sea Food Company Ltd
Torbay Business Park, Woodview Road,
Paignton, Devon TQ4 7HP
Tel: 01803 555777; www.devoncrab.com
This wholesaler also sells to the public, including Devon crab from the Inshore Potting Agreement area. No mail order but they supply some retail outlets locally and in London.

Interfish
Wallsend Industrial Estate, Cattedown,
Plymouth PL4 0RW
Tel: 01752 267261
Processors of fish including Cornish black bream, South Devon brown crab (from the Inshore Potting Agreement area), coley, dab, red gurnard, MSC-certified herring, Cornish otter-trawled lemon sole, MSC-certified mackerel, Cornish sardines, British red mullet and English Channel whiting. No mail order; contact them to find your nearest retail outlet.

M&J Seafoods
1st Floor, The Gatehouse, Gatehouse Way,
Aylesbury, Buckinghamshire HP19 8DB
Tel: 01296 333800; www.mjseafoods.com
A fresh fish wholesaler that also sells to the public. Mail order not available but check their website to locate your nearest outlet. Stocks MSC-certified Burry Inlet cockles, Dover sole, herring and mackerel.

Seafayre Cuisine
Unit E, St Erth Industrial Estate, Hayle,
Cornwall TR27 6LP
Tel: 01736 755961;
www.seafayrecuisine.co.uk
A wholesaler, also selling to the public, that offers South West Handline Fishermen's Association tagged bass and pollack and MSC-certified mackerel.

Seafood retailers

Bleiker's Smokehouse Ltd
Glasshouses Mill, Glasshouses, Harrogate,
North Yorkshire HG3 5QH
Tel: 01423 711411; www.bleikers.co.uk
Traditional dry-cured smoked salmon from fish reared in low-density conditions, plus local trout smoked over Yorkshire oak.

Bridfish Smokery
Unit 1, The Old Laundry Trading Estate,
Sea Road North, Bridport, Dorset DT6 3BD
Tel: 01308 456306;
www.bridfishsmokery.com
Sells hot- and cold-smoked salmon, eels, cod's roe, haddock and fine kippers.

Brown and Forrest
Freepost, BS 6843, Langport, Somerset
TA10 0BP
Tel: 01458 250875; www.smokedeel.co.uk
Smokes West Country eel, trout, mackerel, line-caught bass and pollack, as well as Scottish salmon.

Butley Orford Oysterage
Market Hill, Orford, Suffolk IP12 2LH
Tel: 01394 450277;
www.butleyorfordoysterage.co.uk
Sells fish caught in the North Sea from its own boats. Fresh fish are smoked daily, including trout, mackerel, wild and farmed salmon, kippers, eels and, in season, sprats.

Cley Smokehouse
High Street, Cley, Holt, Norfolk NR25 7RF
Tel: 01263 740282;
www.cleysmokehouse.com
Producers of traditionally smoked fish, including kippers, bloaters, buckling and red herring.

Continental Crayfish
Toll Cottage, Begbroke, Oxfordshire
OX5 1RH
Tel: 01865 377499;
www.signalcrayfishsales.com
Suppliers of live signal crayfish by post.

Fishmongers
11 New Street, Honiton, East Devon
EX14 1HA
Tel: 01404 43464
Family-run business down the road from River Cottage. Sells local lobster and crab from Beer, scallops from Lyme Bay, local line-caught sea bass and pollack, and plaice, lemon sole and monkfish from day boats at Brixham. No mail order.

The Fish Shop
The Old Watch House, Cobb Square,
Lyme Regis, Dorset DT7 3JF
Tel: 01297 444205; www.wetfishshop.com
Harbourside fishmonger selling fresh seafood from Dorset and Devon boats. The website has a fishcam, so you can look at your fish before you buy.

Fowey Fish
37 Fore Street, Fowey, Cornwall PL23 1AH
Tel: 01726 832422; www.foweyfish.com
Fresh fish and shellfish bought daily from the Looe fish market and from local boats. Products include palourdes.

Graig Farm Organics
Dolau, Llandrindod Wells, Powys LD1 5TL
Tel: 01597 851655; www.graigfarm.co.uk
Sells organically farmed trout, salmon, cod, prawns, sea bass and bream.

Steve Hatt
88–90 Essex Road, London N1 8LU
Tel: 020 7226 3963
Very highly regarded North London fishmonger and game dealer. The staff can give you plenty of advice on how to cook your fish. Mail order not available.

W. Harvey & Sons
The Coombe, Newlyn, Penzance, Cornwall
TR18 5HF
Tel: 01736 362983; www.crabmeat.co.uk
Live and cooked Cornish spider crab, brown
crab, lobster and other shellfish.

Richard Haward's Oysters
129 Coast Road, West Mersea, Colchester,
Essex CO5 8PA
Tel/fax: 01206 383284;
www.richardhawardsoysters.co.uk
Colchester native and gigas (rock) oysters.
Available by mail order, or buy at The
Company Shed fishmonger in West Mersea.

Inverawe Smokehouses
Taynuilt, Argyll PA35 1HU
Tel: 0870 423 0236;
www.smokedsalmon.co.uk
Organic smoked salmon, wild smoked
salmon, Loch Etive trout, eel and halibut.

Isle of Skye Seafood Ltd
Broadford, Isle of Skye IV49 9AP
Tel: 01471 822135;
www.skye-seafood.co.uk
Supplies traditionally smoked fish, locally
caught shellfish and organic salmon.

Loch Fyne Oysters
Clachan, Cairndow, Argyll, PA26 8BL
Tel: 01499 600236; www.loch-fyne.com
Oysters, fresh and smoked salmon,
shellfish, kippers and marinated herrings.

Lyme Bay Shellfish
Tel: 07737 208265
Sells rope-grown mussels from Portland
Harbour in Dorset. Mail order not available.

Maldon Oyster and Seafood
Birchwood Farm, Cock Clarks, Chelmsford,
Essex CM3 6RF
Tel: 01621 828699;
www.maldonoyster.com
Sells cultivated pacific and native oysters,
including organic, plus other shellfish.

The Old Smokehouse
Brougham, Penrith, Cumbria CA10 2DE
Tel: 01768 867772;
www.the-old-smokehouse.co.uk
Oak-smoked wild Cumbrian salmon.

The Orkney Herring Company
Garson Food Park, Stromness,
Orkney KW16 3JU
Tel: 01856 850514;
www.orkneyherring.com
Speciality herring cures.

The Pilchard Works
Tolcarne, Newlyn, Cornwall TR18 5QH
Tel: 01736 332112;
www.pilchardworks.co.uk
Traditionally caught fresh local fish,
including pilchards, plus tinned pilchards
and MSC-certified mackerel.

Andy Race Fish Merchants Ltd
Mallaig, Inverness-shire PH41 4PX
Tel: 01687 462626; www.andyrace.co.uk
Supplier of fresh fish as well as traditional,
undyed smoked fish and shellfish,
including Scottish peat-smoked salmon,
finnan haddock and Mallaig kippers.

Rock-a-Nore Fisheries
3–4 Rock-a-Nore Road, Hastings, East
Sussex TN34 3DW
Tel: 01424 445425
Stocks a range of local fish, including
MSC-certified herring, mackerel and
Dover sole.

Samways
9B West Bay, Bridport, Dorset DT6 4EN
Tel: 01308 424496;
www.samwaysfish.com
Main fish supplier for River Cottage.

R. R. Spink & Sons
Sir William Smith Road, Kirkton Industrial
Estate, Arbroath DD11 3RD
Tel: 01241 872023; www.rrspink.com
Specialises in Arbroath smokies.

Swallow Fish Ltd
2 South Street, Seahouses,
Northumberland NE68 7RB
Tel: 01665 721052;
www.swallowfish.co.uk
Runs the last fully operational nineteenth-
century smokehouse in Seahouses, using
traditional methods to smoke kippers and
salmon.

Weyfish Ltd
1 Custom House Quay, Weymouth, Dorset
DT4 8BE
Tel: 01305 761277
Retail and wholesale fishmonger. No mail
order.

The Whitby Catch
1 Pier Road, Whitby, North Yorkshire
YO21 3PT
Tel: 01947 601313;
www.thewhitbycatch.co.uk
Sells fresh fish caught by the Whitby
fishing fleet, plus smoked fish from a local
fourth-generation smokery.

Farmed fish

Aquascot
Fyrish Way, Alness, Ross-shire IV17 0PJ
Tel: 01349 899 800; www.aquascot.com
Farmed salmon and trout, including organic,
sold through Waitrose. No mail order.

Aquavision
Upper Hayne Farm, Blackborough,
Cullompton, Devon EX15 2JD
Tel: 01823 680888;
www.aquavisiononline.com
Organically farmed carp (initially confined to
restaurant trade). Mail order not available.

Carloway Seafoods Ltd
Dunan Station, Carloway, Isle of Lewis,
Western Isles HS2 9AW
Tel: 01851 643288
Organically farmed salmon. No mail order
but they supply to retailers nationwide.

Hebrides Harvest
Gramsdale, Benbecula, Western Isles
HS7 5LZ
Tel: 01870 602081; www.hebridesharvest.com
Organically farmed salmon. No mail order,
but available from Sainsbury's, Marks &
Spencer and other retailers nationwide.

Johnson Sustainable Seafood
Marine Park, Vidlin, Shetland ZE2 9QB
Tel: 01806 242222; www.nocatch.co.uk
Organically farmed cod. No mail order
but available from Sainsbury's, Tesco and
other retailers.

Purely Organic
Longbridge Deverill, Warminster, Wiltshire
BA12 7DZ
Tel: 01985 841093;
www.purelyorganic.org.uk
Organically farmed trout.

Other suppliers

Goodness Direct
Tel: 0871 871 6611;
www.goodnessdirect.co.uk
Online company selling Fish4Ever brand of
sustainably caught tinned fish, including
tuna, sardines, herrings and anchovies.

Japanese Kitchen
77 Spring Road, Feltham TW13 7JA
Tel: 0845 602 3990;
www.japanesekitchen.co.uk
Mail-order supplier of Japanese foods,
including sushi ingredients and equipment.

River Cottage
www.rivercottage.net
For Stinger beer by post.

Sayell Foods
71 Fanshaw Street, London N1 6LA
Tel: 020 7256 1080;
www.sayellfoods.co.uk
Specialist Spanish ingredients, including
coarse wheat flour for coating fish such as
anchovies before frying.

Charities and campaigning bodies

Anglers Conservation Association
Eastwood House, 6 Rainbow Street,
Leominster, Herefordshire HR6 8DQ
Tel: 01568 620447; www.a-c-a.org
Fights pollution and other damage to water
environments throughout the UK.

Association of Rivers Trusts
10 Exeter Street, Launceston, Cornwall
PL15 9EQ
Tel: 08707 740689;
www.associationofriverstrusts.org.uk
Umbrella organisation representing the
rivers trusts of England and Wales.

Bite-Back
www.bite-back.com
UK organisation dedicated to the protection
of sharks, as well as other threatened
marine species.

Finding Sanctuary
Darts Farm, Topsham, Exeter EX3 0QH
Tel: 01392 878327;
www.finding-sanctuary.org
Aims to create a network of Marine
Protected Areas (MPAs) around the coasts
and seas of Southwest England.

Greenpeace
Canonbury Villas, London N1 2PN
Tel: 020 7865 8100;
www.greenpeace.org.uk
International organisation that works to
defend the natural world. Activities include
a far-reaching oceans campaign.

Invest in Fish South West
Barn C, Boswednan Farm, Tremethick
Cross, Penzance, Cornwall TR20 8UA
Tel: 01736 333733; www.investinfish.org
A project that aims to agree the measures
needed to sustain fish stocks within the
Southwest region, taking economic,
social and environmental considerations
into account.

The Marine Conservation Society
Unit 3, Wolf Business Park, Alton Road,
Ross-on-Wye, Herefordshire HR9 5NB
Tel: 01989 566017;
www.mcsuk.org; www.fishonline.org
A UK charity dedicated to the conservation
of our seas and seashores. It runs
fishonline.org, a website that gives clear
and accessible information about the
sustainability of over 150 fish and shellfish.
Also produces lists of 'fish to eat' and 'fish
to avoid', which are available as a wallet-
sized *Pocket Good Fish Guide* and a book,
The Good Fish Guide.

Marine Stewardship Council
3rd floor, Mountbarrow House, 6–20
Elizabeth Street, London SW1W 9RB
Tel: 020 7811 3300; www.msc.org
This independent international charity
promotes the certification of sustainable
fisheries around the world. Its blue-fish tick
label appears on fish products from areas
the MSC has certified as well-managed and
sustainably fished.

Natural England
Northminster House, Peterborough
PE1 1UA
Tel: 0845 600 3078;
www.naturalengland.org.uk
Works to conserve and enhance biodiversity,
landscapes and wildlife in rural, urban,
coastal and marine areas.

Rivers and Fisheries Trusts of Scotland
Tyneham, Harviestoun Road, Dollar
FK14 7PT
Tel: 07799 628666; www.rafts.org.uk
The trusts address the decline in fish
numbers and the management of other
freshwater species in Scottish rivers.

WWF
Panda House, Weyside Park, Godalming,
Surrey GU7 1XR
Tel: 01483 426444; www.wwf.org.uk
The world's largest conservation
organisation, heavily involved in marine
campaigning.

Commercial and fishermen's groups

North Norfolk Shellfishermen's Association
Lone Pine, Sheringwood, Sheringham,
Norfolk NR26 8TS
Tel: 01263 824333
Provides information on sourcing Cromer
crab and Stiffkey blue cockles.

Scottish Quality Salmon
Durn, Isla Road, Perth PH2 7HG
Tel: 01738 587000;
www.scottishsalmon.co.uk
Industry body that monitors Scottish
farmed salmon.

Sea Fish Industry Authority
18 Logie Mill, Logie Green Road,
Edinburgh EH7 4HG
Tel: 01315 583331; www.seafish.org
Works with the UK seafood industry.
Organiser of the annual October
Seafood Week.

The Shellfish Association of Great Britain
Fishmongers' Hall, London Bridge,
London EC4R 9EL
Tel: 020 7283 8305;
www.shellfish.org.uk
Represents the UK shellfish industry. Has
mediated on a range of environmental
issues, ranging from coastal pollution to
stock conservation.

South West Handline Fishermen's Association
www.linecaught.org.uk
Represents over 50 handline fishermen
in Southwest England, catching sea bass,
pollack, squid and MSC-certified mackerel.
Runs a tagging scheme for pollack and
bass – the website enables you to trace
individual fish.

South West Wales Sea Fisheries Committee
Queens Buildings, Cambrian Place,
Swansea SA1 1TW
Tel: 01792 654466; www.swsfc.org.uk
Manages a range of fish and shellfish
species and fishing methods in South
Wales, including the MSC-certified Burry
Inlet cockle fishery.

Fishing and angling federations and clubs

www.anglersnet.co.uk
Site covering all aspects of sea and
freshwater fishing.

Atlantic Salmon Trust
Suite 3/11, King James VI Business Centre,
Friarton Road, Perth PH2 8DG
Tel: 01738 472032;
www.atlanticsalmontrust.org
Funds and sponsors research programmes
tackling the problems facing wild Atlantic
salmon and sea trout. The website is full
of information about these species.

BASS (Bass Anglers' Sportfishing Society)
Shawe Cottage, Shawe, Kingsley Holt,
Cheadle, Staffordshire ST10 2DL
www.ukbass.com
Leads the campaign to restore European
sea bass stocks.

www.britishcongerclub.org.uk
Concerned with conservation of this species.

The British Disabled Angling Association
9 Yew Tree Road, Delves, Walsall, West
Midlands WS5 4NQ
Tel: 01922 860912; www.bdaa.co.uk
A registered charity set up to develop
fishing opportunities for disabled people.

www.catchalot.co.uk
The Scottish Angling homepage promotes
fish conservation and tag-and-release
programmes in Scottish waters. Also
provides information relevant to Scottish
sea angling.

**www.environment-agency.gov.uk/subjects/
fish/**
Issues rod licences for coarse and game
fishing. Website also gives 'where to fish'
guides for local areas, plus details on
commercial netting and licences.

European Anglers Alliance (EAA)
Rue du Luxembourg, 47, B-1050 Brussels,
Belgium
Tel: +32 (0) 2286 5956;
www.eaa-europe.org
Useful organisation if you want to fish in
Europe. Aims to safeguard European fish
stocks (salt and freshwater) and protect the
interests of European recreational anglers.

Fish and Fly
PO Box 47, Norwich NR11 7WY
Tel: 020 7691 7283; www.fishandfly.com
Online club for fly-fishing enthusiasts.

www.fishing-in-wales.com
Provides a guide to all coarse, game and
sea fishing in and around Wales.

www.fishireland.com
For information on sea fishing, freshwater
fishing and private fisheries in Ireland.

International Game Fish Association (IGFA)
300 Gulf Stream Way, Dania Beach, Florida
33004, USA
Tel: +1 (954) 927 2628; www.igfa.org
Dedicated to ethical game fishing. An
excellent source of information if you're
planning to fish overseas.

www.metoffice.gov.uk
Check the UK shipping and inshore
forecasts at the Met Office.

National Federation of Anglers (NFA)
National Water Sports Centre, Adbolton
Lane, Holme Pierrepont, Nottingham
NG12 2LU
Tel: 01283 734735; www.nfadirect.com
Promotes and encourages freshwater
angling through clubs and regional bodies.
Lists all of its affiliated fishing clubs
around the UK and can help with coaching.

National Federation of Sea Anglers
Level 5, Hamlyn House, Mardle Way,
Buckfastleigh, Devon TQ11 0NS
Tel: 01364 644643; www.nfsa.org.uk
Represents more than 30,000 sea anglers.
Website provides information on everything
from coaching contacts to details of
UK competitions.

www.thenationalmulletclub.org
Promotes interest in and conservation
of the three species of mullet found in
British waters.

The Salmon and Trout Association
Fishmongers' Hall, London Bridge, London
EC4R 9EL
Tel: 020 7283 5838;
www.salmon-trout.org
Represents the UK's game anglers and
fishery owners and managers. Interested
in water and habitat management, fish
stock management and promotion of
game angling.

The Scottish Federation of Sea Anglers
Stichill House, Kelso TD5 7TB
Tel: 01592 657520;
www.fishsea.co.uk
Governing body for sea angling in Scotland.

**The Sea Anglers' Conservation Network
(SACN)**
Leon Roskilly, 9 Iversgate Close, Rainham,
Gillingham, Kent ME8 7PA
Tel: 01634 231682;
www.sacn.org.uk
Body of recreational anglers working to
conserve native fish stocks.

UK Shark Tagging
Dr Ken Collins, National Oceanography
Centre, Southampton SO14 3ZH
Tel/fax: 02380 596010;
www.ukshark.co.uk
Works to save the dwindling numbers of
sharks in UK waters.

web.ukonline.co.uk/aquarium
The Aquarium Project's website acts as a
simple guide to the identification of sea
fish caught around the UK.

The Welsh Federation of Sea Anglers
Tel: 01633 853419; www.wfsa.org.uk
Governing body for sea angling in Wales.

Wild Trout Trust
PO Box 120, Waterlooville, Hampshire
PO8 0WZ
Tel: 02392 570985; www.wildtrout.org
Aims to ameliorate the lot of our native wild
brown trout through habitat-improvement
projects. Website includes practical advice,
such as where to fish for trout.

www.worldseafishing.com
One of the largest sea fishing sites on the
net. Excellent resource for all sea anglers,
covering everything from big game to potting.

Charter boats

www.angling.ukf.net/charter/boats.htm
The Charter Boat Directory lists all UK
charter boats, detailing size, capacity,
facilities, types of fishing and how far off
shore they will go.

www.deepsea.co.uk
UK directory of professional angling, diving
and commercial charter boats.

www.fish-anglesey.co.uk
The Anglesey Charter Skipper Association
site.

The Professional Boatmen's Association
Tel: 01243 551927; www.pba.org.uk
Useful site for finding small, commercially
operated boats for fishing and diving
around the country.

www.ukcharterboats.co.uk
Online directory for UK charter fishing boats.

**web.ukonline.co.uk/aquarium/diary/pages/
charterboats/charterboats.html**
The UK Sea Fishing Diary Directory of
Charter Boats offers a comprehensive list of
charter boats in the UK.

www.wcsa.co.uk
Whitby Charter Skippers Association site.

www.westwightskippers.co.uk
The West Wight Charter Skippers
Association site.

Index

Bibliography

Bagenal, T. B.:
The Observer's Book of Sea Fishes
(Frederick Warne and Co, London, 1972)

Bareham, Lindsey:
The Fish Store
(Michael Joseph, London, 2006)

Buckland, Frank:
Natural History of British Fishes
(SPCK, London, 1880)

Clark, Duncan:
The Rough Guide to Ethical Living
(Rough Guides, London, 2006)

Clover, Charles:
The End of the Line
(Ebury Press, London, 2004)

Cutting, Charles L.:
Fish Saving: A History of Fish Processing from Ancient to Modern Times
(Leonard Hill Books, London, 1955)

David, Elizabeth:
Elizabeth David Classics
(Grub Street, London, 1999)

Davidson, Alan:
North Atlantic Seafood
(Macmillan, London, 1979)
Mediterranean Seafood
(Penguin Books, London, 1972)
The Oxford Companion to Food
(Oxford University Press, Oxford, 1999)

Downes, Stephen and Knowelden, Martin:
The New Compleat Angler
(Orbis, London, 1983)

Erlandson, Keith:
Home Smoking and Curing
(Ebury Press, London, 2003)

Fearnley-Whittingstall, Hugh:
A Cook on the Wild Side
(Boxtree, London, 1997)
The River Cottage Cookbook
(HarperCollins, London, 2001)
The River Cottage Year
(Hodder and Stoughton, London, 2003)

Floyd, Keith:
Floyd on Fish
(BBC Books, London, 1985)

Gibbons, Euell:
Stalking the Blue-eyed Scallop
(David McKay, New York, 1964)

Grigson, Jane:
Jane Grigson's Fish Book
(Penguin Books, London, 1993)

Hartley, Dorothy:
Food in England
(Macdonald, London, 1954; republished Little, Brown, London, 1999)

Hix, Mark:
British Regional Food
(Quadrille Publishing, London, 2006)

Houghton, the Rev. W.:
British Fresh-water Fishes
(William McKenzie, London, 1879; republished Webb and Bower, Exeter, 1981)

Jackson, C. J. and Waldegrave, Caroline:
Leiths Fish Bible
(Bloomsbury Publishing, London, 2005)

Jenkins, J. Travis:
The Fishes of the British Isles
(Frederick Warne and Co, London, 1925)

Kurlansky, Mark:
Cod: A Biography of the Fish that Changed the World
(Walker and Company, New York, 1997)

Mabey, Richard:
Food for Free
(Collins, London, 1972)

Mason, Laura and Brown, Catherine:
The Taste of Britain
(Harper Press, London, 2006)

Montagné, Prosper, and Gottschalk, Dr:
Larousse Gastronomique: The Encyclopedia of Food, Wine and Cooking
(Hamlyn, London, 1961)

Naylor, Paul:
Great British Marine Animals
(Sound Diving Publications, Devon, 2003)

Paston-Williams, Sara:
The National Trust Book of Fish Cookery
(National Trust, London, 1988)

Stein, Rick:
Best of British Fish
(in Association with the Royal National Mission for Deep Sea Fishermen) (Mitchell Beazley, London, 2005)
English Seafood Cookery
(Penguin Books, London, 1988)

Yeatman, Marwood:
The Last Food of England (Ebury Press, London, 2007)

PICTURE CREDITS

Acknowledgements

In researching and writing this book we have benefited from a phenomenal amount of help and encouragement, which has been offered in all cases with staggering enthusiasm.

For guiding us through the tangled mesh of conservation issues we are immeasurably grateful to Dr Bryce Beukers-Stewart of the Marine Conservation Society. In particular, we would like to thank Bryce and his colleagues for their permission to use the MCS sustainability rating system. For his patient response to countless ecological queries, many thanks to Dr Tom Pickerell, Fisheries Policy Officer at WWF. For reading our Fish as food chapter and advising us on nutritional issues, we are most grateful to nutritionist Natalie Savona. For reading and commenting most incisively on our salmonid and fish-farming text (and not least for steering HF-W to at least half the salmon he has ever caught), special thanks to Andrew Wallace.

Many other conservationists and marine experts have fielded specific queries, and we are grateful for their time and for the inevitable effect of passing their expertise off as our own. They include: Chris Davis of Natural England; Jeremy Langley, specialist fish buyer at Waitrose; Professor John Walton at Leeds Metropolitan University; Dr Cat Dorey of Greenpeace UK; David Palmer of the Centre for Environment, Fisheries and Aquaculture Science; Peter Tinsley of the Dorset Wildlife Trust; Professor Steve Hawkins of the Marine Biological Association; Dr Clive Askew of the Shellfish Association of Great Britain; Jim Portus of the South Western Fish Producer Organisation; Gordon Goldsworthy of Loch Fyne Seafarms; writer Jon Beer; Dr Euan Dunn of the RSPB; and Bob Kennard of Graig Farm Organics.

For providing us with the very best fish to cook, photograph and (without fail) eat, thanks to all of the following: Geoff Davies at Ocean Fish; Howell Davies at Aquascot; Simon Bennett of the Wet Fish Shop in Lyme Regis; John Gilbertson of Isle of Skye Seafood; Fowey Fish of Cornwall; Falfish, also of Cornwall; Dermot Sanders of Fishmongers in Honiton; Samways of Bridport; Tony Free of Purely Organic; the team at Hooke Springs Trout Farm; Paul and Andrea Crocker for their crayfish; Jimmie and Penny Hepburn of Upper Hayne Organic Carp Farm; Bos Lawson, Janine Gould and Kelvin Moore for some wonderful Weymouth fish and shellfish; everyone at Weyfish; John Patten for supplying us with zander; Rik Nicholls for his deck and angling skills; and Matthew Warr for his Billy Winters and other capital crustaceans.

For sourcing and caring for so much of this outstanding fish, a special thanks to 'Big' Tim Graveson; another to Matt Toms, our skipper on *Dawn Mist*, and his wife Sharon, who are always a pleasure to fish with. For keeping us afloat on our Arvor boat, a big thanks to Nick Barke and all the team at Essexboatyards.com.

Thanks also, for the less fishy elements of the cookery, to our local producers and suppliers, including Bothen Hill Produce; Bridget's Market greengrocers; Brig's Farm Vegetables; Five Penny Farm; Ganesha Wholefoods; Millers Farm Shop; Pat Foxwell of Ourganics; Riverford Organic Vegetables; the Town Mill Bakery; and Washingpool Farm Shop.

For the stunning photography we have to massively thank Simon Wheeler, whose feel for the 'natural moment' has characterised every River Cottage book to date. He has proved to be equally at home on boats and among the fishes as on land among livestock and people.

Huge thanks to Paul Quagliana, whose additional photography has captured the character of many beloved species – a testament to his skills as an angler and photographer. Many lovely images have also come from Marie Derôme (Hugh's wife). She has recorded moments at sea, on the beach and in the kitchen that capture the very essence of a good family relationship with fish. And thanks, of course, for supporting Hugh inexorably throughout the project. Thanks also to Helen Fisher and family for the frequent use of their kitchen, and indeed their bodies, in much of the photography.

And thanks to various angler-photographers who have allowed us to use their pictures: Jon Beer; Richard Brigham; Pat Carlin; Richard Fishbourne; Charles Rangeley-Wilson; Mike Thrussell; and John Tickner. Thanks to Greenpeace and WWF for permission to use their photographs of tuna.

For the televisual incarnation of this book, *River Cottage: Gone Fishing*, hearty thanks are due to the versatile team at Keo, especially Katherine Perry, Larissa Hickey, Freddie Foff-Smith, Belle Borgeaud, Richard Hill and Bryan Johnson. Extra thanks to directors Ben Roy and Tom Beard, editor Simon Beeley, and to Andrew Palmer for executing the project and welcoming us all on Raasay. And thanks to all the fisherfolk of the Channel Islands, Hebrides and Southwest for their hospitality and time.

Collectively, the River Cottage team have been brilliant. Recipes have been honed by our chefs Gill Meller and Daniel Stevens. Photo shoots have been co-ordinated with great resourcefulness by Pip Corbin. The invasion of Park Farm has been effortlessly negotiated by Jessica Harris and Steven Lamb. Hugh has been kept (almost) sane by his incredibly wonderful PA, Jess Upton. The whole team has been buoyed throughout by the leadership of Rob Love.

But two members of the River Cottage team need to be singled out as genuine 'without whoms' for this project: Helen Stiles has researched many aspects of the book, overseeing the logistics of photography, fish and fishermen with equal alacrity and good humour. Nikki Duffy, the River Cottage Food Editor, has supported us from start to finish with her fantastically well-targeted research. She has calmly collated our raw prose, kept a weather eye on the drifting shape of the book, and brought it all together into one sturdy, watertight vessel. Without Helen and Nikki we would all have fallen apart.

A trio of freelancers has also earned a prostrate debt of gratitude. Our editorial guru on the latter stages of the project, Janet Illsley, has quietly set about solving and sorting all the problems and niggles that inevitably accumulate on such a wide-ranging and long-running publishing saga. She's been brilliant.

Our fantastic copy editor and recipe tester Jane Middleton has been as vigilant and constructive as ever. She should have a medal (or several) for her patience, skill and dedication to our cause over the years – so we are delighted that she won a Glenfiddich award for her own writing earlier this year.

Lawrence Morton, our designer, has been a great pleasure to work with, brimming as he is with elegant, eloquent solutions to the knotty problems of designing such a multi-layered monster of a book. And he's done it all with the good cheer and breezy enthusiasm of a man walking on the beach.

At Bloomsbury, the entire team has responded brilliantly to the challenge of producing such a complex tome in what became, in the final months, an increasingly insane schedule: Penny Edwards, Sarah Beal, Colin Midson, Natalie Hunt and Erica Jarnes have all made us feel that this project mattered to them *almost* as much as to us.

On the other hand our editor, Richard Atkinson, really did live, breathe, eat and sleep this book for most of the last year (and we can only hope his wife Sue will forgive us for that). He has worked phenomenally hard to make sure every aspect of it meets his own extraordinarily exacting standards. His proper, old-fashioned editing skills are present, if invisible, on every page.

And a particular thank you to our agent, Antony Topping, at Greene and Heaton. He may have other clients, but he gives a remarkably good impression of caring only about us.

Finally, we would like to thank one man whose contribution to this book is deeper and more valued than he can possibly know. Pat Carlin has taken us on many unforgettable fishing trips and helped us catch many unforgettable fish. But more importantly, throughout all of these deeply enjoyable forays he has imparted his remarkable knowledge about fish, fishing, the sea, wrecks, tides and weather in a truly selfless and always entertaining manner. We admire him immensely and thank him for helping to give us the confidence to write this book.

Hugh and Nick, September 2007

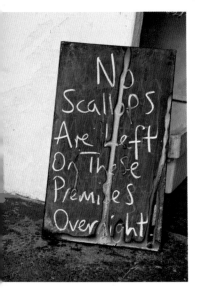

Hugh is a writer, broadcaster and food campaigner. He has been presenting the River Cottage programmes for Channel Four for more than a decade now, and this is the fifth River Cottage book he has written. Hugh lives in Devon with his wife Marie, four children and many animals, some of which they eat when they can't get fish. He shares a boat with his friend Nick.

Nick is a journalist, screenwriter and broadcaster. He presented two angling shows, *Screaming Reels* for Channel Four and *Dirty Tackle* for BBC 5 Live; and he received a BAFTA award for *The Giblet Boys*, a drama series he created for ITV. In a wide-ranging career as a columnist he has been film critic for the *Sun* and agony uncle for *Just Seventeen*; nowadays apart from writing about fishing for the *Shooting Times*, he is mostly busy writing screenplays and stage plays both in the UK and US. Nick lives in Dorset with his wife Helen, four children, various livestock, a lake full of trout and several (leaky) boats.

First published in Great Britain 2007
This edition published 2011

Text © 2007 by Hugh Fearnley-Whittingstall and Nick Fisher
Photography © 2007 by Simon Wheeler
Additional photography © 2007 by Paul Quagliana, Marie Derôme and other contributors (see page 605)

The moral right of the authors has been asserted

Bloomsbury Publishing Plc, 36 Soho Square, London W1D 3QY

A CIP catalogue record for this book is available from the British Library

Paperback ISBN 978 1 4088 1429 1

Hardback ISBN 978 1 4088 1954 8

10 9 8 7 6 5 4 3 2 1

Project editor: Janet Illsley
Design: Lawrence Morton (www.lawrencemorton.com)
Photography: Simon Wheeler (decourcywheeler@gmail.com)

The text of this book is set in Century Schoolbook and Trade Gothic
Printed and bound in Italy by Graphicom

www.bloomsbury.com/rivercottage
www.rivercottage.net